BASIC Programming Today
A Structured Approach

BASIC Programming Today
A Structured Approach

Steven L. Mandell
Bowling Green State University

West Publishing Company
St. Paul   New York   Los Angeles   San Francisco

Copy Editor: Maggie Jarpey
Composition: Carlisle Communications
Artwork: Carlisle Graphics

Cover Image:
"Blue Whale's Hawaii" produced with software by Dynamic Graphics Inc. © 1986; Available through Raven Maps and Images, Medford, Oregon

Chapter Opening Photographs:
Chapter 1: David Bishop; **Chapter 2:** Tom Kovaks; **Chapter 3:** Ken Cooper, The Image Bank; **Chapter 4:** Melvin Prueitt, Computer Graphics Group, Los Alamos National Laboratory; **Chapter 5:** David Bishop; **Chapter 6:** Melvin Prueitt, Computer Graphics Group, Los Alamos National Laboratory; **Chapter 7:** David Bishop; **Chapter 8:** Dominique Sarraute, The Image Bank; **Chapter 9:** Melvin Prueitt, Computer Graphics Group, Los Alamos National Laboratory; **Chapter 10:** David Bishop; **Chapter 11:** Tom Kovaks; **Chapter 12:** Tom Kovaks.

Intext Photographs:
Fig. 1-2: photograph courtesy of AT & Teletype Corporation, Skokie, Illinois;
Fig. 1-3: courtesy of International Business Machines Corporation; **Fig. 1-4:** courtesy of International Business Machines Corporation; **Fig. 1-5:** courtesy of Cray Research Inc.; **Fig. 1-6:** courtesy of International Business Machines Corporation;
Fig. 1-7: courtesy of Digital Equipment Corporation; **Fig. 1-8:** (a) courtesy of Apple Computer Inc., (b) courtesy of Apple Computer Inc., (c) courtesy of International Business Machines Corporation.

COPYRIGHT © 1986   WEST PUBLISHING COMPANY
COPYRIGHT © 1990   WEST PUBLISHING COMPANY
                   50 W. Kellogg Boulevard
                   P.O. Box 64526
                   St. Paul, MN 55164-1003

All rights reserved

Printed in the United States of America

(S) 97 96 95 94 93 92 91 90   8 7 6 5 4 3 2 1 0
(H) 97 96 95 94 93 92 91 90   8 7 6 5 4 3 2 1 0

Library of Congress Cataloging-in-Publication Data

Mandell, Steven L.
    Basic programming today.

    Includes index.
    1. BASIC (Computer program language)   2. Structured
programming.   I. Title.
QA76.73.B3M348   1990   005.13'3   88-33975
ISBN 0-314-47155-3 Hardcover
ISBN 0-314-47602-4 Softcover

CONTENTS-IN-BRIEF

Preface—xvii

CHAPTER 1
Introduction to Computers and Programming with BASIC—1

CHAPTER 2
Structured Problem Solving—19

CHAPTER 3
The Fundamentals of BASIC Programming—35

CHAPTER 4
Input and Output—75

CHAPTER 5
Fundamental Control Statements—117

CHAPTER 6
Looping Statements—171

CHAPTER 7
Modularizing Programs—229

CHAPTER 8
Functions—277

CHAPTER 9
Arrays—377

CHAPTER 10
Data Files—405

CHAPTER 11
Program Testing and Writing User-Friendly Programs—453

CHAPTER 12
Matrix Commands—493

APPENDIX A
Reserved Words—518

APPENDIX B
BASIC Operators—523

APPENDIX C
Numeric Functions—524

APPENDIX D
STRING FUNCTIONS—525

APPENDIX E
ASCII Code—526

APPENDIX F
Getting Started on the VAX—527

APPENDIX G
Getting Started on the Apple IIe and Apple IIgs—532

APPENDIX H
Getting Started with IBM BASIC and Microsoft GW-BASIC—536

APPENDIX I
Getting Started on the Macintosh—540

GLOSSARY—548

INDEX—553

TABLE OF CONTENTS

Preface xvii

CHAPTER 1
Introduction to Computers and Programming with BASIC 1

Objectives 1
Outline 2
Overview 2
What Computers Can Do 2
The Components of a Computer 3
    Input Devices 3
    Central Processing Unit 4
    Output Devices 5
Classification of Computer Systems 6
Introduction to Programming 9
Programming Languages 9
    Machine Language 9
    Assembly Language 11
    High-Level Languages 12
Structured Programming 13
Background on BASIC 13
Translating and Executing Programs 14
Batch vs. Interactive Processing 14
Summary Points 16
Review Questions 17

CHAPTER 2
Structured Problem Solving 19

Objectives 19
Outline 20
Overview 20
Defining and Documenting the Problem 20
Designing and Documenting a Solution 22
    Top-Down Design 23
    Top-Down vs. Bottom-Up Design 25
    The Three Types of Program Structures 26
    Flowcharting 27
    Pseudocoding 29
Writing and Documenting the Program 31
Submitting the Program to the Computer 31

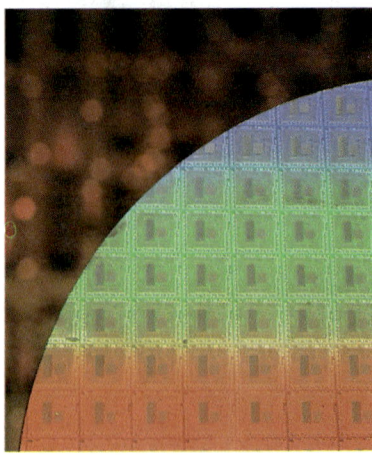

Debugging and Testing the Program 32
Summary Points 33
Review Questions 33

CHAPTER 3
The Fundamentals of BASIC Programming 35

Objectives 35
Outline 36
Overview 36
BASIC Commands 36
    Preparing to Enter a New Program 37
    Listing a Program 37
    Saving a Program 38
    Loading a Program 39
    Executing a Program 39
Line Numbers 40
BASIC Statement Components 43
    Constants 44
    Variables 46
    Reserved Words 49
Simple BASIC Statements 50
    Documenting a Program 50
    The Assignment Statement 53
    The PRINT Statement 56
    The END Statement 59
A Programming Problem 60
    Problem Definition 60
    Solution Design 60
    The Program 61
Avoiding Common Programming Mistakes 63
Summary Points 63
Review Questions 64
Debugging Exercises 66
Additional Programming Problems 67
    Level 1 67
    Level 2 68
    Level 3 70

CHAPTER 4
Input and Output 75

Objectives 75
Outline 76
Overview 76
The INPUT Statement 76
Printing Prompts for the User 79
The READ and DATA Statements 81
The RESTORE Statement 83
Comparing the INPUT and the READ/DATA Statements 84
Printing Results 85
    The Semicolon 85
    Using the Print Zones 87
    The TAB Function 89
    The SPC Function 92
    The PRINT USING Statement 93
Multiple Statements on a Single Physical Line 98
A Programming Problem 99
    Problem Definition 99
    Solution Design 100
    The Program 102
Avoiding Common Programming Mistakes 106
Summary Points 106
Review Questions 107
Debugging Exercises 109
Additional Programming Problems 110
    Level 1 110
    Level 2 111
    Level 3 114

CHAPTER 5
Fundamental Control Statements 117

Objectives 117
Outline 118
Overview 118
Unconditional Transfer: The GOTO Statement 118
Conditional Transfer: The Decision Step 120
    The IF/THEN Statement 121
    The IF/THEN/ELSE Statement 125
    Nested IF Statements 130
    The ON/GOTO Statement 135
    Menus 137
Looping Methods 140
    Trailer Values 143
    Counters 146
A Programming Problem 148
    Problem Definition 148
    Solution Design 148
    The Program 149

Avoiding Common Programming Mistakes 155
Summary Points 155
Review Questions 156
Debugging Exercises 158
Additional Programming Problems 160
    Level 1 160
    Level 2 161
    Level 3 164

CHAPTER 6
Looping Statements 171

Objectives 171
Outline 172
Overview 172
Elements of Looping 172
The FOR/NEXT Loop 174
    Processing Steps of the FOR/NEXT Loop 177
    Flowcharting the FOR/NEXT Loop 182
    Rules for Using the FOR/NEXT Loop 182
    Single Entry and Exit Points 185
Nested FOR/NEXT Loops 190
The WHILE Loop 194
The Importance of Using Loop Structures 196
Logical Operators 201
A Programming Problem 205
    Problem Definition 205
    Solution Design 208
    The Program 208
Avoiding Common Programming Mistakes 212
Summary Points 214
Review Questions 215
Debugging Exercises 217
Additional Programming Problems 219
    Level 1 219
    Level 2 220
    Level 3 222

CHAPTER 7
Modularizing Programs 229

Objectives 229
Outline 230
Overview 230
Importance of Modularizing Programs 230
Writing Subroutines 231
    The GOSUB Statement 231
    The RETURN Statement 231
    A Program Containing Multiple Calls to the Same Subroutine 232
    The ON/GOSUB Statement 232
    Using the Structure Chart to Modularize a Program 239
    Single-Entry, Single-Exit Subroutines 245

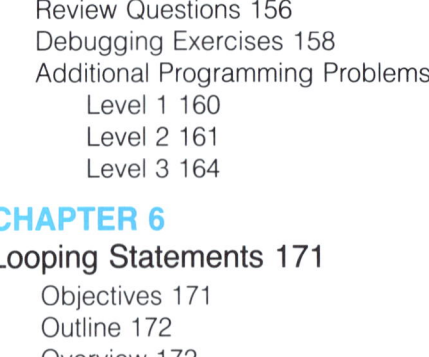

Menus 247
Using Stubs to Enter Programs 247
Checking for Invalid Data 248
A Programming Problem 258
    Problem Definition 258
    Solution Design 259
    The Program 261
Avoiding Common Programming Mistakes 267
Summary Points 267
Review Questions 268
Debugging Exercises 269
Additional Programming Problems 270
    Level 1 270
    Level 2 271
    Level 3 273

CHAPTER 8
Functions 277

Objectives 277
Outline 278
Overview 278
Library Functions 278
    Numeric Functions 279
    String Functions 291
User-Defined Functions 309
A Programming Problem 316
    Problem Definition 316
    Solution Design 317
    The Program 318
Avoiding Common Programming Mistakes 324
Summary Points 324
Review Questions 325
Debugging Exercises 326
Additional Programming Problems 328
    Level 1 328
    Level 2 329
    Level 3 332

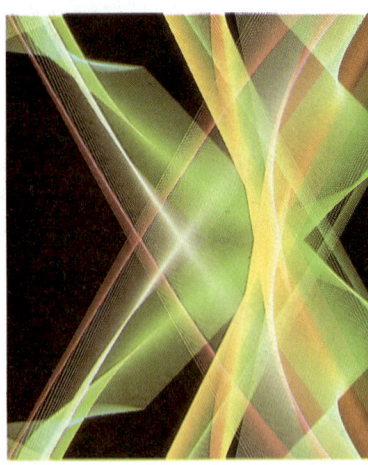

CHAPTER 9
Arrays 337

Objectives 337
Outline 338
Overview 338
Subscripts 339
Dimensioning an Array 341
One-Dimensional Arrays 342
    Reading Data to an Array 342
    Printing the Contents of an Array 343
    Performing Calculations on Array Elements 344
Multi-Dimensional Arrays 347
    Reading and Printing with Two-Dimensional Arrays 349
    Adding Rows 351
    Adding Columns 354
    Totaling a Two-Dimensional Array 354
    Arrays with More Than Two Dimensions 355
Sorting 360
    Bubble Sort 360
    Shell Sort 367
    Merge Sort 369
Searching 377
    Sequential Search 377
    Binary Search 378
A Programming Problem 381
    Problem Definition 381
    Solution Design 382
    The Program 383
Avoiding Common Programming Mistakes 390
Summary Points 390
Review Questions 391
Debugging Exercises 392
Additional Programming Problems 393
    Level 1 393
    Level 2 396
    Level 3 399

CHAPTER 10
Data Files 405

Objectives 405
Outline 406
Overview 406
What Is a File? 407
File Organization 408
Methods of Accessing Files 410
Secondary Storage 410
Using Sequential Files with Sequential Access 413
    Creating and Writing to a Sequential File 415
    Reading from a Sequential File 415
    VAX 416
    Apple 417
    IBM/Microsoft and Macintosh/Microsoft 420
Using Relative Files with Random Access 422
    VAX 423
    Apple 426
    IBM/Microsoft and Macintosh/Microsoft 429
A Programming Problem 433
    Problem Definition 433
    Solution Design 433
    The Programs 435
Avoiding Common Programming Mistakes 442
Summary Points 442
Review Questions 443
Debugging Exercises 444
Additional Programming Problems 446
    Level 1 446
    Level 2 447
    Level 3 449

CHAPTER 11
Program Testing and Writing User-Friendly Programs 453

Objectives 453
Outline 454
Overview 454
More on Structured Programming 454
Program Style 455
    Documentation 455
    The Use of Blank Lines and Spaces 458
The Two Types of Program Errors 460
    Syntax Errors 460
    Logic Errors 460
Program Testing Methods 462
Report Writing 465
Printer Control Characters 472
Writing User-Friendly Programs 472
A Programming Problem 474
Summary Points 483

Review Questions 484
Debugging Exercises 484
Additional Programming Problems 488
    Level 1 488
    Level 2 490

CHAPTER 12
Matrix Commands 493

Objectives 493
Outline 494
Overview 494
Matrix Input/Output 496
Matrix Mathematics 498
    Addition and Subtraction 499
    Matrix Multiplication 499
    Scalar Multiplication 500
    Replacement 501
Matrix Functions 501
    Initialization 501
    The Identity Matrix 502
    Transposition 502
    Inversion 503
A Programming Problem 504
    Problem Definition 504
    Solution Design 504
    The Program 506
Avoiding Common Programming Mistakes 509
Summary Points 509
Review Questions 510
Debugging Exercises 510
Additional Programming Problems 512
    Level 1 512
    Level 2 513
    Level 3 515

APPENDIX A
Reserved Words 518

APPENDIX B
BASIC Operators 523

APPENDIX C
Numeric Functions 524

APPENDIX D
String Functions 525

APPENDIX E
ASCII Code 526

APPENDIX F
Getting Started on the VAX 527
    Signing On 527
    System Commands 528
    The Keyboard 529
    Working in the VAX BASIC Environment 530
    Entering a New Program 530
    Saving and Loading a Program 531
    Executing a Program 531
    Leaving the BASIC Environment 531

APPENDIX G
Getting Started on the Apple IIe and Apple IIgs 532
    Starting BASIC on the Apple IIe 532
    Starting BASIC on the Apple IIgs 532
    Keyboard 533
    Specialized Keys 533
    Manipulating Programs 533
    Special Features 534

APPENDIX H
Getting Started with IBM BASIC and Microsoft GW-BASIC 536
    Starting the Computer 536
    Keyboard 537
    Special Features 538
    Manipulating Programs 538
    Exiting BASIC 539

APPENDIX I
Getting Started on the Macintosh 540
    Starting the Computer 540
    The Microsoft BASIC Screen 540
    Manipulating Programs 542
    Exiting BASIC 545
    Keyboard 545
    Specialized Keys 545
    Additional Features 545
    Print Zones and Width 547

Glossary 548

Index 553

PREFACE

Since 1965, when BASIC was first developed by Drs. John Kemeny and Thomas Kurtz, software design technology has been hugely improved, both on theoretical and practical levels. The introduction of structured programming techniques encouraged the development of better designed, more reliable programs that have readily apparent logic and are easy to maintain and modify. Today such techniques as top-down design, structure charts, and functionally modularized programs continue to advance the sophistication of software.

To help students develop good programming habits, these design techniques have been used throughout the text, with an emphasis on structured problem solving. The principles of structured programming not only facilitate learning at the introductory level, but will serve students well should they move on to more advanced courses. Whenever possible, programs in the text use control structures, such as the WHILE loop and the IF/THEN/ELSE statement, instead of unconditional branches (commonly referred to as "GOTO" statements).

BASIC, the language taught in this text, was chosen because it is easily learned and widely implemented. Students need no prior programming experience to begin learning it. Each new statement is explained with the help of numerous appropriate examples. VAX BASIC, Version 3.2, is the main implementation; all programs were run on a VAX 8530.

Three additional implementations of BASIC—Microsoft BASIC as implemented on the IBM PC, Microsoft BASIC as implemented on the Macintosh, and Applesoft BASIC as implemented on the Apple IIe and Apple IIGS—are also covered. All complete programs include boxes indicating differences between these microcomputer implementations and VAX BASIC. When a control structure is not available on a given system (for example, there is no WHILE loop in Applesoft BASIC), the student is instructed on how to simulate the structure. In addition, the text includes appendixes on each computer system that explain the use of the hardware and various features. When the student arrives at Chapter 3 and begins writing simple programs, he or she should also read the appropriate system appendix.

Numerous examples of well-designed programs are presented throughout the text. Each chapter concludes with a comprehensive programming problem developed using structured design techniques, and the student is taken through this development process step by step.

The importance of making programs reliable and user-friendly cannot be overemphasized. Consequently, coverage of this area has been increased over the first edition, and these themes are woven throughout the text. In addition, an entire chapter (Chapter 11) is devoted to the characteristics of a well-designed program and techniques of debugging and testing. The programmer is continually encouraged to take the user's point of view in considering what features make one program easy and enjoyable to use while another is difficult and awkward. In this way the beginning programmer learns to keep in mind the ultimate purpose of a program.

Helpful features of this text include list of learning objectives at the beginning of each chapter to prepare students for the topics to be covered and learning checks with answers to allow intermittent self-testing throughout the chapter. Numerous review questions and debugging exercises help the student apply what has been learned. Finally, each chapter concludes with a section entitled "Avoiding Common Programming Mistakes."

Each programming chapter (Chapters 3 through 12) concludes with thirty programming problems. In this edition, these problems have been divided into three levels: Level 1 gives the student practice in writing the new statements introduced in the chapter, Level 2 offers problems of medium difficulty, and Level 3 challenges the sophisticated student.

Color coding has been used in programming examples as follows:

Tan shading   Highlighted Statements   (Used to indicate statement currently being discussed.)

Blue   Computer Output

Red   User Response

Acknowledgments

A note of appreciation goes to Irene Bulas for her efforts at making the material "student friendly." A special acknowledgment goes to Sue Baumann, a gifted writer and programmer, whose efforts contributed greatly to the completion of the text book.

I was very fortunate to have had several outstanding college educators serve as reviewers for this project. I wish to again express my thanks to those people who reviewed the manuscript for the first edition of this text:

Marcia A. Merrick
New Hampshire Vocational-Technical College
Claremont, N.H.

John Bujosa
Gonzaga University
Spokane, WA

Edward A. Vondrak
Indiana Central University
Indianapolis, IN

Mike Michaelson
Palomar College
San Marcos, CA

Donald A. Witt
Houston Community College

In preparation of this second edition, the following people provided invaluable comments based on their experience using *BASIC PROGRAMMING TODAY*. My sincere thanks to each of them.

Melissa Artz
Columbia Basin Community College, Washington

Susan Isermann
Illinois Valley Community College

Kenneth W. Jeffreys
Southwest Missouri State University

Douglas W. Knight
University of Southern Colorado

Elaine Rhodes
Illinois Central College

Sandra M. Schleiffers
Colorado State University, Fort Collins

Mohamed Sedighi
Compton College, California
Long Beach College, California

Susan Sliva
Schreiner College, Texas

Steven L. Mandell

BASIC Programming Today
A Structured Approach

CHAPTER

1

INTRODUCTION TO COMPUTERS AND PROGRAMMING WITH BASIC

Objectives

After studying this chapter, you will be able to:
- List the three kinds of tasks a computer can perform.
- Name the three features that make a computer useful.
- Name the three basic components of all computer systems.
- Define input and output.
- Explain the difference between data and information.
- Name the four types of computers, and give characteristics of each type.
- List the three levels of programming languages.
- Name two basic characteristics of structured programming.
- Explain the difference between application and system programs.
- Give a brief history and description of the BASIC programming language.

Outline

Overview
What Computers Can Do
The Components of a Computer
   Input Devices
   Central Processing Unit
   Output Devices
Classification of Computer
    Systems

Introduction to Programming
Programming Languages
   Machine Language
   Assembly Language
   High-Level Languages
Structured Programming

Background on BASIC
Translating and Executing
   Programs
Batch vs. Interactive Processing
Summary Points
Review Questions

Overview

Computer
An electronic machine capable of processing data quickly and accurately in a wide variety of ways.

Program
A series of step-by-step instructions that a computer uses to solve a problem.

Execution
The process in which the computer carries out the instructions submitted to it.

Programming language
A language that a programmer can use to give instructions to a computer.

Computers have become an important force in our society. People use them to perform an ever-increasing variety of tasks, such as banking, locating books in libraries, and making reservations on airline flights. Elementary-school children learn their multiplication tables with the help of computer programs that are entertaining, motivating, and more patient than any human teacher. Everywhere we look, we can find fascinating applications for these versatile machines. The uses for computers are limited only by the creativity of the people who control them.

What is it that makes these machines different from the other machines that we use every day, such as a car or a typewriter? First, a **computer** is an electronic machine that is capable of processing data in a wide variety of ways with an extremely high degree of speed and accuracy. In addition, the versatility of the computer is enhanced by its ability to combine many simple operations into a single, integrated whole. A sequence of instructions that work together to allow the computer to solve a specific problem is called a **program.** A language that a programmer can use to direct the computer to carry out, or **execute,** these instructions is called a **programming language.**

This chapter will introduce some general information about computers and computer programs. At the end of the chapter, a brief discussion of the different types of programming languages will be presented.

What Computers Can Do

The actual tasks that computer systems can perform are quite limited and can be divided into three categories:

1. Arithmetic operations (addition, subtraction, multiplication, and division).
2. Comparison (or logical) operations (determining whether a given value is greater than, equal to, or less than another value).

3. Storage and retrieval operations (such as saving a program on disk so that it can be used later).

What makes the computer particularly useful to people is its ability to perform these tasks with a high degree of speed and accuracy. With care, a person can add 100 numbers and find the correct result, but the chances of making an error somewhere along the way are considerable. Also, it is a boring job. This is the kind of task that is well suited to the computer. It can perform this task quickly and accurately, and it won't get bored. Moreover, it can store the result for future use.

The Components of a Computer

All computers, regardless of their size and complexity, have three basic components: input devices, a central processing unit, and output devices. These physical components are called the **hardware.** Figure 1–1 illustrates how these three components are related.

Hardware
The physical components of a computer.

Input Devices

Programs and data that are entered into a computer to be processed are called **input.** The word **data** refers to facts that have not been organized in any meaningful way. When data is processed, or converted to some meaningful form, the result is **information.** For example, in a national election, the records of all the votes cast for the office of president are data. When these votes are tabulated and the final totals are determined, the result is information.

Input devices are used to enter data into the computer. There are many input devices; some common ones are the keyboard (as shown in Figure 1–2), disk drives, tape drives, and light pens. A computer system can have many different input devices. Some of these devices, such as the keyboard

Input
Data that is submitted to the computer for processing.

Data
Facts that have not been organized in a meaningful way.

Information
Data that has been processed so that it is meaningful to the user.

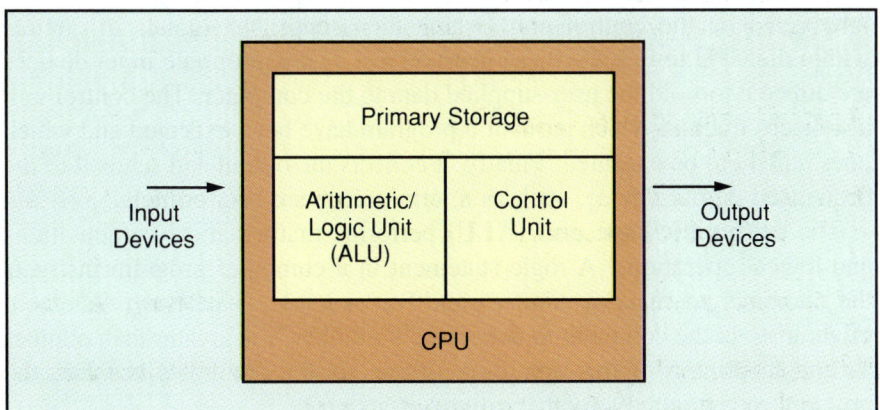

FIGURE 1–1
The Three Basic Components of a Computer System

4 BASIC PROGRAMMING TODAY, A STRUCTURED APPROACH

FIGURE 1–2
A Terminal Keyboard. *The keyboard is a commonly used input device.*

and the light pen, can only be used for input. Others, such as disk and tape drives, can be used for both input and output.

Central Processing Unit

The computer can store data temporarily; it can also perform operations on this data. The component that performs these functions is called the **central processing unit (CPU)**. The CPU can be thought of as the "brain" of the computer. It consists of three major components: the control unit, the arithmetic/logic unit, and the primary storage unit.

The **control unit** is in charge of the activities of the CPU. It does not process or store data itself, but instructs various parts of the computer in performing these tasks. Instructions given to the computer by the user are interpreted by the control unit, which then sends out signals to circuits within the CPU to execute these instructions. The appropriate input devices are directed to send the user-supplied data to the computer. The control unit also keeps track of which parts of a program have been executed and which ones remain to be executed. Finally, it collects the output and sends it to the designated output device, such as a terminal screen or a printer.

The **arithmetic/logic unit (ALU)** performs mathematical computations and logical operations. A logic statement in a computer program instructs the computer to make a comparison. For example, a program statement might instruct the computer to determine if number X is greater than number Y, and to print X if this condition is true. If the condition is false, the program might specify another course of action.

Central processing unit
The "brain" of the computer; it consists of the control unit, the arithmetic/logic unit, and the primary storage unit.

Control unit
The part of the central processing unit that governs the actions of the various components of the computer.

Arithmetic/logic unit
Performs mathematical computations and logical operations.

The **primary storage unit** (also referred to as **main memory, primary memory,** or **internal storage**) holds program instructions, data, and the intermediate and final results of processing. It consists of many storage locations, each of which can hold a small amount of information. Each of these storage locations is assigned a unique address. This address allows the computer to locate items that have been stored in its memory. Large computers have millions of these storage locations.

Primary storage unit
The component of the central processing unit that temporarily stores programs, data, and results.

Output Devices

Output devices such as disk and tape drives are used to transfer data, results, and programs from the primary storage unit to **secondary** (or **auxiliary**) **storage** media such as floppy disks, hard disks, and magnetic tape. A computer system can have many different output devices. For example, the programmer may be able to print the results of a program on paper or transfer them to a magnetic disk for later access. Some of these devices, such as the terminal screen and the printer, can only be used as output devices.

Secondary storage
Storage that is external to the computer and is used to supplement the primary storage unit.

Displaying output on a terminal screen (Figure 1–3) is often convenient. This output, referred to as **soft copy,** is easy for the user to read, but is lost as soon as something else replaces it on the screen. Printing the results on paper saves this information permanently so that the user can refer to it later. This type of output is called **hard copy.** A printer that can be used to obtain hard copy is shown in Figure 1–4.

Soft copy
Output printed on a display screen.

Hard copy
Output printed on paper.

The primary storage unit has only a limited amount of storage space, because this type of memory is expensive. Programs, information, and data that need to be saved for later use can be transferred to secondary storage on

FIGURE 1–3
A Terminal Screen. *A display screen can be used to display output temporarily.*

FIGURE 1–4
A Line Printer. *Hard-copy output can be obtained by using a printer.*

magnetic disk or tape. When the computer needs to process these items again, they can be returned to the computer's primary storage unit. Although it takes more time to access items in secondary storage than those in memory, secondary storage can store enormous quantities of data at a reasonable cost.

Learning Check

1. The three characteristics that make computers different from other machines are their _____, _____, and _____.
2. A computer system consists of three main components: _____, _____, and _____.
3. _____ are facts that have not been organized in any meaningful way.
4. Keyboards, disk drives, light pens are all examples of _____ _____.
5. Output that is printed on paper is _____ _____.

Answers

1. speed, accuracy, ability to store and retrieve programs and data 2. input devices, central processing unit, output devices 3. Data 4. input devices 5. hard copy

Classification of Computer Systems

Computers come in a wide variety of sizes and shapes, ranging from tiny hand-held devices to some that are several feet in height and diameter. Over the years, computers have become smaller and smaller, but they have also become increasingly powerful. Computers can be divided into four categories: supercomputers, mainframes, minicomputers, and microcomputers. These four types differ in price, amount of memory, speed, and processing capabilities.

The most powerful machines available in the late 1980s are the **supercomputers.** They are the fastest and most expensive computers and can perform over a hundred million arithmetic operations per second. The Cray X-MP computer (Figure 1–5), developed by Cray Research, Inc., is a supercomputer system that is used mainly in the scientific areas of weather forecasting, nuclear weapons development, and energy supply and conservation.

For most business applications, the extremely high-speed processing capabilities of a supercomputer are not necessary; a **mainframe** is adequate. Your school may use a mainframe to keep track of student records, handle class scheduling, and prepare staff payrolls. Figure 1–6 shows a popular mainframe.

The distinction between **minicomputers** and mainframes has gradually become blurred. Minicomputers manufactured in the late 1980s are more powerful than mainframes manufactured just ten years earlier. In general, minicomputers (Figure 1–7) are lower-priced, have smaller memories, and process data more slowly than mainframes. They are also generally easier to install. Minicomputers are often used in businesses that do not require the capabilities of a mainframe.

The **microcomputer** is currently the smallest and least costly type of computer. This is the type often found in small businesses and in homes and

Supercomputer
The largest, fastest type of computer currently available; capable of performing several hundred million arithmetic operations per second.

Mainframe
A large computer commonly used in business and industry.

Minicomputer
A computer with many of the capabilities of a mainframe, but generally lower-priced and with a smaller primary storage unit.

Microcomputer
The smallest and least expensive computer currently available; it has a smaller primary storage unit than other types of computers.

FIGURE 1–5
A Supercomputer Configuration. *The Cray X-MP Computer System uses the most advanced technology currently available.*

8 BASIC PROGRAMMING TODAY, A STRUCTURED APPROACH

FIGURE 1–6
A Commonly Used Mainframe. *The IBM 4341.*

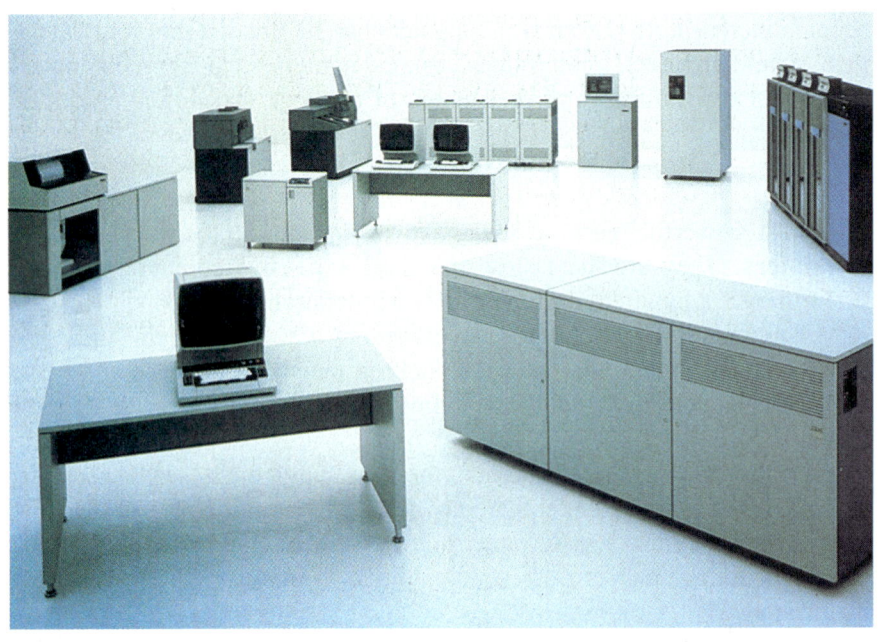

FIGURE 1–7
A Large Minicomputer System. The VAX 8700.

classrooms. Its primary storage unit is usually smaller than that of the other types of computers. Microcomputers are generally less complex and execute programs at slower speeds than minicomputers. Because of the microcomputer's low cost and flexibility of available software packages (commercially written programs that perform specific tasks, such as word processing), its popularity has risen tremendously in the past few years.

In the mid-1970s, when microcomputers were first introduced, they were used primarily for playing games. Since that time, an extremely large number of software packages have been developed for a wide variety of applications, not only in business but also in medicine, education, and just about any other area imaginable. Figure 1–8 shows several popular microcomputers.

Introduction to Programming

Programming is the process of writing instructions (a program) for a computer to use to solve a problem; these instructions must be written in a programming language. A program can be anything from a simple list of instructions that adds a series of numbers together to a large, complex structure with many subsections that calculates the payroll for a major corporation.

Software is a program or a series of programs that tells the computer hardware what to do. Software can be divided into two categories: application programs and system programs. **Application programs** are written to solve a specific user problem. An example would be a program used by a company to keep track of customer accounts. (All of the programs that appear in this book are application programs.) **System programs,** on the other hand, coordinate the operation of computer circuitry and help the computer run quickly and efficiently. For example, one type of system program translates application programs into a form that the computer is able to execute.

Programming
The process of writing instructions for a computer to use to solve a problem.

Software
A program or a series of programs.

Application program
A program that is written to solve a specific user problem.

System program
A program that coordinates the operations of the computer.

Programming Languages

There are three broad categories of programming languages: machine languages, assembly languages, and high-level languages. Each of these types will be discussed here.

Machine Language

Machine language, also called **binary representation,** is the only language that the computer can directly execute. Programs written in any other type

Machine language
The only language that a computer can execute directly; it consists of 1s and 0s.

FIGURE 1–8
Several Popular Microcomputers

a) Apple IIe

c) IBM PC

b) Macintosh SE

of language are translated into machine language by the computer before they are executed. Data represented in binary form is stored in the computer as a series of "high" or "low" electronic states representing binary digits (or *bits*). An "on" bit generally indicates a high voltage whereas an "off" bit represents "low" voltage.

A programmer writing instructions in machine language can specify a "high" bit with the numeral 1 and a "low" bit with the numeral 0. Every operation that the computer is capable of performing (such as addition or storing a value in a given memory location) is indicated by a specific binary code. The programmer must use the proper code for each operation. Also, the memory locations must be accessed by listing their storage address in binary code in the instruction.

Because these 1s and 0s have no intrinsic meaning to humans, writing this type of code is very difficult. The programmer must carefully keep track of which values have been stored in which storage locations. It is easy to reference a wrong location accidentally, or to store a new value in a location that has already been used for something else, thereby losing the previous contents.

Examples of a few machine language statements are shown in Figure 1–9. The equivalent statement in BASIC is shown at the top of the figure. These statements perform the simple task of adding the contents of one storage location to the contents of another. The resulting sum is then stored in a third location.

Machine language is different for each kind of computer, so it is necessary for the programmer to be familiar with the particular computer he or she is programming. Although machine language programs are very tedious to write, they make efficient use of computer time because the computer can quickly and easily execute these instructions.

When computers were first developed, machine language was the only way they could be programmed. The people who worked with these computers quickly realized that this method often led to programming errors. It used computer time efficiently, but it was extremely time-consuming for the programmer.

Assembly Language

Assembly language (referred to as a low-level language) was developed to make programming easier. In assembly language, the programmer uses symbolic names (rather than 1s or 0s) to specify various machine operations. For example, the word ADD might be used to instruct the computer to add the contents of two storage locations. The use of these symbolic names makes assembly language programming much easier than machine language programming. Another important improvement over machine language is the use of names to represent storage locations, so that the programmer no longer has to know the address of the storage location where a particular value is kept.

Assembly language
Uses symbolic names rather than the 0s or 1s of machine language.

```
           HIGH-LEVEL LANGUAGE (BASIC)
      LET  C = A + B
         MACHINE LANGUAGE (MOS-TECH 6502 MACHINE LANGUAGE)
         1010    0000    0000    0000    0000    1101
         1010    1101    0000    1110    0000    1101
         0111    1001    0110    0000    0000    1100
         1101    1000
         1000    1101    0011    1111    0000    1100
```

FIGURE 1–9

A BASIC Statement and Its Machine-Language Equivalent

An assembly language program that performs the task of adding two numbers might look like this:

```
LOAD  A
ADD   B
STORE C
```

These instructions tell the computer to perform the following steps:

1. Get the value contained in address A, and put it in a location in the ALU (called an *accumulator.*).
2. Get the value contained in address B, and add that value to the value in the accumulator.
3. Get the new value in the accumulator and store it in location C.

Like machine language, assembly language is different for each kind of computer. Assembly language is easier for people to understand than machine language, but it must be translated into machine language before the computer can execute the instructions. This translation is accomplished by a special system program called an *assembler*.

High-Level Languages

Although it is much simpler to write a program in assembly language than in machine language, considerable knowledge of the internal operations of the computer is still required. To simplify programming further, other languages have been developed that resemble English even more closely. These languages do not require the programmer to understand the technical details of internal computer operations. Because these languages are strongly oriented toward the programmer rather than toward the computer, they are termed **high-level languages.** Even a person who does not know a particular high-level language can often determine the general purpose of the program statements. Consider the BASIC statement in Figure 1–9:

High-level language
An English-like programming language that must be translated to machine language before execution.

```
LET C = A + B
```

Even a nonprogrammer would have little difficulty in understanding that this statement adds two values together and assigns the sum to C. But, as with assembly language, high-level language programs must be translated into machine language before the computer can execute them. This task is performed by a system program called a *compiler* or *interpreter*.

There are many high-level languages. A few of the more popular ones are COBOL, BASIC, FORTRAN, and Pascal. This book will teach the programming language BASIC.

Structured Programming

When computers were first developed, programming was extremely complex, and programmers were happy simply to get their programs to work. There was little concern over writing programs in a style that was easy for other people to understand. Gradually, however, programmers began to realize that working with such programs was very difficult, particularly when someone other than the original programmer had to alter an existing program. Consequently, programmers began developing ways to make programs easier to understand and modify. These techniques, which have been developed over the last twenty-five years, are referred to as **structured programming.** Structured programming has two basic characteristics: (1) the program logic is easy to follow, and (2) the programs are divided into smaller **subprograms** or **modules,** which in BASIC are referred to as *subroutines*. Thus, structured programming avoids large, complex programs in favor of more manageable subprograms, each designed to perform a specific task. These subprograms are joined together to form the entire program. Because the logic of structured programs is easier to follow than that of unstructured programs, they are more likely to be free of errors and are easier to modify at a later date.

This textbook will emphasize the concepts of structured programming. Chapters 3 through 6 introduce the BASIC statements necessary to write well-structured programs, and Chapter 7 explains how to correctly modularize programs.

Because many versions of BASIC were developed before these concepts of modularization were thoroughly understood, these older versions do not lend themselves to structured programming. We will try to present techniques for working around these difficulties whenever possible.

Structured programming
A method of programming in which programs have easy-to-follow logic and are divided into subprograms, each designed to perform a specific task.

Subprogram
A distinct part of a larger program that is designed to perform a specific task.

Background on BASIC

BASIC, an acronym for Beginner's All-purpose Symbolic Instruction Code, was developed in the mid-1960s at Dartmouth College by Professors John Kemeny and Thomas Kurtz. It is a high-level language that uses English-like words and statements such as LET, READ, and PRINT. It is easy to learn and is considered a general-purpose programming language, because it is useful for a wide variety of tasks.

BASIC, like English and other languages used for communication, includes rules for spelling, grammar, and punctuation. In BASIC, however, these rules are very precise and allow no exceptions. They enable the programmer to tell the computer exactly what to do.

Learning Check

1. The largest, most powerful computers are called _____.
2. Programs written to solve a user problem are _____ _____.
3. Programs that coordinate the operation of computer circuitry are _____ _____.
4. The only language that computers can execute directly is _____ _____.
5. Languages that are English-like are called _____ languages.
6. The ability to divide a program into _____ is an important part of structured programming.

Answers

1. supercomputers 2. application programs 3. system programs 4. machine language 5. high-level 6. subprograms

Translating and Executing Programs

Source program
A program written in assembly or high-level language, which must be translated into machine language before execution.

Interpreter
A system program that translates and executes program statements a line at a time.

Compiler
A system program that translates an entire source program into machine language before execution begins.

Object program
The executable instructions created when a source program is translated into machine language.

Before a program written in a high-level language can be executed, it must be translated into machine language. The program that is to be translated is referred to as the **source program.** This translation is done by a system-program. There are two basic types of system programs that perform this translation: **interpreters** and **compilers.**

The difference between an interpreter and a compiler is that the compiler creates an **object program,** which consists of the entire source program translated into machine language. This object program is then loaded into the computer's memory for execution. An interpreter, on the other hand, translates each program statement into machine language and then submits it to the CPU for execution before going on to the next statement. This approach saves space in the computer's memory. However, interpreters often use more computer time than compilers because program statements that are used more than once must be translated each time they are executed. Most BASIC systems use interpreters, although some use compilers. Figure 1–10 illustrates the compilation and execution process.

Batch vs. Interactive Processing

Batch processing
Processing in which programs wait in line to be executed in a continuous stream without human intervention.

A computer can execute programs in two basic ways: by **batch processing** or by **interactive processing.** In batch processing, the user does not interact directly with the computer during execution. Instead, several user programs are grouped (or "batched") and processed one after another in a continuous stream. Batch processing is usually slow, because programs must wait in line for their turn to be processed. However, batch processing can make

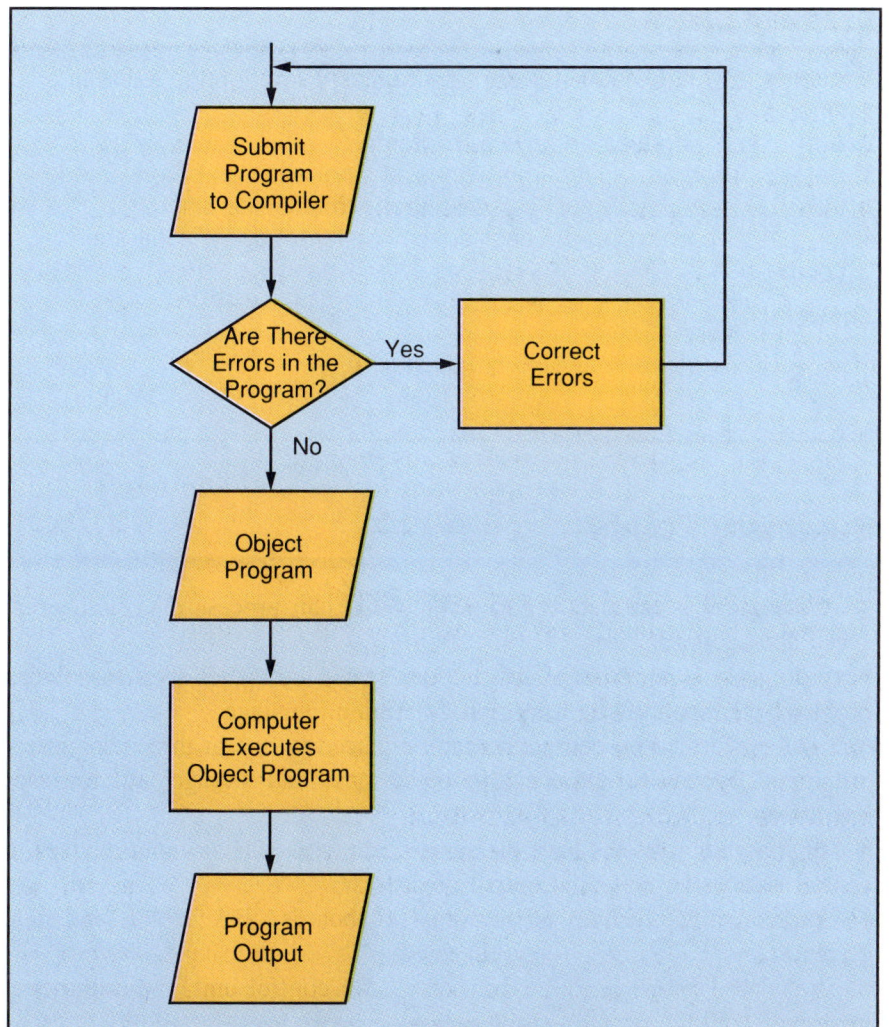

FIGURE 1-10
Compiling and Executing a Program

good use of CPU time. The programs are executed efficiently, and they can be run at times when the system is least busy, such as at night.

By contrast, communicating with the computer during program execution through an input device such as a terminal keyboard may involve direct, or interactive, processing. During interactive processing, programs are translated and executed, and the results returned to the terminal screen, generally in a matter of seconds. Most large computer systems can execute programs using either batch or interactive processing, depending on the needs of a particular situation. Microcomputers generally use interactive processing.

Most large computers are **time-sharing systems.** This means that many terminals are attached to a single central computer, such as a minicomputer or a mainframe. It appears to each terminal user that he or she is the only one using the system, when in reality the computer is dividing its time among all the users.

Interactive processing
Processing in which the user interacts directly with the computer during program execution.

Time-sharing system
A system with many terminals connected to a central computer that divides its time among the users.

Learning Check

1. A(n) _____ translates a program into machine language a line at a time.
2. A(n) _____ creates an object program.
3. Before a program written in a high-level language can be executed, the _____ _____ must be translated into machine language.
4. In _____ processing the user does not interact directly with the computer.

Answers

1. interpreter 2. compiler 3. source program 4. batch

Summary Points

- A computer is an electronic machine that can process data with great speed and accuracy.
- A program is a series of instructions that a computer uses to solve a problem; it must be written in a programming language.
- Tasks performed by computers can be placed in one of three categories: arithmetic operations, comparison operations, and storage and retrieval operations.
- All computer systems have the same basic components: input devices, a central processing unit, and output devices.
- Common input devices are terminal keyboards, disk drives, and tape drives.
- The central processing unit consists of the control unit, the arithmetic/logic unit, and the primary storage unit.
- Common output devices are terminal screens, disk drives, tape drives, and printers.
- Computers are classified as supercomputers, mainframes, minicomputers, or microcomputers.
- Application programs solve specific user problems, while system programs manage the computer's resources so that it can run quickly and efficiently.
- The three levels of programming languages are machine languages, assembly languages, and high-level languages.
- Machine language is the only language that the computer can execute directly. All other languages must be translated into machine language before execution. Machine language is different for each type of computer.
- High-level languages are the most English-like, while assembly language is between machine language and high-level languages.
- Structured programming techniques were developed to encourage the writing of easy-to-understand, more error-free programs. Structured pro-

gramming has two basic characteristics: the logic of the program is easy to follow, and the program is divided into subprograms, each performing a specific task.
- BASIC (Beginner's All-purpose Symbolic Instruction Code) was developed in the mid-1960s at Dartmouth College by Professors John Kemeny and Thomas Kurtz.
- High-level languages such as BASIC are translated into machine language by either an interpreter or a compiler.
- Programs can be executed using either batch or interactive processing. In interactive processing, the user interacts directly with the computer during program execution. In batch processing, the needed programs, data, and so forth are submitted to the computer prior to execution, with no user interaction taking place while the program is being run.
- In a time-sharing system, many terminals access the same central computer. The computer divides its time among the various users.

Review Questions

1. Into what three categories can all functions performed by the computer be divided?
2. Into which of the three categories of computer functions would each of the following be placed?
   a. Finding the square of a number.
   b. Storing a program so that it can be run at a later time.
   c. Determining which of two letters comes first alphabetically.
   d. Calculating a paycheck by multiplying the hours worked by the hourly rate of pay.
3. Explain the difference between computer hardware and computer software.
4. What is the purpose of the central processing unit?
5. List the three parts of the central processing unit, and tell what each does.
6. What is the difference between data and information?
7. Name some common input devices and some common output devices.
8. Define hard copy and soft copy, and name an advantage of each.
9. List the four basic categories of computers, from the largest to the smallest.
10. Name the two types of computer programs, and define each.
11. What is an advantage of using machine language?
12. What are two disadvantages of using machine language?
13. What are two advantages of using high-level languages?
14. What is a disadvantage of using high-level languages?
15. Give a brief history of the BASIC language.

16. Is BASIC a machine language, an assembly language, or high-level language? Explain your answer.
17. Name two characteristics of structured programs.
18. Explain the difference between an interpreter and a compiler.
19. Explain the difference between batch and interactive processing.
20. What is a time-sharing system?

CHAPTER 2

STRUCTURED PROBLEM SOLVING

Objectives

After studying this chapter, you will be able to:
- List the five steps used in problem solving.
- Determine the needed input and output for simple programming problems.
- Give a definition of the term algorithm.
- Draw structure charts for simple programming problem solutions.
- Give three advantages of top-down design.
- Explain how bottom-up design differs from top-down design.
- Give an advantage and a disadvantage of bottom-up design.
- Define the terms flowchart and pseudocode.
- List and explain the purpose of the six flowcharting symbols discussed in this chapter.
- Write flowcharts and pseudocode for simple programming problems.

Outline

Overview
Defining and Documenting the Problem
Designing and Documenting a Solution
    Top-Down Design
        A Sample Problem
Top-Down vs. Bottom-Up Design
The Three Types of Program Structures
Flowcharting
Pseudocoding
Writing and Documenting the Program
Submitting the Program to the Computer
Debugging and Testing the Program
Summary Points
Review Questions

Overview

People who are good programmers are also good problem solvers. Writing a program is a way of using a computer to solve a problem. This chapter will examine problem-solving methods that can help you arrive at solutions in an efficient, logical manner.

People solve problems every day of their lives. Most problems have a number of possible solutions. For example, how many different ways are there to clean a room? Although it may be possible to create a precise listing of the tasks that must be done, many variables can enter into how the tasks are completed. It is usually possible to vary the order in which the tasks are performed and still achieve the desired result. For example, which should be done first—washing the windows or dusting the furniture? Will the floor be cleaned by sweeping it with a broom or with a vacuum cleaner?

The same is true in designing computer programs to solve problems. Many roads may lead to the same solution. Your job will be to find the most feasible road, given the constraints under which you have to work.

To use the computer effectively as a problem-solving tool, you must perform several steps, which together are commonly called the **programming process:**

1. Define and document the problem.
2. Design and document a solution.
3. Write and document the program.
4. Submit the program to the computer.
5. Test and debug the program and revise the documentation if necessary.

Each of these steps will be discussed in this chapter.

Programming process
The steps used to develop a solution to a programming problem.

Defining and Documenting the Problem

It is virtually impossible to get somewhere if you do not know where you are going. Likewise, in programming, a clear and precise statement of the problem must be given before anything else is done. Despite this fact, many programming disasters have occurred because this step has been glossed over. The person who writes the program may not be the same person who will be using it, and communication between these two people (or groups) may be inadequate. Misunderstandings concerning the desired results of the program can lead to programs that do not meet the user's needs. Therefore, before the programmer begins work, the problem must be clearly defined and documented in writing. The documentation and problem definition must be agreed upon by all parties involved. This documentation should include a description of program input and output:

1. What data is necessary to obtain the desired output? From where will this data be obtained? How will this data be entered? The programmer should make it as easy as possible for the user to enter the data that a program needs.

2. All output and the manner in which it is to be formatted must be described. Formatting refers to the way in which the output is to be displayed or printed to make it easy for the user to read and use. For example, placing output in table form with appropriate headings is one way of formatting it.

Let's practice defining and documenting a simple problem. Suppose you need a program to convert a given number of feet to miles. The output is the number of miles in the stated number of feet. The input is the number of feet to be converted. You will also need to know the conversion formula (that is, how many feet there are in one mile). You now have all of the information needed to solve the problem. This information could be documented as follows:

Problem Definition

Write a program to convert a given number of feet to miles.

Needed Input

The number of feet to be converted.

Needed Output

The number of miles in a given number of feet. The output will be formatted like this:

There are xxx.xx miles in xxxx.xx feet.

The programmer must understand the problem thoroughly and must also write the statement of the problem in a clear, concise style. Documenting the problem makes it apparent whether or not the problem is clearly understood. This written documentation should be shown to the potential user(s) of the program (if this is someone other than the programmer) in order to save time and ensure that everyone involved is satisfied with the end product.

Designing and Documenting a Solution

Algorithm
A sequence of steps needed to solve a problem.

Once the programming problem is thoroughly understood and the necessary input and output have been determined, it is time to write the steps needed to obtain the correct output from the input. The sequence of steps needed to solve a problem is called an **algorithm**. Every step needed to solve the problem is listed in the order in which it is to be performed.

Developing an algorithm is an important step in all programming. Indeed, computers are machines designed to execute algorithms. But algorithms are not used only in computer science—we use algorithms in all areas of our lives. In a chemistry course, for example, the steps that are followed when conducting an experiment constitute an algorithm. If you have ever bought an unassembled item, such as a bicycle, the instructions you followed when putting it together were an algorithm. We all know how frustrating it is when these instructions are incomplete or unclear.

Sometimes we are able to figure out what needs to be done even if the instructions are not precise. This is because humans are capable of drawing on past experiences to determine how to perform a task. For example, if the first step in assembling an object is to screw two sections of it together, we know that a screwdriver will be needed. We also know how to use the screwdriver to insert the screws properly. The instructions will not tell us how to do these minor steps; it is assumed that we already know them. However, computers cannot make assumptions or draw on past experiences as humans can. Therefore, an algorithm for a computer must not skip any steps.

Let's develop an algorithm for the problem of converting feet to miles. The steps could be stated like this:

1. Read the number of feet to be converted to miles.
2. Find the number of miles by dividing the number of feet by 5,280 (the number of feet in one mile).
3. Print the number of miles.

Learning Check

1. Any given problem has only one correct solution. True or false?
2. What is the first step in solving a problem?
3. What is the second problem-solving step?
4. A(n) _____ is a sequence of steps needed to solve a problem.
5. The steps in an algorithm can be listed in any order. True or false?

Answers

1. False. 2. Define and document the problem. 3. Design and document a solution. 4. algorithm 5. False.

STRUCTURED PROBLEM SOLVING

Top-Down Design

Using a computer to solve a problem is considerably different than most people think. The programmer needs to know only a little about the computer and how it works, but he or she must know a programming language. The most difficult aspect of programming is learning to organize solutions in a clear, concise way. This is where **top-down design** becomes helpful. Using top-down design in problem solving involves proceeding from the general to the specific. The programmer aims to solve the major problems first and worry about the specific details later.

The process used in top-down design is called **stepwise refinement,** which is the gradual breaking down of a problem into smaller and smaller subproblems. Sometimes this is referred to as the "divide-and-conquer" method, because it is easier to deal with a large job by completing it a small step at a time. This approach prevents the programmer from becoming overwhelmed by the size of the job at hand.

Top-down design
A method of problem solving that proceeds from the general to the specific.

Stepwise refinement
The process of dividing a problem into smaller and smaller subproblems.

A Sample Problem Top-down design can be applied to solving all types of everyday jobs. Making a pizza is a good example. First, the exact type of pizza must be decided upon. In this example, the desired output is a pepperoni and cheese pizza. This decision determines what ingredients are needed. For a pepperoni pizza, the input would look something like this (see also Figure 2–1):

Dough	Toppings
flour	sauce
water	cheese
yeast	pepperoni
salt	

Next, the steps in making the pizza must be listed. In Figure 2–1, the block labeled "Processing" represents these steps.

1. Preheat oven.
2. Prepare dough.
3. Put sauce and toppings on pizza.
4. Cook the pizza.

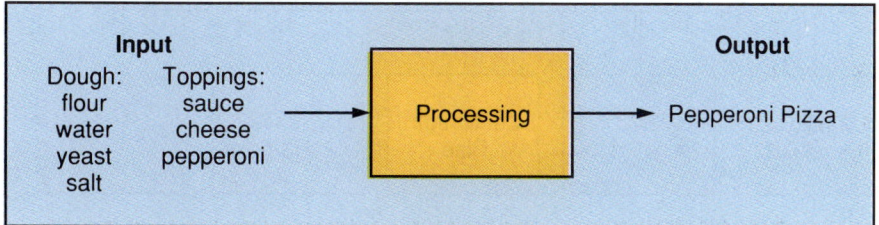

FIGURE 2–1
Input and Ouput for Making a Pizza

These steps are a basic algorithm for solving the problem of making a pizza. This algorithm will need to be further refined, however, by breaking each of the steps into many smaller steps. For example, Step 2 (Prepare dough) could be broken down like this:

1. Read the recipe for making dough.
2. Assemble the ingredients.
3. Measure each ingredient.
4. Mix the ingredients.
5. Let the dough rise.
6. Grease the pan.
7. Spread the dough in the pan.

Even some of these steps could be broken down further. For example, Step 3 could contain many substeps. All these substeps would still come under the heading "Processing" in Figure 2–1.

The diagram in Figure 2–2, called a **structure chart**, graphically represents the stepwise refinement process. Each level represents further refinement of the problem into smaller and smaller subproblems: Level 0

Structure chart
A diagram that shows how a programming problem solution has been divided into related subtasks.

FIGURE 2–2 Structure Chart for Making a Pizza

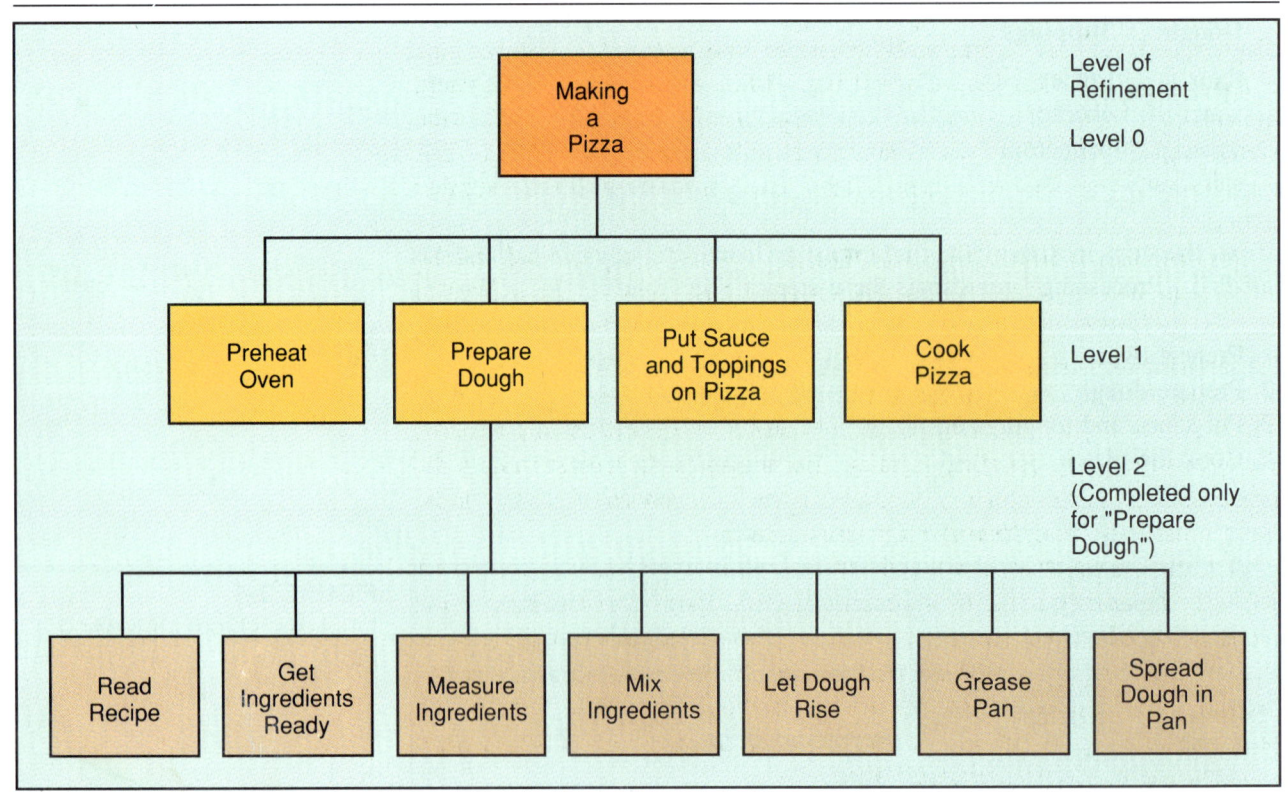

contains the general statement of the problem, Level 1 contains the first level of refinement, and so forth. In Figure 2–2, only one step in Level 1, "Prepare Dough," has been broken down further. Of course, each of these steps could be still further refined. There can be as many levels of refinement as needed to break a problem into manageable subproblems.

Top-Down vs. Bottom-Up Design

The opposite of top-down design is, naturally enough, **bottom-up design;** this term refers to building from the specific to the general. Let's see how these two methods might be applied to a given task, such as building a bookcase.

A top-down approach to this project is to first determine exactly what is wanted. Where is the bookcase to go? How large should it be? How many books should it be able to hold? What kind of wood will be used? What style should it be? Should the finished product be painted or stained? Once these questions (and probably others, depending on the user's needs) are answered, the list of the needed materials can be made. The needed input is tailored exactly to the desired output. Then the supplies are purchased, and the bookcase is built to the stated specifications.

A bottom-up approach to this project would be considerably different. It might start with the builder going down to the basement to see what kind of wood is on hand. Then the bookcase is built from the available materials. The style and overall size are determined as the project progresses. No diagram is drawn ahead of time. Whether the bookcase will be made of pine or oak depends on what kind of wood is available, not on what kind of wood fits into the decor of the room in which the bookcase will be used. When the bookcase is completed, it may or may not exactly meet the user's needs. The user may not like the way it looks, and it may not hold the desired number of books.

Both of these methods have advantages. The bottom-up method has the advantage of using materials already on hand and allowing the builder to start immediately with the actual building of the project. Programmers use this method when they start with an existing program (or part of a program) and attempt to modify it to meet a programming need other than that for which it was originally intended. If only minor modifications are needed, this is often a quick, practical solution. But it may be difficult to modify the program to meet the user's needs, and in the long run this method can be more time-consuming than starting from scratch.

Designing a program in a top-down fashion is more likely to result in a program that satisfies the user because it is designed specifically to meet the user's needs. Another advantage to top-down design is that it increases the likelihood that the programmer will be able to determine early in the programming process whether a given solution will work. It helps the programmer keep his or her eye on the overall program; this leads to more efficient use of the programmer's time.

Bottom-up design
A method of problem solving that proceeds from the specific to the general.

In actuality, most programs are developed using a combination of these two methods. The programmer usually develops a top-down solution to an entire programming problem, but some parts of large programs are nearly always written using the bottom-up method. For example, if the program needs to sort a list of data, there are many well-written and widely used sorting algorithms that can be inserted directly into the program where they are needed. There is no reason to spend time developing a new sorting algorithm if a perfectly acceptable one is readily available.

The Three Types of Program Structures

Computer scientists have determined that all programming problems can be solved using the needed combination of three basic program structures: the sequence, the decision step, and the loop.

A sequence is merely a series of statements that the computer executes in the order in which they are listed in the program. A program that adds three numbers together and determines their average is a sequence.

When a program contains a *decision step* or a *loop*, the program statements are no longer executed in the order in which they occur in the program. For example, certain statements may be skipped over, or a group of statements may be repeated many times. A decision step involves making a comparison. What is done next depends on the result of this comparison. For example, two numbers named X and Y might be compared. If X is the larger number, its value might be printed; otherwise, the value of Y might be printed. A loop is usually the easiest way to perform a repetitive task such as printing a list of several hundred names. A loop allows a series of instructions to be executed as many times as needed. Decision steps and loops are introduced in Chapter 5, and loops are explained in Chapter 6.

Learning Check

1. Top-down design always proceeds from the _____ to the _____.
2. Gradually breaking a problem into smaller and smaller subproblems is called _____ _____.
3. A structure chart may contain a maximum of three levels of refinement. True or false?
4. When a programmer starts with an existing program and modifies it to solve a new programming problem, he/she is using _____.
5. A _____ _____ is a diagram that depicts the levels of refinement of a problem solution.

Answers

1. general, specific 2. stepwise refinement 3. False; there is no maximum. 4. bottom-up design 5. structure chart

Flowcharting

One way of graphically representing the steps necessary to solve a programming problem is by using a **flowchart.** A flowchart shows the actual flow of the logic of a program, whereas a structure chart simply contains statements of the levels of refinement used to reach a solution. The meanings of different flowchart symbols follow. At this point, do not worry if you do not understand them all.

Flowchart
A graphic representation of the solution to a programming problem.

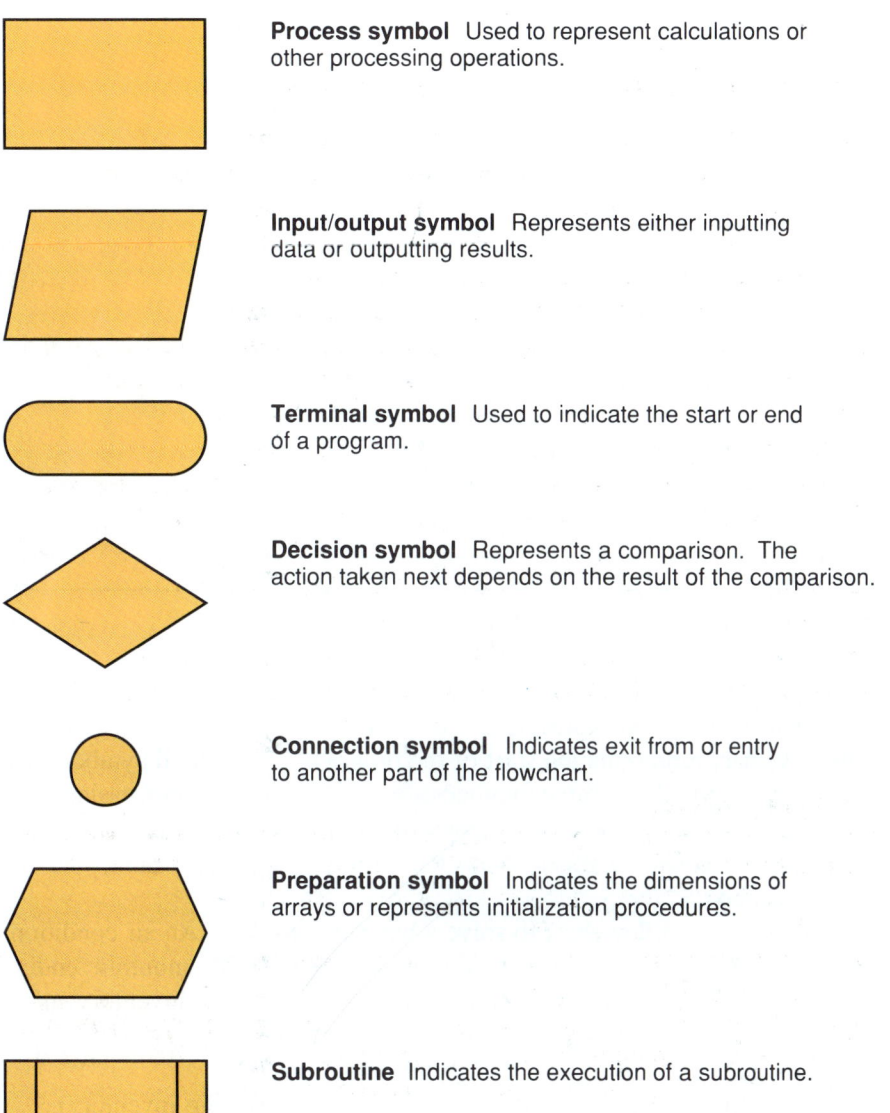

Process symbol Used to represent calculations or other processing operations.

Input/output symbol Represents either inputting data or outputting results.

Terminal symbol Used to indicate the start or end of a program.

Decision symbol Represents a comparison. The action taken next depends on the result of the comparison.

Connection symbol Indicates exit from or entry to another part of the flowchart.

Preparation symbol Indicates the dimensions of arrays or represents initialization procedures.

Subroutine Indicates the execution of a subroutine.

Figure 2–3 shows a sequence flowchart that solves the problem of adding three numbers together. As we already discussed, in a sequence, program statements are executed in the order in which they appear in the program.

FIGURE 2–3
Flowchart to Find a Sum

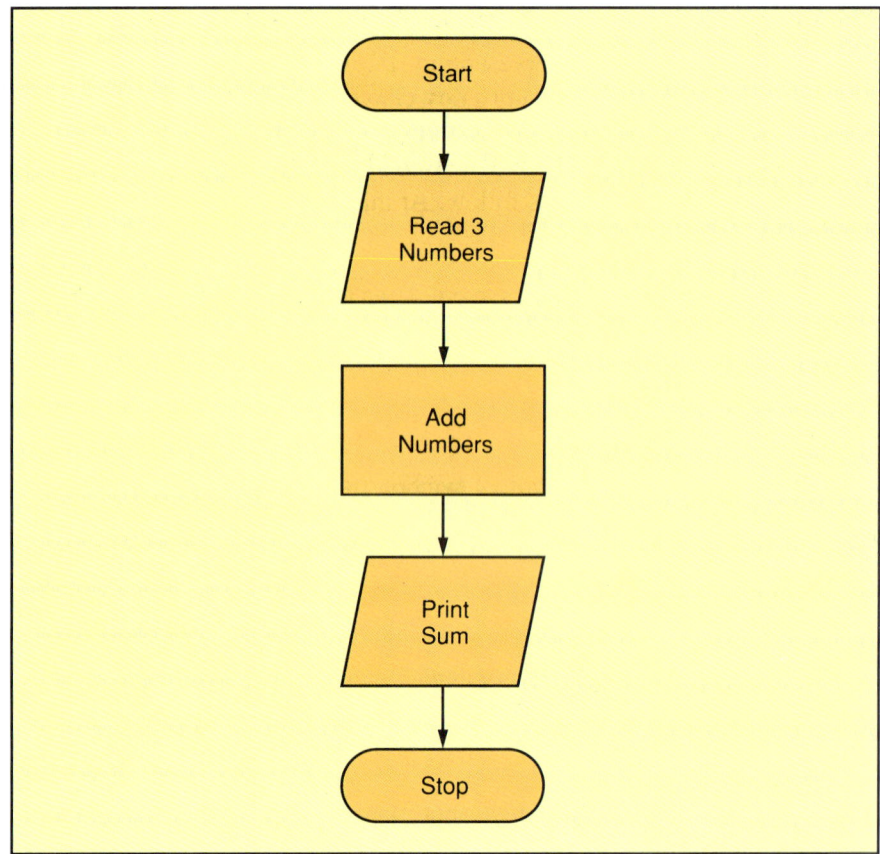

Notice that the arrows indicate the direction of flow. The first symbol in this flowchart represents the start of the program. The second symbol is an input step in which the three numbers are read. Next is the processing step; this is where the work of the program is done. In this case, the three numbers are added together. Then the resulting sum is printed, and the program stops.

Let's develop a flowchart to solve a business problem. An air conditioning company needs a program that will calculate its monthly ending inventory and the value of that inventory. The following inventory information will be used by the program:

1. The inventory at the beginning of the month (beginning inventory).
2. The number of air conditioning units received during the month (receipts).
3. The number of orders placed (orders).
4. The cost of each air conditioning unit (cost per unit).

The ending inventory can be calculated by using the following equation:

Ending Inventory = Beginning Inventory + Receipts − Orders

The value of the ending inventory can then be calculated:

Ending Value = Ending Inventory × Cost Per Unit

A flowchart can be drawn using these equations as a guideline (see Figure 2–4).

Pseudocoding

Pseudocode is an English-like description of the solution to a programming problem. It is a type of algorithm in that all of the steps needed to solve the problem must be listed. However, algorithms can be written to solve all types of problems, whereas pseudocode is developed specifically to solve programming problems. Unlike a flowchart, which is a graphic representation of the solution, pseudocode is similar to the actual program. It lets the programmer concentrate on a program's logic rather than the syntax, or grammatical rules, of a programming language. All of the logic structures present in programs can be written in pseudocode. There are no rigid rules concerning the pseudocode, but once you have developed a style, it is a good idea to follow it consistently.

Pseudocode
An English-like description of the solution to a programming problem.

The problem solution shown in the flowchart in Figure 2–3 could be written in pseudocode like this:

```
Begin
Read the three numbers x, y, z
Calculate sum of the three numbers
Print the sum
End
```

The pseudocode for the inventory problem in Figure 2–4 could be written as follows:

```
Begin
Read the beginning inventory
Read the number of receipts
Read the number of orders
Ending inventory = Beginning inventory + receipts − orders
Ending value = Ending inventory × cost per unit
Print the ending inventory
Print the value of the ending inventory
End
```

FIGURE 2–4
Inventory Flowchart

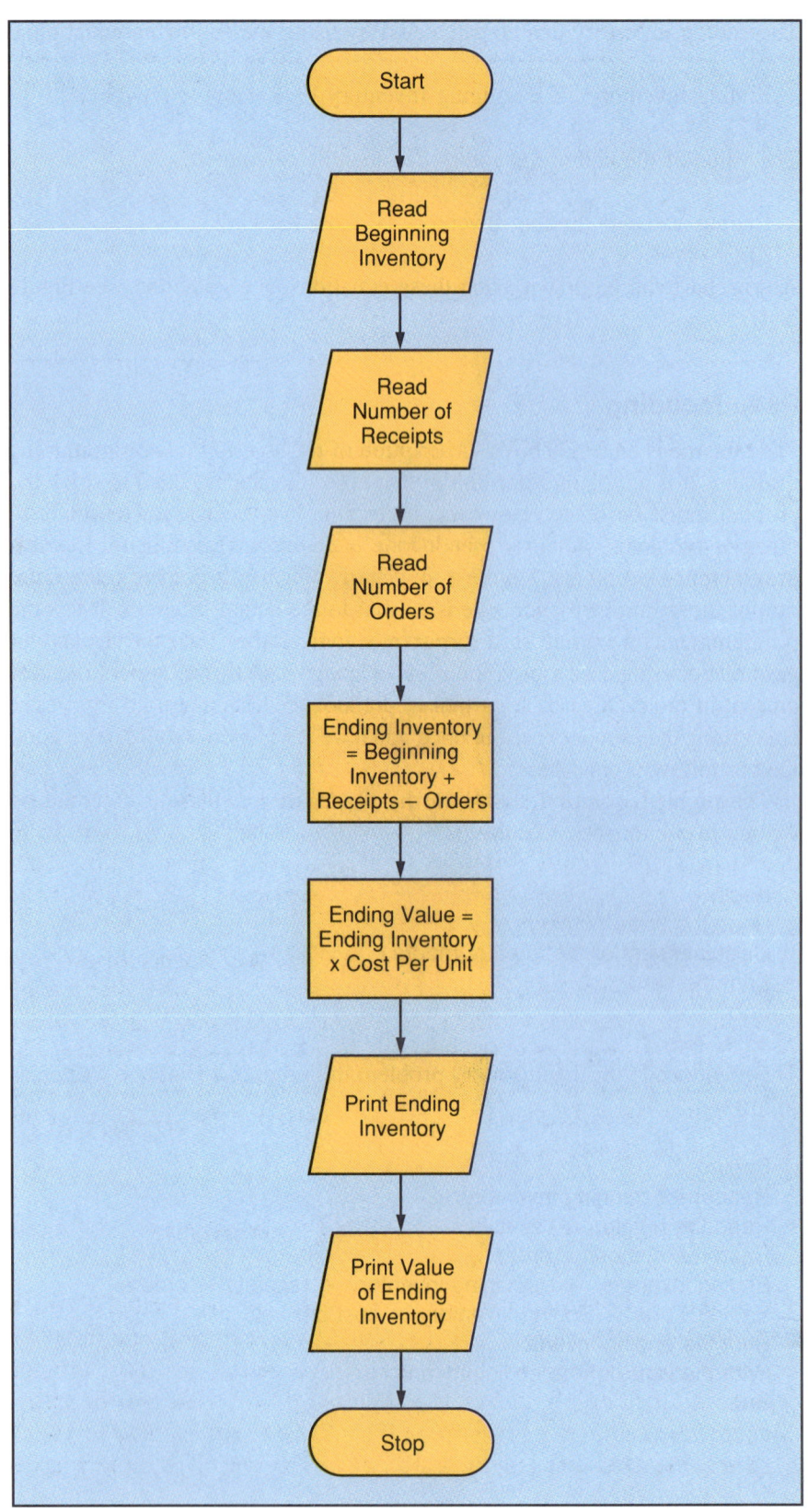

Learning Check

1. A(n) _____ is used to graphically represent a programming problem solution.
2. A(n) _____-shape symbol is always placed at the end of a flowchart
3. A(n) _____ is used to indicate a processing step in a flowchart.
4. An English-like description of a program's logic is given in _____.

Answers

1. flowchart 2. oval 3. rectangle 4. pseudocode

Writing and Documenting the Program

Once a solution to a programming problem has been developed and documented with a flowchart or pseudocode, writing or **coding** the solution in a programming language should be fairly simple, if the programmer is familiar with the language being used.

The programmer should spend some time checking the program before submitting it to the computer. In this process, called **desk checking,** the programmer carefully checks each statement to make sure it follows the syntax rules of the language. In this textbook, you will learn the syntax of BASIC. These rules may seem awkward at first, like the rules for any new language, but they will quickly become second nature. When a programmer desk-checks a program, he or she traces through the program by hand to determine if the logic is correct. This simple process often locates many errors that can easily be corrected before the program is submitted to the computer.

Like the original problem, the program must be documented thoroughly. This kind of documentation consists of comments placed within the program to explain the program to humans; the computer simply ignores these comments. Documenting a program thoroughly is especially important if someone other than the orginal programmer will need to modify an existing program at a later date. This textbook will present many examples of the correct use of comments in program.

Coding
The process of writing a problem solution in a programming language.

Desk checking
A method of tracing through a program by hand to check the correctness of the syntax and logic.

Submitting the Program to the Computer

When students first start programming, they tend to rush through solution development and coding. They want to enter their programs into the computer and see them run. This feedback is one of the most exciting aspects of programming; it is a good feeling to have mastery over such a complex, sophisticated machine. Nonetheless, the beginning student should not hurry the early steps of the programming process. A little time spent carefully developing a solution can help to avoid a lot of frustrating time in the computer lab attempting to correct program errors.

The method used to submit programs to the computer is highly dependent on the system being used. Chapter 3 will discuss this topic in general terms for the computer systems covered in this textbook. For more detailed instructions, consult your instructor, the documentation for your BASIC system, or some other appropriate source.

Debugging and Testing the Program

Structured programming techniques encourage the development of programs with easy-to-follow logic and fewer errors than unstructured programs. Nonetheless, programs of any significant length virtually always contain some errors, and correcting them can account for a large portion of time spent in program development.

Debug
To locate and correct program errors.

Debugging is the process of locating and correcting program errors. The most common errors made by a beginning programmer are simple typing mistakes. Carefully proofreading program statements as they are typed can prevent the majority of these errors.

Once the computer is able to run your program, you will need to test it with a variety of data to determine if the results are always correct. A program may obtain correct results when it is run with one set of data, but incorrect results when run with different data.

Typing errors manifest themselves differently than logic errors. If a typing error is made, the computer usually will not be able to execute the program and an error message will be printed. If the programmer makes a logic error, the program may stop executing prematurely, or it may execute properly but yield incorrect results. Once errors are corrected in a program, the programmer must remember to also revise any corresponding documentation.

Debugging and testing techniques will be mentioned throughout this text, and will be discussed extensively in Chapter 11.

Learning Check

1. _____ is the process of writing a problem solution in a programming language.
2. Tracing through a program by hand in an attempt to locate errors is called _____ _____.
3. The grammatical rules of a language are its _____.
4. _____ is the process of locating and correcting program errors.
5. The computer uses comments to tell it how to execute a program. True or false?

Aswers

1. Coding 2. desk checking 3. syntax 4. Debugging 5. False.

STRUCTURED PROBLEM SOLVING

Summary Points

- There are five basic steps in the programming process
  - —Define and document the problem.
  - —Design and document a solution.
  - —Write and document the program.
  - —Submit the program to the computer.
  - —Test and debug the program, and revise the documentation if necessary.
- Before a problem can be solved, it must be thoroughly understood.
- A clear statement of the problem should be written, including the needed input and output.
- An algorithm should be developed that lists all steps necessary to solve the problem.
- Top-down design is an efficient way of developing a problem solution. This method proceeds from the general to the specific, allowing the programmer to concentrate on major problems first and deal with the details later.
- Stepwise refinement is used to divide a large problem into smaller subproblems.
- Structure charts graphically represent how a problem solution has been broken down into modules.
- In bottom-up design, the programmer proceeds from the specific to the general. Modifying an already existing program (or portion of a program) is an example of bottom-up design.
- When developing most programs, the programmer uses a combination of top-down and bottom-up design.
- Flowcharts are graphic representations of problem solutions. Each symbol in the flowchart has a specific meaning.
- Pseudocode is an English-like description of the solution to a programming problem.
- The actual process of writing a program is called coding, and it is fairly simple if the programmer has already developed a clear solution. After a program is coded, it should be checked for errors by tracing through it by hand (desk-checking).
- The method used to submit a program to the computer depends on the computer system being used. After a program is entered into the computer, the computer will attempt to execute it. If there are any errors, they must be corrected. Once the computer is able to execute the program, it should be tested with a wide variety of data. The results should be carefully checked for accuracy.

Review Questions

1. List the five steps in developing a solution to a programming problem.
2. Think of a task you have performed. What input was needed to complete this task? What was the output? Develop an algorithm for the task.

3. The first step in problem solving is to define and document the problem. What is meant by defining the problem?

4. Why should the programmer consult with the program user when developing a program?

5. Give a definition of the term *algorithm.*

6. Write an algorithm that will evaluate the following expression:

$$\frac{14 + 8}{2} \times \frac{3}{16}$$

7. Sally had $20.00. She went to a movie that cost $3.50 and bought popcorn for $1.10. She then bought three paperback books for $3.25 each plus 6 percent sales tax. Write an algorithm that will determine how much money Sally has left.

8. Complete the structure chart in Figure 2–2 by breaking down the three remaining modules in Level 1 (Preheat Oven, Put Sauce and Toppings on Pizza, and Cook Pizza). Follow the pattern that was used to refine the module titled Prepare Dough.

9. Write an algorithm for accessing the computer system that you will be using for this class. If you don't know the steps necessary to access the system, check with your instructor. Be specific. For example, Step 1 might read, "Turn on the terminal by flipping the rocker switch on the left side of the monitor."

10. Explain how stepwise refinement is used in top-down design.

11. Explain the difference between top-down and bottom-up program design.

12. Explain how you might write a term paper for a class using top-down design.

13. Explain how you might write a term paper using bottom-up design.

14. Compare the two methods of term-paper writing discussed in Questions 12 and 13. List several advantages of each method. Which method do you think will result in the best paper? Why?

15. Develop a flowchart for the process of writing a term paper.

16. Write pseudocode for the process of writing a term paper.

17. List and explain the purpose of each of the seven flowcharting symbols discussed in this chapter.

18. How is a flowchart different from pseudocode?

19. How is debugging a program different from testing it?

20. What is meant by desk-checking a program? Why is this a good idea?

CHAPTER 3

THE FUNDAMENTALS OF BASIC PROGRAMMING

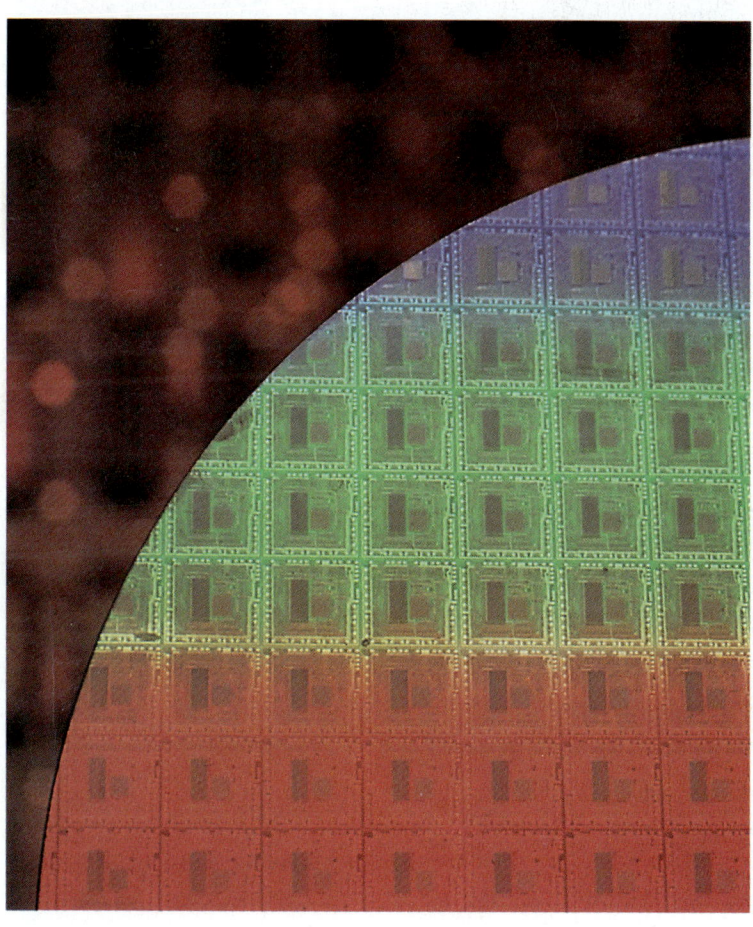

Objectives

After studying this chapter, you will be able to:

- Use the BASIC commands NEW, LIST, SAVE, LOAD, and RUN.
- Differentiate between numeric and character string constants and give examples of each.
- Use numeric and character string constants correctly in programs.
- Explain the purpose of line numbers, and use them correctly when writing programs.
- Explain the purposes of the REM, LET, PRINT, and END statements.
- Use the REM, LET, PRINT, and END statements correctly when writing programs.
- Evaluate arithmetic expressions according to the hierarchy of operations.

Outline

Overview
BASIC Commands
   Preparing to Enter a New
     Program
   Listing a Program
   Saving a Program
   Loading a Program
   Executing a Program
Line Numbers
BASIC Statement Components
   Constants
     Numeric Constants
     Character String Constants
   Variables

Numeric Variables
String Variables
Reserved Words
Simple BASIC Statements
   Documenting a Program
   The Assignment Statement
     Arithmetic Expressions
     Hierarchy of Operations
   The PRINT Statement
     Printing the Value of a
       Variable
     Printing Literals
     Printing the Value of an
       Expression

The END Statement
A Programming Problem
   Problem Definition
   Solution Design
   The Program
   Avoiding Common Programming
     Mistakes
Summary Points
Review Questions
Debugging Exercises
Additional Programming Problems
   Level 1
   Level 2
   Level 3

Overview

When programming in BASIC, it is necessary to use several different types of commands. BASIC commands are used by the programmer to manipulate BASIC programs. They allow the computer to perform such functions as saving a program on disk or clearing a portion of the computer's main memory so that a new program can be entered. The five commands discussed here are NEW, LIST, RUN, SAVE, and OLD (or LOAD); for others, see the BASIC documentation for the computer that you are using.

A second type of commands are called BASIC statements. These are commands placed in the BASIC program itself that tell the computer to perform a task, such as printing some output on the terminal screen. The four BASIC statements covered in this chapter are REM, LET, PRINT, and END. These statements are the foundation for program writing. Therefore, it is important that you clearly understand how to use them. Bear in mind, however, that BASIC commands and statements vary somewhat from one system to another.

BASIC Commands

Immediate-mode command
A command executed as soon as the RETURN key is pressed; it is used without line numbers.

In order to enter, save, execute, or print a program, the programmer must interact with the computer's operating system. BASIC commands are used when performing these tasks. They are usually entered as **immediate-mode** (or **direct-mode**) **commands** that are executed as soon as the carriage control (RETURN or ENTER) key is pressed. Table 3–1 lists the correct formats for some common BASIC commands that can be used with the computers covered in this textbook.

Preparing to Enter a New Program

Before a new program is submitted to the computer, a portion of the computer's main memory must be prepared to store the new program. The NEW command clears a small portion of the computer's main memory by telling the computer to erase any program currently in memory and prepare for a new program to be entered. After typing the NEW command, you can start entering a new program. On the VAX, the name of the new program is also assigned in the NEW command. Therefore,

```
NEW PROGRAM1
```

will not only clear a portion of main memory but also assign the name PROGRAM1 to the new program that is going to be entered. In BASIC used on other systems covered in this text, the command is entered as follows:

```
NEW
```

The program is not assigned a name until it is saved on disk.

Listing a Program

After typing in a program, you may want to view the finished product. To see the program displayed on the terminal screen, use the LIST command.

TABLE 3–1 Common BASIC Commands

PURPOSE	VAX	APPLE	IBM/MICROSOFT	MACINTOSH/ MICROSOFT*
Erase current program from main memory	NEW filename	NEW	NEW	NEW
List a program in main memory	LIST	LIST	LIST	LIST
Execute a program	RUN or RUNNH	RUN	RUN	RUN
Store program on disk	SAVE	SAVE filename	SAVE "filename"	SAVE "filename"
Retrieve program from disk	OLD filename	LOAD filename	LOAD "filename"	LOAD "filename"

*For the Macintosh, commands may also be chosen from menus. See Appendix I for details.

Scrolling
The process by which lines of text move vertically on the terminal screen.

If you have a short program, LIST will display the entire program on the screen. If the program has more lines than the screen is able to display, however, the lines will **scroll** (move vertically) off the top of the screen. For example, if your program has 80 lines but your screen can display only 24 lines at a time, the first 56 lines will scroll off the top of the terminal screen before you can get a chance to read them.

You can solve this problem in one of two ways. One is to suppress the scrolling, that is, to "freeze" the listing temporarily. The method used to do this depends upon the computer system being used, but usually involves pressing one or two keys to freeze the screen and then repeating the same process to resume the listing. Table 3–2 explains how to stop the scrolling for each of the computer systems covered in this textbook. The other method is to display only a part of the program at a time by specifying the line numbers of the statements to be displayed. For example,

```
LIST 150-170
```

will list only lines 150 through 170 of the program currently in main memory.

Saving a Program

After writing a program, usually you will not want to lose it when the computer is turned off or when you enter another program. Because the computer's main memory is used only for temporary storage, you must copy a program that you wish to save to secondary storage. Use the SAVE command to do this. In VAX BASIC the SAVE command is entered like this:

```
SAVE
```

This will cause the current program in main memory to be saved under the file name given in the NEW command.

TABLE 3–2 Keys Necessary to Stop Scrolling

COMPUTER	KEYS USED
VAX (VT-100)	Press NO SCROLL key
Apple	Hold CTRL and S keys down at the same time
IBM/Microsoft	Hold CTRL and NUMLOCK keys down at the same time
Macintosh/Microsoft	*

*See Appendix I for details.

On the other systems used in this book, the SAVE command requires the programmer to supply the name under which the program is to be saved. For example,

```
SAVE PROGRAM1
```

can be used to save the program currently in main memory under the name PROGRAM1. As shown in Table 3–1, some systems (such as the IBM and Macintosh) require that the file name be placed in double quotation marks. (The closing quotation mark is optional.)

```
SAVE "PROGRAM1"
```

Loading a Program

At times you will want to transfer a program from secondary storage to the computer's main memory. This is necessary if you want to edit the program, and on many sytems it is also necessary if you want to execute the program. In VAX BASIC, the OLD command is used to move a designated program from secondary storage into the computer's main memory. This command also erases any program that was previously in main memory. The name of the program to be loaded must be stated in the command. For example, if you needed to load a program named PROGRAM1, the command would look like this:

```
OLD PROGRAM1
```

On the other systems covered in this book, the LOAD command is used instead of the OLD command and works in the same way. The following statement would load PROGRAM1 into main memory on these systems:

```
LOAD PROGRAM1
```

As with the SAVE command, some systems require the name to be placed in double quotation marks.

Executing a Program

After a BASIC program has been entered, it can be executed by using the RUN command. There are two variations of this command on the VAX system: RUN and RUNNH. Both of these commands cause the program in main memory to be executed, but RUN displays a heading giving the time of day and other information in addition to the program output. Using the RUNNH command (short for RUN-No Headings) suppresses these headings. Figure 3–1 shows the listing and output for a program that has been run

FIGURE 3–1 Program Demonstrating Difference between the RUN and RUNNH Commands

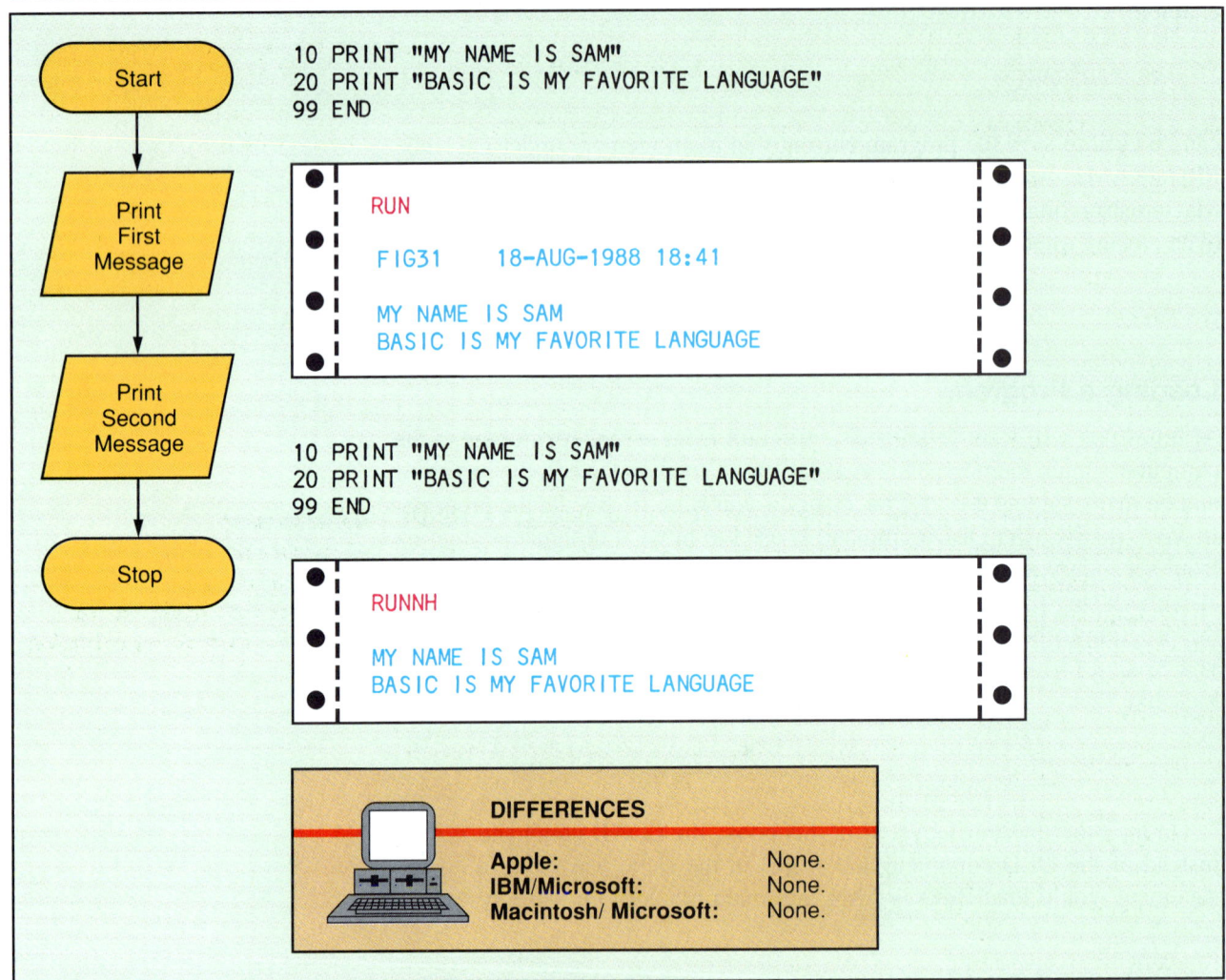

using both methods. Programs presented in this textbook were executed using the RUNNH command.

Line Numbers

Indirect mode
The mode in which statements are not executed until the RUN command is given. The statements must have line numbers.

As we mentioned earlier, BASIC commands are executed in immediate or direct mode. BASIC statements, or instructions, may be executed in either direct mode or **indirect mode**. In indirect mode, the statements are not executed until the RUN (or RUNNH) command is given. **Line numbers** tell the computer that the statements following them are to be executed in indirect mode. Therefore, the computer does not execute these statements until it is instructed to do so.

Learning Check

1. The _____ command causes a program in main memory to be displayed on the screen.
2. In _____ mode, a command is executed as soon as the carriage control key is pressed.
3. _____ occurs when lines of text move from the bottom to the top of the terminal screen.
4. The _____ command tells the computer to erase any program currently in main memory.
5. The _____ command allows a program in main memory to be copied to secondary storage.

Answers

1. LIST 2. direct or immediate 3. Scrolling 4. NEW 5. SAVE

Line numbers also determine the sequence of execution of BASIC statements. (Later on, we will learn ways to alter the order in which statements are executed). Execution starts at the lowest line number and continues in ascending numerical order to the highest number. Line numbers must be integers within a range determined by the system being used (Table 3–3). No commas or embedded spaces can be included in a line number. Table 3–4 contains examples of valid and invalid line numbers. Line numbers in BASIC are often considered labels, because they refer to specific statements in the program. In Figure 3–1, for example, the number 10 is the label for the statement PRINT "MY NAME IS SAM".

In VAX BASIC and Macintosh/Microsoft BASIC, line numbers are optional. These computers could execute both of the following program segments without any problems:

Line number
A number preceding a BASIC statement which is used to reference that statement and determine its order of execution.

```
10 LET NAM$ = "SAM"              LET NAM$ = "SAM"
20 LET MESS$ = "MY NAME IS "     LET MESS$ = "MY NAME IS "
30 PRINT MESS$,NAM$              PRINT MESS$,NAM$
99 END                           END
```

TABLE 3–3 Minimum and Maximum Line Numbers

COMPUTER	LOWEST NUMBER	HIGHEST NUMBER
VAX*	1	32767
Apple	0	63999
IBM/Microsoft	0	65529
Macintosh/Microsoft*	0	65529

*Line numbers are not required.

TABLE 3-4 Valid and Invalid Examples of Line Numbers

VALID	INVALID
10 PRINT "MY NAME IS SAM"	10.5 PRINT "MY NAME IS SAM"
20 LET NME$ = "SAM"	2,000 LET NME$ = "SAM"
99 END	9 99 END

However, because line numbers are required in the other implementations of BASIC discussed here and can be helpful when writing programs, they will be used in the programs in this text.

Line numbers do not have to be in increments of 1. In fact, it is best to use increments of 10 or 20 in order to allow for insertion of lines at a later time if necessary. Instructions need not be entered in ascending numerical order; the computer will rearrange them in this order for execution. This feature of BASIC makes it easy to insert new lines between existing lines. For example, if you type:

```
10 LET NAM$ = "SAM"
20 PRINT MESS$,NAM$
99 END
```

and then realize you forgot a statement that should go between lines 10 and 20, you can simply add the needed statement like this:

```
15 LET MESS$ = "MY NAME IS "
```

Now when the program is listed, it will appear like this:

```
10 LET NAM$ = "SAM"
15 LET MESS$ = "MY NAME IS"
20 PRINT MESS$,NAM$
99 END
```

Because we incremented the line numbers by 10 in this example, it was a simple matter to insert a line. If the statements had been numbered in increments of 1 instead, we would have had to retype the entire program in order to insert a line. For this reason, programmers generally use increments of at least 10.

If you find that you have made an error on a line, simply retype the line number and the correct BASIC statement. This procedure corrects the error because, if two lines are entered with the same line number, the computer saves and executes the most recently typed one. To demonstrate this fact, assume that line 160 should print SUM, but the following was typed instead:

```
160 PRINT SUN
```

THE FUNDAMENTALS OF BASIC PROGRAMMING   43

To correct this, simply retype line 160:

```
160 PRINT SUM
```

The computer will discard the current line 160 and replace it with the newest version of line 160.

BASIC Statement Components

A program is a sequence of instructions that tells the computer how to solve a problem. Figure 3–2 is an example of a BASIC program that calculates the gross pay of an employee who worked 40 hours at $4.50 per hour.

FIGURE 3–2   Program to Compute Gross Pay

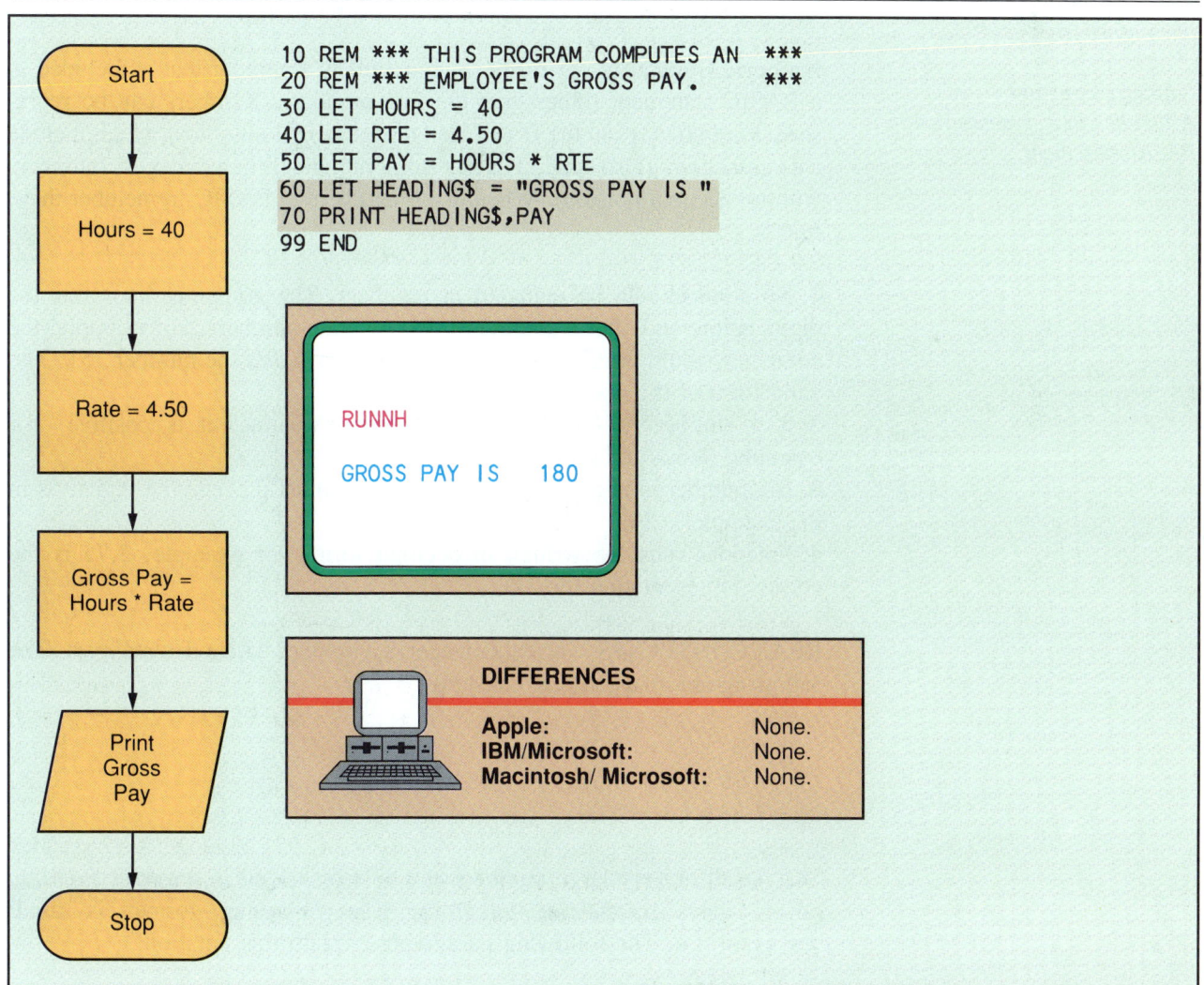

Each line in a BASIC program is called a BASIC statement. All BASIC statements are composed of special programming commands (key words recognized by the BASIC system) and elements of the language: constants, variables, and operators. Basic statements are divided into two general categories: executable statements and nonexecutable statements. Whether or not a line is executable is determined by the command used in the statement. In the example in Figure 3–2, the first two lines of the program are nonexecutable (indicated by the word REM). The computer simply ignores these statements, skipping over them and moving on to the next statement. All of the remaining lines of the program in Figure 3–2 are executable. This means that the computer does something when these lines are encountered.

Constants

Constant
A value that cannot change during program execution.

Constants are values that do not change during the execution of a program. There are two kinds of constants; numeric and character string.

Numeric constant
A number that is contained in a BASIC statement.

Numeric Constants   A **numeric constant** is a number that is included in a BASIC statement (other than the line number). Numbers can be represented in two ways in the BASIC language: as real numbers, which include a decimal point (also called floating-point numbers), or as integers (numbers with no decimal portion). When using numbers in BASIC, remember these rules:

1. No commas can be included in numbers. The computer interprets the digits before and after a comma as two separate numbers. For example, the computer would interpret 3,751 as the number 3 *and* the number 751. The valid form of the number is 3751.
2. If a number has no sign, the computer assumes it is positive. For example, 386 is the same as +386.
3. If a number is negative, the negative sign must precede the digits, as in the example −21.
4. Fractions must be written in decimal form. For example, 2.75 is the correct representation for 2¾.

REAL CONSTANTS   A real constant is a number with a decimal part. The following are all valid real constants:

```
   6.0       6.782
    .95      0.58
 -7.234     -0.09
```

Very small or very large numbers can be represented in *scientific notation* (also called *exponential notation*). The following format is used: ±x.xxxxE±n. The following paragraphs explain this notation.

- The symbol ± represents the sign of the number, positive or negative. The plus sign is optional with positive numbers, but the minus sign is mandatory for negative numbers.
- The symbol x.xxxx is called the *mantissa*, and it represents a number that may be carried to a maximum of eight decimal places.
- The letter E represents the words "times 10 to the power of."
- The expression ±n is the positive or negative exponential value.

For example, the number 3.56E−1 would be 0.356 in regular decimal form.

The following are examples of real constants, some in regular decimal form and some in exponential notation:

```
9.84103E-06     -37.7
6.64            4E+8
8.0E+2          -12543
```

INTEGER CONSTANTS   An integer constant is a number with no decimal portion. The following numbers are examples of integer constants:

```
29      123434
3432    -8
205     -101
```

Character String Constants   A **character string** constant is simply a collection of symbols called **alphanumeric data**. These can include any combination of letters, numbers, and special characters including dashes, commas, blanks, and others. The character string is enclosed in double quotation marks.

You can include single quotation marks within a string constant delimited by double quotation marks. The following are examples of valid character string constants delimited by double quotation marks:

"He said, 'Good morning.' "
"This is a string constant."
"Gary's Tennis Racket"

The following character string constant is invalid:

"The letter "A" is a vowel."

In the last example, the system would recognize the double quotation mark before the letter A as indicating the end of the string. Actually, the quotation mark at the end of the line is supposed to indicate the end of the string. This character string constant could be correctly written as:

"The letter 'A' is a vowel."

Character string
A group of alphanumeric characters enclosed in quotation marks.

Alphanumeric data
Any combination of letters, digits, and/or special characters.

The length of a string constant is determined by counting all of its characters. For example, the two character strings below will not be stored in the computer in the same way:

"SATURDAY   "
"SATURDAY"

The first string will be stored as SATURDAY plus three blanks (the computer can store a blank, just as it can store any other character). The second string will be stored simply as SATURDAY. Therefore, the computer will store eleven characters for the first string and only eight for the second one.

The maximum number of characters allowed in a character string depends upon the system being used. In all of the BASIC systems used in this textbook, the maximum character string length is 255 characters.

Learning Check

1. What are the two parts of a BASIC instruction?
2. The line numbers 101 and 20 are valid in BASIC. True or false?
3. Which of the following are not valid numeric constants?
   a. 354-6957
   b. 1369
   c. 109,493
   d. 12
4. Which of the following are not valid character string constants?
   a. "May 16, 1985"
   b. "Miami, Florida"
   c. '123"
   d. George Smith
5. If two instructions are typed with the same line number, the computer retains only the second. True or false?

Answers

1. A line number and a BASIC statement. 2. True. 3. a and c. 4. c and d. 5. True.

Variables

Before we explain BASIC programming any further, it is important that you understand how data is stored in the primary storage unit of a computer. To visualize a computer's primary storage unit, imagine a block of post office boxes. Each box has an assigned number that acts as an address for that particular box (see Figure 3–3). The addresses of these boxes always remain the same, but their contents will almost certainly change over a period of time. Similarly, the primary storage unit in a computer is divided into many separate storage locations, each with a specific address. A storage location

THE FUNDAMENTALS OF BASIC PROGRAMMING   47

FIGURE 3–3 Post Office Boxes are Similar to Variables

containing a value that can change during program execution is referred to as a **variable**. A variable can contain only one value at a time; when a new value is assigned to a variable, the old value is lost.

These storage locations can be referenced by their addresses, just as post office boxes can be referred to by the number assigned to them. In machine-language programming, a storage location is always referenced by its actual address. It is a difficult task for the programmer to keep track of the address of each location used by a particular program.

Fortunately, in BASIC (and other high-level languages) the programmer is allowed to assign names to storage locations and then refer to each location by its name. In the example in Figure 3–4, HOURS and RTE are **variable names** used to identify specific storage locations. The value (or contents) of the locations named HOURS and RTE are 40 and 4.50 respectively.

The number of characters allowed in a variable name differs from system to system, but most BASIC systems permit variable names of various lengths. Therefore, the programmer can use **descriptive variable names**, that is, names that describe the values they identify. Good programming habits include the use of descriptive variable names, because such names make programs easy to read. For example, the name STUDENT is more descriptive than ST.

There are some BASIC systems, however, that recognize only the first two characters of a variable name (see Table 3–5). These systems would recognize the variables QUANTITY and QUEUE as being identical, for example. When using these computers, the programmer must make sure that the first two characters of each variable name are unique.

Variable
A storage location containing a value that can change during program execution.

Variable name
The name used to represent the memory location where a variable is stored.

Descriptive variable name
A variable name that describes what it represents.

FIGURE 3–4
Variables in Storage

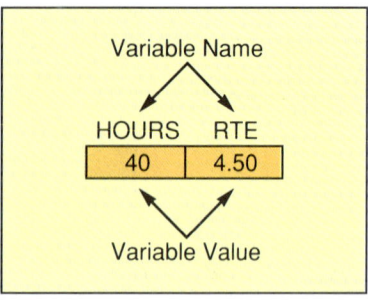

TABLE 3–5 Maximum Number of Characters Recognized in Variable Names

COMPUTER	MAXIMUM ALLOWED	MAXIMUM RECOGNIZED
VAX	31	31
Apple	238	First 2
IBM/Microsoft	Any length	First 40
Macintosh/Microsoft	40	40

The term *program variable* is used to indicate a variable used internally by the program, as compared to *input variables* (those variables that contain values input to the program) and *output variables* (those variables that contain values to be output).

Variables are also classified as *numeric* or *string*. Each of these types will be discussed here.

Numeric variable
A variable used to store a number.

Numeric Variables A **numeric variable** is used to store a number that is either supplied to the computer by the programmer or internally calculated during program execution. A numeric variable name must begin with a letter, followed by letters and/or digits with no embedded blanks. Some BASIC systems also allow other characters, such as the period (.) or the underline character (_), to be included in variable names. On the VAX system, periods may be placed anywhere within a variable name but must not be the first character. Periods are often useful in dividing a variable name in order to make it more readable. For example, the amount of city taxes owed could be represented by the variable name CITY.TAX rather than CITYTAX.

As with numeric constants, there are both integer and real numeric variables. Integer variable names have a percent sign (%) as the last character. Table 3–6 shows some valid and invalid variable names for real and integer numbers.

TABLE 3–6 Valid and Invalid Numeric Variable Names

VALID	INVALID	AND REASON
SUM (real)	225	(Variable name must start with a letter)
M1% (integer)	M2&	(No special characters allowed except those used to designate type of variable)
D6E7 (real)	RT%DAY	(The percent sign must be the last symbol)
BIG47 (real)	B2$	($ symbol used to designate a string variable)
AMT% (integer)	D M6	(Variable name cannot include a blank)

It is possible to assign an integer to a real variable because the computer can convert the integer to a real number without changing its value. For example, the integer 17 can be changed to the real number 17.0. The reverse is not true, however; if a real number is assigned to an integer variable, part of the number is lost. For example, it would be impossible to store 17.65 accurately as an integer. On the VAX system, if a real value is assigned to an integer variable, the value is cut off at the decimal point. Therefore, if the value 17.65 were assigned to the variable X%, it would be stored as 17.

String Variables A **string variable** is used to store a character string, such as a name, an address or a social security number. As with numeric variables, string variables can store only one value at a time.

String variable
A variable used to store a character string.

A string variable name begins with a letter followed by letters or digits and must be terminated with a dollar sign ($). Most computers allow for long, descriptive names, even though some computers recognize only the first two characters of the name. However, all computers require the first character to be alphabetic and the last character to be a dollar sign, which is what enables the computer to distinguish it as a string variable name. Table 3–7 gives examples of string variable names.

In the sample program in Figure 3–2, lines 60 and 70 contain the string variable name HEADING$:

```
60 LET HEADING$ = "GROSS PAY IS "
70 PRINT HEADING$,PAY
```

In line 60, the character string GROSS PAY IS is assigned to the location named HEADING$; in line 70, the value stored in location HEADING$ is printed.

Reserved Words

Certain words have specific meanings to the BASIC compiler or interpreter. These are **reserved words**, which cannot be used as variable names. Table 3–8 lists a few of the most common reserved words. See Appendix A for

Reserved word
A word that has a specific meaning to the BASIC system and therefore cannot be used as a variable name.

TABLE 3–7 Valid and Invalid String Variable Names

VALID	INVALID AND REASON	
C$	$	(First character must be a letter)
HEADING$	4$	(First character must be a letter)
DAY$	E2%	(A string variable name must have a $ as the last character)
EMP$	EM$P	(The $ symbol must be the last character)
M1$	M 1$	(No blanks allowed)
SSNO$	SS-NO$	(Hyphen not allowed)

TABLE 3–8 Common Reserved Words

ABS	EXP	IF	ON	RETURN	TAB
BASE	FN	INPUT	OPEN	RND	TAN
CALL	FOR	INT	PRINT	SIN	THEN
COS	ELSE	LET	PUT	SGN	TO
DATA	GET	LIST	READ	SQR	UNTIL
DEF	GO	LOG	REM	STEP	VAL
DIM	GOSUB	NEXT	RESTORE	STOP	WHILE
END	GOTO				

lists of reserved words for the various BASIC implementations covered in this text.

Some systems, such as the Apple, scan all BASIC statements for reserved words. Any reserved words embedded in a variable name are seen by the computer as reserved words and cannot be used in a variable name. For example, STORE cannot be used as a variable name on such a system because it contains the reserved word TO.

Simple BASIC Statements

The remainder of this chapter discusses four elementary BASIC statements that will be necessary in writing simple programs: REM, LET, PRINT, and END.

Documenting a Program

Documentation
Comments that explain a program to people.

The REM, or remark, statement provides information for the programmer or anyone else reading the program. It is ignored by the computer; in other words, it is a nonexecutable statement. The information is referred to as **documentation,** and its function is to explain to humans the purpose of the program, what the variable names represent, or any special instructions. Because REM statements do not affect program execution, they can be placed anywhere in the program. The only restriction is that the program line must begin with the reserved word REM.

The general format of the REM statement is

line# REM comment

The comment can be any statement that the programmer regards as appropriate documentation. The word REM must be included exactly as shown; ''line#'' indicates that a valid line number must be inserted here.

Learning Check

1. How many values can be stored in a storage location at one time?
2. Which of the following are not valid numeric variable names?
   a. 32
   b. A3%
   c. SUM
   d. BC
   e. PAY
   f. X + Y%
   g. 3RD
   h. DAY$
3. Which of the following are not valid string variable names?
   a. PERSN$
   b. 2$
   c. 4SALE$
   d. BIRTHDAY
   e. Z*A$
   f. PLACE$
   g. ADDRESS$
   h. 4PRICE
4. State whether each of the following would be stored under a numeric or string variable name.
   a. COMPUTER
   b. 1369.48
   c. 379-49-5044
   d. 21
5. A string variable is identified by the use of the _____ _____ as the last character of the variable name.

Answers

1. One. 2. a; f; g; h. 3. b; c; d; e; h. 4. a. String. b. Numeric. c. String. d. Numeric. 5. dollar sign

---

Figure 3–5 is a sample program that uses the REM statement. Lines 10 and 20 describe the purpose of the program. Lines 30 through 70 explain the major variables that are used throughout the program. These seven lines are helpful to someone who may be reading the program but who is not the original programmer. Notice that line 80 contains no comment after the REM statement. This line improves readability by separating the opening remarks from the executable statements listed later in the program.

Notice also the asterisks that surround the comments. Although this device is simply a matter of personal taste, many programmers use it to make the REM statement easily identifiable when the programmer is looking through long program listings.

Remarks may also be placed in the body of the program in order to explain a BASIC instruction or a series of instructions. For example, if an

52 BASIC PROGRAMMING TODAY, A STRUCTURED APPROACH

FIGURE 3–5 Example of a Well-Documented Program

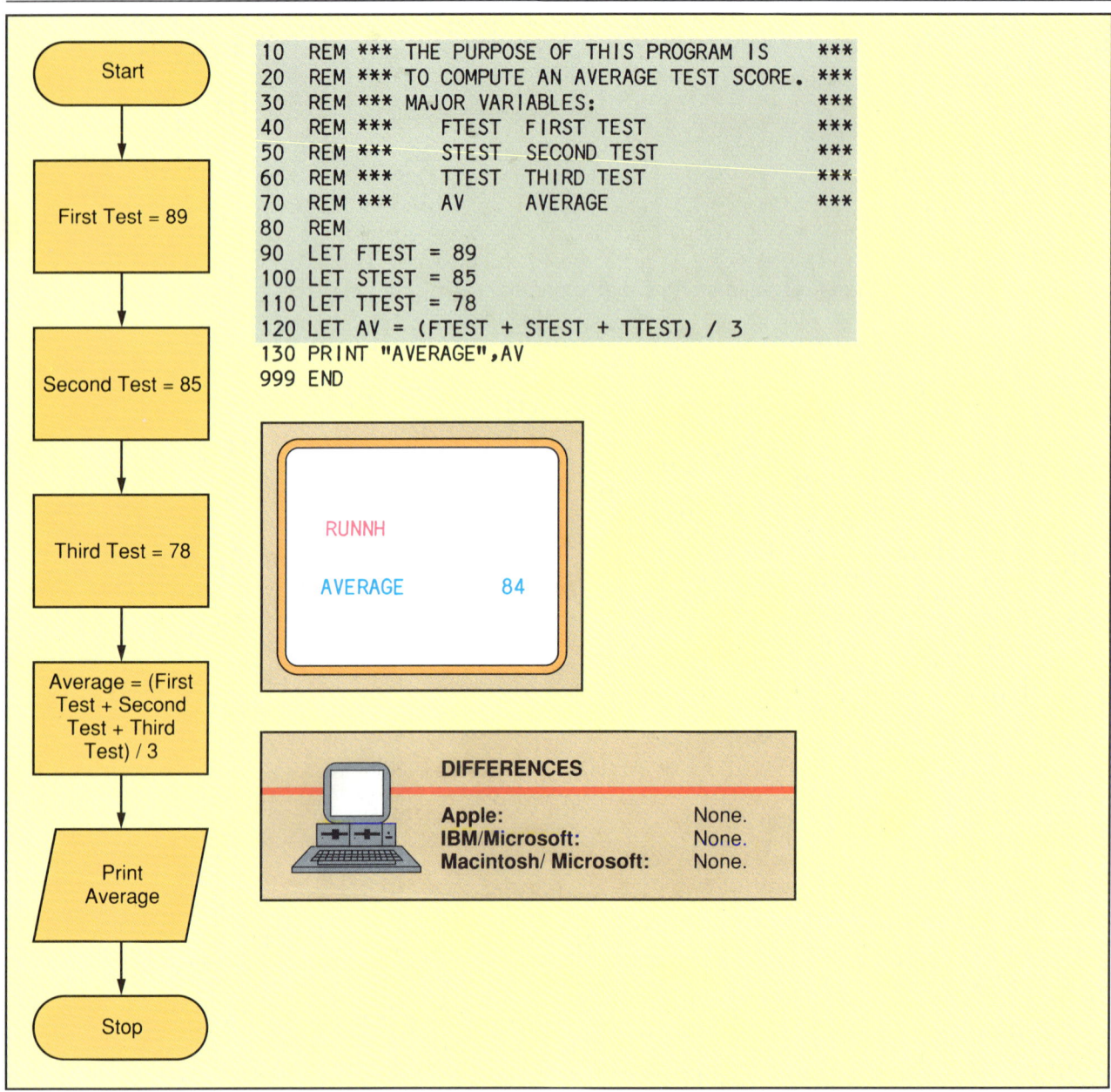

arithmetic calculation is performed, it is sometimes helpful to explain the purpose of that particular calculation immediately before the lines that perform it. We could add the following remark to the sample program in Figure 3–5:

```
115 REM *** COMPUTE AVERAGE OF THREE TEST SCORES. ***
```

A more descriptive remark can be used for more complicated calculations.

Many systems allow comments to be placed on the same line as an executable statement. In these cases, a special symbol must be used to mark the beginning of the comment. On the VAX system this symbol is an exclamation point (!) used as follows:

```
210 PC = AMT * .97     ! CALCULATE THE PERCENTAGE
```

The BASIC system will recognize CALCULATE THE PERCENTAGE as a comment because it is preceded by an exclamation point. This same type of comment can be indicated on the IBM and the Macintosh by the use of a single quotation mark (') like this:

```
210 PC = AMT * .97     ' CALCULATE THE PERCENTAGE
```

Adding a comment at the end of a BASIC statement can be a very useful way to document a program.

The Assignment Statement

The LET statement is an **assignment statement**, that is, a statement that stores a value in main memory in the location allotted to the stated variable. In a flowchart, an assignment statement is illustrated by a processing symbol (☐). The general format of the LET statement is

   line# LET variable = expression

The variable can be a numeric or string variable. If it is a numeric variable, the expression can be a numeric constant, an arithmetic formula, or another numeric variable. If the variable is a string variable, the expression can be either a string constant or another string variable.

The LET statement can be used to assign values to numeric or string variables directly or to assign the result of a calculation to a numeric variable. In either case, the expression on the right side of the equal sign is assigned to the variable on the left side. This operation causes the value of the expression to be placed in the memory location identified by the variable name on the left side of the LET statement.

Here are some of the LET statements from the sample program in Figure 3–5:

```
90  LET FTEST = 89
100 LET STEST = 85
110 LET TTEST = 78
120 LET AV = (FTEST + STEST + TTEST) / 3
```

Lines 90 through 110 assign three numeric constants (in this case, test scores) to three numeric variables. Line 120 assigns the result of an

Assignment statement
A BASIC statement that stores a value in a variable.

arithmetic calculation to the numeric variable AV, which represents the average of the three scores.

The following table lists examples of assignment statements along with short descriptions of how they would be executed.

LET Statement	Computer Execution
100 LET HOURS = 30.5	The numeric value 30.5 is assigned to the storage location called HOURS.
110 LET SUM = A + B	The values in locations A and B are added to together and the result is stored in location SUM. A and B remain unchanged.
120 LET NUMBER = I	The value in location I is also stored in location NUMBER. I remains unchanged.
130 LET EMPL$ = "JON"	The character string enclosed in quotes (but not the quotation marks themselves) is placed in the location called EMPL$.
140 LET CNT = CNT + 1	The value 1 is added to the current value in CNT. This new value replaces the previous value of CNT

Only a variable name is permitted on the left side of the LET statement. For example,

```
130 LET A + 1 = B
```

is *not* a valid statement.

On most BASIC systems, including all those covered in this textbook, the use of the reserved word LET is optional. These systems see the following two statements as identical:

```
10 LET TEST1 = 36
20 TEST1 = 36
```

For simplicity's sake, we will discontinue using LET in programs after this chapter.

Arithmetic Expressions In BASIC, arithmetic expressions are composed of numeric constants, numeric variables, and arithmetic operators. The arithmetic operators that can be used are defined in the following table.

Operator	Operation	Arithmetic Expression	Expression in BASIC
+	Addition	$A + B$	A + B
−	Subtraction	$A - B$	A − B
*	Multiplication	$A \times B$	A * B
/	Division	$A \div B$	A / B
^	Exponentiation	A^B	A ^ B

THE FUNDAMENTALS OF BASIC PROGRAMMING

For example, in the statement

```
50 LET X = Y ^ 3
```

Y would be cubed (Y*Y*Y), and the result would be stored in the location identified by X.

In the example using arithmetic operators, note that we have left a space on each side of the operators. This spacing is not necessary, but it greatly improves the readability of the program.

Hierarchy of Operations When more than one operation is to be performed in a single arithmetic expression, the computer follows a **hierarchy of operations** that states the order in which arithmetic expressions are to be evaluated. When parentheses are used in an expression, the operations inside the parentheses are performed before the operations outside the parentheses. If parentheses are nested, the operations inside the innermost set are done first. Thus, in the expression

$(6 + (5 * 2) / 3.12) + 10$

the first operation to be performed is to multiply 5 by 2.

Hierarchy of operations
The order in which arithmetic operations are performed.

Learning Check

1. Write an assignment statement to do each of the following:
   a. Assign your age to an appropriate variable.
   b. Assign the value 8 cubed to a numeric variable.
   c. Assign the total calories in your lunch to an appropriate variable. (Assume you had three items for lunch containing 100, 65, and 305 calories.)
2. What is documentation?
3. List the hierarchy of operations in BASIC.
4. The LET statement is a(n) _____ statement.
5. Evaluate the following expressions.
   a. 3 * 6 − 12/3
   b. 4 ^ (8/4)
   c. 3 ^ 2 ^ 2
   d. 4 + 6 / (3 * (10 − 9))

Answers

1. a. 100 LET AGE = 22 b. 110 LET AMOUNT = 8 ^ 3 c. 120 LET CAL = 100 + 65 + 305 2. Documentation consists of REM statements placed in a program to explain the program or give instructions to humans. 3. Parentheses; exponentiation; multiplication and division; addition and subtraction. 4. assignment 5. a. 14 b. 16 c. 81 d. 6

Parentheses aside, operations are performed according to the following rules:

Priority	Operation	Symbol
First	Exponentiation	^
Second	Multiplication/division	*, /
Third	Addition/subtraction	+, −

Operations of high priority are performed before operations of lower priority. If several operations are on the same level, they are performed from left to right. Table 3–9 gives some examples of how BASIC evaluates expressions.

The PRINT Statement

The PRINT statement is used to display or print the results of computer processing. It is flowcharted using the input/output symbol (▱). The general form of the PRINT statement is as follows:

line# PRINT { variable / literal / arithmetic expression / any combination of the above }

If more than one item is included in the PRINT statement, the items are separated by commas. These commas are also used to format or arrange the

TABLE 3–9 Examples of Evaluating Arithmetic Expressions

EXPRESSION	EVALUATION PROCESS
1. Y = 2 * 5 + 1	
First: 2 * 5 = 10	Process highest priority
Second: 10 + 1 = 11	Process next priority
Result: Y = 11	
2. Y = 2 * (5 + 1)	
First: 5 + 1 = 6	Perform process within parentheses
Second: 2 * 6 = 12	Perform next priority
Result: Y = 12	
3. Y = (3 + (6 + 2) / 4) + 10 ^ 2	
First: 6 + 2 = 8	Process innermost parentheses
Second: 8 / 4 = 2	Perform next priority
Third: 3 + 2 = 5	Process rest of outer parentheses
Fourth: 10 ^ 2 = 100	Perform next priority
Fifth: 5 + 100 = 105	Perform lowest priority

output; this topic will be discussed in detail in Chapter 4. For now, it is sufficient to know that the commas automatically space the items across the output line.

Printing the Value of a Variable   We can tell the computer to print values assigned to storage locations simply by using the reserved word PRINT with the variable name after it. If there is more than one variable to be printed, the names must be separated by commas:

```
160 PRINT HRS,PERHR,TPAY
```

Printing has no effect on the contents of the storage location being printed. The PRINT statement merely obtains the value of a variable and displays it on the terminal screen.

Printing Literals   A **literal** is a group of characters containing any combination of alphabetic, numeric, and/or special characters. It is essentially the same as a constant. The term *literal*, however, is applied to constants used in PRINT statements. There are two types, character string literals and numeric literals.

A *character string literal* is a group of letters, numbers, and/or special characters enclosed in quotation marks. Whatever is inside the quotation marks is printed exactly as it is. For example,

```
190 PRINT "SAMPLE @%OUTPUT 12"
```

would appear on the screen as

```
SAMPLE @%OUTPUT 12
```

Note that the quotation marks are not printed.

Literals can be used to print headings in output. To print column headings, for example, put each heading in quotation marks and separate them with comas. Here is an example:

```
40 PRINT "NAME","RANK","SERIAL NO."
```

When this statement is executed, the following output will appear on the screen:

```
NAME            RANK            SERIAL NO.
```

Headings can be set off from the rest of the output in two ways: by underlining or by using a blank line. One way to underline headings is by including a separate PRINT statement that contains the necessary underscore lines:

Literal
A group of characters containing any combination of letters, numbers, and/or special characters.

```
40 PRINT "NAME","RANK","SERIAL NO."
50 PRINT "____","____","_____"
```

The output would be

NAME   RANK   SERIAL NO.
____   ____   _____

Note that the underline is slightly separated from the heading. This is caused by the separate PRINT statement.

A blank line in output makes the output more readable, and can be achieved by using a PRINT statement alone:

```
140 PRINT
```

To skip more than one line, simply include more than one such statement:

```
140 PRINT
150 PRINT
```

Numeric literals are numbers placed within the PRINT statement which are to be printed in the output. They do not have to be enclosed in quotation marks. For example, the statement

```
100 PRINT 103
```

will print

103

Printing the Value of an Expression   The computer can print not only literals and the values of variables, but also the values of arithmetic expressions. Look at the following program:

```
10 LET A = 15.00
20 LET B = 26.00
30 PRINT (A + B) / 2, A / B
99 END
```

Each expression in line 30 will be evaluated according to the hierarchy of operations, and the results will be printed:

20.5   .576923

The computer can print only a certain number of digits for each value. Look at the second value printed. In this case, the computer cannot print more than six digits. If the computer did not have this limit, an infinite number of digits would have been printed, because the full answer is

.576923076923076923076 . . .

The last six digits repeat infinitely. An extremely large or small value may may be printed in exponential notation.

The END Statement

The END statement instructs the computer to stop program execution. In a flowchart, it is indicated by the terminal symbol (⌾). The general format of the END statement is

line# END

When the END statement is used, it is always the last line of a program that is executed. On the VAX system, it must also be the last physical line of the program. To make the END statement readily identifiable, many programmers give it a line number of all 9s. All programs in this book will follow this practice.

Learning Check

1. When a variable is printed, the contents of that variable's storage location are changed. True or false?
2. A(n) _____ is an expression consisting of any combination of letters, numbers, or special characters.
3. The _____ statement causes the computer to stop program execution.
4. Write your own statements to do the following:
   a. Print the headings NAME and ADDRESS.
   b. Underline the headings printed in part a.
   c. Print the values of variables N$ and A$.
   d. Print the result of X + Y * Z.
   e. Print the value of A,B, and A ˆ B.
5. Indicate whether the following are valid or invalid PRINT statements.
   a. 110 PRINT B + 1
   b. 110 PRINT NAM$ AND AGE

Answers

1. False. 2. literal 3. END 4. a. 10 PRINT "NAME", "ADDRESS" b. 20 PRINT "_____", "_____" c. 10 PRINT N$,A$ d. 10 PRINT X + Y * Z e. 10 PRINT A, B, A ˆ B 5. a. Valid. b. Invalid.

A Programming Problem

Problem Definition

Smith's Pet Shop is offering a 12 percent discount for any cash purchase. If the purchase totals $38.49 before the cash discount, how much will have to be paid if cash is used?

Input

38.49

Needed Output

RUNNH

THE AMOUNT DUE AFTER THE DISCOUNT IS   33.8712

Solution Design

The regular purchase price will be assigned to a variable by means of a LET statement. This LET statement can be changed if another discount needs to be calculated. Because the discount for cash is always 12 percent, this percentage can be represented as a numeric constant. The program must output the cash amount due after the discount. In order to determine this amount due, multiply the purchase price by the discount rate and then subtract this amount from the purchase price. A program variable can be used to contain the amount of the discount. Thus, the variables needed are listed in the following table. Notice that, after a description of each variable, the table lists the actual variable name that will be used in the program.

Input Variable	Program Variable	Output Variable
price (PURCHASE)	discount (DISCOUNT)	cash owed (CASH)

What operations are needed to determine the cash owed after the discount? First, the purchase price must be assigned to a variable. Once this has been done, the amount of the discount can be computed by multiplying the purchase price by the discount rate of 12 percent (or 0.12). This amount is then subtracted from the original price to obtain the discounted cash price. The output then needs to be printed with an appropriate label.

The stepwise refinement of the algorithm is shown in Figure 3–6. The structure chart showing the three major steps in solving this problem is shown in Figure 3–7. Note that the second step is broken down further into two substeps, one that calculates the actual amount of the discount and another that subtracts this amount from the initial purchase price. Although structure charts and stepwise refinement may be unnecessary with this simple problem, they become very useful as programming problems become more difficult.

THE FUNDAMENTALS OF BASIC PROGRAMMING   61

General Problem: Determine the cash due on a purchase after deducting a 12 percent discount.

Level 1
 A. Assign purchase price.
 B. Compute amount of cash owed.
 C. Print amount of cash owed.

Level 2
 B.1. Compute amount of discount.
 B.2. Subtract discount from purchase price.

FIGURE 3–6
Stepwise Refinement of Cash Discount Problem

FIGURE 3–7 Structure Chart for Cash Discount Problem

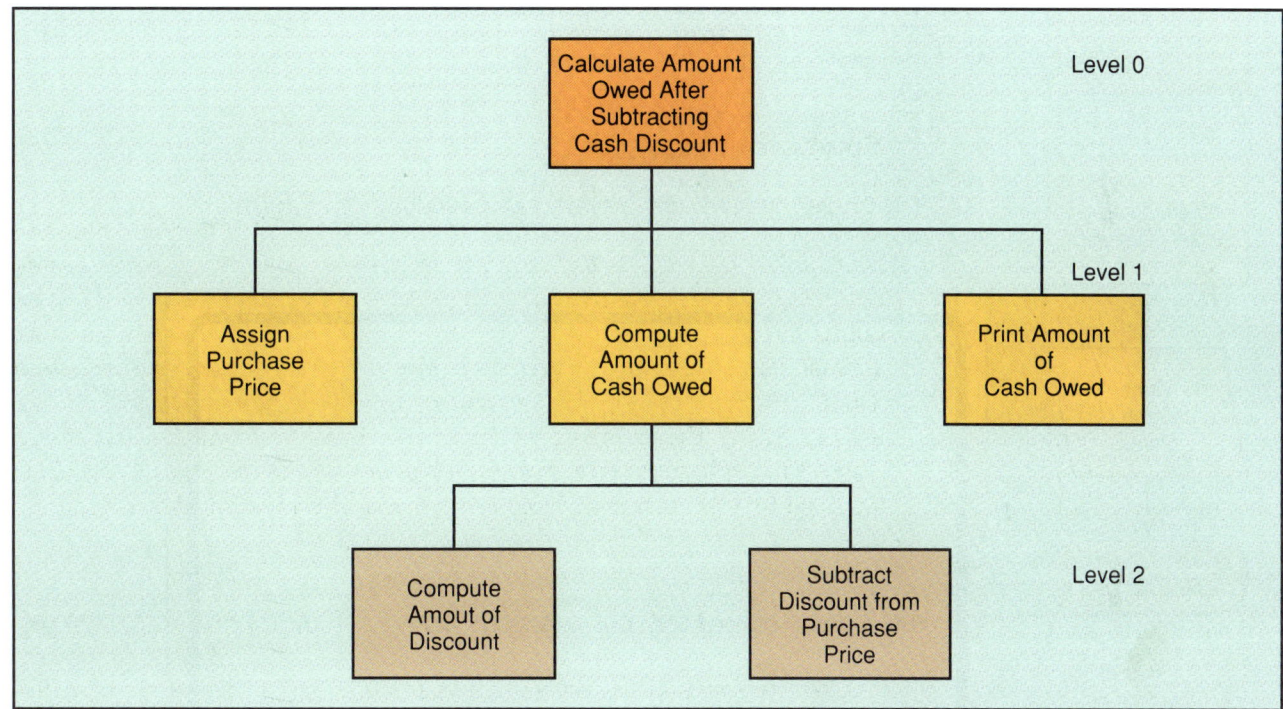

The Program

Figure 3–8 contains the actual program. The REM statements in lines 10 through 60 explain the purpose of the program and the variables used. Line 80 uses a LET statement to assign the purchase price to the variable PURCHASE. Lines 90 and 100 calculate the discount and the cash owed. Line 110 prints an appropriate message and the cash due. The program ends at line 999.

FIGURE 3-8 Cash Discount Program

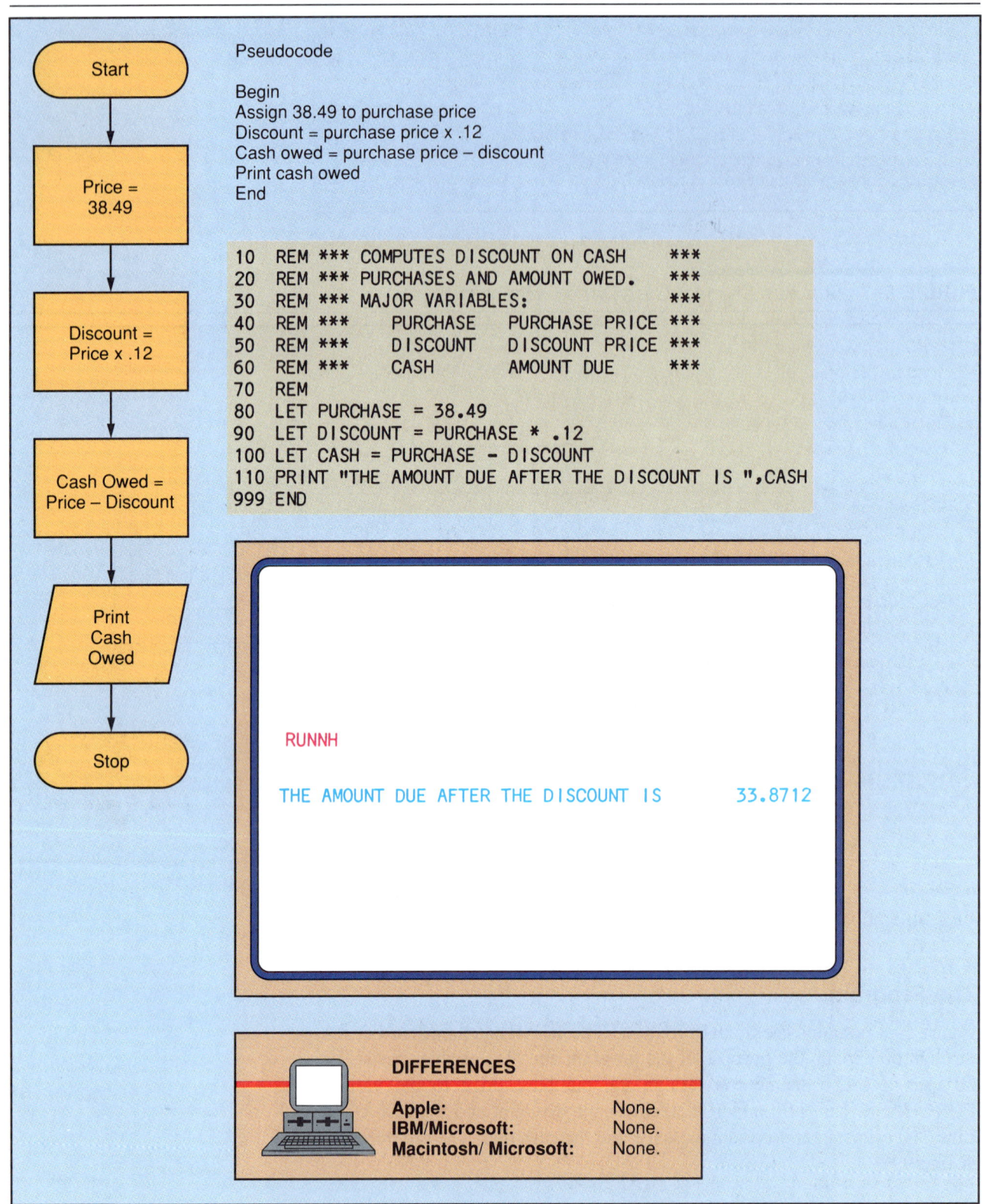

Avoiding Common Programming Mistakes

- Remember that when you type NEW you will lose any BASIC program currently in main memory. To preserve a program currently in memory, use the SAVE command before typing NEW. Be sure to type NEW before entering a new program. If you don't, you will have unexpected results when you list the new program, because both the old and the new statements will be stored in the computer's main memory.
- Remember that BASIC commands usually are used in direct mode and therefore do not have line numbers.
- When you enter a statement in direct mode, it will be executed as soon as you press the RETURN key.
- Be careful not to use reserved words as variable names.
- Check carefully to make sure that the variable name type matches the type of value being assigned to it.
- Be certain that all expressions appear to the *right* of an assignment operator. Only variables may appear on the left side.
- Remember that your program concludes with an END statement.
- Keep the line numbers in a program within the system's range. Do not use the same line number more than once unless you want to replace a line with a new one.
- Increment your line numbers by a large enough margin to allow for insertions if necessary.
- Always enclose character strings in quotation marks.
- When the reserved word REM is used to indicate a comment line, it must always be placed at the beginning of the line.
- Double-check any mathematical expressions to make certain they will be evaluated correctly. Remember that the computer always follows the hierarchy of operations when evaluating arithmetic expressions.

Summary Points

- BASIC commands are used to manipulate BASIC programs. Commonly used BASIC commands are NEW, LIST, SAVE, LOAD, and RUN.
- When NEW is typed, any BASIC program currently in the computer's main memory is erased.
- LIST causes any BASIC program in main memory to be displayed.
- The SAVE command is used to copy a program in main memory to a secondary storage device.
- On the VAX system, the OLD command is used to copy a program from secondary storage to the computer's main memory. The other computers covered in this text use the LOAD command to perform this task.
- The RUN command causes the computer to execute a program in main memory.
- A BASIC program is a series of instructions. Each instruction is composed of a line number and a BASIC statement.

- Line numbers serve to label statements so that they can be referenced, and to specify the order in which instructions are to be executed.
- Using line numbers in large increments, such as 10, permits easy insertion of new statements.
- BASIC statements contain special programming commands (key words), constants, variables, and operators.
- Constants are values that do not change during program execution. A valid numeric constant is any integer or real number. Character strings are alphanumeric data enclosed in quotation marks.
- Variable names are programmer-supplied names that identify storage locations where data values may be stored. Numeric variable names represent numbers. String variables contain alphanumeric values; their names are distinguished from numeric names by the $ symbol used as the last character.
- REM statements are nonexecutable statements that provide information for the programmer or reader. These statements can be placed anywhere in a program.
- The LET statement is used to assign values and results of arithmetic calculations to variables. The word LET is optional on most systems.
- Arithmetic expressions are evaluated according to the following hierarchy of operations: (1) operations in parentheses, (2) exponentiation, (3) multiplication or division, and (4) addition or subtraction. Multiple operations at the same level are evaluated from left to right.
- The PRINT statement enables the user to see the results of a program. It can be used to print the values of variables, literals, arithmetic expressions, or a combination of these.
- The END statement causes program execution to stop.

Review Questions

1. How are each of the following statements indicated in a flowchart?
   a. LET
   b. END
   c. PRINT
2. What is a BASIC command? In what mode are BASIC commands usually executed?
3. Explain the purpose of each of these BASIC commands: NEW, LIST, SAVE, LOAD, and RUN.
4. Convert each of the following arithmetic expressions into a BASIC expression.

   a. $\dfrac{9 \times B + 4^2}{5 + A}$

   b. $\dfrac{A + B + C + (D \times E)}{F}$

c. $\dfrac{X^2}{Y/Z + 5}$

d. $A + 3C - D^2$

e. $(A + 4) \div 6 + (B \times C)$

f. $\dfrac{(X^2 \div 4) + 6}{(L \div M)N}$

5. What are the two main purposes of line numbers?
6. What is the advantage of incrementing line numbers by 10?
7. What is a constant? Name two types of constants.
8. What is a variable? Name two types, and explain how these types differ from each other.
9. Which of the following are illegal variable names and why?
    a. 7$
    b. D
    c. SB
    d. H$
    e. M$
    f. RT
    g. 2009
    h. W*
    i. 25cents
    j. $FACT
10. What is the purpose of the REM statement?
11. In an assignment statement, what are the three forms that the expression on the right side of the equal sign can take if the variable on the left side is a numeric variable?
12. List the arithmetic operators in BASIC. In what order are these operators evaluated?
13. Define a literal, and give three examples.
14. How can a blank line be added to output?
15. Indicate whether each of the following line numbers is valid or invalid.
    a. 0
    b. 136
    c. 2,893
    d. 99999
    e. 234.5
    f. -17
16. Indicate whether each of the following numeric constants is valid or invalid.
    a. 186.75
    b. 93¾
    c. 1,234
    d. 9638
    e. -3896.4
    f. $-586,931$

17. Write a valid assignment statement for each of the following problems:
    a. Add two numbers and store the result.
    b. Store the character string BOOKS in a variable location.
    c. Store the value 3 in a variable location.
    d. Store the value contained in one string variable in a second string variable.

Refer to the following program to answer Questions 18 through 20.

```
100 REM *** COMPUTE PERCENTAGE    ***
110 REM *** FROM FRACTION.        ***
120 REM *** MAJOR VARIABLES:      ***
130 REM ***    N  NUMERATOR       ***
140 REM ***    D  DENOMINATOR     ***
150 REM ***    P  PERCENT         ***
160 LET N = 3
170 LET D = 4
180 LET P = (N / D) * 100
190 PRINT "PERCENT"
200 PRINT -------
210 PRINT P
999 END
```

18. Find and correct the single error in the program above.
19. Draw a flowchart to represent this program.
20. Write a REM statement that would be appropriate to include between lines 170 and 180.

Debugging Exercises

Identify the following programs or program segments that contain errors, and debug them.

1. ```
   10 REM *** PREPARE COMPUTER TO HAVE NEW PROGRAM ENTERED. ***
   20 NEW
   ```
2. ```
   10 REM *** ASSIGN CHARACTER STRINGS TO N$ AND L$. ***
   20 LET N$ = NANCY
   30 LET L$ = LINDA
   40 REM *** OUTPUT N$ AND L$.
   50 PRINT N$,L$
   99 END
   ```
3. ```
   10 REM *** THIS PROGRAM PRINTS
   20 A NAME AND AGE OF A PERSON.
   30 REM
   40 LET A = 21
   50 LET N$ = "STACY"
   60 PRINT N$,A
   99 END
   ```
4. ```
   100 REM *** ADD A TO B AND ASSIGN TO X. ***
   110.5 LET X = A + B
   ```

5. ```
   30 REM *** CONVERT A DISTANCE FROM KILOMETERS TO MILES. ***
   40 LET X = 15.5
   50 LET K = "DISTANCE IN KILOMETERS"
   60 LET Y = X * 1.6
   70 LET M = "DISTANCE IN MILES"
   ```
6. ```
   400 LET A = 3 + 1
   410 LET X + Y = B
   420 PRINT A,B,X, Y
   ```
7. ```
   410 LET AGE% = 17.5
   ```
8. ```
   220 PRINT "COUNTRY" "CONTINENT"
   ```
9. ```
   10 REM *** FIND AVERAGE OF 3 NUMBERS. ***
   20 LET A = 2
   30 LET B = 4
   40 LET C = 6
   50 PRINT (A + B + C) / D
   ```
10. ```
    100 REM *** THIS PROGRAM CALCULATES    ***
    110 REM *** THE AVERAGE OF TWO NUMBERS. ***
    120 LET A = 10
    130 LET B = 15
    140 LET X = A + B / 2
    150 PRINT X
    999 END
    ```

Additional Programming Problems

Level 1

1. Write a program to square the digits 1 through 9, and print the results with appropriate labels.

2. Write a program to cube the digits 1 through 9, and print the results with appropriate labels.

3. The list price of a record that you want is $8.98. A sign in the window says that all $8.98 LPs are on sale for 15 percent off the list prices. Write a program that will calculate the sale price of the record.

4. Write a program to print the following design on the terminal screen. Use asterisks to make the design.

```
*******
* * * *
*******
* * * *
```

5. Write a program that will print the United States flag on the terminal screen. Use asterisks and/or other special characters to print the design.

6. Write a program that will print the name and telephone number of the following people:

```
Linda Jones     818-7081
Anna McGee      223-8764
Leroy Price     449-6062
```

The output should have the following format:

```
NAME            TELEPHONE #
XXXXXXXXXX      XXX-XXXX
```

7. Write a program that will compute the current balance in your checking account. At the beginning of the month the balance was $46.19. During the month, you purchased a record for $8.93, jeans for $15.60, and a book for $14.89. You also deposited $25.00.

8. The local sporting goods store has monthly specials on sporting equipment. The manager has asked you to write a program to calculate the total day's sales for these items:

Item	Sales Price	Units Sold
Hockey stick	$9.95	12
Soccer ball	12.95	5
Baseball gloves	17.95	20

9. Write a program that will convert your weight from pounds to kilograms and your height from inches to centimeters. (There are 2.54 centimeters in an inch and 0.45359 kilograms in a pound.)

10. Assume that the population of Fairfax, Virginia is 600,000 and that it is growing at the rate of 3.5 percent a year. Write a program to calculate what the population will be in four years.

Level 2

1. Your physical education class went on a three-mile hike yesterday. You want to know how many feet you walked, knowing that there are 5,280 feet in one mile. Create a flowchart to solve this problem. Then write a program to find the total number of feet you walked.

2. Johnny Thurn wants to know how much it will cost for gas to get to Fort Lauderdale, Florida and back home. Fort Lauderdale is 2,340 miles from his home. His car gets 28 miles per gallon, and he estimates that gas will cost an average of $1.21 a gallon. Write a program that will produce output similar to the following:

```
DISTANCE    TOTAL COST
XXX         XXX.XX
```

3. Using the formula $C = 5/9 \, (F - 32)$, where C equals the degrees Celsius and F equals the degrees Fahrenheit, write a program that will convert 85 degrees Fahrenheit to its Celsius equivalent. Be sure to document your program.

4. The Time Keeper Manufacturing Corp. needs to know how many hours and seconds there are in a year. Assume that the year is not a leap year. Document your program well, and use appropriate headings.

5. The President of Programs Unlimited needs an employee report listing its three employees, their home addresses, and their phone numbers. The information needed is listed below:

Sam Kessler
61 Rolling Ridge Road
Hackensack, New Jersey 07465
(201) 652-8977

Jennifer Spitz
16-56 202nd Street
Whitestone, New York 12107
(212) 679-9794

Sara John
51 Madison Avenue Apartment #76
New York, New York 10017
(212) 499-7281

Print the output in table form with appropriate headings.

6. Currently, tuition at Famous University is $900.00 per year and room and board fees are $1,500.00 per year. Next fall, tuition is expected to rise by 15 percent, and room and board fees are expected to rise by 10 percent. Karl Perry wants to know what the fees will be and whether he will have enough money to cover them. Karl earns approximately $3,000 during the summer and gets no additional help for his college expenses. Write a program to help Karl. The output should have the following format:

TUITION	ROOM/BOARD	TOTAL	EXCESS
XXXX.XX	XXXX.XX	XXXX.XX	XXX.XX

7. You own a house with nine identically shaped rooms that need carpeting. Each room has a length of 12 feet. The carpet price is $21.95 a square yard. Write a program that will calculate the amount of carpeting needed, as well as the total cost of the carpeting. Document your program thoroughly.

8. To make a circular coil for a magnet, 60 turns of wire are needed. Write a program that will calculate how much wire is needed if the diameter of the coil is 3 inches.

9. Write and document a program to calculate the total sales for a week and the daily average. The sales were:

Monday	75.00	Thursday	95.25
Tuesday	85.00	Friday	100.75
Wednesday	65.00		

The output should appear as follows:

```
TOTAL SALES FOR THE WEEK     XXX.XX
AVERAGE DAILY SALES           XX.XX
```

10. You have been asked to write a program that will calculate the average score of bowling contestants and print each contestant's name, score for each of three games, and average for the three games. Your output should contain column headings. Use the following data:

Name	Game 1	Game 2	Game 3
Bill Davis	113	136	145
Tonya Rae	150	172	167

Level 3

1. The Rich Rug Company's top salesperson is Emmet Mitchell. He earns a base salary of $95.00 per week. In addition, he earns commissions of 6 percent on all Oriental rugs sold and 4 percent on all other items. The total salary is calculated as follows:

Total Salary = Base Salary + Commission

You are to write a program to calculate his salary. Then print his total weekly salary with an appropriate label. Use the following data: Oriental rugs sold, $3892.00; all other sales, $989.00.

2. The Igloo Ice Cream Store would like you to write a program that will calculate the quantities of ice cream, nuts, sauce, and cones that are used on a given day. The following is a list of items they sell and the quantities of ingredients used in each item:

Sundaes	8 oz. ice cream
	1 oz. nuts
	2 oz. sauce
Cones	6 oz. ice cream
	1 cone
Shakes	10 oz. ice cream
	1 oz. sauce

On a given day they sold 104 sundaes, 94 shakes, and 96 cones. Output should be stated in terms of quarts (32 fluid ounces per quart) of ice cream and sauce, pounds of nuts and units of cones.

3. A car dealer agrees to accept an $8,000.00 promissary note at 9 percent interest instead of a cash payment. Write a program to compute the maturity value of the note for a 60-day, a 90-day, and a one-year loan. Have the results displayed with appropriate labels. The formula to compute the maturity value is $V = P \times (1 + I \times N)$ where V is the value, P is the principal, I is the interest rate, and N is the number of years. (For 60 or 90 days, express N as the number of days divided by 365).

4. A local stereo shop is advertising the following discounts:

- 15 percent off the purchase of a receiver and a pair of speakers.
- 20 percent off the purchase of a receiver, a pair of speakers, and a turntable.
- 30 percent off the purchase of a receiver, pair of speakers, turntable, and cassette deck.

Being a small shop, it carries only one model of each item. The price for each is as follows:

Item	Price
Receiver	$423.00
Pair of Speakers	$300.00
Turntable	$185.00
Cassette Deck	$210.00

Before going to the stereo shop, you decide to write a program to tell you the discount price of each of the advertised options. Print these prices with appropriate labels.

5. The President of Welcome, Inc. has asked you to write a program to calculate total department costs for the accounting, finance, and computer services departments. The costs are as follows:

Accounting	Finance	Computer services
$45750.	$67500.	$19900.
$25000.	$12500.	$35000.

Also determine the total cost for all three departments.

6. Frank Mendelle is the father of two teenagers, and lately his telephone bills have been extremely high. To control this expense, he is charging each child $1.00 for every 10 minutes for long distance calls and 25 cents for every 10 minutes for local calls. The following calls were made:

Tom   2 long distance calls (30 minutes each)
                6 local calls (20 minutes each)

Jenny   3 long distance calls (10 minutes each)
60 local calls (20 minutes each)

Compute how much each child owes his or her father, and the total for the two children. Assume the telephone bill totaled $73.62. How much of his own money does Frank owe the telephone company?

7. Lester Lamplight needs to calculate his taxes. He is employed as a brain surgeon at State Medical College and receives $86,000 annually. He deposits $250 per month into a tax-sheltered annuity plan. His effective tax rate is 35 percent. He needs a program to print a report listing his gross salary, the total amount in the annuity account at the end of the year, and the amount of taxes. Use appropriate headings to label the output.

8. Linda Thurston is considering buying a new sports car. Calculate the monthly payment for an installment purchase, using the following formula:

$$P = I(T - D)\left[\frac{(1 + I)^m}{(1 + I)^m - 1}\right]$$

where

P is the monthly payment in dollars
T is the purchase price in dollars
D is the down payment in dollars
I is the monthly interest rate (Determine this value by dividing the annual rate by 12)
M is the number of months

The price of the car is $10,000.00, to be paid for within five years at 15 percent interest. The down payment is 10 percent of the sale price.

9. The water pressure exerted on a diver's eardrums varies directly with the depth at which he or she is swimming. At a depth of 10 feet, the pressure on the eardrums is approximately 4.3 pounds per square inch. It is unsafe for a nonprofessional diver to have more the 65 pounds per square inch of pressure exerted on the eardrums. Write a program that will calculate how deep such a diver can safely swim. Print this depth with an appropriate label.

10. Write a program that will calculate the distance between two points on a plane and the slope of the line between the two points. Use the following formulas:

$$\text{Distance} = (x_2 - x_1)^2 + (y_2 - y_1)^2$$
$$\text{Slope} = (y_2 - y_1) / (x_2 - x_1)$$

Use LET statements to assign the four integer values representing the following coordinates:

$x_1 = 5$
$x_2 = 9$
$y_1 = 8$
$y_2 = 11$

CHAPTER 4

INPUT AND OUTPUT

Objectives

After studying this chapter, you will be able to:

- Use the INPUT statement to allow data to be entered during program execution.
- Use the READ and DATA statements to enter data to programs.
- Explain the advantages and disadvantages of each of these methods of entering data.
- Write programs so that the output is formatted in a readable way.
- Explain how commas and semicolons are used to format program output.
- Use the TAB statement to format output.
- Explain how the PRINT USING statement works, and use it in programs when appropriate.

Outline

Overview
The INPUT Statement
Printing Prompts for the User
The READ and DATA Statements
The RESTORE Statement
Comparing the INPUT and the
    READ/DATA Statements
Printing Results
  The Semicolon
  Using the Print Zones

The TAB Function
The SPC Function
The PRINT USING Statement
Multiple Statements on a Single
    Physical Line
A Programming Problem
  Problem Definition
  Solution Design
  The Program

Avoiding Common
    Programming Mistakes
Summary Points
Review Questions
Debugging Exercises
Additional Programming Problems
  Level 1
  Level 2
  Level 3

Overview

The first part of this chapter explains ways of entering data to a program. The two methods introduced are the INPUT statement and the READ and DATA statements. The INPUT statement allows the user to enter data while the program is running. When the READ and DATA statements are used, the data is entered as part of the program itself. The remainder of the chapter discusses ways of printing program results.

The INPUT Statement

In many programs, the data changes each time the program is executed. For example, think of a program that calculates the gas mileage for your car. Each time you run this program, you will want to be able to enter new values for the number of miles traveled and the amount of gas used. If such a program used assignment statements to assign these values to variables, these statements would have to be rewritten every time you wanted to calculate your gas mileage. A more practical approach to this programming problem is to use the INPUT statement.

The INPUT statement allows the user to enter data at the keyboard while the program is executing. The format of the INPUT statement is

line# INPUT variable1[,variable2]. . .

Take a minute to study the method we are using to present the format of this statement. This method will be used whenever a new statement is introduced in this text. Let's look at each part of this format description:

    line#   A valid line number, such as 210, must be placed here. (In a format description, anything in lowercase repre-

	sents a value to be inserted in the actual statement. In this case, "line#" represents an actual line number.)
INPUT	The statement must begin with the reserved word INPUT. (Uppercase words must be placed in the BASIC statement exactly as they appear in the format description.)
variable1	The reserved word INPUT must be followed by the name of a variable. (Because "variable1" is in lowercase, we know that it is used here to represent something else, in this case an actual variable name.)
[,variable2]...	Additional variables are optional. (Anything placed in brackets is optional.) The dots indicate that as many variable names as are needed may be listed in this statement.

Therefore, by examining this format description, we can determine that the following are all valid INPUT statements:

```
100 INPUT STUDENT$,GPA,YR
110 INPUT ADDRESS$
250 INPUT TPAY,NPAY,TAX
300 INPUT MNTH$,DAY$,YR%
```

The following INPUT statements are not valid:

```
1000 INPUT CITY$ ST$
1010 TABLES,INPUT CHAIRS
```

Note that one or more variables may be listed in a single INPUT statement. If there is more than one, the variables must be separated by commas. The programmer places INPUT statements in a program at the point at which user-entered data is needed, as determined by the logic of the program.

When an INPUT statement is encountered while a program is running, the program temporarily stops executing, and a question mark appears on the terminal screen. The user must then enter the required data and press the RETURN key. After each value entered is stored in its corresponding variable, program execution continues to the next statement.

Consider the following program:

```
10 INPUT CITY$
20 INPUT ST$
30 INPUT PEOPLE
40 PRINT CITY$,ST$,PEOPLE
99 END
```

When this program is executed, the terminal screen might look like this:

```
RUNNH

? CEDAR RAPIDS
? IOWA
? 125000
CEDAR RAPIDS    IOWA            125000
```

Let's trace through what happens as this program is executing. First, the computer executes line 10 and, upon encountering the INPUT statement, prints a question mark and stops. Next, the user enters the value CEDAR RAPIDS and presses the RETURN key. The computer then continues execution, assigning the character string CEDAR RAPIDS to the character string variable CITY$. Execution proceeds to line 20, where another INPUT statement is encountered. Again the computer prints a question mark and stops until the user enters a value and presses the RETURN key. This process is repeated for the last INPUT statement in this program, which assigns the value 125000 to the numeric variable PEOPLE. The values of these three variables are then printed by the PRINT statement to line 40, and the program ends.

Note that the character strings in this example have been entered without quotation marks. Quotation marks are not needed when using the INPUT statement to enter character strings.

In the preceding example, the third data value entered must be a numeric value and will be assigned to the numeric variable PEOPLE. If the user enters a character string instead, an error message is printed, and program execution stops prematurely.

The three INPUT statements in the program could be combined into a single statement like this:

```
10 INPUT CITY$,ST$,PEOPLE
```

Because of the single INPUT statement, only one question mark appears on the screen when the program is run. In this case, the user enters the data in the following format:

```
RUNNH

? CEDAR RAPIDS, IOWA, 125000
```

Note that when more than one data value is entered on a single line, the values must be separated by commas. After the user enters these values and presses the RETURN key, CEDAR RAPIDS is assigned to CITY$, IOWA to ST$, and 125000 to PEOPLE.

The user must enter the exact number of values needed by the INPUT statement. If fewer values are entered than there are variables in the INPUT statement, an error message is printed. For example, if line 10 in the preceding program is executed and the user enters only two values followed by the RETURN key, a message similar to the following appears on the screen:

```
RUNNH

? CEDAR RAPIDS, IOWA
?
```

The computer will continue telling the user that more data is needed until enough data has been entered. Then the program will continue executing.

If the user attempts to enter a character string to a numeric variable, another error message will appear similar to the following:

```
RUNNH

? CEDAR RAPIDS, IOWA, USA
?Redo from start
?
```

The computer cannot assign the string USA to the numeric variable PEOPLE, and therefore an error occurs.

The user can, however, assign a numeric value to a character string variable. The computer treats the numeric value as a string of characters and stores it in the corresponding string variable, but it cannot perform calculations with this value.

Printing Prompts for the User

In the previous example, when the INPUT statement was executed, only a question mark (?) appeared on the terminal screen when it was time for the user to enter data. The user was not told what type of data or how many data items to enter. Therefore, the programmer should also include a **prompt** to tell the user what is to be entered. A prompt can consist of a PRINT statement, placed before the INPUT statement in the program, which tells the user the type and quantity of data to be entered.

Prompt
A message telling the user that data should be entered at this point.

Figure 4–1 shows a short program that calculates the volume of a box. The length, width, and height of the box are entered, and the volume is printed. Note the spelling of the variable names LNGTH and WDTH. It might seem more appropriate to name these variables LENGTH and WIDTH, but all or part of these words are reserved words in at least one of the BASIC implementations covered in this textbook. Therefore, it was necessary to alter these variable names to make them different from the reserved words.

Line 40 of the program in Figure 4–1 contains the prompt,

```
40 PRINT "ENTER THE LENGTH, WIDTH, AND HEIGHT OF THE BOX"
```

FIGURE 4-1 Program Demonstrating the INPUT Statement

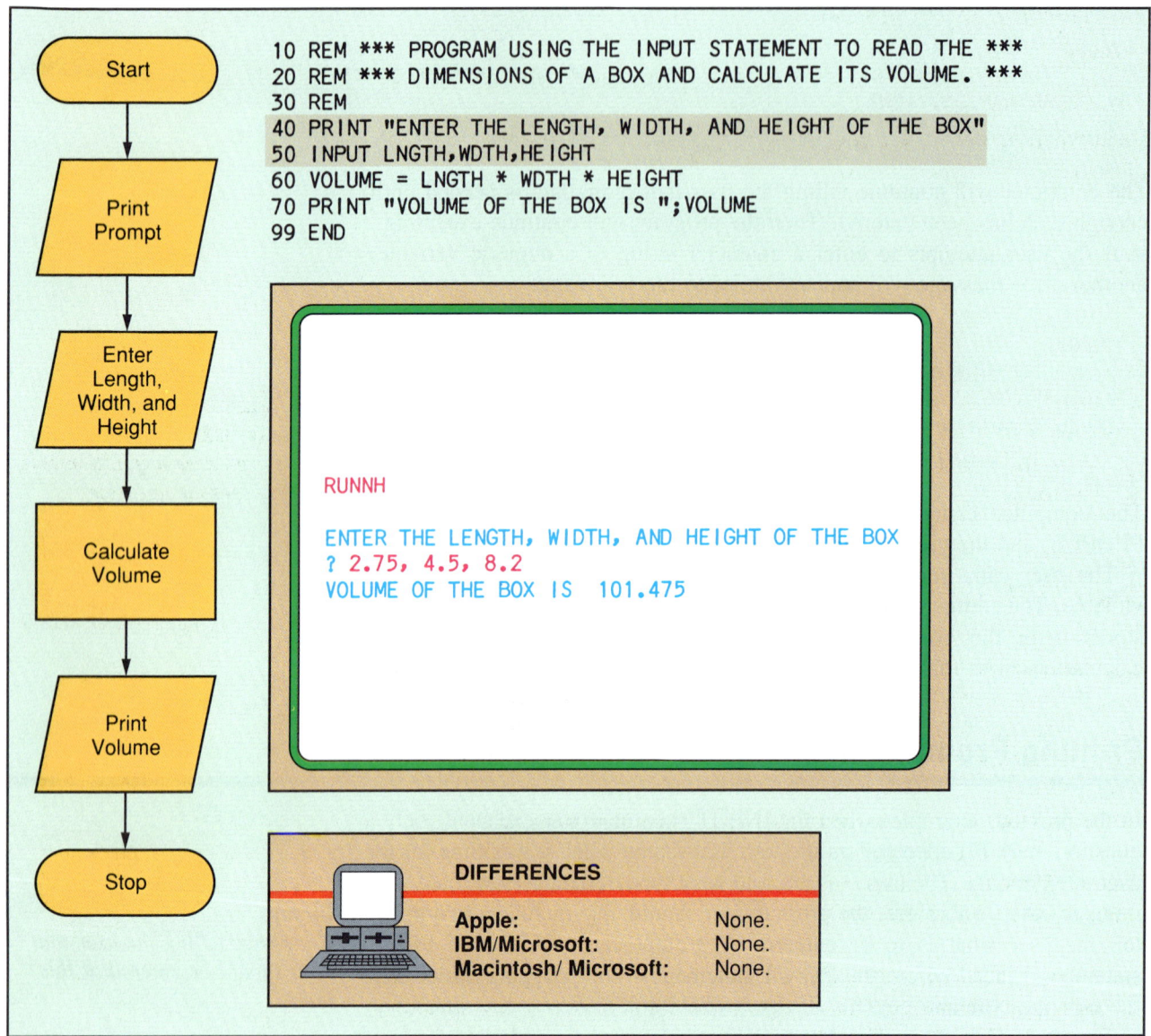

Line 50 is the INPUT statement,

```
50 INPUT LNGTH,WDTH,HEIGHT
```

After line 50 is executed, the computer will stop and wait for the user to enter the desired length, width, and height. Then execution will continue, and the volume of the box will be calculated and printed on the screen.

The prompt can also be contained within the INPUT statement itself. If this were done for the program in Figure 4–1, lines 40 and 50 could be replaced with a single statement:

```
40 INPUT "ENTER THE LENGTH, WIDTH, AND HEIGHT OF THE BOX";LNGTH,WDTH,HEIGHT
```

When this program is run, the question mark and the prompt appear on the same line:

```
RUNNH

ENTER THE LENGTH, WIDTH, AND HEIGHT OF THE BOX? 2.75,4.5,8.2
VOLUME OF THE BOX IS  101.475
```

Using this format simplifies the writing of the program and makes the logic easy to follow.

This method of data entry, in which the user enters a response to a prompt printed on the terminal screen, is called **inquiry-and-response** or **conversational mode.**

Inquiry-and-response mode
A mode of operation in which the program asks a question and the user enters a response.

The READ and DATA Statements

A second method of entering data to a BASIC program is to use the READ and DATA statements. The READ and DATA statements differ from the INPUT statement in that data values are not entered by the user during program execution, but instead are assigned by the programmer within the program itself.

The general formats for the READ and DATA statements are

line# READ variable1[,variable2]...
line# DATA value1[,value2]...

The values in the DATA statement are assigned to the corresponding variables in the READ statement. The following is a list of rules explaining the use of the READ and DATA statements.

- A program may contain any number of READ and DATA statements.
- The placement of READ statements is determined by the logic of a given program. The programmer places them in the program at the point at which data needs to be read.
- DATA statements are nonexecutable and can therefore be placed anywhere in the program before the END statement. This book follows the common practice of placing all data statements immediately before the END statement, so that they are easy to locate.

Data list
A single list containing the values in all of the data statements in a program. The values appear in the order that they occur in the program.

- The computer collects the values from all of the DATA statements in a program and places them in a single list, referred to as the **data list.** This list is formed by taking the values from the DATA statements in order, from the lowest to the highest line number and from left to right within a single statement.
- When more than one data value is placed in a single DATA statement, the values are separated by commas. Character string values may or may not be placed in quotes. However, if the character string contains leading or trailing blanks, commas, or semicolons, it must be enclosed in quotation marks.
- When the program encounters a READ statement, it goes to the data list and assigns the next value from that list to the corresponding variable in the READ statement. If the variable is numeric, the data value must also be numeric. If it is a character string variable, however, the computer will allow a numeric value to be assigned to it, as previously explained for the INPUT statement. Again, computations cannot be performed with numbers that have been assigned to character string variables.
- If there is inadequate data for a READ statement (that is, if there are no more data values in the data list), an OUT OF DATA error message occurs, and the program stops executing at that point.
- If there are more data values than variables, these extra data values simply remain unread.

Figure 4–2 shows a program segment containing READ and DATA statements. When the computer executes this program, it first encounters the READ statement in line 100. The statement instructs it to read four data values from the data list and assign these values to the corresponding variables. Therefore, the values JACOBS, 48, 60, and 53 are assigned to the variables NME$, S1, S2, and S3 respectively. After this task is completed, program execution continues to line 110, where the next value in the data list, GUINARD, is assigned to the variable NME$. This new value of NME$ replaces JACOBS, which was the previous value.

Note that the computer "remembers" where it is in the data list. Whenever it encounters another READ statement, it assigns the next value

FIGURE 4–2
Examples of READ and DATA Statements

			CURRENT VALUE OF VARIABLES		
		AT LINE #:	NME$	S1	S2	S3
100 READ NME$,S1,S2,S3		100	JACOBS	48	60	53
110 READ NME$		110	GUINARD	48	60	53
120 READ S1,S2		120	GUINARD	62	58	53
130 READ S3		130	GUINARD	62	58	54
140 DATA JACOBS,48						
150 DATA 60,53,GUINARD						
160 DATA 62,58						
170 DATA 54						

FIGURE 4–3 Program Demonstrating the READ and DATA Statements

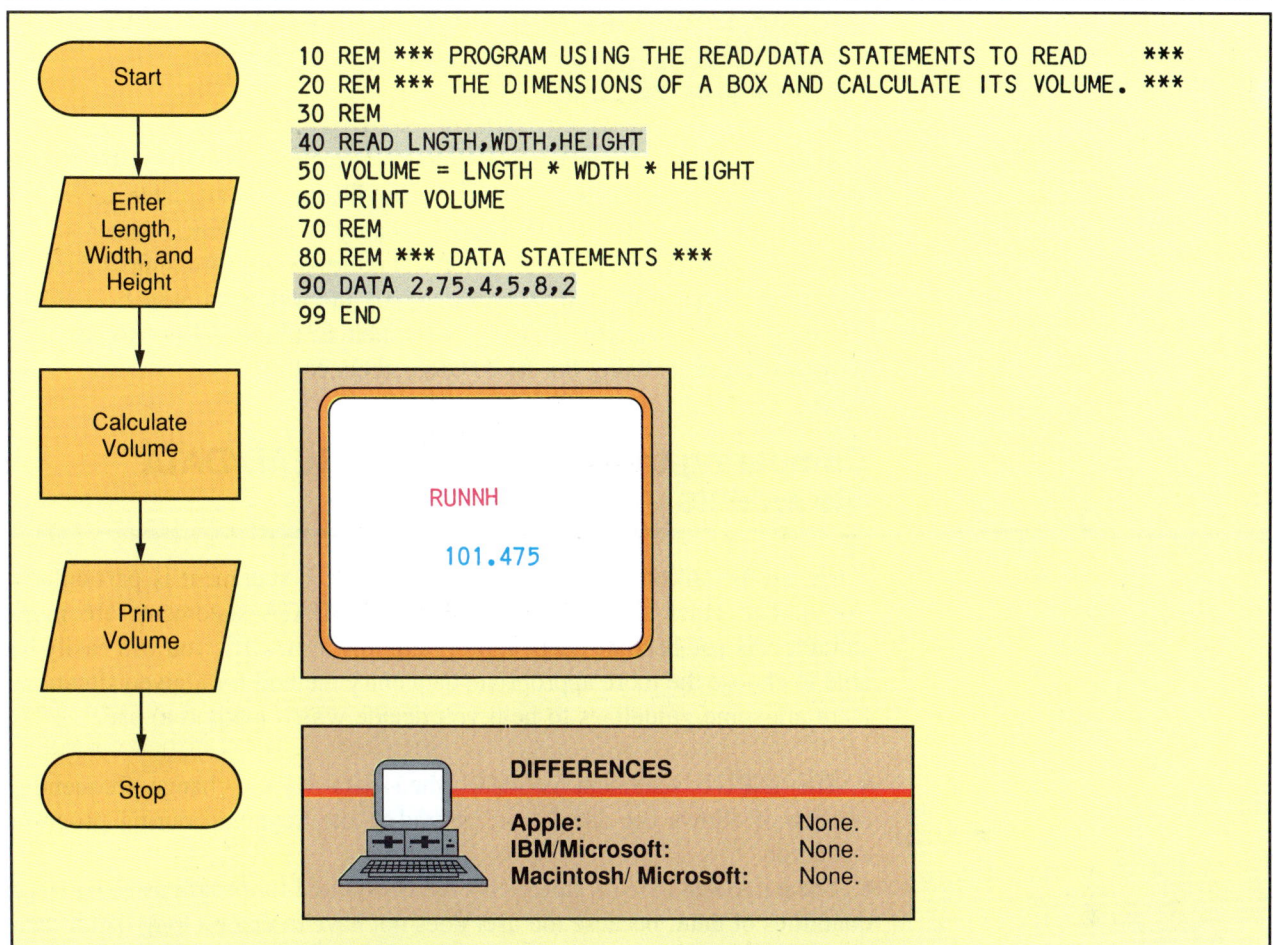

in the list to that variable. Study Figure 4–2 to make certain you understand how the READ and DATA statements are used in reading data values. Notice that the columns on the right side of the figure state the current values of each of the variables for lines 100 through 130.

The program in Figure 4–3 shows how READ and DATA statements can be used to read the dimensions of a box and to calculate and print the volume. Note that line 40 contains a single READ statement that reads all three dimensions of the box. The DATA statement in line 90 contains the three values to be assigned to the three variables in the READ statement.

The RESTORE Statement

Usually, when READ and DATA statements are used, each data value is read only once. If it is necessary to use the same data values more than once, the RESTORE statement can be used. Consider the following program segment:

```
100 READ A,B
110 TT = A + A * B
120 RESTORE
130 READ C,D,E
140 SUM = C + D + E
150 DATA 44,790,1,15,138
```

When line 100 of this program segment is executed, the value 44 will be assigned to A and the value 790 to B. Normally, the next available data value to be read would be 1. However, because a RESTORE statement is encountered in line 120, the computer will return to the beginning of the data list. Thus, when line 130 is encountered, the value 44 will be read to variable C, 790 to variable D, and 1 to variable E. Figure 4–4 contains some program segments using the RESTORE statement.

Comparing the INPUT and the READ/DATA Statements

There are certain situations in which the INPUT statement is particularly useful, and other situations in which READ/DATA statements are more suitable. As you become adept at programming in BASIC, you will easily be able to choose the more appropriate data entry method for a given situation. Here are some guidelines to help you decide which method to use:

- The INPUT statement is ideal when data values change frequently, because it allows the data to be entered at the keyboard during program execution.
- The READ and DATA statements are well suited for programs using large quantities of data, because the user does not have to enter a long list of data values during program execution, as would be necessary with the INPUT statement.

FIGURE 4–4
Program Segments Demonstrating the RESTORE Statement

Program	CURRENT VALUES OF VARIABLES
100 READ A,B,C	A = 14, B = 18, C = 27
110 S1 = A + B + C	S1 = 59
120 RESTORE	
130 READ D,E,F,G	D = 14, E = 18, F = 27, G = 2
140 S2 = D + E + F + G	S2 = 61
150 RESTORE	
160 READ H	H = 14
170 RESTORE	
180 READ I	I = 14
190 S3 = H + I	S3 = 28
200 DATA 14,18,27,2,68	

- The READ and DATA statements are most useful when data values will not be different for each program execution. The main disadvantage of using the READ and DATA statements is that the program itself must be altered when the data values change.

Learning Check

1. When data must be entered to a program while it is executing, a(n) _____ statement is used.
2. A(n) _____ is used to tell the user what kind of data to enter to a program.
3. _____ statements are used to contain the data values that will be assigned to the variables listed in a READ statement.
4. There must be a DATA statement immediately after each READ statement. True or false?
5. The _____ statement causes the next READ statement encountered to start the beginning of the data list.

Answers

1. INPUT 2. prompt 3. DATA 4. False; DATA statements may be anywhere within the program. 5. RESTORE

Printing Results

Chapter 3 explained that the PRINT statement lets us print the results of processing. When more than one item is to be printed on a line, a variety of methods can be used to control the spacing and format of the output.

The Semicolon

The semicolon is often used to separate two or more variables in a single PRINT statement. The semicolon signals the computer to print the next item starting at the next available print position. The following example shows the result when two strings are separated by a semicolon in a PRINT statement.

```
10 PRINT "JOHN";"DRAKE"
```

RUNNH

JOHNDRAKE

The first string is printed, and then the semicolon indicates that the next item should be printed in the next available print position, which is the next column.

To print these strings with a space between them, you can enclose a blank within the quotation marks of one of the strings:

```
10 PRINT "JOHN";" DRAKE"
```

RUNNH

JOHN DRAKE

When numbers are printed, most computers print the number with a preceding space if the number has no sign, such as 104 or 48. If the number has a sign, such as -176 or +32, no preceding space is printed, because the sign is printed in that position. In either case, a space is left after the number for greater readability. Therefore, when numeric values are separated by a semicolon, the printed digits are not adjacent as in the case of the character strings. The following example demonstrates this point:

```
10 PRINT 100;-200;300
```

RUNNH

100 -200 300

Notice that the output shows only one space before -200. This is because the computer left a space after printing the number 100. But there are two spaces before 300: Not only was a space left after -200 was printed, but a space was left for the sign (an assumed positive) of the number 300. However, on the Apple no space is left before or after a number. The programmer can insert blank character strings to insert spaces around numeric output.

A semicolon appearing after the *last* item in a PRINT statement prevents the output of the next PRINT statement from starting on a new line. Instead, the next item printed will appear on the same line at the next available print position:

```
10 PRINT 3567;
20 PRINT "YVONNE";" DRAKE"
```

RUNNH

3567 YVONNE DRAKE

The semicolon at the end of line 10 causes the print position to remain on the same line. When line 20 is encountered, YVONNE DRAKE is printed at the first position after the blank that follows 3567.

Using the Print Zones

The number of characters that can be printed on a line varies with the system being used. On most terminal screens, each output line consists of 80 print positions. Each line is divided into sections called *print zones*. The zone size and the number of zones per line depend on the system. The print zones on the VAX system are 14 characters wide, with five zones per line. The beginning columns of the five print zones are as follows:

ZONE 1:	ZONE 2:	ZONE 3:	ZONE 4:	ZONE 5:
COL 1	COL 15	COL 29	COL 43	COL 57

Commas, like semicolons, can be used within a PRINT statement to control the format of printed output. A comma indicates that the next item to be printed will start at the beginning of the next print zone. The following example shows how this works:

```
10 READ W1$,W2$,W3$
20 PRINT W1$,W2$,W3$
30 DATA "BE","SEEING","YOU"
```

The first item in the PRINT statement is printed at the beginning of the line, which is the start of the first print zone. The comma between W1$ and W2$ causes the computer to space over to the next print zone; then the value in W2$ is printed. The second comma directs the computer to space over to the next zone (Zone 3) and print the value in W3$. The output is as follows:

RUNNH

BE   SEEING   YOU

If there are more items listed in a PRINT statement than there are print zones in a line, the print zones of the next line are also used, starting with the first zone. Notice the output of the following example.

```
10 READ SEX$,AGE,CLASS$,MAJ$,HRS,GPA
20 PRINT SEX$,AGE,CLASS$,MAJ$,HRS,GPA
30 DATA "M",19,"JR","CS",18,2.5
```

RUNNH

M   19   JR   CS   18
2.5

If the value to be printed exceeds the width of the print zone, the entire value is printed, regardless of how many zones it occupies. A following comma causes printing to continue in the next print zone, as shown in the following example:

```
10 SPOT$ = "BAGHDAD"
20 PRINT "YOUR NEXT DESTINATION WILL BE",SPOT$
```

RUNNH

YOUR NEXT DESTINATION WILL BE   BAGHDAD

Table 4–1 presents the formatting differences among the four computer systems discussed in this book. Columns 2 and 3 give the number of print zones per line and zone widths. Note that some systems enable the user to determine the zone dimensions. Columns 4 and 5 indicate whether leading and trailing spaces are provided for numeric values.

A print zone can be skipped by typing consecutive commas:

```
10 PRINT "ARTIST",,"ALBUM"
```

The literal ARTIST will be printed in Zone 1, the second zone will be blank, and the literal ALBUM will be printed in Zone 3:

RUNNH

ARTIST   ALBUM

If a comma appears after the last item in a PRINT statement, the output of the next PRINT statement encountered will begin at the next available print zone. Thus, the statements

```
10 READ NME$,AGE,SEX$,VOICE$
20 PRINT NME$,AGE,
30 PRINT SEX$,VOICE$
40 DATA "SHICOFF",32,"M","TENOR"
99 END
```

produce the following output:

RUNNH

SHICOFF   32   M   TENOR

TABLE 4–1 Computer Display Characteristics

COMPUTER	NUMBER OF PRINT ZONES	ZONE WIDTH	SPACE FOR SIGN?	SPACE AFTER NUMBER?
VAX	5	14	Yes	Yes
Apple	3	16	No	No
IBM/Microsoft	5	14	Yes	Yes
Mac/Microsoft	*	*	Yes	Yes

*Refer to Appendix I for instructions on using print zones on the Macintosh.

Learning Check

1. A semicolon between items in a PRINT statement tells the computer to skip to the next available _____ to print the next item.
2. The _____ is used in PRINT statements to skip to the beginning of the next print zone.
3. 110 PRINT "JOE IS";"NINETY" will result in what output?
4. When a PRINT statement ends with a comma or semicolon, the next value output will always begin _____.
   a. on the next line
   b. on the next page
   c. on the same line, if there is room
5. Which of the following statements will cause a print zone to be left completely blank?
   a. 10 PRINT "YESTERDAY","TODAY"
   b. 20 PRINT "YESTERDAY",,"TODAY"
   c. 30 PRINT "YESTERDAY";;"TODAY"

Answers

1. column 2. comma 3. JOE ISNINETY 4. c. 5. b.

The TAB Function

We have seen that the semicolon causes data to be printed in the next position on the output line, and that the comma causes data to be printed according to predefined print zones. Both formats are easy to use, and many reports can be formatted in this fashion. However, there are times when a report should be structured differently.

The TAB function allows output to be printed in any column in an output line, thus providing the programmer greater flexibility to format printed output. As with the comma and semicolon, one or more TAB functions are used within a PRINT statement. The general format of the TAB function is this:

TAB(expression)

The expression may be a numeric constant, a variable, or an arithmetic expression. When a TAB function is encountered in a PRINT statement, the computer spaces over to the column number indicated in the expression. The next variable value or literal found in the PRINT statement is printed, starting in that column. The TAB function is separated from the items to be printed by semicolons. For example, the statement

```
50 PRINT TAB(10);"HI THERE!";TAB(25);"BYE!"
```

causes the literal HI THERE! to be printed starting in column 10. Then, starting in column 25, the literal BYE! is printed.

It is best to have the expression in the TAB function evaluate as an integer, because this makes it clear in which column the output will start printing. However, it is possible to use a real value for an expression, as in the following statement:

```
50 PRINT TAB(15.7);"HI THERE!"
```

On the VAX system, the number 15.7 will be rounded to 16, and the computer will tab to the sixteenth column.

The program in Figure 4–5 prints a simple table by using the TAB function to place the printed values in columns.

When using the TAB function, it is important to be aware of spacing. On the VAX system, there can be a space between the word TAB and the left parenthesis, because the VAX recognizes the reserved word TAB. On some systems, however—for example, the IBM—there cannot be a space between TAB and the left parenthesis. This is because the reserved word that these systems recognize is TAB(. Without the opening parenthesis following it, TAB is taken as a variable name TAB, and the value in parentheses is taken as an array subscript. (Arrays will be discussed in Chapter 9). The following statement would be invalid on systems that recognize TAB) as a reserved word:

```
10 PRINT TAB (5);"ITEM";TAB (25);"GALLONS"
```

The statement would be correctly written like this:

```
10 PRINT TAB(5);"ITEM";TAB(25);"GALLONS"
```

The TAB function can be used only to advance the print position from left to right; backspacing is not possible. Therefore, if more than one TAB function appears in a single PRINT statement, the column numbers specified should increase from left to right. An example will illustrate this point:

Correct Use of TAB function:

```
20 PRINT TAB(5);3;TAB(15);4;TAB(25);5
```

RUNNH

    3   4   5

Incorrect Use of TAB function:

```
20 PRINT TAB(25);5;TAB(15);4;TAB(5);3
```

FIGURE 4-5 Program Demonstrating the TAB Function

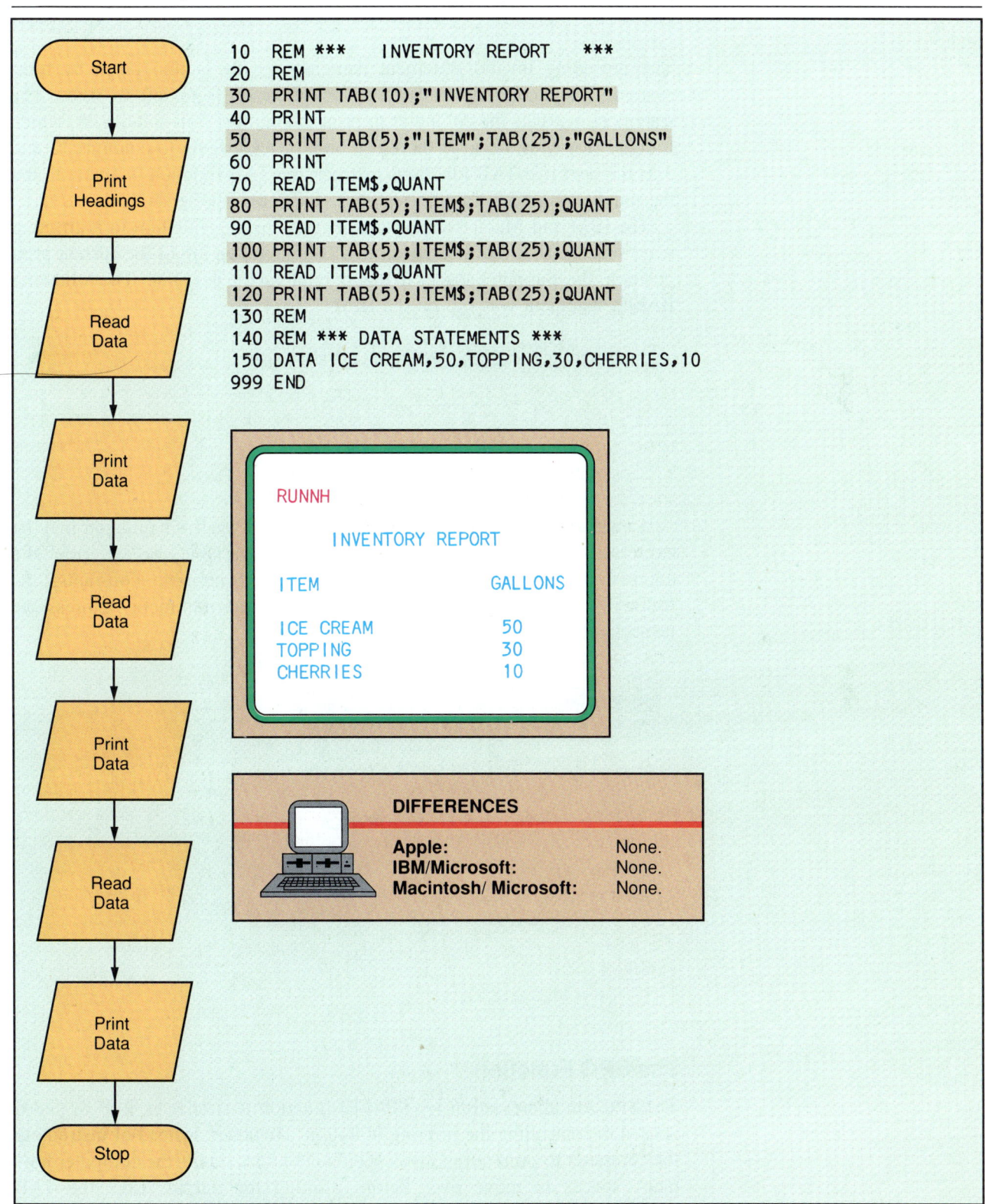

RUNNH

                            5   4   3

The preceding invalid statement demonstrates the action taken by most systems when column numbers do not increase from left to right. The statement instructs the computer to print the number 5 in column 25, which it does. However, because there can be no backspacing to columns 15 and 5 as the next two TAB functions instruct, the TAB function is ignored, and the numbers 4 and 3 are printed where indicated by the semicolons.

The IBM and Macintosh systems respond to this situation in a different way. When a TAB function specifies a column to the left of the current print position, the computer spaces to that column on the next line. The following BASIC statement was run on the IBM:

```
20 PRINT TAB(25);5;TAB(15);4;TAB(5);3
```

RUN

                            5
                  4
        3

As already mentioned, the column number of the TAB function may be expressed as a numeric constant, a numeric variable, or an arithmetic expression. All previous examples have used numeric constants; the following examples use numeric variables and arithmetic expressions respectively:

```
10 Y = 25
20 X = 10
30 PRINT TAB(X);7;TAB(Y);"MONICA"
```

RUNNH

           7   MONICA

```
10 Y = 20
20 X = 15
30 PRINT TAB(X-5);7;TAB(Y+5);"MONICA"
```

RUNNH

           7   MONICA

The SPC Function

The SPC (an abbreviation for SPACE) function is similar to TAB in that it is used in controlling the printing of output. However, instead of instructing the computer to print output in a specified column, it tells the computer how many spaces to move over before printing the output. Like the TAB function, the SPC function should be separated from other items in the PRINT statement by semicolons. For example:

```
40 PRINT "WORD";SPC(10);"LETTER"
```

RUN
WORD   LETTER

When line 40 is executed, WORD is printed in columns 1 through 4; then the computer leaves ten blank spaces between the end of WORD and the beginning of LETTER. Therefore, LETTER is printed starting in column 15.

The SPC function is not available on the VAX system, but it is implemented on all of the other BASIC systems covered in this text.

The PRINT USING Statement

Yet another convenient feature for controlling output, the PRINT USING statement, is especially useful when printing table headings or aligning columns of numbers. All of the computers covered in this text, except the Apple, have a PRINT USING statement. The general format is

line# PRINT USING "format control characters";expression-list

The expression list consists of a sequence of variables or expressions separated by commas, similar to the expression list in any PRINT statement. The PRINT USING statement instructs the computer to print the items in this expression list using the format control characters specified. These format control characters determine how the output will be printed.

PRINT USING statements are useful in aligning columns of numbers. Consider the following program segment:

```
10  READ V1,V2,V3,V4
20  PRINT USING "######.##";V1,V2,V3,V4
30  READ V1,V2,V3,V4
40  PRINT USING "######.##";V1,V2,V3,V4
50  READ V1,V2,V3,V4
60  PRINT USING "######.##";V1,V2,V3,V4
70  READ V1,V2,V3,V4
80  PRINT USING "######.##";V1,V2,V3,V4
90  DATA 14.56,78.90,10234.1,0.03,6.73,12322.4,943.05,17.65
100 DATA 65.56,945.7,125447.80,0.17,175.35,78.92,319.00,4.56
```

The output of this program segment is

RUNNH

14.56	78.90	10234.10	0.03
6.73	12322.40	943.05	17.65
65.56	945.70	125447.80	0.17
175.35	78.92	319.00	4.56

Note that all of the numbers have been aligned at the decimal point. Each "#" symbol represents 1 digit.

A second method of using the PRINT USING statement is to assign the format control characters to a string variable. This variable can then be referred to in the PRINT USING statement. The previous program segment could be rewritten using this method as follows:

```
10   READ V1,V2,V3,V4
20   FMT$ = "######.##"
30   PRINT USING FMT$;V1,V2,V3,V4
40   READ V1,V2,V3,V4
50   PRINT USING FMT$;V1,V2,V3,V4
60   READ V1,V2,V3,V4
70   PRINT USING FMT$;V1,V2,V3,V4
80   READ V1,V2,V3,V4
90   PRINT USING FMT$;V1,V2,V3,V4
100  DATA 14.56,78.90,10234.1,0.03,6.73,12322.4,943.05,17.65
110  DATA 65.56,945.7,125447.80,0.17,175.35,78.92,319.00,4.56
```

Line 20 assigns the format control characters to the string variable FMT$. FMT$ is then referenced in the PRINT USING statements in lines 30, 50, 70, and 90. This method is particularly helpful when a number of output lines need to be formatted in the same way. Table 4–2 contains some commonly used format control characters.

The program in Figure 4–6 illustrates how PRINT USING statements can be used to print a table. Notice the use of the two consecutive dollar signs in line 90:

```
90   PRINT USING "\          \        $$##.##      $$##.##";A$,X,Y
```

This causes the dollar sign to "float," so that it is always printed immediately before the first digit of the number following it.

The PRINT USING statement can easily be used to center character strings within a field. For example, the statements

```
100  PRINT USING "'CCCCCCCCCCCCCCCCCCCCCCCCCCCCCC";
        "HALSTON & LING, INC."
110  PRINT USING "'CCCCCCCCCCCCCCCCCCCCCCCCCCCCCC";
        "ATTORNEYS AT LAW"
120  PRINT USING "'CCCCCCCCCCCCCCCCCCCCCCCCCCCCCC";
        "749 S. MAIN"
130  PRINT USING "'CCCCCCCCCCCCCCCCCCCCCCCCCCCCCC";
        "ALTOONA, MI"
```

will cause the following output:

```
RUNNH

            HALSTON & LING, INC.
              ATTORNEYS AT LAW
                749 S. MAIN
                ALTOONA, MI
```

TABLE 4–2 Format Control Characters for PRINT USING Statement

NUMERIC FORMAT CHARACTERS

CHARACTER	EXPLANATION	EXAMPLE
#	One symbol is used for each digit to be printed; zeros are added to the left of the number to fill the field.	####.##
$	Dollar sign; printed exactly as is.	$###.##
$$	Causes dollar sign to be printed immediately before first digit.	$$##.##
**	Leading asterisks; prints the asterisks in place of blanks.	**#.#
.	Decimal point; printed exactly as is.	##.##
,	Places a comma in front of each group of three digits to the left of the decimal point.	##,###.##

FORMAT CHARACTERS FOR CHARACTER STRINGS

CHARACTER	EXPLANATION	EXAMPLE
\spaces\	Reserves n + 2 spaces for a character string where n is the length of the string. If the string is shorter than the length of the field, it is left-justified.	\ \
C	Centers the string in the field.	'CCCCCCC
L	Left-justifies the string in the field.	'LLLLLLL
R	Right-justifies the string in the field.	'RRRRRRR

Note: C, L, and R are not available on the IBM or Macintosh.

The use of the "C" format control characters causes the output to be centered in a field thirty characters long (there are thirty "C"s in each statement). All format control characters must be enclosed in double quotation marks. In addition, the string format control fields using "C", "L", "R" must be preceded by a single quotation mark (notice that there is a single quotation mark before the first "C" in each of the statements in the previous example).

96 BASIC PROGRAMMING TODAY, A STRUCTURED APPROACH

FIGURE 4-6 Program Demonstrating the PRINT USING Statement

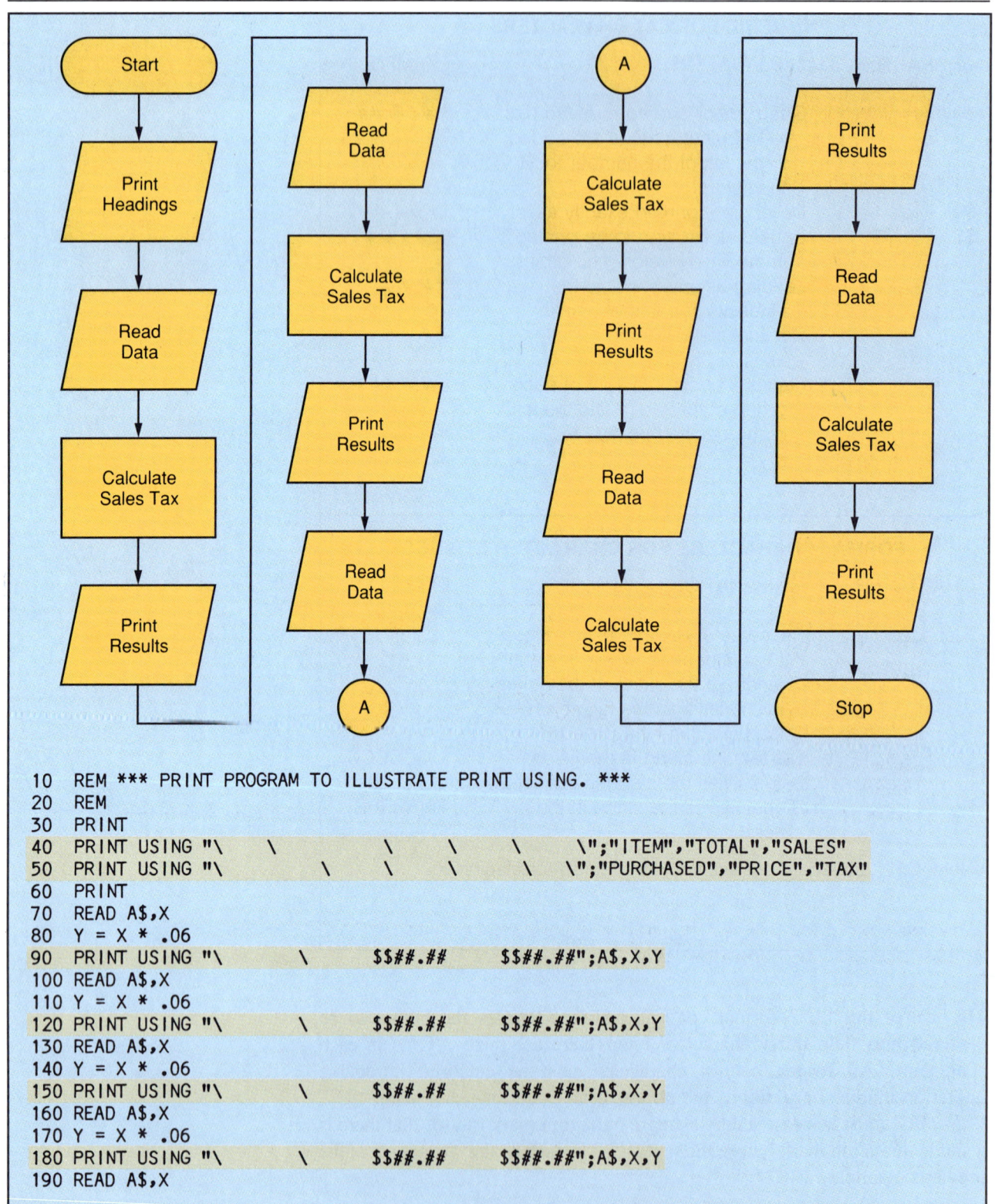

```
10  REM *** PRINT PROGRAM TO ILLUSTRATE PRINT USING. ***
20  REM
30  PRINT
40  PRINT USING "\         \         \         \         \         \";"ITEM","TOTAL","SALES"
50  PRINT USING "\         \         \         \         \         \";"PURCHASED","PRICE","TAX"
60  PRINT
70  READ A$,X
80  Y = X * .06
90  PRINT USING "\         \     $$##.##     $$##.##";A$,X,Y
100 READ A$,X
110 Y = X * .06
120 PRINT USING "\         \     $$##.##     $$##.##";A$,X,Y
130 READ A$,X
140 Y = X * .06
150 PRINT USING "\         \     $$##.##     $$##.##";A$,X,Y
160 READ A$,X
170 Y = X * .06
180 PRINT USING "\         \     $$##.##     $$##.##";A$,X,Y
190 READ A$,X
```

FIGURE 4-6 Continued

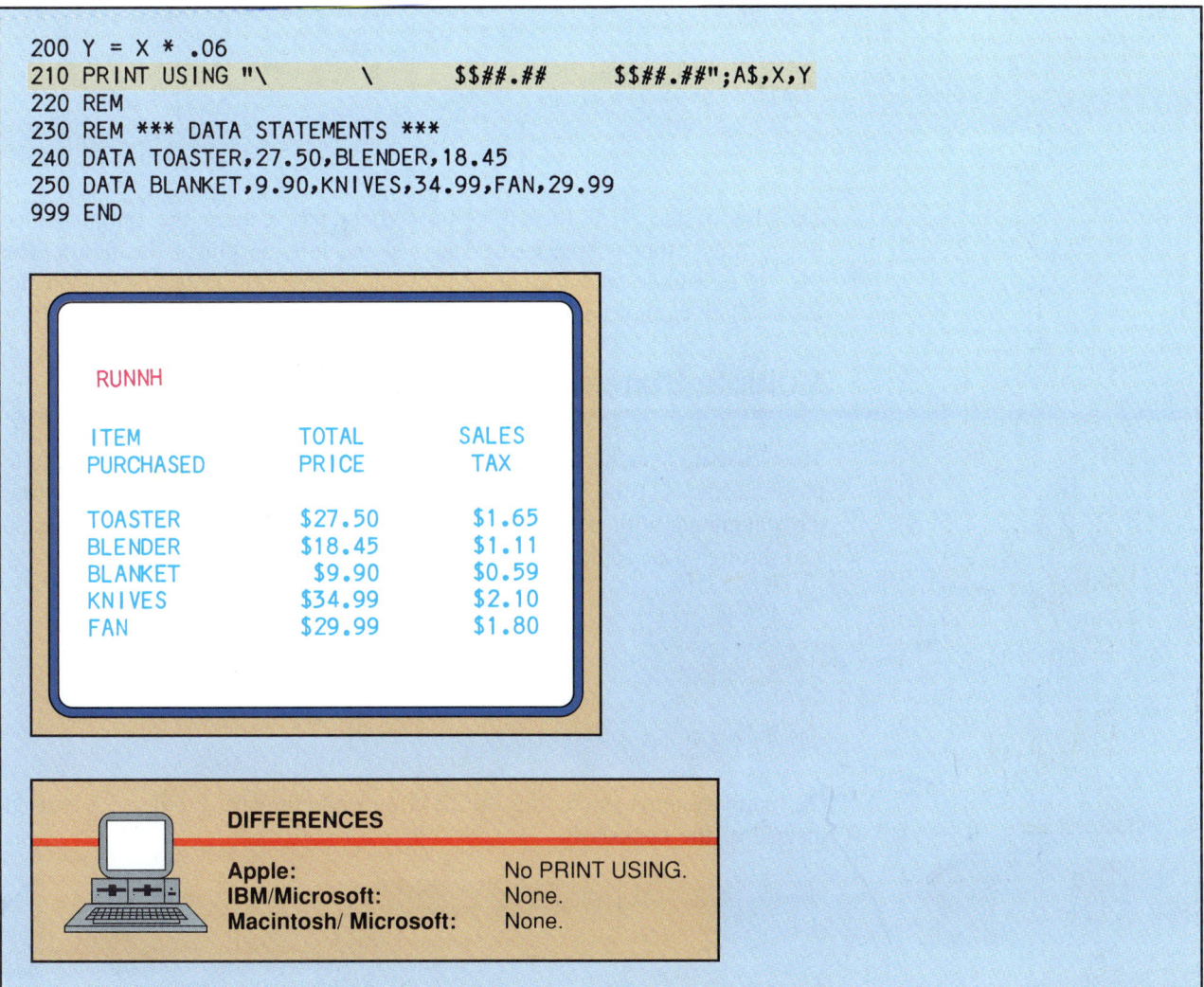

```
200 Y = X * .06
210 PRINT USING "\        \      $$##.##       $$##.##";A$,X,Y
220 REM
230 REM *** DATA STATEMENTS ***
240 DATA TOASTER,27.50,BLENDER,18.45
250 DATA BLANKET,9.90,KNIVES,34.99,FAN,29.99
999 END
```

```
RUNNH

ITEM           TOTAL        SALES
PURCHASED      PRICE        TAX

TOASTER        $27.50       $1.65
BLENDER        $18.45       $1.11
BLANKET         $9.90       $0.59
KNIVES         $34.99       $2.10
FAN            $29.99       $1.80
```

DIFFERENCES

Apple: No PRINT USING.
IBM/Microsoft: None.
Macintosh/Microsoft: None.

Suppose the same program segment is run again, but with the "C" control characters replaced with "L"s:

```
100 PRINT USING "'LLLLLLLLLLLLLLLLLLLLLLLLLLLLLL";
    "HALSTON & LING, INC."
110 PRINT USING "'LLLLLLLLLLLLLLLLLLLLLLLLLLLLLL";
    "ATTORNEYS AT LAW"
120 PRINT USING "'LLLLLLLLLLLLLLLLLLLLLLLLLLLLLL";
    "749 S. MAIN"
130 PRINT USING "'LLLLLLLLLLLLLLLLLLLLLLLLLLLLLL";
    "ALTOONA, MI"
```

the output now looks like this:

```
RUNNH

HALSTON & LING, INC.
ATTORNEYS AT LAW
749 S. MAIN
ALTOONA, MI
```

The use of the "L" format control characters causes the output to be left-justified (that is, the string starts at the left margin of the field). The "C," "L," and "R" format control characters can be used only on the VAX. They cannot be used on the IBM or the Macintosh.

Multiple Statements on a Single Physical Line

Most BASIC systems allow multiple statements to be placed on a single physical line. On the VAX system, this can be accomplished by separating the statements with backslashes (\). The following statements numbered 100 through 120 could be combined as shown in line 130:

```
100 PRINT V1
110 PRINT V2
120 PRINT V3
```

```
130 PRINT V1 \ PRINT V2 \ PRINT V3
```

On many systems (including the IBM and Macintosh), a colon (:) is used instead of the backslash:

```
130 PRINT V1 : PRINT V2 : PRINT V3
```

Learning Check

1. The _____ function causes output to be printed in a column specified by the programmer.
2. What is wrong with this statement?

   ```
   10 PRINT 7;TAB(10 + 12);8;TAB(14);9
   ```

3. The _____, not the _____, is always used with the TAB function.
4. What is the purpose of the comma (,) format control character in a PRINT USING statement?
5. How will the output of the following two statements differ?

   ```
   10 PRINT USING "$###.##";M$
   ```

   ```
   10 PRINT USING "$$###.##";M$
   ```

Answers

1. TAB 2. The column number given in the second TAB is larger than the one given in the third TAB. 3. semicolon; comma 4. To place a comma between each group of three digits that are to the left of the decimal point. 5. In the first statement, the dollar sign will always be in the same position whereas in the second statement it will "float," so that it is always immediately in front of the first digit of the number.

A Programming Problem

Problem Definition

Port Charles, Rhode Island, is holding its mayoral election and would like to analyze the voting by party affiliation at different times of the election day. A program is needed to determine the percentage of voters per party, the total votes cast, and the percentage of voter turnout at three different times of the day.

Input:

Registered Voters

Number of Republicans	Number of Democrats	Number Unaffiliated
372	218	324

Votes Received*

Time	Republican	Democrats	Unaffiliated
7 a.m.	15	16	10
12 p.m.	92	104	143
4 p.m.	260	188	199

*(The above counts are cumulative; in other words, the 92 Republican votes counted at 12 p.m. include the 15 votes received by 7 a.m.)

Needed Output:

```
                    ELECTION DAY VOTING ANALYSIS:
                    BY TIME AND PARTY AFFILIATION

REGISTERED         REP      DEM     UNAFFILIATED      TOTAL
                   ---      ---     ------------      -----
                   372      218         324            914

NUMBER OF VOTES CAST BY:
TIME    REP    %      DEM    %      UNAFF    %      TOTAL    %
----    ---    ---    ---    ---    -----    ---    -----    ---

 7       15    4.03    16    7.34     10    3.09      41    4.49
12       92   24.73   104   47.71    143   44.14     339   37.09
 4      260   69.89   188   86.24    199   61.42     647   70.79
```

Solution Design

There are three basic types of data for this program: (1) the number of voters registered in each classification, (2) the time, and (3) the number of voters in each category who have cast their ballots by the three designated times. READ and DATA statements should be used for the party registration, because these numbers are static. However, INPUT statements should be used for the time and number of ballots cast, so that different values can be entered every time the program is run.

The program needs to output this information along with the total votes cast by the designated times. The percentage for each category and the overall percentage who have voted by the designated time must also be calculated and printed. The problem specifies the format in which the output should be printed. This formatting can be accomplished with the use of the TAB function and the PRINT USING statement.

To determine the percentages, you divide the votes cast in each category by the total number of possible voters in that category and multiply by 100. The total number of ballots cast is determined by adding together all the votes received as of that time. Again, the total percentage is calculated by dividing total votes by total possible votes and multiplying by 100. The following variables are necessary:

Input Variables

Designated time	(TIME#)
Republican votes received within a given time period	(R#VOTE)
Democrat votes received within a given time period	(D#VOTE)
Unaffiliated votes received within a given time period	(U#VOTE)
Number of registered Republicans	(REPREG)
Number of registered Democrats	(DEMREG)
Number of registered unaffiliates	(UNAREG)

Output Variables

Percentage of Republicans voting in a given time period	(P#PER)
Percentage of Democrats voting in a given time period	(M#PER)
Percentage of unaffiliated voting in a given time period	(A#PER)
Total votes in first time period	(FPERIOD)
Total votes in second time period	(SPERIOD)
Total votes in third time period	(TPERIOD)
Percentage of all voters voting within a given time period	(P#PER)
Total number of registered voters	(VOTET)

Note the use of the number symbol (#) in the variable names, such as TIME#. This symbol is used to designate that the number of the correct time period will be inserted at this point. For example, the variable TIME# would be replaced in the program with three variables, one for each of the three time periods: TIME1, TIME2, and TIME3.

The stepwise refinement of the algorithm for this problem is shown in Figure 4–7, and the corresponding structure chart is contained in Figure 4–8.

FIGURE 4–7
Stepwise Refinement of Mayoral Election Problem

General Problem: Calculate the percentage of votes per party, total votes received, and total turnout percentage at three designated times for the mayoral election.

Level 1
A. Print primary headings
B. Process party registrations
C. Print secondary headings
D. Process data for each party at each time

Level 2
B.1. Read party registration
B.2. Print party registration
D.1. Calculate percentage of ballots cast by party affiliation for time period
D.2. Calculate total votes and total percentages for each time period
D.3. Print results

FIGURE 4–8 Structure Chart of Mayoral Election Problem

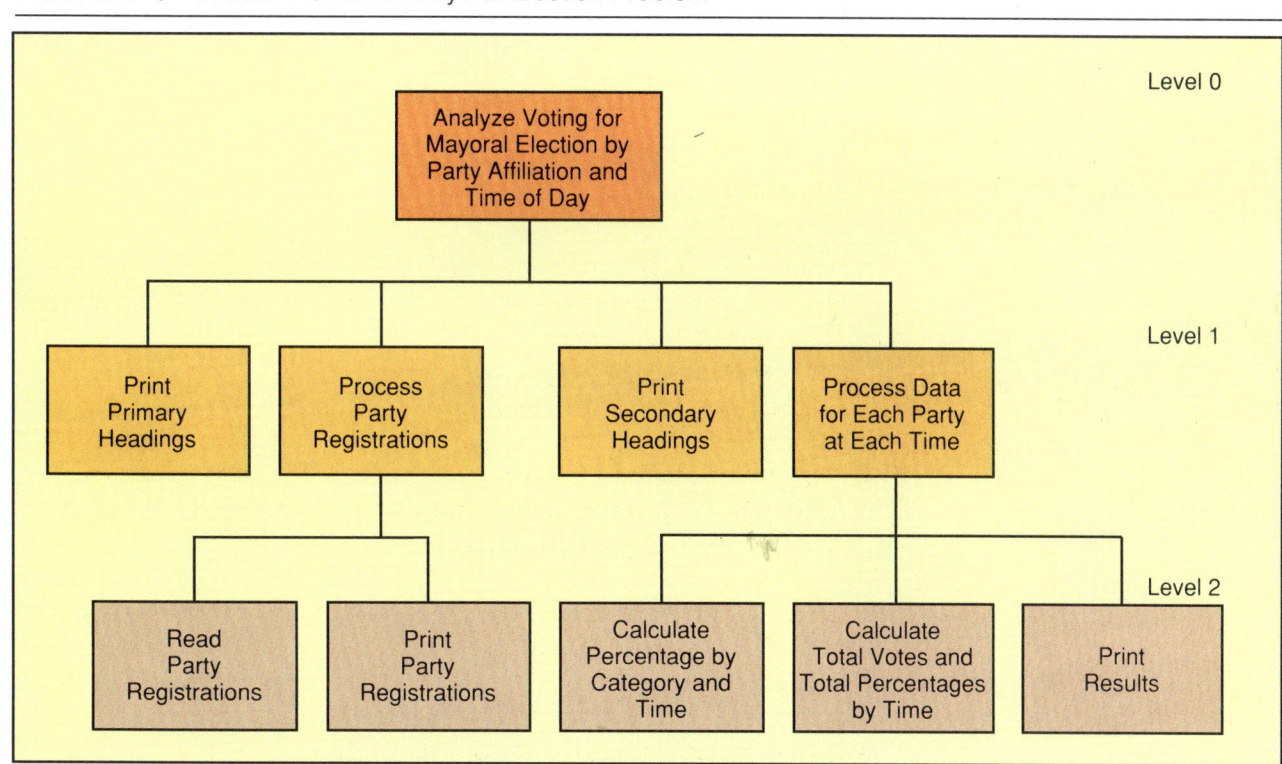

The Program

The solution to the completed program is shown in Figure 4–9. In order to prevent input prompts from occurring within the formatted output, the program has been written so that the times and votes are inputted first (lines 240 through 350), followed by the printing of the headings (line 370 through 590). One line of the headings is the number of registered voters per party. These values are read to the program by using READ and DATA statements because these numbers are static.

The percentage of Republicans having voted at each of the three time periods is calculated in lines 630 through 650. The same is done for the Democrats in lines 680 through 700 and for unaffiliated voters in lines 730 through 750. The format for outputting each of these figures is the same. Therefore, the same format statement (contained in line 860) can be used for each of these PRINT USING statements.

Spend a minute examining the documentation of this program. The first line contains the program name. Next are five lines that explain the overall purpose of the program. The major variables used by the program are described in lines 90 through 210. Documentation is also placed within the body of the program itself. REM statements are placed before each major section. Thoroughly documenting a program makes its logic easier to follow.

INPUT AND OUTPUT 103

FIGURE 4-9 Mayoral Election Program

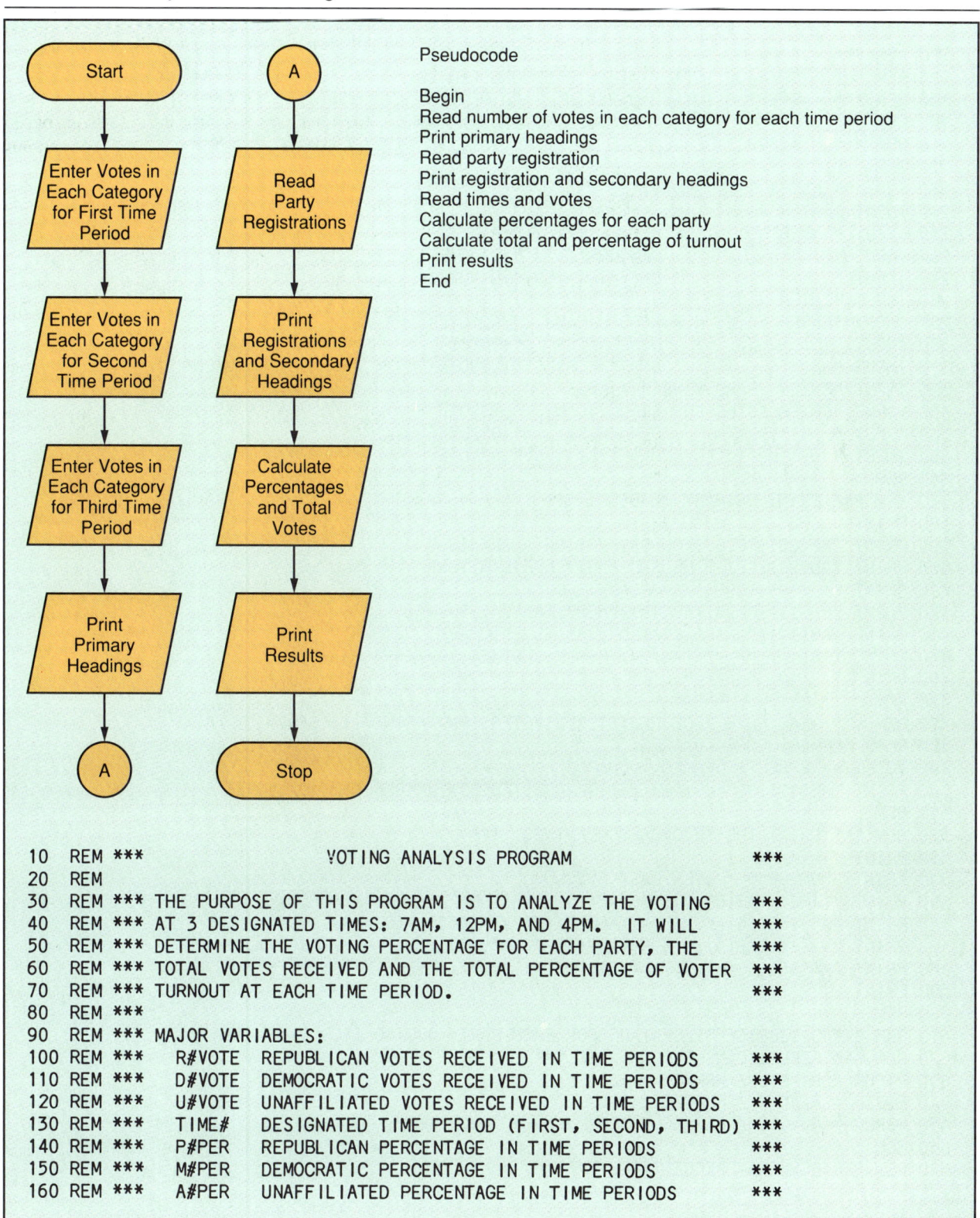

FIGURE 4-9 *Continued*

```
170 REM ***     FPERIOD  TOTAL VOTES IN FIRST PERIOD           ***
180 REM ***     SPERIOD  TOTAL VOTES IN SECOND PERIOD          ***
190 REM ***     TPERIOD  TOTAL VOTES IN THIRD PERIOD           ***
200 REM ***     VOTET    TOTAL POSSIBLE VOTES                  ***
210 REM ***     T#PER    PERCENTAGE OF TOTAL VOTE IN TIME PERIODS ***
220 REM
230 REM *** ENTER TIME AND VOTES CAST. ***
240 INPUT "ENTER FIRST TIME ";TIME1
250 INPUT "ENTER VOTES FOR REPUBLICANS: ";R1VOTE
260 INPUT "                 DEMOCRATS:   ";D1VOTE
270 INPUT "                 UNAFFILIATES:";U1VOTE
280 INPUT "ENTER SECOND TIME ";TIME2
290 INPUT "ENTER VOTES FOR REPUBLICANS: ";R2VOTE
300 INPUT "                 DEMOCRATS:   ";D2VOTE
310 INPUT "                 UNAFFILIATES:";U2VOTE
320 INPUT "ENTER THIRD TIME ";TIME3
330 INPUT "ENTER VOTES FOR REPUBLICANS: ";R3VOTE
340 INPUT "                 DEMOCRATS:   ";D3VOTE
350 INPUT "                 UNAFFILIATES:";U3VOTE
360 REM
370 REM *** PRINT PRIMARY HEADING. ***
380 PRINT
390 PRINT TAB(20);"ELECTION DAY VOTING ANALYSIS:"
400 PRINT TAB(20);"BY TIME AND PARTY AFFILIATION"
410 PRINT
420 PRINT "REGISTERED";TAB(16);"REP";TAB(24);"DEM";
430 PRINT TAB(32);"UNAFFILIATED";TAB(49);"TOTAL"
440 PRINT TAB(16);"---";TAB(24);"---";TAB(32);"------------";
450 PRINT TAB(49);"-----"
460 REM
470 REM *** READ NUMBER OF REGISTERED VOTERS AND PRINT IT. ***
480 READ REPREG,DEMREG,UNAREG
490 VOTET = REPREG + DEMREG + UNAREG
500 PRINT TAB(15);REPREG;TAB(23);DEMREG;TAB(35);UNAREG;TAB(49);VOTET
510 REM
520 REM *** PRINT THE SECONDARY HEADINGS. ***
530 PRINT
540 PRINT "NUMBER OF VOTES CAST BY:"
550 PRINT "TIME";TAB(8);"REP";TAB(16);"%";TAB(22);"DEM";TAB(30);
560 PRINT "%";TAB(36);"UNAFF";TAB(46);"%";TAB(52);"TOTAL";TAB(62);"%"
570 PRINT "----";TAB(8);"---";TAB(15);"---";TAB(22);"---";TAB(29);"---";
580 PRINT TAB(36);"-----";TAB(45);"---";TAB(52);"-----";TAB(61);"---"
590 PRINT
600 REM
610 REM *** DETERMINE PERCENTAGE FOR EACH PARTY DURING EACH TIME. ***
620 REM *** REPUBLICANS PERCENTAGES ***
630 P1PER = R1VOTE / REPREG * 100
640 P2PER = R2VOTE / REPREG * 100
650 P3PER = R3VOTE / REPREG * 100
660 REM
670 REM *** DEMOCRAT PERCENTAGES ***
```

FIGURE 4–9 *Continued*

```
680 M1PER = D1VOTE / DEMREG * 100
690 M2PER = D2VOTE / DEMREG * 100
700 M3PER = D3VOTE / DEMREG * 100
710 REM
720 REM *** UNAFFILIATED PERCENTAGES ***
730 A1PER = U1VOTE / UNAREG * 100
740 A2PER = U2VOTE / UNAREG * 100
750 A3PER = U3VOTE / UNAREG * 100
760 REM
770 REM *** CALCULATE TOTALS AND PERCENTAGE AT TIME INTERVALS. ***
780 FPERIOD = R1VOTE + D1VOTE + U1VOTE
790 T1PER = FPERIOD / VOTET * 100
800 SPERIOD = R2VOTE + D2VOTE + U2VOTE
810 T2PER = SPERIOD / VOTET * 100
820 TPERIOD = R3VOTE + D3VOTE + U3VOTE
830 T3PER = TPERIOD / VOTET * 100
840 REM
850 REM *** PRINT RESULTS. ***
860 F$ = "##      ###  ##.##     ###  ##.##     ###  ##.##     ###  ##.##"
870 PRINT USING F$;TIME1,R1VOTE,P1PER,D1VOTE,M1PER,U1VOTE,A1PER,FPERIOD,T1PER
880 PRINT USING F$;TIME2,R2VOTE,P2PER,D2VOTE,M2PER,U2VOTE,A2PER,SPERIOD,T2PER
890 PRINT USING F$;TIME3,R3VOTE,P3PER,D3VOTE,M3PER,U3VOTE,A3PER,TPERIOD,T3PER
900 REM
910 REM *** DATA STATEMENT ***
920 DATA 372,218,324
999 END
```

```
RUNNH

ENTER FIRST TIME ? 7
ENTER VOTES FOR REPUBLICANS: ? 15
                DEMOCRATS:    ? 16
                UNAFFILIATES:? 10
ENTER SECOND TIME ? 12
ENTER VOTES FOR REPUBLICANS: ? 92
                DEMOCRATS:    ? 104
                UNAFFILIATES:? 143
ENTER THIRD TIME ? 4
ENTER VOTES FOR REPUBLICANS: ? 260
                DEMOCRATS:    ? 188
                UNAFFILIATES:? 199
```

FIGURE 4–9 *Continued*

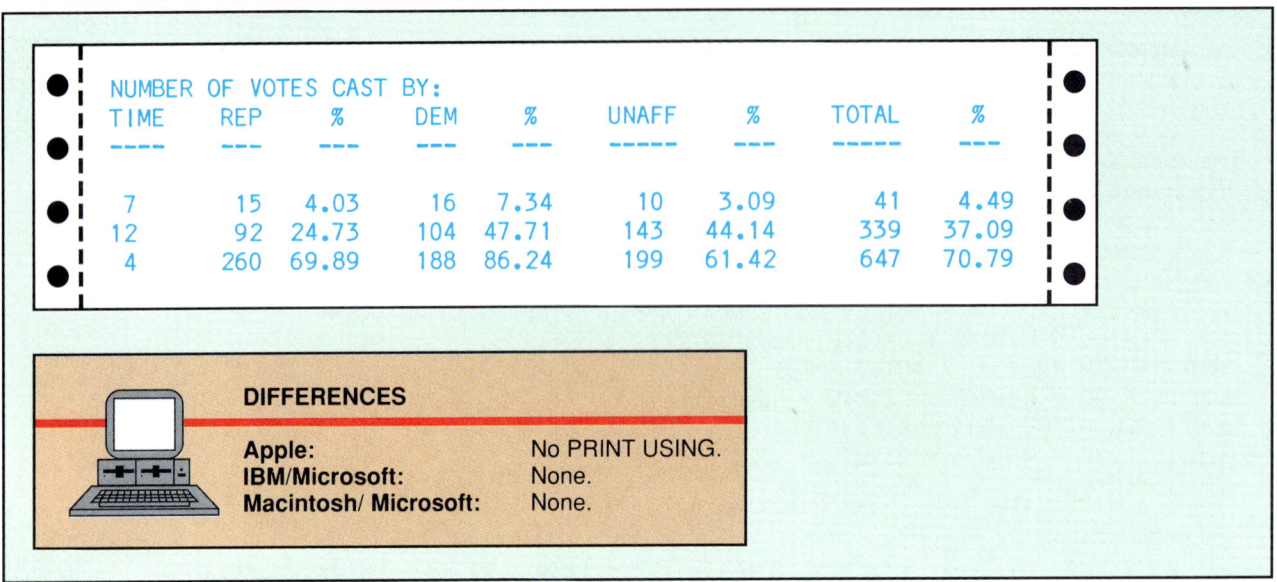

Avoiding Common Programming Mistakes

- Wherever your program contains an INPUT statement, be sure to include a prompt telling the user the number of data values to be entered and the kind of values (numeric or string).
- Make certain that each data value in the DATA statements of a program will be assigned to the correct variable in a READ statement.
- Remember that if a PRINT statement contains more commas than there are print zones, the print zones of the next line will be used.
- Do not use commas in a TAB statement. If you do, the output will be printed in the predefined print zones rather than in the column specified in the TAB statement.
- Remember that the TAB function can be used only to advance the print position. Therefore, each column number in the statement should be larger than the previous one.
- On many systems, there cannot be a space between the reserved word TAB and the left parenthesis. If this is true for your system, be certain that you observe this rule.

Summary Points

- This chapter introduced two methods of entering data to a program: the INPUT statement and the READ and DATA statements.

- The INPUT statement allows the user to enter data while the program is running. Therefore, the values used can change each time the program is run.
- When an INPUT statement is encountered during program execution, the program stops running until the user enters the needed data and presses the RETURN key. Each data value entered is then assigned to the corresponding variable in the INPUT statement.
- When data must be entered by the user, the program should display a prompt telling exactly what data is to be entered.
- The READ and DATA statements are a second method of entering data. The READ statement causes values contained in the DATA statements to be assigned to the variables listed in the READ statement.
- DATA statements are nonexecutable and can be located anywhere in the program. For consistency, they are generally placed at the end of the program. When a program is executed, all of the data values in all of the DATA statements are combined into one listing, called the *data list*.
- READ and INPUT statements are located in a program where the logic of the program dictates.
- The RESTORE statement causes the next READ statement to begin taking values from the top of the data list.
- Numeric values can be assigned to character variables, but character strings cannot be assigned to numeric variables.
- The INPUT statement is ideally suited for programs in which the data changes often, whereas the READ and DATA statements are particularly useful when it is necessary to read large quantities of data.
- When more than one item is to be printed on a single output line, the spacing can be controlled by the use of commas and semicolons.
- The semicolon causes the next item output to be placed in the next available print position.
- Each line of output can be divided into a predetermined number of print zones. The comma causes results to be printed in a particular print zone.
- The TAB function is used to cause output to be printed in a specified column.
- The SPC function is used within the PRINT statement to tell the computer how many spaces to move over before printing the output.
- The PRINT USING statement provides a flexible method of formatting output. The format control characters define how the output will look.

Review Questions

1. What are the advantages of the INPUT statement? What is a disadvantage?

2. What does the computer do when it encounters an INPUT statement?

3. What is a prompt used for? What two things should a prompt tell the user?

4. When are READ and DATA statements best used?

5. How does the programmer determine where to place INPUT and READ/DATA statements in a program?

6. What is a data list, and how is it created?

7. What happens if a program attempts to read a data value when there are no more data values in the data list?

8. How does the RESTORE statement work?

9. What will be printed by the following program segment?

```
100 READ X,Y
110 M = X + Y
120 PRINT M;X;Y
130 RESTORE
140 READ A,B,C
150 PRINT A,B,C
160 RESTORE
170 READ D
180 N = A + B + C + D
190 PRINT D;N
200 DATA 17,80,0,76,14,2,7
```

10. Can a numeric value be assigned to a character string variable? Why or why not? Can a character string be assigned to a numeric variable? Why or why not?

11. What will be the output of the following program segment?

```
230 X$ = "MOUNTAIN"
240 Y$ = "MOLEHILL"
250 PRINT X$;Y$
```

12. What will be the output of the following program segment?

```
200 READ W1$,W2$,W3$
210 READ W4$,W5$,W6$
220 READ W7$,W8$,W9$
230 PRINT W1$,W2$,W3$;
240 PRINT W4$,W5$,
250 PRINT W6$,W7$,W8$,W9$
260 DATA MARY,HAD,A,LITTLE
270 DATA LAMB,ITS,FLEECE,WAS,WHITE
```

13. Write the following statements using the TAB function.

a. Write a statement that will print HI in column 30 and THERE in column 40.

b. Write a statement that will place the digits 1 through 5 in columns 1, 5, 10, 15, and 20 respectively.

14. What happens when a comma is used in a PRINT statement?

15. When using commas, what happens if there are more items listed in a PRINT statement than there are print zones?

16. In which zone will the word RETURNS appear if the following statement is executed?

```
70 PRINT "HAPPY",,"RETURNS"
```

17. What happens when a semicolon is used in a PRINT statement?

18. What will be the output of the following program segment?

```
100 READ W1$,W2$,W3$,W4$
110 PRINT,,W2$
120 PRINT W3$;" ";W4$
130 DATA "WE","WANT","INFORMATION","!"
```

19. How does the PRINT USING statement work?

20. Explain the purpose of three format control characters that can be used with the PRINT USING statement.

Debugging Exercises

Identify the following programs or program segments that contain errors and debug them.

1. ```
   10 REM *** PROMPT THE USER TO ENTER A COUNTRY. ***
   20 PRINT "INPUT THE NAME OF A COUNTRY";CTRY$
   ```
2. ```
   10 REM *** PROMPT THE USER TO ENTER NAME OF SCHOOL. ***
   20 PRINT "ENTER THE NAME OF YOUR SCHOOL"
   30 INPUT SCHOOL
   ```
3. ```
   90  REM *** TOTAL 3 SCORES AND GET PERCENTAGE. ***
   100 READ P1,P2,P3
   110 AMT = (P1 + P2 + P3) / 100
   120 DATA 14,77
   ```
4. ```
   200 READ PLYER$,BTS,HITS
   210 AVE = BTS / HITS
   220 PRINT AVE
   230 DATA "GOMEZ","44",23
   ```
5. ```
   250 READ PLYER$,BTS,HITS
   260 AVE = BTS / HITS
   270 PRINT AVE
   280 DATA SANCHEZ,PETERS,60,44,20
   ```
6. ```
   120 READ A,B
   130 SUM = A + B + C
   140 PRINT SUM
   150 RESTORE
   160 READ X,Y,Z
   170 DATA 14.45,78.90
   ```
7. ```
   50  READ W1$,W2$,W3$
   60  READ X,Y,Z
   70  X = X - 10
   80  Y = Y + 5
   90  PRINT W1$;TAB(X);W2$;TAB(Y);W3$
   100 DATA "WHAT","IS","LIFE?",8,5,15
   ```
   ```

```
 8.  50 READ NMBR$
     60 PRINT "YOU";TAB(6);"ARE";TAB(12),NMBR$
     70 DATA "#6","#2"
 9.  50 READ NME$,SAL
     60 F$ = \        \    $$###.##
     70 PRINT USING F$;NME$,SAL
     80 READ NME$,SAL
     90 PRINT USING F$;NME$,SAL
10.  10 INPUT "ENTER CITY AND STATE:";CITY$,ST
     20 INPUT "AND ZIP CODE",ZIP$
     30 PRINT TAB(5);CITY$;",";TAB(25);ST;
        TAB(35);ZIP$
```

Additional Programming Problems

Level 1

1. Write a program to print your initials in large block letters, using the letters of your initials. For example:

```
SSSSSSSS         JJJJJJJJ       H         H
S                       J       H         H
S                       J       H         H
SSSSSSSS                J       HHHHHHHHHH
       S                J       H         H
       S       J        J       H         H
SSSSSSSS         JJJJJJ         H         H
```

2. Write a program that evaluates the following expression:

$$\frac{16.8 - 8.0}{3.3} + \frac{7.0 + 2}{12.5 \times 2}$$

3. Write a program that uses an INPUT statement to enter the diameters of three circles, and then calculates and outputs each circle's radius, circumference, and area with appropriate labels.

4. Rewrite the program in problem 3 using READ and DATA statements instead of the INPUT statement.

5. Write a program that asks for the name of an object and its weight in pounds. The program should then calculate the weight in kilograms (1 pound = 0.453592 kilograms) and print the name, weight in pounds, and weight in kilograms, each in a different print zone.

6. Write a program to solve the following equation for X:

$$X = \frac{(14 + 4^2) * 8 - 2}{4 + 3}$$

7. The University Health Department needs a program that prints a report listing each student's name, emergency telephone number, and any medical problems that student might have. The program should use READ and

DATA statements to read the data to the program. Use an appropriate format for the report. The input data is as follows:

Name	Emergency Phone Number	Medical Problems
Candi Mullen	(716) 459-0989	none
Joy Jones	(614) 787-8383	none
Polly Cracker	(222) 321-1234	asthma

8. Write a program that calculates a person's age in days and then lists this age in both days and years. Use an INPUT statement to allow the user's name and age in years to be entered. The format of the output should be something like this:

```
NAME              YEARS    DAYS
XXXXXXXXXXXXX      XX      XXXXX
```

9. Write a program to read the following data and print it with the headings NAME, AREA CODE, and TELEPHONE#, using the TAB function: Bob Hoax, 491-535-0101, Janice Freze, 982-453-0748

10. Write a program using the PRINT USING to duplicate the following table.

Company	Assets	Sales	Market Value
CHRYSLER	7,074,365	15,537,788	1,227,533
AT & T	86,716,989	32,815,582	38,570,218
BURROUGHS	2,539,319	1,870,845	3,707,422

Level 2

1. Write a program to list several activities and the number of the calories expended during 15, 30, and 60 minutes of each activity. Use the following data:

Activity	Calories Burned Per Minute
Sleeping	2.3
Jogging	15.0
Sitting	1.7

Output should look similar to the following:

```
ACTIVITY   15 MINUTES   30 MINUTES   60 MINUTES
SLEEPING    xxx.xx       xxx.xx       xxx.xx
JOGGING     xxx.xx       xxx.xx       xxx.xx
SITTING     xxx.xx       xxx.xx       xxx.xx
```

2. Write a program that calculates the batting average of a baseball player. Use INPUT statements to allow the necessary data to be entered. The program should read the times at bat, the number of walks, and the number of hits. Subtract the number of walks from the times at bat and then divide this by the number of hits to calculate the batting average. Output this value with an appropriate label.

3. Write a program that uses the INPUT statement to enable the user to enter any two numbers. The program should then print the sum, difference, product, and quotient of these two numbers. Your output should be as follows:

```
ENTER ANY TWO NUMBERS
(SEPARATE THE NUMBERS WITH A COMMA) XXX,XXX
XXX + XXX = XXX
XXX - XXX = XXXX
XXX * XXX = XXXX
XXX / XXX = XXXX
```

4. Westward College would like a program to calculate the fees owed by each student. Each credit hour costs $98.50, and there is an additional general fee of $160.00. For each student, the student's name and number of credit hours should be read into the program. Use the following data:

BOB BOO	16
JOE DOE	13
SALLY SMITH	10
JIM JONES	15

Output each student's name and amount owed to the College in table form.

5. Mr. Sims purchased a Rolls-Royce four years ago and has decided to sell it. He would like to know the market value of the car today. Using a depreciation rate of 7.63 percent per year, determine the depreciation per year in dollars, total depreciation to date, and the current value of the car. Print the output in table form.

6. Write a program segment to find the weighted average of three test scores. The data will be in the form of an integer test score followed by its associated weight. Use the following input data:

90	0.3
85	0.25
78	0.45

Output the weighted score for each test and the overall weighted score. Each weighted score can be found by multiplying the actual score by its weight. The overall weighted score is found by adding the three individual weighted scores together.

7. Write a program that demonstrates the use of the RESTORE command. Your program should use four data items in one DATA statement, as well as two READ statements. Read and add the first two data items; then read the same DATA statement again and total all four data items. Your output should look similar to this:

```
THE FIRST TWO DATA ITEMS = XXXX
ALL FOUR DATA ITEMS = XXXXX
```

8. The Thriftway Company wants to generate a monthly report for each of its salespeople. The report should print a salesperson's total sales for each item, and his or her total sales overall (on three items). The output should look similar to the following (place three asterisks next to totals):

```
                    THRIFTWAY COMPANY
                    SALES ANALYSIS REPORT

SALESPERSON      PRODUCT   QNTY SOLD   UNIT PRICE   SALE AMT
XXXXXXXXXXXX     XXXXX        XXX        XX.XX       XXX.XX
                 XXXXX        XXX        XX.XX       XXX.XX
                 XXXXX        XXX        XX.XX       XXX.XX
                                                    XXXX.XX***
      .             .          .           .           .
      .             .          .           .           .
      .             .          .           .           .
                                    FINAL TOTAL   XXXXXX.XX***
```

9. Write a program to compute an individual's typing speed. The program should read the following information: person's name, number of words typed, number of minutes spent typing, and the number of errors. The formula to be used for calculating words typed per minute is:

$$\text{WPM} = \frac{\text{Number of Words Typed} - (\text{Number of Errors} * 5)}{\text{Number of Minutes Spent Typing}}$$

10. The Persian Pots Co. is running a sale of 10 percent off all pots and plants for Arbor Day. Write a program that uses READ/DATA and PRINT USING statements to print a table containing the sale prices of the following plants:

Plant	Regular Price
Swedish Ivy	$1.50
Boston Fern	2.00
Poinsettia	5.40
Cactus	1.70

Level 3

1. The Acme Concrete Company has bought a new computer and would like a program to compute the cost of a given amount of concrete and the cost of the labor to pour it. The input should be the length, width, and depth, in feet, of the concrete to be poured. Concrete costs $32 per cubic yard, and labor costs $20 per cubic yard (a cubic yard has 27 cubic feet). The output should appear similar to the following:

```
                    CONCRETE COSTS
IN FEET:            CUBIC    CONCRETE AT    LABOR AT      TOTAL
LEN    WID    DEP   YARDS    $32/CU. YD.    $20/CU. YD.   COST
xx     xx     xx    xxx      $xx.xx         $xx.xx        $xxx.xx
```

2. Jim and Bob have decided to stop smoking and would like to know how much money they will save per week and per year. Bob smokes one and one-half packs a day at $1.25 a pack, and Jim smokes one pack a day at $1.32 a pack. Format your output as follows:

```
SMOKER'S       NO. PACKS     COST         AMT. SAVED    AMT. SAVED
 NAME          PER DAY       PER PACK     PER WEEK      PER YEAR
xxxxxxxx         xx           xx¢          $x.xx         $xxx.xx
```

3. Martha's Dance School charges a flat hourly rate of $6.75. Martha would like a program to determine the total amount owed by each student and the dance school's total income. The output should be in table form. Use READ and DATA statements to read the following data to the program:

Name	Monday	Tuesday	Wednesday	Thursday	Friday
Karen	2	3	3	4	2
Alex	3	2	2	2	3

4. The Rainbow Paint Shop would like a program to determine the cost and number of gallons of paint needed to paint one room, based on the room's width, length, and height. Assume that each gallon of paint covers approximately 250 square feet and the cost is $15.95 a gallon. Write a program that will enable the user to enter the dimensions of the room during program execution and that will print a table containing the desired output. Create your own input to use when testing the program.

5. Plastic Cards, Inc. wants a program to compute the new balance for its credit card customers. The input is the customer's account number, the old balance on the account, the amount of the payment, the new charges, and the finance charge rate. The output should be printed in the following format:

```
              OLD                    INCURRED      NEW
ACCT. NO.     BALANCE    PAYMENT     CHARGES       BALANCE
xxxx          xxx.xx     xx.xx       xx.xx         xxx.xx
```

Create your own input to test the program.

6. Mr. Leady wants to know how much it would cost him to replant the grass in his backyard, which measures 150 by 200 feet. Grass seed costs 93¢ per pound, and one pound covers 50 square yards. He also needs to know how much it would cost if he used Special Blend Grass Seed, which costs 99¢ per pound; one pound of this seed also covers 50 square yards. The program should output the cost of using each and the cost difference between the two.

7. A local pet store, the Pet Palace, is having its annual clearance sale this month. It offers the following pets at the indicated sale prices:

Pet	Sale Price
Fish	$ 0.53
Kittens	9.98
Puppies	28.75
Birds	7.69

During the first two weeks of the sale, the Pet Palace sold 117 fish, 39 kittens, 25 puppies, and 63 birds. Management wants to know the gross sales for each item, as well as the total gross sales for the two-week period. Write a program to print this output in table form with appropriate headings.

8. The owners of the McHenry Farm of Edgar County, Illinois, have purchased a small computer. They want to be able to make profit projections based on expected crop yield and market prices. Soybeans are to be planted in field 1, which contains 100 acres, and corn in field 2, which contains 75 acres. The costs per acre for planting, cultivating, and harvesting the two crops are $105.00 for soybeans and $160.00 for corn. The McHenrys expect to get 40 bushels of soybeans per acre and 100 bushels of corn per acre. The projected selling prices for soybeans and corn at harvest time are $6.80 per bushel and $2.90 per bushel respectively. The output should appear similar to the following:

CROP	FIELD 1 SOYBEANS	FIELD 2 CORN
COST	xxxx.xx	xxxx.xx
INCOME	xxxx.xx	xxxx.xx
PROFIT	xxxx.xx	xxxx.xx

9. Baymont High School would like a program to generate absentee percentages per class. Design the program so that they can run it every day in order to compare the daily figures and determine if there is any pattern. Format the output as follows:

DAILY ABSENCE REPORT FOR (current date)

CLASS	TOTAL NUMBER OF STUDENTS	NUMBER ABSENT	PERCENTAGE ABSENT
xx	xxx	xx	xx
xx	xxx	xx	xx
xx	xxx	xx	xx
xx	xxx	xx	xx

Use INPUT statements to allow the user to enter the current date and the following data:

Class	#Students	#Absent
9	345	4
10	321	28
11	367	10
12	298	32

10. Sharkey's Loan Agency would like a program to determine the monthly payment on loans. Use the following formula to determine this:

$$P = \frac{b(r/12)}{1 - \left(\frac{1}{1 + r/12}\right)^{y*12}}$$

where

b is the amount borrowed.
r is the annual interest rate.
y is the number of years to repay the loan.

Format the output like this:

INSTALLMENT LOAN—AMOUNT OF MONTHLY PAYMENT

AMOUNT BORROWED	ANNUAL INT. RATE	NO. YEARS TO REPAY	MONTHLY PAYMENT
xxxx.xx	.xx	xx	xxx.xx

Use the following input to test your program:

Borrowed	Rate	Years
5000	12%	5
750000	11.5%	35

CHAPTER

5

FUNDAMENTAL CONTROL STATEMENTS

Objectives

After studying this chapter, you will be able to:
- Explain and use the unconditional transfer statement GOTO.
- Use the IF/THEN and IF/THEN/ELSE statements in programs.
- Use nested IF/THEN and IF/THEN/ELSE statements in programs.
- Give examples of single- and double-alternative decision structures.
- Explain and use the conditional transfer statement ON/GOTO in programs.
- Control loops using trailer values and counters.

Outline

Overview
Unconditional Transfer: The GOTO Statement
Conditional Transfer: The Decision Step
  The IF/THEN Statement
  The IF/THEN/ELSE Statement
  Nested IF Statements
  The ON/GOTO Statement
  Menus

Looping Methods
  Trailer Values
  Counters
A Programming Problem
  Problem Definition
  Solution Design
  The Program
Avoiding Common Programming Mistakes

Summary Points
Review Questions
Debugging Exercises
Additional Programming Problems
  Level 1
  Level 2
  Level 3

Overview

Control statements
Statements that allow the programmer to alter the order in which program instructions are executed.

This chapter introduces the control statement, a powerful programming tool that will be used in all programs from this point on. **Control statements** allow the programmer to control the order in which program statements are executed. The GOTO, IF/THEN/ELSE, and ON/GOTO control statements are discussed here, along with the technique of looping and two methods of controlling loop execution.

Unconditional Transfer: The GOTO Statement

All of the programs we have written so far have been executed in a simple sequential manner. That is, the lowest numbered line is executed first, then control passes to the next-lowest numbered line, and so on from the beginning to the end of the program. To solve many programming problems, however, it is necessary to alter the order in which statements are executed. Changing the normal path or flow of program execution is known as **branching,** and a statement that can make such a change is called a *branch*.

Branching
Altering the normal flow of program execution.

An example of a branch is the GOTO statement. Its general format looks like this:

line# GOTO transfer line#

The transfer line number tells the computer the line number of the next statement to be executed, and control transfers to that program line regardless of its location in the program.

When a GOTO statement is executed, there are three possible actions that may be taken:

- If the statement indicated by the transfer line number is executable, it is executed, and execution continues from that point.
- If the statement indicated by the transfer line number is nonexecutable (such as a REM or DATA statement), control passes to the next line after it.
- If the transfer line number is not a line number contained in the program, an error message is displayed, and execution is terminated.

The following is an example of a GOTO statement:

```
100 GOTO 60
```

This statement causes program execution to branch or "go to" line 60, execute it if possible, and continue execution with the line following line 60.

Because control of the execution path *always* changes when the GOTO statement is encountered, such a statement is known as an **unconditional transfer.** Figures 5–1 and 5–2 show how execution paths are controlled with GOTO statements.

In Figure 5–1, the GOTO statement in line 50 causes control to pass to line 70. Therefore, only the value of Y is printed; line 60 is skipped and left unexecuted. In Figure 5–2, control is transferred to line 50 by the GOTO statement. Line 50 contains a nonexecutable statement, so control passes to line 60. Notice that lines 30 and 40 are skipped and left unexecuted.

At this point a word of caution is in order. Although the GOTO statement gives the programmer increased control over the logical flow of a program, unconditional transfers can produce an execution path so complex and unreadable that the logic is virtually impossible to follow, and debugging becomes a nightmare. Later in this chapter and in other chapters, you will be introduced to control statements that are preferable to the GOTO statement. The GOTO should be used only when it is not feasible to use a different control statement.

Unconditional transfer
Program control is always transferred to another point, regardless of any program conditions.

FIGURE 5–1
GOTO Statement: Sample 1

```
30 X = 10
40 Y = 20
50 GOTO 70
60 PRINT X
70 PRINT Y
80 ----
```

Learning Check

1. The term that refers to changing the normal flow of program execution is _____.
2. A statement that always alters the execution path when it is encountered is a(n) _____ transfer statement.
3. An example of the transfer statement described in Question 2 is the _____ statement.
4. A well-written program uses as many GOTO statements as possible. True or false?

Answers

1. branching 2. unconditional 3. GOTO 4. False.

FIGURE 5–2
GOTO Statement: Sample 2

```
10 X = 20
20 GOTO 50
30 ----
40 ----
50 REM *** THIS ISN'T EXECUTED. ***
60 PRINT Y
```

Conditional Transfer: The Decision Step

Conditional transfer
Program control is transferred to another point only if a stated condition is true.

Single-alternative decision step
A specified action is taken only if the comparison is true; otherwise execution proceeds to the next statement.

In an unconditional transfer statement like the GOTO statement, no conditions in the program are considered. A second type of control statement is the **conditional transfer** or **decision step,** in which the computer makes a comparison, and the result of this comparison determines what is done next. Figure 5–3 shows a flowchart for a program that reads a letter and then prints the letter only if it is a consonant. The corresponding pseudocode is also listed in this figure. If the letter is not a consonant, nothing is done. Note that the decision step is represented by a diamond-shaped symbol in the flowchart. This is a **single-alternative decision step.** In contrast, Figure 5–4 shows the flowchart and pseudocode for a **double-**

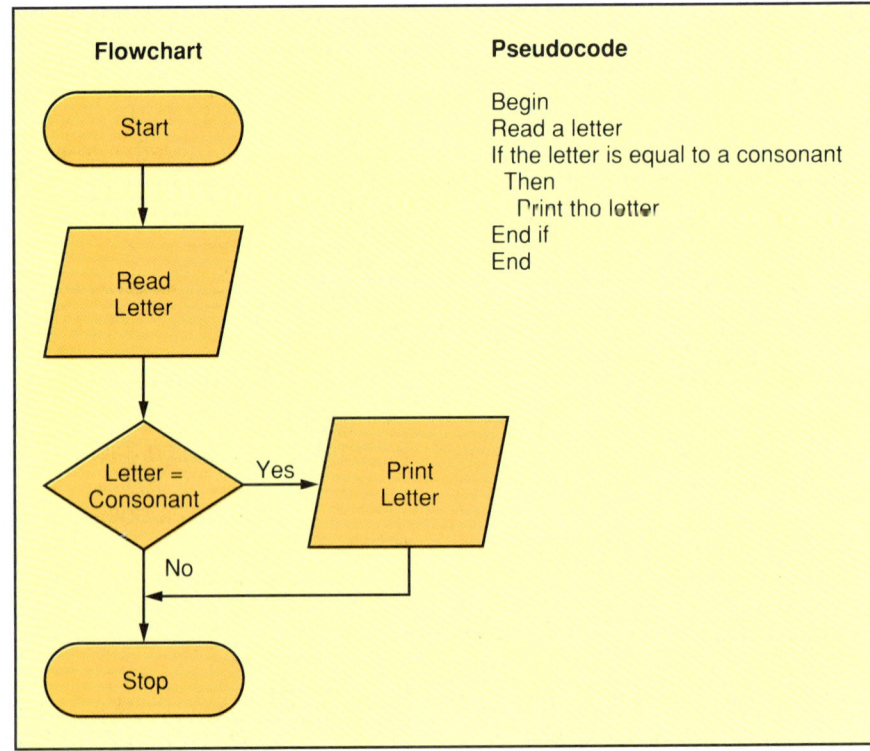

FIGURE 5–3
Flowchart and Pseudocode Showing Single-Alternative Decision Step

FUNDAMENTAL CONTROL STATEMENTS

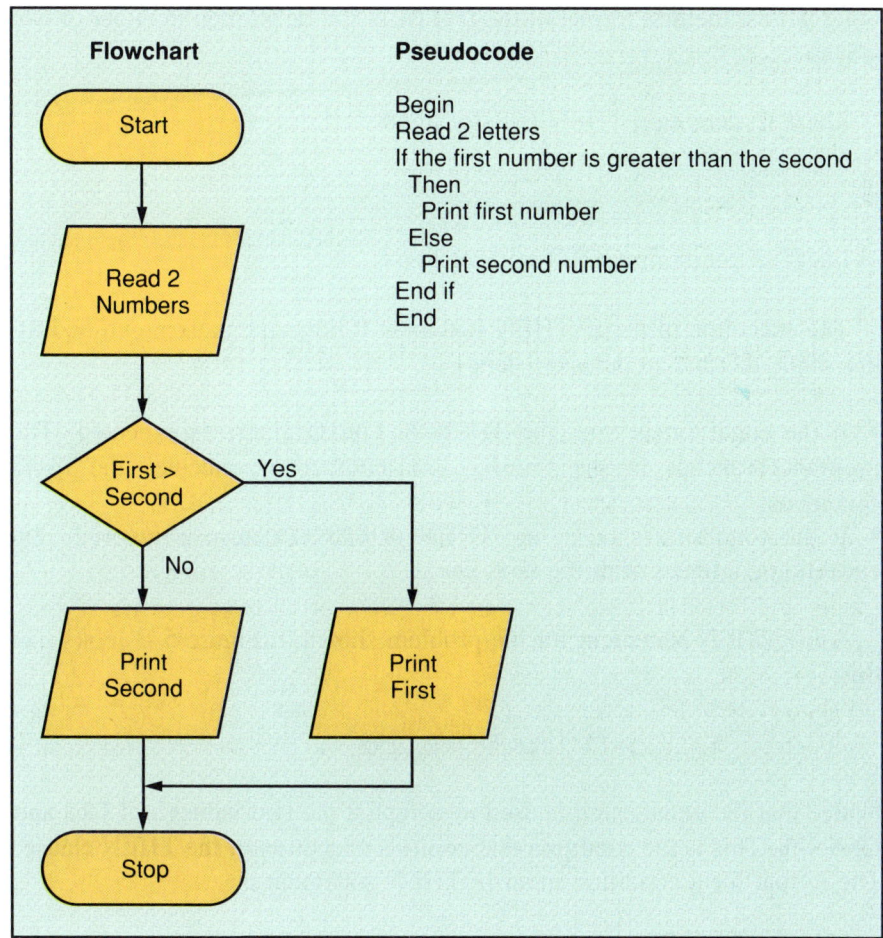

FIGURE 5–4
Flowchart and Pseudocode Showing Double-Alternative Decision Step

alternative decision step, where one action is taken if the comparison is true and another if it is false. In this flowchart, the "Yes" route is taken if the first number is larger than the second. Otherwise, the "No" route is taken.

Double-alternative decision step One action is taken if the comparison is true and another if it is false.

The IF/THEN Statement

A single-alternative decision step can be written by using an IF/THEN statement. There are two general formats for this statement:

line# IF condition $\begin{Bmatrix} \text{THEN} \\ \text{GOTO} \end{Bmatrix}$ transfer line#

line# IF condition THEN statement(s)

Note the use of braces ({ }) in the first format statement. They indicate that one of the enclosed words is to be chosen when writing the statement. In other words, the first format of the IF/THEN can be worded in either of two ways:

line# IF condition THEN transfer line#

or

line# IF condition GOTO transfer line#

The execution of the IF/THEN statement follows the pattern outlined for the single-alternative decision step:

- If the condition is true, the THEN or GOTO clause is executed. The program branches to the transfer line number or executes the listed statements.
- If the condition is false, the THEN or GOTO clause is ignored, and execution continues with the next line.

An IF/THEN statement for the problem shown in Figure 5–3 looks like this:

```
40 IF LTR$ = CNSNT$ THEN PRINT LTR$
```

Notice that the equals sign is used to compare the two values in LTR$ and CNSNT$. This is the condition that controls execution of the THEN clause. The format for a condition in an IF/THEN statement is:

$\text{expression}_1 \quad \text{relational symbol} \quad \text{expression}_2$

The values of the expressions of the condition can be either numeric or character strings (both must be of the same type), and the expressions can be constants, variables, and/or arithmetic expressions. The condition compares the two expressions by means of a **relational symbol,** as defined in the following table:

Relational symbol
Specifies a relationship between two values.

Symbol	Meaning	Example
<	less than	SMALL < BIG
<=	less than or equal to	8 <= 10
		"A" <= "B"
>	greater than	STOCK > 100
>=	greater than or equal to	X + 1 >= Y
=	equal to	NAM$ = "BRUCE"
<>	not equal to	AGE <> 18
		CODE$ <> "OK"

In order to compare two character strings, the computer makes use of the code that represents character data in the computer's main memory. The system assigns an integer value to each character it is capable of recognizing according to a predetermined order known as the **collating sequence.** A commonly used collating system—used by all the computers discussed in this book—is the ASCII (American Standard Code for Information Interchange) code. Table 5-1 shows part of the ASCII collating sequence.

Collating sequence
The order the computer assigns to the set of characters that it is capable of recognizing.

A character string comparison is performed from left to right, one character at a time. The first character of one string is compared to the first character of the other string; then the second character of each string is

TABLE 5-1 ASCII Codes

	CHAR		CHAR		CHAR
32	SPC	64	@	96	'
33	!	65	A	97	a
34	"	66	B	98	b
35	#	67	C	99	c
36	$	68	D	100	d
37	%	69	E	101	e
38	&	70	F	102	f
39	'	71	G	103	g
40	(	72	H	104	h
41	)	73	I	105	i
42	*	74	J	106	j
43	+	75	K	107	k
44	,	76	L	108	l
45	−	77	M	109	m
46	.	78	N	110	n
47	/	79	O	111	o
48	0	80	P	112	p
49	1	81	Q	113	q
50	2	82	R	114	r
51	3	83	S	115	s
52	4	84	T	116	t
53	5	85	U	117	u
54	6	86	V	118	v
55	7	87	W	119	w
56	8	88	X	120	x
57	9	89	Y	121	y
58	:	90	Z	122	z
59	;	91	[	123	{
60	<	92	\	124	|
61	=	93	]	125	}
62	>	94	^	126	~
63	?	95	_	127	⌂

considered, and so on until a character of one string is found to be less than the corresponding character of the other string. One character is determined to be less than another if its ASCII code number is smaller than the other character's code number. Thus a look at the ASCII codes shows the character A to be less than B, because 65 is less than 66. Likewise, the following condition is true:

"MAN"<"MAT"

The ASCII codes of these two strings match up to the last letter; N is found to be less than T.

When two strings of unequal length are compared, and all the letters of the shorter string match the corresponding letters of the longer string, the shorter string is considered to be less than the longer string. Thus the following condition evaluates as true:

"HOPE"<"HOPEFUL"

Be aware also that leading and trailing blanks are significant. Because a blank has a smaller ASCII value than any letter or digit, the following conditions are true:

" CAT "<"CAT "(blank<C)

"CAT"<"CAT "(the second string is longer)

Figure 5–5 shows two different ways of using the IF/THEN statement to accomplish the same purpose. Examine the top program segment. In line 50, the THEN clause is executed if Y is greater than or equal to X. Program control then continues with line 60. The bottom program segment accomplishes this same purpose by using a transfer line number in the IF statement. If Y is less than X, line 60 is skipped; otherwise it is executed. The first example is considered better programming practice than the second. Whenever practical, use the THEN clause rather than the transfer format.

Below is an example of an IF/THEN statement that has three statements in the THEN clause. (Remember that on the IBM and Macintosh, multiple statements are separated by colons. On the Apple, it is not possible to place multiple statements on a single line.)

```
50 IF PTS > 90 THEN MARK$ = "A" \ PRINT NAM$,MARK$ \ TTL = TTL + 1
```

Figure 5–6 shows a program that uses a series of IF/THEN statements to print a class rank. Only one of these conditions will evaluate as true, depending on the value entered for rank. The IF statements will cause the correct message to be displayed.

FIGURE 5-5 Comparison of Two IF/THEN Statements

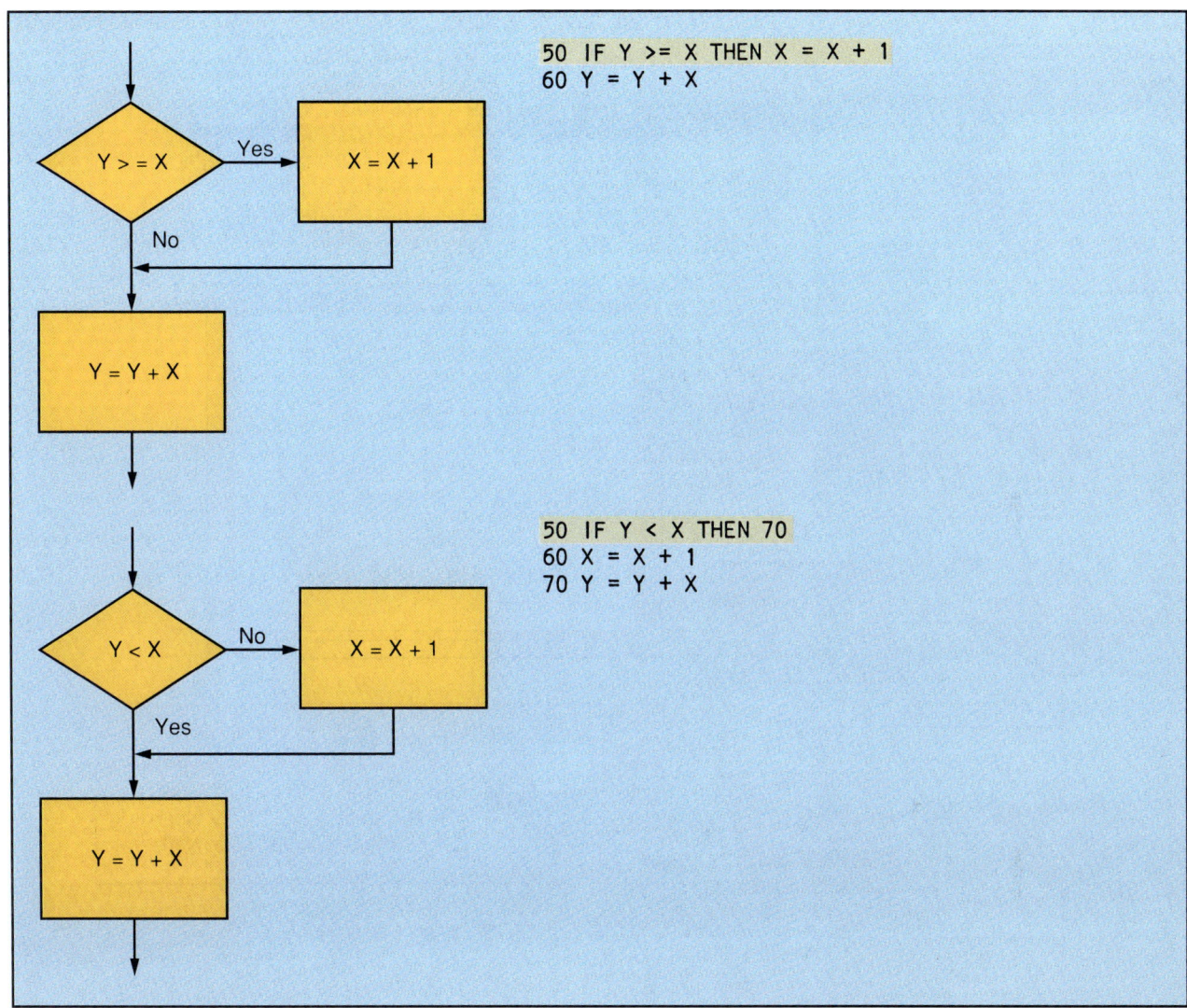

The IF/THEN/ELSE Statement

An extension of the IF/THEN statement which is available on the VAX system, the IBM, and the Macintosh is the IF/THEN/ELSE statement. The IF/THEN/ELSE statement is not available on the Apple. Refer to Figure 5-7 for instructions on simulating the IF/THEN/ELSE on the Apple. Like the IF/THEN statement, it has two formats:

line# IF condition $\left\{ \begin{array}{c} \text{THEN} \\ \text{GOTO} \end{array} \right\}$ transfer line# ELSE $\left\{ \begin{array}{c} \text{transfer line\#} \\ \text{statement(s)} \end{array} \right\}$

line# IF condition THEN statement(s) ELSE $\left\{ \begin{array}{c} \text{transfer line\#} \\ \text{statement(s)} \end{array} \right\}$

126 BASIC PROGRAMMING TODAY, A STRUCTURED APPROACH

FIGURE 5-6 Program Using Successive IF/THEN Statements

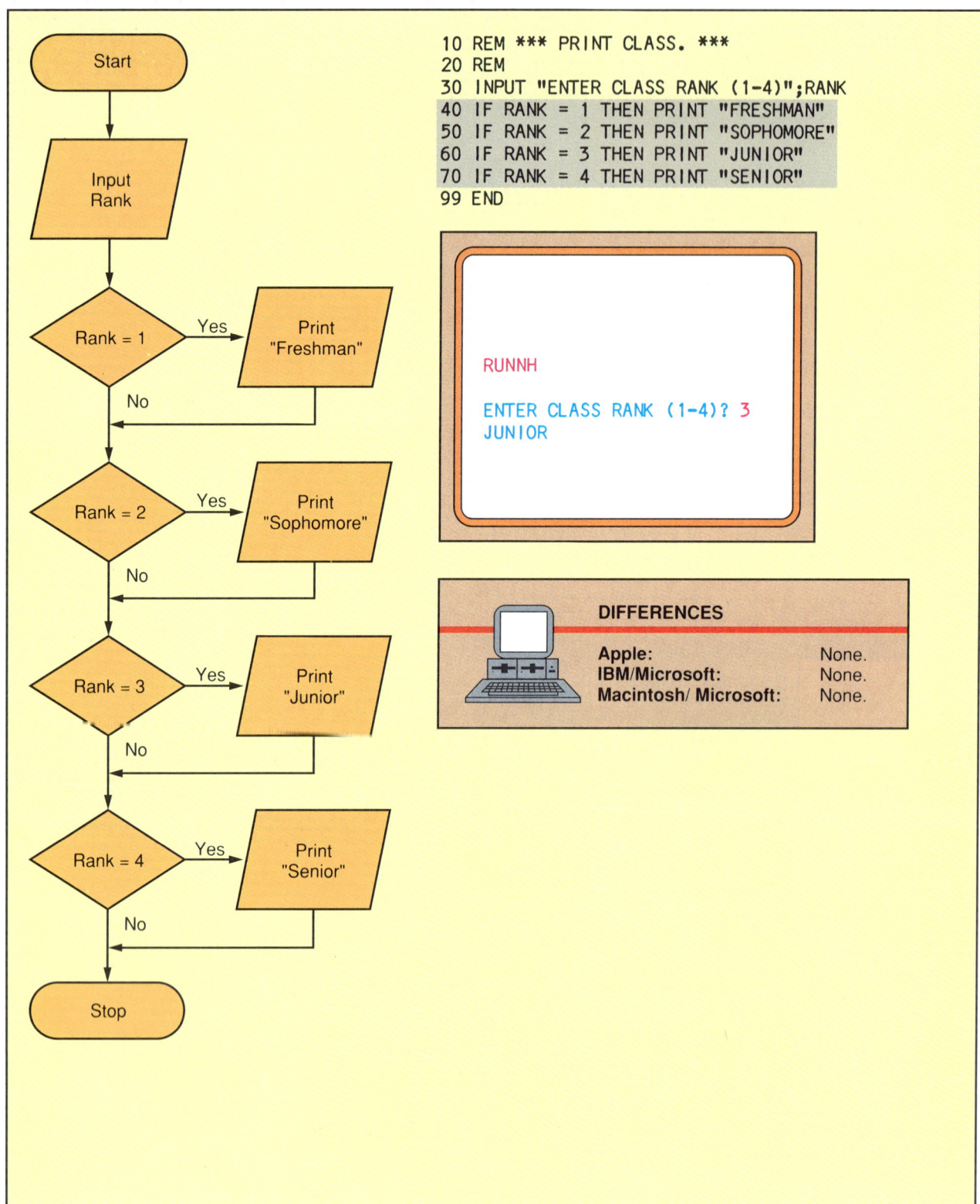

FUNDAMENTAL CONTROL STATEMENTS

FIGURE 5-7 Simulating the IF/THEN/ELSE Statement

For those systems (such as the Apple) that do not provide the IF/THEN/ELSE statement, the logic of the double-alternative decision can be acheived by use of the IF/THEN and GOTO statements. The following flowchart is correct for both of the program segments below:

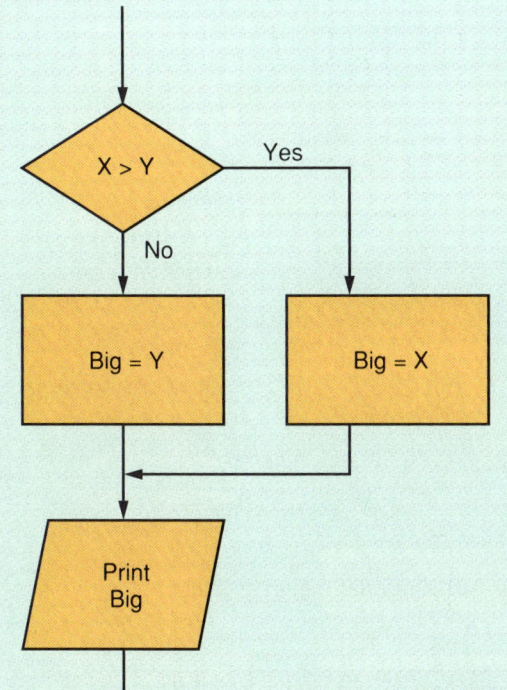

Solution A

```
40 IF X > Y THEN BIG = X ELSE BIG = Y
50 PRINT BIG
```

Solution B

```
40 IF X > Y THEN 70
50 BIG = Y
60 GOTO 80
70 BIG = X
80 PRINT BIG
```

In both segments the condition is the same, and both take the same actions for the true and false conditions. In Solution B the false action is contained in line 50, with a GOTO statement in line 60 to bypass the following THEN action. Notice that, in solution B, control is passed to line 80 after the ELSE action (via line 60) **and** after the THEN action (via normal execution flow). Whether the IF/THEN/ELSE statement or the IF/THEN statement is used, there should be a single common exit point for any double-alternative decision structure.

The IF/THEN/ELSE statement is an example of the double-alternative decision step mentioned earlier in this chapter. It is executed in this way:

- If the condition is true, the THEN clause is executed and the ELSE clause is ignored.
- If the condition is false, the THEN clause is ignored and the ELSE clause is executed.

Some examples of the IF/THEN/ELSE statement are shown in Figures 5–8 and 5–9.

FIGURE 5-8
IF/THEN/ELSE Sample 1

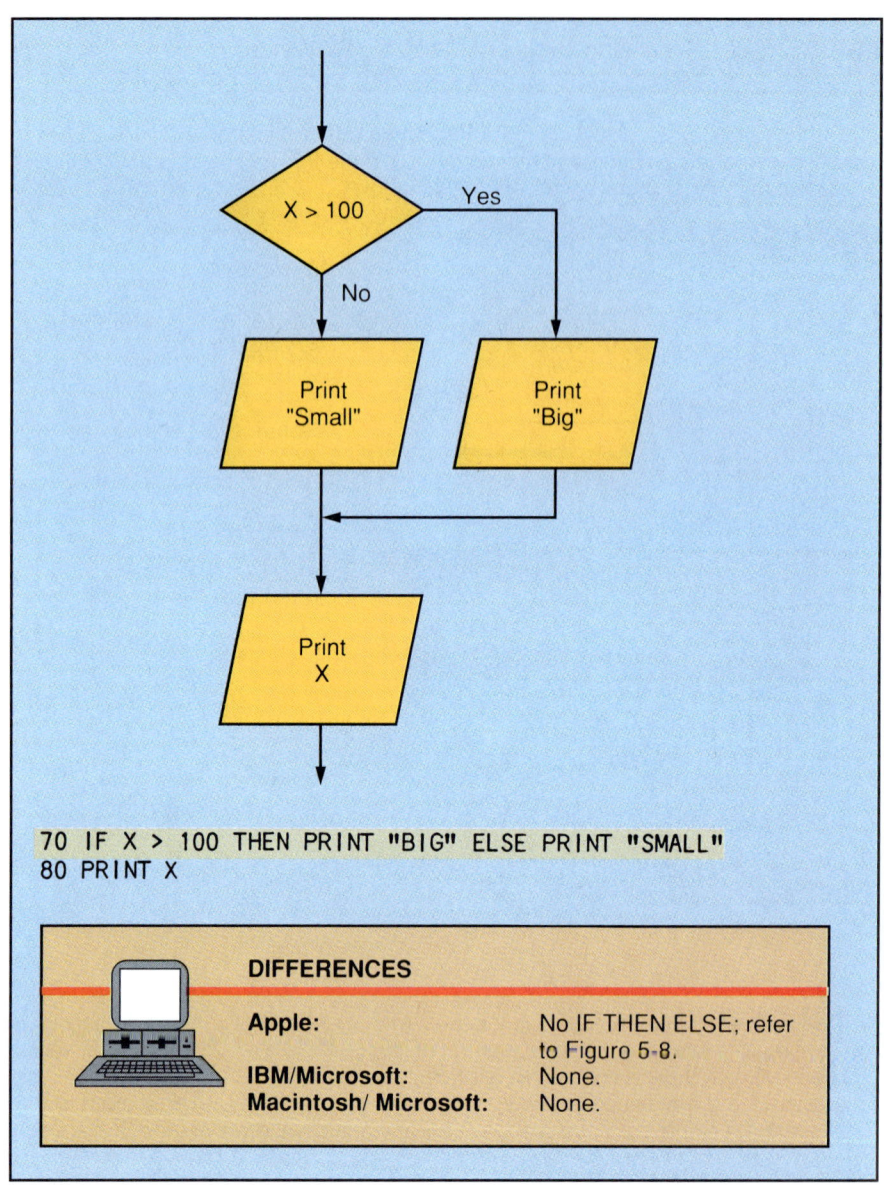

When the THEN and ELSE clauses consist of several statements, the entire IF/THEN/ELSE statement can become rather long, as shown below:

```
10 IF X > Y THEN Y = 0 \ X = X + 5 ELSE X = 0 \ Y = Y + 5
```

In this example, the THEN and the ELSE clauses each contain two statements. On all of the systems covered in this text, the entire IF/THEN/ELSE must appear on a single physical line. (A physical line always ends with a carriage return.) If a statement will not fit on one line, most computers will cause the statement to "wrap around" to the next line without the use of a carriage return. (The Macintosh scrolls to the left to

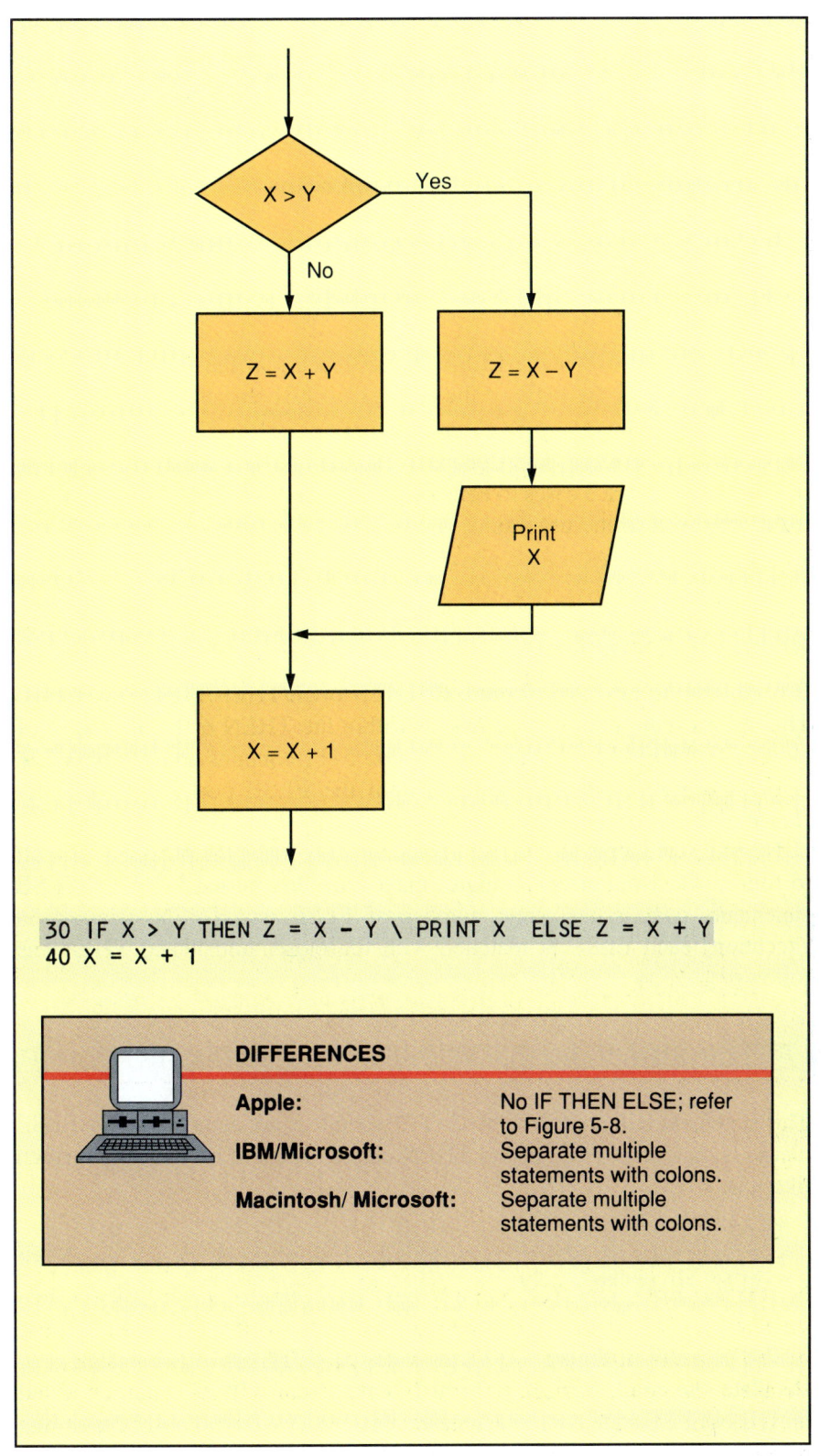

FIGURE 5–9
IF/THEN/ELSE Sample 2

show a line of up to 255 characters.) Because no carriage return has been pressed, the BASIC system correctly sees the statement as being on a single physical line. Many programmers like to use the space bar to insert blanks so that the second line of the statement is indented below the first line. This makes the program more readable. The previous IF/THEN/ELSE statement could be made to "wrap around" as shown below:

```
10 IF X > Y THEN Y + 0 \ X = X + 5
   ELSE X = 0 \ Y = Y + 5
```

Inserting blanks so that the ELSE clause appears at the beginning of the second line makes the logic of the IF/THEN/ELSE easier to understand.

The program in Figure 5–10 converts temperatures from Fahrenheit to Celsius if a 1 is entered, and Celsius to Fahrenheit if a 2 is entered. Because there are two separate cases to consider, the IF/THEN/ELSE statement lends itself very well to the program.

Nested IF Statements

It is possible to nest two or more IF/THEN or IF/THEN/ELSE statements. This means that either can be placed within the THEN or ELSE clause of another IF/THEN/ELSE statement. Figure 5–11 contains an example of an IF/THEN/ELSE statement nested within the ELSE portion of an outer IF/THEN/ELSE statement.

Nesting statements in this manner can quickly make the program difficult to follow. To avoid errors in logic, make sure that nested IF/THEN/ELSE statements contain the same number of ELSE and THEN clauses; on execution, each ELSE is matched with the closet unmatched THEN, as follows:

```
10 IF R = S THEN IF S = T THEN PRINT "R = T" ELSE PRINT "R <> T"
```

This statement will not print "R<>T" when R is not equal to S. The ELSE clause is matched to the second THEN clause. It could be correctly written like this:

```
10 IF R = S THEN IF S = T THEN PRINT "R = T" ELSE PRINT "R <> T"
   ELSE PRINT "R <> T"
```

The program in Figure 5–12 uses a nested IF/THEN/ELSE statement to calculate the total cost of a T-shirt order. Line 110 contains a nested IF/THEN/ELSE statement to determine the cost of a T-shirt order depending on the size of T-shirts needed.

FIGURE 5-10 Program Using IF/THEN/ELSE Statement

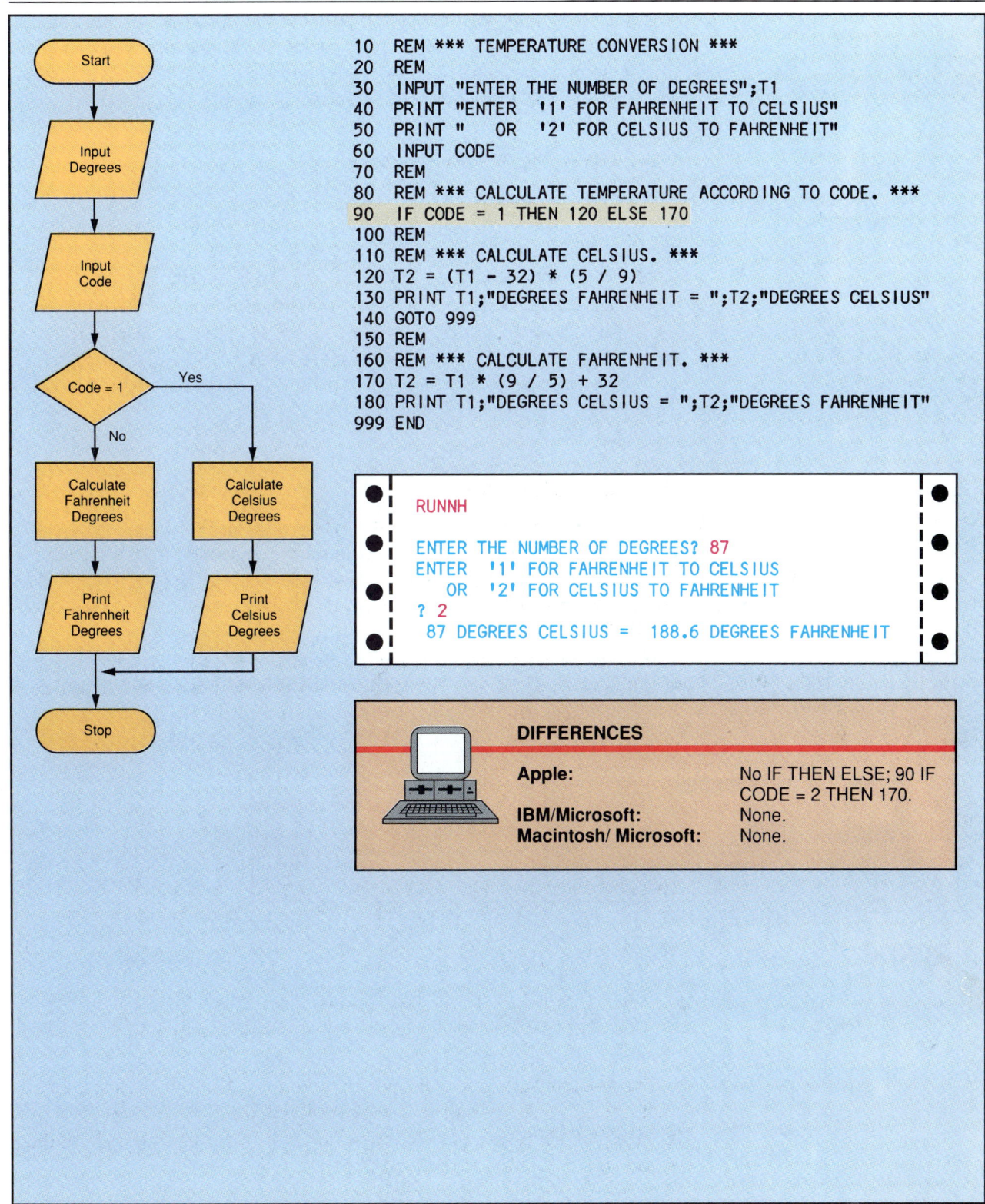

132 BASIC PROGRAMMING TODAY, A STRUCTURED APPROACH

FIGURE 5–11 Nested IF/THEN/ELSE Sample

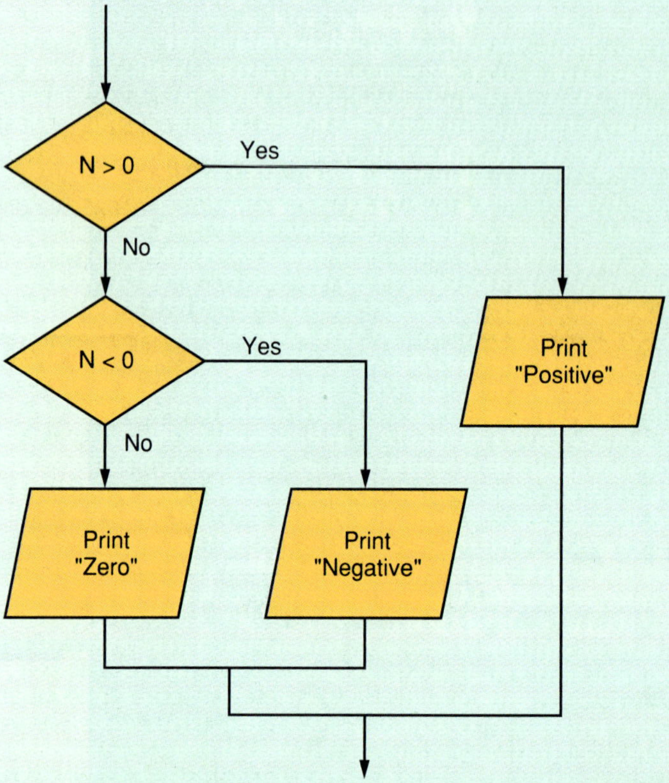

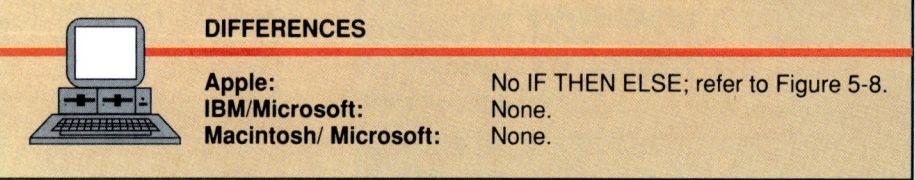

```
10 IF N > 0 THEN PRINT "POSITIVE" ELSE IF N < 0 THEN PRINT "NEGATIVE"
   ELSE PRINT "ZERO"
```

DIFFERENCES

Apple:	No IF THEN ELSE; refer to Figure 5-8.
IBM/Microsoft:	None.
Macintosh/ Microsoft:	None.

FIGURE 5–12 Program Using Nested IF/THEN/ELSE Statement

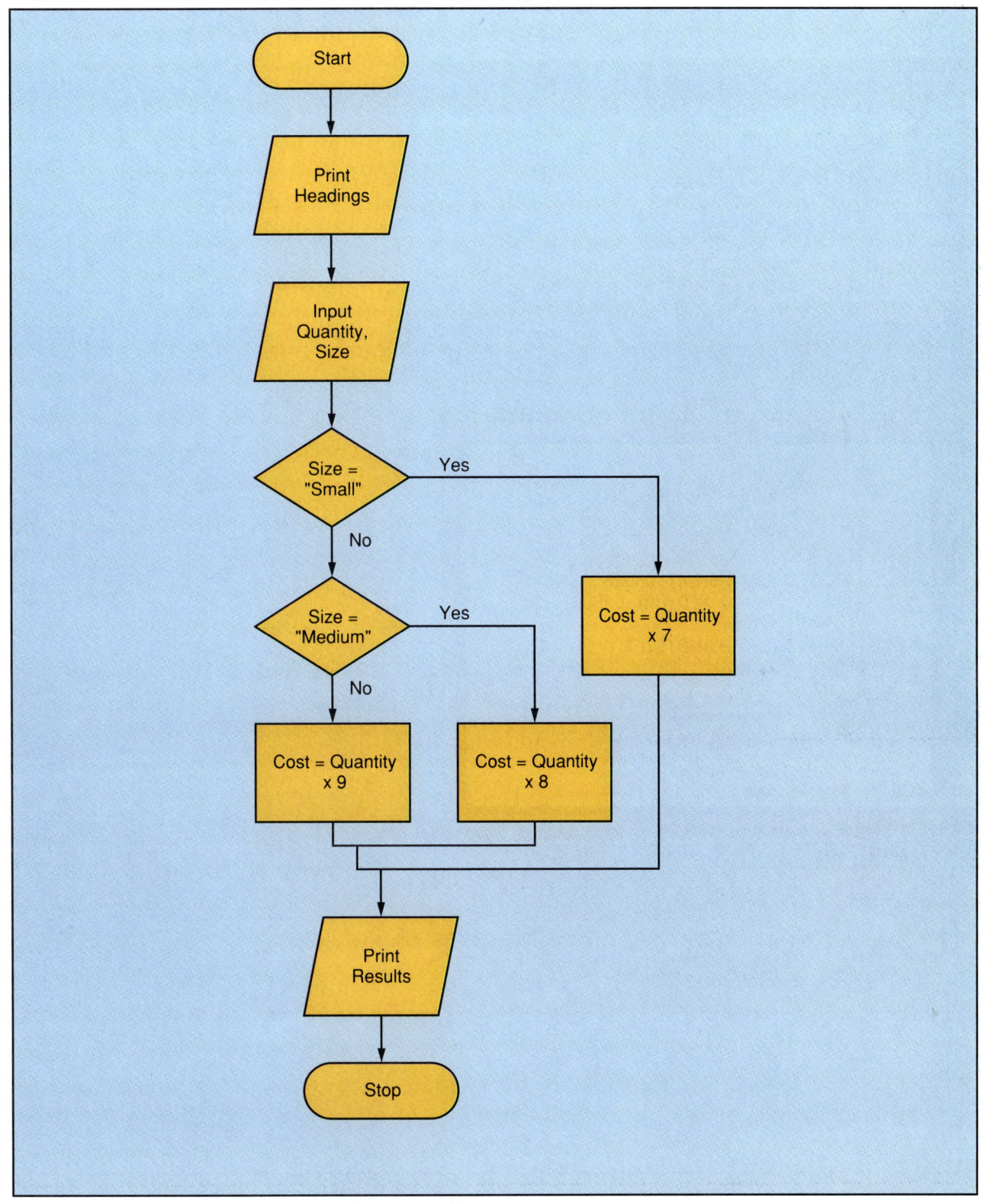

FIGURE 5-12 *Continued*

```
10 REM *** CALCULATE T-SHIRT ORDER. ***
20 REM
30 PRINT TAB(6);"ROCK TOUR T-SHIRT ORDER"
40 PRINT TAB(4);"SIZES:  SMALL, MEDIUM, LARGE"
50 PRINT
60 INPUT "ENTER NUMBER OF T-SHIRTS: ";QUANTITY
70 INPUT "ENTER SIZE: ";SIZE$
80 PRINT
90 REM
100 REM *** CALCULATE COST ACCORDING TO SIZE. ***
110 IF SIZE$ = "SMALL" THEN PAY = 7 * QUANTITY
        ELSE IF SIZE$ = "MEDIUM" THEN PAY = 8 * QUANTITY
            ELSE PAY = 9 * QUANTITY
120 REM
130 PRINT "TOTAL COST FOR ";QUANTITY; " ";SIZE$;" T-SHIRTS = $";PAY
999 END
```

```
RUNNH

     ROCK TOUR T-SHIRT ORDER
   SIZES:  SMALL, MEDIUM, LARGE

ENTER NUMBER OF T-SHIRTS: ? 6
ENTER SIZE: ? SMALL

TOTAL COST FOR  6   SMALL T-SHIRTS = $ 42
```

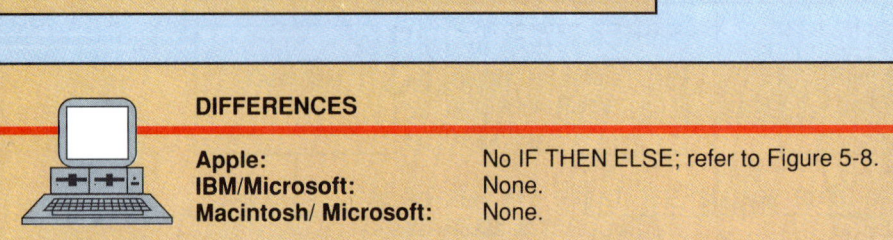

DIFFERENCES

Apple:	No IF THEN ELSE; refer to Figure 5-8.
IBM/Microsoft:	None.
Macintosh/ Microsoft:	None.

Learning Check

1. A control statement that makes a decision based on the values of certain expressions is called a(n) _____ transfer statement.
2. The two types of decision steps are the _____ and _____.
3. Must the condition of the IF/THEN statement evaluate only as true or false?
4. A(n) _____ _____ is the internal ordering of characters by the computer.
5. Is the IF/THEN/ELSE statement a single- or double-alternative decision statement?
6. Is the following statement valid?

   ```
   40 IF X = Z THEN IF Z = Q THEN PRINT "X = Q"
       ELSE PRINT "X <> Q" ELSE PRINT "X <> Z"
   ```

Answers

1. conditional 2. single-alternative, double-alternative 3. Yes. 4. collating sequence 5. Double-alternative. 6. Yes.

The ON/GOTO Statement

The ON/GOTO, or computed GOTO, statement transfers control to other statements in the program based on the evaluation of a mathematical expression. The ON/GOTO operates in the same way as multiple IF/THEN statements: any one of several transfers can occur, depending on the result computed for the expression. Because transfers depend on the expression, the ON/GOTO is another conditional transfer statement. Its general format is this:

   line# ON expression GOTO line#1[,line#2]. . .

The arithmetic expression is evaluated as an integer value. Depending on the system, the computer will either round or truncate the expression value if necessary. (To truncate a real number means to drop its decimal portion.) On the VAX, the value is truncated. Refer to Table 5–2 to determine whether this value will be rounded or truncated on your system.

The execution of the ON/GOTO statement is as follows:

1. The expression is evaluated as an integer.
2. Depending on the value of the expression, control passes to the corresponding line number.
   a. If the value of the expression is 1, control passes to the first line number listed.
   b. If the value of the expression is 2, control passes to the second line number listed.

136 BASIC PROGRAMMING TODAY, A STRUCTURED APPROACH

TABLE 5–2 ON/GOTO Actions

COMPUTER	EXPRESSION IS	ACTION IF EXPRESSION IS ZERO	ACTION IF EXPRESSION IS NEGATIVE OR GREATER THAN MAXIMUM ALLOWED	ACTION IF EXPRESSION IS GREATER THAN NUMBER LINES
VAX	truncated	"ON STMT OUT OF RANGE" error	"ON STMT OUT OF RANGE" error	Error message
Apple	truncated	ON/GOTO bypassed	"ILLEGAL QUANTITY" error	ON/GOTO bypassed
IBM/Microsoft	rounded	ON/GOTO bypassed	"ILLEGAL FUNCTION CALL" error	ON/GOTO bypassed
Macintosh/ Microsoft	rounded	ON/GOTO bypassed	"ILLEGAL FUNCTION CALL" error	ON/GOTO bypassed

c. If the value of the expression is *n*, control passes to the *nth* line number listed.

The following examples demonstrate the execution of the ON/GOTO statement.

Statement	Value of Variable	Execution
`10 ON X GOTO 30,50,70`	X = 1	Control passes to line 30.
	X = 2	Control passes to line 50.
	X = 3	Control passes to line 70.
`10 ON X - 2 GOTO 100,150`	X = 3	3 − 2 = 1. Control passes to line 100.
	X = 4	4 − 2 = 2. Control passes to line 150.
`20 ON X / 3 GOTO 40,60,80`	X = 7	7/3 = 2.33. Result of 2.33 is truncated to 2. Control passes to line 60.

Three additional rules apply to the ON/GOTO statement:

- If the value of the expression is *zero*, the VAX displays an error message. The other systems described in this book ignore the rest of the ON/GOTO statement, and control passes to the next statement.
- If the value of the expression is greater than the number of transfer lines listed (but still within the system's permitted range), the VAX displays an error message, and execution stops. Other systems merely bypass the ON/GOTO.

- If the value of the expression is negative, or if it exceeds the system's permitted maximum, an error message is displayed, and execution stops.

The following table illustrates what happens if the value of the expression is greater than the number of transfer lines listed.

Statement	Value of Variable	Execution
30 ON COUNT GOTO 70,85,100 40 COUNT = COUNT - 1	COUNT = 5	**VAX system** Execution stops. Error message displayed. **Microcomputers** Control passes to line 40.

Table 5–2 shows how different systems handle such conditions.

Menus

A **menu** is a displayed list of the functions that a program can perform. Just as a customer in a restaurant looks at the menu to choose a meal, so a program user looks at a menu displayed on the screen to choose a desired function. The user makes a selection by entering a code, usually a simple number or letter, at the keyboard. Figure 5–10 presented a simple example of a menu. Here is another example:

Menu
A screen display of a program's functions.

```
      MONEY CONVERSION MENU

ENTER NUMBER OF DOLLARS TO BE CONVERTED
? 12.00

PLEASE ENTER ONE OF THE FOLLOWING NUMBERS:
     1  TO CONVERT TO POUNDS
     2  TO CONVERT TO MARKS
     3  TO CONVERT TO FRANCS
     4  TO CONVERT TO LIRA
? 2
THE RESULT =  28.8
```

The ON/GOTO statement is often used in menu programs such as the one in Figure 5–13. After entering the number of dollars to be converted, the user enters a 1, 2, 3, or 4 to indicate the currency desired. The ON/GOTO statement in line 150 then branches to the part of the program that performs

138 BASIC PROGRAMMING TODAY, A STRUCTURED APPROACH

FIGURE 5–13 Menu Using the ON/GOTO Statement

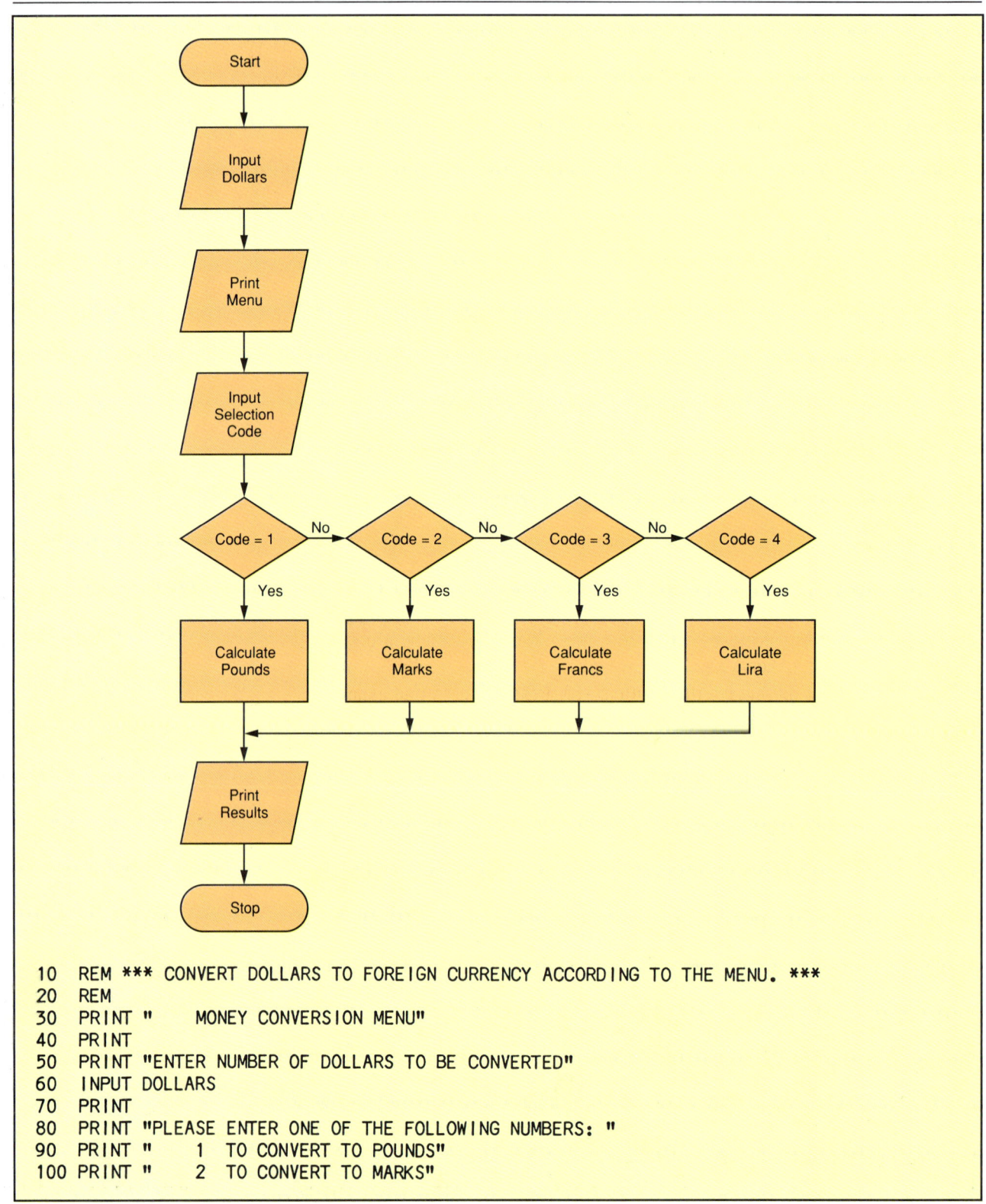

```
10   REM *** CONVERT DOLLARS TO FOREIGN CURRENCY ACCORDING TO THE MENU. ***
20   REM
30   PRINT "     MONEY CONVERSION MENU"
40   PRINT
50   PRINT "ENTER NUMBER OF DOLLARS TO BE CONVERTED"
60   INPUT DOLLARS
70   PRINT
80   PRINT "PLEASE ENTER ONE OF THE FOLLOWING NUMBERS: "
90   PRINT "     1  TO CONVERT TO POUNDS"
100  PRINT "     2  TO CONVERT TO MARKS"
```

FIGURE 5–13 *Continued*

```
110 PRINT "    3   TO CONVERT TO FRANCS"
120 PRINT "    4   TO CONVERT TO LIRA"
130 PRINT
140 INPUT CODE
150 ON CODE GOTO 180,220,260,300
160 REM
170 REM *** POUNDS ***
180 RESULT = DOLLARS * 0.94
190 GOTO 310
200 REM
210 REM *** MARKS ***
220 RESULT = DOLLARS * 2.40
230 GOTO 310
240 REM
250 REM *** FRANCS ***
260 RESULT = DOLLARS * 7.20
270 GOTO 310
280 REM
290 REM *** LIRA ***
300 RESULT = DOLLARS * 1439.00
310 PRINT "THE RESULT = ";RESULT
999 END
```

```
RUNNH

      MONEY CONVERSION MENU

ENTER NUMBER OF DOLLARS TO BE CONVERTED
? 12.00

PLEASE ENTER ONE OF THE FOLLOWING NUMBERS:
    1   TO CONVERT TO POUNDS
    2   TO CONVERT TO MARKS
    3   TO CONVERT TO FRANCS
    4   TO CONVERT TO LIRA

? 2
THE RESULT =  28.8
```

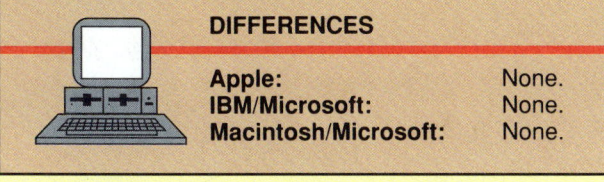

DIFFERENCES

Apple:	None.
IBM/Microsoft:	None.
Macintosh/Microsoft:	None.

the indicated conversion. For example, if a 2 is entered, the ON/GOTO branches to line 220, where the marks conversion section begins.

Looping Methods

Often a situation arises in which a single task must be performed several times. For example, a teacher may need a program to find the average test score of all the students in a given class. The job of processing a single student's data is simple enough:

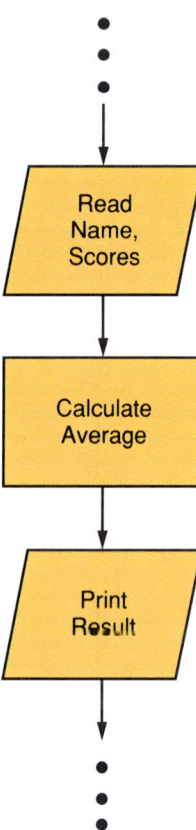

However, consider the problem of repeating these steps for a class of thirty students:

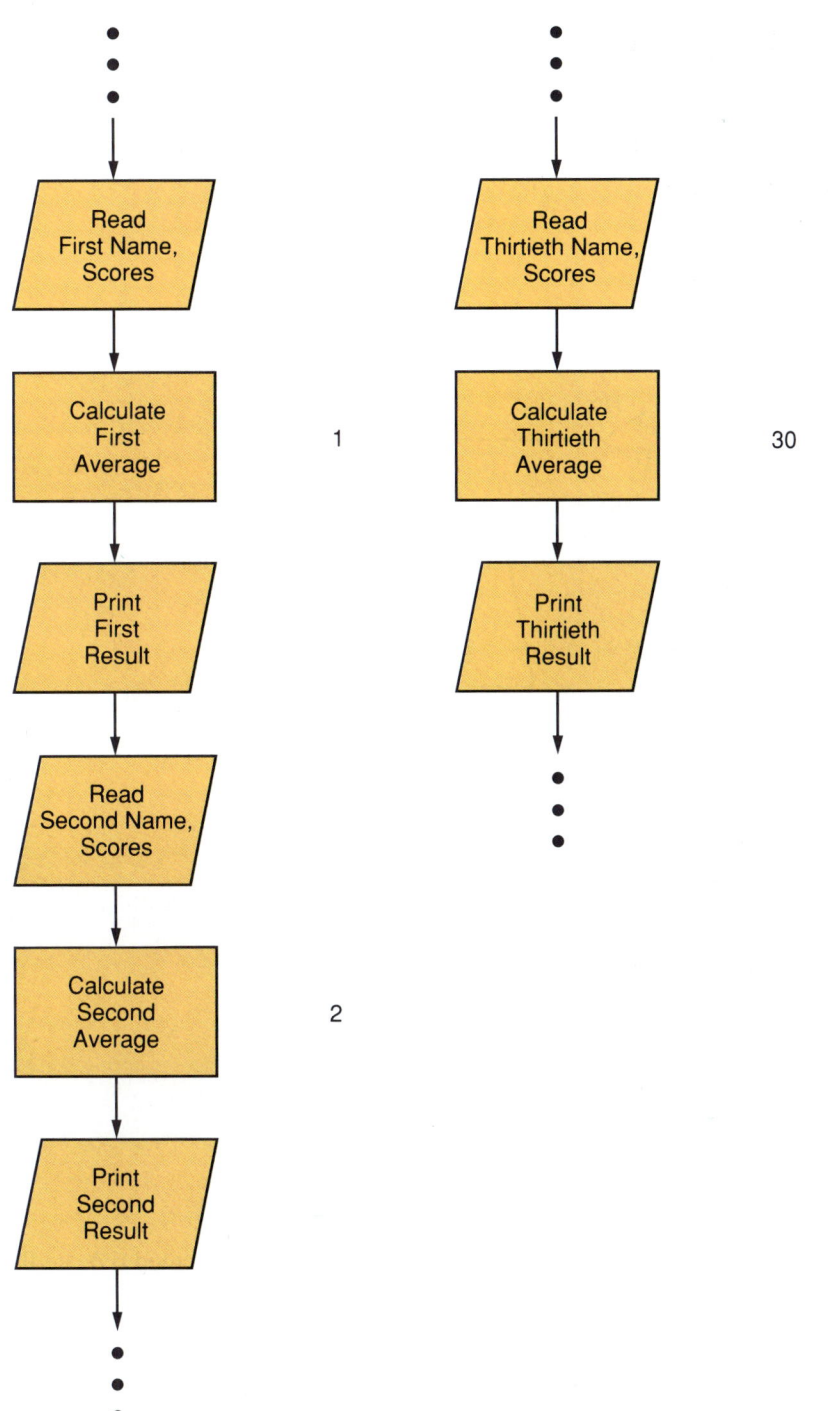

The same three statements to process a single student's data would have to be written thirty times. Although such a solution would be possible, it clearly would be a tedious and taxing job for the programmer. The problem could be greatly simplified by writing the statements to process the data of just one student, then executing those statements as many times as needed. This procedure, called *looping,* is flowcharted as follows:

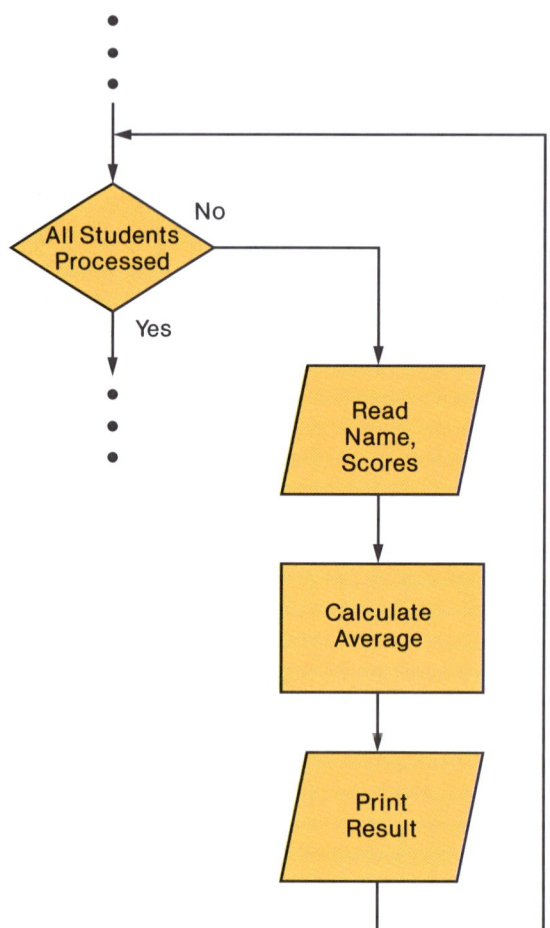

As first mentioned in Chapter 2, a sequence of steps executed repeatedly in this way constitutes a loop. One of the most important uses of control statements is the creation of loops. Control statements can determine which actions are to be repeated and the number of repetitions to made. In the rest of this chapter, we will discuss two ways of writing loops: using trailer values and counters.

Trailer Values

A **trailer value** is a dummy value that follows, or "trails," the data items to be processed. It is sometimes referred to as a **sentinel value.** The trailer value signals to the program that all of the data has been read. The trailer can be either a numeric value or a character string, depending on the type of data being input, but it should always be a value outside the range of the actual data. For example, if a program reads people's ages, a good trailer value might be -1. If names are being read, an example of a good trailer value would be "FINISHED."

A trailer value can control a loop in the following way. Before the loop begins, a READ or INPUT statement reads the first data item or group of data items into a certain variable or variables. The loop begins with an IF/THEN statement that checks one of those variables to see if this value equals the trailer value. If so, then all the data items have been read and program control passes to the first executable statement following the loop. If the variable's value is not equal to the trailer value, however, then the action of the loop is performed. At the end of the loop, the next data item or group of data items is read, and a GOTO statement passes control back to the beginning of the loop.

The program in Figure 5–14 shows a loop controlled by a trailer value. This program calculates the wages of the employees of The Village Hotel. After each employee's data is entered, the following statement tests the name for the trailer value:

```
110 IF NME$ = "DONE" THEN 210
```

If the condition is true, control passes out of the loop to line 210. Otherwise, execution continues on to line 120. The GOTO statement in line 200 marks the end of the loop.

Care is needed when using GOTO statements in loops. An incorrect transfer line number can produce unexpected results. For example, study Figure 5–14 and consider what would happen if the GOTO statement in line 200 were written like this:

```
200 GOTO 120
```

In this case, control would always be passed to the line after the IF/THEN statement. Thus the employees' names would not be tested for the trailer value, and there would be no way for control to pass out of the loop. A loop such as this without an exit is called an **infinite** (or **endless**) **loop.** An infinite loop can either cause an error or prevent the program from continuing to a normal termination. Careful checking of all program branches will help you to avoid infinite loops.

Trailer value
A method of loop control in which a unique value signals the termination of the loop.

Infinite loop
A loop without an exit point.

FIGURE 5–14
Payroll Program with Trailer Value

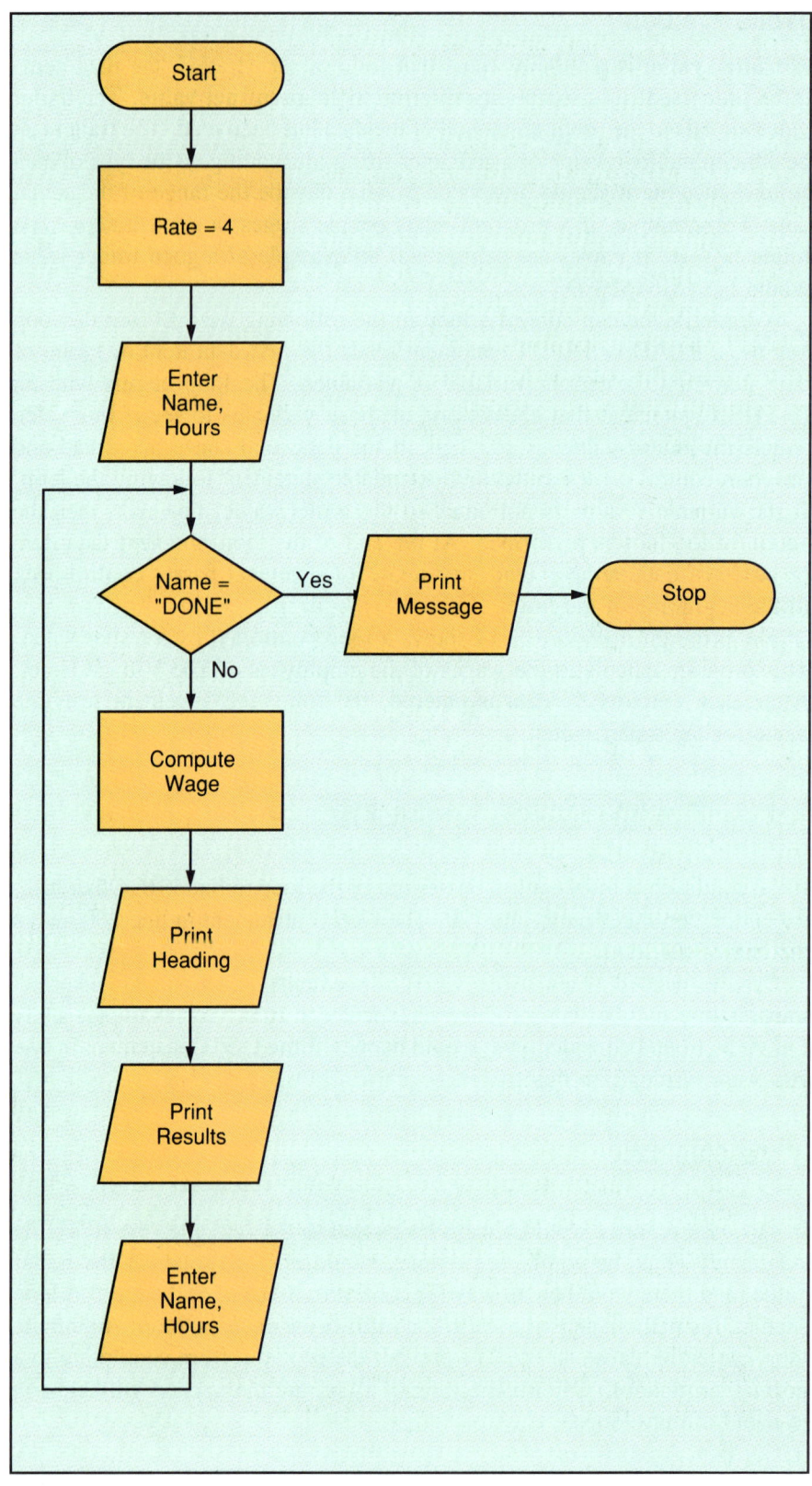

FIGURE 5-14 Continued

```
10   REM *** CALCULATE THE PAYROLL FOR THE VILLAGE. ***
20   REM
30   RTE = 4.00
40   REM
50   REM *** ENTER FIRST DATA. ***
60   PRINT "ENTER NAME, NUMBER OF HOURS"
70   PRINT "TYPE  'DONE,0' TO END"
80   INPUT NME$,HOURS
90   REM
100  REM *** TEST FOR TRAILER VALUE. ***
110  IF NME$ = "DONE" THEN 210
120     WAGE = RTE * HOURS
130     PRINT "NAME","WAGE"
140     PRINT NME$,WAGE
150     PRINT
160     REM *** ENTER NEXT DATA. ***
170     PRINT "ENTER NAME, NUMBER OF HOURS"
180     PRINT "TYPE 'DONE,0', TO END"
190     INPUT NME$,HOURS
200  GOTO 110
210  PRINT "FINISHED"
999  END
```

```
RUNNH

ENTER NAME, NUMBER OF HOURS
TYPE   'DONE,0' TO END
? SMITH,39
NAME           WAGE
SMITH           156

ENTER NAME, NUMBER OF HOURS
TYPE 'DONE,0', TO END
? JONES,43
NAME           WAGE
JONES           172

ENTER NAME, NUMBER OF HOURS
TYPE 'DONE,0', TO END
? DONE,0
FINISHED
```

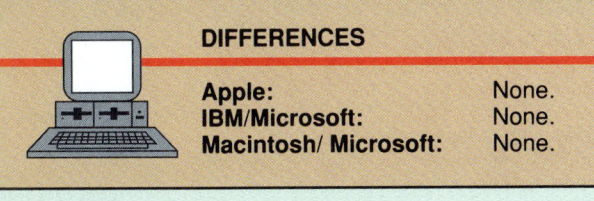

DIFFERENCES

Apple:	None.
IBM/Microsoft:	None.
Macintosh/Microsoft:	None.

Counters

Counter
A method of loop control in which a variable is tested until the stopping value is reached.

A second method of controlling a loop is to create a special variable to keep track of the number of times the loop has been executed. Such a variable is called a **counter.** The counter is increased, or incremented, by a fixed amount (usually 1) each time the loop is executed. When the programmer knows in advance how many times the loop should be performed, the counter can be tested after each loop execution by an IF/THEN statement to see if the proper number has been reached.

To set up a counter for loop control, you should perform the following steps:

1. Initialize the counter (before entering the loop) by setting it to a beginning value.
2. Increment the counter each time the loop is executed.
3. Test the counter each time the loop is executed to see if the loop has been performed the desired number of times.

The program from Figure 5–14 has been rewritten in Figure 5–15 to use a counter rather than a trailer value. There are three employees, so the loop must be executed exactly three times. The counter is initialized to one in line 60 before the loop starts. Line 90 determines if the counter is greater than 3 and exits the loop if the condition is true. Otherwise, the loop is executed and the counter is incremented in Line 160 before a branch to the top of the loop again.

Learning Check

1. The ON/GOTO statement is an example of a(n) _____ transfer statement.
2. The expression in the ON/GOTO statement is always evaluated as a(n) _____.
3. A list of choices shown on the screen from which the user can pick the needed operation is called a(n) _____.
4. A trailer value is a number that tells how many times a loop should be executed. True or false?
5. A loop without an exit is known as a(n) _____ _____.

Answers

1. conditional 2. integer 3. menu 4. False 5. infinite loop

FUNDAMENTAL CONTROL STATEMENTS

FIGURE 5-15 Payroll Program with Counter

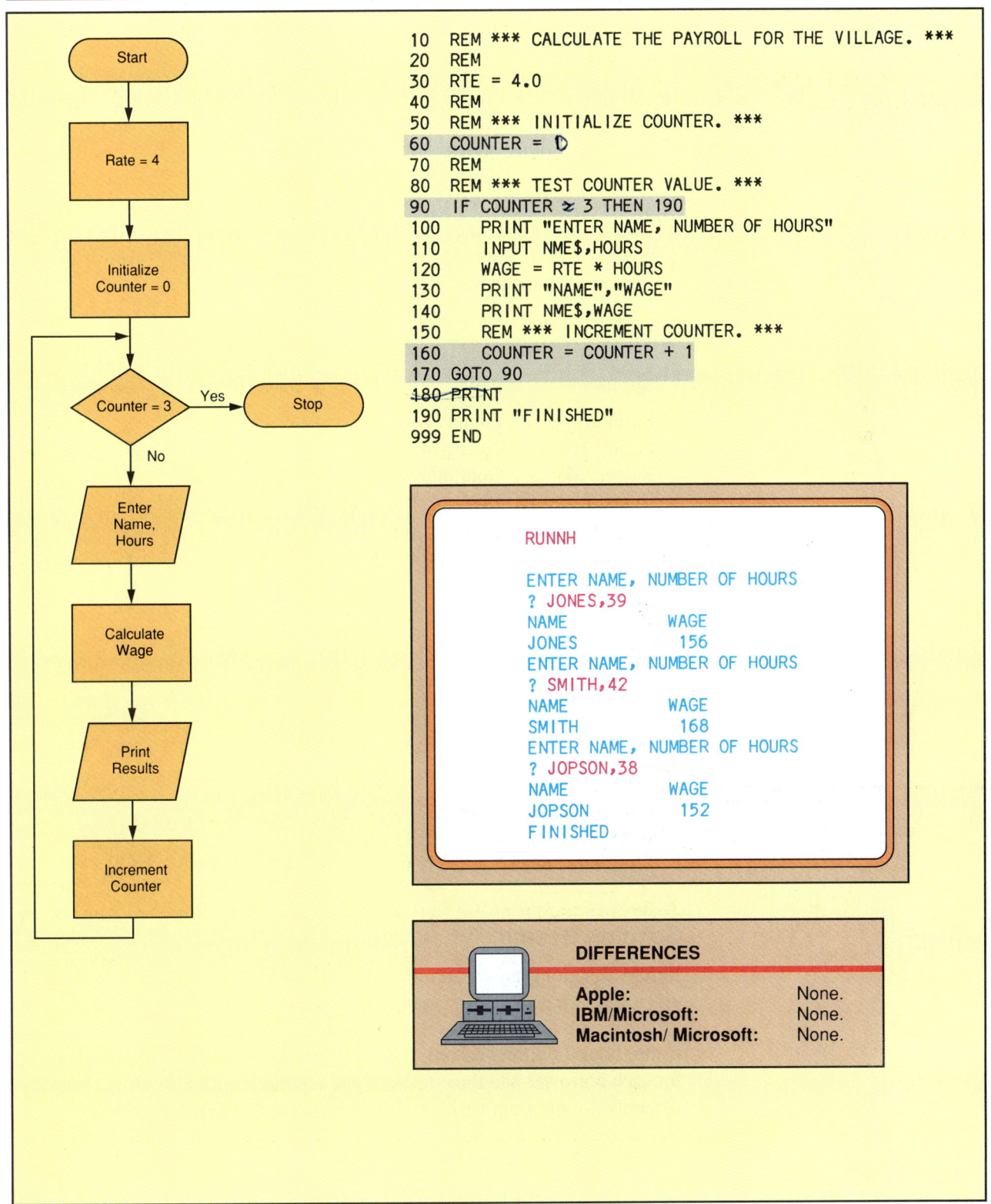

A Programming Problem

Problem Definition

The library is preparing its monthly billing report for overdue books. For books on the high-demand list, indicated in the data by a Y if high-demand and an N if not, the rates are 50¢ a day for the first five days and 75¢ a day after that. For other books, the fines are 25¢ a day for the first five days and 50¢ a day after five days. The program should print each borrower's name, book title, and fine. Also, a summary should be printed giving the total number of books overdue, total number of high-demand books overdue, and total fines owed. A trailer value of "XXXX" for the borrower's name should be used to mark the end of the data.

Input:

Borrower	Book	# Days Overdue	Demand
Pushkin, A.	Eugene Onegin	14	N
Poirot, H.	Third Girl	1	Y
Rainer, M.	Goldfinger	5	N
Bulas, I.	1984	39	Y
Mathey, D.	Desiree	21	N
Lord, P.	Thornbirds	7	Y

Needed Output:

BORROWER	BOOK	FINE
XXXXXXXX	XXXXX	XX.XX
.	.	.
.	.	.
.	.	.

Total Books overdue = XX
Total high-demand books overdue = XX
Total fines owed = XXX.XX

Solution Design

Before designing an algorithm, it is necessary to determine what input is given and what output is required. The input variables for the program should be obvious; they are simply the data items given (the borrower's name, book title, and so on). The problem asks for a fine to be calculated for each borrower and three totals; these are the program's output variables. A number of program variables might be needed to figure the output values. For example, if a book is more than five days overdue, the fine can be broken into two parts: up to five days and after five days. Thus, the following variables are needed:

Input Variables

name of borrower	(NME$)
title of book	(TITLE$)
# days overdue	(DAYS)
demand	(DEMND$)

Program Variables

fine for first five days	(F1)
fine for days after five	(F2)

Output Variables

fine for one book	(FINE)
total fines	(BUCKS)
total # books	(TCOUNT)
total # high-demand	(HICNT)

Looking again at the problem, we see that the program must accomplish two basic jobs: (1) calculate and print the fine for each book, a repeated task suggesting the need for a loop, and (2) calculate and print the total for all books processed. To accomplish the first task, a loop controlled by the trailer value XXXX can be set up to process one book per loop repetition.

What must be done to process each book? First, the fine must be calculated after determining which fine rate applies to the book in question. (This step should suggest decision structures.) Next, because accumulated totals of fines and number of books are needed, these totals should be updated as each book is processed. Finally, the information for the book must be printed. These operations should therefore be included in the loop. The final totals are printed only once, after the loop has processed all books.

This basic algorithm is outlined in Figure 5–16 and diagrammed in Figure 5–17. Make sure you understand how the problem solution has been broken down before proceeding.

The Program

The final solution to the problem is shown in Figure 5–18 with its corresponding pseudocode. After printing the headings in lines 220 and 230, the program initializes the totals to zero in lines 260 through 280. Line 320 marks the beginning of the loop, checking for the trailer value XXXX. Line 330 decides which rates are to be used in calculating the fine. There are two alternatives: if the book is in high demand, then control passes to line 340; otherwise, control passes to line 410. For each type of book there are two additional alternatives. The fine is computed with either one or two rates,

FIGURE 5–16
Stepwise Refinement of Library Fine Program Algorithm

General Problem: Calculate the fines for overdue books at the library.

Level 1
A. Process data for one book at a time.
B. Print totals.

Level 2
A.1. Calculate fine.
A.2. Update totals.
A.3. Print data for book and fine.

Level 3
A. 1. a. Determine which rates to apply in calculating fine.
A. 1. b. Calculate fine with appropriate rate.
A. 2. a. Update total for high-demand books.
A. 2. b. Update overall book totals.

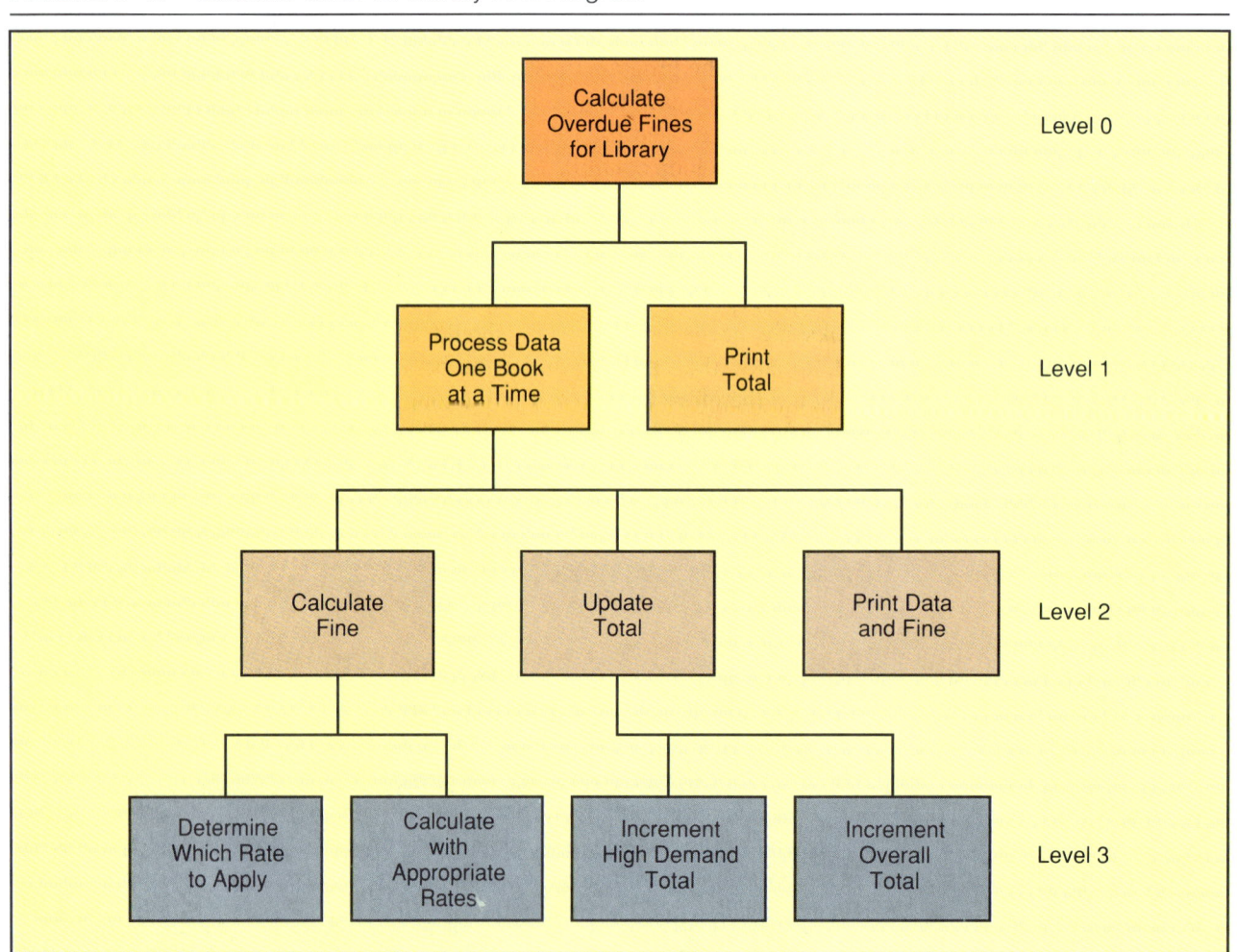

FIGURE 5–17 Structure Chart for Library Fine Program

FUNDAMENTAL CONTROL STATEMENTS 151

FIGURE 5–18 Library Fine Program

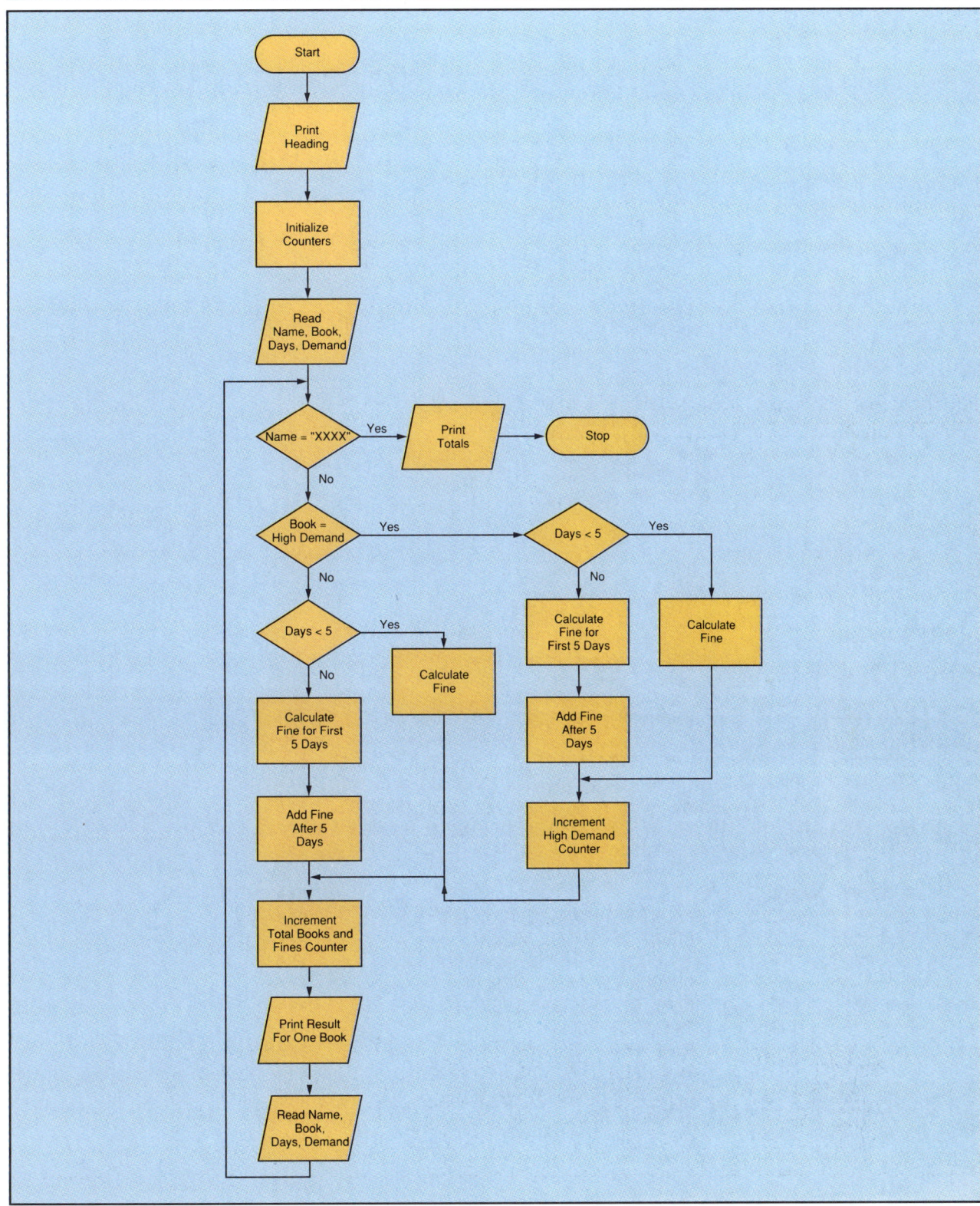

FIGURE 5–18 *Continued*

Pseudocode

```
Begin
Print heading
Initialize counters
Read borrower's name, book title, days overdue
  and high–demand marker
Begin loop, do until end of items
  If book is high–demand
    Then
      If the days overdue are greater than 5
        Then
          Multiply days beyond 5 by $1.00
          Add 5 x 50¢ for first 5 days to give total fine
        Else multiply days by 50¢, giving fine
      End if
      Update high–demand counter
    Else
      If the days overdue are greater than 5
        Then
          Multiply days beyond 5 by 50¢
          Add 5 x 25¢ for first 5 days, giving total fine
        Else multiply days by 25¢, giving fine
      End if
  End if
  Update total books counter
  Print data and fine
  Read borrower's name, book title, days overdue
End loop
Print totals
End
```

```
10  REM ***             LIBRARY FINES REPORT PROGRAM            ***
20  REM
30  REM *** THIS PROGRAM READS DATA FOR ALL OVERDUE BOOKS        ***
40  REM *** AND PRINTS A REPORT CONTAINING THE AMOUNT OWED       ***
50  REM *** FOR EACH BOOK, PLUS A SUMMARY OF TOTAL FINES         ***
60  REM *** AND THE NUMBER OF BOOKS OVERDUE, BOTH HIGH-          ***
70  REM *** DEMAND AND REGULAR.                                  ***
80  REM
90  REM *** MAJOR VARIABLES:                                     ***
100 REM ***     HICNT     COUNT OF HIGH-DEMAND BOOKS             ***
110 REM ***     TCOUNT    COUNT OF TOTAL BOOKS                   ***
120 REM ***     DEMND$    IS BOOK HIGH-DEMAND(Y/N)?              ***
130 REM ***     DAYS      NUMBER OF DAYS OVERDUE                 ***
140 REM ***     NME$      NAME OF THE BORROWER                   ***
150 REM ***     TITLE$    TITLE OF BOOK                          ***
160 REM ***     FINE      FINE FOR ONE BOOK                      ***
170 REM ***     F1        FINE FOR THE FIRST FIVE DAYS           ***
180 REM ***     F2        FINE FOR DAYS AFTER FIVE               ***
190 REM ***     BUCKS     TOTAL FINES                            ***
200 REM
210 REM *** PRINT HEADING. ***
```

FIGURE 5–18 *Continued*

```
220 PRINT "BORROWER","BOOK","FINE"
230 PRINT "--------","----","----"
240 REM
250 REM *** INITIALIZE COUNTERS. ***
260 HICNT = 0
270 TCOUNT = 0
280 BUCKS = 0
290 READ NME$,TITLE$,DAYS,DEMND$
300 REM
310 REM *** LOOP TO PROCESS ONE BOOK PER PASS. ***
320 IF NME$ = "XXXX" THEN 550
330    IF DEMND$ = "Y" THEN 340 ELSE 410
340    REM
350    REM *** PROCESS HIGH-DEMAND BOOK. ***
360    IF DAYS < 5 THEN FINE = DAYS * 0.50 ELSE F1 = 5 * 0.50 \
           F2 = (DAYS - 5) * 0.75 \ FINE = F1 + F2
370    HICNT = HICNT + 1
380    GOTO 440
390    REM
400    REM *** PROCESS REGULAR-DEMAND BOOK. ***
410    IF DAYS < 5 THEN FINE = DAYS * 0.25 ELSE F1 = 5 * 0.25 \
           F2 = (DAYS - 5) * 0.50 \ FINE = F1 + F2
420    REM
430    REM *** UPDATE TOTALS. ***
440    TCOUNT = TCOUNT + 1
450    BUCKS = BUCKS + FINE
460    REM
470    REM *** PRINT BOOK INFORMATION. ***
480    PRINT NME$,TITLE$,FINE
490    REM
500    REM *** CONTINUE LOOP. ***
510    READ NME$,TITLE$,DAYS,DEMND$
520 GOTO 320
530 REM
540 REM *** PRINT TOTALS. ***
550 PRINT
560 PRINT "TOTAL BOOKS OVERDUE = ";TCOUNT
570 PRINT "TOTAL HIGH-DEMAND BOOKS OVERDUE = ";HICNT
580 PRINT "TOTAL FINES OWED = $";BUCKS
590 REM
600 REM *** DATA STATEMENTS ***
610 DATA "PUSHKIN,A.","EUGENE ONEGIN",14,"N"
620 DATA "POIROT,H.","THIRD GIRL",1,"Y"
630 DATA "RAINER,M.","GOLDFINGER",5,"N"
640 DATA "BULAS,I.","1984",39,"Y"
650 DATA "MATHEY,D.","DESIREE",21,"N"
660 DATA "LORD,P.","THORNBIRDS",7,"Y"
670 DATA "XXXX","XXX",0,"X"
999 END
```

FIGURE 5-18 Continued

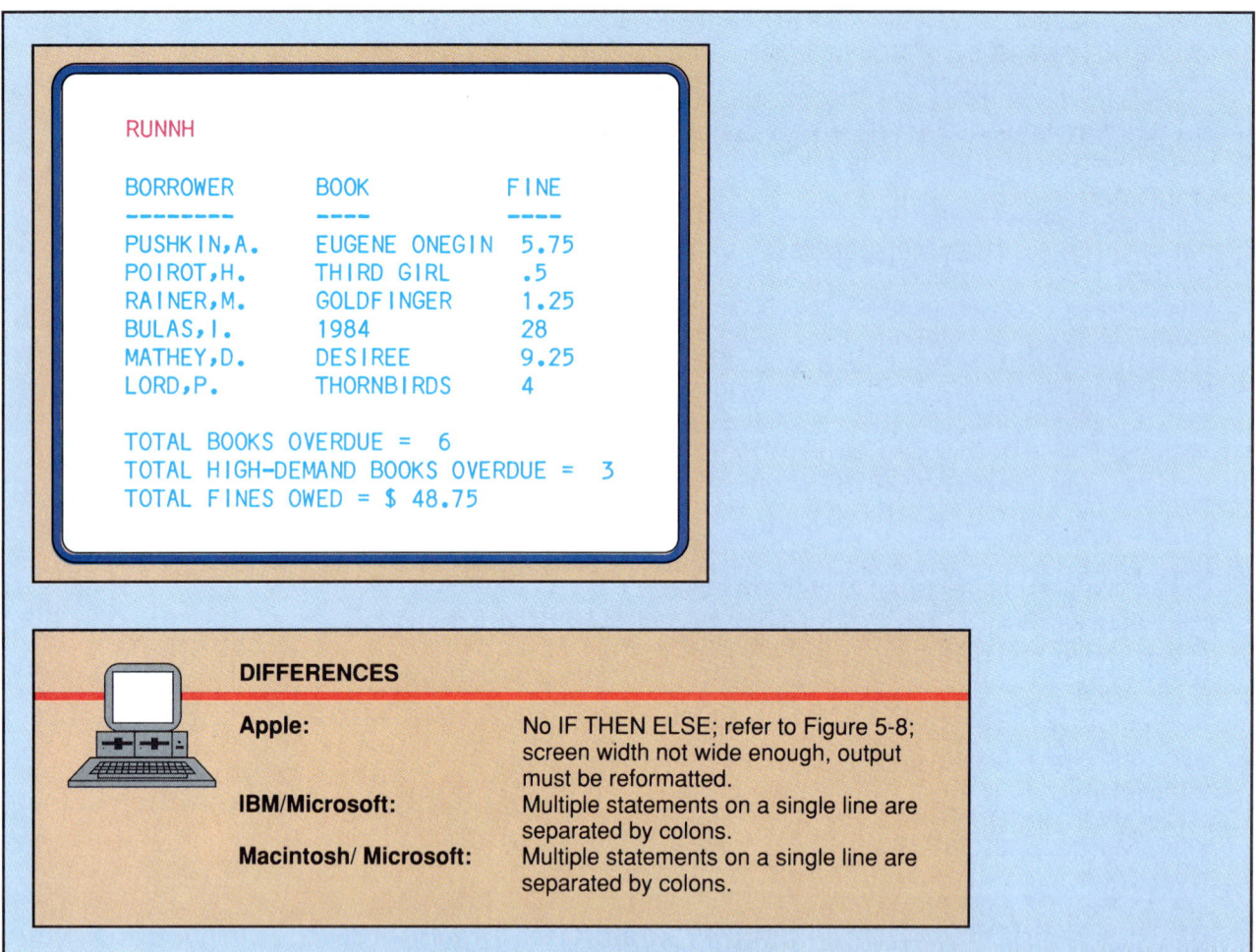

depending on whether the book is more than five days overdue. This condition is tested in lines 360 and 410 for each case. In the high-demand case, the total is updated in line 370 before control passes to line 440 where the general totals are updated. When the trailer value is found, control passes to line 550, where the summary is printed.

Let's take a moment and examine the style of this program. Using good program style makes a program easier to read and understand. A program with good style (1) is well documented, (2) uses blank spaces to make it more readable, and (3) uses meaningful variable names.

A well-documented program should have comments both at the beginning of the program and before each major section of the program. The beginning documentation should explain the overall purpose of the program and list the major variables. Lines 10-190 in Figure 5-18 perform this task. Comments such as the one in line 310 explain portions of the program.

Blank spaces are used to make the program more readable. For example, the loop in lines 320-520 is indented so that it is easily recognizable. Not all BASIC systems allow you to perform this type of indentation, but if yours does, be sure to take advantage of it.

The variable names describe the values they contain. NME$ is used for the name of the borrower, TITLE$ is used to represent the book's title, and so forth. Using meaningful variable names makes the logic of the program easier to follow.

Avoiding Common Programming Mistakes

The following points should be kept in mind when using control statements such as the GOTO, IF/THEN, and ON/GOTO.

- Attempting to transfer control to a nonexistent program line obviously produces an error. Transferring control to the wrong line is not always as obvious, but often creates an infinite loop or results in unexpected execution flow.
- Comparing two variables of different data types in a condition produces an error. For example, a variable containing a real value cannot be compared to another containing a character string.
- An error results when the number and data types of trailer values provided for data do not match the number and data types of items required by the READ or INPUT statement.
- An infinite loop is often created when the value of a variable used to control a loop is not modified somewhere within the loop. For example, a loop that does not have a statement to change the value of its counter will repeat infinitely.
- Nested IF/THEN or IF/THEN/ELSE statements with unequal numbers of THEN and ELSE clauses can produce logic errors. Carefully check the logic of any nested IF statements to verify their correctness.
- Errors using the ON/GOTO statement occur when the expression of the ON/GOTO is not arithmetic, or when the expression evaluates as a negative value or a value larger than the maximum allowed by the system.

Summary Points

- An unconditional transfer statement, such as the GOTO, *always* passes control to a specific program line.
- A conditional transfer statement makes a decision about passing control, depending on the values of certain expressions.
- The IF/THEN/ELSE statement, an extension of the IF/THEN, passes control to the THEN clause if the condition is true and to the ELSE clause if the condition is false. IF/THEN and IF/THEN/ELSE statements can be nested.

- The IF/THEN/ELSE statement is an example of a double-alternative decision step.
- The ON/GOTO is a conditional transfer statement that evaluates an arithmetic expression and, based on this value, branches to various points in the program.
- A menu is a listing of the functions a program can perform. The user enters a code at the keyboard to make a selection. The ON/GOTO statement is often used in menu programs.
- Trailer values and counters can be used to control the number of times a loop is executed.
- The trailer value is a dummy value that follows the data. When the trailer value is read, the loop stops executing.
- A counter can be used to control a loop if the number of desired loop repetitions is known in advance.

Review Questions

1. What is meant by branching?
2. Why is the GOTO statement called an unconditional transfer?
3. Why is the IF/THEN statement called a conditional transfer?
4. The IF/THEN statement is an example of a double-alternative decision. True or false?
5. The THEN clause of an IF/THEN statement is executed when the condition is false. True or false?
6. The condition of the IF/THEN statement compares _____.
   a. numeric constants or character strings
   b. numeric or character variables
   c. arithmetic expressions
   d. numeric or character constants and variables, and arithmetic expressions
7. Which of the following are valid IF/THEN statements?
   a. 10 IF X$ = "FRANCO" THEN M = M + 1
   b. 10 IF Y$ <> "YES" THEN 40
   c. 20 IF Z = "NIENTE" GOTO 100
   d. 70 IF Y THEN 20
   e. 60 IF "HOPELESS" >= "HOPEFUL" THEN 999
8. The ELSE clause of the IF/THEN/ELSE is executed when the condition is _____ (true or false).
9. What is printed when the following statements are executed?

```
20 X = 100
30 IF X > 50 THEN PRINT "HUGE" ELSE IF X < 50 THEN PRINT "SMALL"
   ELSE PRINT "FIFTY"
```

10. Give the statement(s) corresponding to the following flowchart:

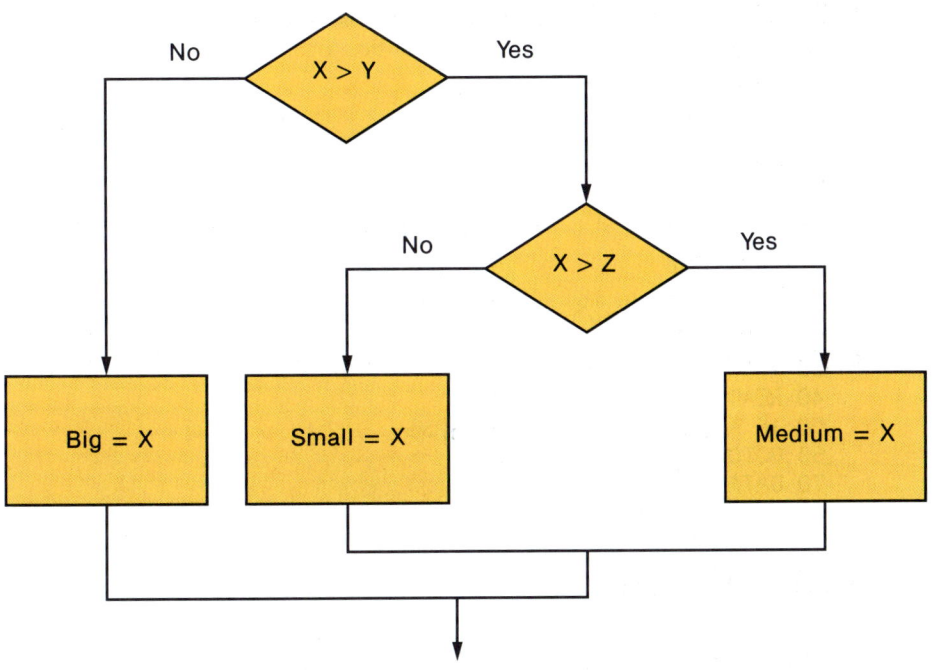

11. The expression of the ON/GOTO statement must evaluate as a(n) _____.

12. Control passes to what line when the following statement is executed if SUM = 21?

```
10 ON SUM / 7 GOTO 50,80,110
```

13. What is a menu?
14. What is a trailer value?
15. The trailer value is sometimes called a sentinel value. Explain why this name is appropriate.
16. What is a counter?
17. Give the three steps involved in using a loop control counter.
18. Rewrite the following program, using a loop controlled by a trailer value:

```
10 PRINT "GRAFFITI"
20 READ N1NAM$,N2NAM$
30 PRINT N1NAM$;"LOVES";N2NAM$
40 READ N1NAM$,N2NAM$
50 PRINT N1NAM$;"LOVES";N2NAM$
60 READ N1NAM$,N2NAM$
70 PRINT N1NAM$;"LOVES";N2NAM$
80 DATA "JOAN","BOBBY","MONICA","TONY"
90 DATA "BRUCE","IRENE"
99 END
```

19. Rewrite the program in question 18 using a counter-controlled loop.
20. What are three ways to control repetition of a loop?

Debugging Exercises

Identify the following programs or program segments that contain errors, and debug them.

1.
```
10 REM *** READ DATA AND PRINT NAMES IF OVER 18. ***
20 CNT = 1
30 IF CNT > 3 THEN 99
40 READ NAM$,AGE
50 IF AGE > 18 THEN PRINT NAM$
60 GOTO 20
70 DATA IRENA,23,DAVE,27
80 DATA CAROLYN,22
```
2.
```
10 REM *** IF X > 10, PRINT X. ***
20 INPUT X
30 X = X + 10
40 IF X THEN 99
50 PRINT X
99 END
```
3.
```
10 REM *** PRINT MESSAGE STATING WHETHER NUMBER ***
20 REM *** IS POSITIVE, NEGATIVE, OR ZERO.        ***
30 INPUT NMBR
40 IF NMBR > 0 PRINT "POSITIVE"
      ELSE PRINT "ZERO" ELSE PRINT "NEGATIVE"
```
4.
```
10  REM *** READ NAME AND MARITAL STATUS. ***
20  MARRIED = 0
30  SNGLE = 0
40  READ NAM$,STAT
50  IF NAM$ = "DONE" THEN 999
60  IF STAT = 2 THEN 80
70  REM *** PRINT CORRECT MARITAL STATUS. ***
80  PRINT NAM$;" : MARRIED"
90  MARRIED = MARRIED + 1
100 PRINT NAM$;" : SINGLE"
110 SNGLE = SNGLE + 1
120 GOTO 40
130 DATA SUSAN JONES,1,MARILYN MCCARTHY,1
140 DATA YVONNE RENKA,2,ROSE MARIE,2,DONE,0
999 END
```
5.
```
10  REM *** PRINT CORRECT CHOICE, DEPENDING ON VALUE OF S. **
20  READ Q,R
30  S = Q - R
40  ON S GOTO 40,60,80
50  PRINT "CHOICE 1"
60  GOTO 10
70  PRINT "CHOICE 2"
80  GOTO 10
90  PRINT "CHOICE 3"
100 DATA 13,12,1,-1,2,3
999 END
```

6.  ```
    10   REM *** PRINT WORLD CUP STANDINGS. ***
    20   PRINT TAB(7);"WORLD CUP STANDINGS"
    30   PRINT
    40   PRINT TAB(5);"NAME";TAB(26);"POINTS"
    50   PRINT
    60   READ NAM$,PTS
    70   IF NAM$ = "DONE" THEN 999
    80   PRINT TAB(5);NAM$;TAB(26);PTS
    90   READ NAM$,PTS
    100  GOTO 50
    110  DATA BILL JOHNSON,192,PHIL MAHRE,131
    120  DATA INGMAR STENMARK,47,DONE
    999  END
    ```

7.  ```
    10 REM *** CALCULATES AVERAGE OF FIVE SCORES. ***
    20 CNT = 1
    30 IF CNT > 5 THEN 80
    40 INPUT "ENTER SCORE";PTS
    50 TT = TT + PTS
    60 GOTO 30
    70 AVG = TT / 5
    80 PRINT "THE AVERAGE IS ";AVG
    99 END
    ```

8.  ```
    10   REM *** PRINT MEMBERS OF CHOIR. ***
    20   PRINT 1 = SOPRANO
    30   PRINT 2 = ALTO
    40   PRINT 3 = TENOR
    50   PRINT 4 = BASS
    60   INPUT "ENTER NAME AND VOICE CODE";NAM$,CODE
    70   ON CODE GOTO 80,90,100,120
    80   PRINT NAM$;" IS A SOPRANO" \ GOTO 999
    90   PRINT NAM$;" IS AN ALTO" \ GOTO 999
    100  PRINT NAM$;" IS A TENOR" \ GOTO 999
    110  PRINT NAM$;" IS A BASS"
    120  GOTO 60
    999  END
    ```

9.  ```
    10 REM *** PRINT INVENTORY REPORT. ***
    20 PRINT "INVENTORY UPDATE"
    30 PRINT
    40 INPUT "ENTER NUMBER OF ITEMS SOLD";NMBR
    50 IF T1 - NMBR > 0 THEN T1 = T1 - NMBR ELSE
       IF T1 - NMBR = 0 THEN PRINT "NOW OUT OF STOCK"
       ELSE PRINT "INSUFFICIENT STOCK"
    60 PRINT "THE CURRENT NUMBER IN STOCK IS ";T1
    99 END
    ```

10. ```
    10 REM *** CALCULATE SUM OF 20 NUMBERS. ***
    20 Y = 1
    30 IF Y > 20 THEN 80
    40 PRINT "ENTER NUMBER"
    50 INPUT NMBR
    60 SUM = SUM + NMBR
    70 GOTO 20
    80 PRINT "SUM = ";SUM
    99 END
    ```
    ```

Additional Programming Problems

Level 1

1. Write a program to input three values, and print the largest. If all three are equal, print that value.

2. Write a program segment to read and compare two numbers. Place the larger in a variable named LARGE and the smaller in a variable named TINY.

3. Write a program segment to read three integers. If the first is negative, output the product of all three. Otherwise, output the sum of all three.

4. Write a program segment using a nested IF/THEN/ELSE statement to assign the price of the following three items: sweater, slacks, and shorts. The prices are $50, $23, and $15 respectively. Assume the item has already been read to variable ITEM$. Then output the price and name of the item with an appropriate label.

5. Write a program that uses nested IF/THEN/ELSE statements to determine if an employee is eligible for a promotion. An employee is eligible if he or she has been with the company for more than four years and is employed as a salesperson. Have the program output a message that states whether the employee will be eligible for the promotion.

6. The local paint store wants a program that will conveniently list its best-selling shades of a given color. Use a menu to display the choices available. The ON/GOTO statement should be used, and the data is as follows:

Color	Shades
Blue	Cote d'Azur, Periwinkle, Cornflower
Brown	Mocha, Sandalwood
Green	Kelly, Forest, Key Lime
Yellow	Mellow, Iced Lemon, True Saffron

7. Write a program to compute how much a person would weigh on the moon and on the planets listed in the following table:

Planet	Percentage of Earth Weight
Moon	16
Jupiter	264
Venus	85
Mars	38

8. Write a program that will search a school's records to find students eligible for honors on graduation day. The student must be a senior with at least a 3.5 cumulative grade point average out of a possible 4.0. The program will read the school's records, which consist of the name, class, and grade point average of each student. Use the following input:

SUE BARTELL	SENIOR	3.42
TOM BIX	JUNIOR	3.60
JENNY SOOD	SENIOR	3.63

9. Using a trailer value, write a program to calculate the squares of the following numbers:

4, 17, 6, 10.

10. Your geometry teacher has asked you to calculate the perimeter for several shapes—squares, pentagons, hexagons, and octagons—given the length of one side. (Assume that the polygons are regular.) Write a program that uses a loop to calculate the various answers. Include a menu within the loop to ask the shape. Enter the length of one side by using the INPUT statement. The output should indicate the name of the shape and its perimeter.

Level 2

1. Write a program to calculate the gas mileage for a car for each of four weeks, and print each week's starting date and average miles per gallon.

Week of	Gallons	Miles
Jan. 1	5.0	173
Jan. 8	4.5	121
Jan. 15	6.0	201
Jan. 22	4.5	142

2. A program contains an unknown number of DATA statements. Each DATA statement contains an employee's name, number of years of experience, position code, and weekly pay. Each employee is assigned a Christmas bonus based on the following rules:

Position Code	Bonus
1	1 week's pay
2	2 weeks' pay; maximum $700
3	1½ weeks' pay

Employees with more than ten years experience are to receive an additional $100. Employees with fewer than two years of experience are to receive half the usual bonus. Write a program to compute each employee's bonus.

3. Write a program to compute the area of a triangle given three sides *a*, *b*, and *c*, using the formula:

$$\text{area} = s(s-a)(s-b)(s-c)$$

where $s = \dfrac{a+b+c}{2}$

4. The metric system is being used more and more in the United States. Write a program that converts from the metric to the English system or from the English system to the metric system. Identify all results with appropriate headings. The formulas for metric conversions are as follows:

Fahrenheit to Centigrade: (Fahrenheit − 32) × 5/9
Inches to centimeters: inches × 2.54
Miles to kilometers: miles × 1.609
Pounds to kilograms: pounds × .45359

5. The marketing division of a cookie manufacturer wants a program to report the results of a customer survey of its four kinds of cookies. Customers gave each kind a rating of 0 to 10 (10 = most favorable, 0 = least). The program should average the ratings for each kind and print the results, with a message for any type receiving the unsatisfactory average of 4 or less.

Chocolate Chip	Oatmeal	Lemon	Licorice
7	4	7	2
8	7	9	5
10	9	6	3
9	6	4	1
9	5	5	1
7	4	3	0
6	5	6	4
8	7	5	3
8	6	4	4
7	6	7	2

6. As a very conscientious student, you want a program that will calculate your projected semester grade point average, based on your anticipated grades for each class you are currently taking. To calculate the semester grade point average, you assign each letter grade a point value (A = 4.0, B = 3.0, C = 2.0, D = 1.0, F = 0.0), which is multiplied by the number of credit hours for that course. This is done for each class, the results are totaled, and the total is divided by the total credit hours. Use a loop controlled by a counter. Two variables should be used to keep track of the total credit hours and letter grade point values. Test the program with the following data:

Class	Credit Hrs.	Anticipated Grade
Art 101	3	C
Bowling 121	5	A
Physics 201	5	B
Computer Science	3	D

7. The Drake Encyclopedia Company is processing the monthly checks for its door-to-door sales agents. Each agent receives a 35 percent commission on his or her monthly sales. An agent whose sales exceed $800 receives a $50 bonus, and an agent whose sales are less than $300 must pay a $25 processing charge, which is subtracted from that month's check. Each set of encyclopedias sells for $150. Write a program that will calculate each agent's total sales, straight commission, bonus or deduction if necessary, and check total. A report should print each agent's name, straight commission, bonus or deduction adjustment, and total amount to be paid. Use following data:

Agent	Number of Sets Sold
Drake, J.	10
Emerson, R.	3
Bond, J.	1
McKinniss, S.	5

8. The Wastenot Utility Company charges customers for electricity according to the following scale:

Kilowatt Hours (KWH)	Cost
0–300	$5.00
301–1000	$5.00 + .03 for each KWH above 300
1001 or above	$35.00 + .02 for each KWH above 1000

Write a program that accepts as input the customer's name and old and new meter readings, and then calculates the amount of the bill. The output should include the customer's name, the old and new readings, the number of KWH used, and the amount of the bill.

Name	Old Reading	New Reading
Sally Smith	938	1,243
Joe College	43,930	46,930
Mike Cool	1,001	1,031
Jim Brown	9,934	10,286

9. Write a program that reads the social security number, sex code (1 = male, 2 = female), and yearly salary for an unknown number of employees. The program should be written so that this information is entered at the keyboard. When the user is finished entering the data, he or she should enter a value of 0 for the social security number. The program should print the number of males earning more than $30,000 and the social security numbers of all females earning less than $35,000. Use the following data:

Social Security #	Sex	Salary
284-70-9932	M	$30,000
787-70-3394	M	$28,500
920-79-3394	F	$52,000
274-33-5770	M	$42,000
293-48-6934	F	$28,500
293-48-6935	F	$19,800
202-70-0010	M	$23,500

10. To encourage its new customers to maintain healthy savings accounts, a local bank gives away free gifts according to the account averages over the first three months. Use the following data:

Name	Month 1	Month 2	Month 3
Ahmad, A.	17,550	21,700	30,225
Corleone, M.	4,730	12,485	20,310
Smith, J.	514	729	999
Poirot, H.	25,415	20,050	18,539

Print a report listing each customer's name, average savings, and the gift he or she receives according to the following scale:

Savings	Gift
$20,000 and up	Jacuzzi
$5000–20,000	Microwave oven
$1000–5000	Toaster
Less than $1000	Bank T-shirt

Level 3

1. An income tax agent is checking wage earners in the income bracket $20,000 to $30,000. Write a program that will allow the user to enter the amount of a wage earner's income and the amount of taxes paid. If taxes paid are below 27.5 percent of gross earnings, compute the additional amount due, and print a stern message to the wage earner, specifying the amount due. If the amount due is over $5,000.00, add a penalty charge of 1.5 percent to the amount due. Reject entries with incomes below $20,000 or above $30,000.

Earnings	Tax Paid
23,000	6279.00
34,000	9282.00
30,000	8000.00
28,540	2791.42

2. The present value of an investment P invested at interest rate R for T years with interest compounded N times per year is given by the formula

$$P*(1+R/N)^{T*N}$$

For input amounts P, R, and N, determine the number of years required to at least double the investment. Test your program with the following data:

P	R	N	T (years)
100	.10	12	7
100	.15	365	5
100	.18	1	5

3. Write a program to find the number of quarters, nickels, and pennies required to equal a given amount of change, using the smallest possible number of coins. Assume that the value entered will always be less than a dollar. For example, if 73 is entered, the output should be similar to the following:

Quarters	Dimes	Nickels	Pennies
2	2	0	3

4. A school has information concerning the grades given to students for different sections of a particular course. The data specifies the section number, number of students in that section, and each student's grade. Write a program to determine the percentage of passing grades for each section (passing grades are above 60). Provide a listing of grades by section number as follows:

SECTION 102
GRADES
90
80
73
.
.
.

```
                    PASSING GRADES = XXX
                    PASSING PERCENTAGE = XXX

                         SECTION 103
                           GRADES
                             22
                             32
                             10
                              .
                              .
                              .
```

Use the following data:

Section	No. of Grades	
102	18	90 80 73 84 69 59 70 43 49 20 94 88 73 60 59 88 87 90
103	10	90 73 14 23 50 64 83 84 87 66

5. The Happy Hedonist Health Club needs a program to handle its monthly billing. Visitors are charged per visit, and members are charged additional membership dues. A report should print each customer's name, address, and total bill, the total numbers of members and nonmembers, and the total of all money due to the club. Use the following data:

Name	**Address**	**Visits**	**Membership Status**
Bulas, Irene	129 Park Ave.	10	Member
Stevens, Jacqueline	1472 Holly Dr.	7	Member
Dillion, Robert	73 W. Fourth St.	3	Nonmember
Rainer, Monica	141 E. Ninth	5	Nonmember

Rates

Member	$20
Nonmember	$35

Membership Dues

$50 per month

6. Acme Rental charges customers for use of its rental cars based on type of car, insurance purchased, mileage used, and number of days. The company leases three types of cars:

Type	Daily Charge	Mileage Charge
1	$ 8.00	.06
2	$10.00	.08
3	$15.00	.12

The company offers two insurance plans:

Plan	Cost
1	20 percent of the combined daily + mileage charge
2	$20 per day of use

Write a program to read the type of car, the insurance plan selected, the mileage, and the number of days the car is rented. The program must print a report that displays this information and the total charge. Use the following data:

Car	Plan	Mileage	Days
1	1	500	1
1	2	500	4
2	1	10	2
3	1	1000	10
3	1	1000	2

7. The wrestling coach at Musclebound High School has a tryout camp each year for the wrestling team. The coach likes to divide the potential team members into three groups, based on this chart:

Weight	Class
Less than 100 pounds	Lightweight
100–199 pounds	Middleweight
200 pounds or more	Heavyweight

Then a coach is assigned to each group in order to make the practice more productive.

Write a program that indicates in which weight class each person belongs. Additionally, the total number of wrestlers in each weight class should be calculated, as well as the total of all people trying out. Because any number of individuals might attend the camp, a trailer value should be used for loop control. Use the following data:

Name	Weight
Dave Johnson	98
Ralph Long	158
Joe Jones	256
Jim Jackson	175
Tim Holden	95
Dick Nickels	210
Bob Brynes	166
Mike Murphy	184
Mark Bartel	238
Rick Leeds	148

8. Your school is presenting its first play of the season this weekend. Ticket sales have been booming. The director would like a report listing total sales to date, as well as the sales for each different type of ticket. The types of tickets, their prices, and the number sold for each follow:

Type	Price	Sold
Adults	$3.55	206
Senior Citizens	$3.15	33
Students	$1.75	105
Children	$1.05	103

The report should be similar to the following:

```
                TICKET SALES
TYPE                PRICE       SALES
XXXXXXXXXXXX        $X.XX       $XXX.XX
XXXXXXXXXXXX        $X.XX       $XXX.XX

TOTAL SALES                     $XXX.XX
```

9. Write an interactive program that converts a given time in one time zone to the corresponding time in another zone. The user should select the original zone from a menu and enter the time to be converted, then select the new time zone. The time entered should consist of an integer value (for the hour) and a string of either "AM" or "PM." The program should make the conversion by first changing the given time to a 24-hour clock time (for example, 3 p.m. is 15 hours), adjusting to the new zone, and then changing back to a.m./p.m. time to print it out. Use your own data to test the program. Here are examples of the time differences in three U.S. time zones:

Zone	Sample Times
Atlantic	11 AM
Central	10 AM
Pacific	8 AM

10. In automobile racing, championships are awarded to the driver with the most accumulated points earned throughout the racing season. The Las Vegas Grand Prix is the final race of the season, and points are awarded to drivers finishing in the first six positions as follows:

Place	Points
1	9
2	6
3	4

4	3
5	2
6	1

The judges need a program to determine the total points for each of the drivers listed in the following table:

Name	Accumulated Points	Place in L.A. Grand Prix
Carlos Reuteman	49	4
Nelson Pequet	48	5
Jacque Laffite	43	2
Marko Mallony	50	3
Jesse Reese	40	8
Mike Racer	48	1
Jackie Stewart	50	6
Al Macleiwski	42	7

CHAPTER 6

LOOPING STATEMENTS

Objectives

After studying this chapter, you will be able to:
- Set up loops using the FOR and NEXT statements.
- Use the single-entry/single-exit point principle in setting up any loop.
- Write programs using nested FOR/NEXT loops.
- Set up loops using the WHILE and NEXT statements.
- List the three logical (Boolean) operators discussed here, and explain how each functions.
- Correctly evaluate expressions containing logical operators.
- Use logical operators correctly in programs.
- Use stubs in developing programs.

Outline

Overview
Elements of Looping
The FOR/NEXT Loop
   Processing Steps of the
     FOR/NEXT Loop
   Flowcharting the FOR/NEXT
     Loop
   Rules for Using the FOR/NEXT
     Loop
   Single Entry and Exit Points

Nested FOR/NEXT Loops
The WHILE Loop
The Importance of Using Loop
   Structures
Logical Operators
A Programming Problem
   Problem Definition
   Solution Design
   The Program

Avoiding Common Programming
   Mistakes
Summary Points
Review Questions
Debugging Exercises
Additional Programming Problems
   Level 1
   Level 2
   Level 3

Overview

Chapter 5 introduced the concept of the loop and presented two methods of loop control: trailer values and counters. Chapter 6 takes a closer look at the basic components of the loop and introduces a third and more efficient method of loop control, the FOR and NEXT statements. More complex looping is demonstrated in the section dealing with nested loops. The WHILE loop is also introduced.

Elements of Looping

Loop control variable
A variable whose value is used to determine the number of loop repetitions.

Loop body
The statement(s) that constitute the action to be performed by the loop.

The loop is an extremely powerful and vital programming tool. Many looping methods exist among the myriad of programming languages used today, but all share some basic components. A **loop control variable,** for example, is used to determine the number of times a loop will be repeated. The counter variable presented in Chapter 5 is an example of this. All loops contain some action that may be performed repeatedly; the statements that perform such an action make up the **loop body.**

Execution of the basic loop structure consists of the following five steps:

1. The loop control variable is initialized to a particular value before loop execution begins.
2. The program tests the loop control variable to determine whether it should execute the loop body or exit the loop.
3. The loop body, consisting of any number of statements, is executed.
4. At some point during loop execution, the value of the loop control variable must be modified to allow an exit from the loop.
5. The loop is exited when the decision of Step 2 determines that the right number of loop repetitions has been made. Execution continues with the next statement following the loop.

Research has determined that the first statement of a loop should always contain Step 2, the condition controlling loop repetition. Therefore, the branch at the bottom of the loop transfers program control to this statement. This makes the boundaries of the loop readily identifiable. Also, the execution path of the loop becomes more tightly controlled and therefore easier to follow, because no actions of the loop can be performed unless the controlling condition is satisfied. To illustrate this concept, consider the following loop:

```
10 READ AGE
20 IF AGE > 18 THEN 99
30 PRINT AGE
40 GOTO 10
99 END
```

The preceding loop begins with a READ statement, because the GOTO statement at the end of the loop always branches to line 10. The READ statement initializes and modifies the value of variable AGE, but does not test it. This same loop is better designed in the following example:

```
10 READ AGE
20 IF AGE > 18 THEN 99
30 PRINT AGE
40 READ AGE
50 GOTO 20
99 END
```

The extra READ statement within the loop body makes line 20 the first statement of the loop, thus satisfying good programming principles. Keep this rule in mind whenever setting up a loop.

Figure 6–1 pictures the elements of a loop in the form of a flowchart. The section on counters in Chapter 5 gave three steps for setting up a counter:

1. Initialize the counter to give it a beginning value.
2. Test the counter to see if the desired number of repetitions has been performed.
3. Increment the counter each time the loop is executed.

These three steps correspond to steps 1, 2, and 4 in the flowchart shown in Figure 6–1. The flowcharts for the sample counter and trailer value programs of Chapter 5 (Figures 5–14 and 5–15) are shown in Figures 6–2 and 6–3, with the five loop elements identified by step number in each.

Keep in mind the five loop elements as the next section presents another way to control a loop: the FOR and NEXT statements.

FIGURE 6–1
Flowchart of Loop Elements

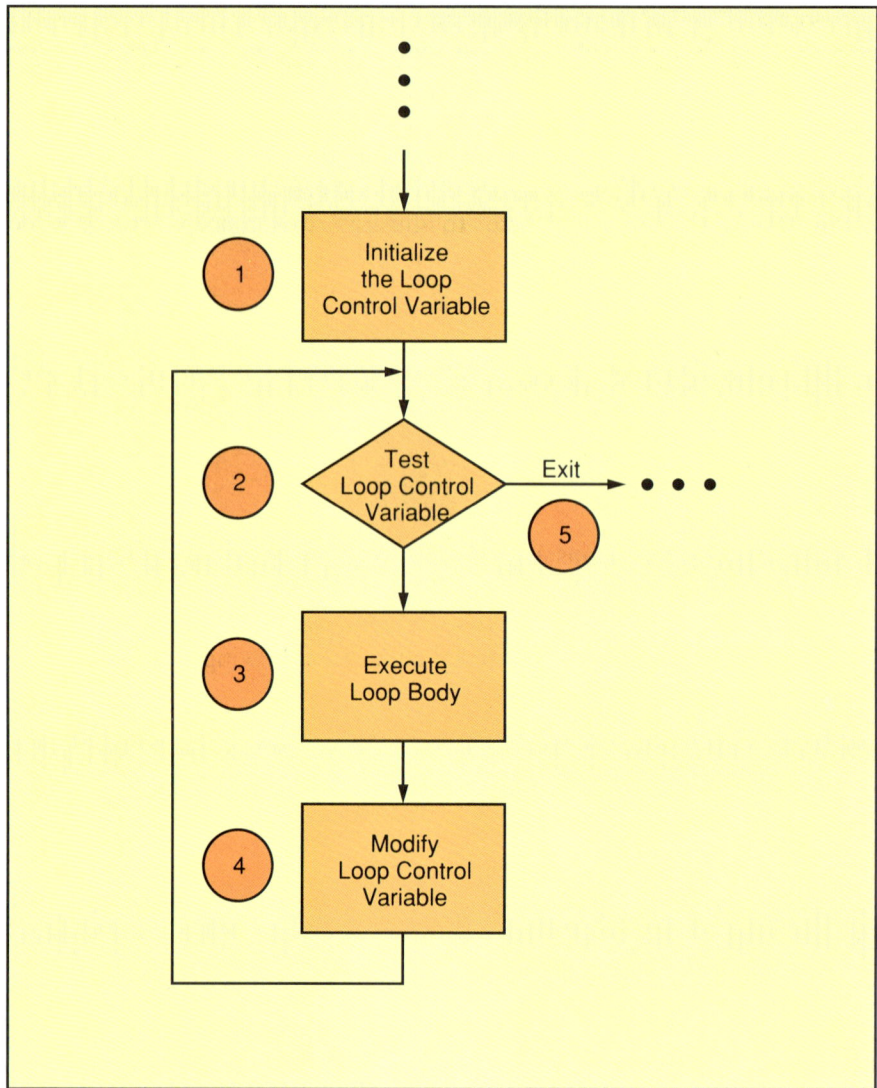

The FOR/NEXT Loop

The FOR and NEXT statements are used together to form a loop that is executed a given number of times. The general format is as follows:

line# FOR loop control variable = initial value TO terminal value
          [STEP step value]
     .
     .
     .

line# NEXT loop control variable

FIGURE 6-2 Flowchart of a Loop with a Trailer Value

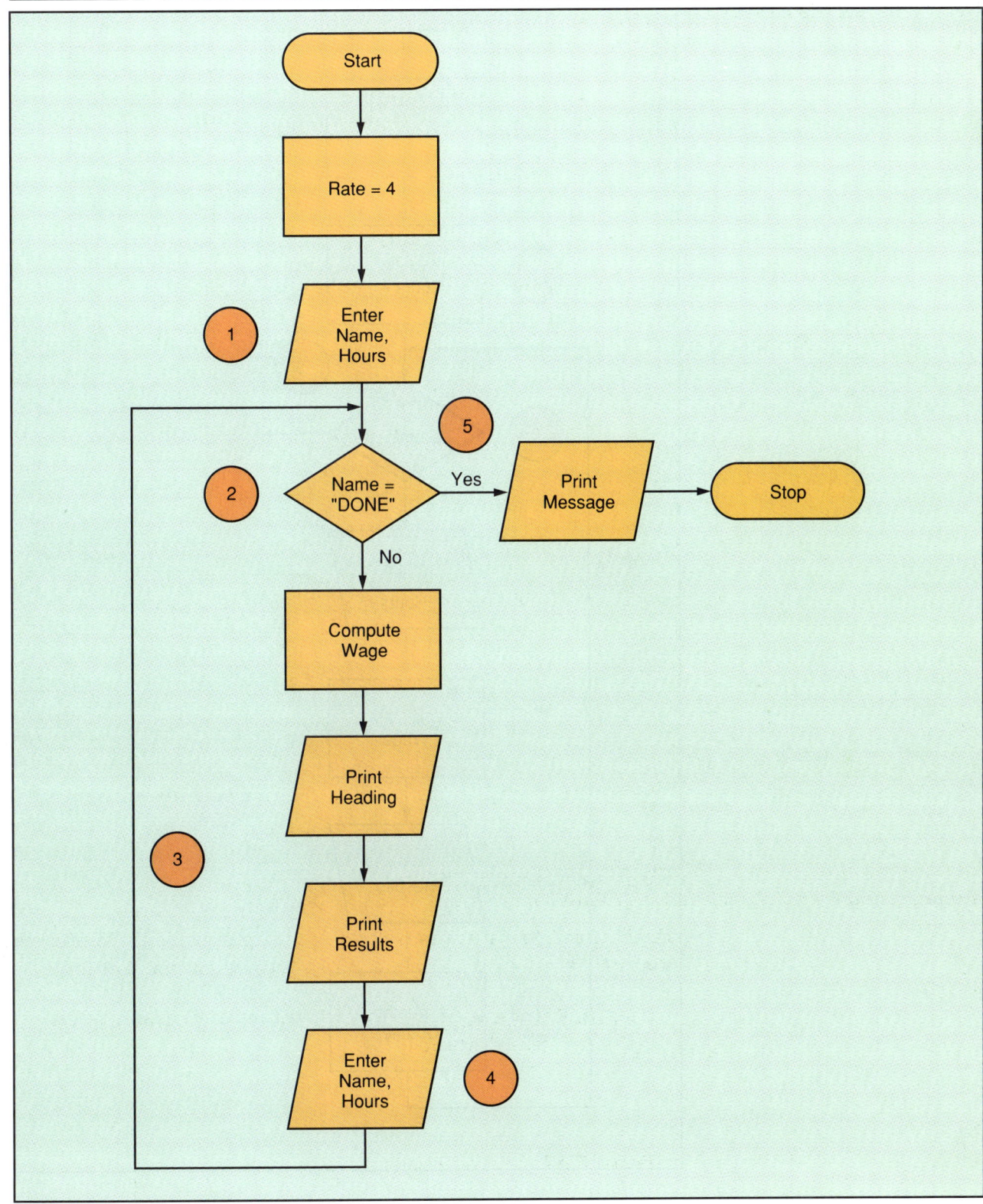

FIGURE 6-3
Elements of a Loop with Counter

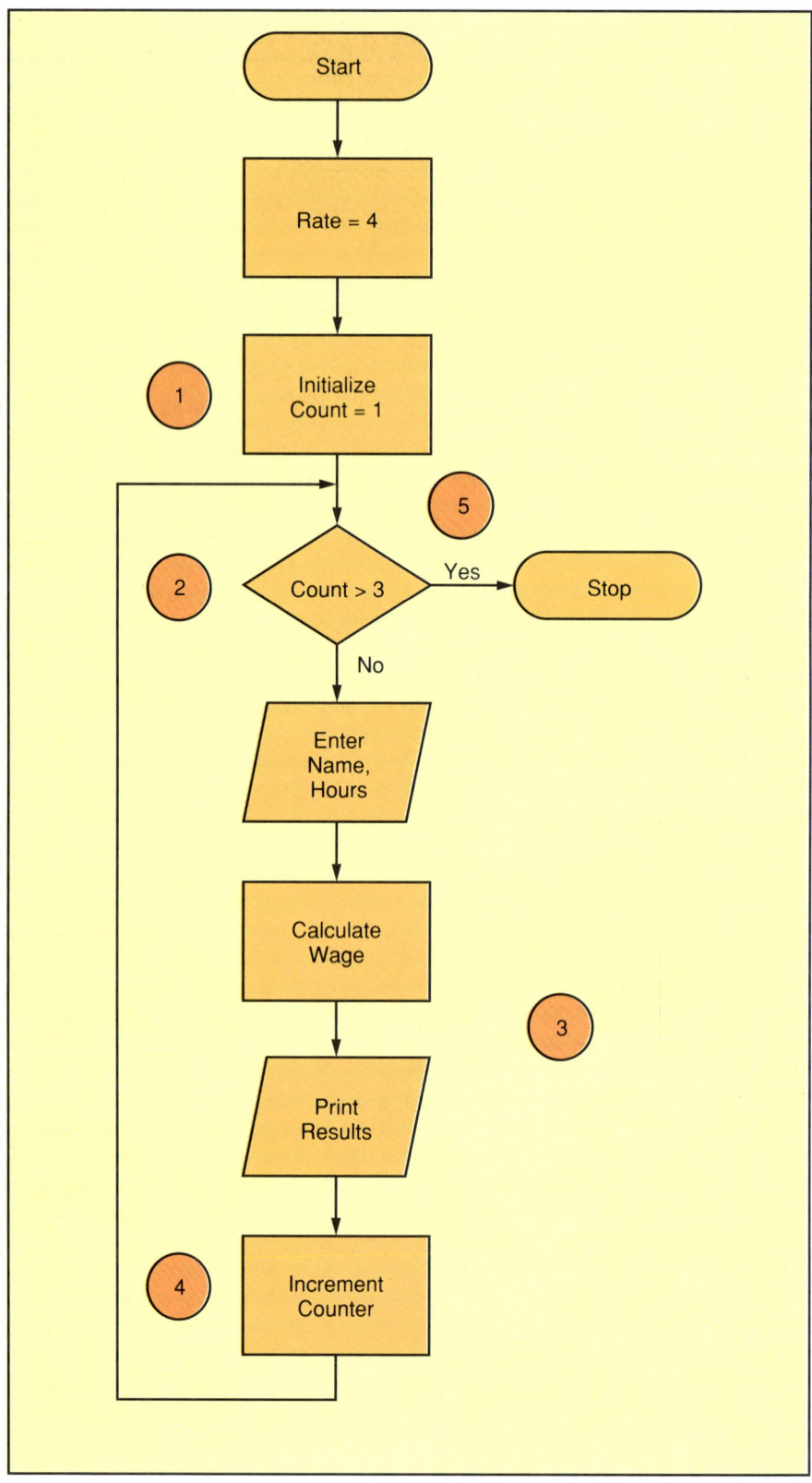

The loop control variable can be any numeric variable. The initial and terminal values and the optional step value must all be numeric. They can consist of any of the following:

Example

- constants
- variables

```
FOR I = 1 TO 3 STEP 1
FOR I = SMALL TO BIG STEP X
```

- expressions

```
FOR I = (A + B) TO (C - D) STEP K + 1
```

The FOR statement marks the beginning of the loop, and the NEXT statement marks the end. Any statements between the two make up the loop body. Figure 6–4 shows sample FOR and NEXT statements with their components labeled.

Processing Steps of the FOR/NEXT Loop

A number of actions are taken when a FOR statement is first encountered:

1. The initial, terminal, and (if given) step value expressions are evaluated.
2. The loop control variable is assigned the initial value.
3. The value of the loop control variable is tested against the terminal value.
4. If the loop control variable is less than or equal to the terminal value, then the loop body is executed.
5. If the loop control variable is greater than the terminal value, the loop body is skipped and control passes to the first statement following the NEXT

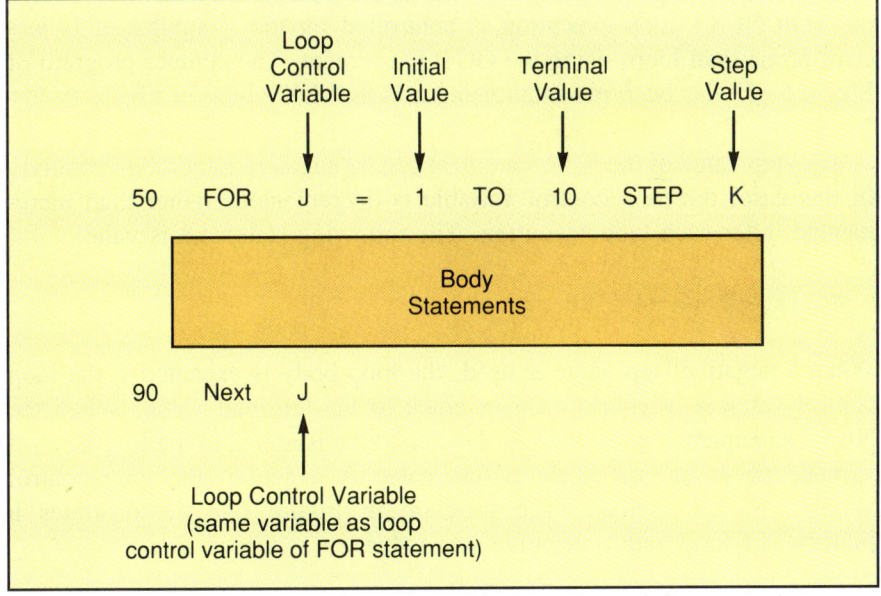

FIGURE 6–4
FOR/NEXT Components

statement. This means that the loop will not be executed at all. (The Apple is an exception here—it always executes a FOR/NEXT loop at least once.)

Here is what happens when the NEXT statement is found:

1. The step value indicated in the FOR statement is added to the loop control variable. If the step value is omitted, a +1 is added.
2. A check is performed to determine if the value of the loop control variable exceeds the terminal value.
3. If the loop control variable is less than or equal to the terminal value, control is transferred back to the statement after the FOR statement, and the loop is repeated. Otherwise, the loop is exited, and execution continues with the statement following the NEXT statement.

Figures 6–5 and 6–6 each show a program that prints the numbers 1 through 5. Notice that the program in Figure 6–5 uses two statements to initialize the loop control variable (the counter) and test its value, while the program in Figure 6–6 achieves the same results with a single FOR statement. Similarly, lines 60 and 70 of Figure 6–5 increment the loop control variable and pass control to the top of the loop, while the second program uses one NEXT statement in line 50 for the same purpose. Thus the FOR/NEXT loop is seen to perform the same task as a loop with an IF/THEN and a GOTO statement, but more efficiently.

Also, it is important to note that the FOR/NEXT loop eliminates the need for using an unconditional branch. Rather than the programmer writing a branching statement into the program, the branch is performed automatically by the NEXT statement. In writing structured programs, it is always preferable to use looping statements such as the FOR/NEXT instead of loops developed by the programmer with the help of GOTO statements. Because the FOR/NEXT loop execution is controlled by the computer, it is less error-prone than loops using the GOTO statement. The counter program of Figure 5–15 has been rewritten using a FOR/NEXT loop in Figure 6–7.

The step value of the FOR statement can be negative rather than positive. In this case, the loop control variable is decremented, rather than incremented, after each loop execution. The following statement is valid:

```
FOR I = 8 TO -4 STEP -2
```

When a negative step value is used, the loop body is executed if the loop control variable is greater than or equal to the terminal value. When the NEXT statement is encountered, the step value is added to the loop control variable as usual; and because this value is negative, the loop control variable is decremented. The program in Figure 6–8 demonstrates a FOR/NEXT loop with a negative step value.

FIGURE 6-5
Loop with GOTO

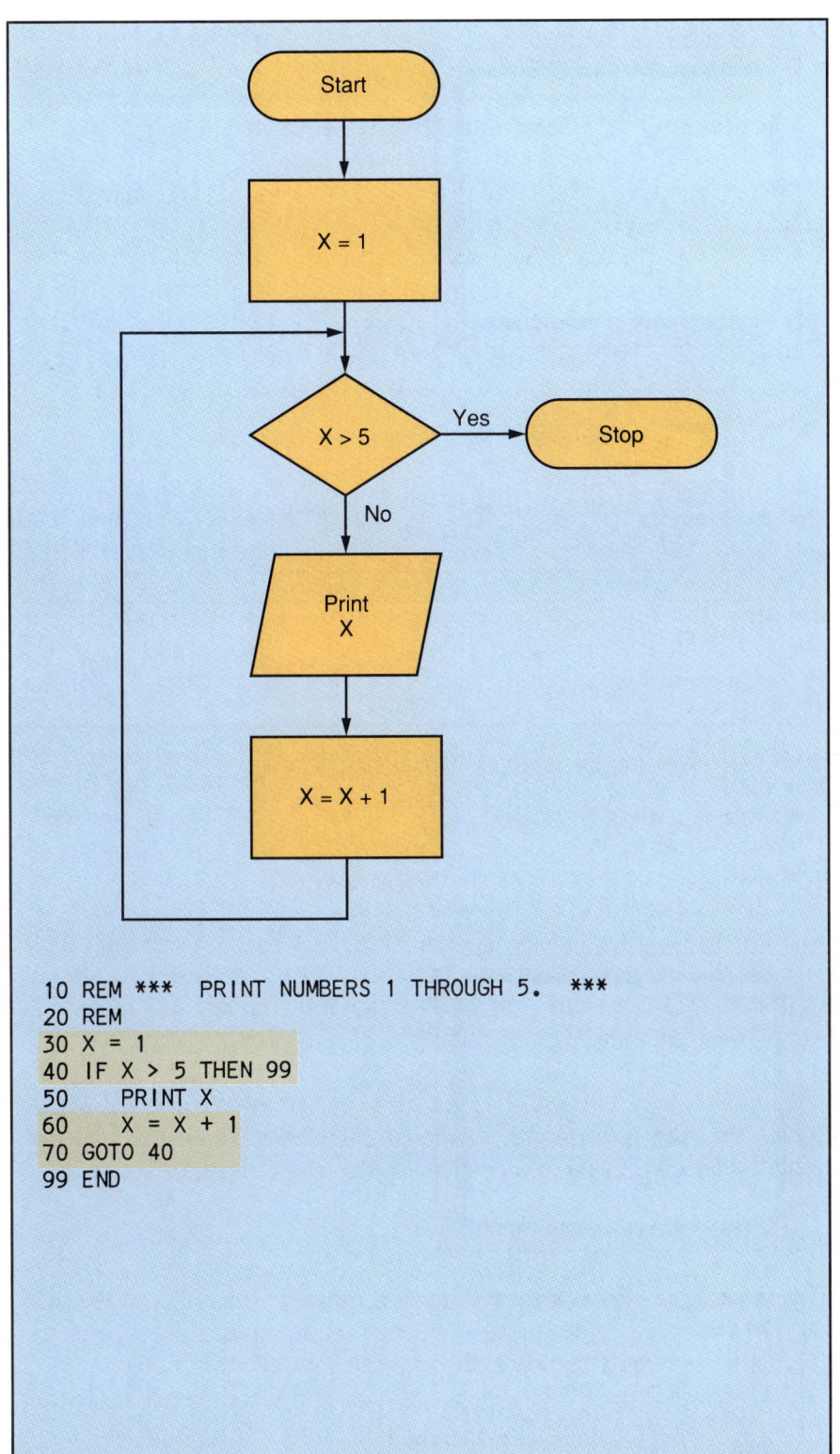

FIGURE 6–5
Continued

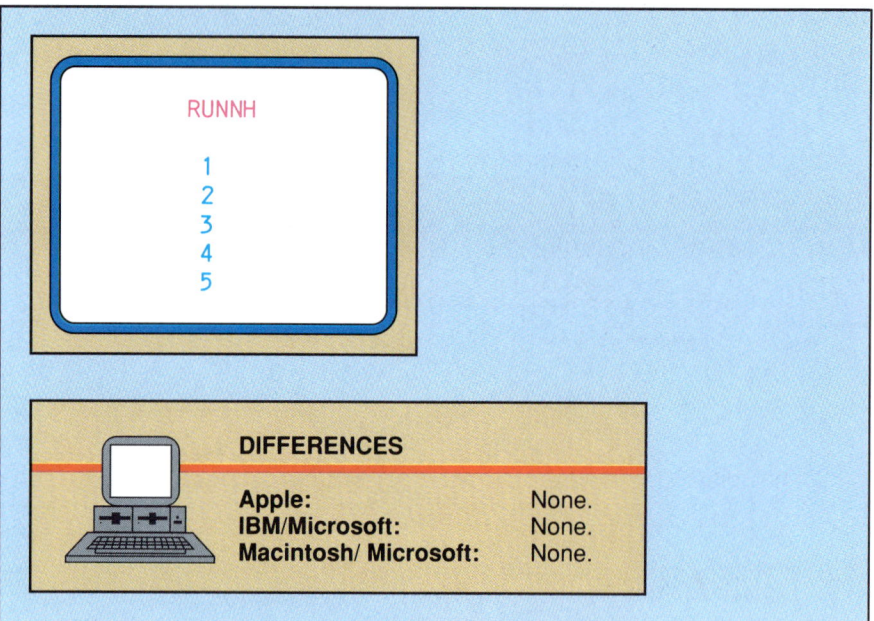

FIGURE 6–6
Loop with FOR/NEXT

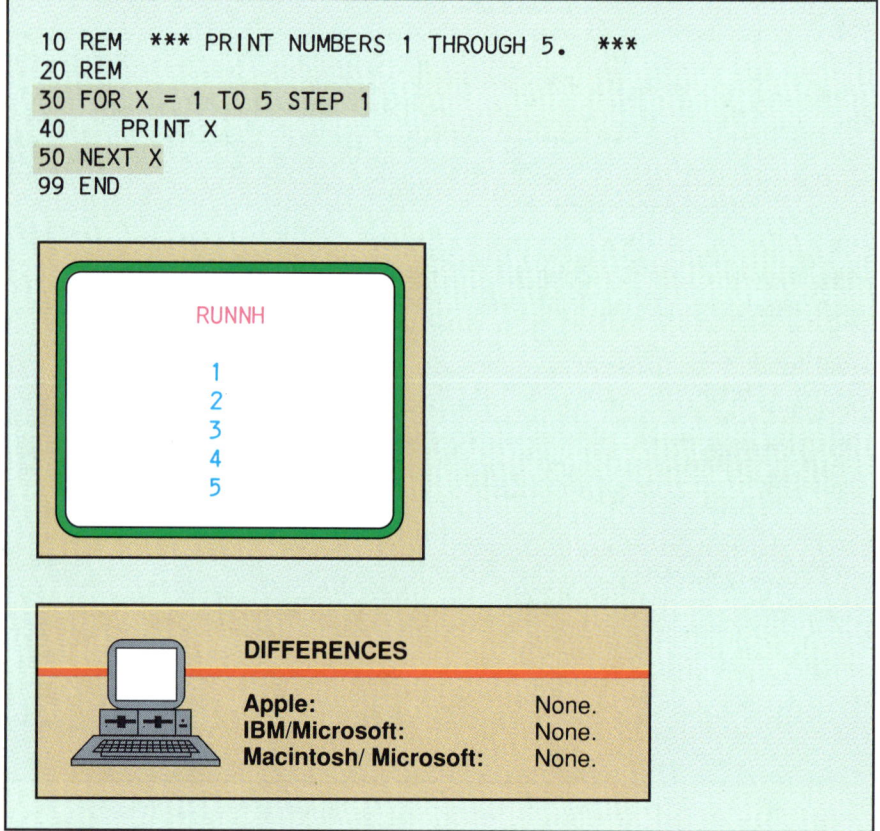

```
10   REM ***  THE VILLAGE PAYROLL.  ***
20   REM
30   RTE = 4
40   REM
50   REM *** LOOP TO PROCESS 3 EMPLOYEES. ***
60   FOR COUNTER = 1 TO 3
70      PRINT "ENTER NAME, NUMBER OF HOURS"
80      INPUT NME$,HOURS
90      WAGE = RTE * HOURS
100     PRINT "NAME","WAGE"
110     PRINT NME$,WAGE
120  NEXT COUNTER
130  REM
140  REM *** PRINT MESSAGE. ***
150  PRINT
160  PRINT "FINISHED"
999  END
```

FIGURE 6-7
Counter Program with FOR/NEXT Loop

```
RUNNH

ENTER NAME, NUMBER OF HOURS
? FETTERMAN,78
NAME            WAGE
FETTERMAN       312
ENTER NAME, NUMBER OF HOURS
? HOSSLER,32
NAME            WAGE
HOSSLER         128
ENTER NAME, NUMBER OF HOURS
? BULAS,25
NAME            WAGE
BULAS           100

FINISHED
```

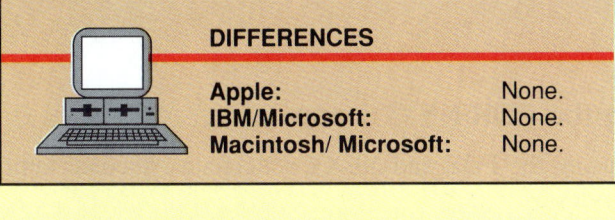

DIFFERENCES

Apple:	None.
IBM/Microsoft:	None.
Macintosh/Microsoft:	None.

FIGURE 6–8 FOR/NEXT with Negative Step

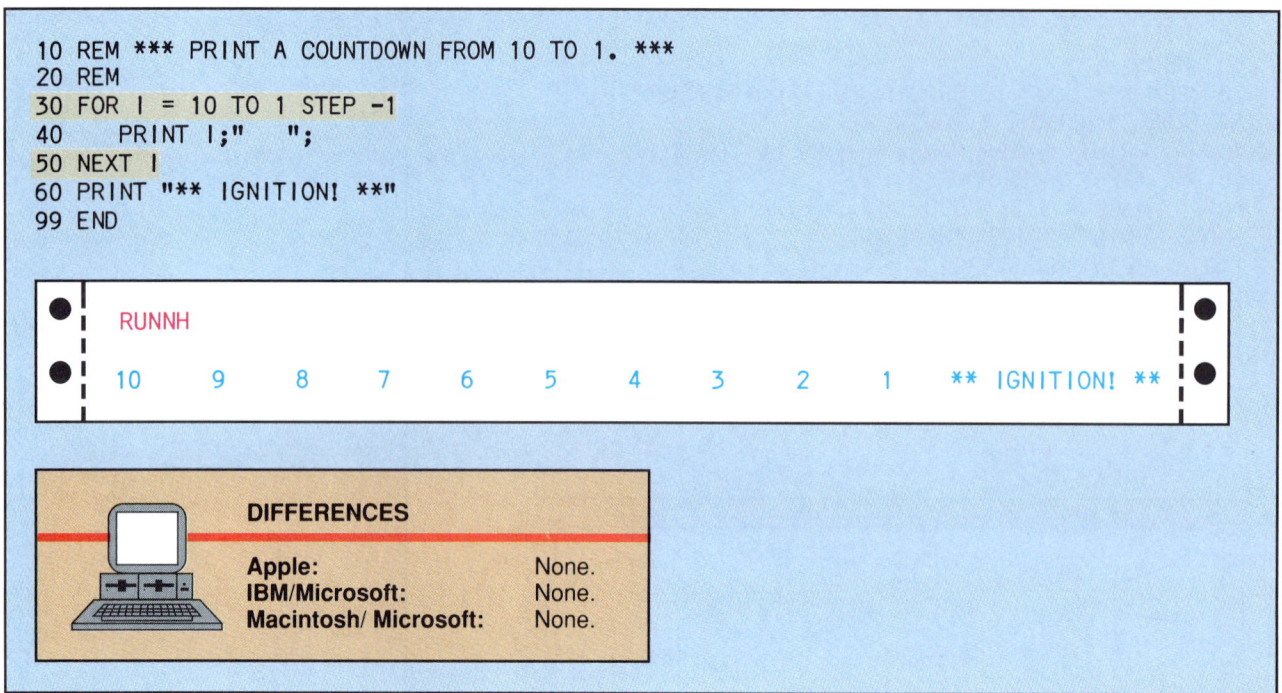

Flowcharting the FOR/NEXT Loop

Figure 6–9a shows the common method of flowcharting a FOR/NEXT loop. An alternate method, shown in Figure 6–9b, shows a convenient shorthand symbol that we have developed to indicate the initial, terminal, and step values. The symbol represents the actions of both the FOR and NEXT statements. As long as the terminal condition (indicated on the right portion of the symbol) is false, the execution path containing the loop body is followed. The arrow from the last loop body action to the step value portion of the symbol indicates the action of the NEXT statement. When the terminal condition is true, the path containing the actions following the loop is taken.

Rules for Using the FOR/NEXT Loop

To avoid errors in using the FOR and NEXT statements, become familiar with the following rules:

- The body of the loop is not executed if the initial value is greater than the terminal value when using a positive step, or if the initial value is less than the terminal value when using a negative step. For example, a loop containing either of the following statements would not be executed at all:

FIGURE 6-9 FOR/NEXT Flowchart Symbol

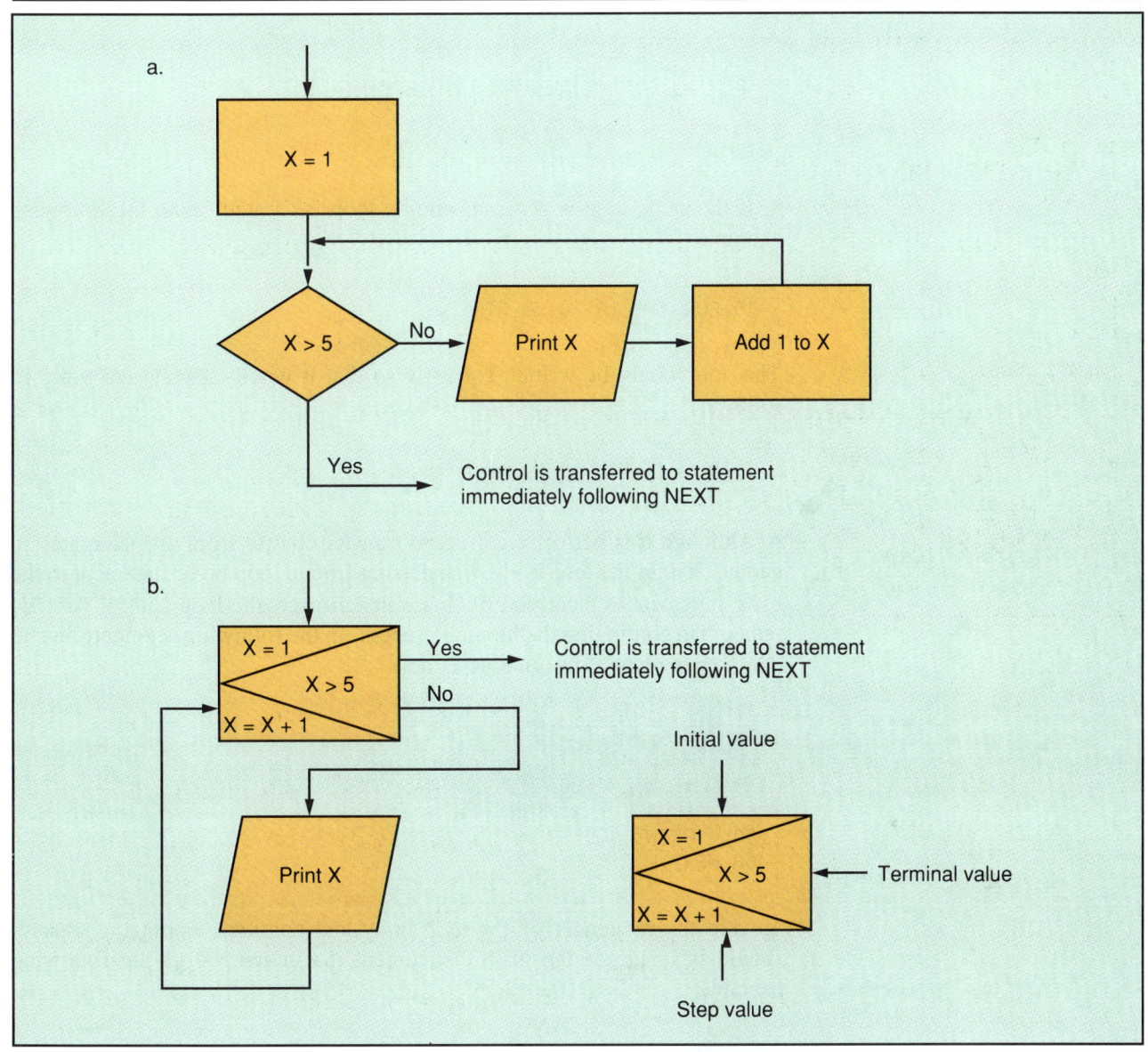

```
10 X = 10 TO 5 STEP 2
20 COUNT = 4 TO 6 STEP -1
```

However, on the Apple, a FOR/NEXT loop is always executed at least once.

- The initial, terminal, and step values cannot be modified in the loop body.
- It is possible to modify the loop control variable in the loop body, *but this should never be done.* Note how unpredictable the execution of the

following program loop would be. The value of I is dependent on the integer entered by the user.

```
30 FOR I = 1 TO 10
40     INPUT "ENTER AN INTEGER";X
50     I = X
60 NEXT I
```

- If the step value is zero, an infinite loop is created, as in the following example:

```
10 FOR X = 10 TO 20 STEP 0
```

This loop could be written correctly so that it would execute ten times as follows:

```
10 FOR X = 10 TO 20 STEP 1
```

- Although it is perfectly correct to transfer control from one statement to another within the loop body, transferring from a loop body statement to the FOR statement is incorrect. Such a transfer resets the loop control variable rather than continuing the looping process. In the following segment, line 30 is a proper branch, but line 40 is not:

```
10 FOR K = 1 TO 10
20     READ AGE
30     IF AGE < 20 THEN 50
40     IF AGE > 20 THEN 10
50     PRINT AGE
60 NEXT K
```

To skip the remainder of the loop body and continue looping, a transfer should be made to the NEXT statement, as in line 40 of the following example:

```
10 FOR K = 1 TO 10
20     READ AGE
30     IF AGE < 20 THEN 50
40     IF AGE > 20 THEN 60
50     PRINT AGE
60 NEXT K
```

- Each FOR statement should be associated with a corresponding NEXT statement.

Remember from Chapter 5 that in order to control a loop with a counter, the exact number of needed repetitions must be known before starting the loop. The FOR/NEXT is a loop with a built-in counter, so the same rule applies to it. Thus the FOR/NEXT loop is not an appropriate choice for reading an unknown amount of data, but it is very efficient for a job such as processing sales data for a given week. The FOR/NEXT loop is used in this way in Figure 6–10. The program reads candy sales data, updates a sales total, and prints the number of the day and amount sold for each of seven days. It then prints the total and average sales for the week. The value of the loop control variable is not modified within the loop body, but its value is printed during each loop repetition to indicate the number of the day.

Single Entry and Exit Points

An important principle of structured programming is that a program structure (such as a loop or decision step) must have only one entry point and only one exit point. The entry point should be the first statement of the structure, and the exit point should be the last statement. Restricting the entry and exit points in this way limits the number of different execution paths the program can follow, thus making the logic easier to follow and errors easier to detect.

In FOR/NEXT loops, the FOR statement is the proper entry point. In other words, no statement outside the loop should branch around the FOR statement to a statement in the loop body. The program and flowchart shown in Figure 6–11 demonstrate a poorly designed FOR/NEXT loop with multiple entry points. When X is greater than 10, control passes from line 60 directly to line 90 within the loop body, skipping the FOR statement. Because I is initialized in the FOR statement, it may not have a valid value when a branch like this takes place. Also, on some systems an error will occur when the NEXT statement is encountered, because no corresponding FOR statement has been found.

Similarly, the NEXT statement should be the only exit point for the loop. That is, no statement within the loop body should branch out of the loop, bypassing the NEXT statement. Figure 6–12 shows an example of a poorly designed loop with multiple exit points. Note that there are two ways of exiting the loop: (1) through the NEXT statement and (2) from line 20 when J is equal to 6. The loop will not continue until J is greater than 8, but will stop after only two loop executions. The FOR/NEXT loop should ideally be used in such a way that the number of actual loop executions equals the number specified by the initial and terminal values.

Keep in mind that the single-entry, single-exit point principle applies to all kinds of loops, not just the FOR/NEXT. It is good programming practice to make sure that all program structures, or modules, satisfy this rule.

FIGURE 6-10
FOR/NEXT Sales Program

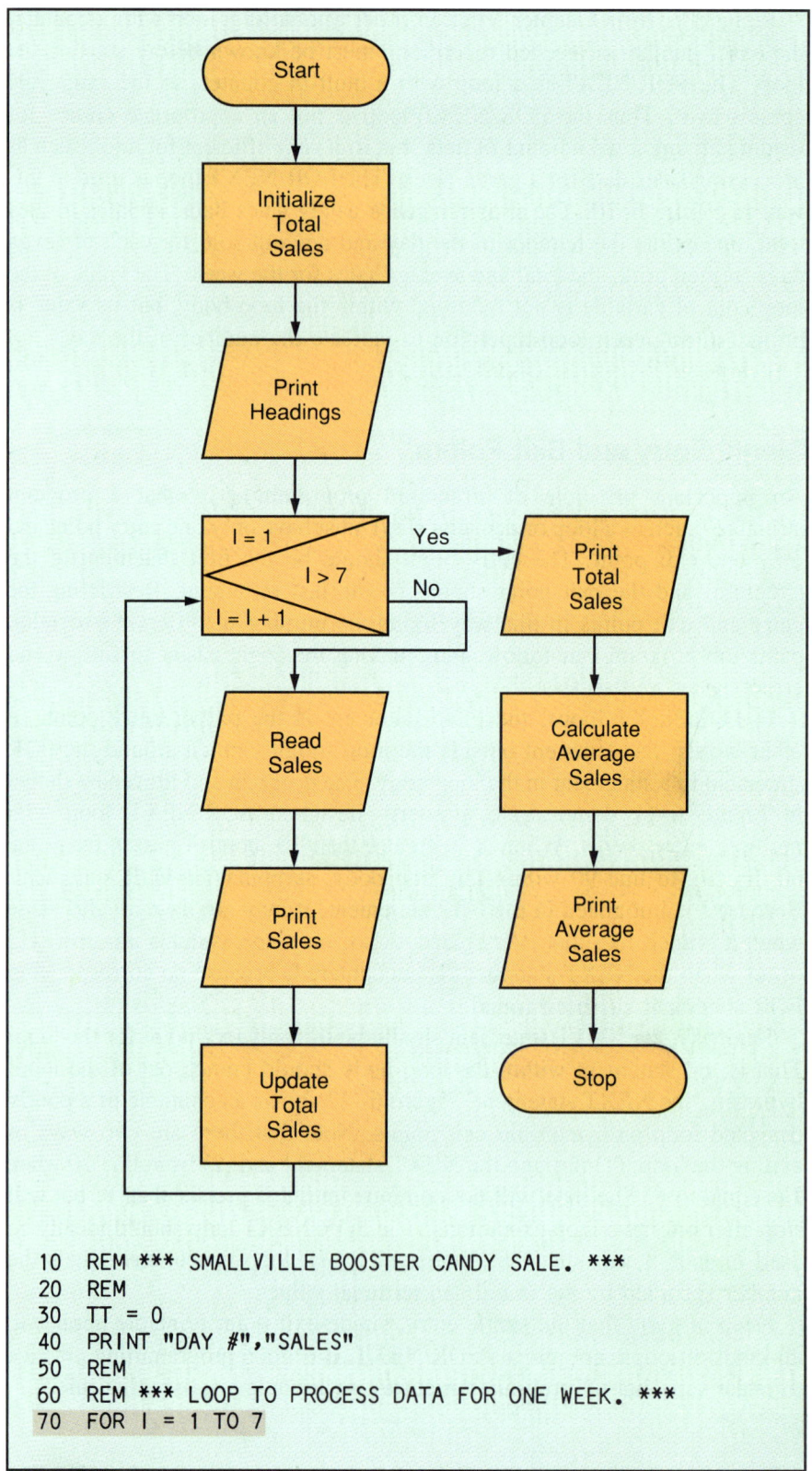

FIGURE 6–10
Continued

```
80      READ SALES
90      PRINT I,SALES
100     TT = TT + SALES
110 NEXT I
120 REM
130 REM *** PRINT TOTAL AND AVERAGE SALES. ***
140 PRINT
150 PRINT "TOTAL SALES = $";TT
160 AVE = TT / 7
170 PRINT "AVERAGE SALES = $";AVE
180 REM
190 REM *** DATA STATEMENTS ***
200 DATA 27.50,41.00,19.00,23.50,28.75,54.25,33.25
999 END
```

```
RUNNH

DAY #           SALES
 1               27.5
 2               41
 3               19
 4               23.5
 5               28.75
 6               54.25
 7               33.25

TOTAL SALES = $ 227.25
AVERAGE SALES = $ 32.46429
```

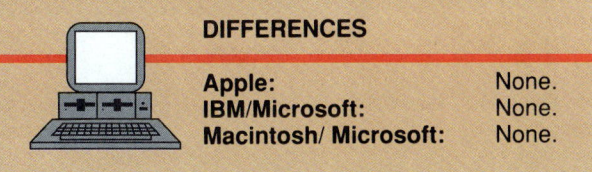

DIFFERENCES

Apple:	None.
IBM/Microsoft:	None.
Macintosh/Microsoft:	None.

FIGURE 6–11
Incorrectly Written Loop With Multiple Entry Points

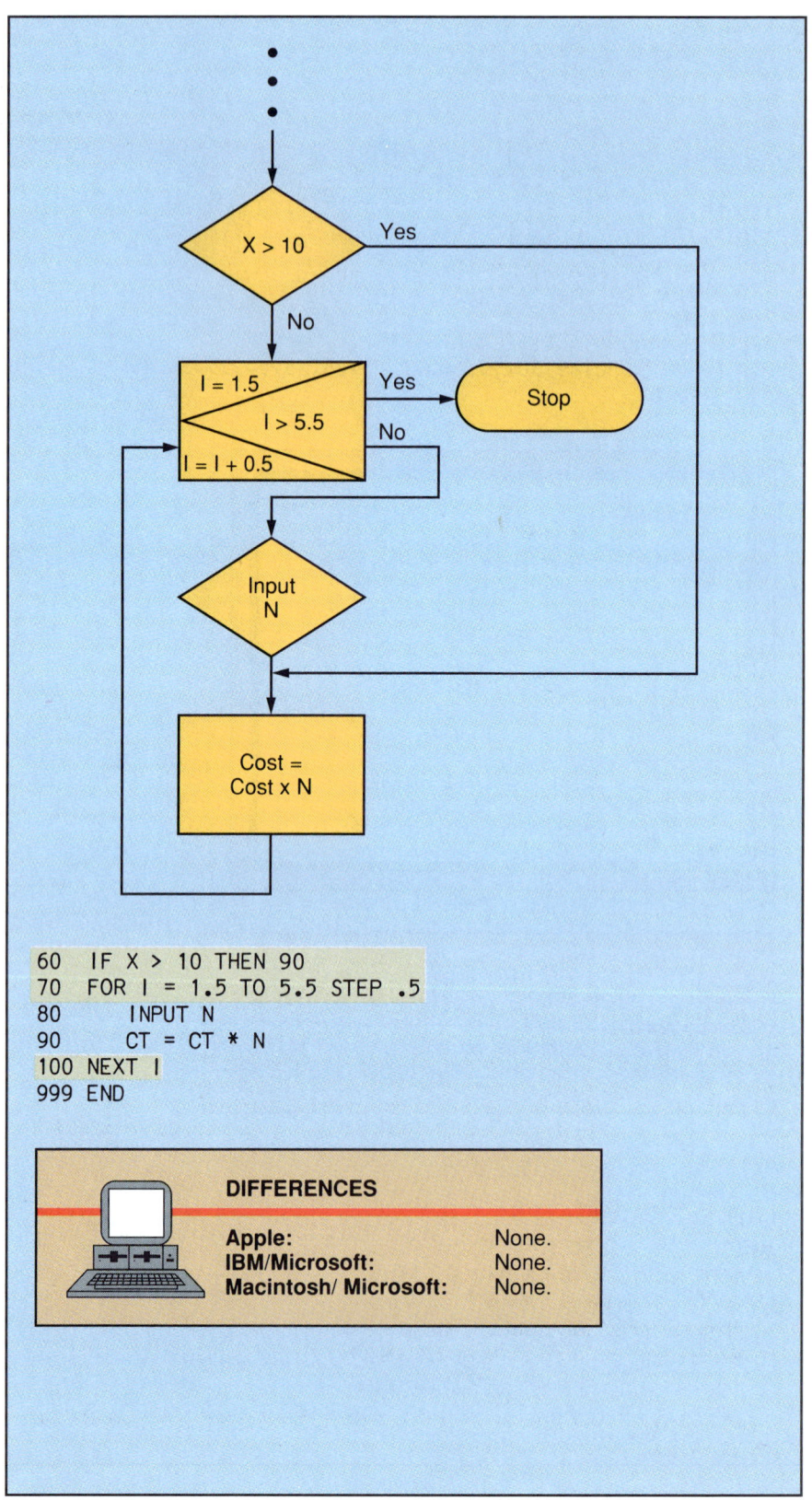

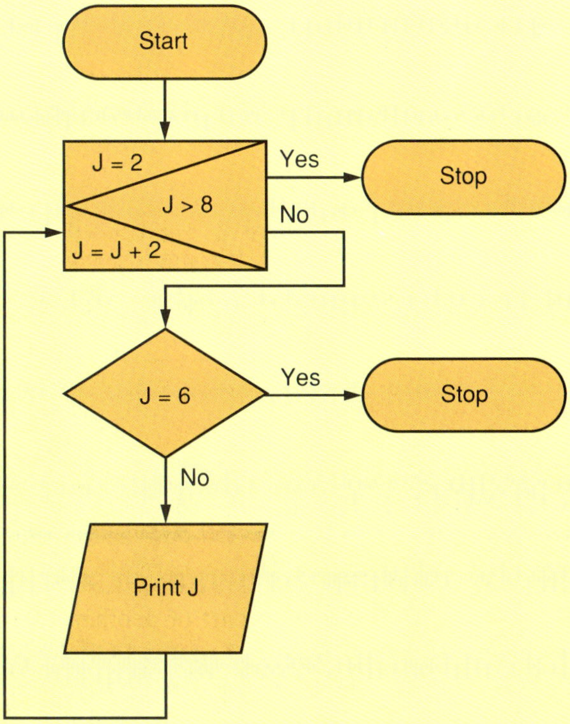

FIGURE 6-12
Incorrectly Written Loop With Multiple-Exit Points

```
10 FOR J = 2 TO 8 STEP 2
20    IF J = 6 THEN 99
30    PRINT J
40 NEXT J
99 END
```

DIFFERENCES

Apple:	None.
IBM/Microsoft:	None.
Macintosh/Microsoft:	None.

Learning Check

1. Name the five elements of the loop structure.
2. The FOR statement serves to _____.
   a. initialize the loop control variable
   b. increment the loop control variable by the step value
   c. pass control to the NEXT statement
3. How many times would a loop containing the following statement be executed?

   120 FOR I = 30 TO 12 STEP −5

4. When the terminal value is exceeded in a FOR/NEXT loop (using a positive step value), control passes to what statement?
5. When no step value is specified in a FOR statement, it is assumed to be _____.
6. The only entry point of a FOR/NEXT loop should be what statement?

Answers

1. a. Loop control variable is initialized. b. Loop control variable is tested for exit condition. c. Loop body is executed. d. Loop control variable is modified to allow an exit. e. Loop is exited. 2. a. 3. 4 times. 4. The first statement following the NEXT. 5. +1 6. The FOR statement.

Nested FOR/NEXT Loops

Chapter 5 showed how IF/THEN and IF/THEN/ELSE statements can be nested, so that one statement makes up part of another statement. Similar nesting can be done with loops. A pair of nested FOR/NEXT loops looks like this:

```
FOR I = 1 TO 4
    FOR J = 1 TO 2
        .
        .
        .
    NEXT J
NEXT I
```

Nested loops should be indented as shown to make the structure more readable. In this case, each time the outer loop (loop I) is executed once, the inner loop (loop J) is executed twice, since J varies from 1 to 2. When the inner loop has terminated, control passes to the first statement after the NEXT J, which in this case is the statement NEXT I. This statement causes I to be incremented by 1 and tested against the terminal value of 4. If I is still less than or equal to 4, the body of loop I is executed again. The J loop is again encountered, the value of J is reset to 1, and the inner loop is executed until J is greater than 2. Altogether, the outer loop is executed I times (four times in this case), and the inner loop is executed I × J times (4 × 2 = 8 times).

The following rules should be remembered when using nested FOR/NEXT loops.

- Each loop must have a unique loop control variable. The following example is invalid, because execution of the inner loop modifies the value of the outer loop control variable:

```
FOR I = X TO Y STEP 2
    FOR I = Q TO R
        .
        .
        .
    NEXT I
NEXT I
```

These nested loops should be rewritten so that each uses a unique loop control variable:

```
FOR I = X TO Y STEP 2
    FOR J = Q TO R
        .
        .
        .
    NEXT J
NEXT I
```

- The NEXT statement for an inner loop must appear within the body of the outer loop, so that one loop is entirely contained within another.

Incorrect

```
FOR I = 1 TO 5
    FOR J = 1 TO 10
        .
        .
        .
NEXT I
    NEXT J
```

Correct

```
FOR I = 1 TO 5
    FOR J = 1 TO 10
        .
        .
        .
    NEXT J
NEXT I
```

Notice that in the invalid example, the J loop is not entirely inside the I loop but extends beyond the NEXT I statement.

- It is possible to nest many loops within each other. (Beware of improper nesting, however, as in the preceding invalid example.) Figure 6–13 illustrates multiple nested loops.

Loop 1 is executed three times, loop 2 is executed twelve times ($3 \times 4 = 12$), and loop 3 is executed twenty-four times ($3 \times 4 \times 2 = 24$). Each loop is completely contained within its outer loop. Following this rule upholds the single-entry/single-exit principle.

The program segment and accompanying table shown in Figure 6–14 demonstrate the execution of nested loops. The outer loop is executed three times, because I varies from 1 to 3, and the inner loop is executed twelve times ($3 \times 4 = 12$).

FIGURE 6-13
Multiple Nested Loops

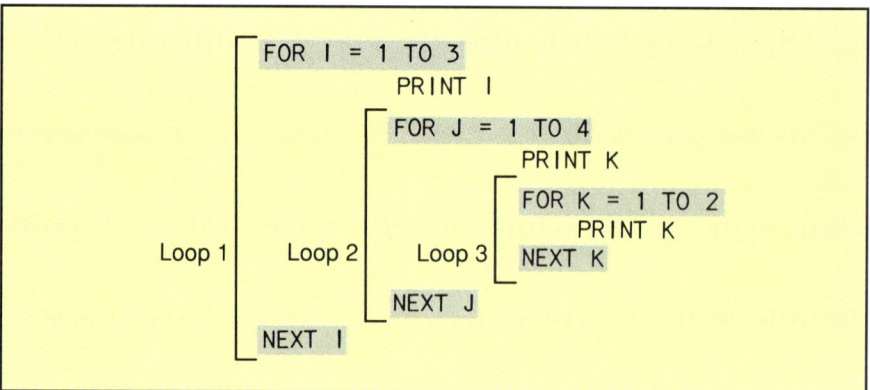

Figure 6-15 shows an application of nested FOR/NEXT loops. The program prints the multiplication tables for the numbers 1, 2, and 3, with each table in a single column. The inner loop, loop S, controls the printing in each of the three columns, while the outer loop R controls the printing of rows. The first time the outer loop is executed, the first row is printed; the inner loop prints three statements on that row. The first time the S loop is executed, R = 1 and S = 1, so the printed statement is "1 * 1 = 1". The comma at the end of line 90 causes a space to appear before the next output.

FIGURE 6-14
Example of Nested Loops

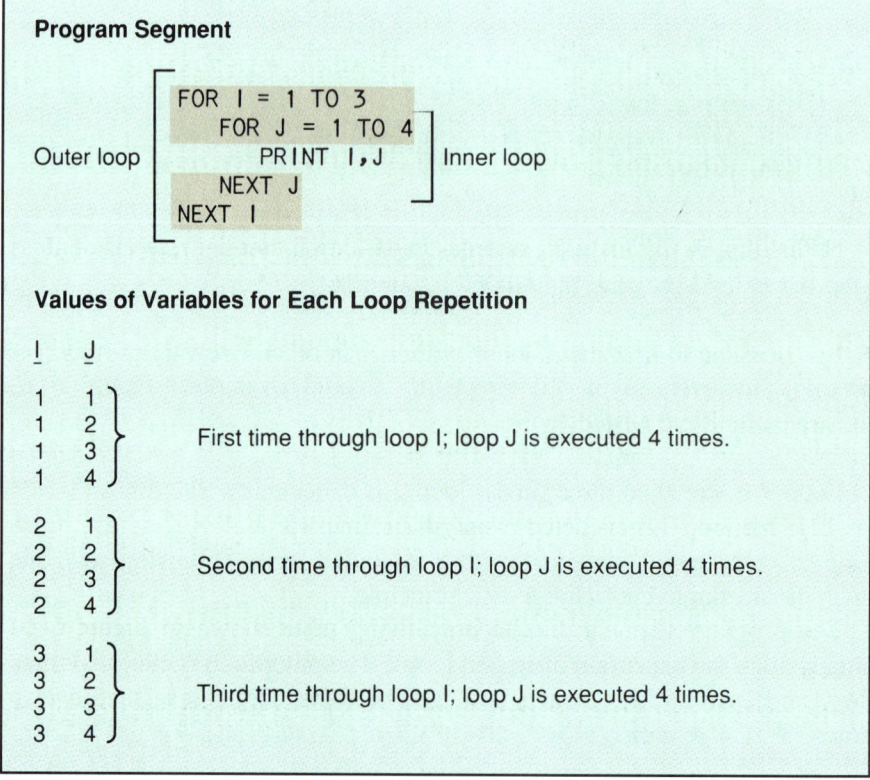

FIGURE 6-15 Multiplication Program

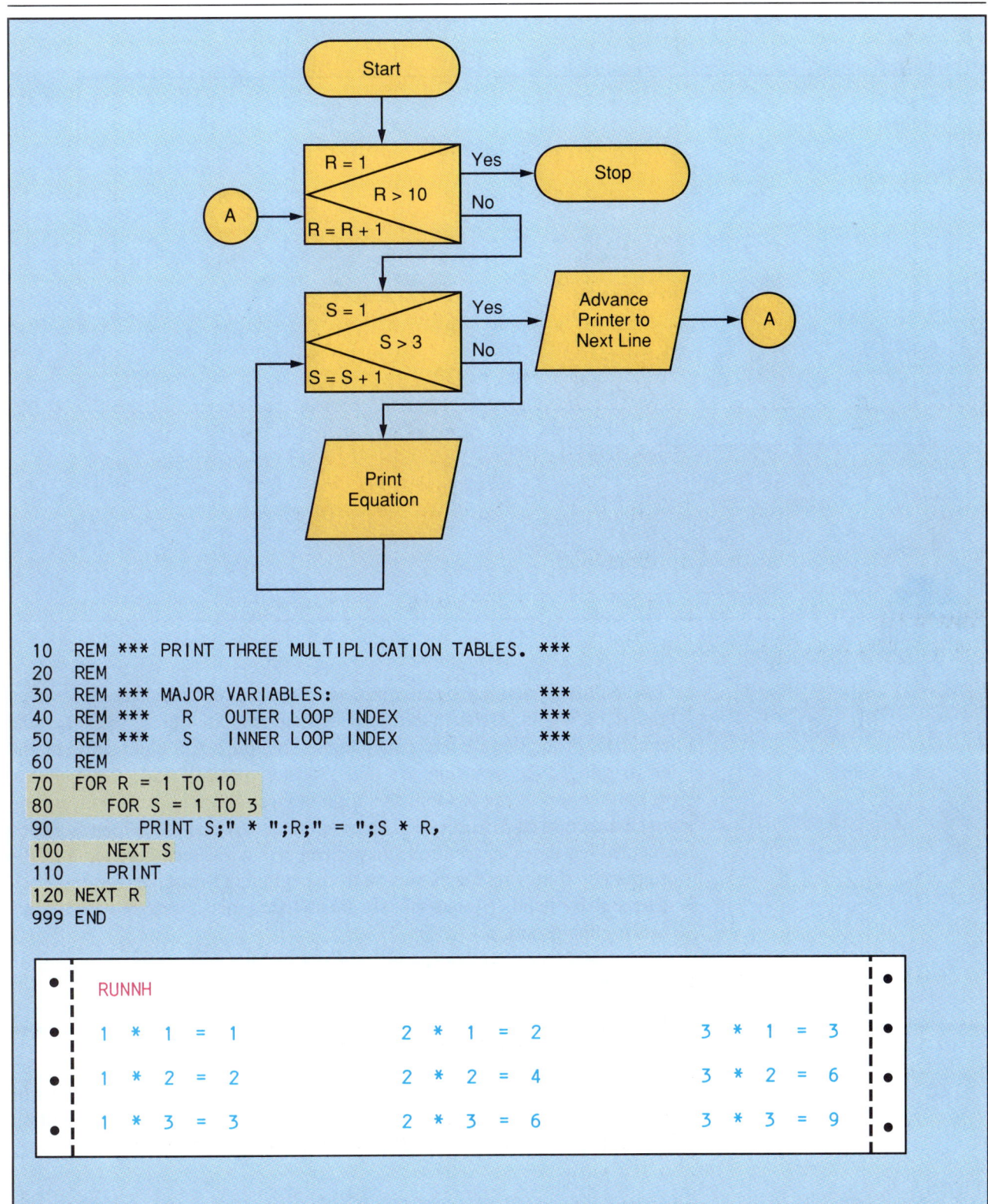

```
10  REM *** PRINT THREE MULTIPLICATION TABLES. ***
20  REM
30  REM *** MAJOR VARIABLES:                     ***
40  REM ***    R    OUTER LOOP INDEX             ***
50  REM ***    S    INNER LOOP INDEX             ***
60  REM
70  FOR R = 1 TO 10
80     FOR S = 1 TO 3
90        PRINT S;" * ";R;" = ";S * R,
100    NEXT S
110    PRINT
120 NEXT R
999 END
```

```
RUNNH

1 * 1 = 1         2 * 1 = 2         3 * 1 = 3

1 * 2 = 2         2 * 2 = 4         3 * 2 = 6

1 * 3 = 3         2 * 3 = 6         3 * 3 = 9
```

FIGURE 6–15 *Continued*

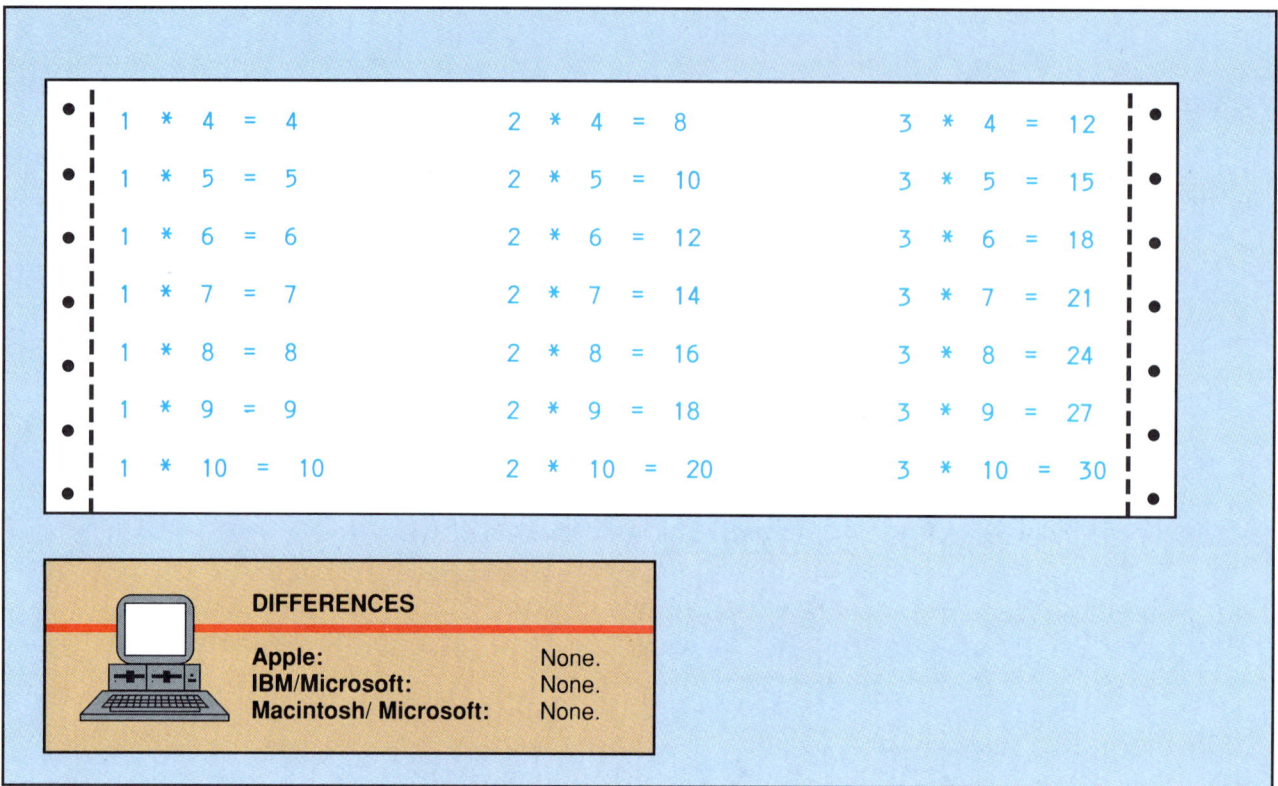

When the S loop has been completed (when three statements have been printed on the first row), the PRINT statement in line 110 causes the remainder of the first row to remain blank, and the next output starts on the left margin on the next line. As line 120 increments R and passes control back to the top of the R loop, this loop begins a second execution, during which a second row is printed. The program ends when the R loop has been executed ten times and ten rows have been printed. Check the output of the program by following the execution from beginning to end, performing each statement by hand. (As previously mentioned, this is referred to as *desk checking* the program.)

The WHILE Loop

Another type of loop available on many BASIC implementations is the WHILE loop. Unlike the FOR/NEXT, which executes a specified number of times, the WHILE loop continues to execute as long as a certain condition is true. The format of the WHILE loop on the VAX is as follows:

line# WHILE expression
    .
    .
    .
line# NEXT

Some implementations of BASIC (such as the IBM and Macintosh) create WHILE loops with the WHILE/WEND rather than the WHILE/NEXT statements. The format of the WHILE/WEND follows:

line# WHILE expression
    .
    .
    .
line# WEND

Both versions of the WHILE loop work the same way. The only difference is that on the VAX the end of the loop is marked by the NEXT statement, whereas on the IBM and Macintosh it is marked by the WEND statement. There is no WHILE loop on the Apple.

The WHILE loop executes according to the following steps:

1. The expression, which can be a numeric expression or numeric variable, is evaluated as true or false. If the expression is a variable, it is true if the variable is not equal to zero.
2. If the expression is true, the loop body statements are executed until the NEXT (or WEND) statement is encountered; if the expression is false, control passes to the first statement after the NEXT (or WEND).
3. When the NEXT (or WEND) is encountered, control passes back to the WHILE statement, and the expression is checked again.
4. If the condition is still true, the loop is executed again; if false, the loop is exited to the statement following the NEXT (or WEND).

In contrast to the FOR/NEXT loop, the WHILE loop involves no automatic initialization or incrementing of the loop control variable. A statement before the WHILE statement must initialize the control variable, and another statement within the loop body must at some point change the value of the control variable so that the expression of the WHILE statement can become false and end the loop. Otherwise an infinite loop results, as shown here:

```
10 WHILE CNT < 50
20     PRINT CNT
30 NEXT
```

This loop could be correctly written:

```
10 CNT = 1
20 WHILE CNT < 50
30     PRINT CNT
40     CNT = CNT + 1
50 NEXT
```

A comparison of the FOR/NEXT and WHILE loops can be made by studying Figures 6–8 and 6–16. Notice that in the second program in Figure 6–16 the expression consists of a single variable; thus the condition is true as long as the variable's value is not equal to zero. This expression is equivalent to the more familiar condition format of the first program.

Figure 6–17 shows how the programs shown in Figure 6–16 would look if they were written using the WHILE/WEND instead of the WHILE/NEXT loop. As previously mentioned, the WHILE/WEND is used on the IBM and the Macintosh. Notice that the only difference is the use of the WEND statement in line 60.

The WHILE loop can always be used in place of the FOR/NEXT loop, but the reverse is not true. The FOR/NEXT loop executes a prespecified number of times, as given by the initial and terminal values of the loop control variable. The WHILE loop can also execute a given number of times, if the programmer initializes the loop control variable before the loop begins and tests for the given value in the WHILE statement. However, the WHILE loop can also be used when the final number of desired loop executions is not known, such as when a trailer value is used. In such a situation, a properly structured FOR/NEXT loop would not be appropriate. For those systems such as the Apple that do not have a WHILE loop, refer to Figure 6-18 for information on simulating this loop.

The Importance of Using Loop Structures

Spaghetti program
A program with convoluted logic, often resulting from the use of numerous GOTO statements.

As already discussed, one of the features of structured programming is that it uses concise, easy-to-follow logic. Because of this, the GOTO statement should be avoided whenever possible. The GOTO makes program logic very difficult to follow, particularly when a number of GOTO statements are used, as in a nested loop. Programs with convoluted logic, often resulting from the use of many GOTO statements, are referred to as **spaghetti programs.** The logic is all tangled together, like a large plate of spaghetti. Therefore, it is always preferable to use one of the looping structures such as the FOR/NEXT or the WHILE loops. These structures make the loop's logic readily apparent and greatly enhance program readability. Also, they are generally more efficient for the computer to execute.

If you are forced to create a loop using GOTOs because of the lack of looping structures in your implementation of BASIC, it is imperative that

FIGURE 6–16 WHILE/NEXT Examples

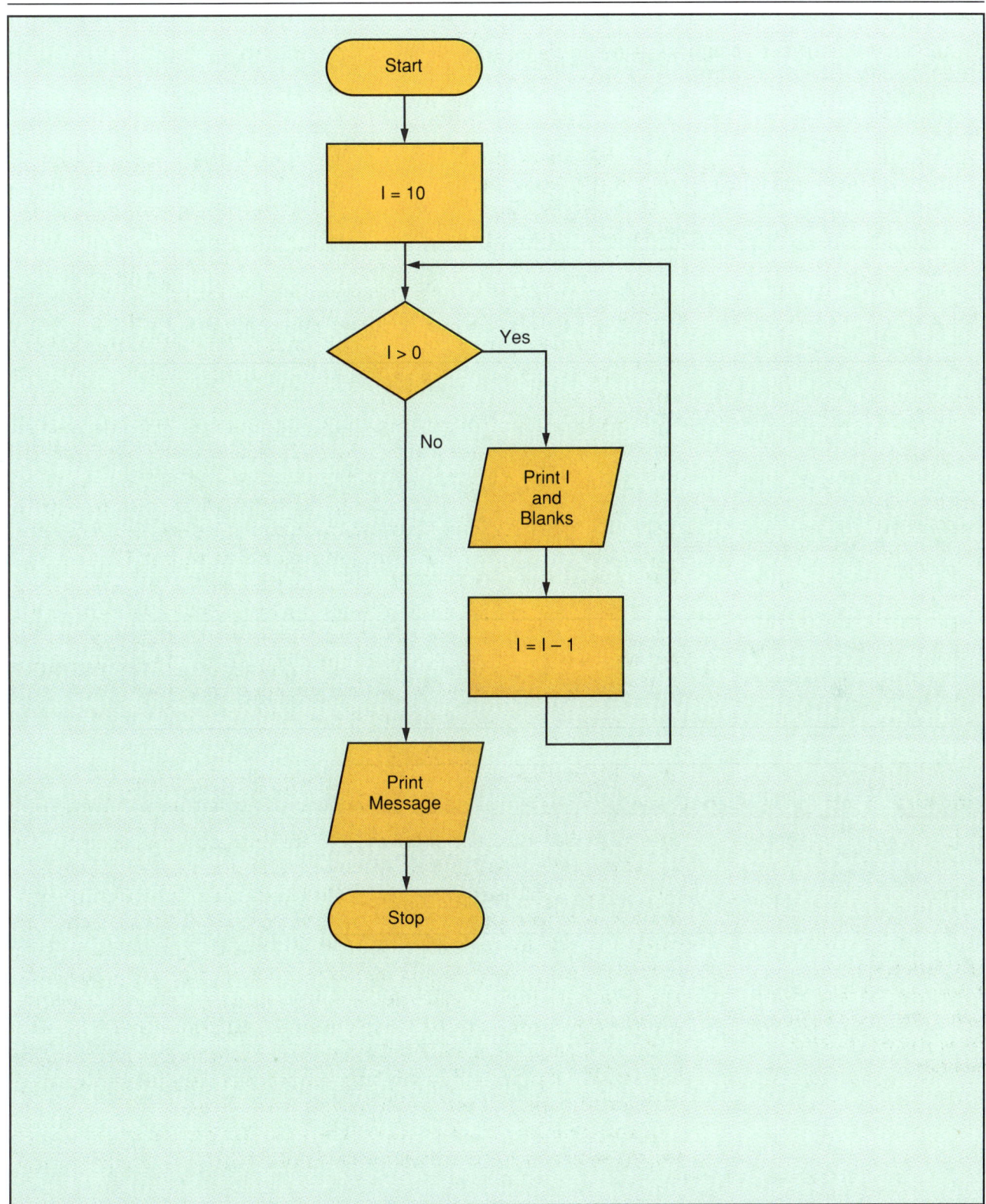

198 BASIC PROGRAMMING TODAY, A STRUCTURED APPROACH

FIGURE 6–16 *Continued*

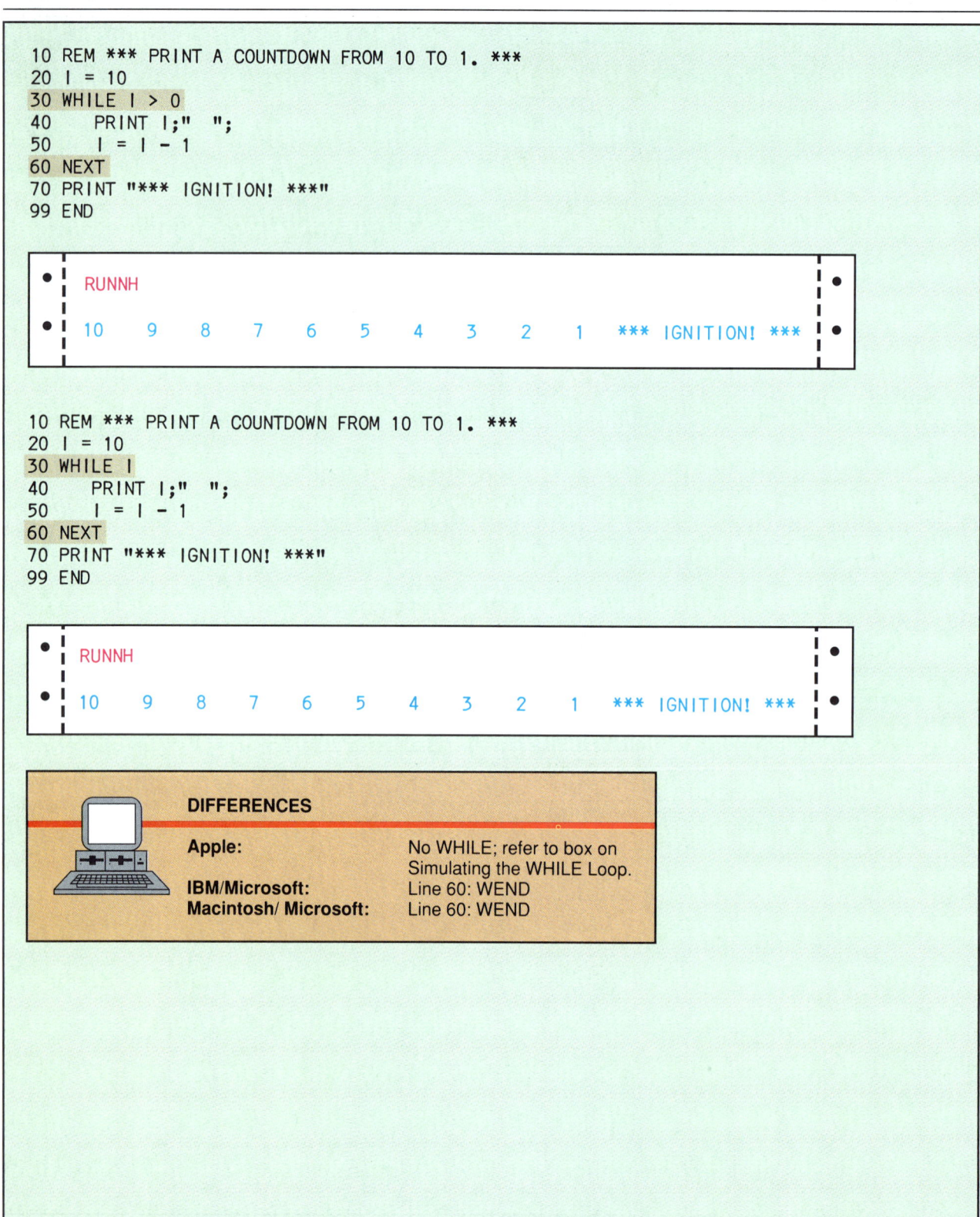

FIGURE 6-17 WHILE/WEND Examples

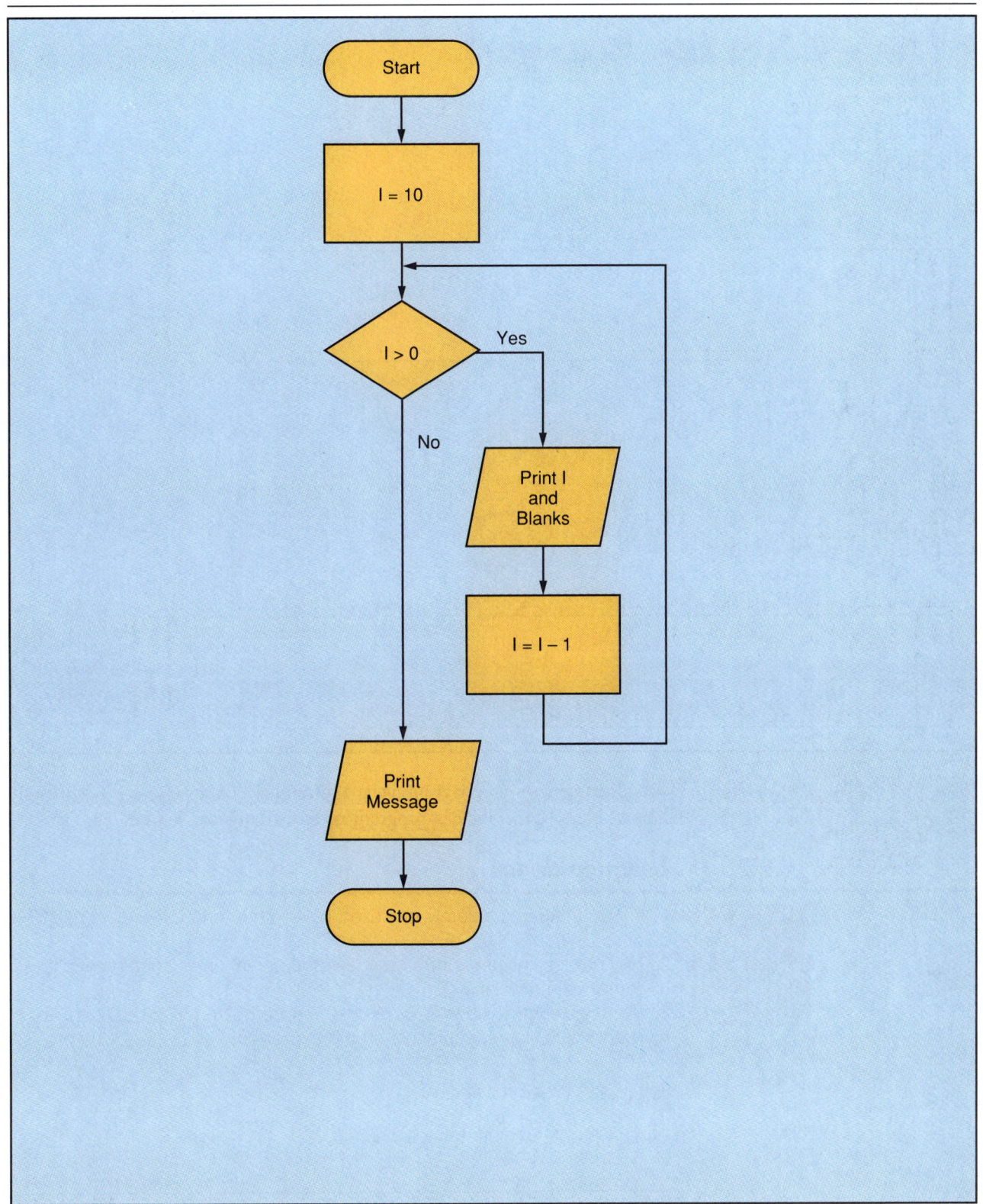

FIGURE 6–17 Continued

```
10 REM *** PRINT A COUNTDOWN FROM 10 TO 1. ***
20 I = 10
30 WHILE I > 0
40    PRINT I;" ";
50    I = I - 1
60 WEND
70 PRINT "*** IGNITION! ***"
99 END
```

```
RUN
 10  9  8  7  6  5  4  3  2  1  *** IGNITION! ***
```

```
10 REM *** PRINT A COUNTDOWN FROM 10 TO 1. ***
20 I = 10
30 WHILE I
40    PRINT I;" ";
50    I = I - 1
60 WEND
70 PRINT "*** IGNITION! ***"
99 END
```

```
RUN
 10  9  8  7  6  5  4  3  2  1  *** IGNITION! ***
```

you document your program very thoroughly. Otherwise, it is virtually impossible to understand a program of any significant length.

Learning Check

1. A loop that is completely enclosed by another loop is called a(n) _____ loop.
2. Two or more nested loops can have the same loop control variable name. True or false?
3. The maximum number of loops that can be nested is _____.
4. The WHILE loop executes when the expression is _____ (true or false).

Answers

1. nested 2. False 3. unlimited 4. true

FIGURE 6–18
Simulating the WHILE Loop

> On systems (such as the Apple) that do not provide the WHILE loop, the same program logic can be obtained by using the IF/THEN and GOTO statements. The following programs both print a countdown from 5 to 1:
>
> a.
> ```
> 10 REM *** COUNTING WITH THE WHILE/NEXT. ***
> 20 REM
> 30 CNT = 5
> 40 WHILE CNT > 0
> 50    PRINT CNT
> 60    CNT = CNT - 1
> 70 NEXT
> 99 END
> ```
>
> b.
> ```
> 10 REM *** COUNTING WITHOUT THE WHILE. ***
> 20 REM
> 30 CNT = 5
> 40 IF CNT = 0 THEN 99
> 50    PRINT CNT
> 60    CNT = CNT - 1
> 70 GOTO 40
> 99 END
> ```
>
> Any WHILE loop can be simulated with the IF/THEN and GOTO statements, as in example b. Take care that the condition used in the IF/THEN statement is the correct one for the loop execution you desire. However if your system provides a WHILE loop, it is always preferrable to use it instead of the IF/THEN and GOTO statements.

Logical Operators

So far in this text, the arithmetic operators (^, *, /, +, −) and the relational operators (=, <>, <, >, <=, >=) have been covered. Now a third group of operators will be discussed: the **logical**, or **Boolean, operators.** A logical operator acts on one or more expressions that evaluate as true or false to produce a statement with a true or false value. The three most commonly used logical operators are AND, OR, and NOT.

The operator AND combines two expressions and produces a value of true only when both of these conditions are true. For example, the combined logical expression in the statement

```
20 IF (HEIGHT > 72) AND (WEIGHT > 150) THEN PRINT NME$
```

evaluates as true only if the expressions HEIGHT > 72 and WEIGHT > 150 are both true. If one or the other is false, the entire statement is false, and the THEN clause of the statement is ignored. The parentheses in the preceding statement are not necessary, but they improve the readability of the statement.

Logical operator
An operator that acts on one or more conditions to produce a value of true or false.

The logical operator OR also combines two expressions, but only one of these expressions needs to evaluate as true for the entire statement to be true. Thus, the statement

```
20 IF (HEIGHT > 72) OR (WEIGHT > 150) THEN PRINT NME$
```

evaluates as true if either HEIGHT $>$ 72 *or* WEIGHT $>$ 150 is true, or if both are true. The entire condition is false only if the expressions HEIGHT $>$ 72 and WEIGHT $>$ 150 are both false. Table 6–1 shows the results for all possible values of two expressions combined by AND and OR.

The third logical operator, NOT, is a **unary operator** (an operator used with only one operand) and therefore is used with a single expression. The effect of NOT is to reverse the logical value of the expression it precedes. For example, if the variable PET$ has the value DOG, the condition of the following statement is false:

Unary operator
An operator used with one operand.

```
20 IF NOT (PET$ = "DOG") THEN 90
```

Because the condition PET$ = ''DOG'' evaluates as true, the NOT operator reverses this value to false, making the final result of the entire condition false. If PET$ contained any other value, the condition PET$ = ''DOG'' would evaluate as false, and the NOT would make the value of the entire condition true.

Logical operators can be combined in a single statement, and they are evaluated in the following sequence:

1. NOT
2. AND
3. OR

For example, the following statement combines AND and OR:

```
50 IF (PET$ = "DOG") OR (AGE = 3) AND (WT = 10) THEN 90
```

TABLE 6–1 The AND and OR Logical Operators

CONDITION 1	CONDITION 2	CONDITION 1 AND CONDITION 2	CONDITION 1 OR CONDITION 2
true	true	true	true
true	false	false	true
false	true	false	true
false	false	false	false

Given the predefined order of evaluation, the following diagram shows how the preceding statement would be evaluated if PET$ = "DOG", AGE = 3, and WT = 9:

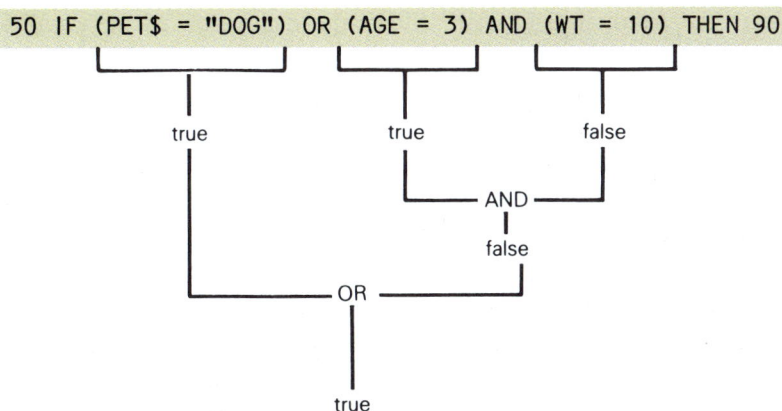

The AND portion of the IF/THEN statement is evaluated first. That result is then combined with the OR portion of the statement to determine the final value of the entire condition. In this case, the statement condition is true, so control is passed to line 90.

The precedence of logical operators (like that of arithmetic operators) can be altered using parentheses. The previous example, using the same variable values as before, could be rewritten as

```
50 IF ((PET$ = "DOG") OR (AGE = 3)) AND (WT = 10) THEN 90
```

In this example, the OR portion of the expression is evaluated before the AND portion. Thus the parentheses can change the final result of the evaluation, as shown in the following diagram. Compare the evaluation of this statement with the previous diagram.

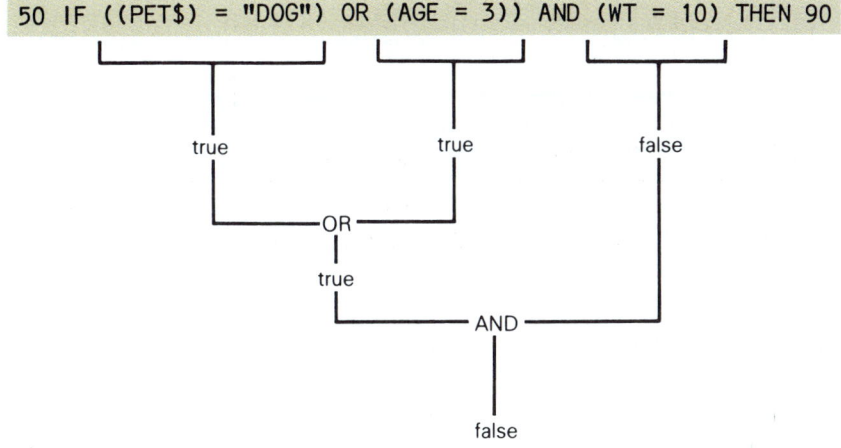

Even if the order of evaluation desired in a condition is the same as the predefined order, it is good programming practice to use parentheses in order to make the logic easier to follow.

NOT can also be combined with AND and OR in a single statement, as shown in the following diagram. Study the evaluation of the condition, making sure that you understand how the use of parentheses and the predefined order of operators has determined the final result of the evaluation. Assume that PET$ = "PIG", AGE = 6, and WT = 1500.

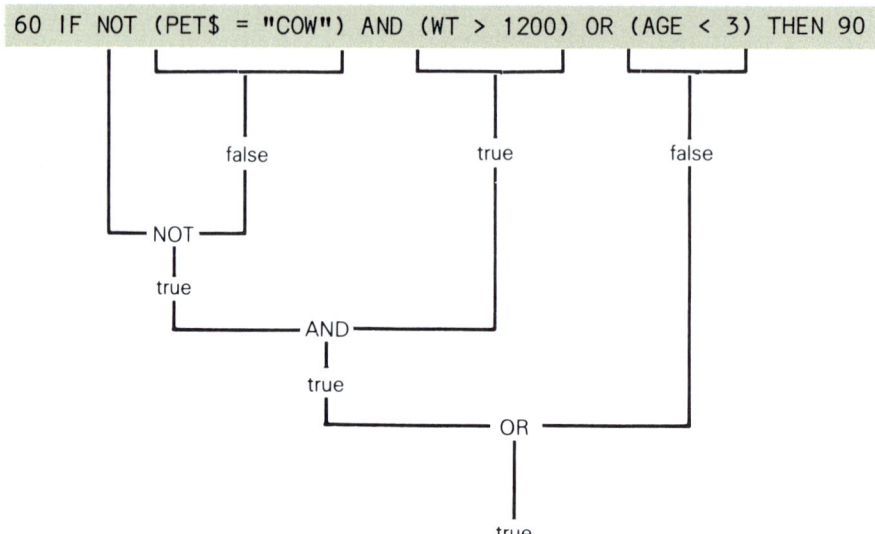

Table 6–2 shows the order in which all types of BASIC operators are evaluated. Further examples involving these operators are shown in Table 6–3.

The program shown in Figure 6–19 demonstrates how logical operators can be used to determine if a triangle is scalene, isosceles, or equilateral. Notice that the condition of the first test uses the AND operator to determine if all three sides are equal:

```
80 IF (S1SIDE) = S2SIDE) AND (S2SIDE = S3SIDE)
```

TABLE 6–2 Order of Precedence

1. Anything in parentheses
2. Exponentiation (^)
3. Unary plus and minus (+, −)
4. Multiplication and division (*, /)
5. Addition and subtraction (+, −)
6. Relational operators (=, <>, <, >, <=, >=)
7. NOT
8. AND
9. OR

Note: Operators on the same level are evaluated left to right.

TABLE 6–3 Examples of Conditions Using Logical Operators

CONDITION	EVALUATES AS
NOT (1 * 4 = 5)	TRUE
(18 < 16) OR (7 + 2 = 9)	TRUE
(18 < 16) AND (7 + 2 = 9)	FALSE
((2 + 8) <= 11) AND (17 * 2 = 34)	TRUE
NOT (12 > 8 − 2)	FALSE

Learning Check

1. The three logical operators, in their order of evaluation, are _____, _____, and _____.
2. The unary logical operator is _____.
3. With the _____ operator, only one of the conditions listed must evaluate as true for the entire expression to be true.
4. In the following condition, which of the logical operators is evaluated first? (LTR <> "X") AND (NOT (TREE > 10))
5. Evaluate the following:
   a. ("Y" <> "X") AND (143.55 < 143.55)
   b. (0 = 14) OR (6 ^ 2 − 3 <= 4 / 2 + 8)
   c. NOT (6 = 7) AND (44 > 33)

Answers

1. NOT, AND, OR 2. NOT 3. OR 4. NOT 5. false, false, true

The test for an isosceles triangle is more complex and involves checking for three different conditions. Only one of these conditions needs to be true for the triangle to be isosceles; therefore, this test involves the OR operator. If none of these conditions is true, the triangle must be scalene. As shown by this program, logical operators allow for a variety of conditions to be checked efficiently and simultaneously.

A Programming Problem

Problem Definition

The local library wants a program to produce a weekly listing of its new books. The numbered list should include each book's title, author, and a critic's rating of 1 to 5 asterisks (to be represented in the data as an integer

FIGURE 6-19 Program Demonstrating the Use of Logical Operators

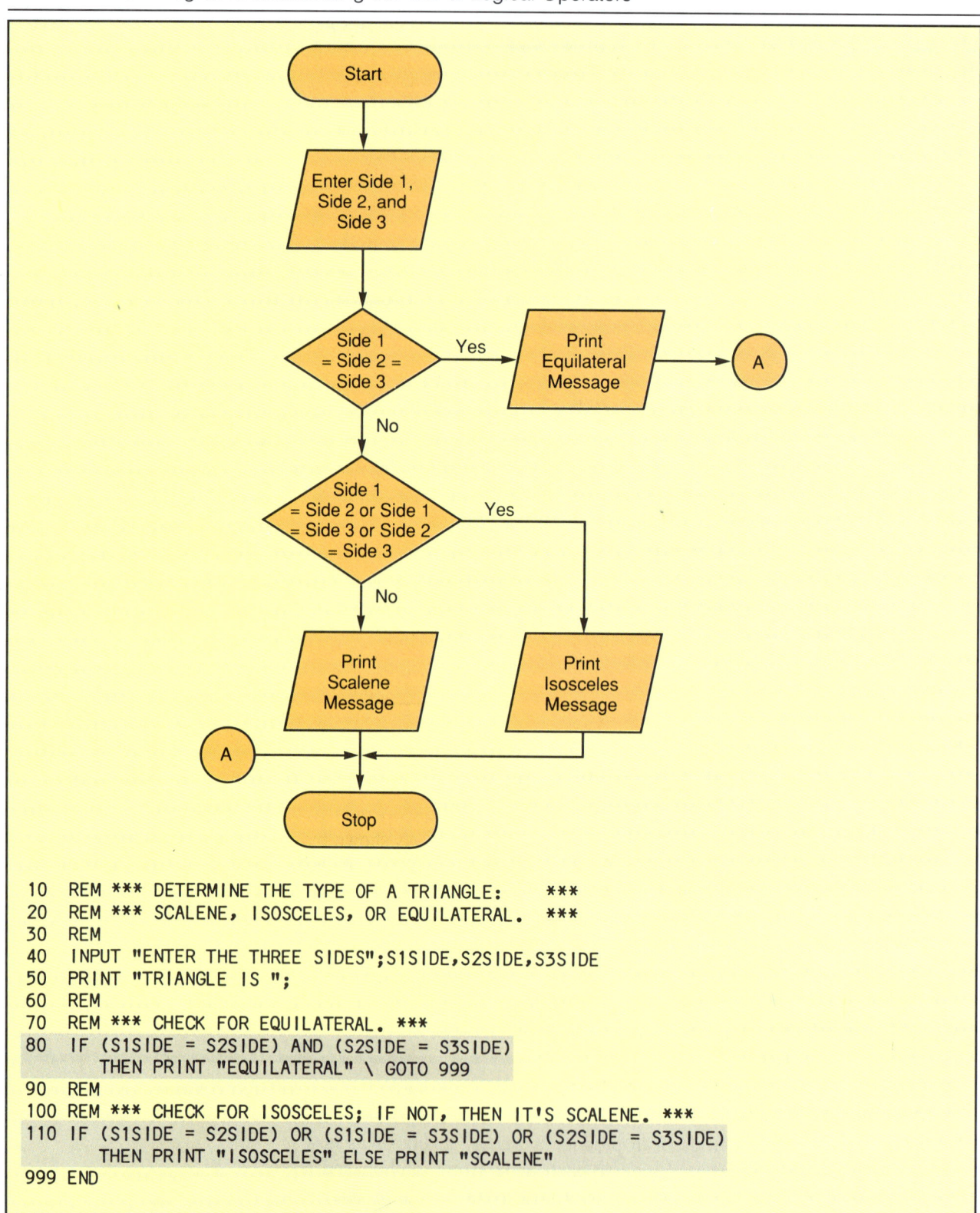

```
10   REM *** DETERMINE THE TYPE OF A TRIANGLE:     ***
20   REM *** SCALENE, ISOSCELES, OR EQUILATERAL.   ***
30   REM
40   INPUT "ENTER THE THREE SIDES";S1SIDE,S2SIDE,S3SIDE
50   PRINT "TRIANGLE IS ";
60   REM
70   REM *** CHECK FOR EQUILATERAL. ***
80   IF (S1SIDE = S2SIDE) AND (S2SIDE = S3SIDE)
         THEN PRINT "EQUILATERAL" \ GOTO 999
90   REM
100  REM *** CHECK FOR ISOSCELES; IF NOT, THEN IT'S SCALENE. ***
110  IF (S1SIDE = S2SIDE) OR (S1SIDE = S3SIDE) OR (S2SIDE = S3SIDE)
         THEN PRINT "ISOSCELES" ELSE PRINT "SCALENE"
999  END
```

FIGURE 6–19 *Continued*

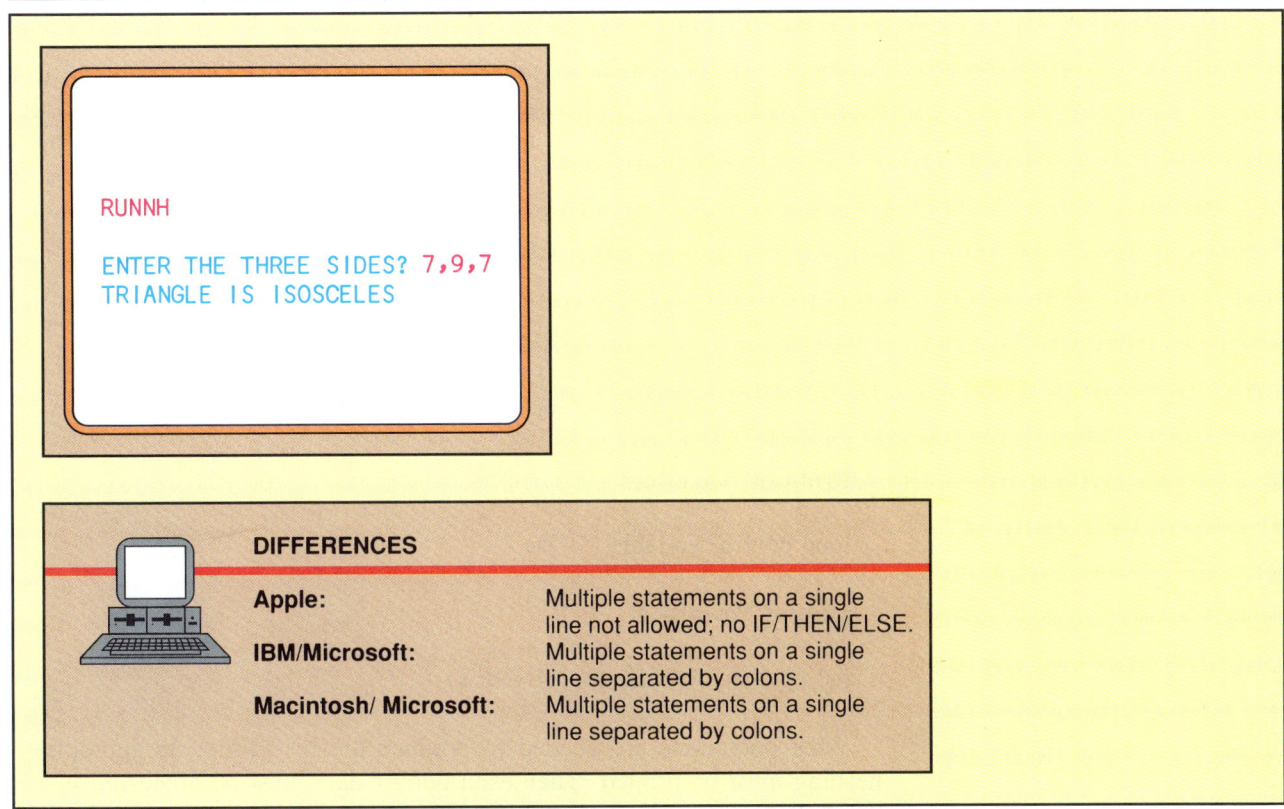

between 1 and 5). The program should be able to handle any number of books. Sample input is shown below.

Input:

Title	Author	Rating
Competitive Tanning	Harris, Z.	1
Bombay	Goodtime, C.	2
Death in Crete	Kay, M.	4
Learning to Love C.	Lord, P.	5
The Survivor	Bulas, I.	3
Don't Look Now	Poirot, H.	1
Neon Sun	Rainer, A.	4

Needed Output:

	TITLE	AUTHOR	RATING
1.	Bombay	Goodtime, C.	**
	.	.	.
	.	.	.
	.	.	.

Solution Design

The input variables for this program are the data items given for each book; the program must output the values of those items. In addition, a variable is needed to assign a number to each book in the list. The problem also specifies that a row of asterisks should be printed that corresponds to the book's numeric rating. This task is well suited to a loop, so a program variable will be needed to control that loop. The following variables are to be used:

Input Variables

    title   (TITLE$)
    author   (AUTHR$)
    rating number   (BNUM)

Program Variables

    loop control variable   (I)

Output Variables

    list number of books   (INDEX)

What operations are needed to produce the list? First, an appropriate heading must be printed. Then each book's data must be processed in the same way, by means of a loop. Because an unknown number of books is to be read, a WHILE loop can be used to check for a trailer value. To process each book,

1. Its number in the list is printed.
2. Its title and author are printed.
3. The proper number of asterisks are printed to show the rating.

Because the rating number tells exactly how many times an asterisk should be printed, it would be appropriate to use a FOR/NEXT loop to print a single asterisk during each loop execution. This basic algorithm is outlined in Figure 6–20 and diagrammed in Figure 6–21.

The Program

The final solution is shown in Figure 6–22. After the list heading is printed, the index that numbers the book list is initialized to zero. A WHILE loop is used to read an undetermined number of books. The book title serves as the loop control variable, which is checked for the trailer value ''XXX'' in the WHILE statement of line 200. The loop control variable TITLE$ is initialized to the first book title in line 170. Within the loop body the index, title, and author are printed. To print the rating, a FOR/NEXT loop is set up in line 240 that uses the rating number as the terminal value and prints a single asterisk for each loop execution. The loop control variable of the main loop is modified by reading the next book's data in line 280, and the loop control variable is tested again for the trailer value at the top of the loop in line 200.

General Problem: Print a listing of all new books at the library.

Level 1
    A. Print list heading.
    B. Process data for each book.

Level 2
    B.1. Update and print the number of the book.
    B.2. Print title.
    B.3. Print author.
    B.4. Print rating as asterisks.

FIGURE 6–20
Stepwise Refinement of Library New Books Problem

FIGURE 6–21 Structure Chart of Library New Books Problem

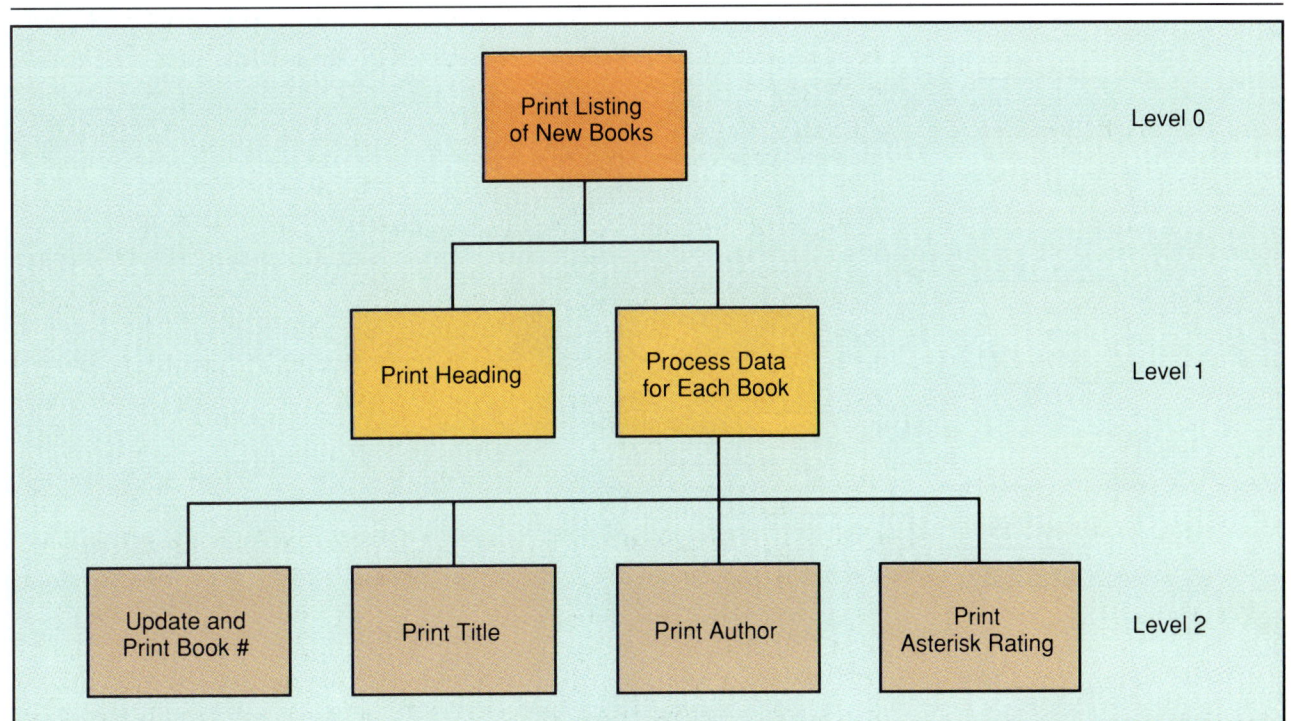

210 BASIC PROGRAMMING TODAY, A STRUCTURED APPROACH

FIGURE 6–22 Library New Books Program

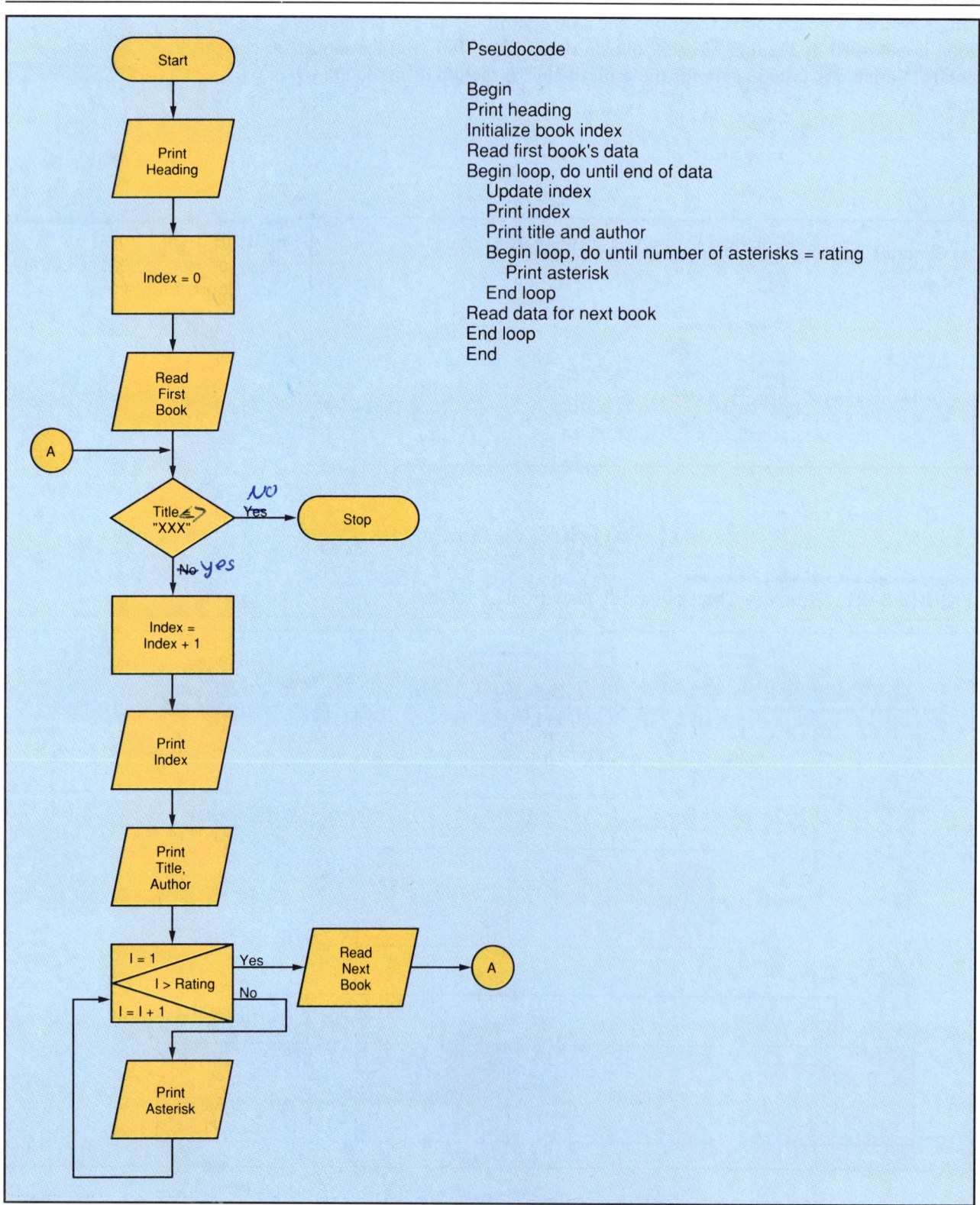

FIGURE 6-22 *Continued*

```
10  REM ***           LIBRARY LISTING OF NEW BOOKS              ***
20  REM
30  REM *** THIS PROGRAM READS DATA FOR ALL NEW BOOKS AND        ***
40  REM *** PRINTS A LISTING OF THEM.                            ***
50  REM
60  REM *** MAJOR VARIABLES:                                     ***
70  REM ***     TITLE$     BOOK TITLE                            ***
80  REM ***     AUTHR$     BOOK'S AUTHOR                         ***
90  REM ***     BNUM       NUMERIC RATING OF BOOK                ***
100 REM ***     INDEX      LISTING NUMBER OF BOOK                ***
110 REM
120 REM *** PRINT HEADING. ***
130 PRINT TAB(6);"TITLE";TAB(30);"AUTHOR";TAB(42);"RATING"
140 REM
150 REM *** INITIALIZE VARIABLES. ***
160 INDEX = 0
170 READ TITLE$,AUTHR$,BNUM
180 REM
190 REM *** LOOP TO PROCESS ONE BOOK PER PASS. ***
200 WHILE TITLE$ <> "XXX"
210     INDEX = INDEX + 1
220     PRINT INDEX;". ";
230     PRINT TAB(6);TITLE$;TAB(30);AUTHR$;TAB(42);
240     FOR I = 1 TO BNUM
250        PRINT "*";
260     NEXT I
270     PRINT
280     READ TITLE$,AUTHR$,BNUM
290 WEND
300 DATA "COMPETITIVE TANNING","HARRIS,Z.",1,"BOMBAY","GOODTIME,C."
310 DATA 2,"DEATH IN CRETE","KAY,M.",4,"LEARNING TO LOVE C"
320 DATA "LORD,P.",5,"THE SURVIVOR",BULAS,I.",3
330 DATA "DON'T LOOK NOW","POIROT,H.",1,"NEON SUN",RAINER,A."
340 DATA 4,"XXX","XXX",0
999 END
```

FIGURE 6-22 *Continued*

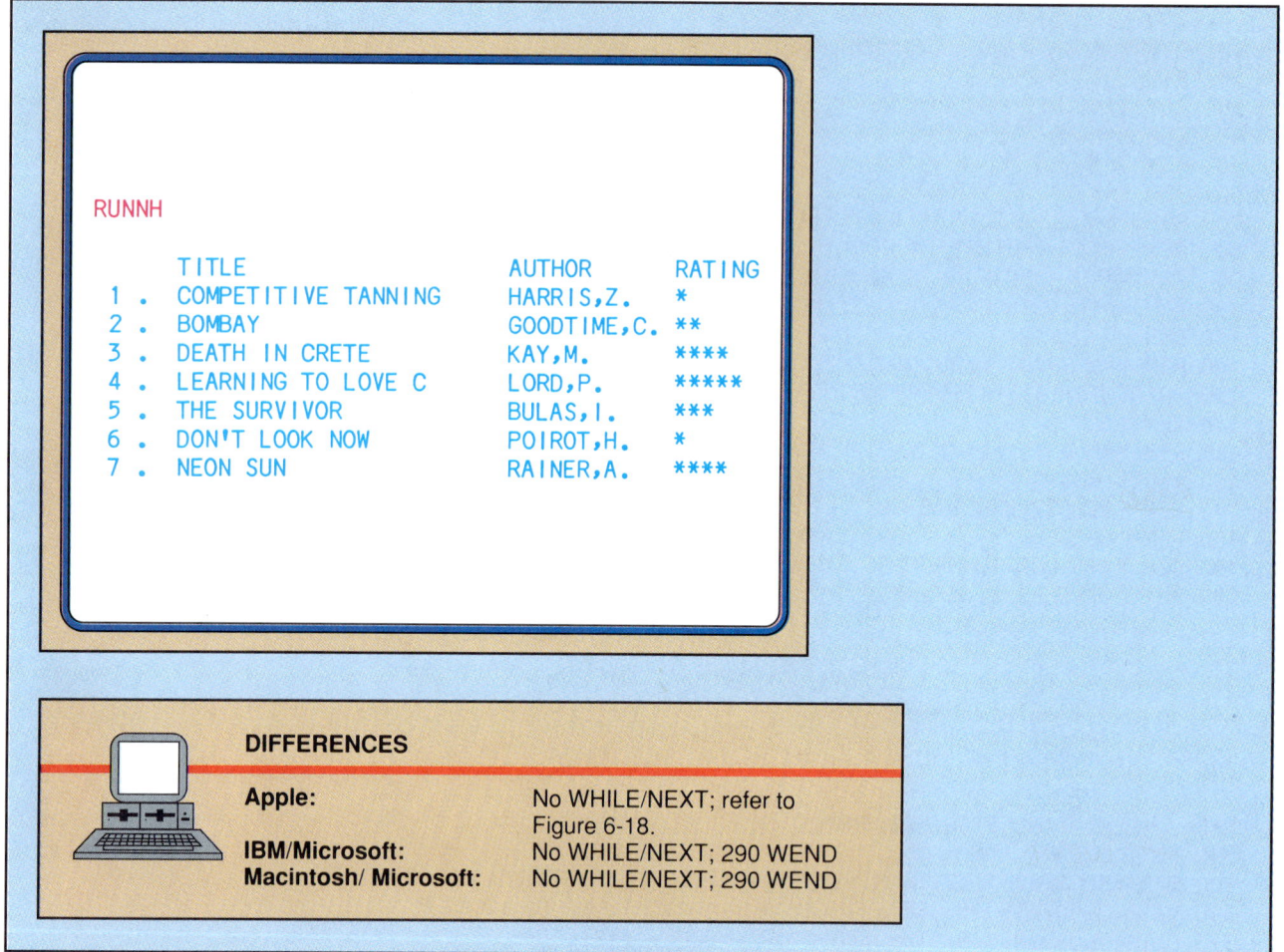

Avoiding Common Programming Mistakes

The following points should be kept in mind when using looping structures such as the FOR/NEXT, and WHILE loops.

- Care must be taken that the initial, terminal, and step values of the FOR statement are all numeric, and that the proper values have been specified to produce the desired number of loop executions.
- An attempt to modify the initial, terminal, or step values within the FOR/NEXT loop produces an error.
- The loop control variable should never be modified within the FOR/NEXT loop.
- Branching from within the loop body to the FOR statement resets the value of the loop control variable, which upsets the logic of the loop.

LOOPING STATEMENTS **213**

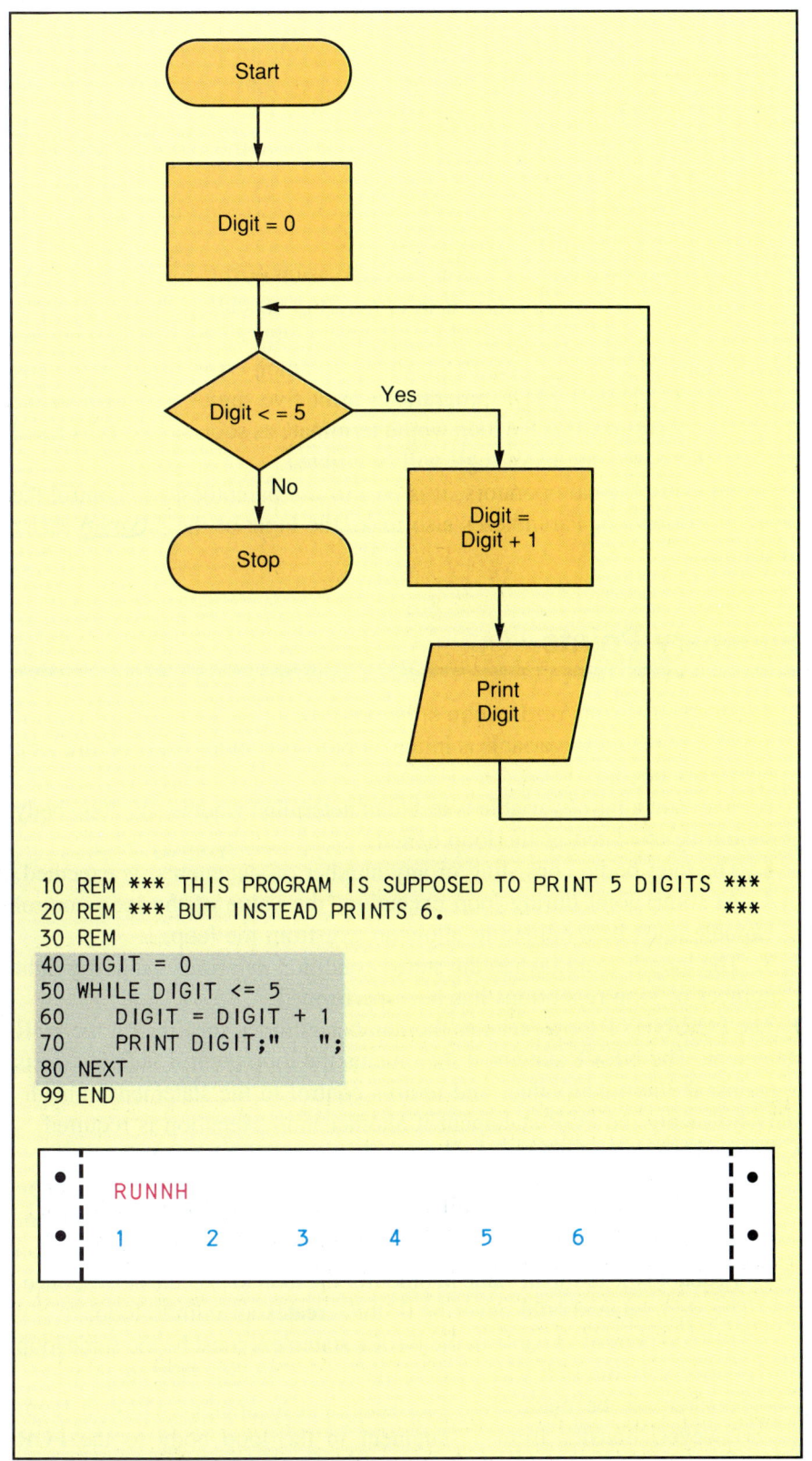

FIGURE 6–23
Example of Incorrectly Written WHILE Loop

```
10 REM *** THIS PROGRAM IS SUPPOSED TO PRINT 5 DIGITS ***
20 REM *** BUT INSTEAD PRINTS 6.                       ***
30 REM
40 DIGIT = 0
50 WHILE DIGIT <= 5
60     DIGIT = DIGIT + 1
70     PRINT DIGIT;"   ";
80 NEXT
99 END
```

```
RUNNH
1    2    3    4    5    6
```

- Special care should be given to nested FOR/NEXT loops; overlapping loops or missing FOR or NEXT statements result in an error.
- The loop control variable of the WHILE loop must be initialized before entering the loop.
- If the loop control variable is not modified within the WHILE loop body, an infinite loop is created.
- The NEXT (or WEND) statement of the WHILE loop does *not* contain the name of the loop control variable.
- The WHILE loop executes until the expression of the WHILE statement is tested and found to be false. It does *not* stop executing the moment the loop control variable is modified in the loop body, making the expression false. Figure 6–23 is an example of a very common error. Many beginning programmers would write a program to print five digits as shown in the example and assume that the loop would terminate as soon as DIGIT is equal to 5. In this case, one extra digit will be printed.
- When using logical operators, it is best to use parentheses to control the order of evaluation. Parentheses also make the logic of the program easier to follow.

Summary Points

- The basic elements of the loop structure follow:
    1. The loop control variable is initialized to a particular value before loop execution begins.
    2. The loop control variable is tested to determine whether the loop body should be executed or the loop exited.
    3. The loop body, consisting of any number of statements, is executed.
    4. At some point during loop execution, the value of the loop control variable must be modified to allow an exit from the loop.
    5. The loop is exited when the stated condition determines that the right number of loop repetitions has been performed.
- The FOR/NEXT loop executes the number of times specified in the FOR statement. The NEXT statement increments the loop control variable, tests it against the terminal value, and returns control to the statement immediately following the FOR statement if another loop execution is required.
- Some rules to remember for using FOR and NEXT loops follow:
    —The initial value must be less than or equal to the terminal value when using a positive step value. Otherwise, the loop will never be executed.
    —The step value can be negative. If it is, the initial value must be greater than or equal to the terminal value in order for the loop to execute at least once.
    —The step value should never be 0; this creates an infinite loop.
    —The loop control variable in the NEXT statement must be the same loop control variable that was used in the corresponding FOR statement.
    —Transfer can be made from one statement to another within a loop. However, transfer from a statement in the loop body to the FOR statement is poor programming practice.

—The value of the loop control variable should not be modified by program statements within the loop.
—The initial, terminal, and step expressions can be composed of any valid numeric variable, constant, or mathematical formula.
—Each FOR statement must be accompanied by a NEXT statement.
—FOR/NEXT loops can be nested.
—The NEXT statement of the nested inner loop must come before the NEXT statement of the outer loop.
- Good programming practice dictates that all program structures have a single entry point and a single exit point.
- The WHILE statement repeats execution of its loop body as long as the given condition in the WHILE statement is true.
- The logical operators NOT, AND, and OR are used with conditions. NOT is a unary operator that negates a condition. An expression containing AND evaluates as true when both conditions joined by the AND are true. A condition containing OR is true if at least one of the joined conditions is true.

Review Questions

1. When should a loop structure be used in a program?
2. What are the five elements of a controlled loop?
3. Which of the following FOR statements will execute at least once?

   a. 20 FOR I = 8 TO 7
   b. 100 FOR K = 15 TO 20 STEP 6
   c. 500 FOR N = 3 TO 5 STEP 1
   d. 420 FOR X = −2 to −1 STEP −1
   e. 160 FOR I = 1 TO 100 STEP 20

4. What is the output from the following statements?

   ```
   50 X = 7
   60 FOR X = 1 TO 4
   70     PRINT X
   80 NEXT X
   ```

5. When the step value is negative, will a loop terminate when the loop control variable is greater or less than the terminal value?
6. What happens when the step value of a FOR statement is zero?
7. Is the following FOR/NEXT loop valid?

   ```
   10 FOR K = 10 TO 5 STEP −1
   20     PRINT "K =";K
   30     INPUT N
   40     K = N
   50 NEXT K
   ```

8. Is the following FOR/NEXT loop valid?

```
10 FOR T = 1 TO 20 STEP 4
20     IF T < 5 THEN 50
30     INPUT X
40     C = T + X
50 NEXT T
```

9. If no step value is specified in a FOR/NEXT loop, what happens?

10. In a FOR/NEXT structure, which of the following can be arithmetic expressions?
- **a.** initial value
- **b.** terminal value
- **c.** step value

11. What happens when a NEXT statement is encountered?

12. When is a WHILE loop a more appropriate choice than a FOR/NEXT loop?

13. Why is the use of the single-entry/single-exit point rule considered good structured programming?

14. How many times is the following inner loop executed? How many times is the outer loop executed?

```
10 Q = 10
20 W = 5
30 L1 = 4
40 FOR L1 = (Q - W) TO 1 STEP -1
50     FOR L2 = 1 TO W STEP 1
60         PRINT L1, L2
70     NEXT L2
80 NEXT L1
```

15. How many times are each of the following loops executed?

```
     ⎧ FOR I = 50 TO 10 STEP -5
     ⎪    ⎧ FOR J = 1 TO 6 STEP 2
     ⎪    ⎪    ⎧ FOR K = 5 TO 5
3 ⎨  2 ⎨  1 ⎨
     ⎪    ⎪    ⎩ NEXT K
     ⎪    ⎩ NEXT J
     ⎩ NEXT I
```

16. What type of value does the expression of a WHILE statement evaluate as?
   a. numeric
   b. character string
   c. true or false

17. What is the difference between a FOR/NEXT loop and a WHILE loop?

18. Is the following a valid nested loop structure?

```
30 FOR R = 1 TO 10 STEP 2
40     PRINT R
50     FOR K = 7 TO -3 STEP -1
60         PRINT K
70         Q = K + 3
80         FOR Q = 2 TO 10
90             T = Q + K
100            PRINT T
110            PRINT Q
120        NEXT Q
130        PRINT Q; "=INNERMOST LOOP"
140    NEXT R
150    PRINT R
160 NEXT K
```

19. Evaluate the following expressions, assuming that $X = 4$, $Y = 3$, and $Z = 12$:
   a. (Z - X ^ 3 > 12) AND (NOT (X > 3))
   b. (X ^ Y * 2 < 20) OR ((X <= 12) AND (Z - Y <> 9))
   c. NOT (Y - X > 0) AND (Y ^ Y >= 4)
   d. NOT ((Z - 6 > X + Y) OR (Y + X < Z / 2))

20. The Happy Hedonist Health Club has updated its requirements for membership. New members must be between the ages of 21 and 55, with an income of no less than $50,000 a year. The income requirement is waived if the prospective member has credit for at least $5,000 with a major credit agency. Write a condition expressing these requirements.

Debugging Exercises

Identify the following programs and program segments that contain errors and debug them.

1.
```
10 REM *** LOOP TO DISPLAY EACH VALUE FROM HIGH TO LOW. ***
20 FOR H = HI TO LO STEP -1
30     PRINT H
40     INPUT AMT
50     IF AMT < LO THEN PRINT "--";AMT
           ELSE H = AMT - LO
60 NEXT H
```

2. ```
10 REM *** READ AND COUNT LIST OF NAMES. ***
20 C = 0
30 FOR X = 4.5 TO .5 STEP -.5
40   INPUT N$
50   IF N$ <> "N" THEN 20
60   C = C + 1.0
70 NEXT
```

3. ```
10 REM *** EXECUTE LOOP 8 TIMES. ***
20 FOR I = 7 TO 4 STEP 0.5
30     PRINT I
40     M = M + 1
50     IF M > 10 THEN PRINT "M > 10"
60     PRINT M
70 NEXT I
```

4. ```
10 REM *** EXECUTE LOOP TEN TIMES AND PRINT ***
20 REM *** R IF IT IS GREATER THAN 15.   ***
30 T = 0
40 UP = T
50 R = 5
60 FOR R = 10 TO 20 STEP UP
70   IF R > 15 THEN 70
80   PRINT R
90 NEXT R
```

5. ```
10   REM *** READ NAMES OF 5 ACCOUNTS. IF THE ***
20   REM *** AMOUNT OWED IS $20 OR MORE, PRINT ***
30   REM *** THE NAME AND AMOUNT.              ***
40   K = 1
50   WHILE K < 5
60       PRINT K
70       INPUT N$,AMT
80       IF AMT < 20.0 THEN 70
90       PRINT N$,AMT
100      K = K + 1
110  NEXT
```

6. ```
10   REM *** EXECUTE X LOOP 5 TIMES, Y LOOP 10 ***
20   REM *** TIMES, AND Z LOOP 20 TIMES.   ***
30   FOR X = 1 TO 5
40   FOR Y = 1 TO 10
50   FOR Z = 1 TO 20
60   PRINT X,Y,Z
70   PRINT "*","*","*"
80   SUM = X + Y + Z
90   PRINT SUM
100   NEXT Y
110   PRINT "Z = ";Z
120   NEXT Z
130   PRINT "X = ";X
140 NEXT X
```
```

7.
```
10 T = 10
20 S = 20
30 WHILE S > 19.5
40     PRINT S
50     T = S + T
60     PRINT T
70     IF T < 19.5 THEN S = S + 1
80 NEXT
```

8.
```
10  REM *** READ AND PRINT NAMES OF CITIES. ***
20  P = 4
30  R = 1
40  FOR L = 1 TO P
50      PRINT L
60      FOR K = R TO L STEP 2
70          PRINT K
80          READ P$
90          PRINT P$
100     NEXT K
110 NEXT L
```

9.
```
10  A = 25
20  B = 35
30  C = 40
40  FOR X = 1 TO (A + 5) STEP 5
50      PRINT X
60      FOR Y = (A + 5) TO (B + 5) STEP 5
70          PRINT Y
80          IF A + 5 >= 40 THEN 60
90          PRINT "A + 5 < 40"
100     NEXT Y
110 NEXT X
```

10.
```
10 REM *** READ RATE AND TIME FOR EACH JOB. ***
20 K = 10
30 FOR S = 5 TO (K - 5) STEP 5
40     PRINT S
50     READ R,T
60 NEXT S
```

Additional Programming Problems

Level 1

1. Write a FOR/NEXT loop that will print the even integers between 1 and 21.

2. Write a WHILE loop that will print the even integers between 1 and 21.

3. Write a program segment that will read data until it encounters a negative number.

4. Write a WHILE loop that will read data until it encounters the trailer value 1.

5. Write a nested FOR/NEXT loop that will read ten numbers. Each number should be added to itself twenty times.

6. Write a WHILE loop to count by 5s until a given value is reached. For example, if the value read is 49, output should be similar to the following:

5 10 15 20 25 30 35 40 45

7. Write a program that prints five rows of periods followed by five rows of asterisks, each row containing eighty characters. *nest for next loop*

8. Write a program that uses a FOR/NEXT loop to output the following pattern:

```
         *
       * * *
     * * * * *
   * * * * * * *
     * * * * *
       * * *
         *
```

9. Write a program that reads an integer i and calculates $i + (i - 1) + (i - 2) + \ldots + 1$. For example, if the integer read was 6, the calculation would look like this:

6 + 5 + 4 + 3 + 2 + 1 = 21

10. Write a program to print the following design:

```
        *
        *
        *
        *
* * * * * * * *
        *
        *
        *
        *
```

Level 2

1. Write a program to print the multiples of 3 that are less than or equal to any given positive integer entered by the user. For example, if the user entered a 20, the following numbers would be output:

3 6 9 12 15 18

Allow the user to continue entering integers as long as desired. Use two WHILE loops.

2. Write a program to display a multiplication table. The user should be allowed to enter the upper and lower limits of the table. Use the following format for the table:

X	1	2	3	4
1	1	2	3	4
2	2	4	6	8
3	3	6	9	12
4	4	8	12	16

3. Mr. Williams came up with a way of saving money to donate to his favorite charity. He wants to start with a penny on the first day and double the amount he gives for each subsequent day. Write a program to determine how much he will have donated after fifteen days.

4. The computer science department needs a program that will display, in a horizontal bar graph, the number of students enrolled in each class section 300 through 309:

Section	Students
300	20
301	15
302	32
303	17
304	28
305	35
306	26
307	29
308	19
309	27

The graph should have appropriate headings, and should be marked off in increments of 10.

5. Write a program that will display a table of factorials. The user should be prompted for the upper and lower limits of the table, with 0 the lowest number allowed. Remember that $0! = 1$, and that if N is greater than 0, $N! = 1 \times 2 \times 3 \times \ldots N$. The table should consist of two columns.

6. The Happy Hedonist Health Club has opened a new branch in your town recently. The Club is offering two types of membership: "weight-training" membership and "all facilities" membership. The manager has asked you to write a program to print a list of the new members of the club and the types of memberships they hold. A report with appropriate headings should be printed. Use the following input data. An A indicates an all facilities membership, and W indicates a weight-training membership.

David Toth, A
Irene Bulas, A
John Drake, A
Bob Szymanski, W
Mike Costarella, W
Eileen Riley, A
Tom Neanderthal, W

7. A high school assigns students to counselors on the basis of the students' last names. Students with last names beginning with A through J are assigned to Mr. Krebs; those with names K through R are assigned to Mrs. Kraus; and those with names S through Z are assigned to Mrs. Klink. Write a program that will read twenty names listed in alphabetical order, and print three lists of students, each under the name of that group's counselor.

8. Write a program to calculate X^N. This value should be found by multiplying X times itself N number of times (e.g., $X^4 = X*X*X*X$). Use the following values for X and N to test your program:

X	N
1	2
6	3
5	4
2	6

The output should have the following format:

X raised to the $N = R$.

A trailer value should be used to determine the end of data.

9. You just bought a new car and already you're looking to the future, wondering just how much your car will be worth in the coming years. Write a program that will provide you with a chart of depreciated values for rates of 7 percent, 10 percent, and 12 percent. The program should ask for the current value of your car and the number of years you want to consider, then print a chart with appropriate headings. The depreciation for each year should be calculated according to the previous year's value.

10. Write a program to print the first fifteen terms of the Fibonacci sequence. This sequence is created by assigning the value 1 to the first two terms, and calculating the next term by adding the two previous terms. The beginning of the Fibonacci sequence is as follows: 1, 1, 2, 3, 5, 8, 13, 21, . . .

Level 3

1. The trustees of Bowling Green High School are considering a measure to give the ten full-time teachers a 4 percent, 4.5 percent, or 5 percent pay raise. To make their decision, they want to know how much additional money they would need in each of the three cases. Write a program to show sample salaries of $12,000 to $18,000 (by $1,000) and the three proposed increased salaries for each. Create a table like the following:

SALARY	+4%	+4.5%	+5%
12,000	XXXX	XXXX	XXXX
13,000	XXXX	XXXX	XXXX
.	.	.	.
.	.	.	.
.	.	.	.

2. Modify the program for problem 1 so that an extra line of summary information is included at the bottom of the chart. This line should give the total of the seven sample salaries and the totals of each of the three increased salary columns. Also, print the difference between the sample salary total and each of the three increased totals. A sample summary follows:

.	.	.	.
.	.	.	.
.	.	.	.
18,000	XXXXX	XXXXX	XXXXX
XXXXXX	XXXXXX	XXXXXX	XXXXXX

+4% gross difference = XXXXX
+4.5% gross difference = XXXXXX
+5% gross difference = XXXXX

3. Your professor has asked you to write a program that will read the name and three test scores for each student in the class. The program should provide a listing of the test averages and then display a breakdown of the class averages according to the following format:

NAME	AVG
XXXXX	XXX
.	.
.	.
.	.

RANGE	NUMBER OF SCORES
90–100%	XX
80–90%	XX
70–80%	XX
60–70%	XX
0–60%	XX

Use the following data with a trailer value:

John Drake	99,100,98	Romana Who	100,100,100
Giselle Dunn	80,93,70	Phyllis Romig	51,42,30
Bob Tahiti	99,91,100	Patricia Lord	65,75,79
Jim Roberts	65,71,80	Brett Tuski	81,88,81
Robert Zimmer	50,41,49	Mike Chepay	65,75,88
Steve Smith	73,72,79	Claude Hyde	77,78,79
Navid Dadfar	61,68,59	Raoul Ramirez	82,80,73

4. Write a program to print in a column the binary equivalent for the base ten numbers 0 through 15. Each number should be printed to four places.

5. Iconia College needs a program to determine the late enrollment for its CS 101 class. The input data includes the student's name, class rank, and the class for which he or she is registered. From this data, the program must generate a report containing a horizontal bar graph that depicts the late enrollment of CS 101 by the students' class ranks and by the total as a whole.

The input data is listed below. Note there are twenty students.

John Drake	Senior	CS 101
Harry Mudd	Freshman	CS 101
James Kirk	Junior	MGMT 300
Reni Gade	Senior	SOC 100
Tom Baker	Freshman	SOC 100
Romana Who	Senior	CS 101
Robert Dillon	Freshman	CS 101
Stewart Birsch	Senior	MIS 200
John Koenig	Senior	CS 101
Helena Russel	Junior	CS 101
Ellen Karaway	Freshman	MATH 124
Millie Travers	Sophomore	CS 101
Tony Vedeccio	Sophomore	CS 101
Sheila Ravassio	Junior	CS 101
Zosha Meir	Sophomore	CS 101
Dawn Matthey	Freshman	CS 101
Arnie Guthrie	Senior	CS 101
Chloe Tully	Senior	CS 101
Pat Lord	Junior	CS 101
Bruce Brawn	Sophomore	CS 101

6. The Olympic Judging Committee has asked you to write a program for the diving competition. The program must read a diver's name and seven scores in the range 0.0 through 10.0. The highest and lowest scores are thrown out; then the total and average of the remaining five scores are calculated. The diver's name, average, and total scores should be output.

Use the following input:

Apollo Creed	7.5,	5,5,	6.5,	6.0,	5.7,	6.1,	8.0
Yani Petrok	3.1,	4.5,	3.8,	5.0,	4.9,	4.5,	3.9
Petro Valecia	5.7,	6.1,	6.9,	5.9,	6.8,	4.9,	6.4
Igor Stravinski	8.0,	8.2,	7.0,	9.1,	7.5,	8.3,	9.2
Thomas Kerry	6.5,	6.6,	6.5,	4.8,	5.7,	6.8,	6.0
Gino Balducci	9.1,	8.5,	9.9,	8.1,	8.8,	4.6,	7.8
Mietek Petrowski	7.7,	8.3,	6.5,	6.9,	7.5,	7.7,	8.0
Johann Mueller	2.1,	1.8,	3.0,	3.1,	2.8,	0.8,	2.5
Claude Bernard	5.5,	6.8,	3.1,	9.7,	8.5,	2.3,	7.5

7. A local company has decided to sell three new products. The accounting department of the company has asked you to write a program to determine the break-even quantities of each of the products. The break-even formula is given as follows:

$$n = \frac{fc}{sp - vc}$$

Where

sp = selling price/unit
fc = fixed costs
vc = variable costs/unit
n = break-even quantity

The following information will be necessary to write this program:

Product	Selling Price	Fixed Costs	Variable Costs
A	$25.00/unit	$ 650.00	$12.00
B	$15.00/unit	$ 275.00	$ 8.00
C	$38.00/unit	$1200.00	$15.00

The output should be formatted similar to the following:

PRODUCT	SELLING PRICE	FIXED COST	VARIABLE COSTS	BREAK-EVEN QUANTITY
X	$XX.XX/unit	$XXX.XX	$XXX.XX	$XX.XX
.	.	.	.	.
.	.	.	.	.
.	.	.	.	.

8. Stewart and Sons Jewelers needs a program to accept its salespersons' sales for each of four months. Output the total sales and average sales for each person, and the total sales for all four months. Use the following data:

Stewart Birsch	7,457.90	5,071.63	4,921.16	5,717.05
Monica Bulas	1,125.16	927.19	1,674.84	1,970.15
Carolyn Carstons	2,257.08	3,716.84	2,116.93	1,877.45
David Toth	871.69	1,199.72	1,299.60	941.38
Irene Drake	4,412.77	2,128.91	3,008.97	2,364.33
Anne Swetlick	2,740.08	3,165.75	2,981.39	1,886.40
XXX	0	0	0	0

The output should look similar to this:

```
SALESPERSON     TOTAL      AVERAGE
XXXXXXXX        $XXXX      $XXXXX
TOTAL SALES = $XXXXXX
```

9. The Hottimes Company just completed its first year of production of its newest model of hot tub. The president would like you to write a program that will produce a bar chart of production costs for each of the last twelve months. Production costs per unit vary depending on the volume produced:

Production Volume	Cost Per Unit
0–50	.8
51–100	.4
101 and up	.2

The following numbers of tubs were produced during the last twelve months:

Jan.	50	July	40
Feb.	10	Aug.	20
Mar.	15	Sept.	50
Apr.	5	Oct.	120
May	20	Nov.	66
June	30	Dec.	98

The output should appear similar to the following:

```
MONTH     HOT TUB PRODUCTION COSTS
          1   10   20   30
JAN       **********  . . .
FEB       ********  . . .
  .
  .
  .
DEC       ******  . . .
```

10. Given last month's checking account balance, write a program to list this month's checks and the new balance. The output should appear similar to the following:

		BALANCE
PREVIOUS MONTH:		$XXX.XX
CHECK #	AMOUNT	
101	XX.XX	XXX.XX
.	.	.
.	.	.
.	.	.

The program should read the withdrawals as long as the balance is not negative. If the account is overdrawn, the listing should stop, and a message should be printed. Then the program should read and total the remaining check amounts and print the amount overdrawn. Otherwise, a message should be printed at the end of the listing giving this month's balance. A check number of 000 marks the end of the data. Use the following data:

Last month's balance: 209.62

Check #	Amount
201	132.00
202	14.06
203	10.25
204	52.37
205	1.69
206	10.69
207	23.15
000	–0

CHAPTER

7

MODULARIZING PROGRAMS

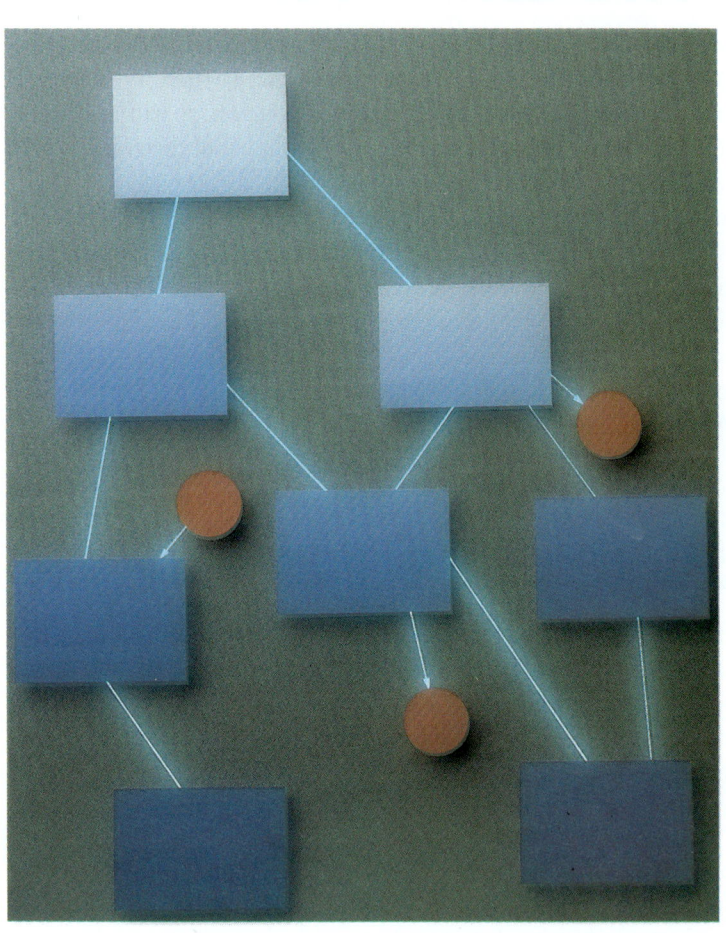

Objectives

After studying this chapter, you will be able to:
- Write correctly modularized programs.
- Use both the GOSUB and the ON/GOSUB statements in programs.
- Use the RETURN statement when it is needed.
- Use structure charts to help you in modularizing programs.
- Explain what a driver program is, and write driver programs when appropriate.
- Explain the single-entry, single-exit subroutine principle.
- Use the ON/GOSUB statement with menus.

Outline

Overview
Importance of Modularizing
   Programs
Writing Subroutines
  The GOSUB Statement
  The RETURN Statement
  A Program Containing Multiple
    Calls to the Same Subroutine
  The ON/GOSUB Statement
  Using the Structure Chart to
    Modularize a Program

Single-Entry, Single-Exit
   Subroutines
Menus
Using Stubs to Enter Programs
Checking for Invalid Data
A Programming Problem
  Problem Definition
  Solution Design
  The Program

Avoiding Common Programming
   Mistakes
Summary Points
Review Questions
Debugging Exercises
Additional Programming Problems
  Level 1
  Level 2
  Level 3

Overview

Subroutine
A module in a BASIC program containing a sequence of statements designed to perform a specific task.

We have previously discussed the two main characteristics of structured programs: (1) they incorporate easy-to-follow logic (which is achieved mainly by using decision and looping structures whenever possible, instead of using GOTO statements), and (2) they are divided into subprograms, each of which is designed to perform a specific task.

Decision and looping structures were introduced in the two previous chapters. This chapter will explain how programs are divided into subprograms or modules, which in BASIC are called **subroutines.** The GOSUB and ON/GOSUB statements are the two methods of executing a subroutine in BASIC, and both will be covered here.

Logical operators, which allow for more than one condition to be checked in a single BASIC statement, will also be introduced in this chapter.

Importance of Modularizing Programs

Dividing a program into modules is useful for two basic reasons:
1. Programs that are divided into modules, each performing a distinct task, make the logic of the program easier to follow.
2. The same module can be executed any number of times. For example, if the program needs to perform the same task at two different points in the program, the subroutine that performs this task may simply be executed twice.

Without the subroutine, the programmer would have to write the same program segment twice. Well-modularized programs are an important characteristic of structured programming.

Writing Subroutines

A subroutine is a sequence of statements typically located after the main body of the program. Two statements in BASIC can be used to **call** a subroutine, that is, to cause it to be executed: the GOSUB and the ON/GOSUB statements.

Call
To cause a subroutine to be executed.

The GOSUB Statement

The GOSUB statement transfers the flow of program control from the calling program to a subroutine. A subroutine can be called either from the main program or from another subroutine. The format of the GOSUB statement is

line# GOSUB transfer line#

The transfer line number must be the first line number of the subroutine to be executed. This is very important, because the computer will not detect an error if it is instructed to branch to an incorrect line. It will detect an error only if the transfer line number does not exist in the program. The GOSUB statement causes an unconditional branch to this specified line number. For example, the following statement will always cause a branch to the subroutine starting at line 1000:

```
100 GOSUB 1000
```

The RETURN Statement

After a subroutine is executed, the RETURN statement causes program control to return to the line following the one that contained the GOSUB statement. The format of the RETURN statement is

line# RETURN

Note that no transfer line number is needed in the RETURN statement. The computer automatically returns control to the statement immediately following the GOSUB statement that called the subroutine. If the line returned to is a nonexecutable statement, such as a REM statement, the computer simply skips it. Each subroutine must contain a RETURN statement; otherwise, the program cannot branch back to the point from which the subroutine was called. The difference between the GOSUB and the GOTO statement is that when a GOSUB is used, the BASIC system keeps track of the line number to which program control will branch when the RETURN statement is encountered.

A Program Containing Multiple Calls to the Same Subroutine

Look at the program in Figure 7–1. This program prints a simple multiplication table. It contains a subroutine that prints a row of asterisks to divide the multiplication table into sections to make it more readable. The subroutine is called from three places in the main program: line 70, line 90, and line 190. Each time this subroutine is called, program control transfers to line 1000. Because lines 1000 through 1030 are nonexecutable statements, execution skips down to line 1040. Lines 1040 through 1060 contain a FOR/NEXT loop that is used to print a line of 80 asterisks. Then program control returns to the line following the statement that called the subroutine. In Figure 7–1, both the main program and the subroutine are labeled. Arrows are drawn to show the flow of execution of the program.

In this example, the subroutine is very short, so it would be easy to repeat the necessary series of statements each time they are needed. If the subroutine were ten, twenty, or more lines long, however, it would be tedious and wasteful to type it three times. Using the subroutine simplifies the program logic by organizing specific tasks into neat, orderly subsections.

Notice that the subroutine in Figure 7–1 begins at line 1000. To make programs more readable, programmers often start subroutines at readily identifiable line numbers, such as multiples of 1000. For example, the first subroutine might start at line 1000, the second at line 2000, and so on. This practice of starting at readily identifiable line numbers will be followed in this textbook.

In Figure 7–1, when program execution reaches the last line of the main program (line 200), it is ready to stop. We do not want to execute the subroutine again at this point, because it has already been called where it was needed in the program. Therefore, it is necessary to branch to the END statement, which has a line number of 9999. This branch statement will skip over any subroutines that have been placed between the end of the main program and the END statement.

On the VAX system, the END statement must be at the end of the entire program and must also have the highest line number. Not all BASIC implementations have these requirements. On many systems, the END statement may be placed immediately after the last statement of the main program and before the subroutines. If this is possible on your system, it is recommended that you use this method because it avoids the use of a GOTO statement.

The ON/GOSUB Statement

Because the GOSUB statement is an unconditional transfer statement, it always transfers program control to the subroutine starting at the indicated line number. Sometimes, however, it is necessary to branch to one of several

FIGURE 7–1 Program Demonstrating Multiple Calls to a Subroutine

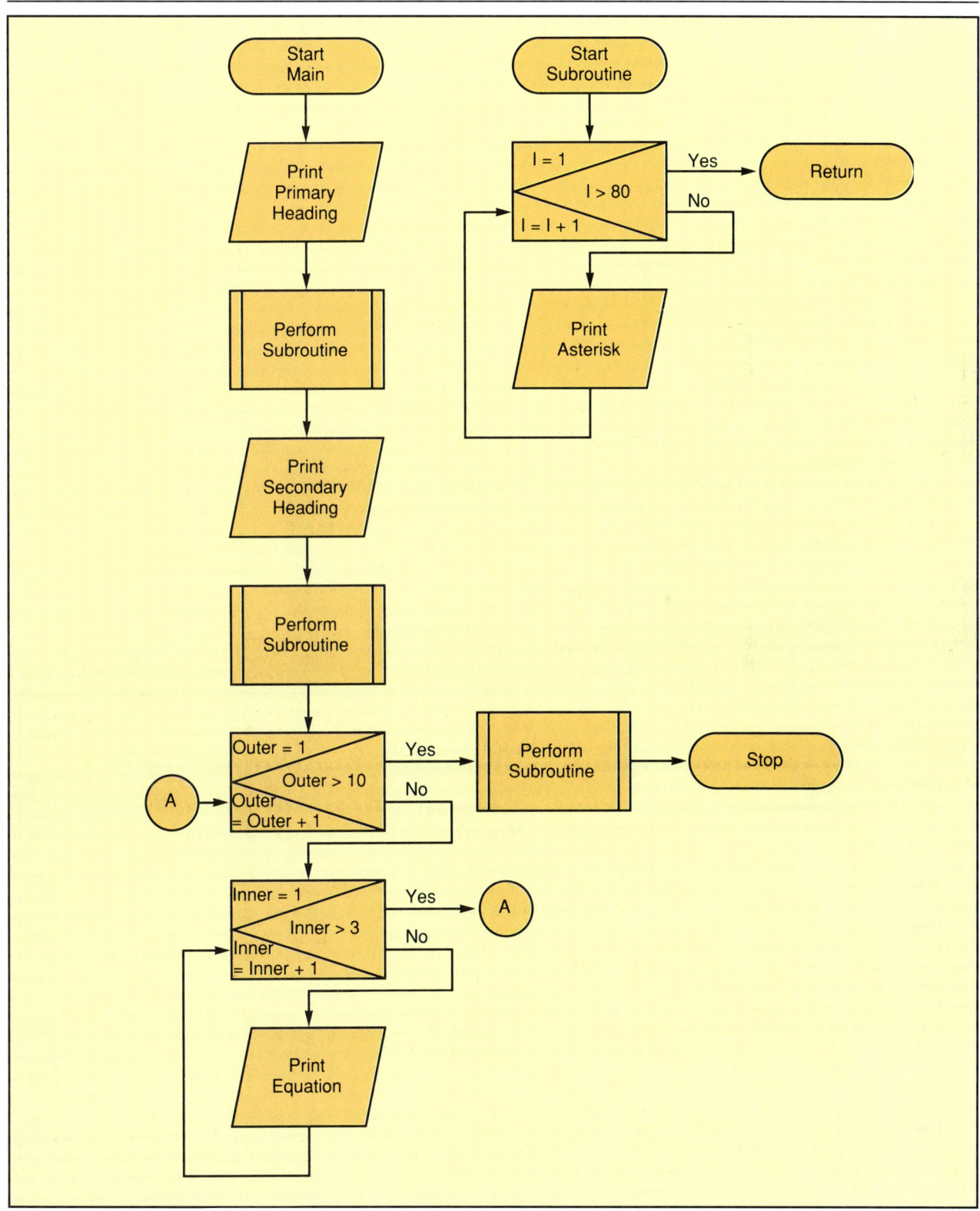

FIGURE 7-1 *Continued*

```
10  REM ***           MULTIPLICATION PROGRAM        ***
20  REM *** THE PURPOSE OF THIS PROGRAM IS TO DEMON- ***
30  REM *** STRATE MULTIPLE CALLS TO A SINGLE SUB-   ***
40  REM *** ROUTINE.                                 ***
50  REM
60  PRINT TAB(30);"MULTIPLICATION TABLE"
70  GOSUB 1000
80  PRINT TAB(5);"ONE";TAB(33);"TWO";TAB(59);"THREE"
90  GOSUB 1000
100 REM
110 REM *** DISPLAY THE TABLE. ***
120 FOR OUTER = 1 TO 10
130    FOR IN = 1 TO 3
140       PRINT OUTER;" * ";IN;" = ";OUTER * IN,
150    NEXT IN
160    PRINT
170 NEXT OUTER
180 PRINT
190 GOSUB 1000
200 GOTO 9999    End
1000 REM
1010 REM ************************************************
1020 REM ***            ASTERISK SUBROUTINE            ***
1030 REM ************************************************
1040 FOR I = 1 TO 80
1050    PRINT "*";
1060 NEXT I
1070 PRINT
1080 RETURN
9999 END
```

(Lines 70, 90, 190, 1000–1080 are the Subroutine; the rest is the Main Program.)

```
RUNNH
                    MULTIPLICATION TABLE
********************************************************************************
     ONE                        TWO                         THREE
********************************************************************************
  1 * 1 =  1              1 * 2 =  2                  1 * 3 =  3

  2 * 1 =  2              2 * 2 =  4                  2 * 3 =  6

  3 * 1 =  3              3 * 2 =  6                  3 * 3 =  9

  4 * 1 =  4              4 * 2 =  8                  4 * 3 = 12

  5 * 1 =  5              5 * 2 = 10                  5 * 3 = 15

  6 * 1 =  6              6 * 2 = 12                  6 * 3 = 18

  7 * 1 =  7              7 * 2 = 14                  7 * 3 = 21

  8 * 1 =  8              8 * 2 = 16                  8 * 3 = 24
```

FIGURE 7–1 *Continued*

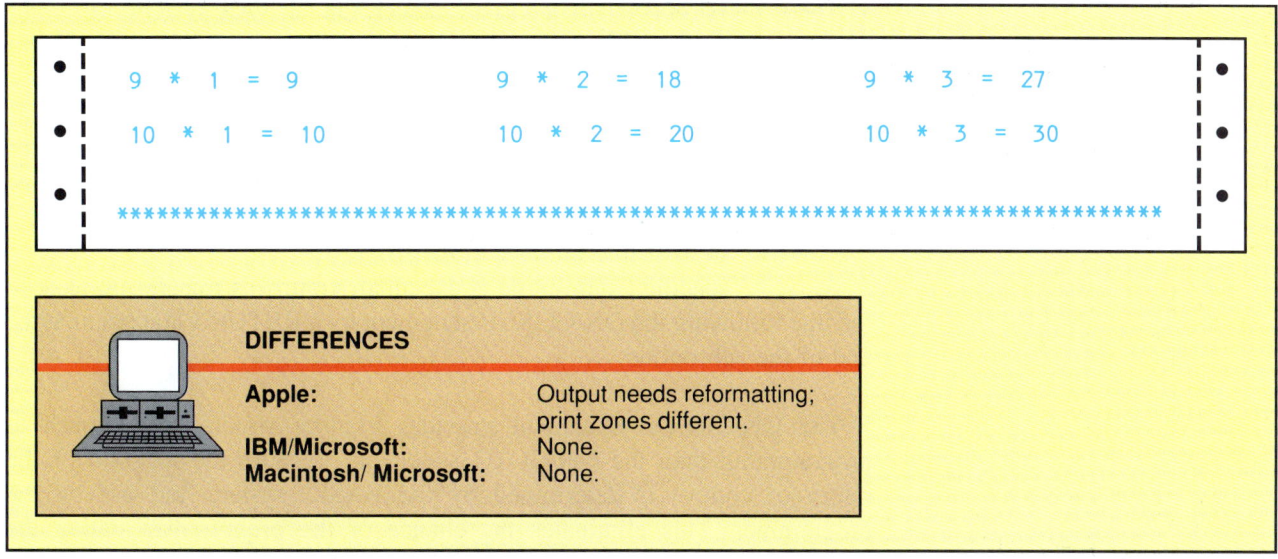

subroutines, depending on existing conditions. The ON/GOSUB statement allows for such conditional transfer of program control. Its format is

line# ON expression GOSUB transfer line#1[,transfer line#2]. . .

The ON/GOSUB is similar to the ON/GOTO statement (Chapter 5) in that it uses an expression to determine the line number to which program control will transfer. This expression must be arithmetic. The transfer line numbers in the ON/GOSUB statement, however, are not within the calling program. Each transfer line number indicates the beginning of a subroutine.

Learning Check

1. Subprograms in BASIC are called _____.
2. A(n) _____ statement causes an unconditional branch to a subroutine.
3. A(n) _____ to a subroutine causes it to be executed.
4. The _____ statement causes control to be transferred from a subroutine back to the calling program.
5. How many times can a given subroutine be called in a program?

Answers

1. subroutines 2. GOSUB 3. call 4. RETURN 5. There is no limit.

The general execution of the ON/GOSUB proceeds as follows:

1. The expression is evaluated as an integer. On the VAX system, this value is truncated if it is a real number. See Table 7–1 for system differences in this respect.
2. Depending on the value of the expression, control passes to the subroutine starting at the corresponding line number. If the value of the expression is *n,* control passes to the subroutine starting at the *n*th line number listed. (For example, if the expression evaluates as 1, control transfers to the first line number in the list.)
3. After the specified subroutine is executed, control is transferred back to the line following the ON/GOSUB statement by a RETURN statement at the end of the subroutine.

The ON/GOSUB statement provides a more structured approach to programming than the ON/GOTO statement, because the location of the return of control is determined by the BASIC system and not by the programmer. This eliminates the chance of the programmer stating the incorrect line number in the GOTO statement.

On the VAX system, if the expression in an ON/GOSUB statement evaluates as a number larger than the number of transfer line numbers indicated, an error message is printed and program execution terminates. The other systems covered here simply skip to the next executable statement. Table 7–1 explains how different systems handle this situation.

Figure 7–2 demonstrates a simple use of the ON/GOSUB statement. The user enters an integer value representing his or her year in college (1, 2, 3,

TABLE 7–1 ON/GOSUB Differences

COMPUTER	ACTION TAKEN IF EXPRESSION IS GREATER THAN NUMBER OF LINE NUMBERS	EXPRESSION TRUNCATED OR ROUNDED?
VAX System	"ON statement out of range at line 120"	Truncated
Apple	Control is passed to next executable statement	Truncated
IBM/Microsoft	Control is passed to next executable statement	Rounded
Macintosh/Microsoft	Control is passed to next executable statement	Rounded

FIGURE 7–2 Program Using the ON/GOSUB Statement

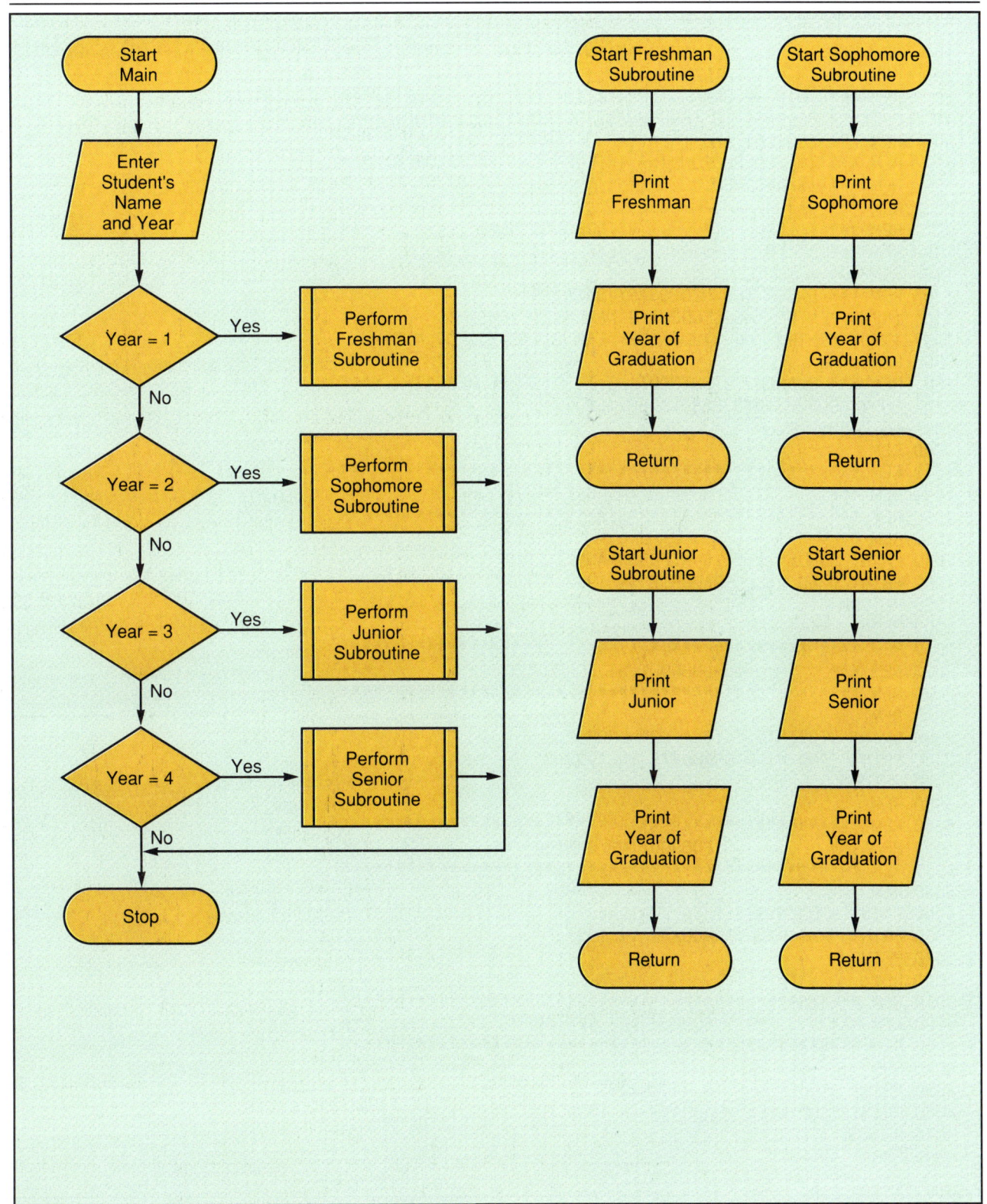

FIGURE 7–2 *Continued*

```
10   REM ***                GRADUATION PROGRAM           ***
20   REM ***                                             ***
30   REM *** THIS PROGRAM DISPLAYS THE CLASS A STUDENT   ***
40   REM *** BELONGS TO (FRESHMAN, SOPHOMORE, JUNIOR,    ***
50   REM *** SENIOR) AND THE YEAR OF GRADUATION WHEN     ***
60   REM *** THE CORRESPONDING INTEGER (1, 2, 3, OR 4)   ***
70   REM *** IS ENTERED.                                 ***
80   REM *** MAJOR VARIABLES:                            ***
90   REM ***      STUDENT$       STUDENT'S NAME          ***
100  REM ***      YR             YEAR                    ***
110  REM
120  REM *** ENTER THE NECESSARY DATA. ***
130  INPUT "ENTER THE STUDENT'S NAME";STUDENT$
140  INPUT "ENTER THE STUDENT'S YEAR (1, 2, 3, OR 4)";YR
150  REM
160  REM *** BRANCH TO SUBROUTINE TO DISPLAY MESSAGE. ***
170  ON YR GOSUB 1000,2000,3000,4000
180  GOTO 9999    End
1000 REM
1010 REM ******************************************************
1020 REM ***                SUBROUTINE FRESHMAN            ***
1030 REM ******************************************************
1040 REM
1050 PRINT STUDENT$;" IS A FRESHMAN"
1060 PRINT "AND WILL GRADUATE IN 1993."
1070 RETURN
2000 REM
2010 REM ******************************************************
2020 REM ***                SUBROUTINE SOPHOMORE           ***
2030 REM ******************************************************
2040 REM
2050 PRINT STUDENT$;" IS A SOPHOMORE"
2060 PRINT "AND WILL GRADUATE IN 1992."
2070 RETURN
3000 REM
3010 REM ******************************************************
3020 REM ***                SUBROUTINE JUNIOR              ***
3030 REM ******************************************************
3040 REM
3050 PRINT STUDENT$;" IS A JUNIOR"
3060 PRINT "AND WILL GRADUATE IN 1991."
3070 RETURN
4000 REM
4010 REM ******************************************************
4020 REM ***                SUBROUTINE SENIOR              ***
4030 REM ******************************************************
4040 REM
4050 PRINT STUDENT$;" IS A SENIOR"
4060 PRINT "AND WILL GRADUATE IN 1990."
4070 RETURN
9999 END
```

FIGURE 7–2 Continued

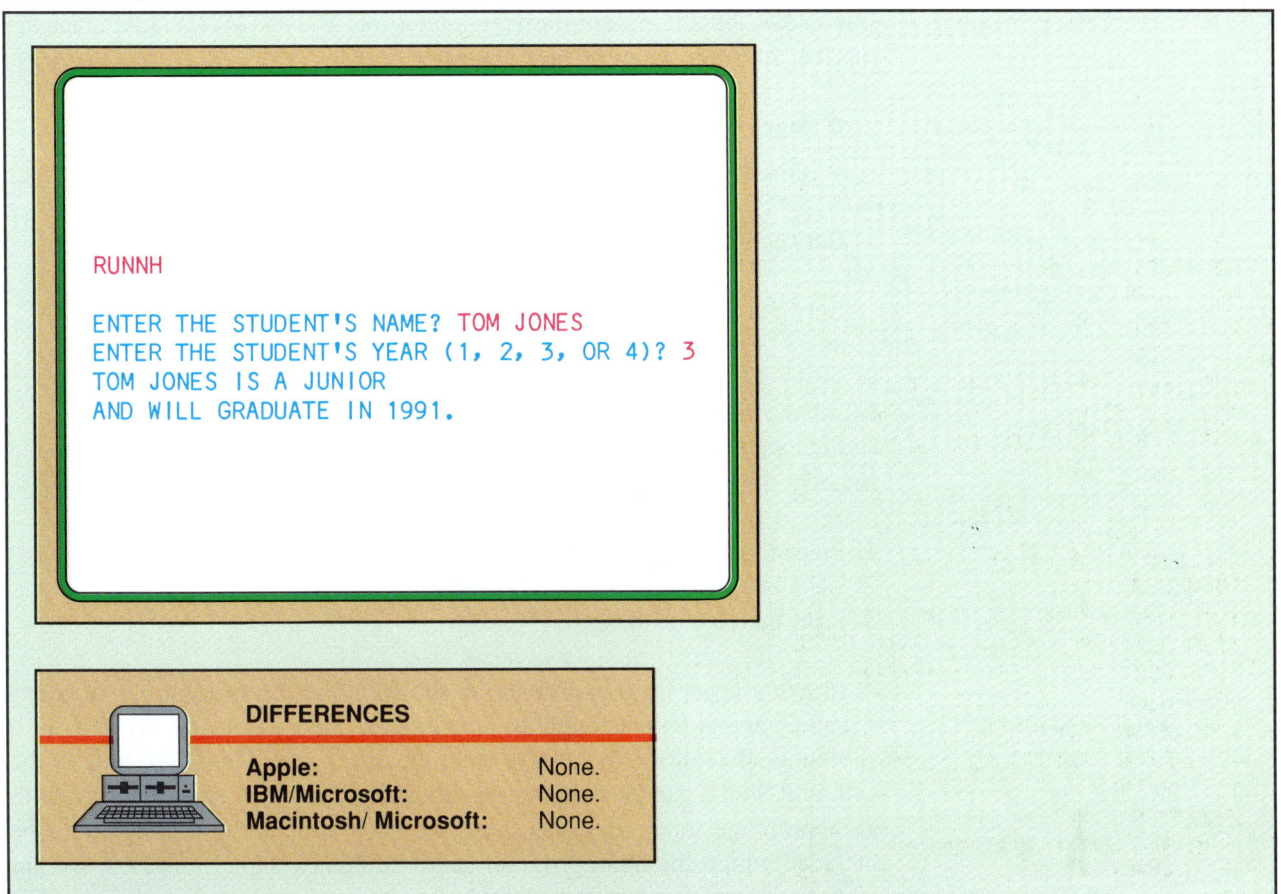

or 4). This integer value is assigned to the variable YR, which is then used to determine which subroutine will be executed. If YR = 1, the subroutine starting at line 1000 will be executed; if YR = 2, the subroutine starting at line 2000 will be executed; if YR = 3, the subroutine starting at line 3000 will be executed; and if YR = 4, the subroutine starting at line 4000 will be executed. After the appropriate subroutine is executed, control is returned to the main program, which then stops executing.

Using the Structure Chart to Modularize a Program

So far in this textbook, we have been using structure charts to help analyze the steps necessary to solve programming problems. Structure charts enable us to visualize the specific tasks a program must perform to achieve the desired overall result. Because structure charts represent the subtasks involved in solving a problem, they are very useful in developing modularized programs. Once the tasks of a program are identified, each of these can be implemented in the program as a separate subroutine.

We will illustrate the use of structure charts with a simple problem. We are going to write a program that will calculate the cost of a long-distance phone call, based on the following table (note that the user should enter the number of miles as an integer value):

Distance of Call	Cost Per Minute
Within 99 miles	12¢ per minute for first 5 minutes, 10¢ per minute thereafter
Between 100 and 199 miles	15¢ per minute for first 5 minutes, 13¢ per minute thereafter
Between 200 and 299 miles	18¢ per minute, regardless of length of the call

No phone calls can be placed outside the 299-mile radius.

First we need to develop an algorithm for this problem. The steps needed to solve this problem could be listed like this:

1. Enter the distance and length of time of the call.
2. Calculate the cost of the call based on the distance.
3. Print the cost of the call.

A structure chart for this problem is shown at the top of Figure 7–3. Steps 1 and 3 are simple enough to implement: Step 1 can be written as a subroutine that allows the user to enter the distance and length of time of the call, and Step 3 can be written as a subroutine that prints the final cost with an appropriate label. Because these are such simple steps, they could be included within the main program itself. In this example, however, we are including them as subroutines to demonstrate how every task in the program can be modularized.

Step 2 is more complex. We want the program to use one of three rates in determining the cost, depending on the distance. This is a situation that is well suited to the ON/GOSUB statement; three subroutines can be used to perform these calculations, as shown in Figure 7–3. The following ON/GOSUB statement will cause program control to be transferred to the needed subroutine, if the computer system being used is one that truncates the value of the ON/GOSUB expression, as the VAX and Apple do.

```
120 ON (DIST + 100) / 100 GOSUB 2000,3000,4000
```

Let's test this expression by assuming that the number of miles entered is 199. With this value substituted, the statement would look like this:

```
120 ON (199 + 100) / 100 GOSUB 2000,3000,4000
```

The expression (199 + 100) / 100 is equal to 2.99. This number is truncated to 2, so the program will branch to the second subroutine, which starts at

FIGURE 7–3 Program Using a Calculated Value in the ON/GOSUB Statement

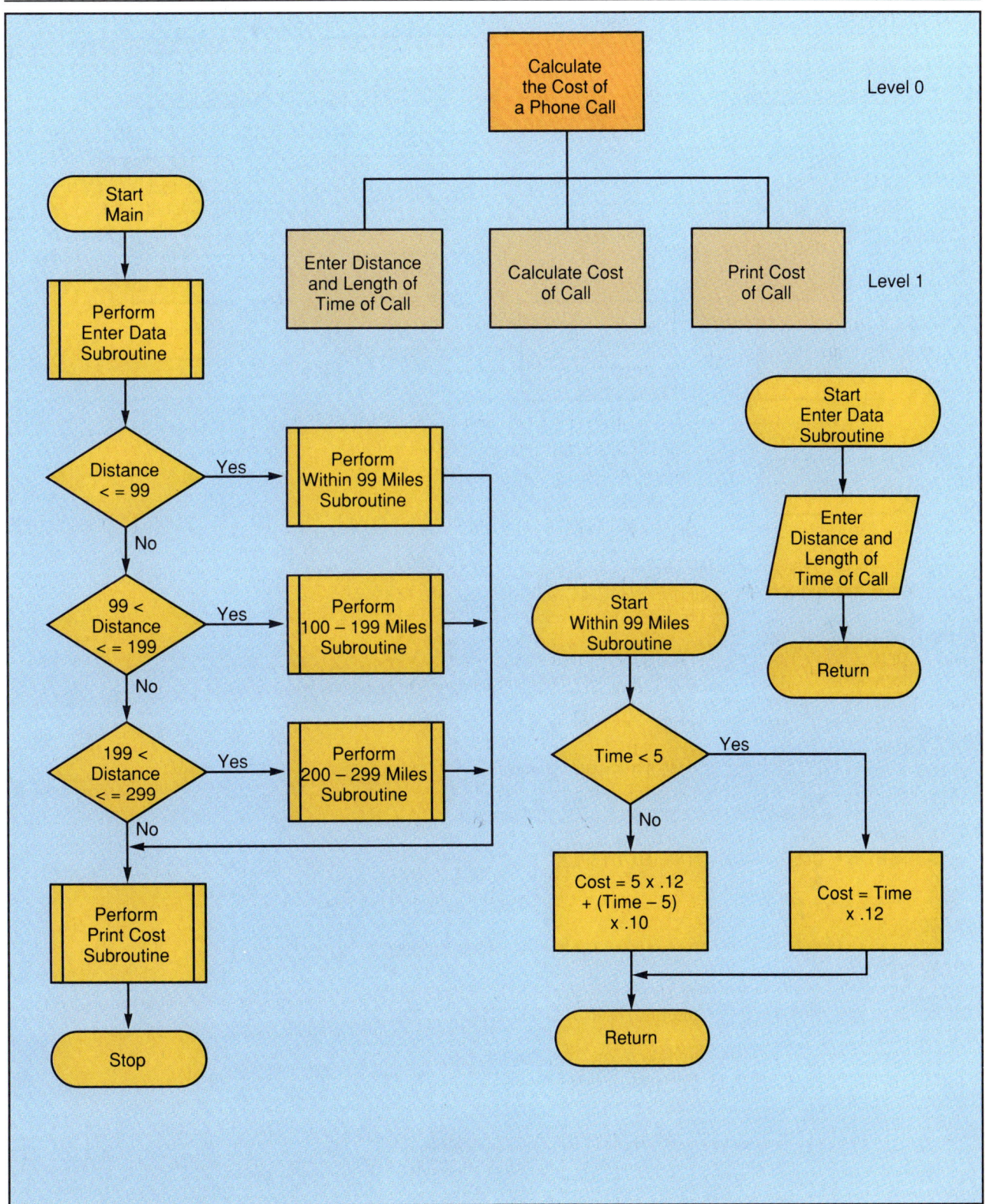

FIGURE 7-3 Continued

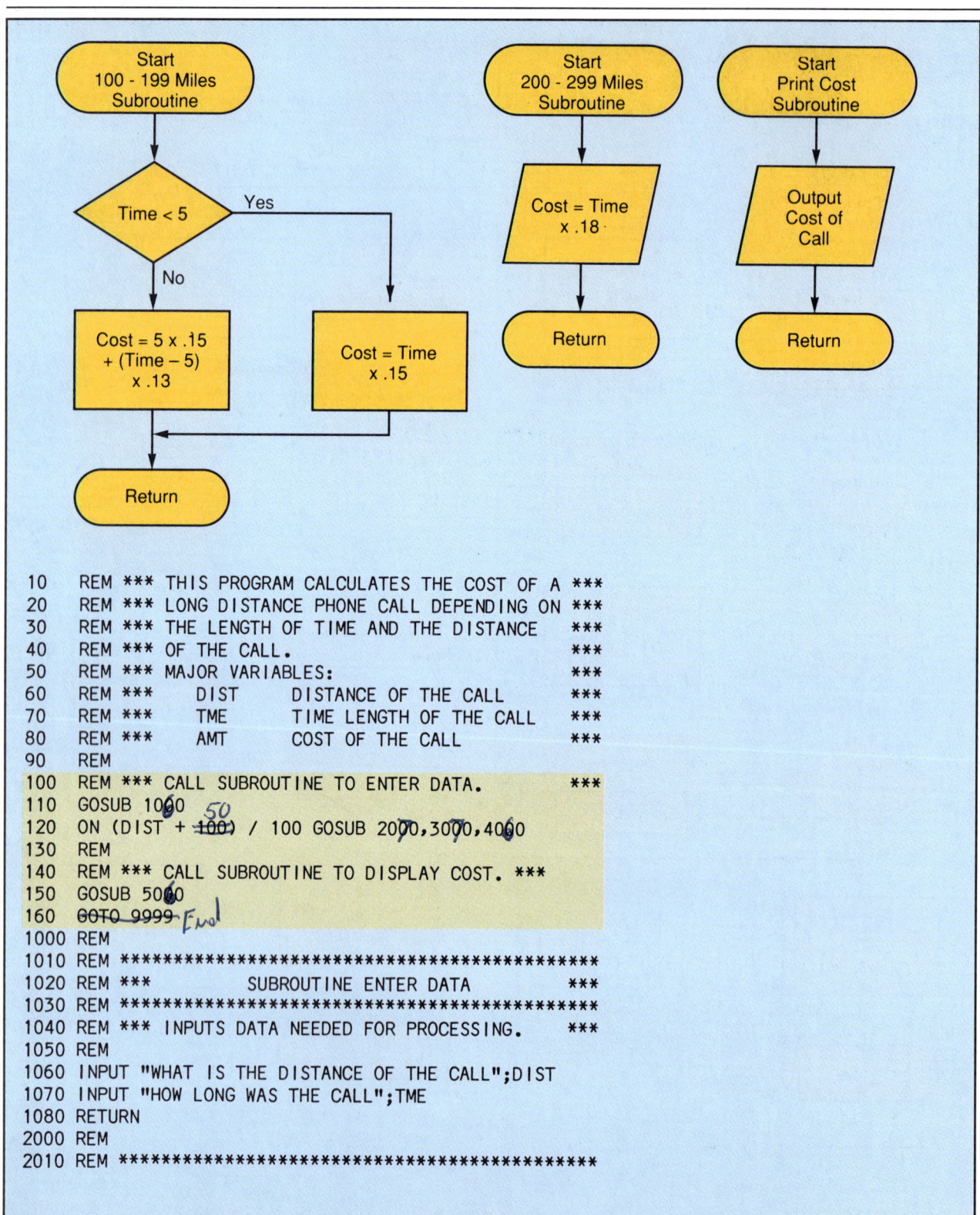

```
10   REM *** THIS PROGRAM CALCULATES THE COST OF A     ***
20   REM *** LONG DISTANCE PHONE CALL DEPENDING ON     ***
30   REM *** THE LENGTH OF TIME AND THE DISTANCE       ***
40   REM *** OF THE CALL.                              ***
50   REM *** MAJOR VARIABLES:                          ***
60   REM ***     DIST     DISTANCE OF THE CALL         ***
70   REM ***     TME      TIME LENGTH OF THE CALL      ***
80   REM ***     AMT      COST OF THE CALL             ***
90   REM
100  REM *** CALL SUBROUTINE TO ENTER DATA.            ***
110  GOSUB 1000
120  ON (DIST + 100) / 100 GOSUB 2000,3000,4000
130  REM
140  REM *** CALL SUBROUTINE TO DISPLAY COST. ***
150  GOSUB 5000
160  GOTO 9999
1000 REM
1010 REM ***********************************************
1020 REM ***           SUBROUTINE ENTER DATA          ***
1030 REM ***********************************************
1040 REM *** INPUTS DATA NEEDED FOR PROCESSING.       ***
1050 REM
1060 INPUT "WHAT IS THE DISTANCE OF THE CALL";DIST
1070 INPUT "HOW LONG WAS THE CALL";TME
1080 RETURN
2000 REM
2010 REM ***********************************************
```

(Handwritten annotations: line 110 "50" written over "00"; line 120 "100" crossed out and replaced with "50", the "00" in 2000, 3000, 4000 overwritten with "70,70,60"; line 150 "00" changed to "60"; line 160 "GOTO 9999" crossed out and "End" written.)

FIGURE 7–3 Continued

```
2020 REM ***        SUBROUTINE WITHIN 99 MILES       ***
2030 REM *********************************************
2040 REM *** CALCULATES COST OF CALL WITHIN 99        ***
2050 REM *** MILES.                                   ***
2060 REM
2070 IF TME < 5 THEN AMT = TME * .12 ELSE AMT = 5 * .12 + (TME - 5) * .10
2080 RETURN
3000 REM
3010 REM *********************************************
3020 REM ***        SUBROUTINE 100 - 199 MILES        ***
3030 REM *********************************************
3040 REM *** CALCULATES COST OF CALL IN 100 - 199     ***
3050 REM *** MILE RANGE.                              ***
3060 REM
3070 IF TME < 5 THEN AMT = TME * .15 ELSE AMT = 5 * .15 + (TME - 5) * .13
3080 RETURN
4000 REM
4010 REM *********************************************
4020 REM ***        SUBROUTINE 200 - 299 MILES        ***
4030 REM *********************************************
4040 REM *** CALCULATES COST OF CALL IN 200 - 200     ***
4050 REM *** MILE RANGE.                              ***
4060 AMT = TME * .18
4070 RETURN
5000 REM
5010 REM *********************************************
5020 REM ***           SUBROUTINE PRINT COST          ***
5030 REM *********************************************
5040 REM *** PRINTS COST OF THE TELEPHONE CALL.       ***
5050 REM
5060 PRINT "THE COST OF THIS PHONE CALL IS ";AMT
5070 RETURN
9999 END
```

```
RUNNH

WHAT IS THE DISTANCE OF THE CALL? 274
HOW LONG WAS THE CALL? 24
THE COST OF THIS PHONE CALL IS  4.32
```

DIFFERENCES

Apple: No IF/THEN/ELSE.
IBM/Microsoft: ON/GOSUB expression rounded.
Macintosh/Microsoft: ON/GOSUB expression rounded.

line 3000. This is the subroutine used to calculate phone bills in the 100- to 199-mile radius.

Test this program yourself, using different values for the distance. If your BASIC system rounds the expression rather than truncating it (as the IBM and Macintosh do), the expression must be written differently:

```
120 ON (DIST + 50) / 100 GOSUB 2000,3000,4000
```

To check this statement, let's again assume that 199 has been entered as the value for DIST:

```
120 ON (199 + 50) / 100 GOSUB 2000,3000,4000
```

The expression evaluates as 2.49, which rounds to 2. This value will cause the program to branch to the subroutine starting at line 3000, which is exactly what we want it to do.

It is often possible to use expressions similar to the preceding one in ON/GOSUB statements. Although they can often simplify the programming process, they must be thoroughly tested to make certain that they will always evaluate as expected.

The complete program is shown in Figure 7–3. Note that this main program contains only four executable statements, three of which are used to call subroutines; the fourth statement branches to the end of the program. This is an example of a **driver program,** which calls the subprograms. These subprograms then perform the actual processing.

Driver program
A program that calls the subroutines that do the actual work of the program.

Learning Check

1. The ON/GOSUB is a(n) _____ transfer statement.
2. To what line will control be transferred when the following program segment is executed?

   50 A = 14 / 7 + 2
   60 ON A GOSUB 3000,4000,5000,6000

3. Why is this program segment invalid:

   100 VOWEL$ = "E"
   110 ON VOWEL$ GOSUB 2000

4. Every subroutine should have a(n) _____ _____ _____ and a(n) _____ _____ _____.

5. What programming principle does the following subroutine violate?

   3000 REM *** SUBROUTINE TO CALCULATE OVERTIME PAY ***
   3010 IF HRS <= 40 THEN RETURN

FIGURE 7–4 Demonstration of Single-Entry Subroutine Principle

```
100   INPUT "ENTER YOUR SCORE";PTS
110   IF PTS > 80 THEN GOSUB 1000 ELSE GOSUB 1060
120   GOTO 9999
1000  REM
1010  REM ***************************************************
1020  REM ***                 SUBROUTINE                  ***
1030  REM ***************************************************
1040  REM
1050  PRINT "YOU DID VERY WELL!"
1060  PRINT "YOU PASSED THE COURSE."
1070  RETURN
9999  END
```

Incorrectly Written Program Segment With Branch to the Middle of Subroutine

```
100   INPUT "ENTER YOUR SCORE";PTS
110   GOSUB 1000
120   GOTO 9999
1000  REM ***************************************************
1010  REM ***                 SUBROUTINE                  ***
1020  REM ***************************************************
1030  REM
1040  IF PTS > 80 THEN PRINT "YOU DID VERY WELL!"
1050  PRINT "YOU PASSED THE COURSE."
1060  RETURN
9999  END
```

Correctly Written Program Segment With a Single-Entry Point to Subroutine

```
3020  PAY = PAY + (HRS - 40) * PAY * 0.5
3030  RETURN
```

Answers

1. conditional 2. Line 6000. 3. The expression in an ON/GOSUB statement must be numeric. 4. single-entry point; single-exit point 5. The single-exit point principle.

Single-Entry, Single-Exit Subroutines

Chapter 6 discussed the fact that program structures such as loops, decisions, and subroutines should have only one entry point and one exit point. This is an important principle of structured programming.

A subroutine may be called any number of times in a given program, but it should always be entered at the first line of the subroutine. Branching to the middle of a subroutine makes program logic virtually impossible to follow and often leads to errors.

FIGURE 7–5 Demonstration of Single-Exit Subroutine Principle

```
100  INPUT "ENTER YOUR SCORE";PTS
110  GOSUB 1000
120  GOTO 9999
1000 REM
1010 REM *************************************************
1020 REM ***                  SUBROUTINE               ***
1030 REM *************************************************
1040 REM
1050 IF PTS < 80 THEN PRINT "YOU FAILED" \ RETURN ELSE PRINT "YOU PASSED"
1060 CREDITHR = CREDITHR + 4
1070 ST$ = "OK"
1080 RETURN
9999 END
```

Incorrectly Written Program Segment With Multiple RETURNs

```
100  INPUT "ENTER YOUR SCORE";PTS
110  GOSUB 1000
120  GOTO 9999
1000 REM
1010 REM *************************************************
1020 REM ***                  SUBROUTINE               ***
1030 REM *************************************************
1040 REM
1050 IF PTS < 80 THEN PRINT "YOU FAILED" \ GOTO 1080 ELSE PRINT "YOU PASSED"
1060 CREDITHR = CREDITHR + 4
1070 ST$ = "OK"
1080 RETURN
9999 END
```

Correctly Written Program Segment With a Single RETURN

Figure 7–4 illustrates two program segments, both of which perform the same task. The top segment is incorrectly written, because the IF/THEN/ELSE statement in line 110 can allow control to be passed either to the first line of the subroutine (line 1000) or to the middle of the subroutine (line 1060). The bottom example shows this segment correctly written. Note that an IF/THEN statement within the subroutine is used to control execution.

Likewise, a subroutine should contain only one RETURN statement, which should be the last statement of the subroutine. This rule is referred to as the single-exit point principle. At the top of Figure 7–5 is a program segment that is incorrectly written because it contains two RETURN statements, one in line 1050 and one in line 1080. The bottom program segment accomplishes the same task by using an IF/THEN statement (line 1050) to branch to the RETURN statement at the end of the subroutine.

Menus

Many programming applications require that the user be presented with a list of tasks that the program is able to perform. The use of menus for this purpose has already been discussed in connection with the ON/GOTO statement. The ON/GOSUB statement is also well suited for use with menus. The user can enter a value based on the choices offered in the menu, and the correct subroutine can be executed to perform the desired task.

Figure 7–6 contains a program that uses the ON/GOSUB statement with a menu. When this program is executed, the user is asked to enter a code number depending on the food item desired. Then the statement in line 220 causes the correct subroutine to be executed depending on the item chosen. Each subroutine prompts the user for the desired quantity of that particular item, calculates the cost, and then adds it to the total cost of the food purchased. If the user enters code number 5, the total bill is printed, and the program stops executing. Otherwise, the menu is displayed again so that the user can enter another choice.

Using Stubs to Enter Programs

So far, considerable attention has been given to top-down development of programming problem solutions. It is also possible to use a top-down method when entering a program to the computer. Indeed, when writing a large program that contains many subroutines, it is poor programming practice to enter the entire program at one time. A far wiser approach is to start by entering the main program (the driver) and one or two subroutines.

Subroutines that are not yet implemented are called, but each of these nonimplemented subroutines consists merely of a **stub.** A stub contains a PRINT statement that indicates a given subroutine has been called but is not yet implemented. The stub must also contain a RETURN statement to return control to the main program. The idea is to enter the program in manageable segments, which can then be executed and tested for errors in an orderly way. As segments of the program work properly, more can gradually be added and tested.

Stub
A subroutine containing only a PRINT statement, which indicates that the subroutine has not yet been implemented, and a RETURN statement.

Let's see how the program in Figure 7–6 might have been developed in this manner. First, the main program would be typed into the computer. Next, subroutine 1 could be entered and executed to determine if the menu is properly displayed. At this point the programmer might also want to enter subroutines 5 and 6. The number of subroutines entered at one time is entirely dependent upon the judgment of the programmer. We have chosen to enter a subroutine that calculates the cost of one of the food items (in this case, soft drinks), and also the subroutine that prints the total bill so that we can check to see if the results obtained by the program are accurate.

Let's assume that lines 10 through 1190 and lines 5000 through 9999 are entered exactly as they appear in Figure 7–6. The rest of the program could be entered like this:

```
2000 PRINT "SUBROUTINE 2 NOT YET IMPLEMENTED"
2010 RETURN
3000 PRINT "SUBROUTINE 3 NOT YET IMPLEMENTED"
3010 RETURN
4000 PRINT "SUBROUTINE 4 NOT YET IMPLEMENTED"
4010 RETURN
```

Therefore, it is possible for the user to order soft drinks and have the total cost of the soft drinks printed. If the user attempts to order hamburgers, the following message will appear on the screen:

SUBROUTINE 2 NOT YET IMPLEMENTED

Control will then return to line 230 of the main program. The user will not be prompted to enter the number of hamburgers desired, nor will any value be added to the variable containing the total cost of the order (TTCST). This same thing will happen if the user attempts to order cheeseburgers or french fries.

The programmer is now able to determine if the main program, the menu subroutine, the soft drink subroutine, and the final printing subroutine are working properly. If the total cost printed is incorrect, or if there is some other error, it is much easier to pinpoint the problem than if the entire program had been entered at once. When the programmer is certain that the program is working properly, more subroutines can be gradually added and tested. This method of entering and testing programs greatly simplifies the debugging process, particularly for large programs.

Checking for Invalid Data

Interactive programs should check to make certain that data entered by the user is valid. If the data is invalid, the program should ask the user to reenter it. For example, in the program in Figure 7–6, the user is asked to enter an integer between 1 and 5. If the user entered a number that was less than 1 or more than 5, the program would not be able to execute properly. In order to protect the program from such an occurrence, the program should check the data entered and make certain that it falls within the allowable range.

Figure 7–7 shows how this checking can be accomplished. A WHILE loop (lines 1190 to 1240) is used to determine if the value of FOOD is within the valid range. This condition is checked using the logical operator OR:

```
1190 WHILE FOOD < 100 OR FOOD > 5
```

This loop will be executed only if the value of FOOD is either less than 1 or greater than 5. Otherwise, the loop will be skipped. If the loop is executed, the user is instructed to reenter a code number, making certain that the number is between 1 and 5.

FIGURE 7–6 Using the ON/GOSUB Statement with a Menu

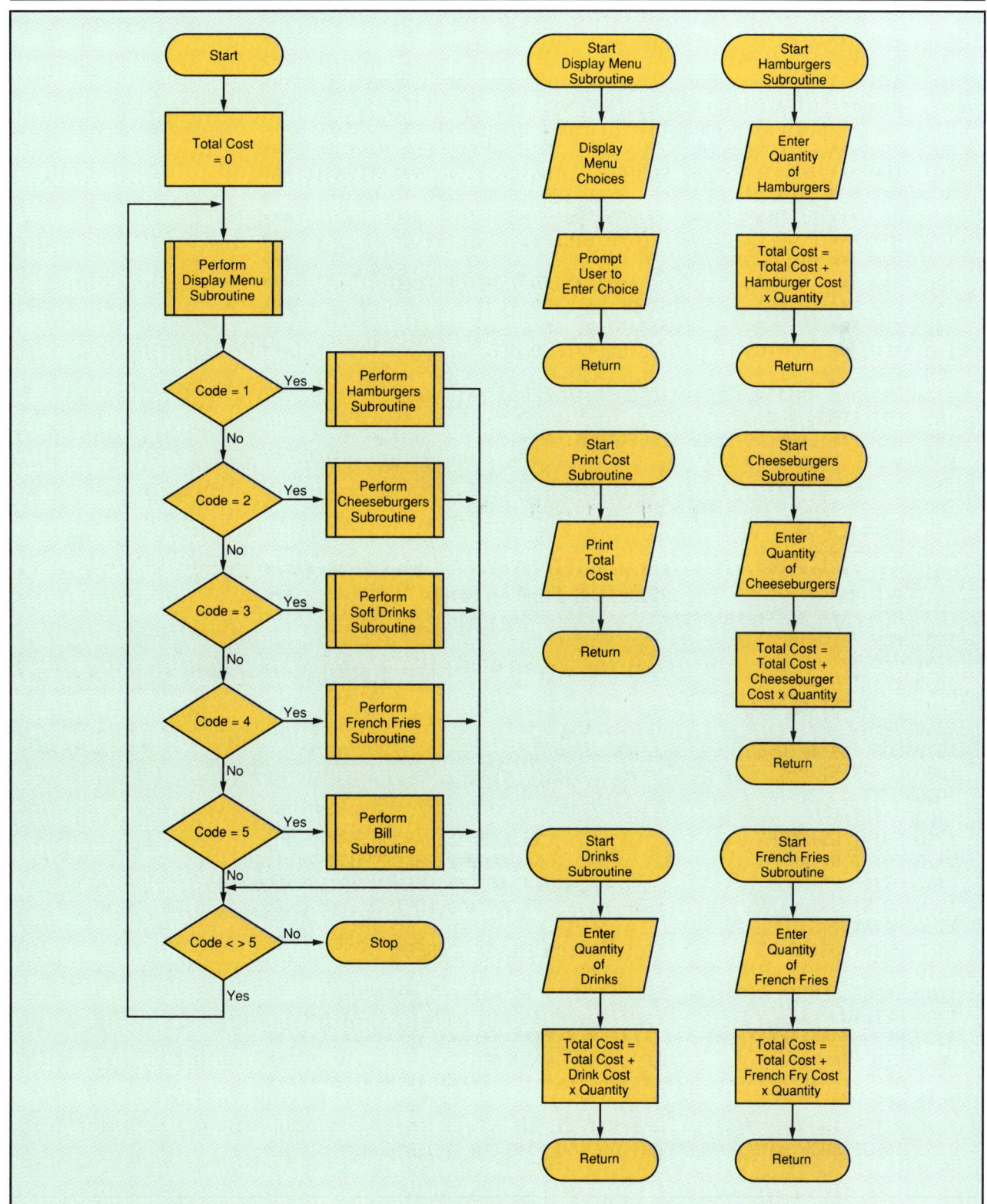

FIGURE 7–6 *Continued*

```
10   REM ***                PROGRAM MEAL COST                ***
20   REM ***                                                 ***
30   REM *** THIS PROGRAM CALCULATES THE COST OF A PURCHASE  ***
40   REM *** AT A FAST FOOD RESTAURANT. THE USER IS PROMPTED ***
50   REM *** TO ENTER AN INTEGER REPRESENTING THE ITEM TO BE ***
60   REM *** BE PURCHASED.  THE USER THEN ENTERS HOW MANY OF ***
70   REM *** THAT ITEM ARE DESIRED. THE COST OF THAT ITEM IS ***
80   REM *** THEN CALCULATED.  THE USER IS ALLOWED TO ORDER  ***
90   REM *** AS MANY ITEMS AS DESIRED.  WHEN THE ORDER IS    ***
100  REM *** COMPLETED, THE TOTAL BILL IS DISPLAYED.         ***
110  REM *** MAJOR VARIABLES:                                ***
120  REM ***     FOOD     CODE INDICATING TYPE OF FOOD       ***
130  REM ***     CST      COST OF AN ITEM                    ***
140  REM ***     NMBR     QUANTITY OF AN ITEM                ***
150  REM ***     TTCST    TOTAL COST OF ORDER                ***
160  REM
170  REM *** INITIALIZE TOTAL COST TO ZERO. ***
180  LET TTCST = 0
190  REM *** LOOP TO MAKE SELECTIONS. ***
200  WHILE FOOD <> 5
210     GOSUB 1000
220     ON FOOD GOSUB 2000,3000,4000,5000,6000
230  NEXT    wend
240  GOTO 9999    END
1000 REM ***************************************************
1010 REM ***             SUBROUTINE DISPLAY MENU           ***
1020 REM ***************************************************
1030 REM
1040 PRINT
1050 PRINT USING "\             \    \             \";"ITEM",
     "COST OF ITEM"
1060 PRINT
1070 FOR I = 1 TO 60
1080    PRINT "-";
1090 NEXT I
1100 PRINT
1110 PRINT USING "\             \    $#.##";"1 HAMBURGER",1.00
1120 PRINT USING "\             \    $#.##";"2 CHEESEBURGER",1.25
1130 PRINT USING "\             \    $#.##";"3 FRENCH FRIES",0.80
1140 PRINT USING "\             \    $#.##";"4 SOFT DRINK",0.75
1150 PRINT
1160 PRINT USING "\             \";"5 END OF ORDER"
1170 PRINT
1180 INPUT "ENTER CODE FOR FOOD ITEM (5 TO FINISH) ";FOOD
1190 RETURN
2000 REM ***************************************************
2010 REM ***             SUBROUTINE HAMBURGERS             ***
2020 REM ***************************************************
2030 REM
2040 CST = 1.00
2050 INPUT "HOW MANY HAMBURGERS DO YOU WANT TO ORDER";NMBR
```

FIGURE 7–6 *Continued*

```
2060 TTCST = TTCST + (CST * NMBR)
2070 RETURN
3000 REM ****************************************************************
3010 REM ***                   SUBROUTINE CHEESEBURGERS              ***
3020 REM ****************************************************************
3030 REM
3040 CST = 1.25
3050 INPUT "HOW MANY CHEESEBURGERS DO YOU WANT TO ORDER";NMBR
3060 TTCST = TTCST + (CST * NMBR)
3070 RETURN
4000 REM ****************************************************************
4010 REM ***                   SUBROUTINE FRENCH FRIES               ***
4020 REM ****************************************************************
4030 Rem
4040 CST = 0.80
4050 INPUT "HOW MANY FRENCH FRIES DO YOU WANT TO ORDER";NMBR
4060 TTCST = TTCST + (CST * NMBR)
4070 RETURN
5000 REM ****************************************************************
5010 REM ***                   SUBROUTINE DRINKS                     ***
5020 REM ****************************************************************
5030 REM
5040 CST = 0.75
5050 INPUT "HOW MANY SOFT DRINKS DO YOU WANT TO ORDER";NMBR
5060 TTCST = TTCST + (CST * NMBR)
5070 RETURN
6000 REM ****************************************************************
6010 REM ***                   SUBROUTINE BILL                       ***
6020 REM ****************************************************************
6030 PRINT
6040 PRINT USING "\                    \    $$###.##";
          "TOTAL AMOUNT DUE IS";TTCST
6050 RETURN
9999 END
```

```
RUNNH


ITEM                COST OF ITEM
_____

1 HAMBURGER         $1.00
2 CHEESEBURGER      $1.25
3 FRENCH FRIES      $0.80
4 SOFT DRINK        $0.75

5 END OF ORDER

ENTER CODE FOR FOOD ITEM (5 TO FINISH) ? 2
HOW MANY CHEESEBURGERS DO YOU WANT TO ORDER? 2
```

FIGURE 7–6 Continued

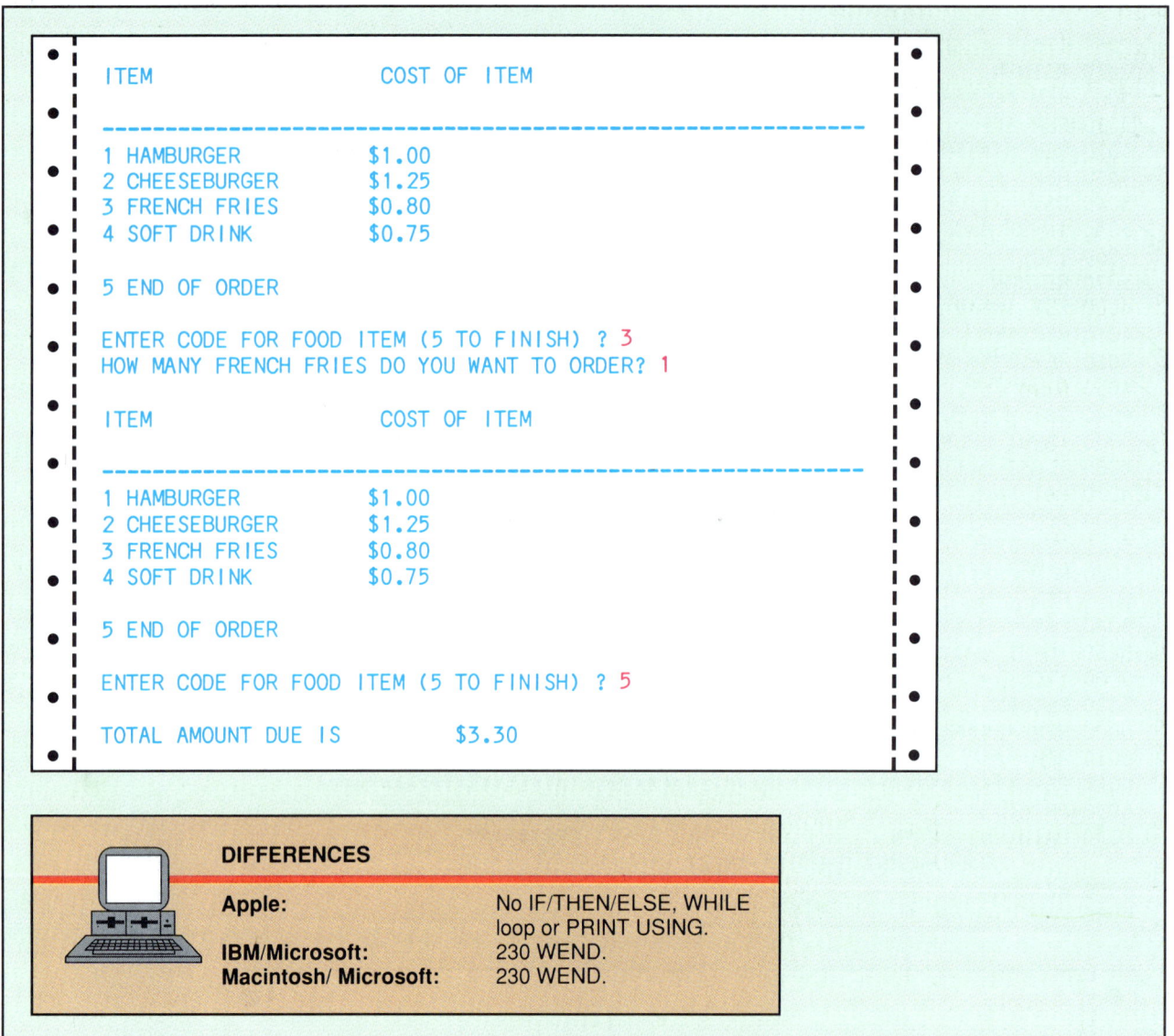

In programs that are not interactive, invalid data must be handled in a different manner. Suppose that the program in Figure 7–6 had been written using READ/DATA statements instead of INPUT statements. How could the programmer handle data outside the allowable range?

One method is to ignore the invalid data item and go on to the next item. An error message could be printed, stating that an invalid data item was encountered and ignored. Another method is to print an error message and stop program execution prematurely. For example, if the value 7 was entered in this example, a message such as INVALID VALUE ENTERED TO

FIGURE 7-7 Checking for Invalid Input

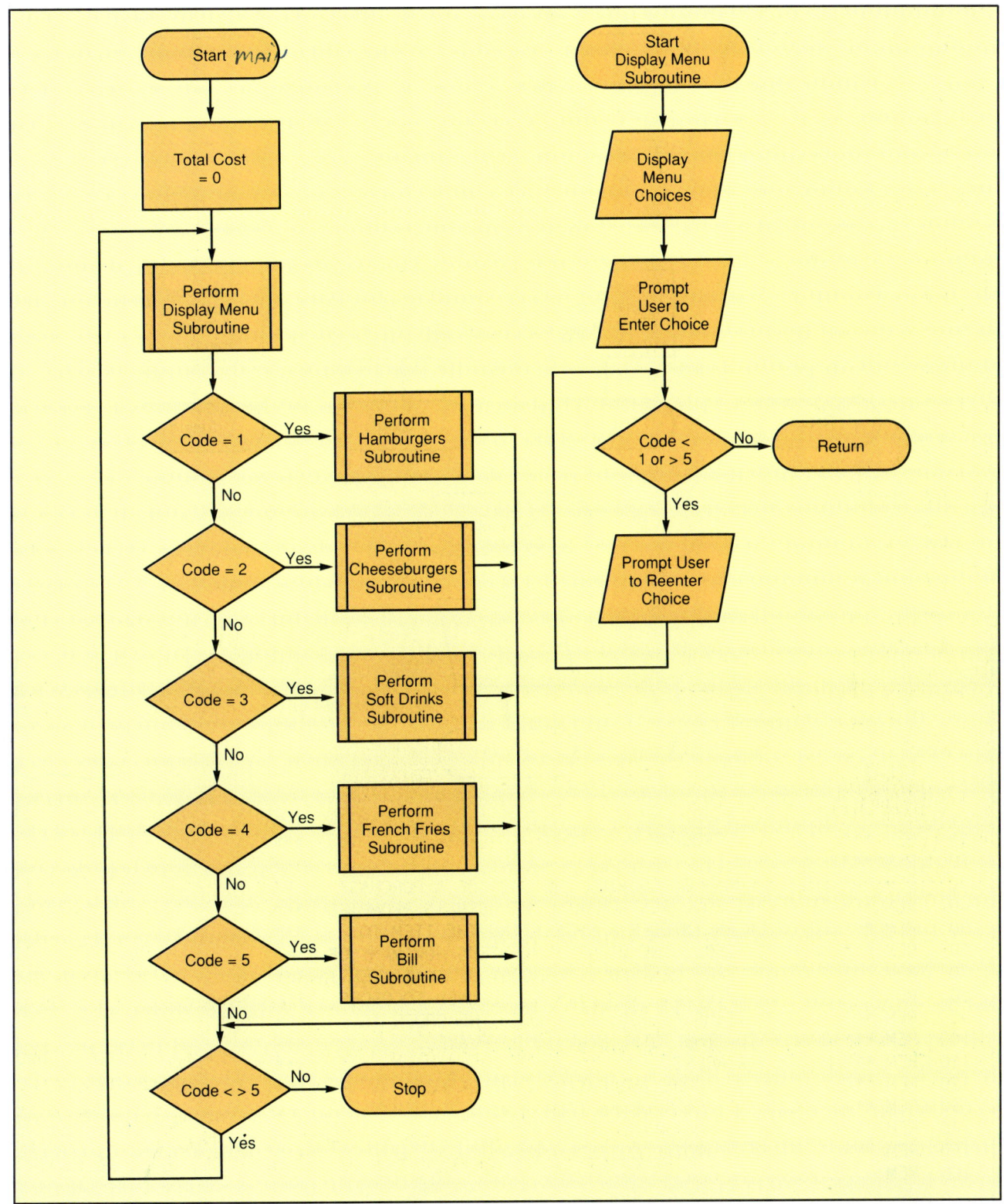

FIGURE 7–7 Continued

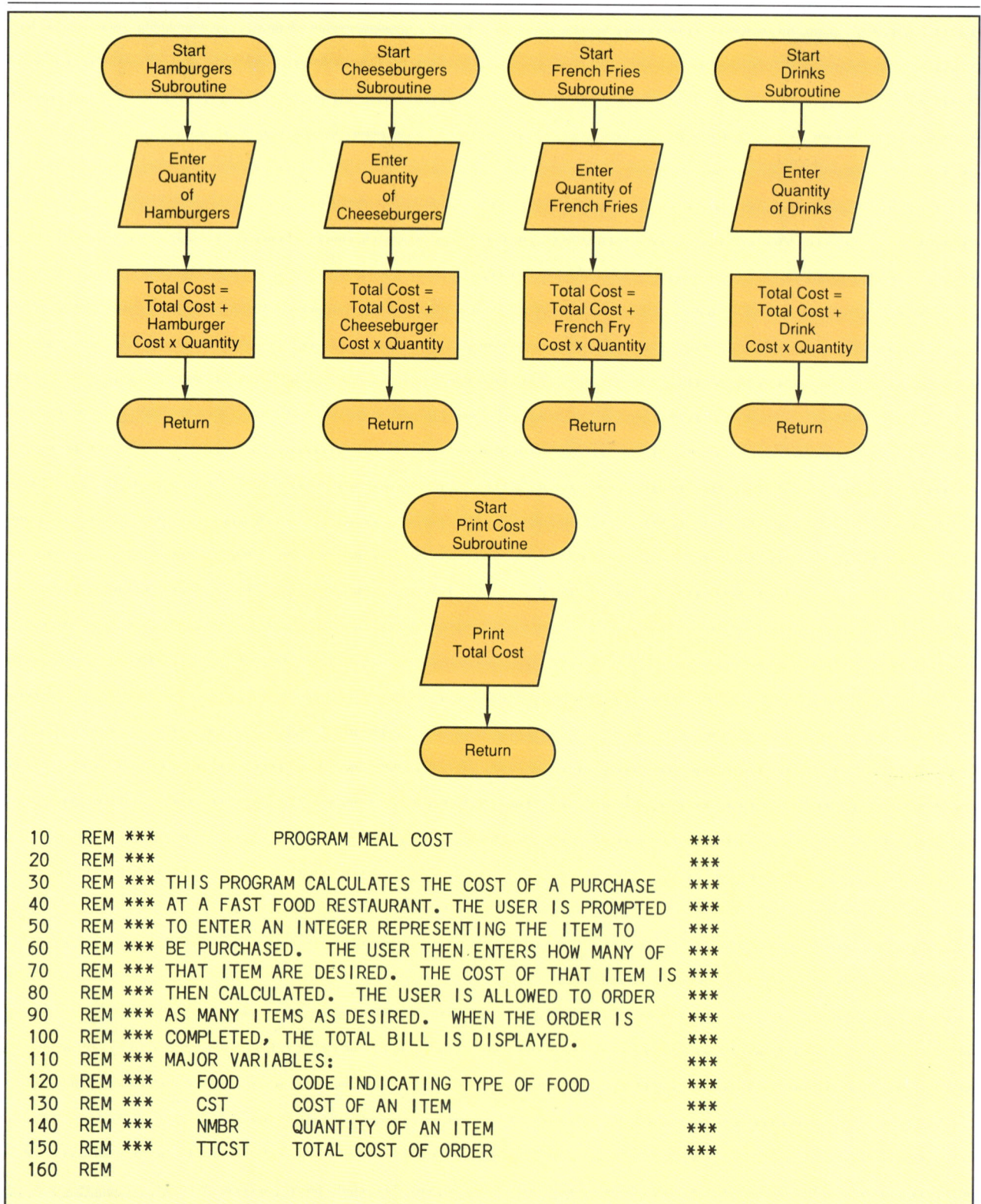

```
10    REM ***              PROGRAM MEAL COST                  ***
20    REM ***                                                 ***
30    REM *** THIS PROGRAM CALCULATES THE COST OF A PURCHASE  ***
40    REM *** AT A FAST FOOD RESTAURANT. THE USER IS PROMPTED ***
50    REM *** TO ENTER AN INTEGER REPRESENTING THE ITEM TO    ***
60    REM *** BE PURCHASED.  THE USER THEN ENTERS HOW MANY OF ***
70    REM *** THAT ITEM ARE DESIRED.  THE COST OF THAT ITEM IS***
80    REM *** THEN CALCULATED.  THE USER IS ALLOWED TO ORDER  ***
90    REM *** AS MANY ITEMS AS DESIRED.  WHEN THE ORDER IS    ***
100   REM *** COMPLETED, THE TOTAL BILL IS DISPLAYED.         ***
110   REM *** MAJOR VARIABLES:                                ***
120   REM ***     FOOD     CODE INDICATING TYPE OF FOOD       ***
130   REM ***     CST      COST OF AN ITEM                    ***
140   REM ***     NMBR     QUANTITY OF AN ITEM                ***
150   REM ***     TTCST    TOTAL COST OF ORDER                ***
160   REM
```

FIGURE 7–7 Continued

```
 170 REM *** INITIALIZE TOTAL COST TO ZERO. ***
 180 LET TTCST = 0
 190 REM *** LOOP TO MAKE SELECTIONS. ***
 200 WHILE FOOD <> 5
 210    GOSUB 1000
 220    ON FOOD GOSUB 2000,3000,4000,5000,6000
 230 NEXT
 240 GOTO 9999
1000 REM ************************************************************
1010 REM ***              SUBROUTINE DISPLAY MENU                 ***
1020 REM ************************************************************
1030 REM
1040 PRINT
1050 PRINT USING "\                \    \              \";"ITEM",
        "COST OF ITEM"
1060 PRINT
1070 FOR I = 1 TO 60
1080    PRINT "-";
1090 NEXT I
1100 PRINT
1110 PRINT USING "\             \     $#.##";"1 HAMBURGER",1.00
1120 PRINT USING "\             \     $#.##";"2 CHEESEBURGER",1.25
1130 PRINT USING "\             \     $#.##";"3 FRENCH FRIES",0.80
1140 PRINT USING "\             \     $#.##";"4 SOFT DRINK",0.75
1150 PRINT
1160 PRINT USING "\             \";"5 END OF ORDER"
1170 PRINT
1180 INPUT "ENTER CODE FOR FOOD ITEM (5 TO FINISH) ";FOOD
1190 WHILE FOOD < 1 OR FOOD > 5
1200    PRINT
1210    PRINT "CODE NUMBER MUST BE AN INTEGER"
1220    PRINT "BETWEEN 1 AND 5."
1230    INPUT "PLEASE REENTER CODE";FOOD
1240 NEXT
1250 RETURN
2000 REM ************************************************************
2010 REM ***                SUBROUTINE HAMBURGERS                 ***
2020 REM ************************************************************
2030 REM
2040 CST = 1.00
2050 INPUT "HOW MANY HAMBURGERS DO YOU WANT TO ORDER";NMBR
2060 TTCST = TTCST + (CST * NMBR)
2070 RETURN
3000 REM ************************************************************
3010 REM ***               SUBROUTINE CHEESEBURGERS               ***
3020 REM ************************************************************
3030 REM
3040 CST = 1.25
3050 INPUT "HOW MANY CHEESEBURGERS DO YOU WANT TO ORDER";NMBR
3060 TTCST = TTCST + (CST * NMBR)
3070 RETURN
```

FIGURE 7–7 Continued

```
4000 REM ***************************************************************
4010 REM ***             SUBROUTINE FRENCH FRIES                     ***
4020 REM ***************************************************************
4030
4040 CST = 0.80
4050 INPUT "HOW MANY FRENCH FRIES DO YOU WANT TO ORDER";NMBR
4060 TTCST = TTCST + (CST * NMBR)
4070 RETURN
5000 REM ***************************************************************
5010 REM ***                 SUBROUTINE DRINKS                       ***
5020 REM ***************************************************************
5030 REM
5040 CST = 0.75
5050 INPUT "HOW MANY SOFT DRINKS DO YOU WANT TO ORDER";NMBR
5060 TTCST = TTCST + (CST * NMBR)
5070 RETURN
6000 REM ***************************************************************
6010 REM ***                  SUBROUTINE BILL                        ***
6020 REM ***************************************************************
6030 PRINT
6040 PRINT USING "\                    \    $$###.##";
        "TOTAL AMOUNT DUE IS";TTCST
6050 RETURN
9999 END
```

```
RUNNH

ITEM                COST OF ITEM
--------------------------------------------------
1 HAMBURGER         $1.00
2 CHEESEBURGER      $1.25
3 FRENCH FRIES      $0.80
4 SOFT DRINK        $0.75

5 END OF ORDER

ENTER CODE FOR FOOD ITEM (5 TO FINISH) ? 2
HOW MANY CHEESEBURGERS DO YOU WANT TO ORDER? 2

ITEM                COST OF ITEM
--------------------------------------------------
1 HAMBURGER         $1.00
2 CHEESEBURGER      $1.25
3 FRENCH FRIES      $0.80
4 SOFT DRINK        $0.75

5 END OF ORDER
```

FIGURE 7-7 Continued

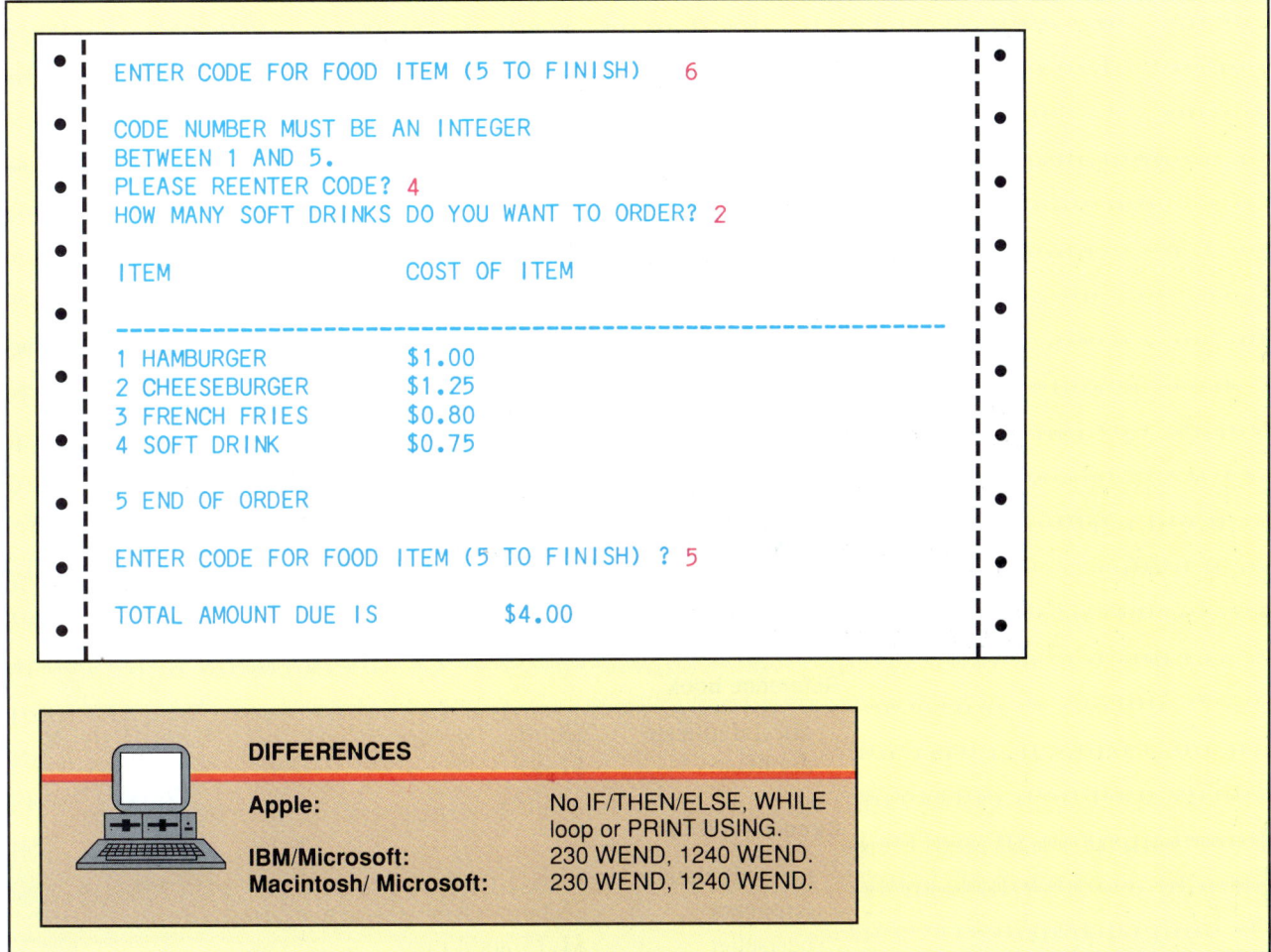

VARIABLE FOOD could be printed. Program execution could then be terminated by the STOP statement, which has the following format:

line# STOP

The STOP statement differs from the END statement in that STOP can appear as often as necessary in a program, whereas the END statement can appear only once. Also, on the VAX system, the END statement must have the highest line number, whereas the STOP statement can have any line number. When the STOP statement is executed, the computer prints a message similar to the following:

Break In 310

This type of error checking is a feature of any well-written program. From this point on, you should attempt to write programs that are protected as much as possible from invalid input.

A Programming Problem

Problem Definition

The public library needs a program to calculate the total cost of the books it adds to its collection. This cost includes not only the purchase price of the book but also the cost of processing the book. The program should be interactive, allowing the librarians to enter the data at the keyboard. The total book cost should then be printed on the terminal screen.

Processing costs are dependent upon two factors: (1) the type of book (reference, circulating, or paperback) and (2) whether or not the book is a duplicate of one already in the library. It is cheaper to process books that are duplicates of those already in the library's collection, because cards for these books are already in the card catalog and the cost of card production is saved. Processing costs are as follows:

Reference book

not a duplicate	$8.50
duplicate	$7.40

Circulating Book

not a duplicate	$7.82
duplicate	$6.60
bestseller	$1.75 additional

Paperback

not a duplicate	$4.60
duplicate	$3.10

The type of book should be entered using an integer code:

1—Reference
2—Circulating
3—Paperback

Note the additional $1.75 cost for processing circulating books that are also best-sellers. This cost is for a plastic cover to give the book extra protection. The necessary input and output for this program are shown in the following example:

Input:

Price	Type of Book	Duplicate	Bestseller
			(applies to code 2 only)
25.39	2	N	N

Needed Output:

TOTAL COST: $33.21

Solution Design

Each time this program is executed, it will calculate the total cost (purchase price plus processing cost) of one book. The program needs four input variables: one numeric variable for the price of the book, another numeric variable to represent the book code, a character string variable to store a Y if the book is a duplicate and an N if it is not, and, if the book code entered is a 2, a character string variable to indicate whether the book is a bestseller. The output variable will be a numeric variable containing the total cost. The needed variables are summarized in the following table:

Input Variables
price of book	(PRICE)
code for type of book	(CODE)
duplicate indicator	(DUP$)
bestseller indicator	(SELLER$)

Program Variables
processing cost	(PRCST)

Output Variables
total cost	(TTCST)

Three basic steps are necessary to determine the total book costs:

1. Enter the data for the book.
2. Calculate the correct processing cost.
3. Determine the total cost.

The stepwise refinement and structure chart for this program are shown in Figures 7–8 and 7–9 respectively.

Step 1 can be divided into three substeps that ask the user to enter the price of the book, the code for the type of book, and the duplicate indicator. This step should also include checking to make certain that the values entered for the book code and the duplicate indicator are valid. If an invalid value has been entered, the user should be prompted to reenter that value. Since each of these substeps is relatively simple, we will include them all in a single subroutine when we write the program.

FIGURE 7–8
Stepwise Refinement of Book Processing Cost Problem

General Problem: Calculate total cost of book to library.

Level 1
  A. Enter data for the book.
  B. Calculate the processing cost.
  C. Determine total cost.

Level 2
  A.1. Enter the price of the book.
  A.2. Enter the code for the type of book.
  A.3. Enter the duplicate indicator.
  C.1. Add processing cost to book price.
  C.2. Print the total cost.

FIGURE 7–9 Structure Chart for Book Processing Cost Problem

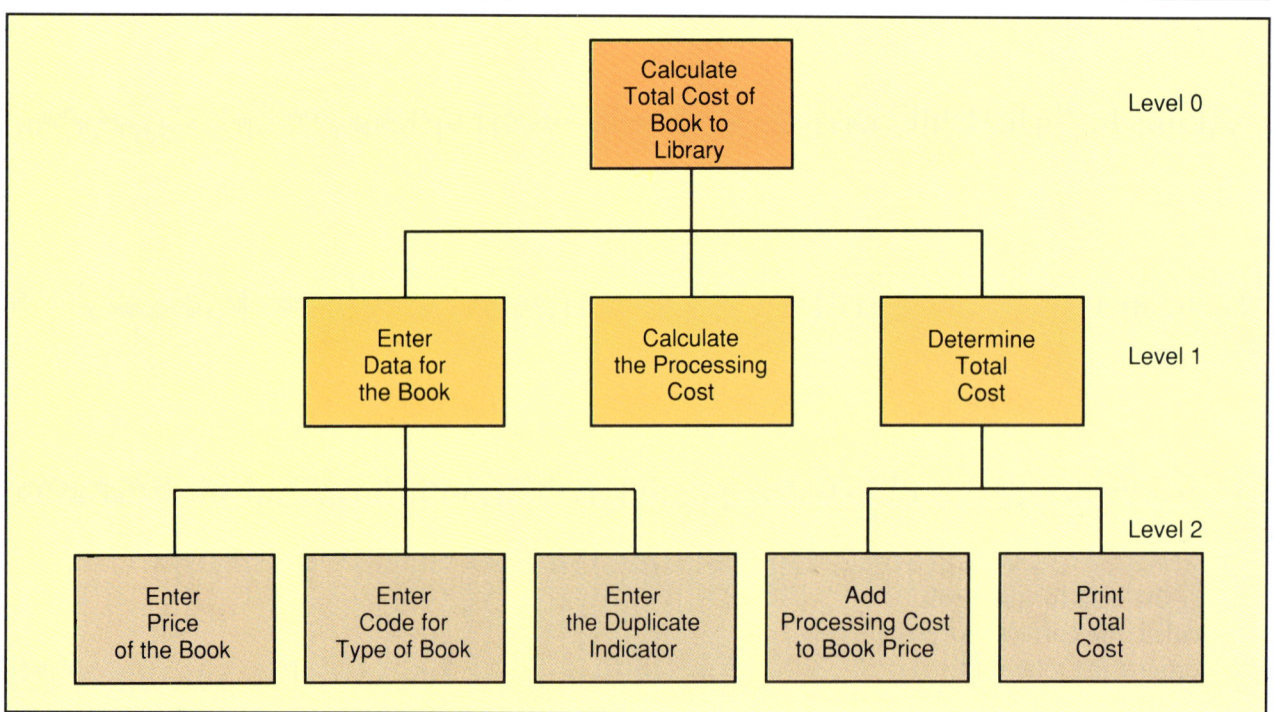

Step 2 is the most difficult part of this problem. It involves performing one of three options, depending on whether a reference, circulating, or paperback book is being processed. Because only one of these options will be executed, this is an ideal solution for a conditional branch to one of three subroutines, each of which will calculate the cost for a particular type of book. The book-type code can be used as the controlling expression in an ON/GOSUB statement to transfer program control from the main program to the appropriate subroutine.

Step 3 involves adding the processing cost to the purchase price of the book and printing this total.

The Program

Study the complete program as shown in Figure 7–10. Note that the main body of the program is a driver program and is therefore quite short.

The first subroutine enables the user to enter the necessary data. This subroutine contains two WHILE loops that check for invalid data. The first loop (lines 1150–1180) allows the user to reenter the value of the type code if an invalid code has been entered. The second loop (lines 1220–1250) makes certain that the user has entered either a Y or an N as the duplicate book indicator. If a different value has been entered, the user is asked to reenter the data.

The value entered for the book type code must be a 1, 2, or 3. This value is then used in the ON/GOSUB statement in line 310 to determine which one of the three subroutines will be executed. Each of the subroutines calculates the processing cost for one type of book. The circulating book subroutine is a little more complicated than the other two, because it must ask the user if the book is a bestseller and include an additional charge if it is. After the processing cost of the book has been determined, control returns to the main program, where the final subroutine is called to add the processing cost to the purchase price and print the total cost.

FIGURE 7–10 Book Processing Cost Program

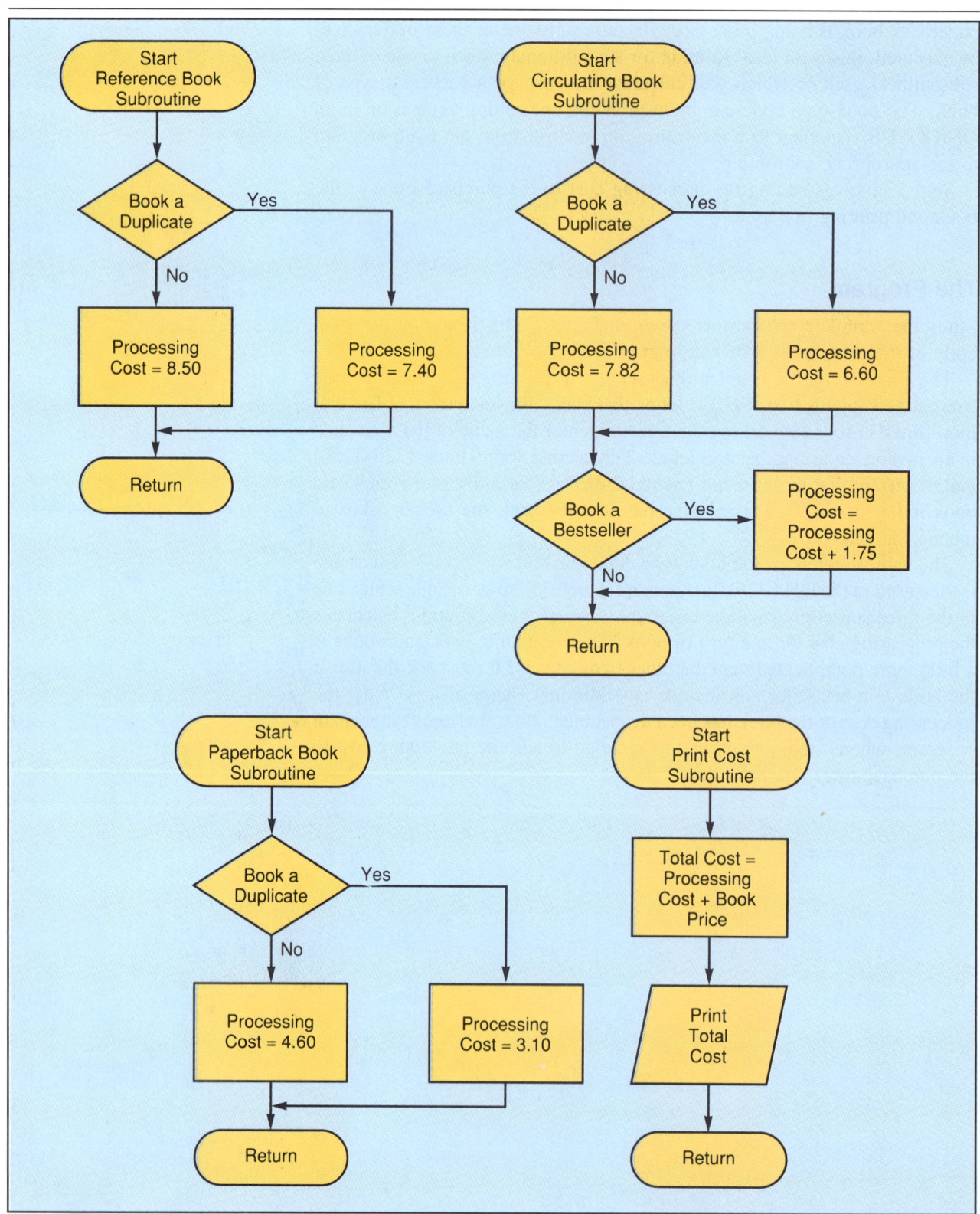

FIGURE 7–10 *Continued*

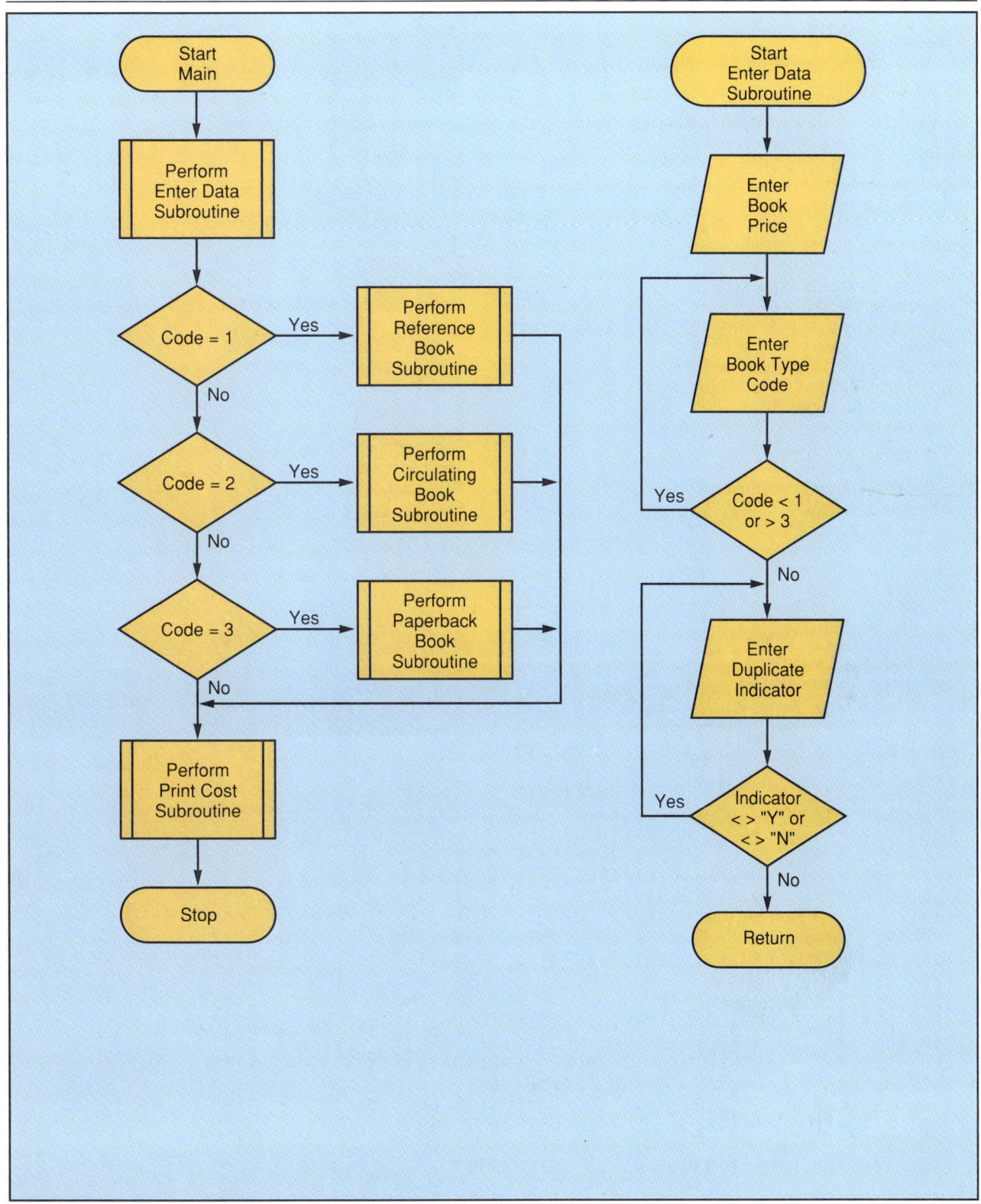

FIGURE 7–10 Continued

Pseudocode

Begin main program
Perform enter data subroutine
If type code = 1 perform reference book subroutine
If type code = 2 perform circulating book subroutine
If type code = 3 perform paperback book subroutine
Perform print cost subroutine
End main program

Begin enter data subroutine
Prompt user to enter price
Prompt user to enter type code
Begin loop, do until code >= 1 and <= 3
   Prompt user to reenter type code
End loop
Prompt user to enter duplicate indicator
Begin loop, do until indicator is equal to "Y" or "N"
   Prompt user to reenter duplicate code
End loop
End enter data subroutine

Begin reference book subroutine
If book is duplicate
   Then processing cost = 7.40
   Else processing cost = 8.50
End if
End reference book subroutine

Begin circulating book subroutine
If book is duplicate
   Then processing cost = 6.60
   Else processing cost = 7.82
End if
Prompt user to enter bestseller indicator
If book is a bestseller
   Then add 1.75 to processing cost
End if
End circulating book subroutine

Begin paperback book subroutine
If book is duplicate
   Then processing cost = 3.10
   Else processing cost = 4.60
End if
End paperback subroutine

Begin print cost subroutine
Total cost = processing cost + book price
Print total cost
End print cost subroutine

```
10   REM ***                    PROGRAM BOOKCOST                  ***
20   REM
30   REM *** THIS PROGRAM CALCULATES THE TOTAL COST OF A           ***
40   REM *** BOOK.  THE TOTAL COST IS OBTAINED BY ADDING           ***
50   REM *** THE PRICE OF THE BOOK TO THE PROCESSING COST,         ***
60   REM *** WHICH IS BASED ON THE TYPE.                           ***
70   REM ***     1.  REFERENCE BOOK                                ***
80   REM ***            NOT A DUPLICATE     $8.50                  ***
90   REM ***            DUPLICATE           $7.40                  ***
100  REM ***     2.  CIRCULATING BOOK                              ***
110  REM ***            NOT A DUPLICATE     $7.82                  ***
120  REM ***            DUPLICATE           $6.60                  ***
130  REM ***            BESTSELLER          $1.75                  ***
140  REM ***     3.  PAPERBACK                                     ***
150  REM ***            NOT A DUPLICATE     $4.60                  ***
160  REM ***            DUPLICATE           $3.10                  ***
170  REM
180  REM *** MAJOR VARIABLES:                                      ***
190  REM ***     PRICE     PRICE OF THE BOOK                       ***
200  REM ***     CODE      TYPE OF BOOK AS ABOVE                   ***
210  REM ***     DUP$      IS BOOK A DUPLICATE(Y/N)?               ***
220  REM ***     PRCST     PROCESSING COST                         ***
230  REM ***     SELLER$   IS BOOK A BESTSELLER (Y/N)?             ***
240  REM ***     TTCST     TOTAL COST OF BOOK                      ***
250  REM
260  REM *** CALL SUBROUTINE TO ENTER DATA.                        ***
```

FIGURE 7–10 Continued

```
270   GOSUB 1000
280   REM
290   REM *** CALL APPROPRIATE SUBROUTINE TO CALCULATE       ***
300   REM *** THE PROCESSING COST.                           ***
310   ON CODE GOSUB 2000,3000,4000
320   REM
330   REM *** CALL SUBROUTINE TO ADD PROCESSING COST TO      ***
340   REM *** BOOK PRICE AND PRINT TOTAL COST.               ***
350   GOSUB 5000
360   GOTO 9999   END
1000  REM
1010  REM ************************************************************
1020  REM ***                 SUBROUTINE ENTER DATA                ***
1030  REM ************************************************************
1040  REM *** SUBROUTINE TO ALLOW USER TO ENTER DATA.              ***
1050  REM
1060    INPUT "ENTER PRICE OF THE BOOK";PRICE
1070  PRINT
1080  PRINT
1090  PRINT
1100  PRINT "1 - REFERENCE BOOK"
1110  PRINT "2 - CIRCULATING BOOK"
1120  PRINT "3 - PAPERBACK"
1130  INPUT "ENTER TYPE CODE FOR THE BOOK, USING THE CODE LISTED ABOVE";CODE
1140  REM
1150  REM *** LOOP TO ALLOW INVALID CODE TO BE REENTERED. ***
1160  WHILE CODE < 1 OR CODE > 3
1170     INPUT "TYPE CODE MUST BE A 1, 2, OR 3.  PLEASE REENTER CODE";CODE
1180  NEXT  wend
1190  PRINT
1200  INPUT "IS BOOK A DUPLICATE (Y/N)";DUP$
1210  REM
1220  REM *** LOOP TO ALLOW INVALID DUPLICATE INDICATOR TO BE REENTERED. ***
1230  WHILE DUP$ <> "Y" AND DUP$ <> "N"
1240     INPUT "IS BOOK A DUPLICATE?  PLEASE ENTER A 'Y' OR AN 'N'";DUP$
1250  NEXT  wend
1260  RETURN
2000  REM
2010  REM ************************************************************
2020  REM ***              SUBROUTINE REFERENCE BOOK               ***
2030  REM ************************************************************
2040  REM *** SUBROUTINE TO CALCULATE PROCESSING COST OF           ***
2050  REM *** REFERENCE BOOK.                                      ***
2060  REM
2070  IF DUP$ = "Y" THEN PRCST = 7.40 ELSE PRCST = 8.50
2080  RETURN
3000  REM
3010  REM ************************************************************
3020  REM ***             SUBROUTINE CIRCULATING BOOK              ***
3030  REM ************************************************************
3040  REM *** SUBROUTINE TO CALCULATE PROCESSING COST OF           ***
3050  REM *** CIRCULATING BOOK.                                    ***
3060  REM
3070  IF DUP$ = "Y" THEN PRCST = 6.60 ELSE PRCST = 7.82
3080  INPUT "IS THE BOOK A BESTSELLER (Y/N)";SELLER$
```

FIGURE 7–10 *Continued*

```
3090 IF SELLER$ = "Y" THEN PRCST = PRCST + 1.75
3100 RETURN
4000 REM
4010 REM **************************************************************
4020 REM ***              SUBROUTINE PAPERBACK BOOK                 ***
4030 REM **************************************************************
4040 REM *** SUBROUTINE TO CALCULATE PROCESSING COST OF             ***
4050 REM *** PAPERBACK BOOK.                                        ***
4060 REM
4070 IF DUP$ = "Y" THEN PRCST = 3.10 ELSE PRCST = 4.60
4080 RETURN
5000 REM
5010 REM **************************************************************
5020 REM ***                 SUBROUTINE PRINT COST                  ***
5030 REM **************************************************************
5040 REM *** SUBROUTINE TO CALCULATE AND PRINT TOTAL COST.          ***
5050 REM
5060 TTCST = PRCST + PRICE
5070 PRINT
5080 PRINT USING "\                        \        $$###.##";
                 "***     TOTAL COST:",TTCST
5090 RETURN
9999 END
```

```
RUNNH

ENTER PRICE OF THE BOOK? 25.39


1 - REFERENCE BOOK
2 - CIRCULATING BOOK
3 - PAPERBACK
ENTER TYPE CODE FOR THE BOOK, USING THE CODE LISTED ABOVE? 2

IS BOOK A DUPLICATE (Y/N)? J
IS BOOK A DUPLICATE?  PLEASE ENTER A 'Y' OR AN 'N'? N
IS THE BOOK A BESTSELLER (Y/N)? N

***     TOTAL COST:           $33.21
```

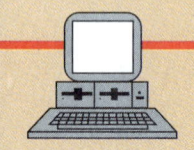

DIFFERENCES

Apple:	No IF/THEN/ELSE, WHILE loop or PRINT USING.
IBM/Microsoft:	1180 WEND, 1250 WEND.
Macintosh/Microsoft:	1180 WEND, 1250 WEND.

Avoiding Common Programming Mistakes

- When branching to a subroutine, be careful that program control is being transferred to the correct line number. A common programming error is to place incorrect line numbers in GOSUB and ON/GOSUB statements. This error can lead to unpredictable behavior when the program is executed.
- When using the ON/GOSUB statement, make certain that the numerical expression will evaluate as expected. Find out whether your system willtruncate or round this value, as this process will affect how you write the ON/GOSUB expression.
- All subroutines must have a single exit point and a single entry point. This rule is fundamental to good structured programming. The last line of a subroutine should always be the RETURN statement.
- In interactive programs, data entered by the user should be checked for its validity. If invalid data is entered, the program should allow the user to reenter the data. Programs that are not interactive can print an error message when invalid data is encountered.

Summary Points

- Modularizing programs involves dividing them into subprograms, each of which performs a specific task. In BASIC, these subprograms or modules are referred to as *subroutines*.
- The use of subroutines makes program logic easier to follow. Also, a given subroutine can be called any number of times.
- Two BASIC statements can be used to call subroutines: GOSUB and ON/GOSUB.
- The GOSUB statement is an unconditional branch that causes the flow of execution to be passed to the line number contained in the GOSUB statement.
- The RETURN statement causes control to be transferred back to the statement after the one that called the subroutine.
- The ON/GOSUB statement allows for a conditional branch to one of several stated subroutines, depending on the evaluation of the expression in the ON/GOSUB statement. If the value of the expression is n, control passes to the subroutine starting at the nth line number listed.
- An important role in structured programming is that all subroutines should have a single entry point and a single exit point. Otherwise, the possibility of an error in the program is greatly increased. Also, entering or exiting from the middle of a subroutine makes the logic of the program convoluted and difficult to follow.
- Menus often use the ON/GOSUB statement, which provides a simple way for the program to branch to the correct subroutine depending on the code number entered by the user.

- Stubs allow a program to be developed in a methodical fashion. Rather than entering a program to the computer all at once, the programmer can add and test subroutines gradually. Once the parts already entered work properly, more of the program can be entered. This procedure makes it easier to locate program errors.
- All programs should check for invalid data and print an error message if any is found. In interactive programs, the user can be prompted to reenter the data.

Review Questions

1. Name two advantages of modularizing programs.
2. How can a structure chart help in modularizing a program?
3. Why doesn't the RETURN statement contain a transfer line number? That is, how is it possible that program control can be transferred back to the correct statement even though no transfer line number is specified in the RETURN statement?
4. Where are RETURN statements placed in programs?
5. Why is the GOSUB statement referred to as an unconditional branching statement?
6. What happens if the transfer line number in a GOSUB statement is a nonexecutable statement?
7. Why is it important that a subroutine have only one entry point and one exit point?
8. Explain how the ON/GOSUB statement works. How is it different from the GOSUB statement?
9. Where will program control be transferred if the following statements are executed?

    260 X = 4 + 23
    270 N = X / 8 + 1
    280 ON N GOSUB 1000,2000,3000,4000

10. Rewrite the following program segment using a single ON/GOSUB statement.

    350 IF X = 1 THEN GOSUB 2000
    360 IF X = 2 THEN GOSUB 3000
    370 IF X = 3 THEN GOSUB 4000

11. How is the ON/GOSUB statement useful in writing programs with menus?
12. What is a driver program?
13. What is a stub?
14. How can stubs be used when entering programs to the computer?
15. Explain the format of the statement used to call a subroutine.

16. Write a program segment that will prompt the user to enter a letter of the alphabet. If the user does not enter a letter, he or she should be prompted again.

17. Explain how the STOP statement works.

18. In interactive programs, what should the program do if an invalid value has been entered?

19. What subroutine will be executed for each of the values of TTL given in parts a through c.

    410 ON TTL/2 GOSUB 2000,3000,5000,7000

    a. LET TTL = 8 / 2
    b. LET TTL = 4 + 2
    c. LET TTL = 4 * 2

20. Give an example of a situation in which a programmer might need to write a program that checks for invalid data.

Debugging Exercises

Identify the following programs and program segments that contain errors and debug them.

1.
```
90   REM *** EXECUTE APPROPRIATE SUBROUTINE ***
100  REM *** DEPENDING ON GRADE.             ***
110  INPUT "ENTER THE STUDENT'S GRADE";GD$
120  ON GD$ GOSUB 2000,3000,4000,5000
```

2.
```
250  X = 14
260  Y = 7
270  Z = (X + Y) / 20
280  ON Z GOSUB 1000,2000,3000
```

3.
```
40  REM *** EXECUTE APPROPRIATE SUBROUTINE    ***
50  REM *** DEPENDING ON CURRENT VALUE OF I.  ***
60  FOR I = 1 TO 6
70      ON I GOSUB 2000,3000,4000,5000
80  NEXT I
```

4.
```
10    REM *** EXECUTE SUBROUTINE TO DETERMINE ***
20    REM *** TOTAL QUANTITY.                 ***
30    GOSUB 1000
40    PRINT X
         .
         .
         .
1000  REM ***    SUBROUTINE    ***
1010  REM
1020  X = 12 * 77
9999  END
```

5. ```
   20 REM *** EXECUTE APPROPRIATE SUBROUTINE ***
   30 REM *** DEPENDING ON VALUE OF X.         ***
   40 X = 14 - T
   50 IF X <= 4 ON GOSUB 1000,2000,3000,4000
   ```

6. ```
   20 REM *** PRINT CORRECT VALUE. ***
   30 IF (X > 10) AND (Y + X) THEN PRINT X
         ELSE PRINT Y
   ```

7. ```
   40 REM *** READ INVENTORY. ***
   50 WHILE (ITEM <> X) AND (X > 0)
   60    READ ITEM,STK
   70    IF (STK > 0) NOT (STK < 10) THEN PRINT "OK"
   80 NEXT
   ```

8. ```
   100 REM *** PRINT AN EMPLOYEE'S NAME IF   ***
   110 REM *** AGE > 40 AND SALARY > 28000.  ***
   120 INPUT "ENTER NAME, AGE, AND SALARY";
           EMP$,AGE,SALARY
   130 IF (AGE > 40) OR (SALARY > 28000)
           THEN PRINT EMP$
   ```

9. ```
   90    REM *** IF SIZE IS SMALL, INCREMENT ***
   100   REM *** APPROPRIATE COUNTER.        ***
   110   IF SIZE < 45 THEN GOSUB 1030
            .
            .
            .
   1000 REM *** THIS PACKAGE IS A SMALL SIZE. ***
   1010 REM
   1020 SMALL = SMALL + 1
   1030 PRINT "THIS PACKAGE IS A SMALL SIZE"
   1040 RETURN
   ```

10. ```
    10 REM *** PROMPT USER TO ENTER VALID INTEGER ***
    20 REM *** REPRESENTING A MONTH OF THE YEAR.  ***
    30 INPUT "ENTER THE INTEGER VALUE OF THE MONTH";
          MNTH
    40 WHILE (MNTH > 1) OR (MNTH > 12)
    50    PRINT "PLEASE ENTER THE INTEGER"
    60    PRINT "BETWEEN 1 AND 12 THAT"
    70    INPUT "REPRESENTS THE MONTH";MNTH
    80 NEXT
    90 PRINT MNTH
    ```

Additional Programming Problems

Level 1

1. Assume that a numeric variable named AMT can contain the value 1, 2, or 3. Write a program segment that asks the user to enter a value to AMT. The program should then call one of three subroutines, depending on the value of AMT. If the value of AMT is 1, the subroutine starting at line 1000 should be executed. If the value of AMT is 2, the subroutine starting at line 2000 should be executed. If the value of AMT is 3, the subroutine starting at line 3000 should be executed.

2. Rewrite problem 1, this time checking that the value entered for AMT is valid. If a value other than 1, 2, or 3 is entered, prompt the user to reenter the value.

3. Assume that the numeric value of a variable named DIST can be 200, 400, or 600. Write an ON/GOSUB statement that will cause program control to transfer to the subroutine starting at line 2000 if DIST is 200, to line 3000 if DIST is 400, and to line 4000 if DIST is 600.

4. Write a program segment to accomplish the same task as in problem 3, but this time use IF/THEN and GOSUB statements to do the job.

5. Write a subroutine to find the surface area and volume of a cube.

6. Write a subroutine to convert a person's weight from pounds to kilograms.

7. Look at the program in Figure 7–2. Add a series of statements that will protect this program if the user enters an invalid value for the variable YR. Use a prompt to allow the user to reenter this value.

8. Write a program that determines the unit price (cents per ounce) of different boxes of laundry detergent. The input should include the weight in pounds and ounces and the total price. The output should state the price per ounce.

9. Write a subroutine to calculate the area of a triangle.

10. Write a program that will allow Coach Kramer to determine if a student is a likely candidate for his football team. According to Coach Kramer, students who are likely candidates should be male, at least 5' 10" tall, and have a grade point average of at least 2.5. The program should use logical operators to determine if a student is a likely candidate and then print an appropriate message.

Level 2

1. Think of a song you know that contains a refrain. Write a program that will print the words to this song. Use a different subroutine for each of the verses and a subroutine for the refrain. Then, after each verse is printed, call the refrain subroutine to print the refrain.

2. Rewrite the program for problem 1 of Level 3 in Chapter 6, using at least two subroutines.

3. In the streams of Montana there are four types of trout. For each type, a daily limit has been designated.

Type	Limit
Brookie	8
Brown	4
Rainbow	6
Cutthroat	4

Using the ON/GOSUB statement, write a program to allow program execution to branch to a subroutine that will print the limit for each type of trout entered by the user.

4. Write a program that will tell a bicyclist how long it will take to travel a given distance under certain weather conditions. The bicyclist is able to travel at the following rates:

Weather	Speed
EXCELLENT	—25 miles an hour
GOOD	—18 miles an hour
POOR	—14 miles an hour

The program should be written so that the user enters the current weather conditions (EXCELLENT, GOOD, or POOR) and the number of miles to be traveled. The program should use subroutines to determine the approximate time needed to complete the trip. This time should then be printed with an appropriate label.

5. Urbank's Well Drilling Company drills water and oil wells for businesses and individuals. A water well costs $15 a foot to drill. An oil well costs $20 a foot to drill for the first 10,000 feet; below that, it costs $35 a foot. Write a subroutine that calculates the cost of drilling a given well.

6. Write a program that will print the number of days in a given month. The user should enter the name of the month, and the program should call a subroutine to print the correct number of days in that month.

7. The Interior Furniture Company wants you to write a program that will help them color-coordinate furniture with room color for their customers. Three main colors can be used as room colors: blue, yellow, and tan. The program should allow the user to enter the room color and should then print appropriate color schemes for that room. This output will enable the customer to choose appropriate room furnishings. The following coordinating colors should be printed, depending on the room color entered:

Room Color	Coordinating Colors
Blue	Soft Peach, Sunshine Yellow, Passionate Purple, Creamy Biege
Yellow	Halo Blue, Soft Peach, Spring Green, Burnt Orange
Tan	Amber Brown, Crimson, Soft Peach, Sierra Blue

8. Being a working person, you want a program to help you plan meals. This program should allow you to select one of several main entrees and then print the appropriate side dishes. Use the following data or develop your own.

Main Entree	Side Dishes
Pork Chops	Mashed potatoes, peas, baked apples
Chicken	Baked potatoes, stuffing, applesauce, green beans
Hamburgers	Potato salad, french fries, pickles, fruit salad
Lasagna	Tossed salad, Jell-O, garlic bread

9. Program 8 was designed to help you decide what to serve for dinner. Now write a program that will make a grocery list for the chosen dinner. The menu should display the four main dinner entrees, enable you to select one, and print the grocery items and supplies that you will need to purchase. Use the following data or develop your own.

Main Entree	Ingredients and Supplies for Meal
Pork chops	Pork chops, potatoes, flour, peas, apples, salt, pepper, butter, milk, cinnamon sugar
Chicken	Chicken, potatoes, stuffing mix, applesauce, green beans, aluminum foil, salt, pepper
Hamburgers	Ground beef, potato salad, frozen french fries, pickles, apples, bananas, oranges
Lasagna	Lasagna noodles, hamburger, tomato sauce, cheese, lettuce, carrots, cucumbers, salad dressing, garlic bread, Jell-O, fruit

10. Write a program that acts as a computerized address book. When the user selects a person's name, the program should print that person's address, phone number, and birthdate. The name should be chosen from a menu of five to ten names. The program should then branch to a subroutine to print the address, phone number, and birthdate. Develop your own data for the program.

Level 3

1. Fun Rental provides clowns for parties, seasonal celebrations, and other special occasions. The basic fee is $45.00 for the first hour and $25.99 for every additional hour. The company needs a program to help calculate its clients' bills. The program should call a subroutine to do the actual calculating, and use a loop to allow as many bills to be calculated as desired.

2. Write a program that will allow the user to enter a request to add, subtract, multiply, or divide two numbers. The operations should be listed in a menu. After the operation is chosen, the program should ask for two numbers. Then it should use a subroutine to perform the computation and print the result.

3. Busbee's Department Store wants a computer program that will help its customers in selecting appropriate gifts. A menu should be printed to allow the user to select the type of person the gift is for. Then an appropriate listing of gifts should be printed. Use the following data:

Person	Gift Suggestions
Man	Wallet, socks, fishing equipment, bathrobe, watch, shirt
Woman	Key chain, purse, golf clubs, slippers, stationery, nightgown
Boy	Records, board game, sporting equipment, pajamas, books
Girl	Board game, records, books, sporting equipment, sweats, bicycle

After the user has read a list of gift ideas, he or she should be able to press any key in order to return to the main menu. In this way, the program will be ready for another customer to make a selection.

4. Double D Travel Agency wants a program that displays a menu with a list of cities to which it has charter flights. After the user enters the name of a particular city, the program should print all flights and their times to and from that city. Use the following data:

City	Flight Leaves	Flight Returns
San Francisco, California	May 10, 8:30 a.m.	May 20, 9:10 p.m.
	June 2, 4:15 p.m.	June 12, 3:00 p.m.
	Dec. 20, 3:00 p.m.	Dec. 28, 10:45 p.m.
Houston, Texas	Jan. 5, 10:00 p.m.	Jan. 15, 8:00 p.m.
	March 10, 11:45 a.m.	March 17, 11:45 a.m.
	Aug. 25, 3:35 p.m.	Sept. 3, 8:30 p.m.
Denver, Colorado	Jan. 3, 6:30 a.m.	Jan. 10, 8:40 p.m.
	Sept. 5, 2:45 p.m.	Sept. 14, 10:45 p.m.
	Nov. 12, 10:00 a.m.	Nov. 20, 9:00 a.m.
New York, New York	May 1, 12:35 p.m.	May 16, 8:00 p.m.
	June 28, 1:00 p.m.	July 15, 1:30 a.m.
	Oct. 12, 10:15 a.m.	Oct. 26, 12:30 p.m.

5. The Birds Airways wants a program to determine the flight cost for passengers to various cities. The cost per person for the following cities is

Columbus	$ 39.00
Denver	142.00
New York	108.00
New Orleans	158.00

A menu should display the names of the cities and ask how many people would like to purchase tickets. If the customers want first-class tickets, there is an additional $30 flat fee. The cost of the needed tickets should be calculated in subroutines. Develop your own data to test the program.

6. Shangri-La Realty needs a program to assist its agents in keeping track of the various apartments available for rent. Write a program using subroutines that will give the user a choice of a studio, one-bedroom, or two-bedroom apartment. The monthly rent depends on the size of the apartment and whether it is to be furnished or unfurnished (this data should also be entered by the user). Use the following data:

Type	Deposit	Rent Furnished	Rent Unfurnished
Studio	$ 75	$150	$135
One-bedroom	150	275	250
Two-bedroom	200	325	315

The program should print the apartment description, required deposit, and monthly rent according to the choices entered, using the following format:

```
Description  :   One-bedroom furnished
    Deposit  :   $150
       Rent  :   $275
```

7. Mr. Cray's sixth-grade class of twelve students has been assigned group research projects, with four students per group. Write a program that prints a report for each group, listing the name and score of each member plus the group average. Use one subroutine to print the report heading and another to print the group average. The format of your output should be similar to the following:

```
      TEAM 1
NAME        SCORE
XXXXX        xx
XXXXX        xx
  .           .
  .           .
  .           .

Team Score: xx

      TEAM 2
NAME        SCORE
  .           .
  .           .
  .           .
```

Use the following data (teams are separated by asterisks):

| Joe Furillo | 82 |
| Mike De la Serna | 93 |

Phil Barth	83
Ellen Kumata	96
*	
Kathy Shieh	93
Anna Banana	86
Joe Cool	90
Lisa Rae	88
*	
Miguel De la Serna	79
Patrick Rielly	82
Leonard Hall	76
LaVerne Heidemann	75

8. Stan's Television Corporation needs a program to help with the billing of its customers. The user should be able to enter the due date for all bills to be processed. For each customer, enter a name, address, and the applicable charges selected from the following list:

Standard Service	$7.00
Cable service	4.00
Home Cinema Channel	2.00
Continual Cartoon Channel	2.00

All customers receive the standard service. The program should print an itemized bill showing the total amount due and the amount owed for late payment, which is the total plus 5 percent. Use your own test data. Your output should resemble the following:

Name:
Address: Due Date:

Services:

Standard service	$7.00
Cable service	4.00
Continual Cartoon Channel	2.00
Total amount due:	$13.00
After due date:	$13.65

9. Write a subroutine that will determine if a given year is a leap year. Note: If a year is evenly divisible by 4, it is a leap year, except for the last year of the century. Even though the last year of the century is always evenly divisible by 4, it is not a leap year unless it is also evenly divisible by 400. Therefore, 1900 was not a leap year, but the year 2000 will be.

10. The greatest common divisor of two positive integers is the largest integer that evenly divides them both. For example, the greatest common divisor of 16 and 24 is 8. Write a program that asks the user to enter two positive integers and then uses a subroutine to determine their greatest common divisor. The program should then print this result.

CHAPTER 8

FUNCTIONS

Objectives

After studying this chapter, you will be able to:
- Explain and use the common numeric and string library functions.
- Write user-defined functions to meet specific programming needs.

Outline

Overview
Library Functions
  Numeric Functions
    Trigonometric Functions
    Exponential Function
    Natural Logarithm Function
    Square Root Function
    Integer Function
    Sign Function
    Absolute Value Function
    Random Number Function
  String Functions
    Concatenation
    LEN Function
    LEFT$ and RIGHT$ Functions
    MID$ Function
    ASCII and CHR$ Functions
    VAL and STR$ Functions
  User-Defined Functions
A Programming Problem
  Problem Definition
  Solution Design
  The Program
Avoiding Common Programming
  Mistakes
Summary Points
Review Questions
Debugging Exercises
Additional Programming Problems
  Level 1
  Level 2
  Level 3

Overview

Function
A subprogram that performs a specific task and results in a single value.

Library function
A function that is prewritten as part of the language.

User-defined function
A function that is written by the programmer.

A useful feature of BASIC is the **function,** a subprogram designed to perform a specific task and return a single value. BASIC has numerous **library functions,** or built-in functions, which perform common mathematical operations, such as finding the square root of a number or its absolute value. Other library functions operate on character strings, performing tasks such as finding the length of a string. These functions are also called **intrinsic** or **predefined functions.** They spare the programmer the necessity of writing the sequence of statements otherwise needed to perform these operations. In some cases, however, it is useful for the programmer to write a function to meet a particular need. These functions written by the programmer are called **user-defined functions.** This chapter discusses both library functions and user-defined functions.

Library Functions

Library functions are those that have been built into the BASIC language and included in the BASIC language library, where the programmer can easily reference them. In order to use a library function in a program, the programmer must call or reference the function, just as a subroutine must be called by the main program. The general format of a function call is as follows:

    function name (argument)

Argument
A value used by a function to obtain its final result.

The **argument** required within the parentheses is the value needed by the function to obtain a result, and can consist of

- A constant
- A variable
- Another function
- Expressions involving any of the preceding

The type of argument depends on the function used. The function performs its specific task, using the argument value, and returns a single value to the calling program.

A function call can be used in a BASIC statement in the place of a constant, a variable, or an expression. A function call evaluates as a single value and cannot be used to the left of an equal sign. For example, the function that finds the square root of a number, SQR, could be used in the following statement which assigns the value 5 (2 + 3) to the variable SUM:

```
60 SUM = SQR(4) + 3
```

The following statement would be invalid, however, because it attempts to assign the value of SUM plus 3 to the value 2 (the square root of 4):

```
60 SQR(4) = SUM + 3
```

When a function call occurs in a statement, it is evaluated before any other operations in the statement are evaluated. Therefore, a function call has a higher priority than arithmetic, relational, and logical operators.

There are two categories of BASIC library functions: numeric functions and string functions. Some of the numeric functions available on most systems will be discussed first.

Numeric Functions

Table 8–1 shows eleven common numeric functions that are available on most systems and used by all of the systems discussed in this text.

Trigonometric Functions Four of these functions—SIN, COS, TAN, and ATN—are trigonometric functions used in mathematical, engineering, and scientific applications. The argument for these functions is an angle measure given in radians; however, often a trigonometric problem is more easily understood using degrees. You may convert from one unit to the other as follows:

Radians to degrees:
  1 radian = 57.29578 degrees
  N radians = $N \times 57.29578$ degrees

To convert 2.5 radians to degrees, for example, multiply 2.5 by 57.29578. The product is approximately 143 degrees.

TABLE 8–1 Numeric Functions

FUNCTION	OPERATION
ABS (X)	Absolute value of X
ATN (X)	Trigonometric arc tangent of X radians
COS (X)	Trigonometric cosine of X radians
EXP (X)	e^x
INT (X)	Greatest integer less than or equal to X
LOG (X)	Natural logarithm (if $x = e^y$, LOG (X) = Y)
RND	Random number between 0 and 1
SGN (X)	Sign of X: $+1$ if $X > 0$, 0 if $X = 0$, -1 if $X < 0$
SIN (X)	Trigonometric sine of X radians
SQR (X)	Square root of X
TAN (X)	Trigonometric tangent of X radians

Degrees to radians:
   1 degree = 0.01745 radians
   N degrees = $N \times 0.01745$ radians

To convert 180 degrees to radians, multiply 180 by 0.01745. The result is equal to π (approximately 3.14 radians).

Exponential Function The exponential, or EXP, function performs the calculation $EXP(X) = e^x$. The constant e is equal to approximately 2.718. For example, the following statement assigns the value e^x to Y:

```
50 Y = EXP(X)
```

Natural Logarithm Function The natural logarithm, or LOG, function is the reverse of the EXP function. For example, if $X = e^y$, then $LOG(X) = Y$. In other words, Y (the natural logarithm of X) is the power that e is raised to in order to find X. If we know X but need to know the value of Y, we can use the following statement to assign the natural logarithm of X to Y:

```
30 Y = LOG(X)
```

The argument of the LOG function must be a positive real number.

Square Root Function The square root, or SQR, function determines the positive square root of its argument. In most BASIC implementations, the argument must be greater than or equal to zero. (On the Apple, the argument must be greater than zero). The following examples illustrate the SQR function:

Statement	Result
20 Y = SQR(X)	$Y = \sqrt{X}$
50 Z = SQR(SQR(16))	$Z = 2$
30 T = SQR((A * B) / (A - C))	$T = \sqrt{\frac{AB}{A-C}}$

Integer Function The integer, or INT, function computes the largest integer less than or equal to the argument value. For example:

X	INT (X)
8	8
5.34	5
16.9	16
−2.75	−3
−0.5	−1

If the argument is a positive value with a fractional part, the digits to the right of the decimal point are truncated (cut off). Notice from the preceding examples that truncation does not occur when the argument is negative. For instance, when the argument equals −2.75, the INT function returns −3, the largest integer *less than or equal to* that value. This fact can be seen on the number line, where the farther to the left a number lies, the less value it has:

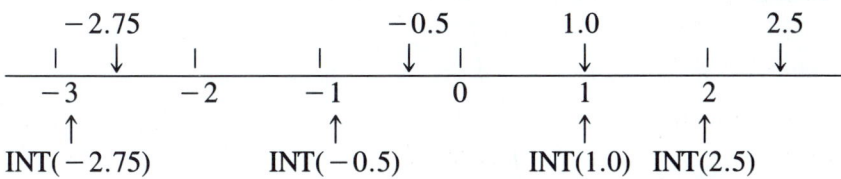

Although the INT function alone does not round its argument, it can be used in an expression that rounds to the nearest integer, nearest tenth, or nearest hundredth, or to any other degree of accuracy desired. The program in Figure 8–1 rounds a number to the nearest integer, as shown in line 50. Line 60 rounds the same number to the nearest tenth, by adding 0.05 to the number and multiplying the result by 10. Then the INT function is applied, and the result is divided by 10. The steps to round the number to the nearest hundredth follow the same pattern in line 70, adding 0.005 and multiplying the result by 100.

The INT function can also be used to determine if a number is divisible by another number. The program in Figure 8–2 tests a number to see if it can be divided evenly by 5.

FIGURE 8–1 Rounding with the INT Function

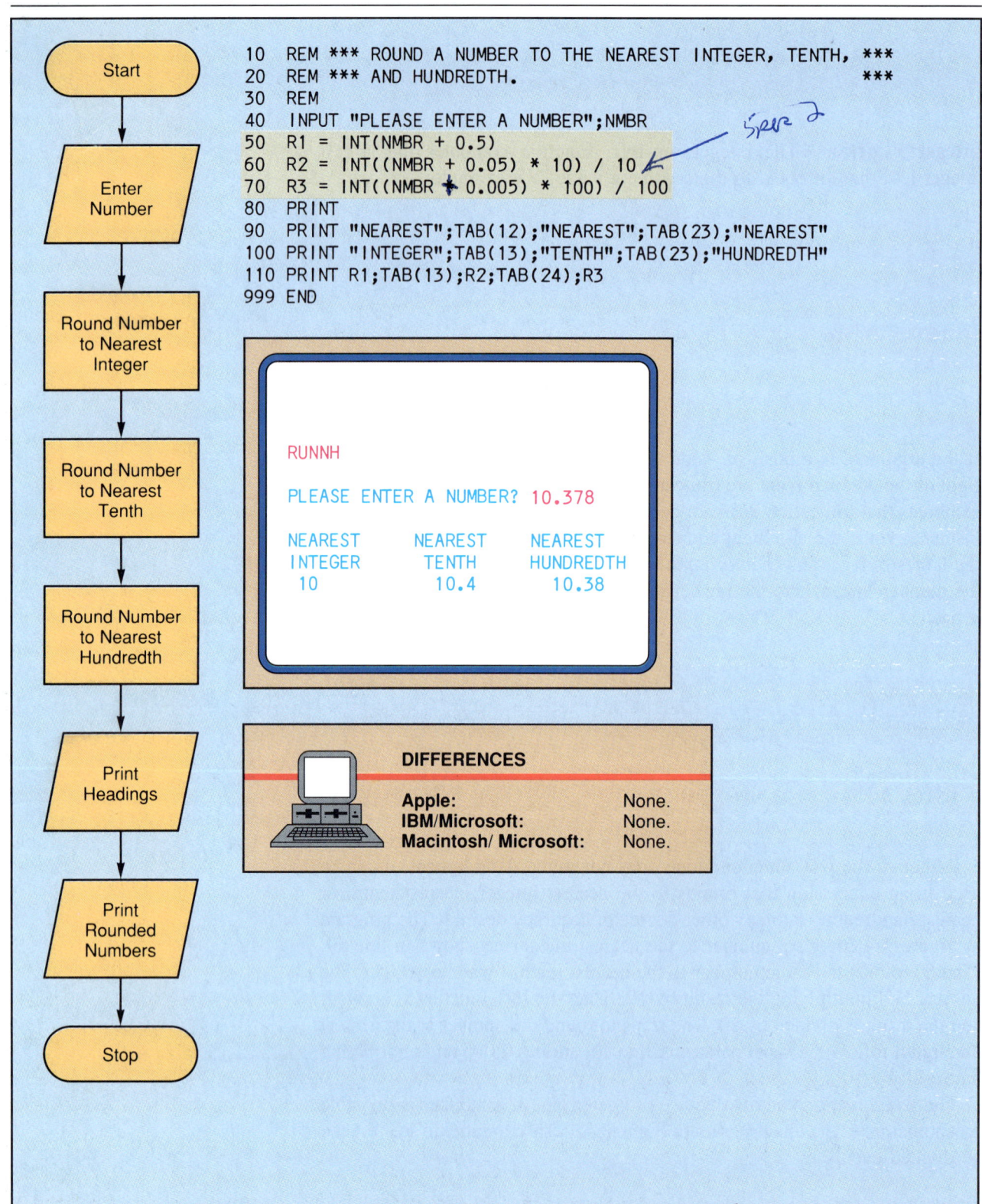

FIGURE 8-2 Testing Divisibility with the INT Function

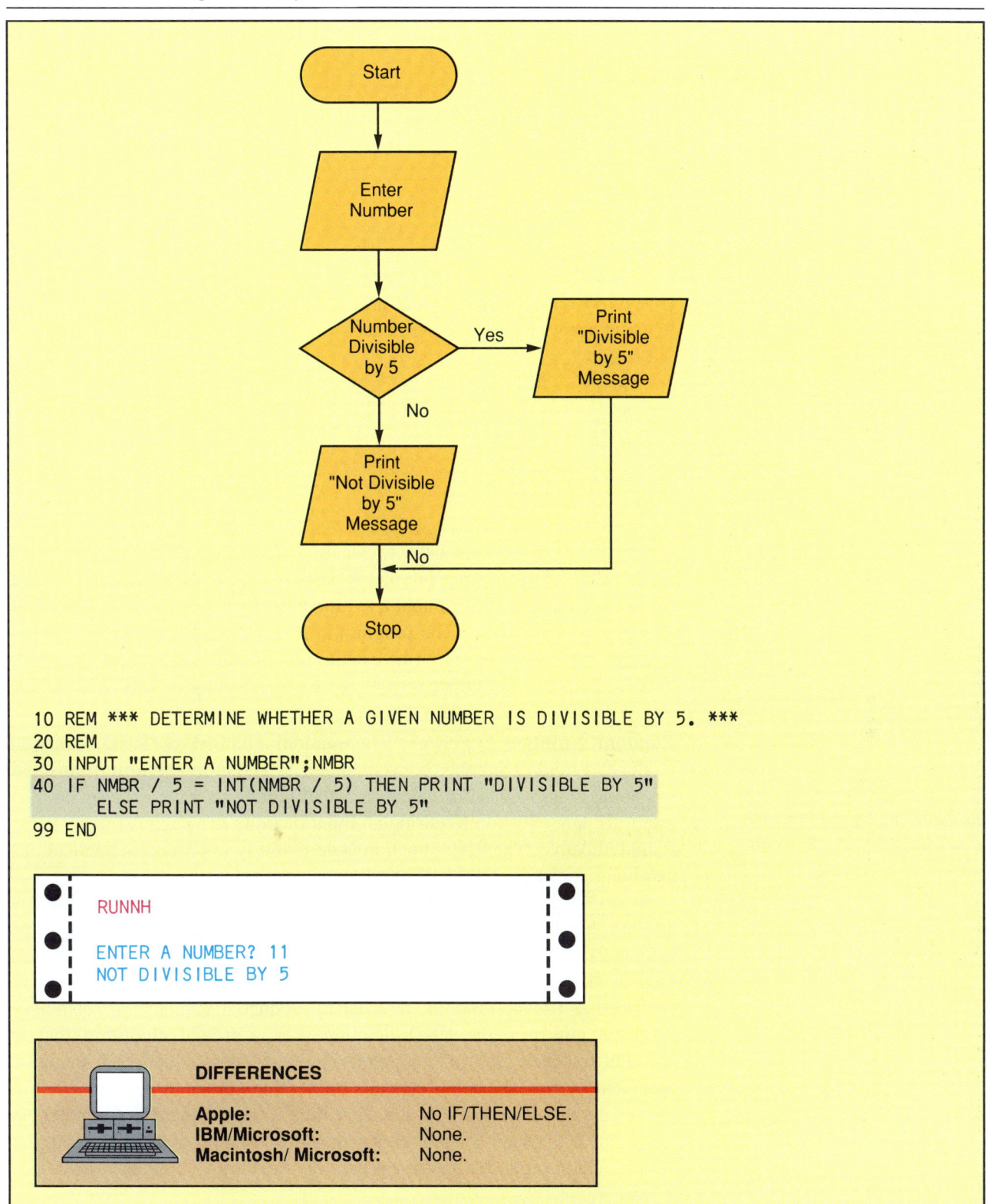

Sign Function The sign, or SGN, function determines the sign of a number. If $X > 0$, then $SGN(X) = 1$; if $X = 0$, then $SGN(X) = 0$; and if $X < 0$, then $SGN(X) = -1$. For example:

X	SGN (X)
8.5	1
0	0
−5.02	−1
−1005	−1

Absolute Value Function The absolute value, or ABS, function returns the absolute value of its argument. Remember that the absolute value is always positive or zero; if the argument has a negative value, the ABS function serves to remove the negative sign. For example:

X	ABS (X)
−2	2
0	0
3.54	3.54
−2.75	2.75

This function is often used to identify significant differences between given values. Suppose the Internal Revenue Service wants to know which individuals owe the government a substantial sum or are owed a substantial sum by the government. The program in Figure 8–3 demonstrates how the absolute value function might be used to identify such individuals. Line 50 tests for persons who either owe or are being refunded at least $1,000.00.

Random Number Function The random number, or RND, function produces a random number between 0 and 1. The term **random** means that any value in a given set of values is equally likely to occur. The function is useful for any situation requiring an input quantity of which the exact value is unpredictable. The RND function is particularly important in applications involving statistics, computer simulations, and games.

At first it might not seem hard to produce random values. This task is difficult, however, for machines of very precise structure and logic (such as computers). The numbers produced by a computer are not truly random, such as those resulting from a throw of dice, but are more accurately described as pseudo-random. In order to produce a sequence of seemingly unrelated numbers, the RND function uses a special algorithm that is different for each type of computer. The particular sequence of numbers generated by this algorithm depends on a value known as a *seed*. When a new seed value is supplied to the algorithm, a new sequence of numbers is produced. If the seed is never changed, however, a program containing the RND function produces the same series of "random" numbers each time it is run.

Random
A term describing a set (for example, numbers) in which every member has an equal chance of occurring.

FIGURE 8–3 Program Demonstrating the ABS Function

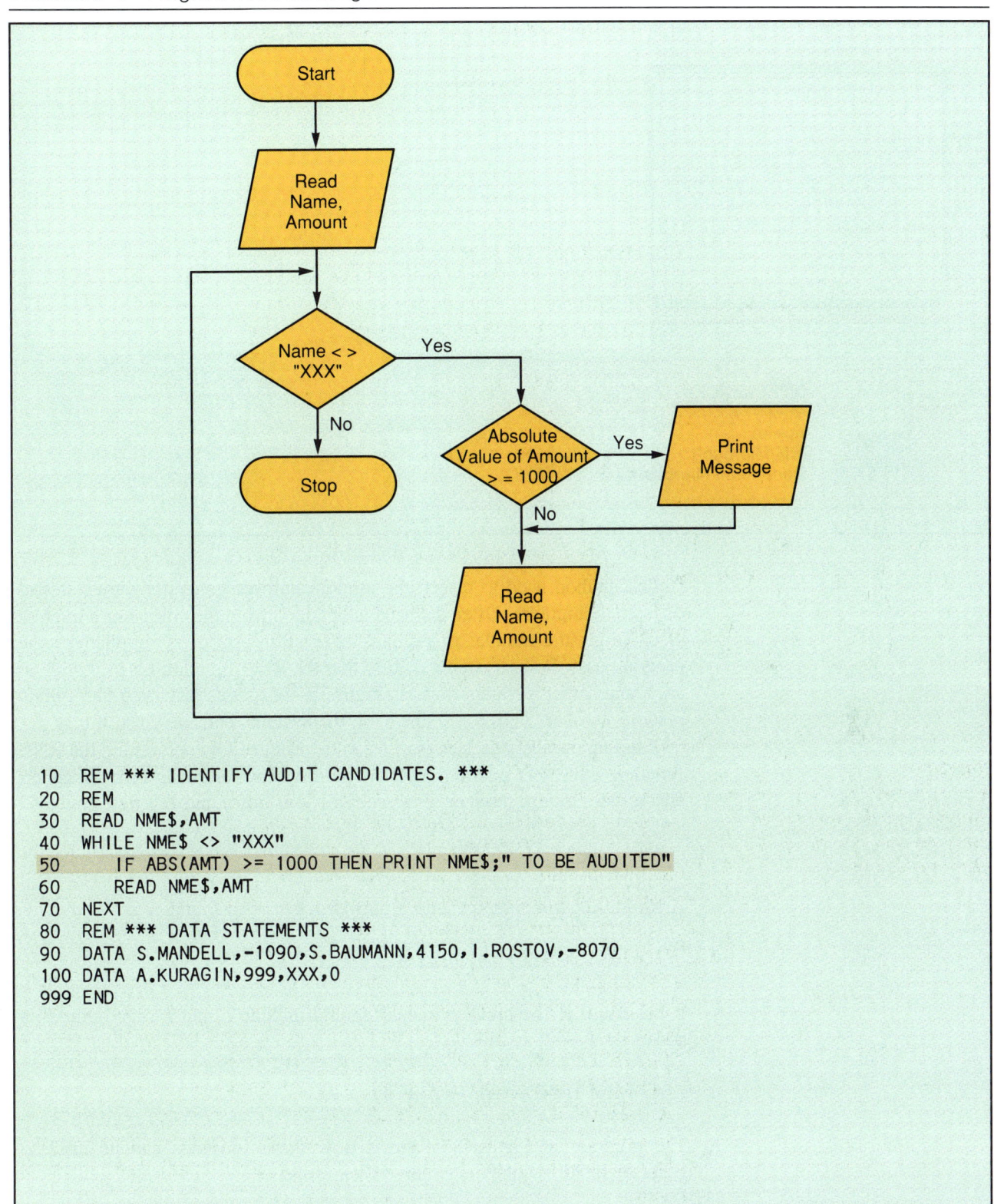

```
10   REM *** IDENTIFY AUDIT CANDIDATES. ***
20   REM
30   READ NME$,AMT
40   WHILE NME$ <> "XXX"
50      IF ABS(AMT) >= 1000 THEN PRINT NME$;" TO BE AUDITED"
60      READ NME$,AMT
70   NEXT
80   REM *** DATA STATEMENTS ***
90   DATA S.MANDELL,-1090,S.BAUMANN,4150,I.ROSTOV,-8070
100  DATA A.KURAGIN,999,XXX,0
999  END
```

FIGURE 8–3 *Continued*

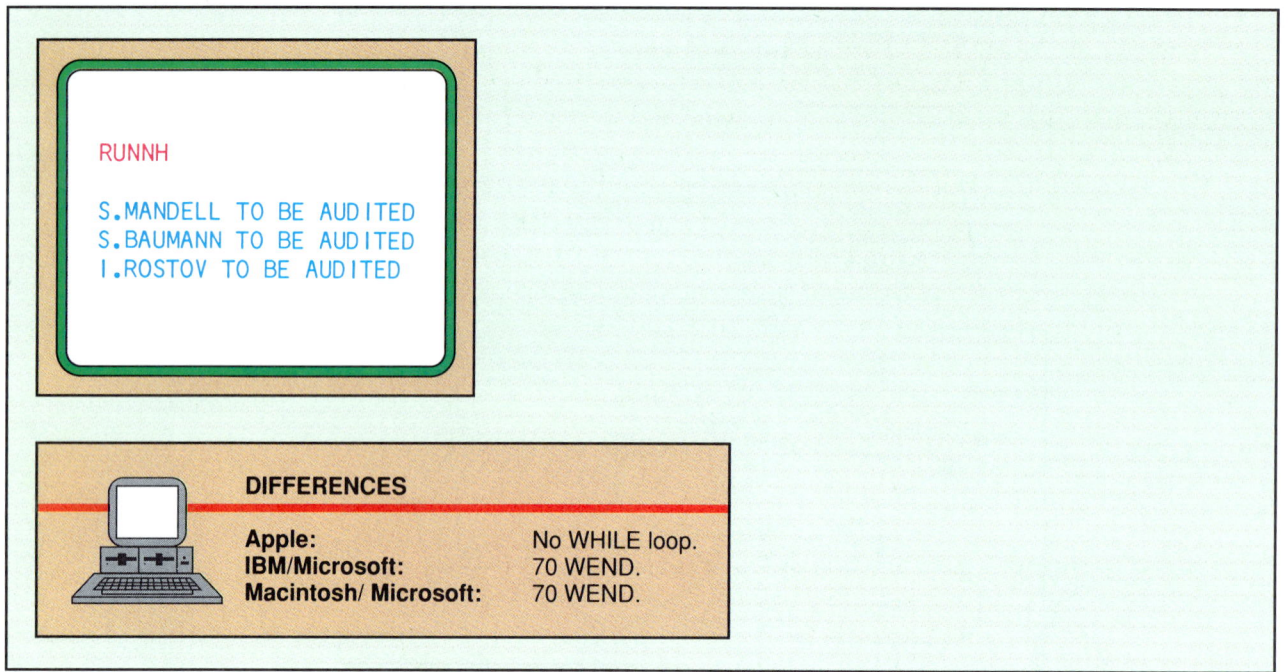

The method used to reseed the random number generator varies among different computers. Often the seed is obtained from the computer's internal clock (e.g., the number of seconds after midnight) or is supplied by the program user. Some systems require that the RND function be used with an argument; other systems do not. Figure 8-4 explains how you can obtain random numbers between 0 and 1 on the systems considered in this text.

Random numbers greater than 1 can be produced by combining the RND function with other mathematical operations. The following formula generates a real random number R between L (low limit) and H (high limit):

$$R = \text{RND} * (H - L) + L$$

A formula to generate a random integer I, between L and H is

$$I = \text{INT}(\text{RND} * (H - L) + L)$$

If the range of the random integer should include L and H, the value 1 is added to $H - L$ as follows:

$$I = \text{INT}(\text{RND} * (H - L + 1) + L)$$

The program in Figure 8–5 shows how these formulas can be used to generate random numbers in any given range.

FIGURE 8-4
Generating Random Numbers

Random numbers between 0 and 1 can be obtained as follows:

VAX System The RND function returns a number greater than or equal to zero. This function needs no argument when used with the VAX system. The function gives the same numbers each time the program is run unless it is reseeded; therefore, these numbers are not truly random. Once a program is working correctly, the RANDOMIZE statement can be inserted before the statement containing RND. The RANDOMIZE statement automatically reseeds the random number generator, thus causing the RND function to produce different numbers each time the program is run. An example follows:

```
30 RANDOMIZE
      .
      .
      .
60 X = RND
```

Apple Only one statement is needed with the Apple computer to produce different numbers each time the program runs. The RND function requires one argument; the sign and value of the argument affect the result. A positive argument, as in the following example, returns a random real number greater than or equal to 0 and less than 1:

```
10 X = RND(3)
```

If the argument is 0, as in the following example, the most recently generated random number is returned.

```
10 X = RND(0)
```

If the argument is negative, a particular random number sequence is started that is the same every time RND is used with that negative argument:

```
10 X = RND(-4)
```

If a RND call with a positive argument follows a RND call with a negative argument, it will generate the particular, repeatable sequence of numbers peculiar to the negative argument. Each different negative argument starts a different repeatable sequence.

IBM and Macintosh When the RND function is used alone on the IBM, it produces the same sequence of numbers each time the program runs. Used without an argument or with an optional positive argument, the RND function generates a random number between 0 and 1.

FIGURE 8–4
Continued

An argument of 0 gives the last random number generated, and a negative argument begins a particular sequence that is the same every time that negative argument is used.

The RANDOMIZE statement is needed to provide a new random number seed and therefore give a truly random result. The format of this statement is as follows:

RANDOMIZE [integer]

or

RANDOMIZE TIMER

The integer, if used, must be changed each time the program runs to produce new numbers. If the integer is omitted, the prompt message

Random Number Seed (−32768 to 32767)?

asks the user to enter a number within this range.

If the function name TIMER is specified, a new number seed determined by the computer's clock is generated for each program run and no prompt appears. For example:

```
10 RANDOMIZE TIMER
20 PRINT RND
```

Learning Check

1. _____ _____ are functions that have been built into the BASIC language.
2. In BASIC, the argument of a function must be a single constant or variable. True or false?
3. The _____ function returns the largest integer less than or equal to the value specified as the argument.
4. The _____ function is used to generate unpredictable numbers.
5. What are the values of the following expressions?
   a. INT((2 − 4) / 4)
   b. SQR(4 * 3 + 4)
   c. ABS(INT(4 / 5) − 1)
   d. SGN(ABS(4 ^ 2 - 20))

Answers

1. Library functions 2. False 3. INT 4. RND 5. a. −1 b. 4 c. 1 d. 1

FIGURE 8-5 Generating Random Numbers in a Given Range

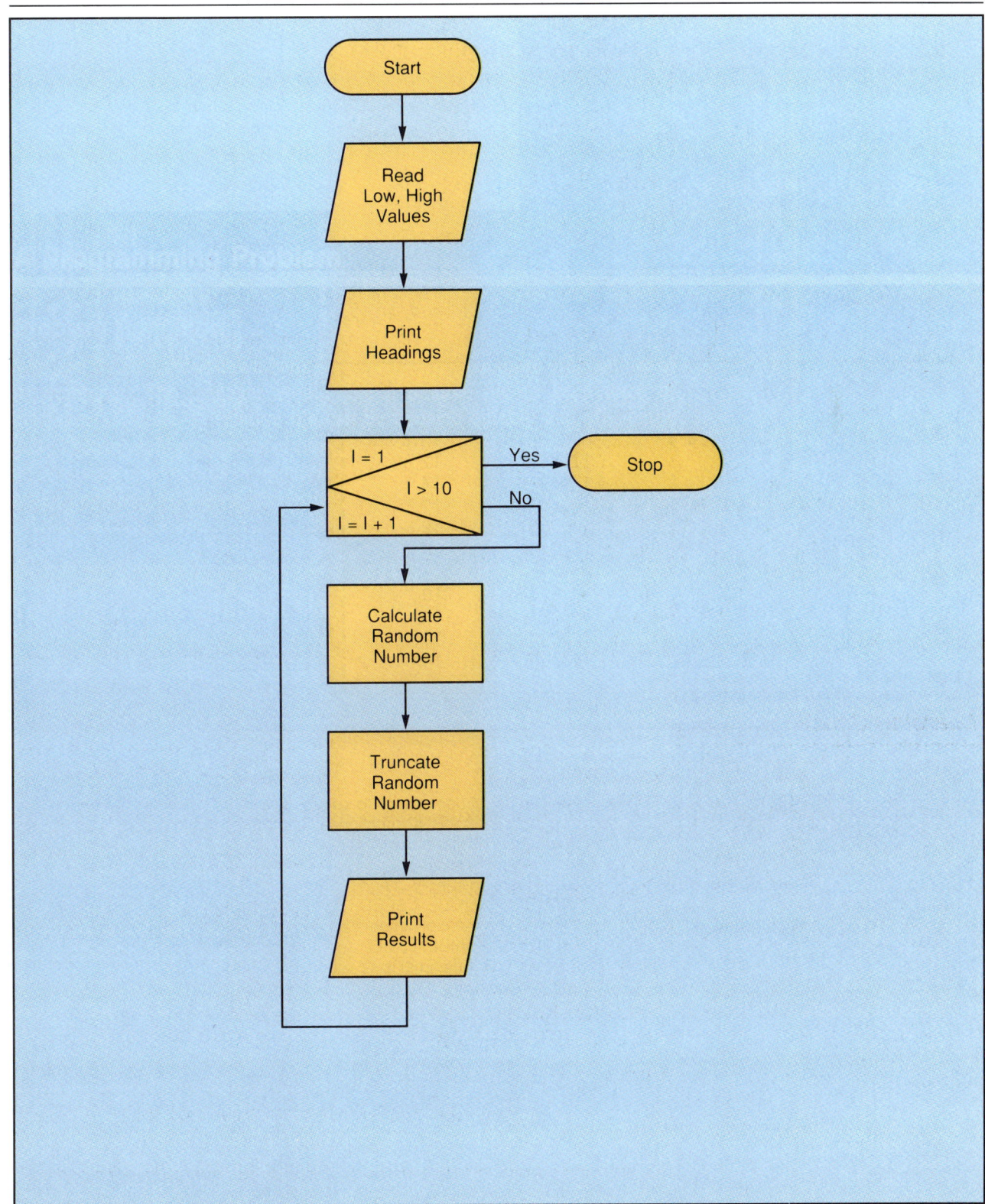

FIGURE 8–5 *Continued*

```
100 REM *** GENERATE RANDOM NUMBERS FOR A GIVEN RANGE. ***
110 REM
120 RANDOMIZE
130 READ LO,HI
140 PRINT "BETWEEN ";LO;" AND ";HI;":"," REAL"," INTEGER"
150 FOR I = 1 TO 10
160     R1 = RND * (HI - LO) + LO
170     R2 = INT(R1)
180     PRINT,,R1,R2
190 NEXT I
200 REM *** DATA STATEMENTS ***
210 DATA 10,20
999 END
```

```
RUNNH

BETWEEN  10  AND  20 :        REAL            INTEGER
                              12.8487         12
                              14.4943         14
                              17.4336         17
                              19.7787         19
                              18.0591         18
                              14.596          14
                              10.0685         10
                              14.003          14
                              10.017          10
                              14.3686         14
```

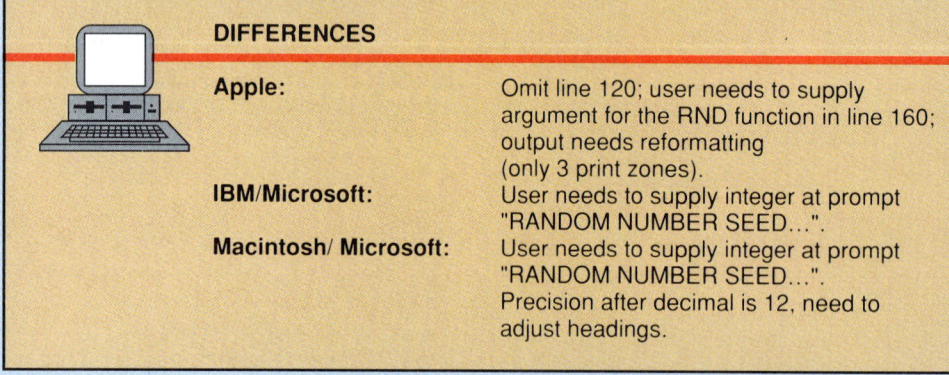

DIFFERENCES

Apple: Omit line 120; user needs to supply argument for the RND function in line 160; output needs reformatting (only 3 print zones).

IBM/Microsoft: User needs to supply integer at prompt "RANDOM NUMBER SEED...".

Macintosh/Microsoft: User needs to supply integer at prompt "RANDOM NUMBER SEED...". Precision after decimal is 12, need to adjust headings.

String Functions

Up to this point, we have manipulated numbers but have done little with strings except to print them or compare them in IF/THEN statement tests. Many programming applications require more sophisticated manipulations of strings.

BASIC string functions allow programmers to modify, **concatenate** (join together), compare, and analyze the composition of strings. These functions are useful for sorting lists of names, determining subject matter in text, printing mailing lists, and so forth. For example, the use of string functions can enable a program to determine that John J. Simmons is the same as Simmons, John J. The most common string functions are listed in Table 8–2.

Concatenation
The joining of data items, such as strings, to form a single item.

Concatenation Concatenation serves to join two strings end to end, forming a new string. It is not a library function, as are the other string

TABLE 8–2 String Functions

FUNCTION	OPERATION	EXAMPLE
string1 + string2	Concatenation; joins two strings	"KUNG" + " FU" is "KUNG FU"
ASCII (string) or ASC (string)	Returns the ASCII code for the first character in the string	IF A$ = "DOG", THEN ASCII (A$) is 68
CHR$ (integer expression)	Returns the string representation of the ASCII code of the expression	CHR$(68) is "D"
LEFT$ (string, integer expression)	Returns the specified number of leftmost characters of a string specified by the expression	LEFT$("ABCD",2) is "AB"
LEN (string)	Returns the length of a string	IF N$="HI THERE", then LEN(N$) is 8
MID$ (string, expression1, expression2)	Starting with the character at expression1, returns the number of characters specified by expression2	MID$("MARIE",2,3) is "ARI"
RIGHT$(string, expression)	*VAX:* Returns the rightmost characters of a string, starting with character specified by the expression	RIGHT4("ABCDE",2) is "BCDE"
	Micros: Returns the number of rightmost characters specified by the expression	RIGHT$("ABCDE",2) is "DE"
STR$(expression)	Converts a number to its string equivalent	STR$(123) is "123"
VAL (string)	Returns the numeric value of a number string	IF N$ = "352 63" THEN VAL(N$) is 35263

FIGURE 8-6
Program Demonstrating Concatenation

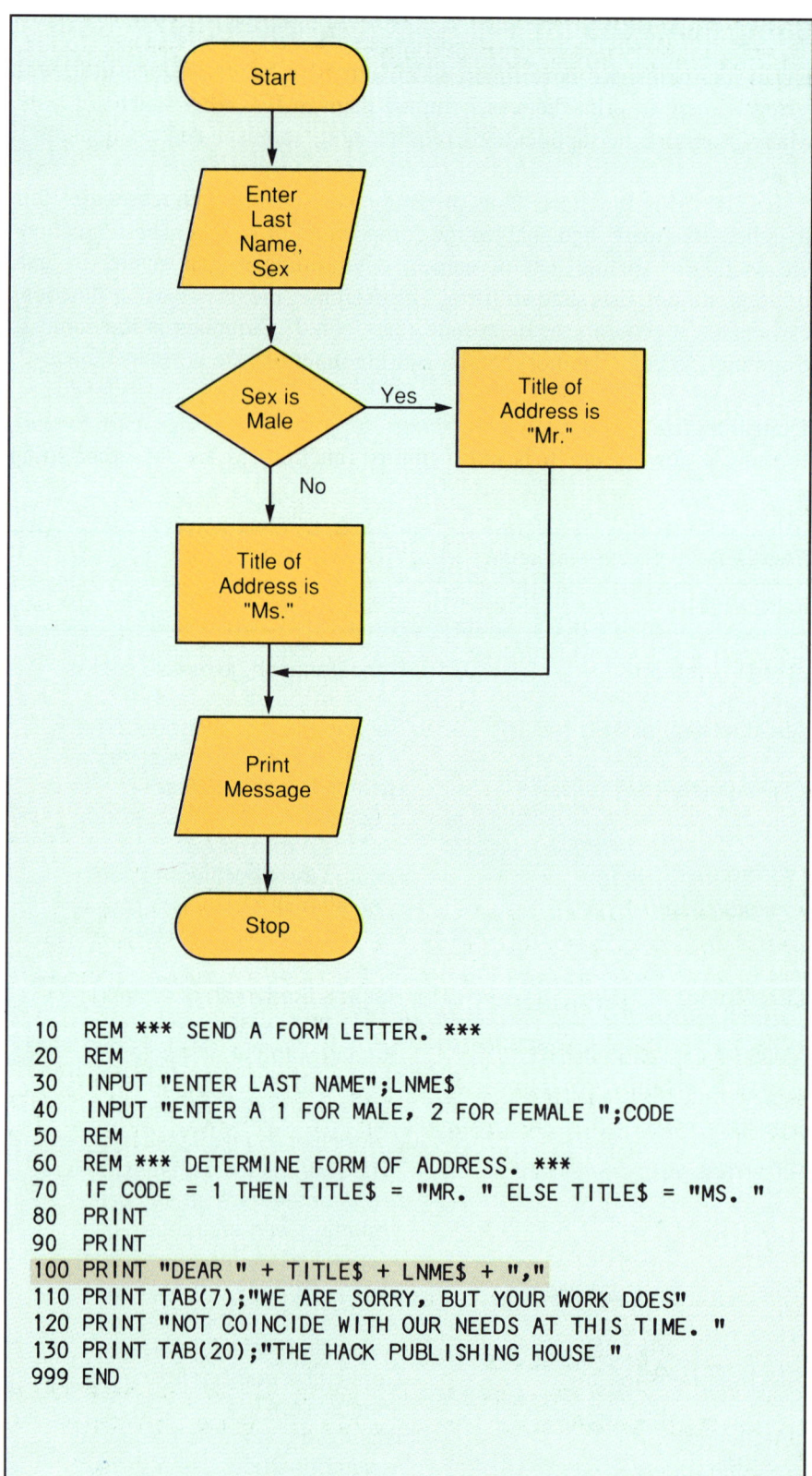

FIGURE 8–6
Continued

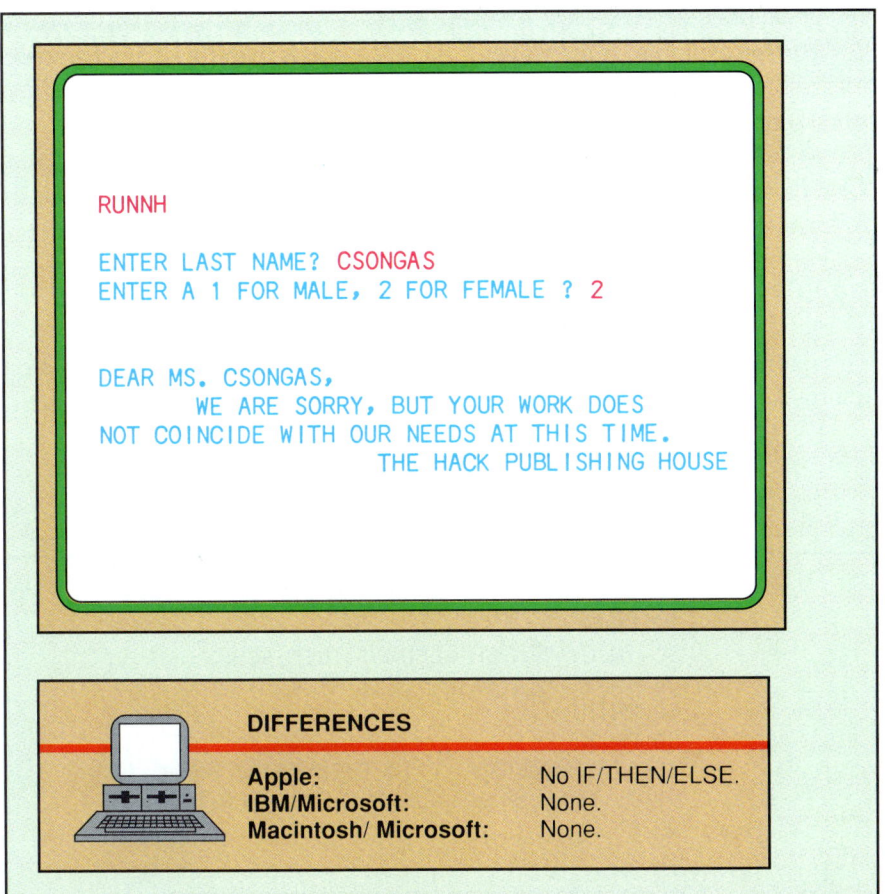

functions discussed here; instead it is an operation performed on two string operands, just as the arithmetic operators +, −, *, and / act on two numeric values. The plus sign (+) serves as the concatenation operator. For example, the statement

```
20 A$ = "NIGHT" + "MARE"
```

assigns the string NIGHTMARE to the variable A$. Similarly, the following segment results in X$, containing the value SAN FRANCISCO:

```
20 A$ = "SAN "
30 B$ = "FRAN"
40 C$ = "CISCO"
50 X$ = A$ + B$ + C$
```

The program in Figure 8–6 demonstrates the use of concatenation.

LEN Function The length, or LEN, function returns the number of characters in the single string that is its argument. (Remember that blanks in quoted strings are counted as characters.) Its format is as follows:

LEN (string)

An example of how the LEN function might be used is given in Figure 8–7. In this example, if the value of ALBM$ is less than fourteen characters long, this string and the associated price can be printed within the predefined print zones. Otherwise, the TAB function is used to print the price.

LEFT$ and RIGHT$ Functions The format of the LEFT$ function is as follows:

LEFT$ (string, expression)

The expression in parentheses has an integer value. The LEFT$ function returns a string that consists of the leftmost portion of the string argument,

FIGURE 8–7 The LEN Function

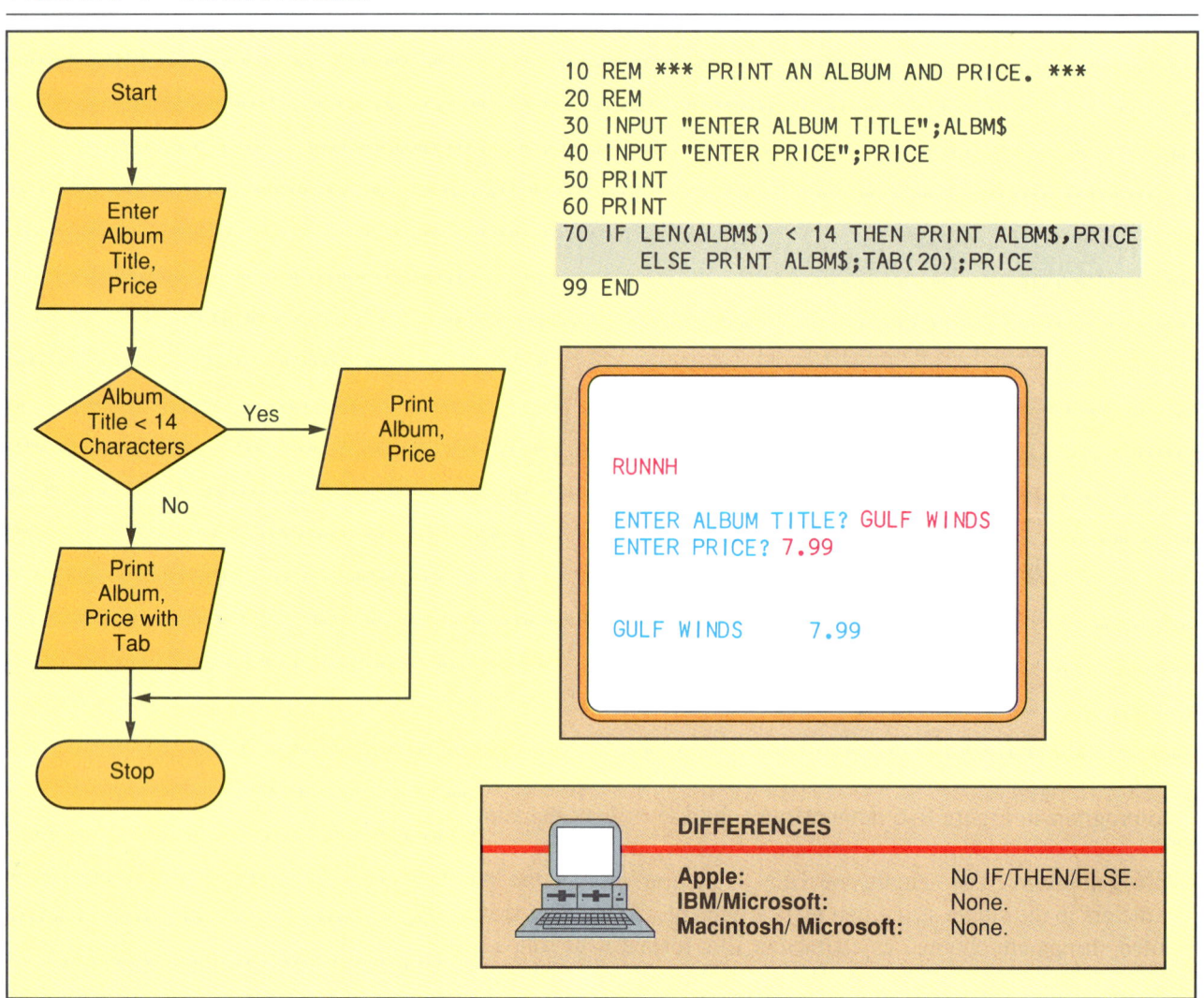

from the first character to the character position specified by the expression. For instance, the following statement assigns to X$ the value BE SEEING:

```
30 X$ = LEFT$("BE SEEING YOU!",9)
```

The LEFT$ function is used in the program in Figure 8-8.

The format of the RIGHT$ function is similar to that of the LEFT$ function:

RIGHT$ (string, expression)

The microcomputers discussed in this book handle the RIGHT$ function differently than the VAX system does. On the VAX system, the RIGHT$ function returns the rightmost part of the string, from the *character position* given by the expression to the end of the string. Thus the following statement assigns the value SEEING YOU! to X$:

```
30 X$ = RIGHT$("BE SEEING YOU!",4)
```

With the microcomputers, however, this function returns the *number of characters* specified by the expression from the right end of the string. On these systems, the following instruction would assign to X$ the last nine characters of the string, in this case the value EING YOU!:

```
30 X$ = RIGHT$("BE SEEING YOU!",9)
```

The programs in Figures 8-9 and 8-10 demonstrate the RIGHT$ function as used on the VAX system and the microcomputers respectively. Notice how line 60 differs between the two programs to produce the same output.

The LEFT$ function is often useful when comparing character strings. Suppose a program asks the user to answer a yes or no question, but does not specify whether the question should be answered by typing the entire word YES or NO or just the first letter, Y or N. The LEFT$ function can compare just the first character of the user's response, allowing the user to type either YES/NO or Y/N. The program in Figure 8-11 illustrates this.

MID$ Function The MID$ function has the following format, where the two expressions are integer expressions:

MID$ (string,expression1 [,expression2])

The function returns the portion of the string beginning at the character position defined by *expression1* and extending for the number of characters given by *expression2*. On many systems (including all those considered here except the VAX system), *expression2* can be omitted; in this case the characters from the starting position of *expression1* to the end of the string

FIGURE 8–8
The LEFT$ Function

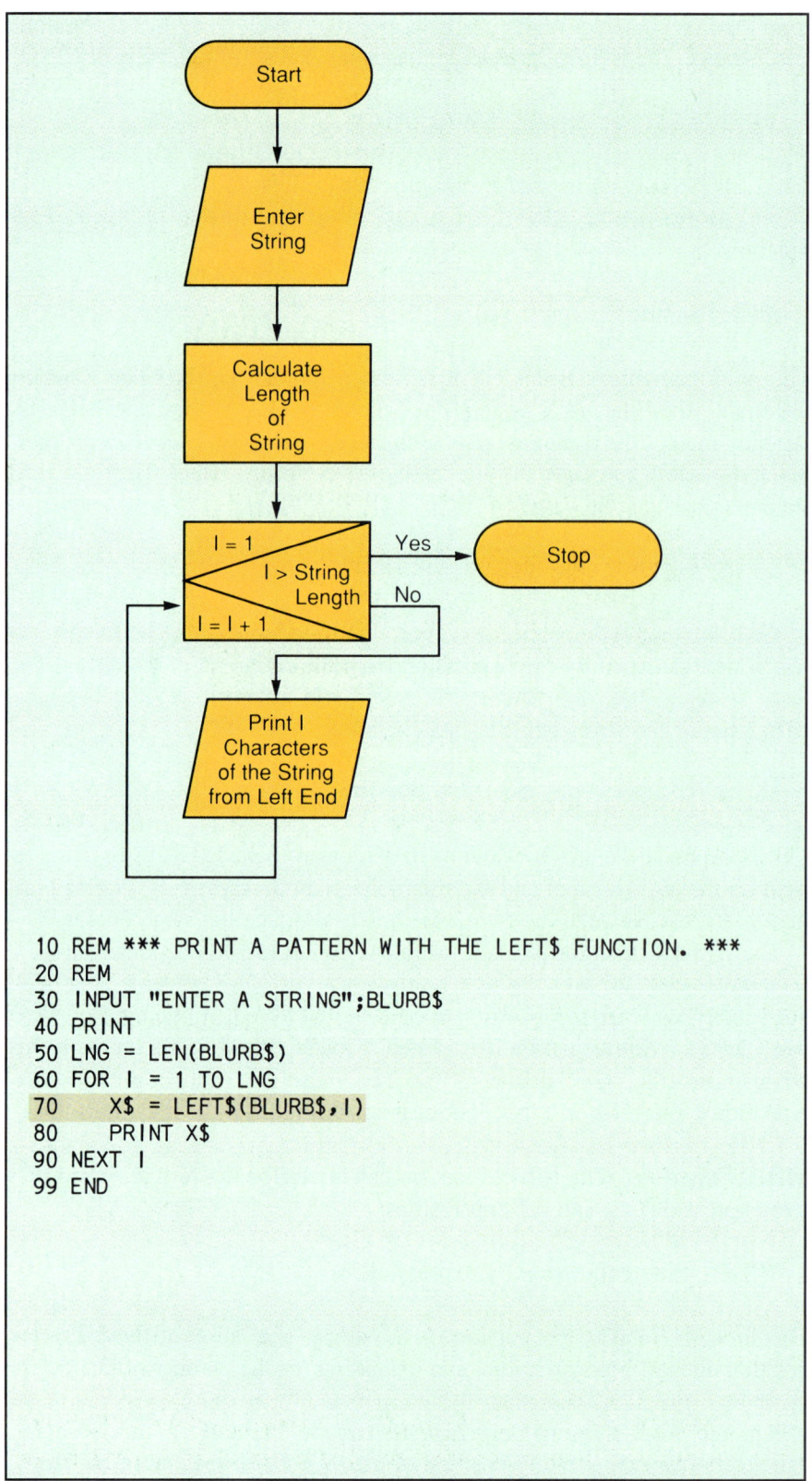

```
10 REM *** PRINT A PATTERN WITH THE LEFT$ FUNCTION. ***
20 REM
30 INPUT "ENTER A STRING";BLURB$
40 PRINT
50 LNG = LEN(BLURB$)
60 FOR I = 1 TO LNG
70    X$ = LEFT$(BLURB$,I)
80    PRINT X$
90 NEXT I
99 END
```

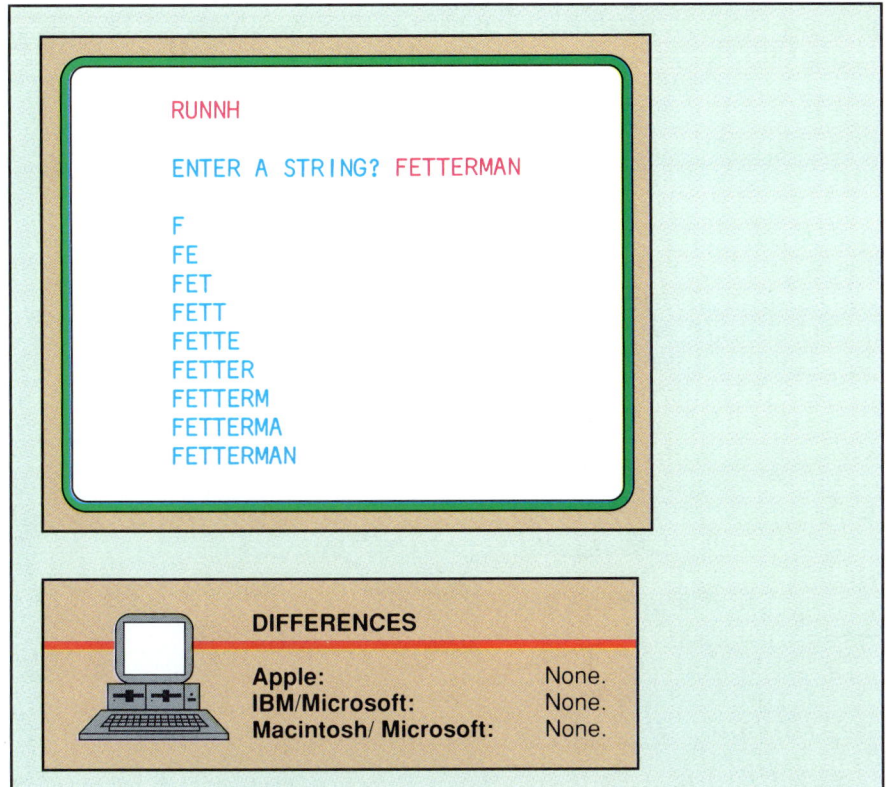

FIGURE 8-8
Continued

are returned. The following statement assigns to X$ a string four characters long, starting at the fifth character: PHAL.

```
20 X$ = MID$("ENCEPHALITIS",5,4)
```

The MID$ function is useful for examining some middle characters of a string. Assume you have a file of telephone numbers and you want to print only those with a prefix of 352. Here are the numbers:

491-354-1070
491-353-0011
491-352-3520
491-352-1910
491-352-7350
491-353-9822

The program in Figure 8-12 compares the exchange to 352 and prints the numbers that qualify.

ASCII and CHR$ Functions The ASCII function returns the ASCII value of the first character of its string argument. The format of the ASCII function

FIGURE 8-9
The RIGHT$ Function on the VAX System

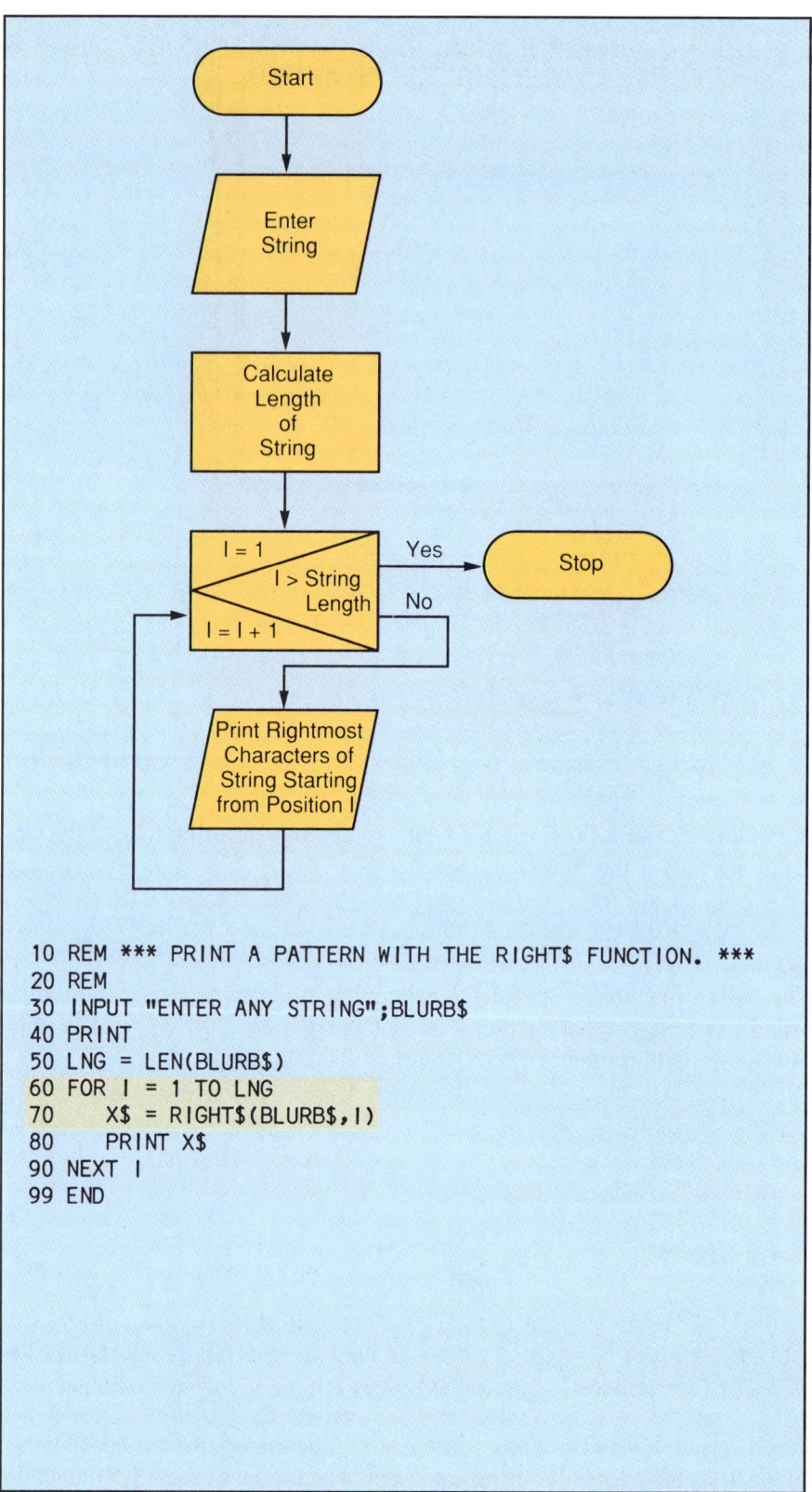

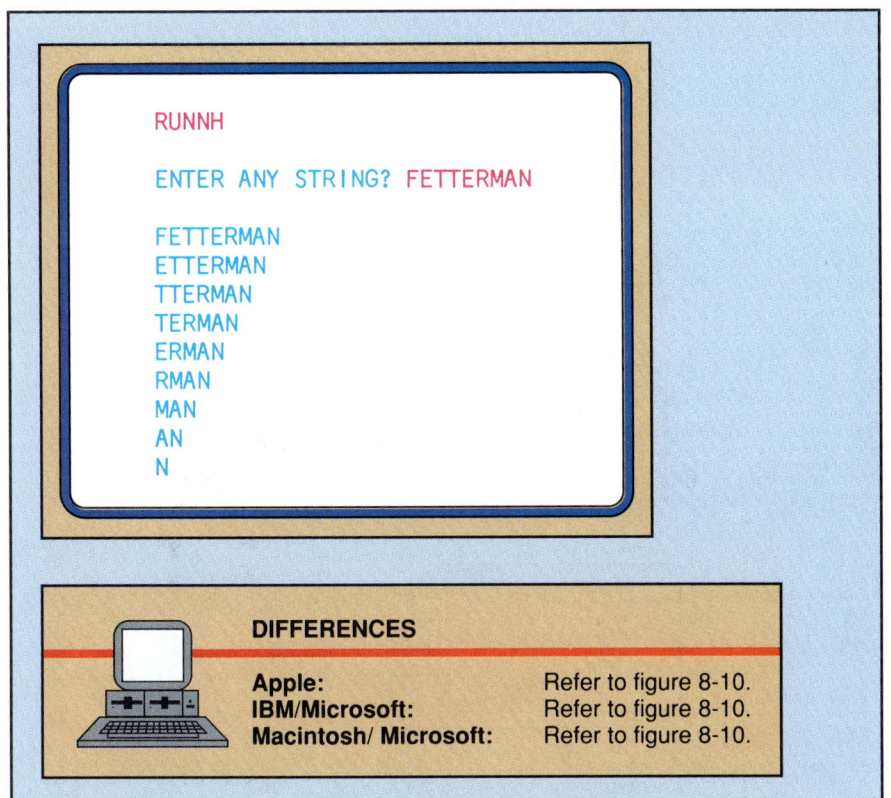

FIGURE 8-9
Continued

is as follows, where the argument is a string constant, variable, or expression.

ASCII (string)

On the VAX, the function name is ASCII; the same function on the microcomputers discussed in this text is called ASC, and its format is the same as for the VAX. Appendix E lists characters and their corresponding ASCII values. For example, the following statement examines the first character of the argument, R, and assigns its ASCII value of 82 to the variable RVALUE:

```
30 RVALUE = ASCII("RETURN A VALUE")
```

The CHR$ function performs the reverse operation of the ASCII function: it returns the single character that corresponds to a given ASCII value. The format of the function is as follows, where the expression evaluates as an integer in the range 0 through 255:

CHR$ (expression)

FIGURE 8–10
The RIGHT$ Function on the IBM, Macintosh, and Apple

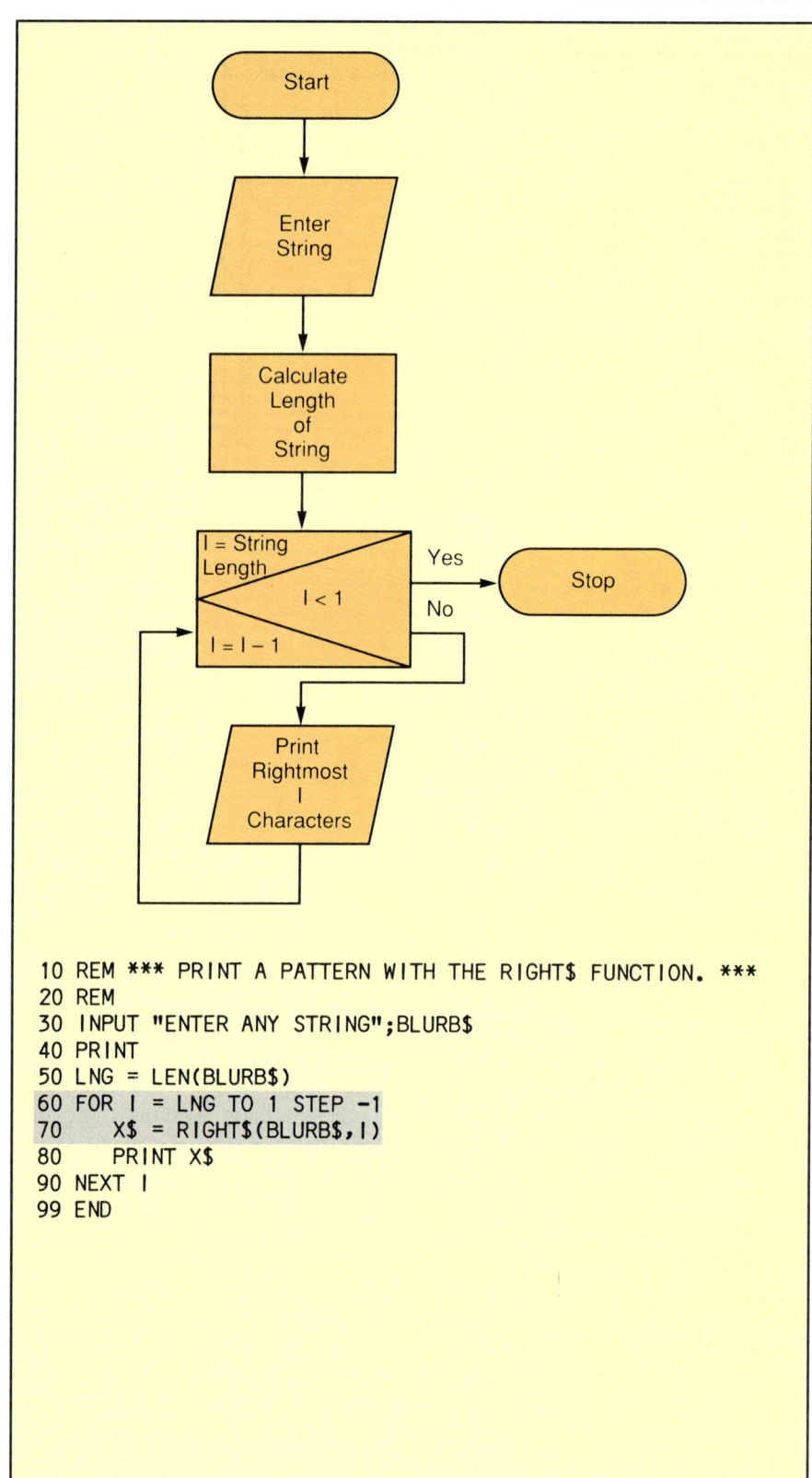

```
10 REM *** PRINT A PATTERN WITH THE RIGHT$ FUNCTION. ***
20 REM
30 INPUT "ENTER ANY STRING";BLURB$
40 PRINT
50 LNG = LEN(BLURB$)
60 FOR I = LNG TO 1 STEP -1
70    X$ = RIGHT$(BLURB$,I)
80    PRINT X$
90 NEXT I
99 END
```

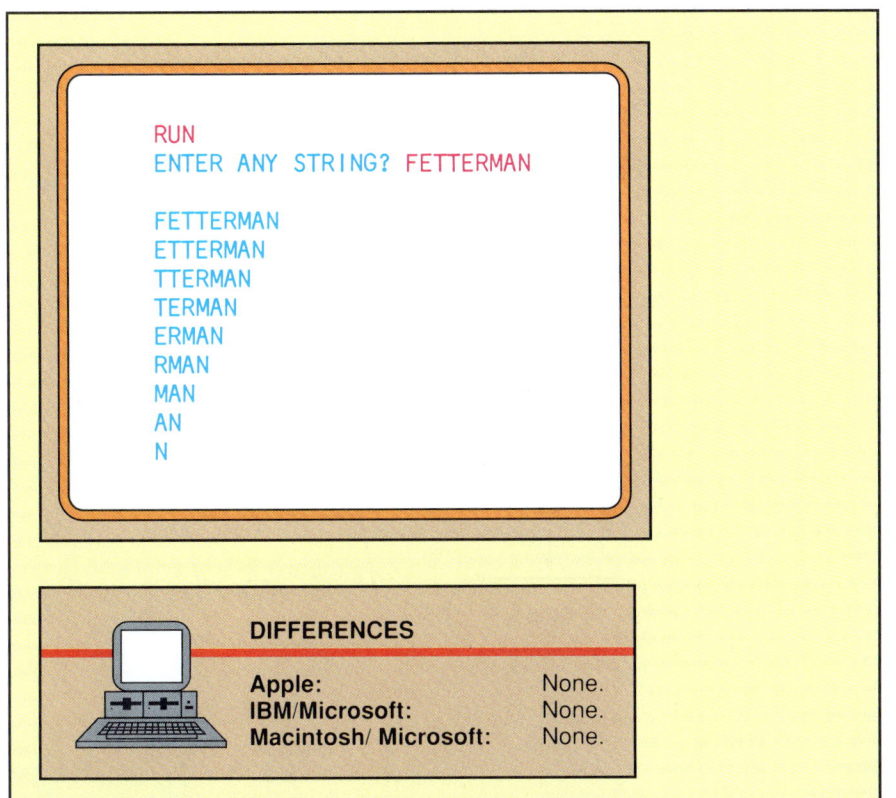

FIGURE 8–10
Continued

The following statement assigns to MES$ the value HI!:

```
70 MES$ = CHR$(72) + CHR$(73) + CHR$(33)
```

The ASCII and CHR$ functions are demonstrated in the program in Figure 8–13, which prints a listing of the alphabet with its corresponding ASCII values.

The ASCII and CHR$ functions are helpful in allowing programs to respond to both lowercase and uppercase input. Using these functions, a program can allow the user to answer a yes or no question with y, Y, n, or N. Appendix E shows that the codes for the lowercase letters range from 97 through 122, and those for uppercase letters range from 65 through 90. An IF/THEN statement can be used to compare the ASCII value of the user response to 96. If the value is greater than 96, a lowercase letter has been typed; if the value is less than 96, the letter is uppercase.

Once the program has determined the type of letter, it can convert the letter to either uppercase or lowercase for comparison. An uppercase letter can be changed to lowercase by adding 32 to the ASCII value, and a lowercase letter can be made uppercase by subtracting 32. The program

FIGURE 8–11
Comparing Character Strings with the LEFT$ Function

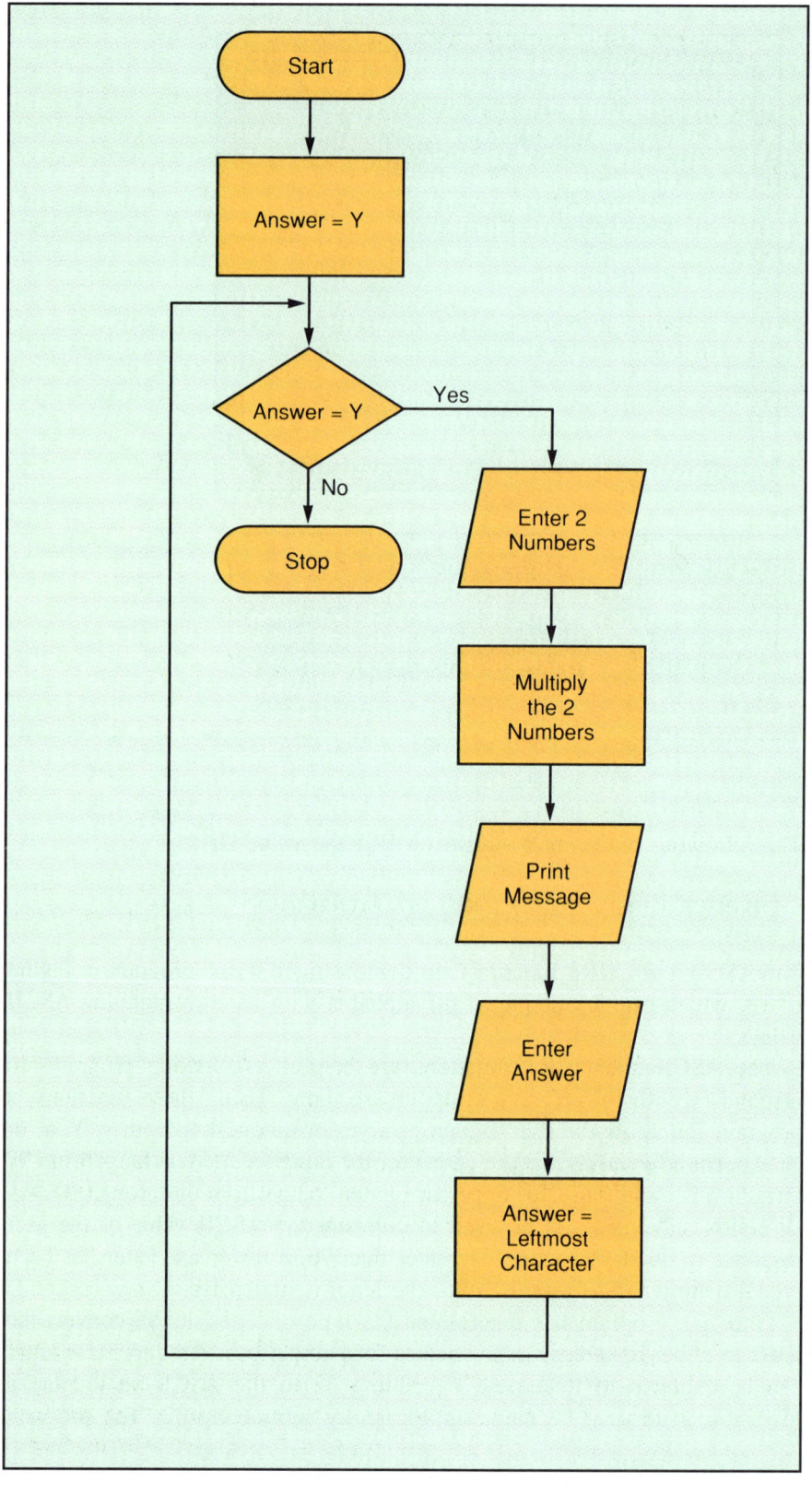

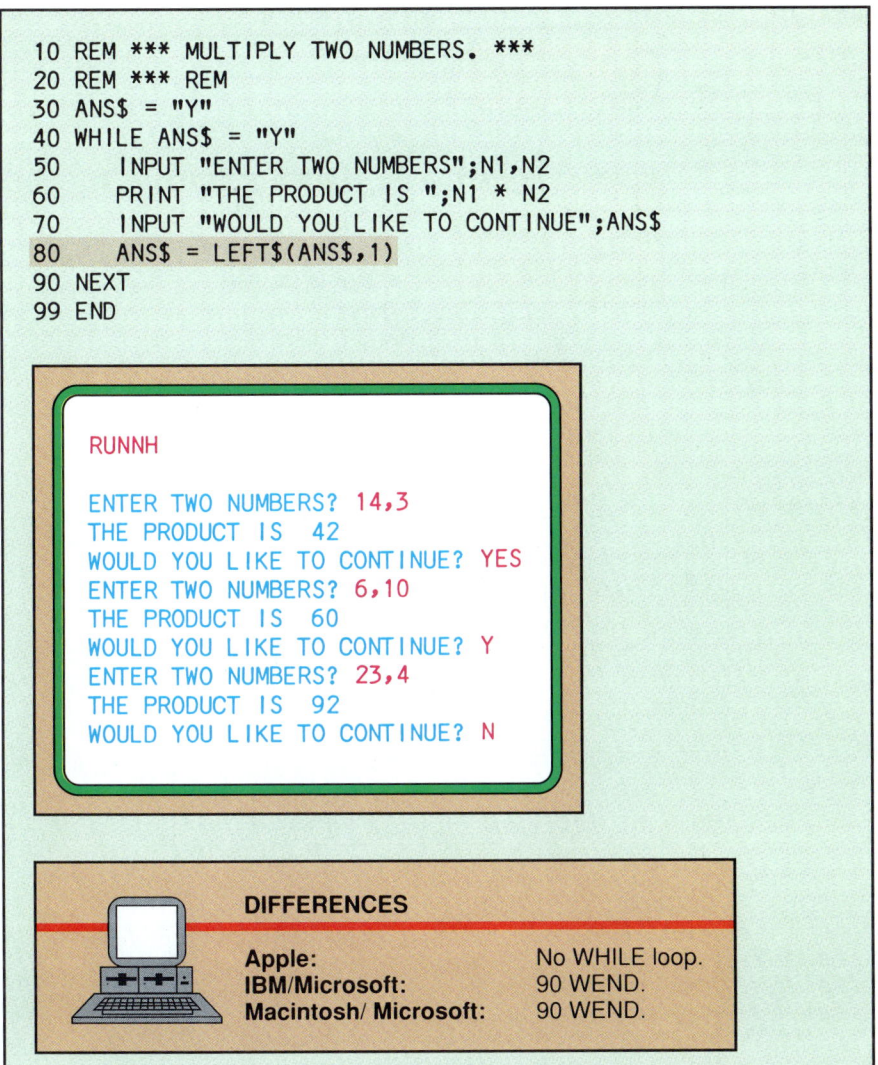

FIGURE 8–11
Continued

segment in Figure 8–14 checks a user's reply and converts it to uppercase if necessary in order to compare it.

VAL and STR$ Functions   The VAL function converts a numeric string expression (such as ''12.34'') to its equivalent numeric value. Its format is as follows, where the string consists of numeric characters:

   VAL(string)

These characters can include the digits 0 through 9, the plus and minus signs, and the decimal point. Any leading blanks in the string are ignored. The microcomputers discussed in this book also allow the string argument to contain non-numeric characters. Figure 8-15 explains the manner in which different systems handle the VAL function.

FIGURE 8–12
The MID$ Function

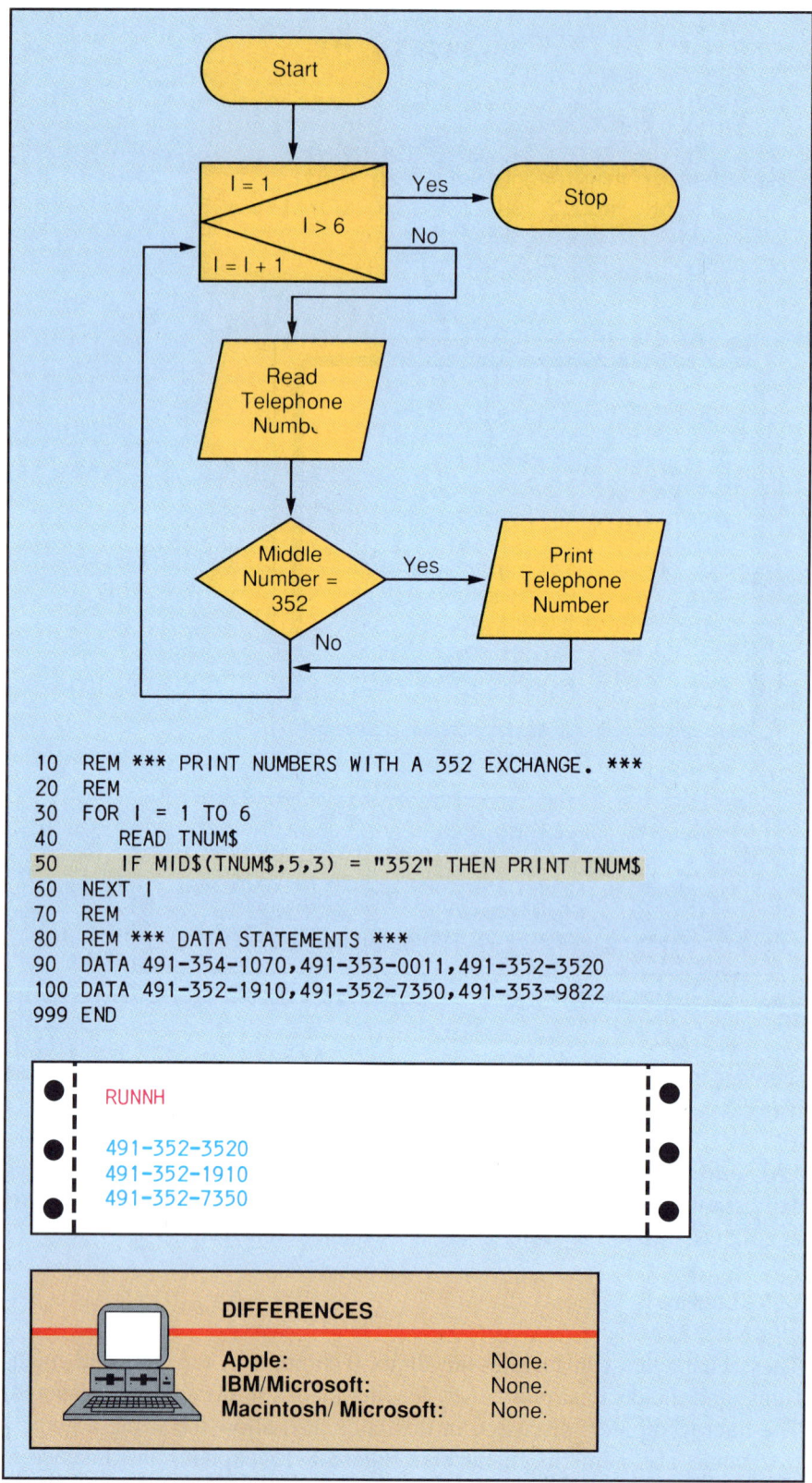

FUNCTIONS **305**

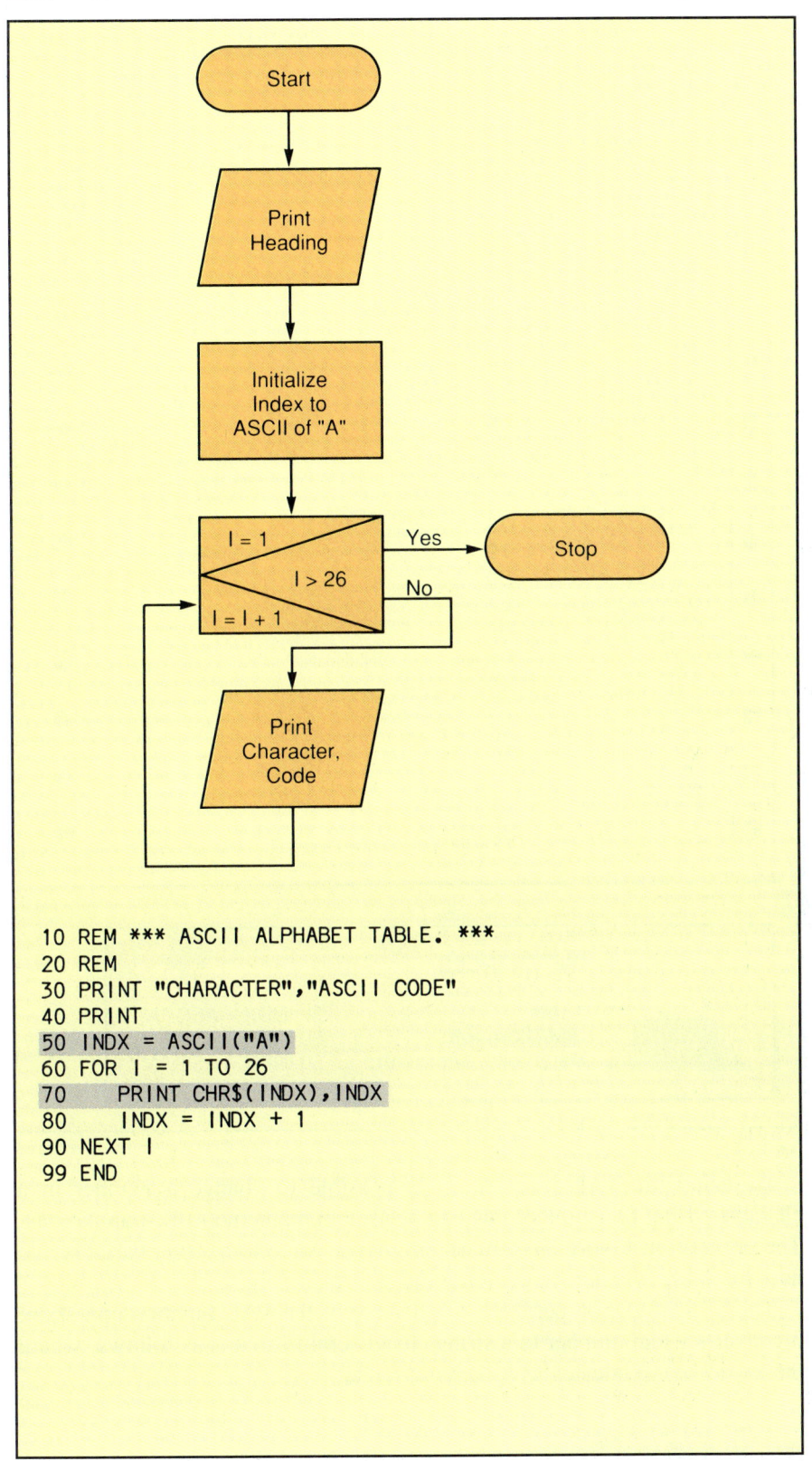

FIGURE 8–13
The ASCII and CHR$ Functions

```
10 REM *** ASCII ALPHABET TABLE. ***
20 REM
30 PRINT "CHARACTER","ASCII CODE"
40 PRINT
50 INDX = ASCII("A")
60 FOR I = 1 TO 26
70     PRINT CHR$(INDX),INDX
80     INDX = INDX + 1
90 NEXT I
99 END
```

FIGURE 8–13
Continued

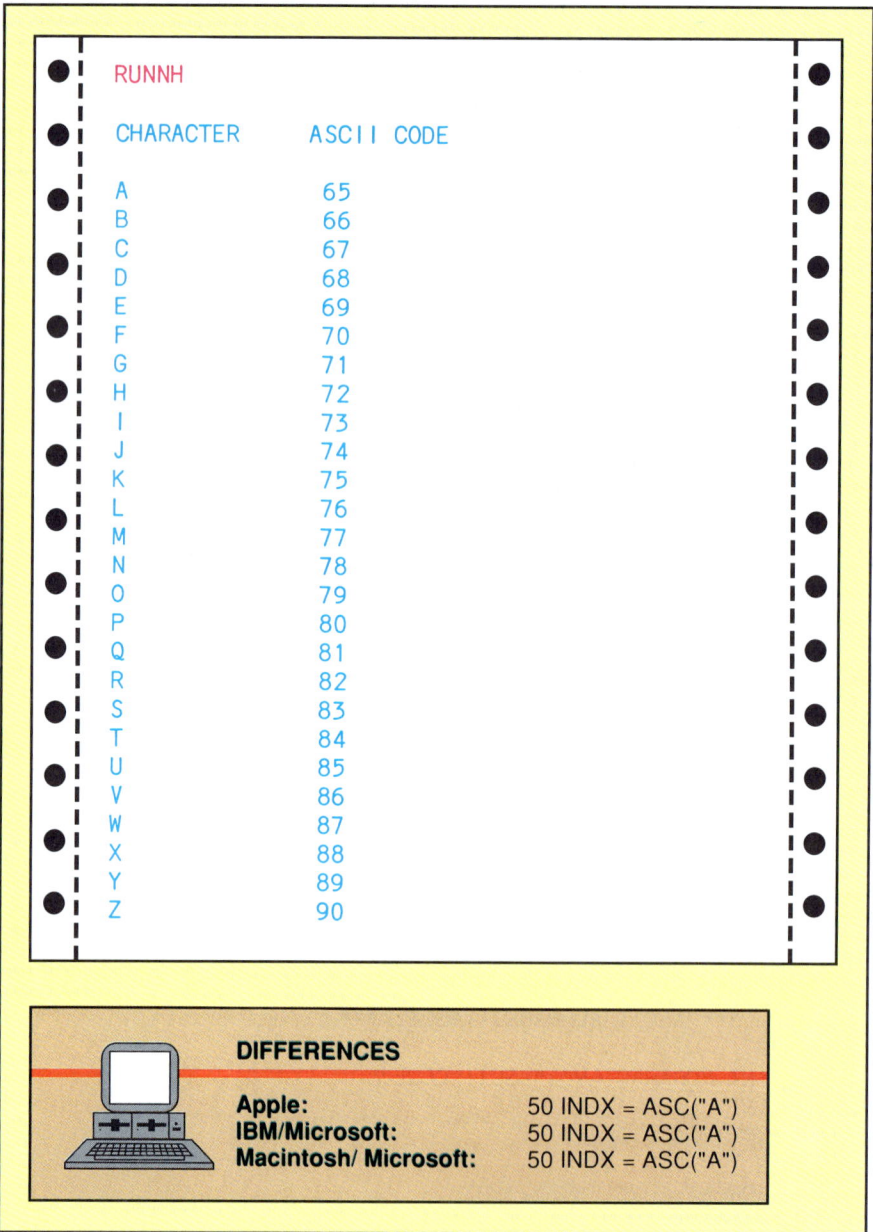

By using the VAL function, it is possible to change a number in a character string to a number that can be used in mathematical computations. The program in Figure 8–16 reads an integer value to a string variable and uses the VAL function to compute the sum of its digits.

The STR$ function performs the reverse of the VAL function operation: it converts a real number to a string. Its general format is as follows, where the expression evaluates as a numeric value:

STR$ (expression)

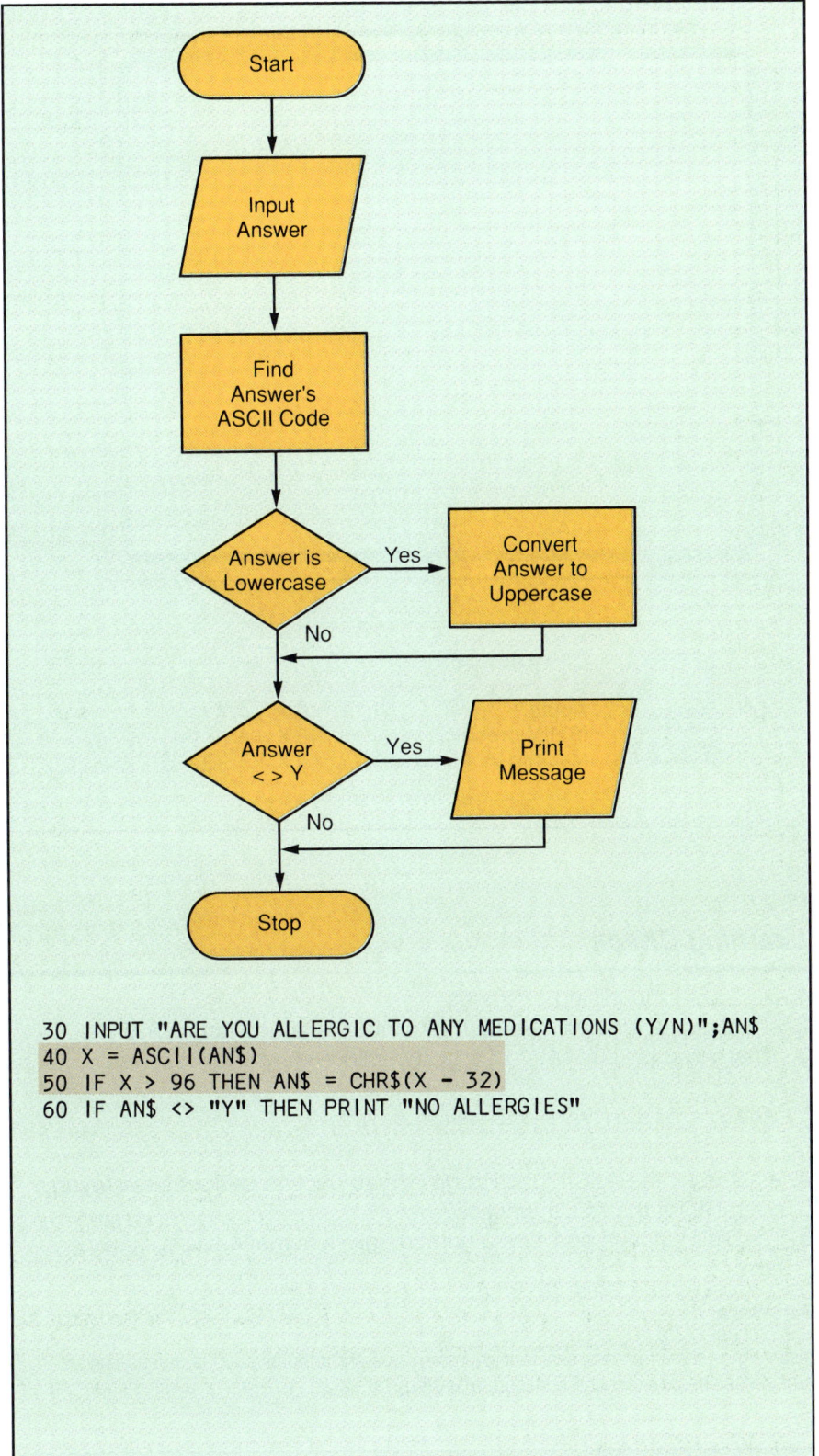

FIGURE 8–14
Converting Lowercase Letters to Uppercase

```
30 INPUT "ARE YOU ALLERGIC TO ANY MEDICATIONS (Y/N)";AN$
40 X = ASCII(AN$)
50 IF X > 96 THEN AN$ = CHR$(X - 32)
60 IF AN$ <> "Y" THEN PRINT "NO ALLERGIES"
```

FIGURE 8–14
Continued

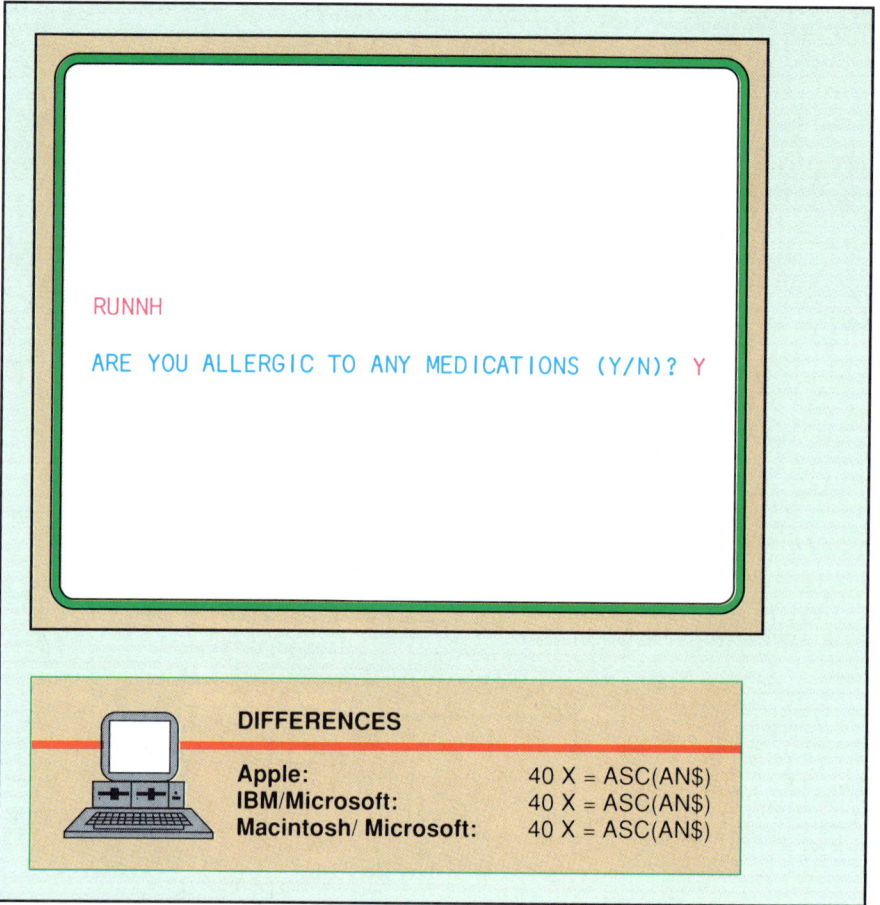

Learning Check

1. _____ is the joining of strings.
2. The _____ function returns the number of characters in a string.
3. What value is assigned to T$ by the following instruction?

   10 T$ = MID$("491–352–4448",5,3)

4. What does the ASCII function do? What function performs the reverse operation of the ASCII function?
5. The VAL function converts a number into a numeric string. True or false?

Answers

1. Concatenation 2. LEN 3. "352" 4. The ASCII function returns the ASCII value of the first character of its string argument. The CHR$ function does the reverse. 5. False.

> **FIGURE 8-15**
> VAL Function Differences
>
> If the string argument of the VAL function contains non-numeric characters (other than leading blanks), the VAX system gives an error message. Such a string is handled differently on the Apple, IBM, and Macintosh: If the first non-blank character of the string is non-numeric, the function returns a value of zero. For example, the following statement would output 0:
>
> ```
> 70 PRINT VAL(" BG, OH 43402")
> ```
>
> Otherwise, the function examines the string one character at a time until an unacceptable character is encountered. On all of the systems mentioned above, a blank is acceptable within a numeric string; it is simply ignored. The following statement would be valid and would assign to N1 the value 1084:
>
> ```
> 70 N1 = VAL(" 1084 WELSH VIEW DR.")
> ```

The program in Figure 8-17 demonstrates the STR$ function. Remember that once a number has been converted to a string, it can no longer be used in mathematical computations unless it is converted back to a numeric value.

User-Defined Functions

The DEF, or definition, statement can be used by the programmer to define a function not already included in the BASIC language. Once a function has been defined, the programmer can use it as many times as necessary in the program. The DEF statement can be placed anywhere in the program before the function is first called, but in the interests of clarity and organization, all DEF statements should appear near the beginning of the program. The general format of the DEF statement is as follows:

  line# DEF function name (argument list) = expression

The function name consists of the letters FN followed by a valid variable name (e.g., FNROUND, FNAREA, or FNX). The arguments are one or more variables that are replaced by values given when the function is called (the Apple allows only one argument). The expression contains the operations performed by the function; it evaluates as a single value, which is returned by the function. The entire DEF statement cannot exceed one logical line.

FIGURE 8–16
The VAL Function

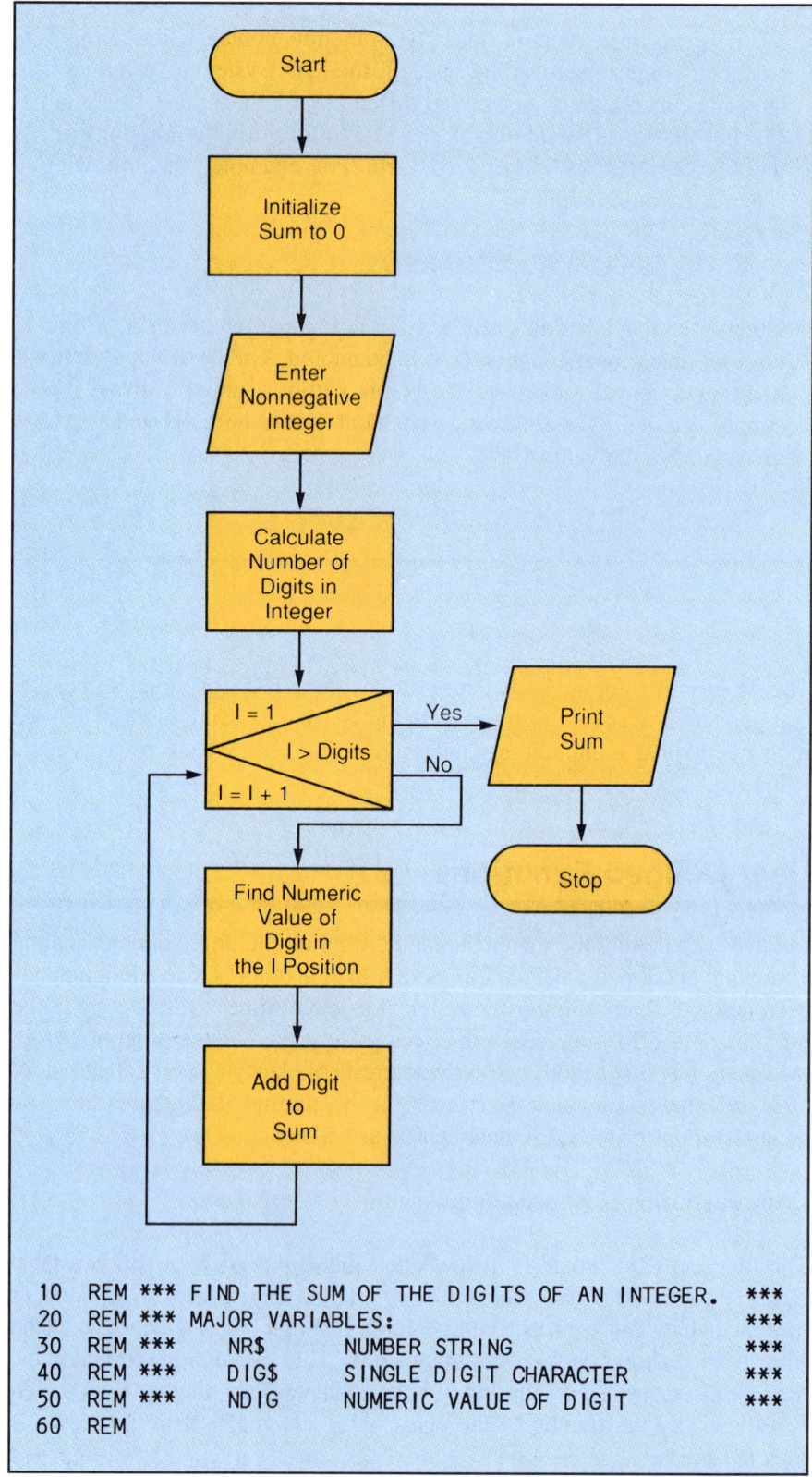

```
 70  SUM = 0
 80  INPUT "ENTER A NON-NEGATIVE INTEGER";NR$
 90  LNG = LEN(NR$)
100  FOR I = 1 TO LNG
110     DIG$ = MID$(NR$,I,1)
120     NDIG = VAL(DIG$)
130     SUM = SUM + NDIG
140  NEXT I
150  PRINT "SUM = ";SUM
999  END
```

```
RUNNH

ENTER A NON-NEGATIVE INTEGER? 7540
SUM =  16
```

DIFFERENCES

Apple:	None.
IBM/Microsoft:	None.
Macintosh/Microsoft:	None.

FIGURE 8–16
Continued

A call to a user-defined function has the following format:

function name (expression list)

The function name matches a function name appearing in a previous DEF statement. The one or more expressions are evaluated, and the results are used to replace the arguments of the DEF statement on a one-to-one basis.

The following segment demonstrates the use of a simple user-defined function. When the computer encounters line 10, it stores in memory the definition for the function FNR. Line 20 initializes PRICE to 5.50. When the computer encounters line 30, it evaluates the expression in parentheses

FIGURE 8–17 The STR$ Function

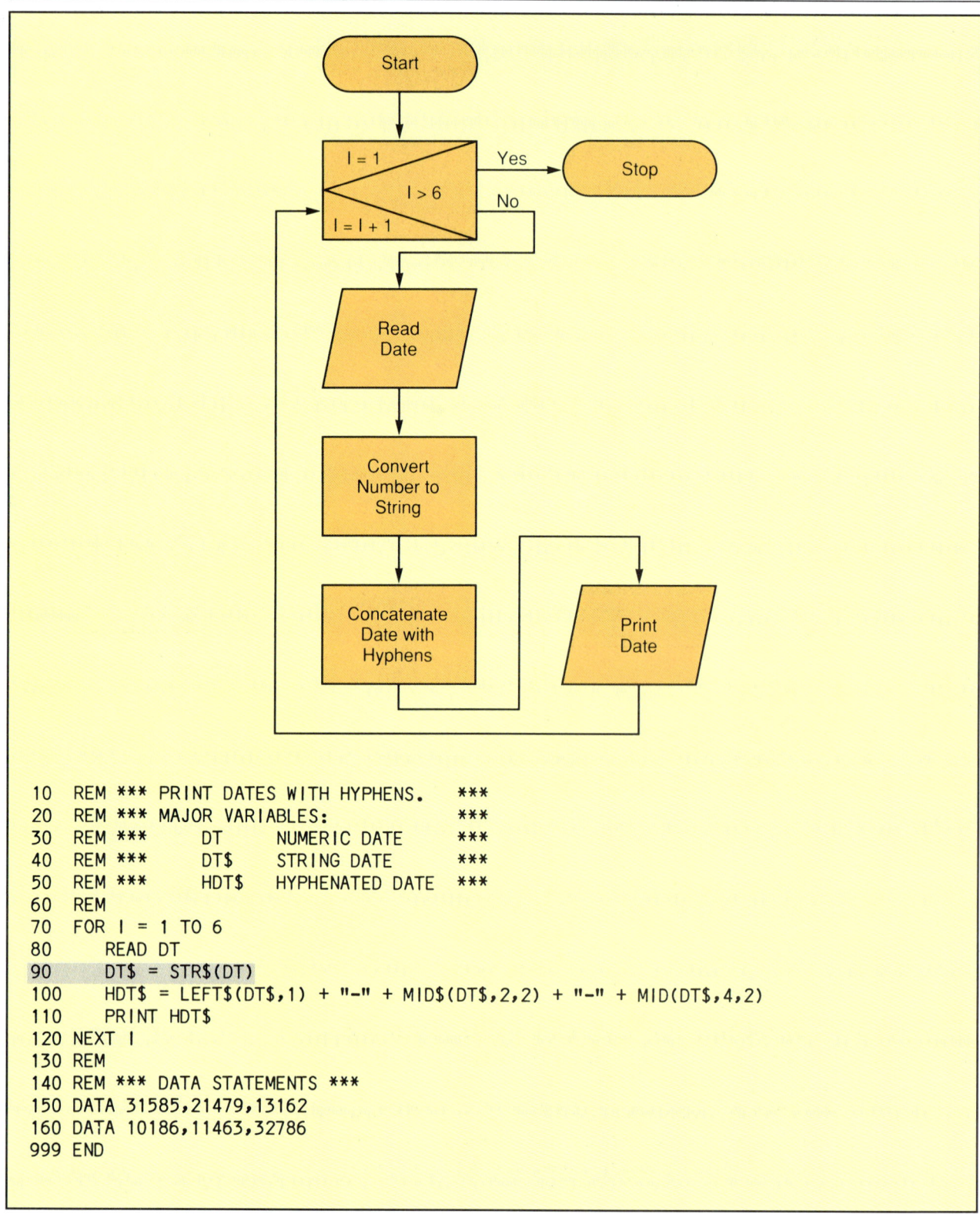

```
10   REM *** PRINT DATES WITH HYPHENS.   ***
20   REM *** MAJOR VARIABLES:            ***
30   REM ***     DT     NUMERIC DATE     ***
40   REM ***     DT$    STRING DATE      ***
50   REM ***     HDT$   HYPHENATED DATE  ***
60   REM
70   FOR I = 1 TO 6
80       READ DT
90       DT$ = STR$(DT)
100      HDT$ = LEFT$(DT$,1) + "-" + MID$(DT$,2,2) + "-" + MID(DT$,4,2)
110      PRINT HDT$
120  NEXT I
130  REM
140  REM *** DATA STATEMENTS ***
150  DATA 31585,21479,13162
160  DATA 10186,11463,32786
999  END
```

FIGURE 8-17 Continued

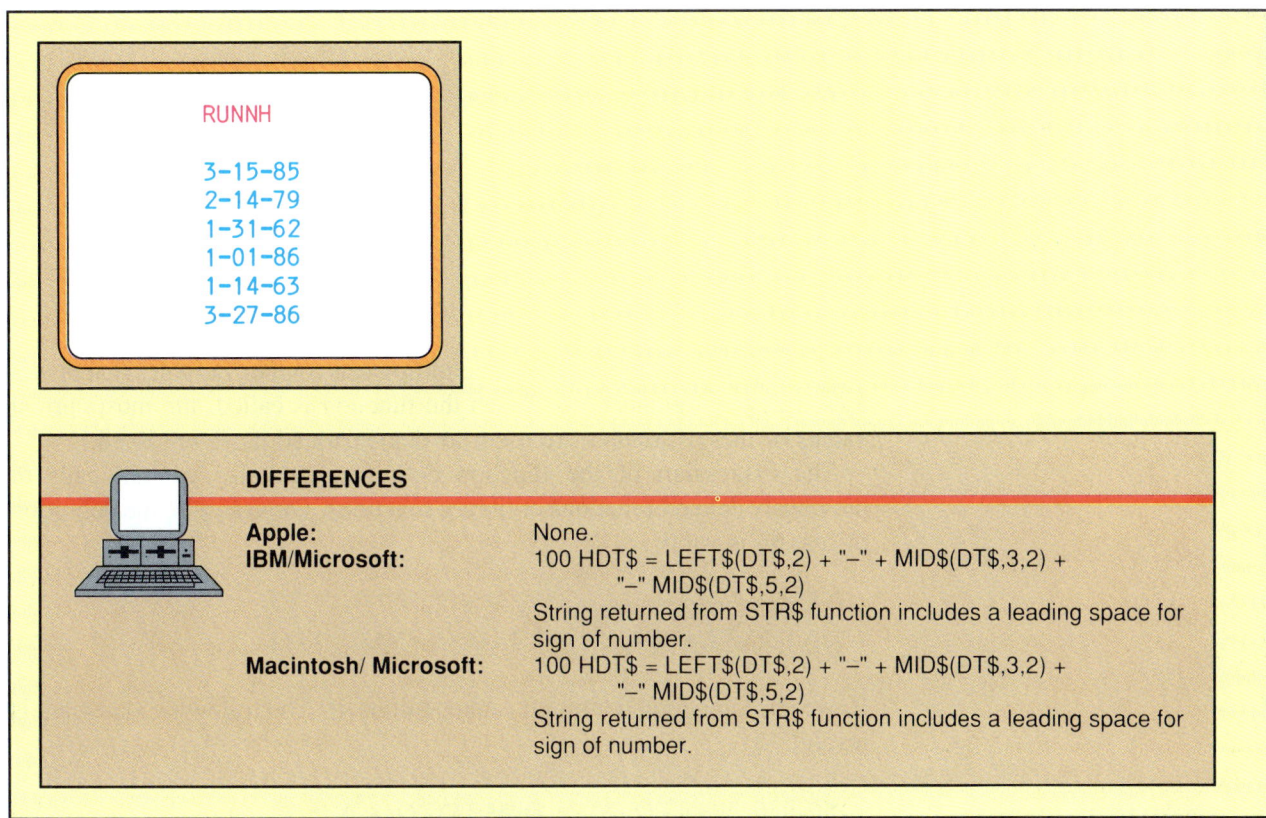

as 5.50; then, using the definition for FNR, it substitutes this value for *X*. Therefore, the expression (*X* + 20)/2 evaluates as 12.75. This value becomes the function value, which is printed by line 30.

```
10 DEF FNR(X) = (X + 20) / 2
20 PRICE = 5.50
30 PRINT FNR(PRICE)
```

RUNNH

12.75

The arguments in the DEF statement are sometimes called *dummy arguments* because they have no real values; they only show how the input values of the function will be used. A dummy argument can have the same name as a regular program variable without affecting the value of the regular variable, as shown in the following example. (However, this is not recommended because it makes the program logic difficult to follow.)

```
10 N = 3
20 DEF FNCUBE(N) = N * N * N
30 PRINT N
40 Y = 4
50 PRINT FNCUBE(Y)
60 PRINT N
```

RUNNH

3
64
3

The expression of the function definition can contain variables that do not appear in the argument list. When the function is called, the most current values of these variables are used, as demonstrated in Figure 8–18.

The expression of the function definition can also contain calls to previously defined functions or library functions. For example, the definition of line 60 is valid:

```
50 DEF FNMULT(X,Y) = (X * Y)
60 DEF FNCALC(X,Y) = SGN(X) + FNMULT(X,Y)
```

However, a function definition cannot call itself. The following statement is invalid:

```
60 DEF FNMULT(X,Y) = FNMULT(X,Y) + X + Y
```

Many systems (including those discussed in this book, with the exception of the Apple) also allow the programmer to define string functions. The type of a function, like that of a variable, is indicated by its name. For example, the function FNA$ specifies a string function, while FNA is a numeric function. Figure 8–19 demonstrates a user-defined string function that prints a name in the format of last name, first initial.

Learning Check

1. _____ _____ are functions defined by the programmer which are not already included in the BASIC language library.
2. The DEF statement can be placed _____.
   a. after the reference to the function
   b. anywhere before the first reference to the function
   c. only on the line immediately preceding the reference to the function
   d. none of the above
3. A function definition _____.
   a. cannot exceed one line
   b. may be up to four lines long
   c. may be any length

FIGURE 8–18 User-Defined Numeric Function

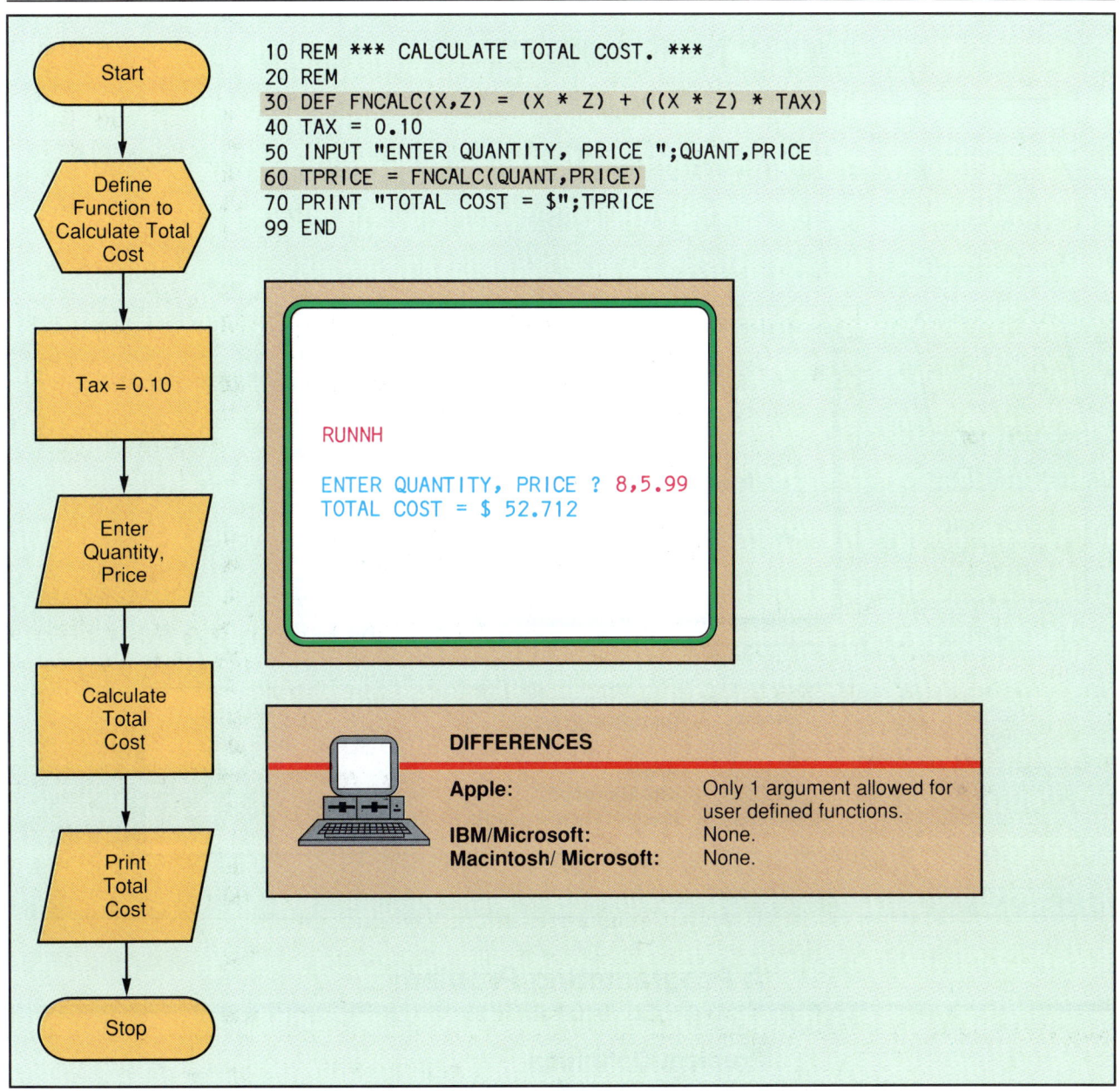

4. Which of the following statements are valid?
   a. 60 DEF FN1A(X) = X + 5
   b. 30 DEF FNA(X) = X / 3 + FNA(X)
   c. 40 DEF FNPAY(X) = (X + Y) / SIN (X)
   d. 50 DEF FNAN$(X) = CHR$(X)

Answers

1. User-defined functions 2. b 3. a 4. c and d

FIGURE 8-19 User-Defined String Function

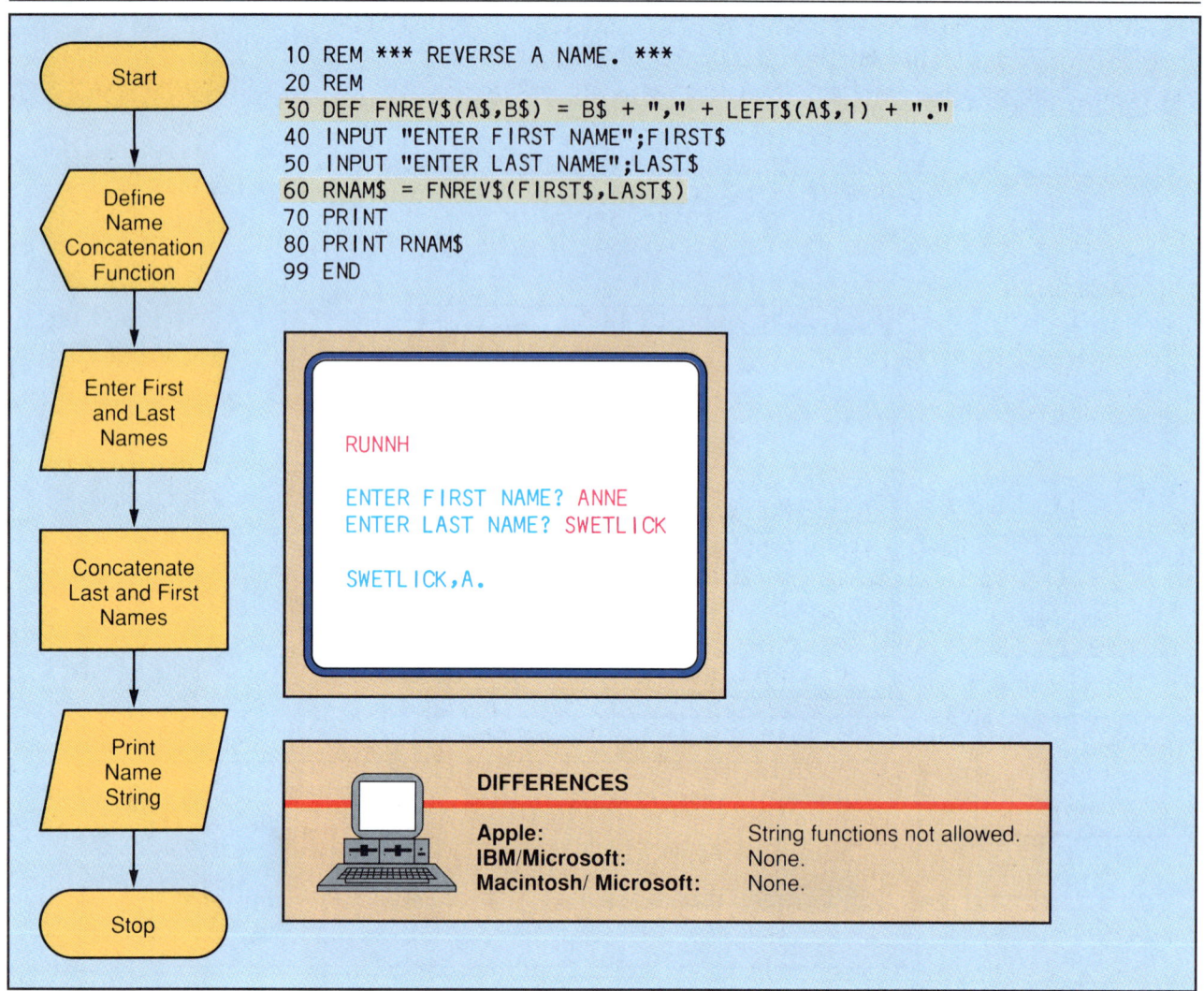

A Programming Problem

Problem Definition

Create an interactive program that generates a mathematical sequence and allows a player to guess the next number in the sequence. The program should show the player the first three numbers of the sequence and offer him or her the option of seeing the next number and as many numbers thereafter as he or she requests. The player should then be asked for a guess as to the next number, and the program should print appropriate messages in response to the guess. If the guess is correct, the game is over; otherwise, the player is again given the option of seeing more numbers.

The program should allow for upper- or lowercase responses of either a full word or a first letter, and guesses should be entered as character strings to guard against an error in case the player enters a non-numeric guess. The values of the sequence should be such that the nth member is generated by itself and adding to it the value $n - 1$. A sample game is shown below:

```
RUNNH
CURRENT SEQUENCE
   1    5    11
 DO YOU WANT TO SEE THE NEXT NUMBER ? Y
CURRENT SEQUENCE
   1    5    11   19
 DO YOU WANT TO SEE THE NEXT NUMBER ? N
 ENTER YOUR GUESS ? 29
 THAT'S CORRECT
```

Solution Design

Because this is an interactive program, it is helpful to consider what steps must be taken to enable the player to enter a correct guess—the action that ends the program. In order to begin, the player must be able to see a part of the sequence. Each element is calculated according to the same formula, so a user-defined function could be used in generating the sequence.

The second major step, and therefore a second subroutine of the program, must give the player the option of seeing another number. In order to do this, the program must prompt the player with a yes or no question. The player's response at this point could be converted to a Y or N and checked by another subroutine. If the answer is yes, then the first step of the program (printing the current number sequence) must be performed again. This process of prompting the player and displaying the sequence can continue until the player answers no; the repetition should suggest a loop.

The third major step of the program is to allow a guess to be entered. This step involves prompting the user, checking to see if the guess is correct (and therefore generating the next number of the sequence), and then printing an appropriate message. A correct guess ends the game; otherwise, the program must continue to offer the player more numbers and accept guesses until a correct guess is entered. These two processes could therefore be initiated within a loop.

This algorithm is outlined in Figure 8–20 and diagrammed in Figure 8–21. Each of the steps on the second level of the diagram represents a subroutine. Notice that the subroutine offering the player another number calls two other subroutines, and that one of these is a subroutine that has already been called by the main program.

The variables needed by the program are relatively few. The input variables consist of the user's input, a Y/N response to the question of whether another number is to be displayed, and the user's guess. Program variables needed are a counter to keep track of the numbers in the currently displayed sequence, and a flag to indicate a correct guess. The only output

FIGURE 8–20
Stepwise Refinement of Number Game Problem

General Problem: Create a game allowing the player to guess the next number of a mathematical sequence.

Level 1
 A. Print first three numbers of sequence
 B. Offer to show the player the next number
 C. Offer the player the chance to guess

Level 2
 B.1. Convert player response
 B.2. Print next number in sequence

FIGURE 8–21
Number Game Structure Chart

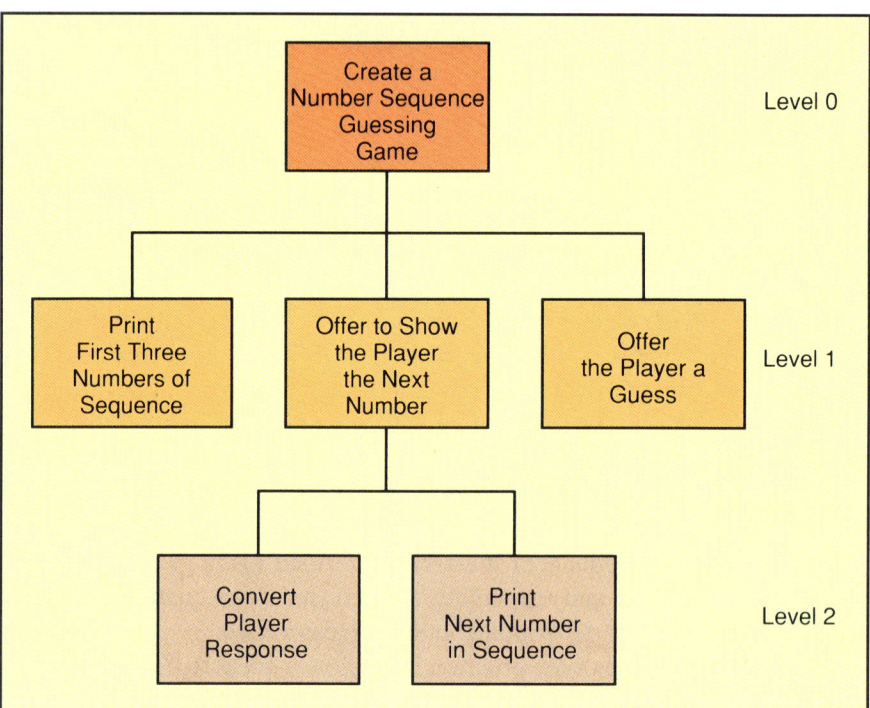

is a message to the user, so no variable is required. The needed variables are summarized below:

Input variables

player response   (AN$)
player guess   (GUES$)

Program variables

count of numbers generated   (CNT)
flag for correct guess   (OK$)

The Program

The program in Figure 8–22 uses four subroutines and one user-defined function (defined in line 90) to solve the problem. The variable CNT is used

FUNCTIONS 319

FIGURE 8-22 Number Game Program

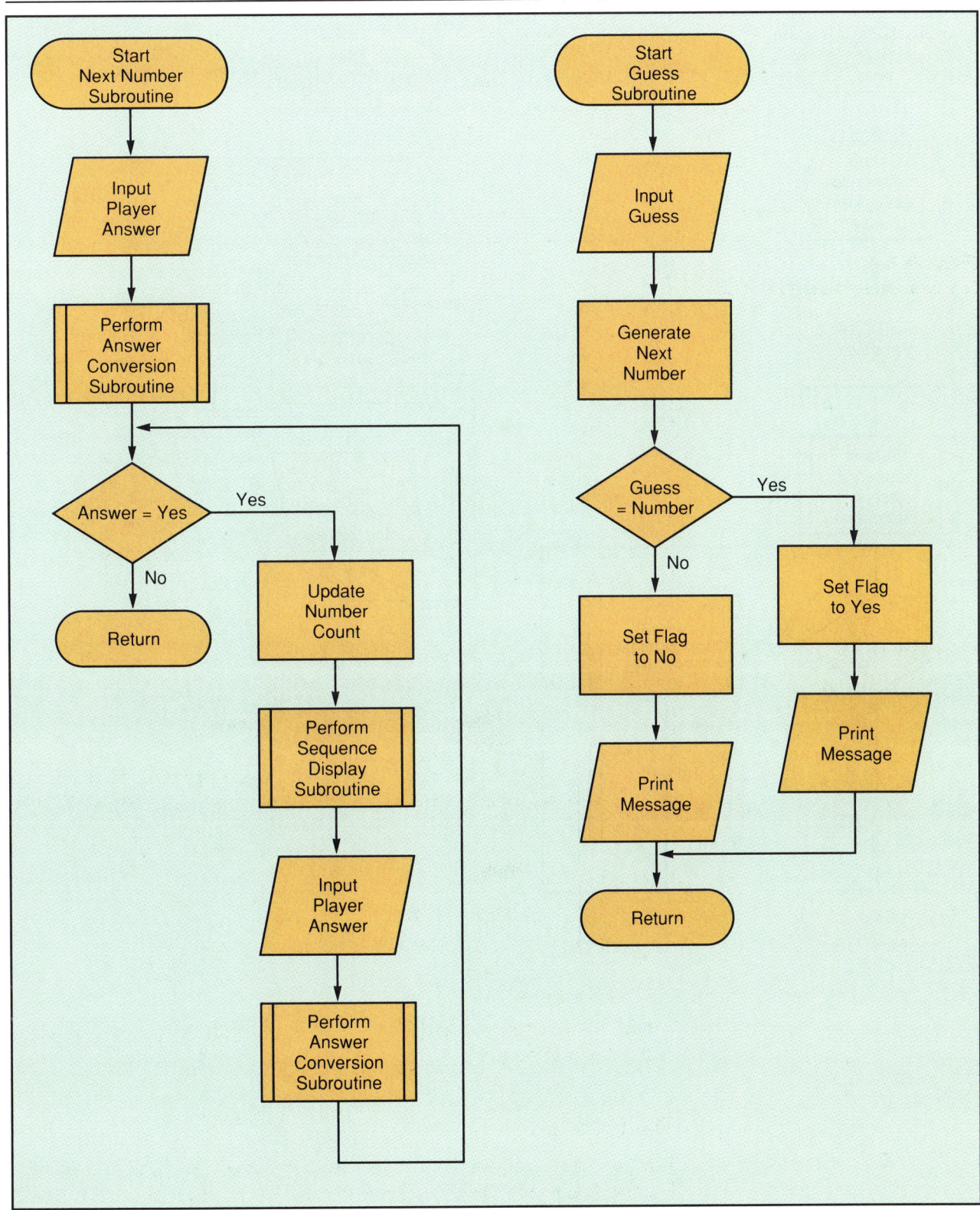

FIGURE 8–22 *Continued*

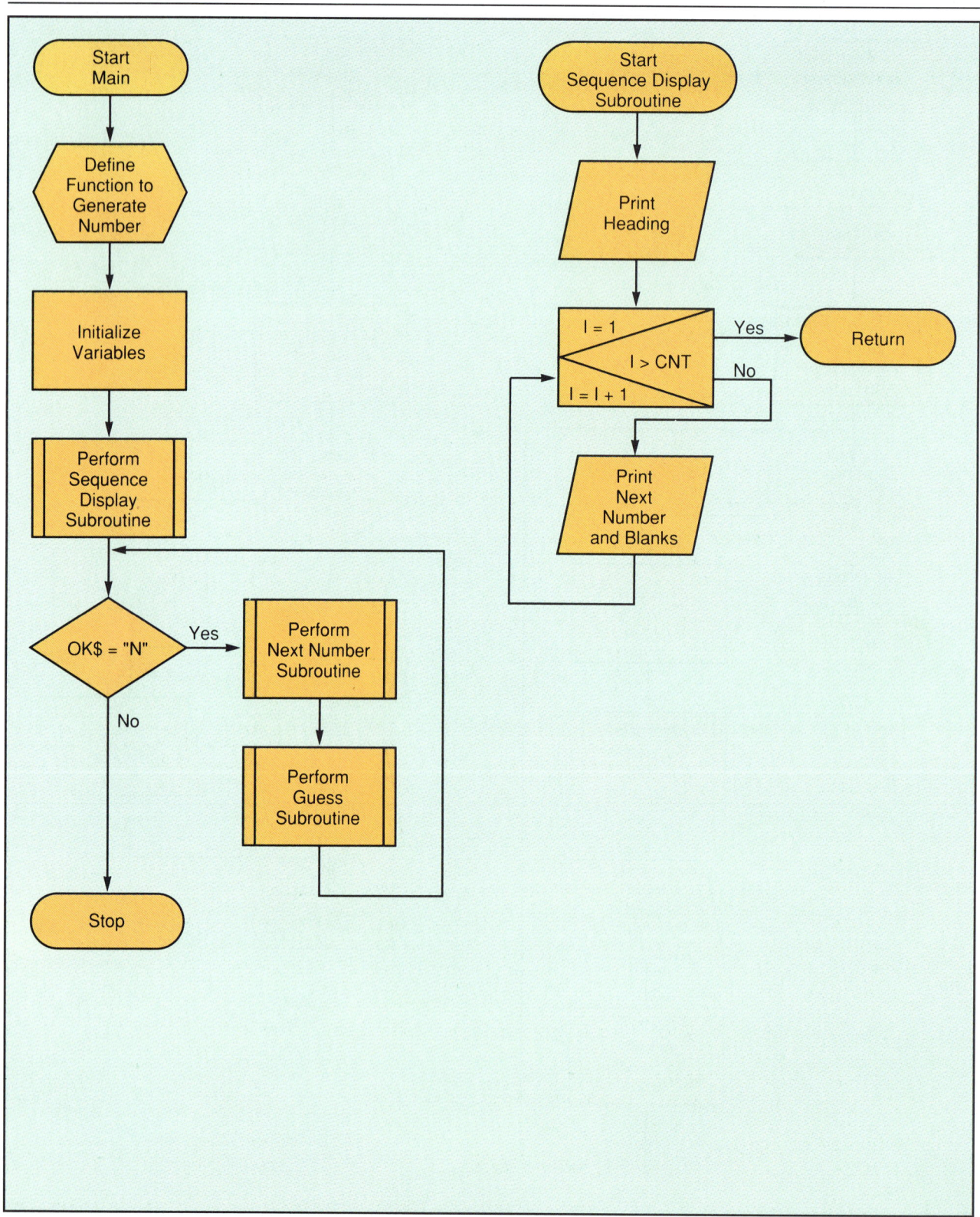

FIGURE 8-22 Continued

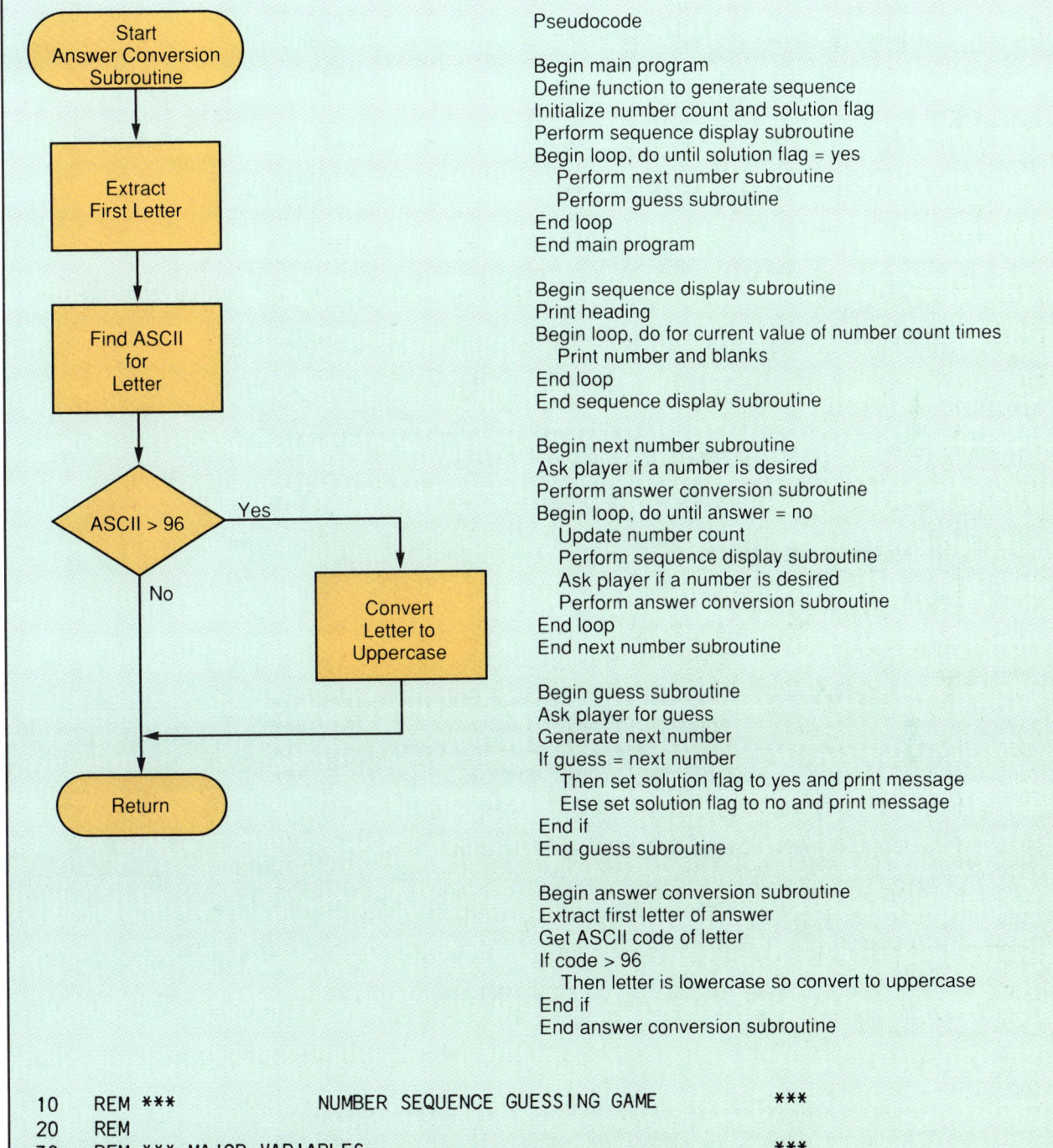

FIGURE 8–22 *Continued*

```
80   REM
90   DEF FNXT(X) = (X * X) + (X - 1)
100  REM
110  REM *** INITIALIZE VARIABLES. ***
120  CNT = 3
130  OK$ = "N"
140  REM
150  REM *** DISPLAY INITIAL SEQUENCE. ***
160  GOSUB 1000
170  REM
180  REM *** LOOP TO DISPLAY NUMBERS AND ACCEPT GUESSES UNTIL CORRECT. ***
190  WHILE OK$ = "N"
200     GOSUB 2000
210     GOSUB 3000
220  NEXT
230  GOTO 9999
1000 REM
1010 REM ************************************************************
1020 REM ***              SUBROUTINE SEQUENCE DISPLAY            ***
1030 REM ************************************************************
1040 REM ***                DISPLAY CURRENT SEQUENCE             ***
1050 REM
1060 PRINT "CURRENT SEQUENCE"
1070 FOR I = 1 TO CNT
1080    PRINT FNXT(I);"  ";
1090 NEXT I
1100 RETURN
2000 REM
2010 REM ************************************************************
2020 REM ***                 SUBROUTINE NEXT NUMBER              ***
2030 REM ************************************************************
2040 REM ***              PROVIDE ADDITIONAL NUMBERS.            ***
2050 REM
2060 PRINT
2070 INPUT "DO YOU WANT TO SEE THE NEXT NUMBER";AN$
2080 GOSUB 4000
2090 WHILE AN$ = "Y"
2100    CNT = CNT + 1
2110    GOSUB 1000
2120    PRINT
2130    INPUT "DO YOU WANT TO SEE THE NEXT NUMBER";AN$
2140    GOSUB 4000
2150 NEXT
2160 RETURN
3000 REM
3010 REM ************************************************************
3020 REM ***                    SUBROUTINE GUESS                 ***
3030 REM ************************************************************
3040 REM ***             ACCEPT AND TEST PLAYER'S GUESS          ***
3050 REM
3060 INPUT "ENTER YOUR GUESS";GUES$
```

FIGURE 8–22 Continued

```
3070 REM
3080 REM *** GENERATE NEXT NUMBER AND TEST GUESS. ***
3090 TEMP = CNT + 1
3100 NXT$ = STR$(FNXT(TEMP))
3110 IF NXT$ = GUES$ THEN OK$ = "Y" \ PRINT "THAT'S CORRECT" \
        ELSE OK$ = "N" \ PRINT "SORRY, INCORRECT"
3120 RETURN
4000 REM
4010 REM ************************************************************
4020 REM ***              SUBROUTINE ANSWER CONVERSION            ***
4030 REM ************************************************************
4040 REM ***            CONVERT PLAYER RESPONSE TO Y/N            ***
4050 REM
4060 AN$ = LEFT$(AN$,1)
4070 B = ASCII(AN$)
4080 IF B > 96 THEN AN$ = CH$(B - 32)
4090 RETURN
9999 END
```

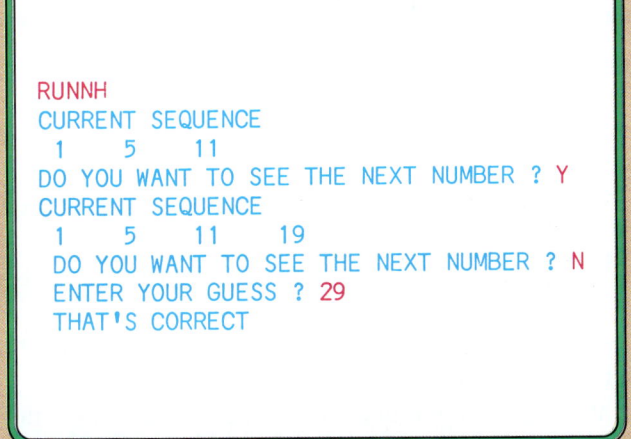

```
RUNNH
CURRENT SEQUENCE
  1    5    11
DO YOU WANT TO SEE THE NEXT NUMBER ? Y
CURRENT SEQUENCE
  1    5    11    19
DO YOU WANT TO SEE THE NEXT NUMBER ? N
ENTER YOUR GUESS ? 29
THAT'S CORRECT
```

DIFFERENCES

Apple:	No WHILE loop; No IF/THEN/ELSE; 4070 B = ASC(AN$)
IBM/Microsoft:	220 WEND; 2150 WEND; 4070 B = ASC(AN$)
Macintosh/Microsoft:	220 WEND; 2150 WEND; 4070 B = ASC(AN$)

to keep track of the quantity of numbers which have been displayed; this is initially set to 3 in line 120 to begin the game. The variable OK$, initialized to N, is used as a flag that indicates whether a correct guess has been given and the game is to end.

The WHILE loop of lines 190 through 220 allows the player to see numbers and make guesses until the answer flag equals Y. The subroutine of lines 1000 through 1100 displays the current sequence by calling the user-defined function FNNXT. The second subroutine asks the player if another number is needed; the answer is converted to a Y or N by calling the fourth subroutine in lines 4000 through 4090. Each time the player responds to a yes/no question, his or her answer is checked in this way.

When the player does not want to see more numbers, the subroutine beginning at line 3000 is called to accept a guess, which is entered as a string in line 3060. The next number of the sequence is computed in line 3100 and converted to a string to be compared to the guess. In line 3110, the flag OK$ is set to reflect a correct or incorrect guess, and control is passed back to the main program at line 220. The WHILE statement then checks the flag and either repeats the entire process or terminates the game.

Avoiding Common Programming Mistakes

- Remember that a function definition must appear in the program before a reference to that function occurs.
- Be aware of the restrictions placed on the arguments of the various functions.
- Remember that a function reference cannot appear to the left of an equal sign.
- A function cannot appear on the right side of the equal sign in its own definition.
- A function is evaluated as a single value immediately; it has a higher priority than arithmetic, relational, and logical operators.
- Remember that the INT function does not round to the nearest integer; instead, it returns the largest integer less than or equal to its argument.
- For most systems to produce a truly random number, the RANDOM or RANDOMIZE statements must be used in conjunction with the RND function. If your system requires the RANDOM or RANDOMIZE statements, these statements must precede the first RND reference.

Summary Points

- The BASIC language includes several library functions that can make complicated mathematical operations easier to program.
- The trigonometric functions are SIN (X), COS (X), TAN (X), and ATN (X), where X is in radians.

- The exponential, or EXP, function calculates $EXP(X) = e^x$, and the natural logarithm or LOG (X) function is the reverse of that function.
- The SQR (X) function returns the square root of its argument.
- The INT (X) function computes the greatest integer less than or equal to the value specified as the argument.
- The SGN (X) function produces a 1, 0, or −1, depending on whether the argument is positive, zero, or negative respectively.
- The ABS (X) function returns the absolute value of its argument.
- BASIC string functions permit modification, concatenation, comparison, and analysis of the composition of strings.
- The concatenation operation (+) joins two strings together.
- The LEN function is used to find the number of characters in a string.
- The LEFT$ function returns a specified number of leftmost characters of a string.
- The RIGHT$ function returns the specified rightmost characters of a string.
- The MID$ function enables the programmer to gain access to characters in the middle of a string.
- The ASCII (ASC on the microcomputers) function returns the ASCII code for the first character in a string.
- The CHR$ function returns the string representation of the ASCII code of the expression.
- The VAL (X) function is used to find the numeric equivalent of a string expression.
- The STR$ function acts as a reverse of the VAL (X) function by converting a number to its string equivalent.
- The programmer can define functions by using the DEF statement. A user-defined function definition cannot exceed one line and must precede any reference to it in a program.

Review Questions

1. What is a function?
2. What are the two types of functions available in BASIC?
3. What are the allowable arguments of a function?
4. How many values can be returned by a function?
5. Angles, when used as arguments to trigonometric functions, are measured in _____.
6. What are the four trigonometric functions?
7. What does the EXP (X) function do?
8. Which function is the reverse of the EXP (X) function?
9. The argument X in SQR (X) can be _____.
   a. any number
   b. any non-negative number
   c. only a positive whole number
   d. any negative number

10. What is the result of INT (−3.4)?
11. Write a BASIC statement using the INT (X) function to round a number to the nearest hundredth.
12. What possible values can SGN (X) return?
13. The function ABS (X) always returns _____.
    a. a number greater than or equal to 0
    b. a number less than or equal to 0
    c. a whole number
    d. an even number
14. The RND function generates a random number between what two values?
15. What BASIC statement is needed to define a user-defined function?
16. What are the rules for naming a user-defined function?
17. What limits, if any, are placed on the length of a function definition?
18. Where is the function definition placed in a program?
19. What is meant by string concatenation?
20. The _____ function returns the number of characters in a string.
21. Explain the use of the LEFT$, RIGHT$, and MID$ functions.
22. What is the restriction placed on an argument of the ASCII function?
23. What two functions help programs respond to both lowercase and uppercase input?
24. What function changes a number in character string format to a real number?
25. What does the STR$ function do?

Debugging Exercises

Identify the following programs and program segments that contain errors and debug them.

1. ```
   10 REM *** PRINT THE COSINE OF X. ***
   20 READ X
   30 Y = COS(X)
   40 PRINT Y
   50 REM *** DATA IS IN DEGREES. ***
   60 DATA 60
   ```

2. ```
   10 REM *** PRINT THE SQUARE ROOT OF A. ***
   20 READ A
   30 B = SQR(A)
   40 PRINT B
   50 DATA -22
   ```

3. ```
   10 INPUT "T = ";T
   20 M = EXP(T,X)
   30 PRINT M
   ```
   ```

4. ```
10 REM *** CALCULATE TOTAL. ***
20 DEF FR(M,T) = M * T + 2
30 READ M1
40 READ T1
50 ANSWR = FNR(M1,T1)
60 PRINT ANSWR
70 DATA 10,5
```
5. ```
10 READ X
20 PRINT FNA(X)
30 DEF FNA(Y) = EXP(Y) + 5
40 DATA 22
```
6. ```
10 REM *** PRINT "CHOP SUEY." ***
20 X$ = "CHOP"
30 Y$ = "SUEY"
40 Z$ = X$ + Y$
50 PRINT Z$
```
7. ```
10 REM *** CONVERT 5 STRING VALUES TO NUMBERS ***
20 REM *** AND DIVIDE THEM IN HALF.           ***
30 FOR I = 1 TO 5
40    READ N$
50    N = STR$(N$)
60    N = N * .5
70    PRINT N
80 NEXT I
```
8. ```
10 REM *** PRINT ASCII VALUE OF FIRST LETTER ***
20 REM *** IN A CHARACTER STRING.   ***
30 N$ = "HELLO"
40 PRINT ASCII(N$)

RUNNH
 79
```
9. ```
10  REM *** LIST PEOPLE WITH MIDDLE INITIAL A. ***
20  FOR J = 1 TO 5
30     READ N$
40     K = LEN(N$)
50     FOR I = 1 TO 5
60        L$ = LEFT$(N$,I)
70        R$ = RIGHT$(L$,I - 1)
80        IF R$ = " " THEN 90
90     NEXT I
90     IF MID$(N$,I,1) = "A" THEN PRINT N$
100 NEXT J
110 DATA MITCH ANTHONY MARCSON
120 DATA TONY WILLIAM REHMER
130 DATA JEREMIAH ALLEN SORENSON,MIKE DAVID LOUGHMAN
140 DATA JOSIE MARIE VALENZUELA
999 END
```
10. ```
10 REM *** DETERMINE LENGTH OF A CHARACTER STRING.
20 N$ = "NEW WORLD"
30 X = LEN(N$)
40 PRINT X

RUNNH
  8
```
```

Additional Programming Problems

Level 1

1. Write a line of code that will transfer program execution to line 100, 200, or 300 depending on the sign of a value in the numeric variable *A*.

2. Write a program that will read a positive integer as a character string and print it with commas inserted where appropriate if the number has four or more digits. (Hint: Concatenate digits with commas starting from the right end of the number.) Use the following data:

    45
    1345623
    100000
    0
    999
    3900

3. Write a program that will print the alphabet twice, in uppercase and in lowercase letters, with slashes (/) between the letters. Use the CHR$ function. A subroutine should be called by a GOSUB statement to concatenate the letter with the slash. The output should have the following format:

    ALPHABET
    A/B/C/. . ./Z

    alphabet
    a/b/c/d/e/. . ./z

4. Write an interactive program that accepts a Celsius temperature and prints the Fahrenheit equivalent. Define one function to use the following formula:

    F = (C * 9 / 5) + 32

A second function should round the results to the nearest tenth of a degree. Let the user enter temperatures as long as desired. Test the program with the following data: 0, 10, 100.

5. Write a program that will print all Social Security numbers with the fourth and fifth digits 64. Read each data line as a character string. Use the following data:

    316642789
    341425632
    278428909
    341648902
    316645430

The output should have the following format:

XXX-XX-XXXX

6. Write a program to generate a random number between 1 and 1,000. Find the square root of this number. Print the random number and its square root.

7. Write a program that will print the absolute value of a number and a plus or minus sign after the number, depending on whether the number is positive or negative.

8. Write a program that will read a sentence and delete the word "IF" wherever it occurs, replacing it with "**". Print the original sentence and the new sentence. Use the following sentence for your input data:

DELETE THE WORD IF WHEREVER IT OCCURS

9. A shoe store has devised a system to help detect errors in recording inventory. The last two digits of every stock number must be the sum of the preceding three digits. For example, the stock number QB412.07 is valid because 07 is the sum of 4 + 1 + 2. Write a program that reads in stock numbers and prints a list of any invalid numbers. Use the following data:

QB371.11	QA919.17
UT491.14	QB497.20
UT307.11	UT410.05
AT478.19	AT731.11
QB115.08	

10. The town of Micropolis has taken a poll of its ten families to determine the average number of television sets per family. Write a program to read the poll data, then calculate and print the average. Define a function to round the result to the nearest whole TV. Use the following test data: 1, 0, 4, 3, 2, 3, 7, 2, 3, 4.

Level 2

1. The Weight Control Center has asked you to write a program to keep track of its customers' weights. Implement this program using a WHILE loop that will execute until customer = " + ". Read each customer's name and current weight as a character string and the weight gained or lost as a numeric value. Use the following data:

Customer's Current Record		Gained	Lost
Betty Green	180	10	
Allen Beech	210		30

John Forbes	250	5	
Kerry Lendall	195		5
Tracy Abbott	175	15	
+	0	0	

The output should consist of the customers' names and present weights.

2. Write a program to print the trigonometric functions sine, cosine, and tangent for 1° to 15°. Define a function to convert degrees to radians and another function to round the results to four decimal places. The output should be printed in a format similar to this:

DEGREES	SIN X	COS X	TAN X
X	X.XXXX	X.XXXX	X.XXXX

3. Write a program to demonstrate that the following statement is true, using sample data:

$$\sqrt{a^2 + a^2} = a\sqrt{2}$$

Define three functions: one to solve the left side of the equation above, a second to solve the right side, and a third to round the value of each side to two decimal places. Use the following test data for *a:* 4, 17, 9, 20, 5.

4. Write a program to simulate the tossing of a coin ten times. After the ten tosses, print the total number of heads and tails. Generate random numbers to represent the tosses, where 1 = heads and 2 = tails. Define a function to generate the needed random numbers.

5. Write a program that reads a sentence and switches all lowercase letters to capitals and all uppercase letters to lowercase. Print the original and converted sentences. Use the following data:

"Miss B. was seen Saturday at Serendipity with a British musician."
"Late Night with David Letterman is broadcast from the NBC studios."

6. Write a program to find the range of the values in a group of ten numbers (that is the highest and lowest values) and the mean (or average) value. Define functions as appropriate. Use the following data to test your program:

10.5   18.4   33.0   40.8   72.1   16.3   93.3   21.9   17.5   83.0

7. The brightness of heavenly bodies can be represented by an apparent magnitude value. The brightest objects have negative magnitudes and the faintest have positive magnitudes. Write a program that reads sample magnitudes and prints a chart classifying them according to brightness: negative values are bright, zeros are medium, and positive values are faint. Also, calculate the average magnitude rounded to the nearest tenth and print it. Use the SGN function and the following data:

Object	Magnitude
Sun	−26.5
Vega	0.0
Sirius	−1.4
Uranus	5.5
Neptune	7.8
Mars	−2.7
Jupiter	−2.6
Pluto	15.0

8. Write a program that will insert three asterisks on either side of a comment in a REM statement. Use the following data:

```
10 REM EXAMPLE PROGRAM
20 FOR I = 1 TO 10
30 REM PRINT THE VALUE OF I
40 PRINT I
50 REM GO TO TOP OF LOOP
60 NEXT I
```

The output should look like this:

```
10 REM *** EXAMPLE PROGRAM ***
20 FOR I = 1 TO 10
30 REM *** PRINT THE VALUE OF I ***
40 PRINT I
50 REM *** GO TO TOP OF LOOP ***
60 NEXT I
```

9. Write a program that will accept four names and print their initials. Use the following data:

Merlin Michael Mueller
Kara Lee Martin
Mary Lynn Deep
Pamela Ann Kim

The initials should be in caps and printed in the following format:

X.X.X.

A subroutine should be called by a GOSUB statement to concatenate the initials.

10. Write a program that will print the intersection of two lowercase character strings (i.e., the characters that the two strings have in common). The output should have the following format:

STRING1 INTERSECTS STRING2 = {X,X,X,X, . . . X}

The set should contain no duplicates.

Level 3

1. Your deadly bacteria culture experiment for biology is out of control. Write a program to calculate the population of the culture after 30, 60, 90, and 120 minutes if you started with 500 bacteria. Use the formula

$$P = (P_0 * e)^{kt}$$

where P_0 is the initial population size, t is the elapsed time in minutes, and k is the constant 0.032. Use a FOR/NEXT loop to read the time values and print the population for each time.

2. Write a program to produce a table comparing the exponential and natural logarithm functions of a given value Y. Define a function to round the results to four decimal places. Use the numbers 1 through 10 to test the program, and format the output similar to the following:

If Y is	EXP (Y)	LOG(Y)
1	e^1 = X.XXXX	1 = X.XXXX
2	e^2 = X.XXXX	2 = X.XXXX
.	.	.
.	.	.
.	.	.

3. Write a program that generates a random integer X in the range 1 through 10 and calculates a Y value according to the following formula:

$$Y = e^x + \sqrt{8X - 7}$$

Define functions to generate the integer X and to perform the calculation. Print two columns showing the X and Y values.

4. Write a program that will use the following formulas to determine a numeric value for each of the listed letters occurring in a given word. The ordinal value of a letter refers to its position in the alphabet (e.g., ordinal value of A = 1.)

A = (ordinal value of A) * 2
E = ((ordinal value of E) / 3) + 5
R = (ordinal value of R) / 2
T = (ordinal value of T) + 10
C = (ordinal value of C) − 20
D = ((ordinal value of D) / 12) * 3

Object	Magnitude
Sun	−26.5
Vega	0.0
Sirius	−1.4
Uranus	5.5
Neptune	7.8
Mars	−2.7
Jupiter	−2.6
Pluto	15.0

8. Write a program that will insert three asterisks on either side of a comment in a REM statement. Use the following data:

```
10 REM EXAMPLE PROGRAM
20 FOR I = 1 TO 10
30 REM PRINT THE VALUE OF I
40 PRINT I
50 REM GO TO TOP OF LOOP
60 NEXT I
```

The output should look like this:

```
10 REM *** EXAMPLE PROGRAM ***
20 FOR I = 1 TO 10
30 REM *** PRINT THE VALUE OF I ***
40 PRINT I
50 REM *** GO TO TOP OF LOOP ***
60 NEXT I
```

9. Write a program that will accept four names and print their initials. Use the following data:

Merlin Michael Mueller
Kara Lee Martin
Mary Lynn Deep
Pamela Ann Kim

The initials should be in caps and printed in the following format:

X.X.X.

A subroutine should be called by a GOSUB statement to concatenate the initials.

10. Write a program that will print the intersection of two lowercase character strings (i.e., the characters that the two strings have in common). The output should have the following format:

STRING1 INTERSECTS STRING2 = {X,X,X,X, . . . X}

The set should contain no duplicates.

Level 3

1. Your deadly bacteria culture experiment for biology is out of control. Write a program to calculate the population of the culture after 30, 60, 90, and 120 minutes if you started with 500 bacteria. Use the formula

$$P = (P_0 * e)^{kt}$$

where P_0 is the initial population size, t is the elapsed time in minutes, and k is the constant 0.032. Use a FOR/NEXT loop to read the time values and print the population for each time.

2. Write a program to produce a table comparing the exponential and natural logarithm functions of a given value Y. Define a function to round the results to four decimal places. Use the numbers 1 through 10 to test the program, and format the output similar to the following:

If Y is	EXP (Y)	LOG(Y)
1	e^1 = X.XXXX	1 = X.XXXX
2	e^2 = X.XXXX	2 = X.XXXX
.	.	.
.	.	.
.	.	.

3. Write a program that generates a random integer X in the range 1 through 10 and calculates a Y value according to the following formula:

$$Y = e^x + \sqrt{8X - 7}$$

Define functions to generate the integer X and to perform the calculation. Print two columns showing the X and Y values.

4. Write a program that will use the following formulas to determine a numeric value for each of the listed letters occurring in a given word. The ordinal value of a letter refers to its position in the alphabet (e.g., ordinal value of $A = 1$.)

A = (ordinal value of A) * 2
E = ((ordinal value of E) / 3) + 5
R = (ordinal value of R) / 2
T = (ordinal value of T) + 10
C = (ordinal value of C) − 20
D = ((ordinal value of D) / 12) * 3

Ignore any characters other than the ones above. The program should sum the calculated letter values to determine a final numeric value for the word. A subroutine should be called by a GOSUB statement to calculate the value of each word. Use the READ/DATA statement to enter the following data. Each word should be in capital letters. Use the trailer value /*.

```
CHARACTER
ARISTOCRAT
SINGER
REPUBLICAN
DEMOCRAT
/*
```

The output should have the following format:

THE VALUE FOR THE WORD "XXX" IS "X".

5. The Chintz Toy Company needs to know how much to charge for its four new products in order to make a 120 percent profit. The cost of making the toys is calculated with the following formula, where X is a combination of various production factors.

$$COST = (X^3 / 16) - (X^2 / 2) + 4$$

Write a program that will read the X values for four new toys and calculate the production costs. Then calculate the final sale prices of the toys at 120 percent of the production costs. Define a function to figure the cost to Chintz and round the final sale prices to the nearest cent. The values of X to be used as test data are 10, 15, 9, and 7.

6. Write a program to see if a given input string is a *palindrome* (a word, phrase, or sentence that reads the same backward and forward). The program should accept character strings from the user, printing a message for each input which tells whether or not it is a palindrome. The user may input any number of strings. The only characters appearing on the input string besides letters will be blanks. Use the following data to test your program:

```
NAME NO ONE MAN
A MAN A PLAN A CANAL PANAMA
BANANA BOAT
```

7. AAA wants you to write a program that will help the customers in the state of Ohio determine in which month their license plates need to be renewed and the amount due. The month is determined by the first character in the customer's last name. The following information should be used:

Membership of AAA $19.00
Non-membership $22.00

A–F	January
G–L	February
M–Q	March
R–Z	April

Subroutines should be called by a GOSUB statement to determine the amount due. Use the ASCII code to determine the month. The output should have the following format:

License Bureau

PLEASE ENTER YOUR LAST NAME: XXX
DO YOU BELONG TO AAA? X
AMOUNT DUE IS $XX.XX
RENEWAL MONTH IS XXXX

8. Write a program that simulates the drawing of fifteen cards from a deck. Two random numbers should be generated: one for the suit (1 = hearts, 2 = diamonds, 3 = clubs, 4 = spades) and one for the values 2 through 10 (the face cards have been removed). Each card should be printed like this:

2 OF HEARTS
5 OF CLUBS
   .
   .
   .

After the fifteen cards have been drawn, print messages telling each suit's percentage of the cards drawn, as in the following examples:

20% of the cards were spades
50% of the cards were hearts

Define a function to calculate the percentages and round them to the nearest whole percent. For this simulation we will allow duplicate cards to be generated.

9. The Lotto Bank has the unusual policy of drawing lots for its customer's interest rates on timed certificates. Rates can range from 3 percent to 20 percent. Interest is compounded continually according to the formula

$$A = Pe^{rt}$$

where A is the final amount, P is the principal, r is the interest rate, t is the time in years, and e is the constant 2.718. Write a program that generates a random interest rate for each customer and computes that customer's new balance. Use the following data:

Name	Principal	Time (years)
Pia Christianson	$4,100	1
Irene Paplas	$2,000	3
Tony Rainer	$620	3
Doug Ausome	$150	2
Dale Smith	$4,300	3
NONAME	$0	0

Print each customer's name and new balance with appropriate headings.

10. You have been hired to write a program to evaluate teachers. You have come up with a formula that will evaluate the teacher on the following scale:

negative number	bad teacher
zero	average teacher
positive number	good teacher

The formula operates on four variables, A, B, C, and X, which are evaluations of the teacher's performance. The rating is calculated as follows:

Rating $= 5 + Z * 0.85$

where $Z = X + A - (X * B) + (C/X)$. Write a program that will read the teacher's name and rating variables X, A, B, and C, and calculate the rating. Define a function to calculate the rating. Use the following data:

Teacher	X	A	B	C
Dixon	5	10	7	4
Meronk	10	1	1	6
Hastings	2	10	3	1
Mishler	10	9	3	7

Print each teacher and rating with appropriate headings.

CHAPTER 9

ARRAYS

Objectives

After studying this chapter, you will be able to:
- Explain the purpose of subscripts.
- Use the DIM statement to dimension arrays.
- Read data to, print, and manipulate arrays.
- Sort arrays using both the bubble and Shell sorts.
- Use the merge sort to merge two sorted arrays.
- Search for data items in an array using both the sequential and binary searches.

Outline

Overview
Subscripts
Dimensioning an Array
One-Dimensional Arrays
   Reading Data to an Array
   Printing the Contents of an Array
   Performing Calculations on Array Elements
Multi-Dimensional Arrays
   Reading and Printing with Two-Dimensional Arrays
   Adding Rows

Adding Columns
Totaling a Two-Dimensional Array
Arrays with More Than Two Dimensions
Sorting
   Bubble Sort
   Shell Sort
   Merge Sort
Searching
   Sequential Search
   Binary Search

A Programming Problem
   Problem Definition
   Solution Design
   The Program
Avoiding Common Programming Mistakes
Summary Points
Review Questions
Debugging Exercises
Additional Programming Problems
   Level 1
   Level 2
   Level 3

Overview

All of our programs thus far have used simple variables such as LBS, TITLE$, or HRS to represent single values. If a program was required to handle many single values of the same type (such as 100 student scores), a loop was used to allow one variable to represent these values one at a time. Now consider the problem of a television network poll. A program is needed to read and retain the daily viewing times of ten random viewers, calculate the average viewing time, and print the difference between each person's viewing time and the average in the following format:

NAME	HRS	DIFFERENCE FROM AVG
P. BUSCH	1	−3
C. CARSTENS	5	1
J. DRAKE	0	−4
H. POIROT	2	−2
M. BULAS	7	3
D. ZONGAS	3	−1
C. HASTINGS	4	0
T. ZEKLY	11	7
S. MCKINNIS	3	−1
G. BALDUCCI	4	0

AVERAGE VIEWING TIME = 4

Our past procedure for calculating averages has been to set up a loop to read and accumulate each value in a single variable. Each time a new value is read by this method, however, the previous value stored in the variable is lost. Thus, in the problem involving the television poll, we would not be able to compare each person's viewing time with the calculated average viewing time. To make the comparison, we must store each person's viewing time in a separate memory location. It is possible to use ten different variables to hold these values, but this is a cumbersome solution that would be even more impractical when dealing with a larger number of values.

There is an easier way: BASIC permits us to deal with many related data items as a group by means of a structure known as an **array.** This chapter shows how arrays can be used in a situation such as the television poll program, in which groups of data items must be stored and manipulated efficiently. Various methods of sorting and searching arrays are also discussed.

Array
An ordered collection of related data items.

Subscripts

The individual data items within an array are called **elements.** An array consists of a group of consecutive storage locations in memory, each location containing a single element. The entire array is given one name, and the programmer indicates an individual element in the array by referring to its position in the array. To illustrate, suppose that there are five test scores to be stored: 97, 85, 89, 95, 100. The scores could be put in an array called TESTS, which we might visualize like this:

Element
An individual value stored in an array.

97	85	89	95	100
TESTS(1)	TESTS(2)	TESTS(3)	TESTS(4)	TESTS(5)

The array name TESTS now refers to all five storage locations containing the test scores. To gain access to a single test score within the array, an array **subscript** or **index** is used. A subscript is a value enclosed in parentheses that identifies the position of a given element in the array. For example, the first element of array TESTS (containing the value 97) is referred to as TESTS(1). The second test score is in TESTS(2), the third test score is in TESTS(3), and so on. Therefore, the following statements are true:

Subscript
A value enclosed in parentheses that identifies the position in an array of a particular element.

TESTS(1) = 97
TESTS(2) = 85
TESTS(3) = 89
TESTS(4) = 95
TESTS(5) = 100

The subscript enclosed in parentheses does not have to be an integer constant; it can consist of any valid numeric expression. When an array element subscript is indicated by an expression, the computer carries out the following steps:

- It evaluates the expression within the parentheses.
- It converts the result to an integer value. (This is done either by truncation, as on the VAX system and the Apple, or by rounding, as on the IBM and Macintosh.
- It accesses the indicated element in the array. Keep in mind that the subscript value of an array element is entirely different from the contents of that element. In the previous example, the value of TESTS(4) is 95; the subscript 4 tells where the value 95 is located in the array.

Variables that refer to specific elements of arrays (such as TESTS(4)) are called **subscripted variables.** In contrast, simple variables such as we have used in previous chapters are called **unsubscripted variables.** Both kinds of variables store a single value, numeric or string, and both can be used in BASIC statements in the same manner. The important difference between the two is that a subscripted variable refers to one value in a group; it is possible to access a different value in the group simply by changing the subscript. An unsubscripted variable, on the other hand, does not necessarily have any special relationship to the values stored before or after it in memory.

The same rules that apply to naming simple variables also apply to naming arrays. Remember that only numeric values can be stored in arrays with numeric variable names, and that character string arrays can contain only string values. It is possible to use the same name for both a simple variable and an array in a program, but this is not good programming practice, because it makes the logic of the program difficult to follow.

Assume that the array X and the variables A and B have the following values:

$$X(1) = 2 \quad A = 3$$
$$X(2) = 15 \quad B = 5$$
$$X(3) = 16$$
$$X(4) = 17$$
$$X(5) = 32$$

The following examples show how the various forms of subscripts are used.

Example	Reference
X(3)	Third element of X, or 16.
X(B)	B = 5; thus the fifth element of X, or 32.
X(X (1))	X(1) = 2; thus the second element of X, or 15.
X(B − SQR (X (3)))	X(3) = 16, SQR (16) = 4, B − 4 = 1; thus the first element of X, or 2.

Subscripted variable
A *variable that refers to a specific element of an array.*

Unsubscripted variable
A *simple variable; one that does not refer to an array element.*

Dimensioning an Array

When a subscripted variable is found in a program, the BASIC system recognizes it as part of an array and automatically reserves a standard number of storage locations for the array. On most systems (including all those discussed here), space is set aside for eleven array elements, the subscripts of which run from 0 through 10. The programmer does not have to fill all of the reserved array storage spaces with values; it is illegal, however, to refer to an array element for which space has not been reserved.

The DIM, or dimension, statement enables the programmer to override this standard array space reservation and reserve space for an array of any desired size. A DIM statement is not required for arrays of eleven or fewer elements, but it is good programming practice to specify DIM statements for all arrays to help document the array usage.

The general format of the DIM statement follows:

line# DIM variable1(limit1)[, variable2(limit2)]...

The variables are the names of arrays. Each limit is an integer constant that specifies the maximum subscript value possible for that particular array. For example, if space is needed to store twenty-five elements in an array ITEM$, the following statement reserves the necessary storage locations:

```
10 DIM ITEM$(24)
```

Although it may seem that this statement sets aside only twenty-four positions, remember that array positions 0 through 24 are actually equal to twenty-five locations. For the sake of clarity and program logic, programmers often ignore the zero element. If we choose not to use the zero position, we would dimension the array ITEM$ as shown below in order to have twenty-five positions:

```
10 DIM ITEM$(25)
```

There is no problem if fewer than twenty-five values are read into array ITEM$. Array subscripts can vary in the program from 0 to the limit declared in the DIM statement, but no subscript can exceed that limit.

As indicated in the statement format, more than one array can be declared in a DIM statement. For example, the following statement declares ACCNT, NAM$, and OVERDRWN as arrays:

```
10 DIM ACCNT(100),NAM$(150),OVERDRAWN(50)
```

Array ACCNT may contain up to 101 elements, NAM$ up to 151 elements, and OVERDRWN up to 51 elements. Or, ignoring the zero position, 100, 150, and 50.

DIM statements must appear in a program before the first references to the arrays they describe; a good practice is to place them at the beginning of the program. The following standard preparation symbol is often used to flowchart the DIM statement:

One-Dimensional Arrays

Reading Data to an Array

A major advantage of using arrays is the ability to use a variable rather than a constant as a subscript. Because a single name such as TESTS(I) can refer to any element in the array TESTS, depending on the value of I, this subscripted variable name can be used in a loop that varies the value of the subscript I. A FOR/NEXT loop can be an efficient method of reading data to an array if the exact number of items to be read is known in advance. The following program segment reads a list of five numbers into the array TESTS:

```
10 FOR I = 1 TO 5
20    READ TEST(I)
30 NEXT I
40 DATA 85,71,63,51,99
```

The first time this loop is executed, the loop variable I equals 1. Therefore, when line 20 is executed, the computer reads the first number from the data list (which is 85) and stores it in TESTS(I), which evaluates as TESTS(1) during this loop execution. The second time through the loop, I equals 2. The second number is read to TESTS(I), which now refers to TESTS(2)—the second location in the array. The loop processing continues until all five numbers have been read and stored. This process is outlined as follows:

For I =	Action	Array TESTS:
1	READ TESTS(1)	85
2	READ TESTS(2)	85 71
3	READ TESTS(3)	85 71 63
4	READ TESTS(4)	85 71 63 51
5	READ TESTS(5)	85 71 63 51 99

An array can also be filled with values using an INPUT statement or an assignment statement within a loop. To initialize an array of ten elements to zero, the following statements could be used:

```
50 FOR I = 1 TO 10
60     SCORES(I) = 0
70 NEXT I
```

It is often possible to read data to several arrays within a single loop. In the following segment, each data line contains data for one element of each of three arrays:

```
10 DIM NAM$(5),AGE(5),SSN$(5)
20 FOR I = 1 TO 5
30     READ NAM$(I),AGE(I),SSN$(I)
40 NEXT I
50 DATA "TOM BAKER",41,"268-66-1071"
60 DATA "LALLA WARD",28,"353-65-2861"
70 DATA "MASADA WILMOT",33,"269-59-9064"
80 DATA "PATRICK JONES",52,"379-44-8184"
90 DATA "BERYLE JONES",49,"271-55-1773"
```

When the exact number of items to be read to an array is unknown, a WHILE loop and a trailer value can be used. This method is demonstrated in the following segment, where the data contains a trailer value of −1. Care must be taken, however, that the number of items read does not exceed the size of the array.

```
10 DIM X(50)
20 I = 1
30 INPUT X(I)
40 WHILE (I < 50) AND (X(I) <> -1)
50     I = I + 1
60     INPUT X(I)
70 NEXT
```

Printing the Contents of an Array

A FOR/NEXT loop can be used to print the contents of the array TESTS, as shown in the following segment.

```
70 FOR T = 1 TO 5
80     PRINT TESTS(T)
90 NEXT T
```

RUNNH
85
71
63
51
99

Because there is no punctuation at the end of the PRINT statement in line 80, each value will be printed on a separate line. The values could be printed on the same line instead by placing a semicolon at the end of the line:

```
70 FOR T = 1 TO 5
80    PRINT TEST(T);
90 NEXT T
```

RUNNH
85 71 63 51 99

As the loop control variable T varies from 1 to 5, so does the value of the array subscript, and the computer prints elements 1 through 5 of array TESTS.

Performing Calculations on Array Elements

Now consider again the problem of the television network viewing poll presented earlier in this chapter. The output format required that each line contain the viewer's name, number of viewing hours, and the difference between those hours and the average hours of all the viewers. This problem is solved in the program in Figure 9–1. The solution can be broken into the following steps:

1. Read the data to two arrays: a character string array for the names and a numeric array for the hours.
2. Calculate the average viewing hours.
3. Calculate for each viewer the difference between his hours and the average; these differences can be stored in a third array.
4. Print the required information from the three arrays.

The viewers' names and hours are read to their appropriate arrays in line 200 as part of a FOR/NEXT loop. Line 210 performs an accumulation of all the elements of the array HRS. As I varies from 1 to 10, the elements 1 through 10 of HRS are added to the total hours (THRS). Therefore, when this loop is exited, the arrays NME$ and HRS are filled with values, and the unsubscripted variable THRS contains the sum of all the values contained in HRS. The average number of viewing hours is then calculated in line 230.

The FOR/NEXT loop starting in line 260 calculates the difference from the average viewing time for each viewer and stores the results in the array DAVG. Thus the first element of each array contains information about the first viewer, the second element of each array concerns the second viewer, and so on. All of the information can then be printed in the required format by the FOR/NEXT loop of lines 320 through 340.

Sometimes not every element of an array needs to be manipulated in the same way. If we wanted to find the product of only the odd-numbered entries

FIGURE 9–1 TV Poll Program

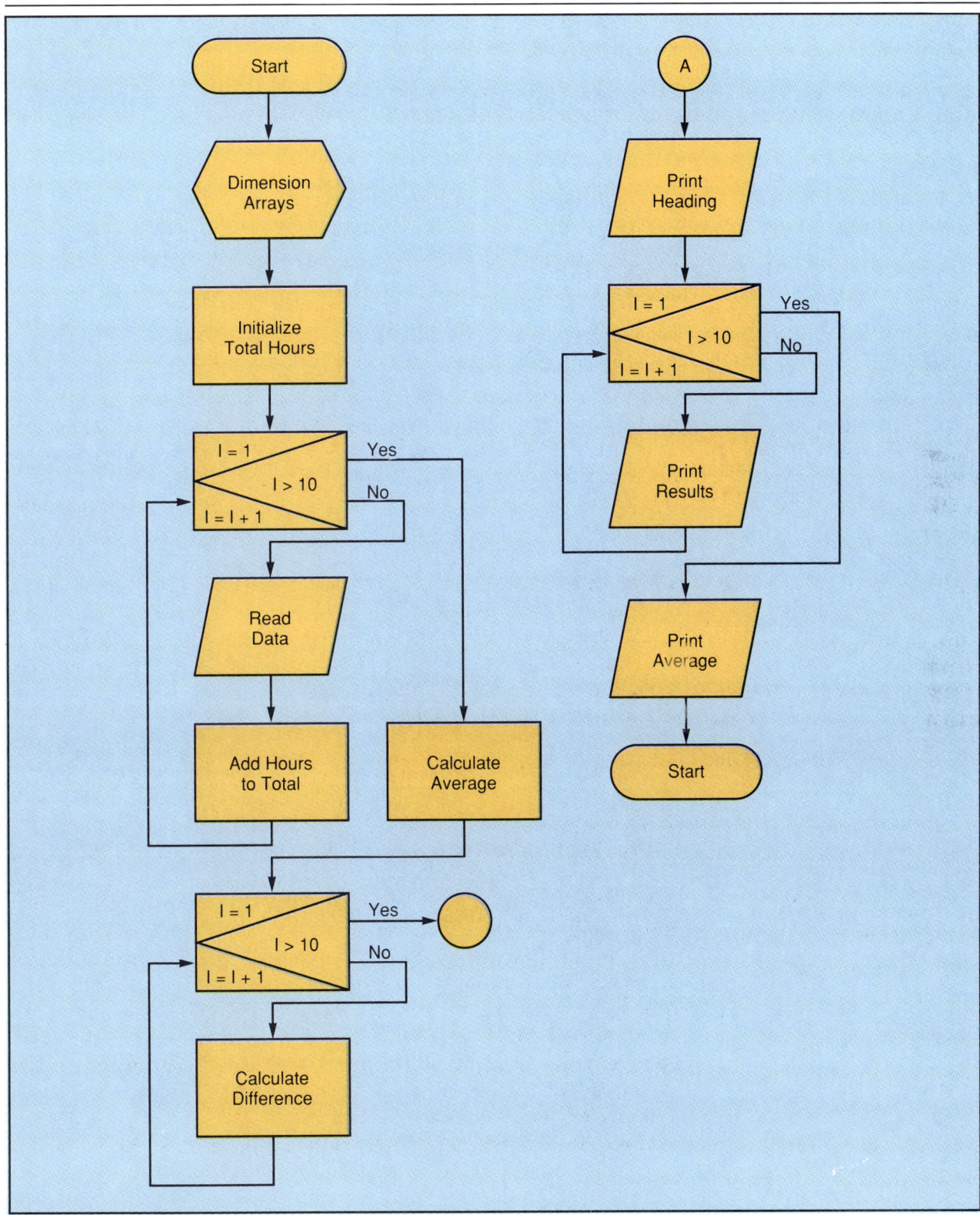

FIGURE 9-1 *Continued*

```
10  REM ***            NETWORK VIEWING TIME SURVEY         ***
20  REM
30  REM *** THIS PROGRAM DETERMINES THE AVERAGE VIEWING    ***
40  REM *** TIME BY A GROUP OF VIEWERS. IT THEN DETER-     ***
50  REM *** MINES THE DIFFERENCE FOR EACH VIEWER FROM      ***
60  REM *** THE AVERAGE AND THEIR ACTUAL VIEWING TIME.     ***
70  REM *** MAJOR VARIABLES:                               ***
80  REM ***     NME$     ARRAY OF VIEWERS                  ***
90  REM ***     HRS      ARRAY OF HOURS                    ***
100 REM ***     DAVG     ARRAY OF DIFFERENCES FROM AVG     ***
110 REM ***     AVG      AVERAGE VIEWING HRS               ***
120 REM ***     THRS     TOTAL VIEWING HRS                 ***
130 REM
140 REM *** DIMENSION THE ARRAY SIZES. ***
150 DIM NME$(10),HRS(10),DAVG(10)
160 THRS =: 0
170 REM
180 REM *** READ DATA AND CALCULATE TOTAL HOURS. ***
190 FOR I = 1 TO 10
200    READ NME$(I),HRS(I)
210    THRS = THRS + HRS(I)
220 NEXT I
230 AVG = THRS / 10
240 REM
250 REM *** CALCULATE DIFFERENCES. ***
260 FOR I = 1 TO 10
270    DAVG(I) = HRS(I) - AVG
280 NEXT I
290 REM
300 REM *** PRINT RESULTS. ***
310 PRINT "NAME","HRS";TAB(22);"DIFFERENCE FROM AVG"
320 FOR I = 1 TO 10
330    PRINT NME$(I),HRS(I),DAVG(I)
340 NEXT I
350 PRINT
360 PRINT "AVERAGE VIEWING TIME = ";AVG
370 REM
380 REM *** DATA STATEMENTS ***
390 DATA P. BUSCH, 1, C. CARSTENS, 5, J. DRAKE, 0, H. POIROT, 2
400 DATA M. BULAS, 7, D. CSONGAS, 3, C. HASTINGS, 4, T. ZEKLY, 11
410 DATA S. MCKINNIS, 3, G. BALDUCCI, 4
999 END
```

FIGURE 9–1 *Continued*

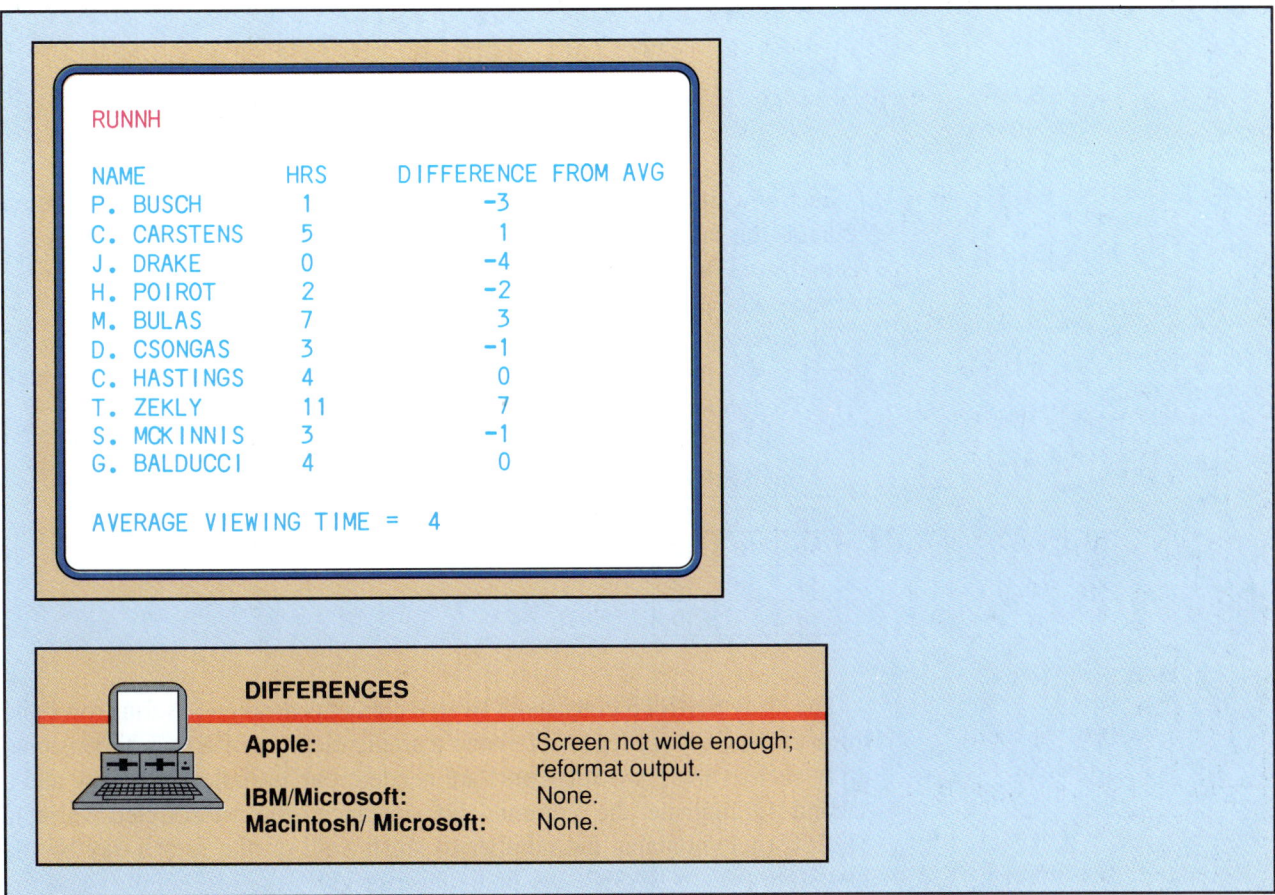

in an array, K, containing twenty-five numbers, we could use the following statements:

```
 90   PROD = 1
100   FOR I = 1 TO 25 STEP 2
110      PROD = PROD * K(I)
120   NEXT I
```

Multi-Dimensional Arrays

The arrays shown so far in this chapter have all been one-dimensional arrays; that is, arrays that store values in the form of a single list. Two-dimensional arrays enable a programmer to represent more complex groupings of data. For example, suppose that a fast-food restaurant chain is running a four-day promotional T-shirt sale at its three store locations. It might keep the following table of data concerning the number of shirts sold by each of the three restaurants.

		Store		
		1	2	3
	1	12	14	15
Day	2	10	16	12
	3	11	18	13
	4	9	9	10

Each row of the data refers to a specific day of the sale, and each column contains the sales data for one store. Thus, the number of shirts sold by the second store on the third day of the sale (18) can be found in the third row, second column.

Data items that can be grouped into rows and columns such as this can be stored easily in a two-dimensional array. A two-dimensional array named SHIRTS containing the preceding data can be pictured like this:

Array SHIRTS

12	14	15
10	16	12
11	18	13
9	9	10

The array SHIRTS consists of twelve elements arranged as four rows and three columns. In order to reference a single element of a two-dimensional array such as this, two subscripts are needed: one to indicate the row and a second to indicate the column. For instance, the subscripted variable SHIRTS(4,1) contains the number of shirts sold on the fourth day by the first store (9). In BASIC, the first subscript gives the row number and the second subscript gives the column number.

The rules regarding one-dimensional arrays also apply to two-dimensional arrays. Two-dimensional arrays are named in the same way as other variables and cannot use the same name as another array (of any dimensions) in the same program. A two-dimensional array can contain only one type of data; numeric and character string values cannot be mixed.

As with one-dimensional arrays, subscripts of two-dimensional arrays can be indicated by any legal numeric expression:

```
SHIRTS(3,3)
SHIRTS(1,2)
SHIRTS(I,J)
SHIRTS(1,I + J)
```

Assume that I = 4 and J = 2, and that the array X contains the following sixteen elements:

Array X:

10	15	20	25
50	55	60	65
90	95	100	105
130	135	140	145

The following examples show how the various forms of subscripts are used:

Example	Refers to
X(4,I)	X(4,4)—The element in the fourth row, fourth column of X, which is 145.
X(J,I)	X(2,4)—The element in the second row, fourth column of X, which is 65.
X(3,J + 1)	X(3,3)—The element in the third row, third column, which is 100.
X(I − 1,J − 1)	X(3,1)—The element in the third row, first column, which is 90.

As with one-dimensional arrays, most computers automatically reserve space for a two-dimensional array. Usually this default reservation allows for eleven elements (0 through 10) for each dimension, making eleven rows and eleven columns. Thus the default space for a two-dimensional array is usually $11 \times 11 = 121$ elements. As mentioned earlier, often the 0 elements (those in the 0 row and 0 column) are ignored.

The DIM statement can also be used to set the dimensions of a two-dimensional array. The general format of such a DIM statement is as follows:

line # DIM variable (limit1,limit2)

where the variable is the array name, and the limits are the highest possible values of the subscripts for each dimension. For example, the following statement reserves space for the two-dimensional character array STDNT$, with up to sixteen rows and six columns, for a total of $16 \times 6 = 96$ elements (or $15 \times 5 = 75$ elements if the subscripts begin at 1):

```
30 DIM STDNT$(15,5)
```

Reading and Printing with Two-Dimensional Arrays

Recall from the previous sections of this chapter that a FOR/NEXT loop is a convenient means of accessing all the elements of a one-dimensional array. The loop control variable of the FOR statement is used as the array subscript, and as the loop control variable changes value, so does the array subscript:

```
30 DIM X(5)
40 FOR I = 1 TO 5
50     READ X(I)
60 NEXT I
```

FOR/NEXT loops can also be used to read data to and print information from a two-dimensional array. It may be helpful to think of a two-dimensional array as a group of one-dimensional arrays, with each row making up a single one-dimensional array. A single FOR/NEXT loop can read values to one row. This process is repeated for as many rows as the array contains; therefore, the FOR/NEXT loop that reads a single row is nested within a second FOR/NEXT loop controlling the number of rows being accessed.

The array SHIRTS of the previous example can be filled from the sales data table one row at a time, moving from left to right across the columns. The following segment shows the nested FOR/NEXT loops that do this:

```
30  FOR I = 1 TO 4
40      FOR J = 1 TO 3
50          READ SHIRTS(I,J)
60      NEXT J
70  NEXT I
80  DATA 12,14,15
90  DATA 10,16,12
100 DATA 11,18,13
110 DATA 9,9,10
```

Notice that each time line 50 is executed, one value is read to a single element of the array; the element is determined by the current values of I and J. This statement is executed 4 × 3 = 12 times, which is the number of elements in the array.

The outer loop (loop I) controls the rows, and loop J controls the columns. Each time the outer loop is executed once, the inner loop is executed three times. While I = 1, J becomes 1, 2, and finally 3 as the inner loop is executed. Therefore, line 50 reads values to SHIRTS(1,1), SHIRTS(1,2), and SHIRTS(1,3), and the first row is filled:

	J = 1	J = 2	J = 3
I = 1	12	14	15

While I equals 2, J again varies from 1 to 3, and line 50 reads values to SHIRTS(2,1), SHIRTS(2,2) and SHIRTS(2,3) to fill the second row:

	J = 1	2	3
	12	14	15
I = 2	10	16	12

I is incremented to 3 and then to 4, and the third and fourth rows are filled in the same manner.

To print the contents of the entire array, the programmer can substitute a PRINT statement for the READ statement in the nested FOR/NEXT loops. The following segment prints the contents of the array SHIRTS, one row at a time:

```
40   BLANK = 10
50   FOR I = 1 TO 4
60     FOR J = 1 TO 3
70       PRINT TAB(BLANK * J);SHIRTS(I,J);
80     NEXT J
90     PRINT
100  NEXT I
```

The semicolon at the end of line 70 tells the computer to print the three values on the same line. After the inner loop is executed, the blank PRINT statement in line 90 causes a carriage return so that the next row is printed on the next line. The program in Figure 9–2 shows how the data table for the T-shirt sales results can be read to a two-dimensional array and printed in table form with appropriate headings.

Adding Rows

Once data has been stored in an array, it is often necessary to manipulate certain array elements. For instance, the sales manager in charge of the T-shirt promotional sale might want to know how many shirts were sold on the last day of the sale.

Because the data for each day is contained in a row of the array, it is necessary to total the elements in one row of the array (the fourth row) to find the number of shirts sold on the fourth day. The fourth row can be thought of by itself as a one-dimensional array. One loop is therefore required to access all the elements of this row:

```
30 D4SALES = 0
40 FOR J = 1 TO 3
50   D4SALES = D4SALES + SHIRTS(4,J)
60 NEXT J
```

352 BASIC PROGRAMMING TODAY, A STRUCTURED APPROACH

FIGURE 9–2 Two-Dimensional Array

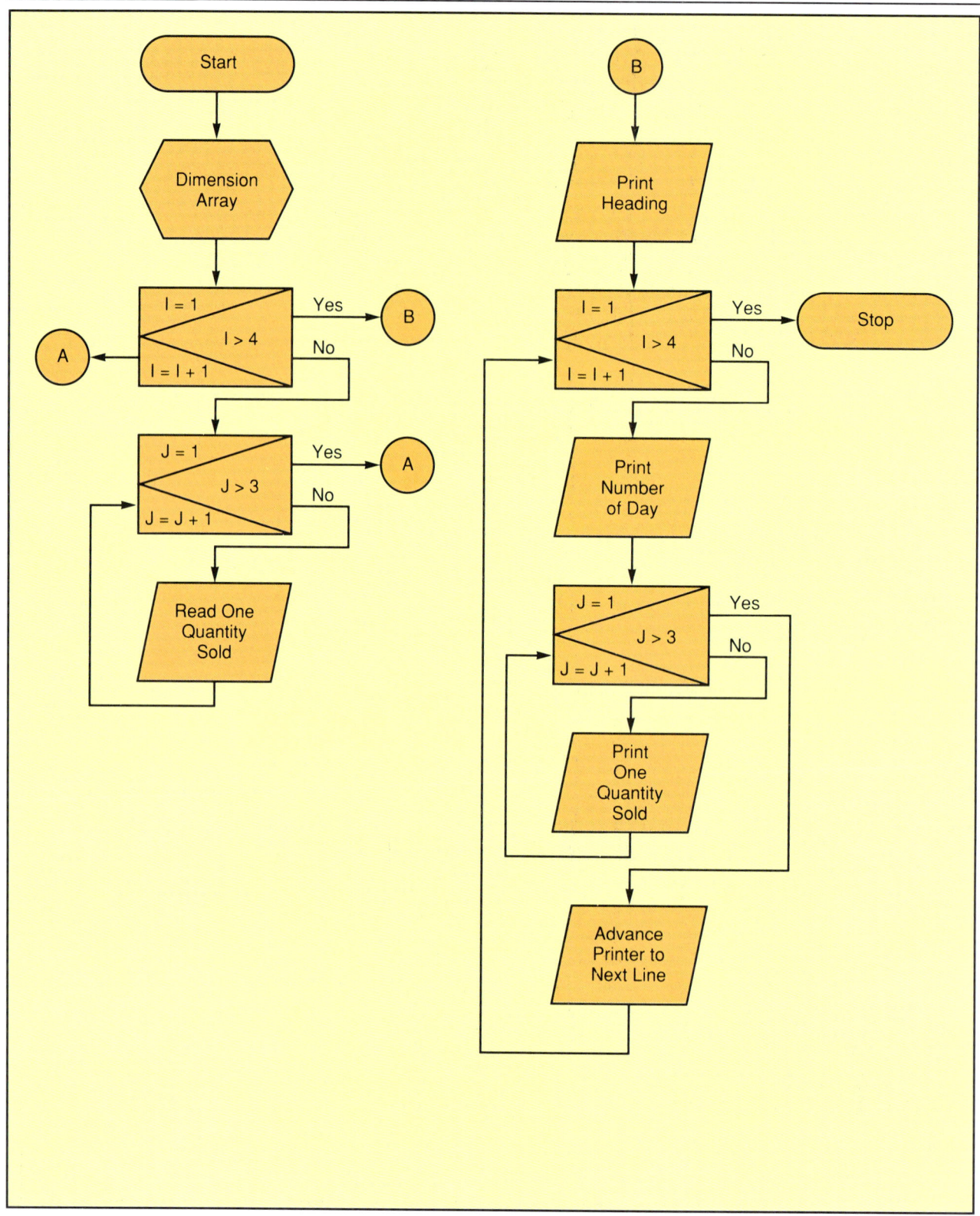

FIGURE 9-2 *Continued*

```
10  REM ***                T-SHIRT SALES REPORT                ***
20  REM
30  REM *** THIS PROGRAM PRINTS A REPORT ON THE NUMBER OF      ***
40  REM *** T-SHIRTS SOLD PER STORE FOR 4 DIFFERENT DAYS.      ***
50  REM *** MAJOR VARIABLES:                                   ***
60  REM ***     TSHIRT        ARRAY OF T-SHIRTS SOLD           ***
70  REM ***     I,J           LOOP CONTROLS                    ***
80  REM
90  REM *** DIMENSION ARRAY. ***
100 DIM TSHIRT(4,3)
110 REM
120 REM *** READ THE DATA. ***
130 FOR I = 1 TO 4
140     FOR J = 1 TO 3
150         READ TSHIRT(I,J)
160     NEXT J
170 NEXT I
180 REM
190 REM *** PRINT TABLE OF QUANTITIES SOLD. ***
200 PRINT "DAY #";TAB(10);"STORE 1";TAB(20);"STORE 2";TAB(30);"STORE 3"
210 FOR I = 1 TO 4
220     PRINT I;
230     FOR J = 1 TO 3
240         PRINT TAB(J*10);TSHIRT(I,J);
250     NEXT J
260     PRINT
270 NEXT I
280 REM
290 REM *** DATA STATEMENTS ***
300 DATA 12,4,15,10,6,12,11,8,13,9,9,10
999 END
```

```
RUNNH

DAY #      STORE 1     STORE 2     STORE 3
 1          12          4           15
 2          10          6           12
 3          11          8           13
 4           9          9           10
```

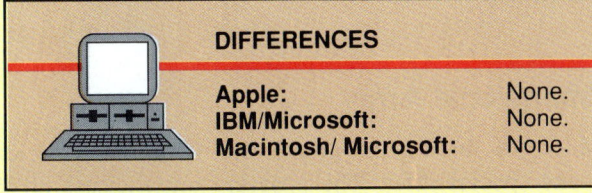

DIFFERENCES

Apple: None.
IBM/Microsoft: None.
Macintosh/Microsoft: None.

Notice that the first subscript of SHIRTS(4,J) restricts the computations to the elements in row 4, while the column J varies from 1 to 3. The process performed in line 50 is pictured in the following diagram:

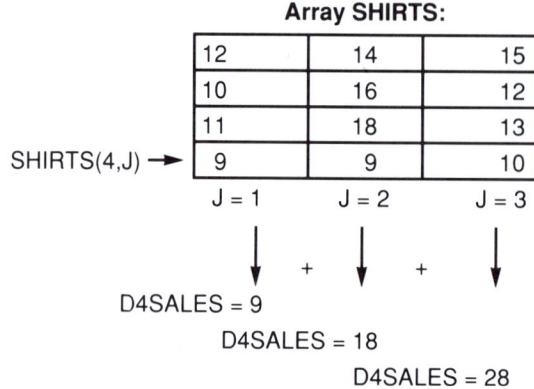

Adding Columns

To find the total number of T-shirts sold by the third store, it is necessary to total the elements in the third column of the array. This time we can think of the column by itself as a one-dimensional array of four elements. This operation calls for a FOR/NEXT loop, as shown here:

```
40 S3SHOP = 0
50 FOR I = 1 TO 4
60    S3SHOP = S3SHOP + SHIRTS(I,3)
70 NEXT I
```

In line 60, the second subscript (3) restricts the computations to the elements in the third column, while the row I varies from 1 to 4. This process is pictured in the following diagram:

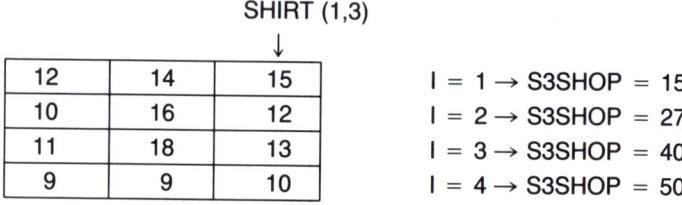

Totaling a Two-Dimensional Array

Consider now the problem of finding the grand total of all T-shirts sold during the entire four-day special offer. The program must access all the elements of the array one at a time and add them to the grand total. Remember that nested FOR/NEXT loops were used to print or read values to a two-dimensional array. This same method can be used to total the elements of an array by substituting an addition operation for the READ or PRINT statement:

```
50   TSHIRT = 0
60   FOR I = 1 TO 4
70      FOR J = 1 TO 3
80         TSHIRT = TSHIRT + SHIRTS(I,J)
90      NEXT J
100  NEXT I
```

This segment adds the elements in a row-by-row sequence. While I equals 1, the inner loop causes J to vary from 1 to 3, thus adding the contents of the first row elements to the total accumulated in TSHIRTS. When the outer loop terminates, the contents of all four rows will have been added to the total.

This totaling of all the elements of the array can also be performed in a column-by-column sequence:

```
50   TSHIRT = 0
60   FOR J = 1 TO 3
70      FOR I = 1 TO 4
80         TSHIRT = TSHIRT + SKIRTS(I,J)
90      NEXT I
100  NEXT J
```

Note that the two loops have been interchanged from the first example. Now the outer loop, loop J, controls the columns, and the inner loop, loop I, controls the rows. While J equals 1, I varies from 1 to 4, and the elements of the first column are added to the total: SHIRTS(1,1), SHIRTS (2,1), SHIRTS(3,1) and SHIRTS(4,1). J is then incremented to 2, the second column is added, and so on.

Arrays with More Than Two Dimensions

It is possible to have arrays with more than two dimensions. The maximum size of each dimension must be specified in the DIM statement using the following format:

line# DIM variable (limit1,limit2,...limit*n*)

For example, the following array, named RD, has three dimensions and can contain up to eighty elements (if the zero subscripts are ignored):

```
10 DIM RD(5,4,4)
```

Three subscripts are needed to access each element in a three-dimensional array. A simple way of illustrating such an array is by using a book, as shown in Figure 9–3. The pages of the book correspond to the first subscript. Each line (or row) of writing refers to the second subscript and each position (or column) in a particular line refers to the third subscript.

The program in Figure 9–2 reported on the T-shirt sales at three different stores for four days. Therefore, it was a two-dimensional array:

```
100 DIM SHIRTS(4,3)
```

What if the T-shirt company expanded and had a total of six stores, three in one city and three in a second city? A three-dimensional array would be useful to keep track of the sales. It could be dimensioned as follows:

```
110 DIM SHIRTS(4,2,3)
```

The first dimension refers to the day (1 through 4), the second is the city (there are two cities), and the third is the store (there are three stores in each city). This array can have a maximum of twenty-four elements. Reading data to this array will be a little more complicated than in the program in Figure 9–2. This new program could be written as shown in Figure 9–4. Notice that lines 140 through 190 contain three nested FOR loops, one for each dimension of the array. After all the data is read to the array, it is printed in two tables: one for the first city (Elmwood) and the other for the second city (North Liberty). This is accomplished by keeping the second array subscript constant during the printing of each table as demonstrated in line 280:

```
280 PRINT TAB(K*10);TSHIRT(I,1,K);
```

FIGURE 9–3
Book Illustration of a Three-Dimensional Array

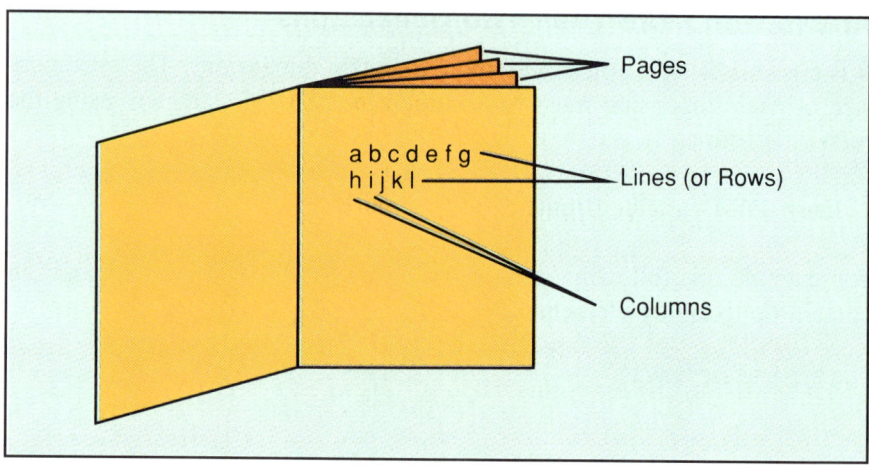

FIGURE 9-4 Program Demonstrating a Three-Dimensional Array

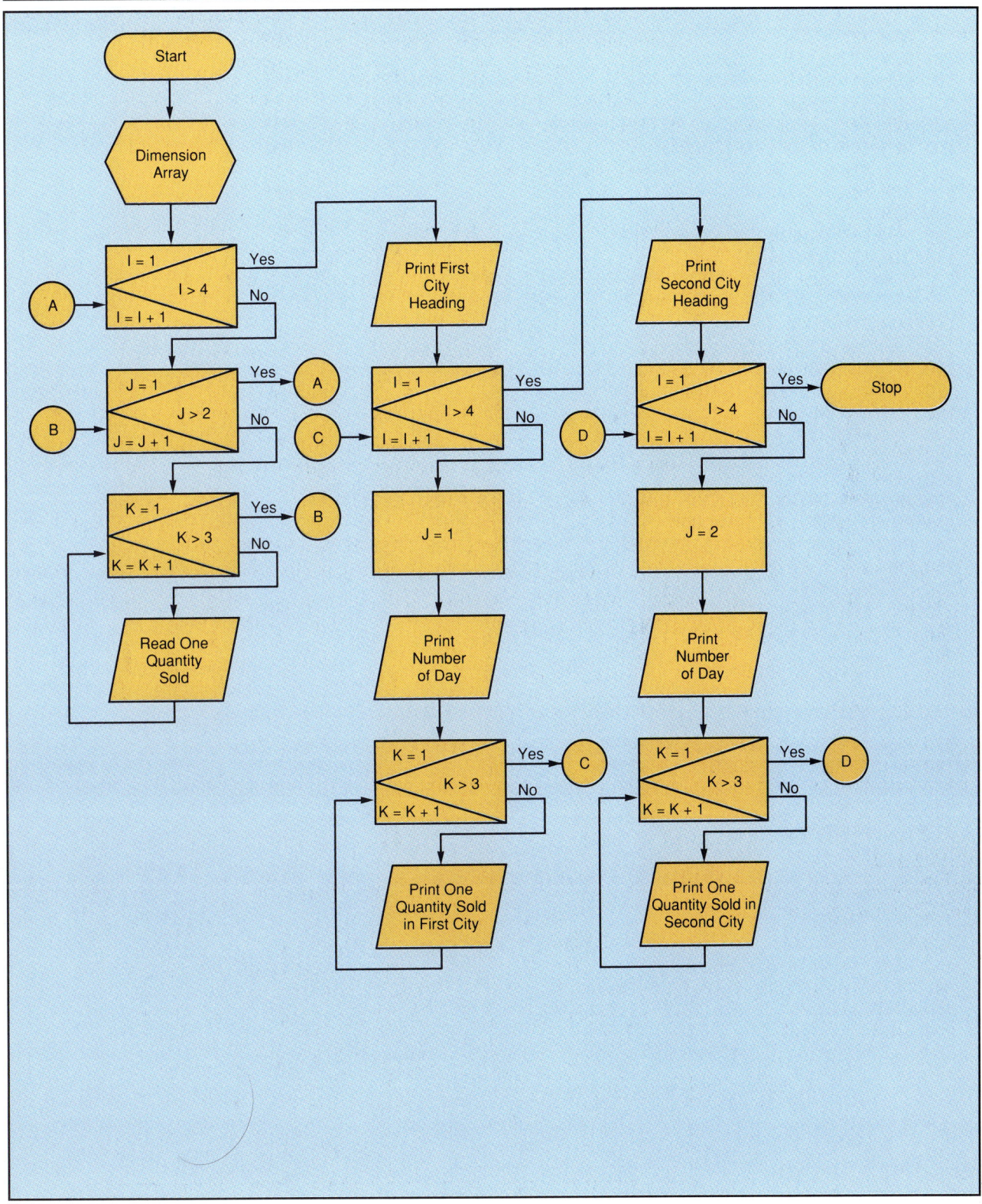

FIGURE 9–4 *Continued*

```
10  REM ***                  T-SHIRT SALES REPORT                ***
20  REM
30  REM *** THIS PROGRAM PRINTS A REPORT ON THE NUMBER OF         ***
40  REM *** T-SHIRTS SOLD FOR A 4-DAY PERIOD IN 6 DIFFER-         ***
50  REM *** ENT STORES (2 CITIES HAVING 3 STORES EACH).           ***
60  REM *** MAJOR VARIABLES:                                      ***
70  REM ***     TSHIRT        ARRAY OF T-SHIRTS SOLD              ***
80  REM ***     I,J,K         LOOP CONTROLS                       ***
90  REM
100 REM *** DIMENSION ARRAY. ***
110 DIM TSHIRT(4,2,3)
120 REM
130 REM *** READ THE DATA. ***
140 FOR I = 1 TO 4
150     FOR J = 1 TO 2
160         FOR K = 1 TO 3
170             READ TSHIRT(I,J,K)
180         NEXT K
190     NEXT J
200 NEXT I
210 REM
220 REM *** PRINT TABLE OF QUANTITIES SOLD IN FIRST CITY. ***
230 PRINT "CITY 1: ELMWOOD"
240 PRINT "DAY #";TAB(10);"STORE 1";TAB(20);"STORE 2";TAB(30);"STORE 3"
250 FOR I = 1 TO 4
260     PRINT I;
270     FOR K = 1 TO 3
280         PRINT TAB(K*10);TSHIRT(I,1,K);
290     NEXT K
300     PRINT
310 NEXT I
320 REM
330 REM *** PRINT TABLE OF QUANTITIES SOLD IN SECOND CITY. ***
340 PRINT "CITY 2: NORTH LIBERTY"
350 PRINT "DAY #";TAB(10);"STORE 1";TAB(20);"STORE 2";TAB(30);"STORE 3"
360 FOR I = 1 TO 4
370     PRINT I;
380     FOR K = 1 TO 3
390         PRINT TAB(K*10);TSHIRT(I,2,K);
400     NEXT K
410     PRINT
420 NEXT I
430 REM *** DATA STATEMENTS ***
440 DATA 12,4,15,10,6,12,11,8,13,9,9,10
450 DATA 17,8,6,12,10,8,13,11,4,7,15,14
999 END
```

FIGURE 9–4 *Continued*

```
RUNNH

CITY 1: ELMWOOD
DAY #      STORE 1    STORE 2    STORE 3
 1           12          4          15
 2           11          8          13
 3           17          8           6
 4           13         11           4
CITY 2: NORTH LIBERTY
DAY #      STORE 1    STORE 2    STORE 3
 1           10          6          12
 2            9          9          10
 3           12         10           8
 4            7         15          14
```

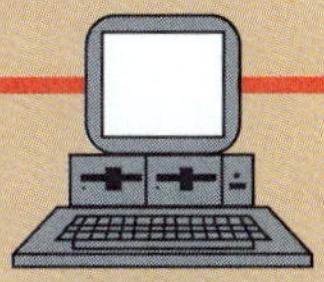

DIFFERENCES

Apple:	None.
IBM/Microsoft:	None.
Macintosh/Microsoft:	None.

Because the second subscript (the J subscript) is always equal to 1, only the data for the first city is printed. In the same manner, line 390 prints the data for the second city because the second subscript is always 2.

Learning Check

1. The _____ tells the computer the position of an element in an array.
2. The _____ statement reserves storage space for the elements in an array.
3. The subscript can consist of any legal numeric or character expression. True or false?
4. If an array is dimensioned as follows, it must contain twenty elements. True or false?

   10 DIM TBL(20)

5. A(n) _____ stores values as a table of rows and columns.
6. The first subscript of a two-dimensional array refers to the _____ of the element, and the second subscript refers to the _____.

Answers

1. subscript 2. DIM 3. False 4. False 5. two-dimensional array 6. row; column

Sorting

Many programming applications require data items stored in arrays to be sorted or ordered in some way. For example, names must be alphabetized, social security numbers must be arranged from lowest to highest, sports statistics must be arranged by numeric value, and so on.

Of course, when dealing with short lists of data, it is no problem to arrange the items mentally in their proper order. In the following example, test scores are to be arranged from lowest to highest:

Array 1 (unsorted)	Array 2 (sorted)
75	55
92	66
66	75
100	92
55	100

If there were 100 test scores to sort, however, the operation would be quite tedious and time-consuming. Fortunately, the computer is well suited to this task. There are various methods the programmer can use to sort data items, some more efficient than others. We'll look at the bubble sort first, as it is relatively easy to understand.

Bubble Sort

Bubble sort
A sort that progressively sorts elements by a series of comparisons of adjacent array values.

The basic idea behind the **bubble sort** is to arrange the elements of an array progressively in ascending or descending order by making a series of comparisons of the adjacent values in an array. If the adjacent values are out of sequence, they are exchanged.

When arranging an array in ascending order, the bubble sort "bubbles" the smallest values to the top of the array. The values of adjacent array elements are compared and are switched if the value of the first element is larger than the value of the second. Then the next pair of adjacent elements is compared and switched if necessary.

This sequence of comparisons (called a *pass*) is then repeated, starting from the beginning of the array. After each complete pass through the array, however, the element moved to the end of the array need not be included in the comparisons of the next pass, because it is now in its proper position. Successive passes are continued through the array until no elements are switched, indicating that the entire array is sorted.

To illustrate this bubbling procedure, an array consisting of five integers is sorted into ascending order in Figure 9–5. Notice that, after each pass is completed, the largest of the numbers compared in that pass is moved to the end of those numbers. After one pass through the array, some of the numbers are closer to their proper positions, but the array is not yet completely ordered. The largest value, the 7, has been successfully positioned at the end of the array and is therefore not included in the comparisons of the following passes.

After each pass is made through the array, the program checks a flag that indicates whether the array is in its final order. After a fourth pass through this array, the array is completely arranged in ascending order, but another pass is required to set the flag value to indicate this fact.

From this illustration, we get an idea of the steady "bubbling" process involved in this sorting routine. Now let's take a look at the actual code for a bubble sort, as illustrated in Figure 9–6.

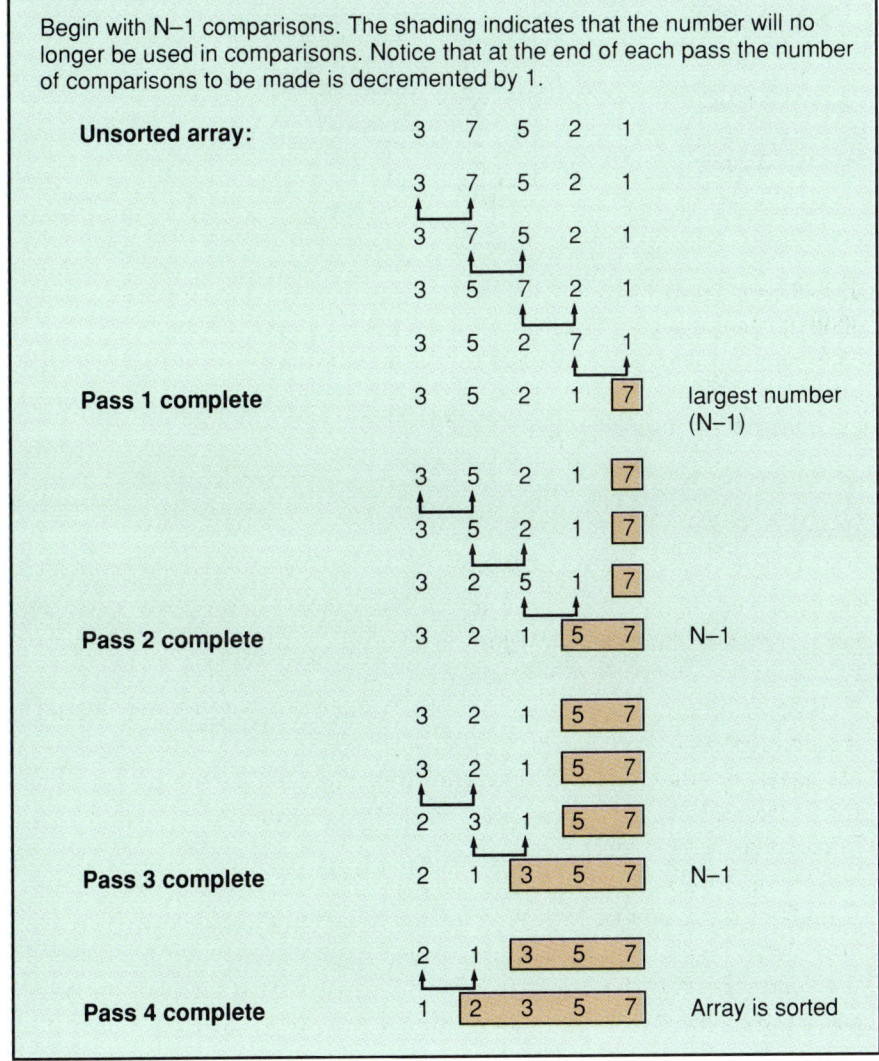

FIGURE 9–5
Bubble Sort Process

FIGURE 9-6 Bubble Sort Program

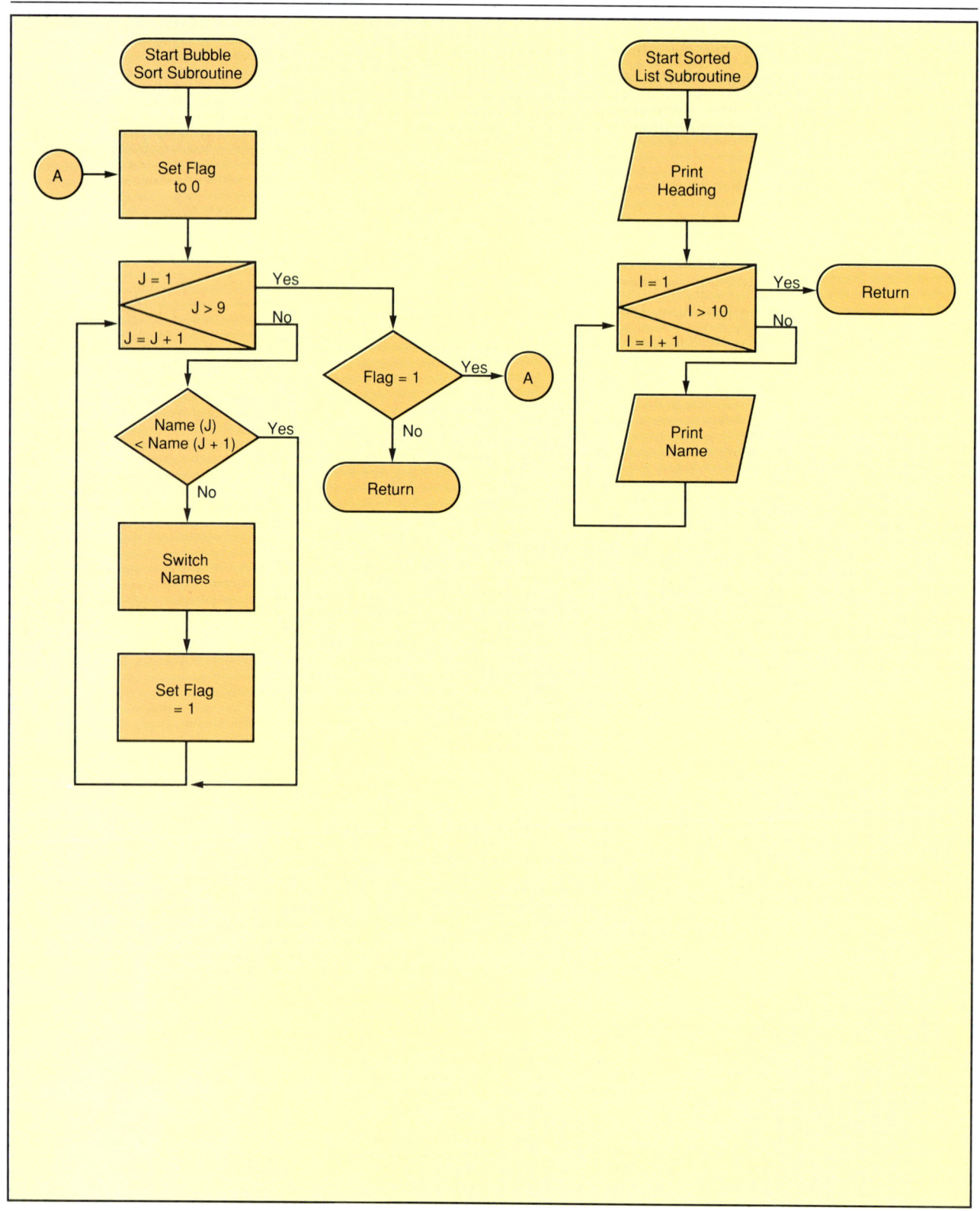

ARRAYS 363

FIGURE 9-6 *Continued*

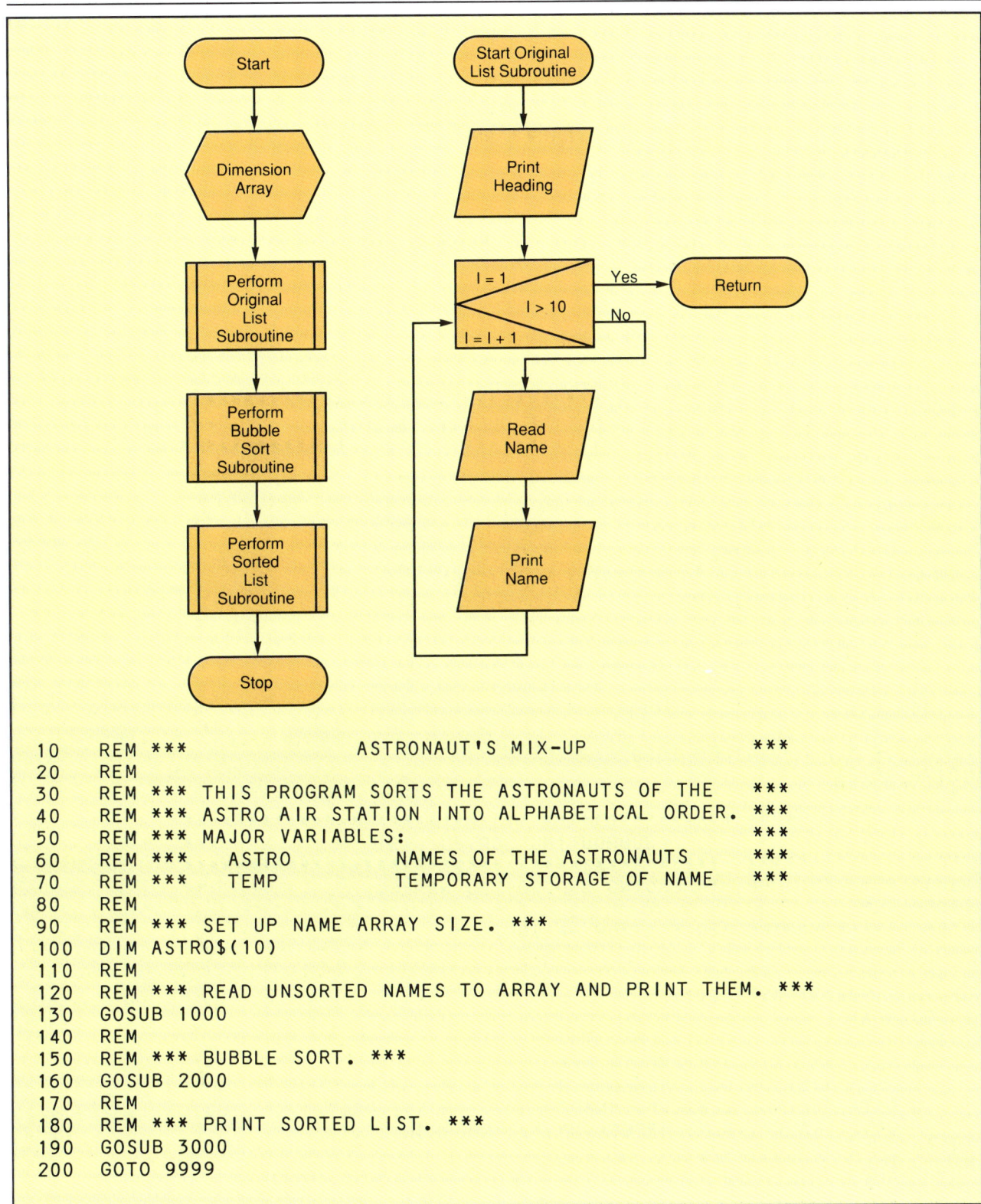

```
10      REM ***              ASTRONAUT'S MIX-UP                ***
20      REM
30      REM *** THIS PROGRAM SORTS THE ASTRONAUTS OF THE        ***
40      REM *** ASTRO AIR STATION INTO ALPHABETICAL ORDER.      ***
50      REM *** MAJOR VARIABLES:                                ***
60      REM ***     ASTRO          NAMES OF THE ASTRONAUTS      ***
70      REM ***     TEMP           TEMPORARY STORAGE OF NAME    ***
80      REM
90      REM *** SET UP NAME ARRAY SIZE. ***
100     DIM ASTRO$(10)
110     REM
120     REM *** READ UNSORTED NAMES TO ARRAY AND PRINT THEM. ***
130     GOSUB 1000
140     REM
150     REM *** BUBBLE SORT. ***
160     GOSUB 2000
170     REM
180     REM *** PRINT SORTED LIST. ***
190     GOSUB 3000
200     GOTO 9999
```

FIGURE 9–6 Continued

```
1000 REM
1010 REM ************************************************************
1020 REM ***              SUBROUTINE ORIGINAL LIST              ***
1030 REM ************************************************************
1040 REM ***    READ NAMES INTO ARRAY AND PRINT THEM.           ***
1050 REM
1060 PRINT "ASTRO AIR STATION--UNSORTED"
1070 PRINT
1080 FOR I = 1 TO 10
1090    READ ASTRO$(I)
1100    PRINT ASTRO$(I)
1110 NEXT I
1120 PRINT
1130 PRINT
1140 RETURN
2000 REM
2010 REM ************************************************************
2020 REM ***              SUBROUTINE BUBBLE SORT                ***
2030 REM ************************************************************
2040 REM
2050 FINL = 9
2060 FLAG = 0
2065 J = 1
2070 WHILE J <= FINL
2080    IF ASTRO$(J) <= ASTRO$(J + 1) THEN 2130
2090    TEMP$ = ASTRO$(J)
2100    ASTRO$(J) = ASTRO$(J + 1)
2110    ASTRO$(J + 1) = TEMP$
2120    FLAG = 1
2130    J = J + 1
2140 NEXT
2150 FINL = FINL - 1
2160 IF FLAG = 1 THEN 2060
2170 RETURN
3000 REM
3010 REM ************************************************************
3020 REM ***              SUBROUTINE SORTED LIST                ***
3030 REM ************************************************************
3040 REM ***    PRINT HEADING AND SORTED NAMES.                 ***
3050 REM
3060 PRINT "ASTRO AIR STATION -- SORTED"
3070 PRINT
3080 FOR I = 1 TO 10
3090    PRINT ASTRO$(I)
3100 NEXT I
3110 RETURN
3120 REM *** DATA STATEMENTS ***
3130 DATA "JETSON,G.", "SOLONG,H.", "QUIRK,J."
3140 DATA "SKYWALTZER,L.", "MADER,D.", "MCSOY,DR."
3150 DATA "KANOBI,B.", "SPECK,MR.", "OHORROR,LT."
3160 DATA "CHECKUP,V."
9999 END
```

FIGURE 9–6 *Continued*

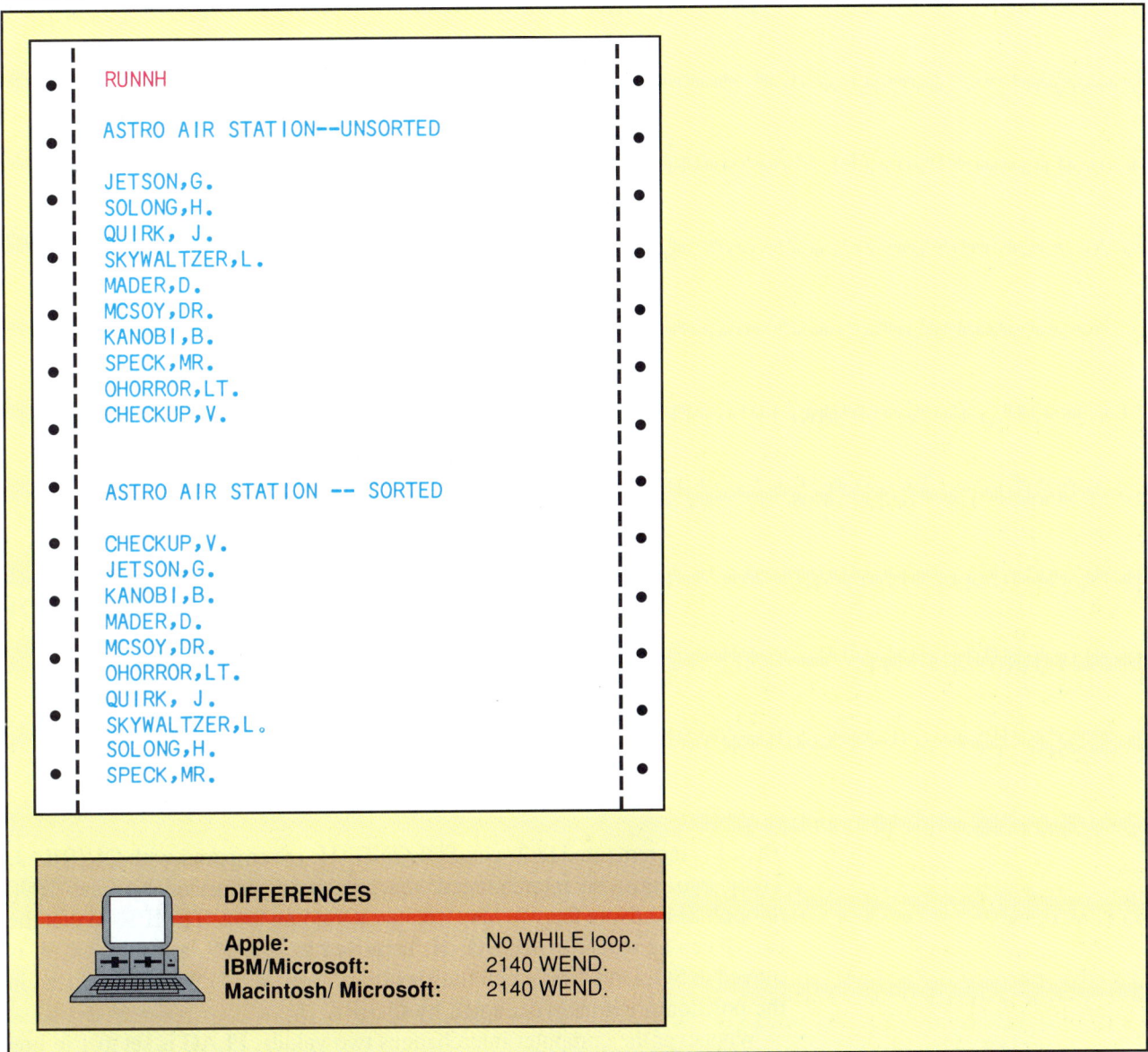

This program sorts ten astronaut names into alphabetical order. Because the computer automatically assigns a collating (or ASCII) sequence value to every character it is capable of representing, it compares the ASCII values for each letter to determine that the letter A is less than the letter B, B is less than C, and so on. The subroutine starting at line 1000 simply reads the astronauts' names into an array ASTRO$ and prints them. The subroutine starting at line 2000 performs the bubble sort. Let us examine them carefully to see what happens.

Line 2060 refers to the variable FLAG. It is initialized to 0; its value is later checked by the computer to determine if the entire array has been sorted.

Notice that FINL is set to one less than the number of items to be sorted. This is because two items at a time are compared. J varies from 1 to 9, which means that the computer eventually will compare item 9 with item 9 + 1. If the terminal value were 10 (the number of names), the computer would try to compare item 10 with item 11, which does not exist in the array.

The IF/THEN statement in line 2080 tells the computer whether to interchange two compared values. For example, when J = 1, the computer compares JETSON, G. with SOLONG, H. Because J is less than S, there is no need to switch these two items:

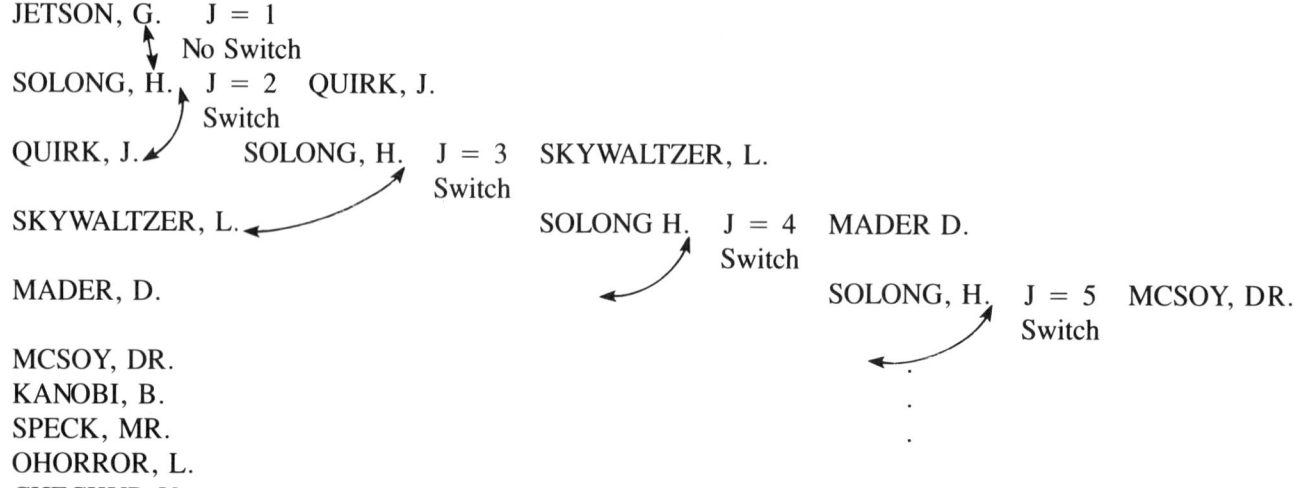

Then J is incremented to 2, and SOLONG, H. is compared with QUIRK, J. These two must be interchanged; the switch is performed by lines 2090 through 2110. Note that we have created a holding area, TEMP$, so that the switch can be made. SOLONG, H. is moved to TEMP$, and QUIRK, J. is moved to SOLONG, H.'s previous position. Now SOLONG, H. is placed in the position previously occupied by QUIRK, J.

Whenever the computer interchanges two values, FLAG is set to 1 in line 2120. This loop continues until every item in the array has been examined. After one pass through this entire loop, the array ASTRO$ looks like this:

JETSON, G.
QUIRK, J.
SKYWALTZER, L.
MADER, D.
KANOBI, B.
SOLONG, H.

OHORROR, L.
CHECKUP, V.
SPECK, MR.

Although several switches have been made, the list is not sorted completely. That is why we need line 2160. As long as FLAG equals 1, the computer knows that switches have been made, and the sorting process must continue. When the loop is completed without setting FLAG equal to 1—that is, when no switches are made—the computer finds FLAG equal to 0 and knows that the list is ordered. Numbers can also be sorted by this same method.

Shell Sort

The bubble sort is very simple to understand and code. It is not very efficient, however, because the bubble sort can only exchange adjacent elements of the list being sorted. If an element is far from its proper position in the list, many exchanges will be necessary to bring it to the correct position. The **Shell sort,** named after its inventor, Donald Shell, avoids this difficulty.

A comparison of the sequence of an array after one pass through a bubble sort and after one pass through a Shell sort gives an indication of the greater efficiency of the Shell sort:

Shell sort
A sort that groups elements into progressively larger sublists, ordering each sublist independently.

Original list:	75	35	48	55	12	5	63	42
Bubble sort pass 1:	35	48	55	12	5	63	42	75
Shell sort pass 1:	12	5	48	42	75	35	63	55

Notice that, after passing through the Shell sort, numbers far from their proper positions have made much greater progress toward their final places than those passed once through the bubble sort. Figure 9–7 shows how one version of the Shell sort works.

After defining the list to be sorted, a gap is chosen that is equal to one-half the size of the list. In the example in Figure 9–7, the gap is equal to 4. The elements of the list to be sorted are separated by the chosen gap and grouped into sublists. The first sublist begins with the first element of the list. The next member of the first sublist is the fifth element, four positions away. The next member would be the ninth element if the list contained that many elements, and so on. The second sublist begins with the second element of the list. The sixth element, four positions away, completes the second sublist. This grouping process continues until each element belongs to a sublist. Our example has four sublists, each consisting of two elements (see Figure 9–7a).

The sublists are sorted independently of one another; the results are shown at the bottom of Figure 9–7a. Notice that the elements of any given sublist are in their proper order. The sorting proceeds rapidly because the

FIGURE 9-7
Shell Sort Process

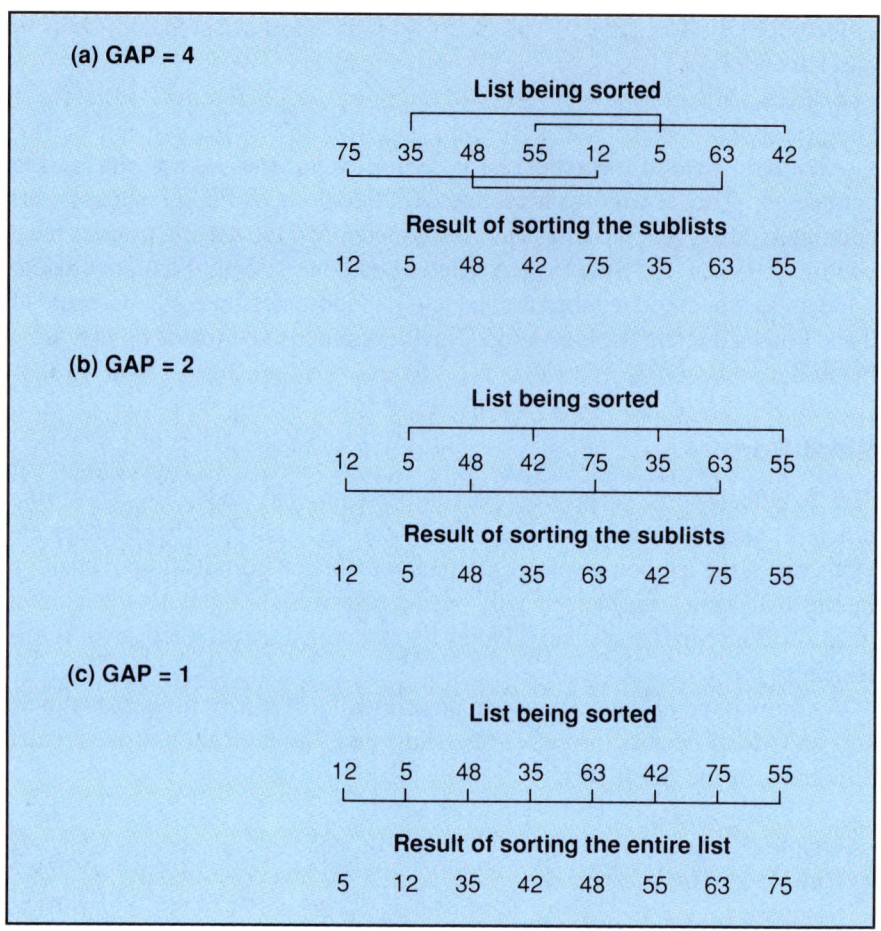

sublists are short. Because the gap between the elements in each sublist is large, elements far out of place make large movements toward their final positions.

Next, the gap is divided in half, and the previously described process is repeated with a gap of 2. This gives us two sublists, one consisting of all the elements in odd-numbered positions and another comprising elements in even-numbered positions. Each sublist is sorted independently; the results are shown in Figure 9-7b.

The final step involves dividing the gap in half again, giving a gap of 1. This leaves us with only one sublist, which gives us the final result shown in Figure 9-7c.

At first glance, the Shell sort may appear less efficient than the bubble sort. In fact, however, the entire sequence of sorts called for by the Shell sort takes much less time than a single bubble sort applied to the same list. As already mentioned, the beginning steps of the Shell sort quickly order several short sublists, and this preliminary sorting makes the longer sublists that follow easier to sort. As the length of the list to be sorted increases, the greater efficiency of the Shell sort over the bubble sort becomes more apparent. Generally speaking, the Shell sort is more efficient than the bubble sort when sorting lists of 100 or more elements.

There are a number of different versions of the Shell sort, each using a different method to sort the sublists. The version of the Shell sort presented here uses the bubble sort to sort the sublists. Figure 9–8 shows the coding for this version. A bubble sort is used, but the program compares and exchanges N(I) and N(I + GAP) instead of N(I) and N(I + 1).

The subroutine starting at line 1000 reads the unsorted numbers to the array N and prints them out. The actual Shell sort is contained in the subroutine starting at line 2000. We will take a closer look at this code.

Line 2050 indicates that there are eight elements in the array to be sorted. Line 2060 initially sets the gap to one-half the size of the array, in this case 4. As long as the gap is not equal to zero (indicating that the array has been sorted), lines 2070 through 2180 will continue to be executed. Lines 2080 through 2160 contain the modified bubble sort that sorts the sublists. After the current sublist is sorted, line 2170 is executed, reducing the size of the gap by one-half, and the entire process is repeated. The subroutine beginning at line 3000 prints the sorted array.

The Shell sort is presented here as a good compromise between speed and simplicity. There are other sorting algorithms that are faster, but they are generally more complex to use.

Merge Sort

The **merge sort** is yet another type of sort. It merges, or combines, two sorted lists into one larger sorted list. Suppose that two sorted integer arrays, array A and array B, need to be merged into array C:

Merge sort
A sort that combines two sorted arrays into a single sorted array.

Array A
| 2 | 4 |

Array B
| 1 | 2 | 3 |

To begin, the first elements in each array are compared to each other and the smaller integer is placed in array C. Because 1 is less than 2, array C looks like this:

Array C
| 1 | | | | |

The integer placed into array C is not considered again. Next, the integer 2 in array A is compared to the integer 2 in array B. They are of equal value, so the array B is chosen arbitrarily to supply the next element of array C. The 2 in array B is no longer considered. Array C now appears this way:

Array C
| 1 | 2 | | | |

FIGURE 9-8 Shell Sort Program

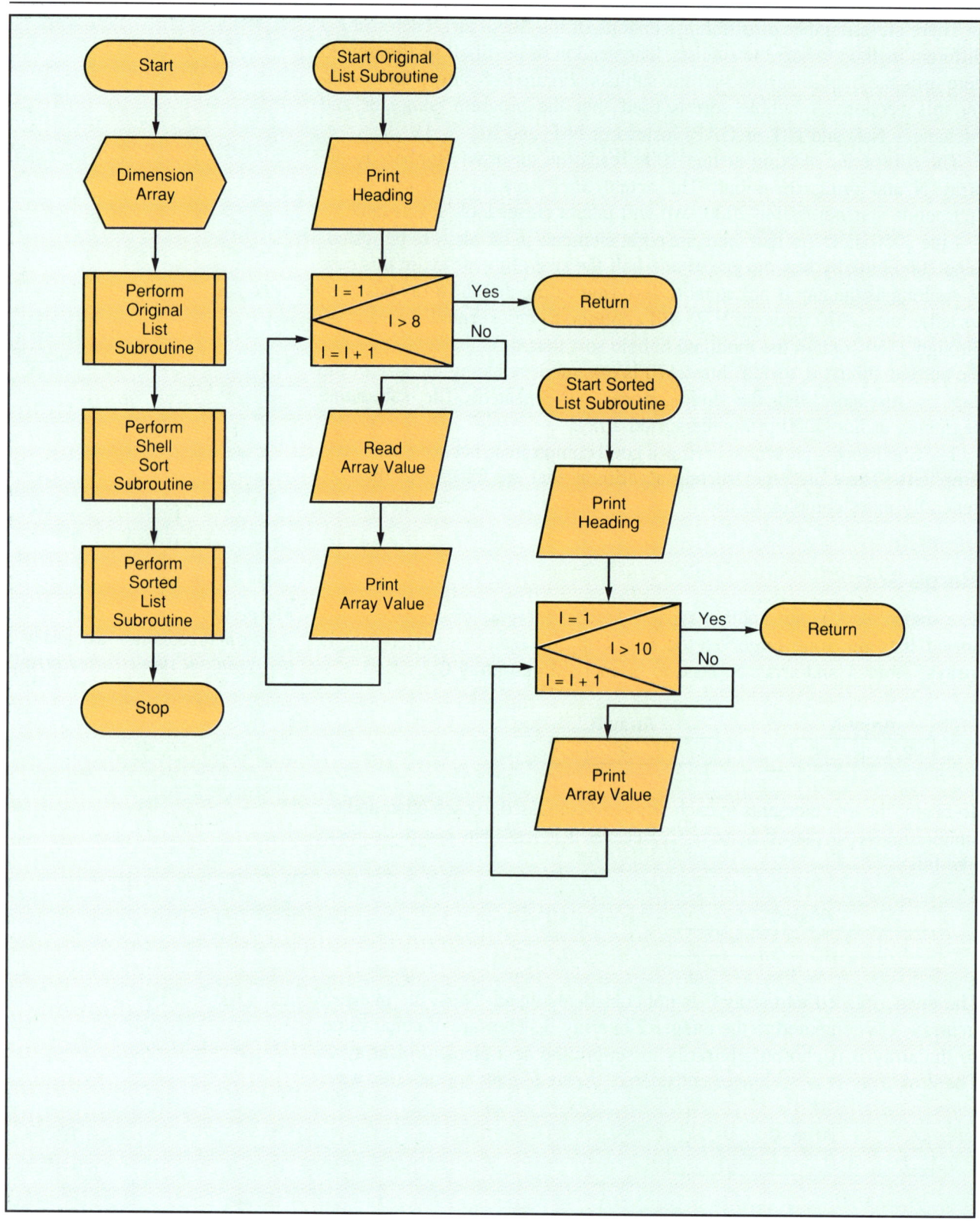

ARRAYS

FIGURE 9-8 Continued

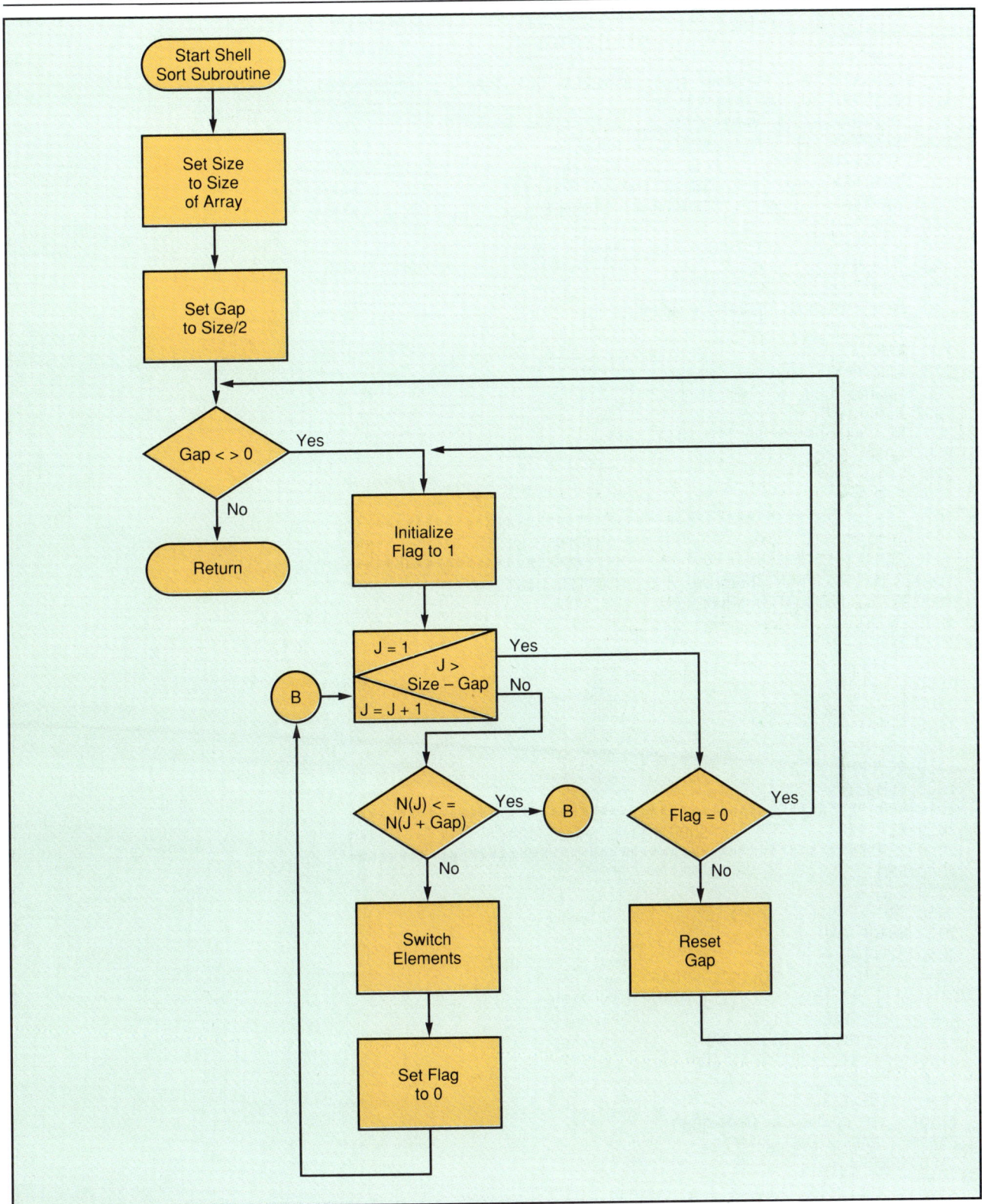

FIGURE 9–8 *Continued*

```
10   REM ***                    SHELL SORT                    ***
20   REM
30   REM *** THIS PROGRAM SORTS NUMBERS INTO NUMERIC ORDER ***
40   REM ***   USING A SHELL SORT.                         ***
50   REM *** MAJOR VARIABLES:                              ***
60   REM ***    N         ARRAY OF NUMBERS                 ***
70   REM ***    SZE       # OF ELEMENTS IN LIST            ***
80   REM ***    GAP       SPLITTING OF THE LIST            ***
90   REM ***    TEMP      TEMPORARY STORAGE                ***
100  REM
110  REM *** DECLARE ARRAY SIZE. ***
120  DIM N(10)
130  REM
140  REM *** READ UNSORTED NUMBERS AND PRINT THEM. ***
150  GOSUB 1000
160  REM
170  REM *** SORT LIST. ***
180  GOSUB 2000
190  REM
200  REM *** PRINT SORTED LIST. ***
210  GOSUB 3000
220  GOTO 9999
1000 REM
1010 REM ***********************************************************
1020 REM ***              SUBROUTINE ORIGINAL LIST               ***
1030 REM ***********************************************************
1040 REM ***   PRINT HEADING AND UNSORTED LIST.                  ***
1050 PRINT "UNSORTED NUMBERS"
1060 PRINT
1070 FOR I = 1 TO 8
1080    READ N(I)
1090    PRINT N(I)
1100 NEXT I
1110 PRINT
1120 PRINT
1130 RETURN
2000 REM
2010 REM ***********************************************************
2020 REM ***              SUBROUTINE SHELL SORT                  ***
2030 REM ***********************************************************
2040 REM
2050 SZE = 8
2060 GAP = INT(SZE / 2)
2070 WHILE GAP <> 0
2080    FLAG = 1
2090    FOR J = 1 TO (SZE - GAP)
2100       IF N(J) <= N(J + GAP) THEN 2150
2110       TEMP = N(J)
2120       N(J) = N(J + GAP)
2130       N(J + GAP) = TEMP
2140       FLAG = 0
2150    NEXT J
2160    IF FLAG = 0 THEN 2080
2170    GAP = INT(GAP / 2)
2180 NEXT
```

FIGURE 9–8 *Continued*

```
2190 RETURN
3000 REM
3010 REM ************************************************************
3020 REM ***           SUBROUTINE SORTED LIST               ***
3030 REM ************************************************************
3040 REM *** PRINT HEADING AND SORTED LIST.                 ***
3050 REM
3060 PRINT "SORTED NUMBERS"
3070 PRINT
3080 FOR I = 1 TO 8
3090    PRINT N(I)
3100 NEXT I
3110 RETURN
3120 REM
3130 REM *** DATA STATEMENTS ***
3140 DATA 75,35,48,55,12,5,63,42
9999 END
```

```
RUNNH

UNSORTED NUMBERS

 75
 35
 48
 55
 12
  5
 63
 42


SORTED NUMBERS

  5
 12
 35
 42
 48
 55
 63
 75
```

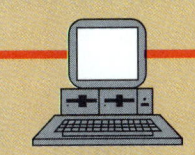

DIFFERENCES

Apple:	No WHILE loop.
IBM/Microsoft:	2180 WEND.
Macintosh/ Microsoft:	2180 WEND.

The integers 2 of array A and 3 of array B are now compared. Because 2 is less than 3, 2 is moved into array C:

Array C

| 1 | 2 | 2 | | |

The 2 in array A is no longer considered. Now 3 and 4 are compared, and 3 is moved into array C:

Array C

| 1 | 2 | 2 | 3 | |

At this point, all of array B has been transferred into array C. The remaining element of array A is now moved to array C; if array A were larger, many integers would need to be moved. Array C finally contains all the elements of both A and B, in sorted order:

Array C

| 1 | 2 | 2 | 3 | 4 |

Figure 9–9 presents a subroutine that performs a merge sort. It is assumed that the sizes of arrays A and B have been established in the main program, and that array C is large enough to hold the elements of both arrays. The loop of lines 1110 through 1140 places values into C until either A or B has no more elements left to be considered.

As indicated in the preceding traced example, if two compared integers are equal, the integer from array B is placed in array C. This comparison and the appropriate move into C are made in line 1120. The WHILE loop of lines 1170 through 1210 adds the remaining elements of array A (if any) to the end of C. If values of A run out before those of B, the loop of lines 1230 through 1270 adds the remaining values of B to array C.

Learning Check

1. What is indicated when a bubble sort makes an entire pass without making an exchange?
2. The _____ sort compares elements separated by a chosen gap and grouped into sublists, and then exchanges them according to the desired order.
3. How does the sort described in question 2 choose the initial gap to be used, according to the version presented here?
4. The _____ sort combines two sorted lists into a single sorted list.
5. A Shell sort is more efficient than the bubble sort when sorting arrays of 100 or more elements. True or false?

Answers

1. The array is sorted. 2. Shell 3. The gap originally equals one-half the array size. 4. merge 5. True.

ARRAYS

FIGURE 9-9 Merge Sort Subroutine

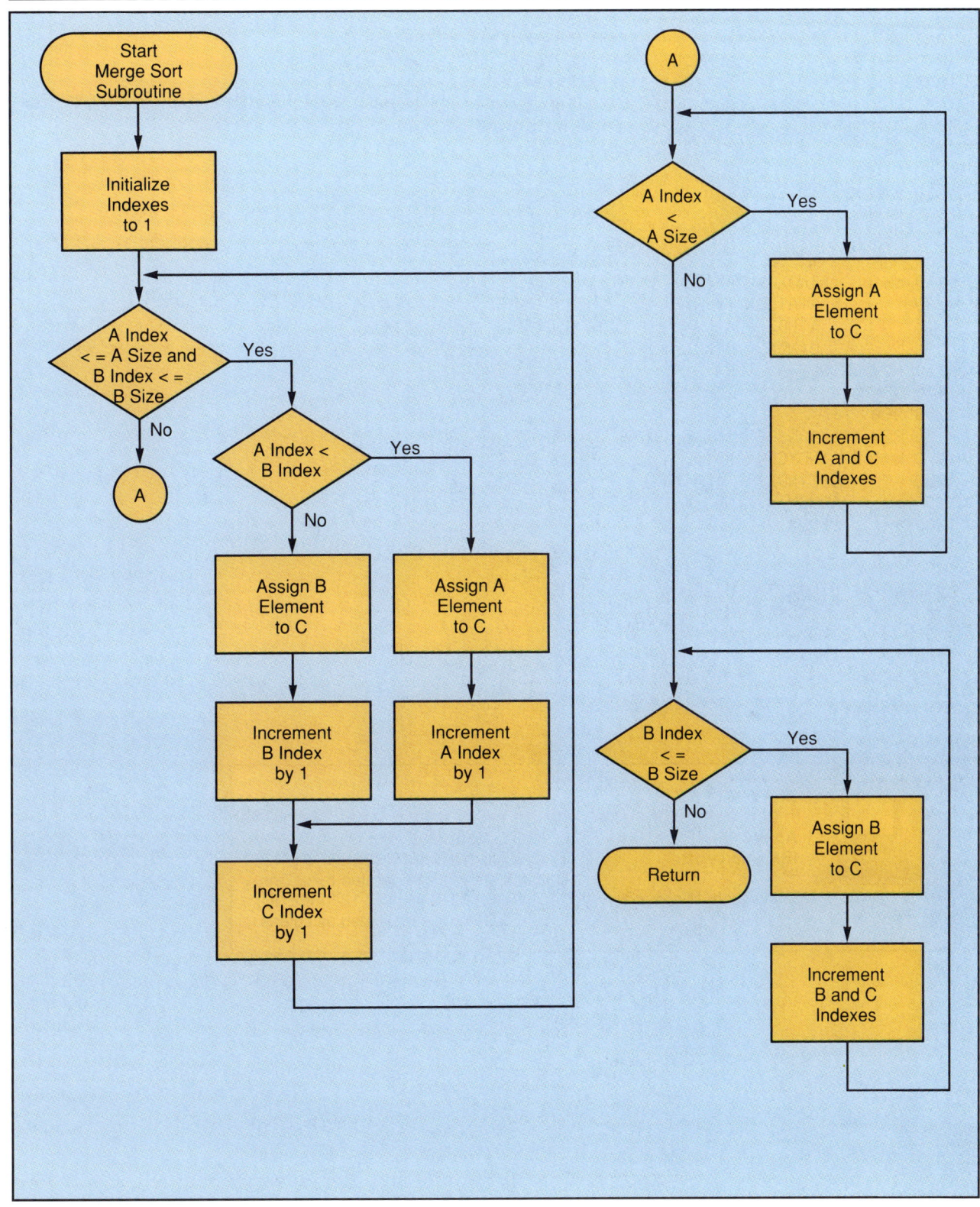

376 BASIC PROGRAMMING TODAY, A STRUCTURED APPROACH

FIGURE 9–9 *Continued*

```
1000 REM *******************************************
1010 REM ***          SUBROUTINE MERGE SORT         ***
1020 REM *******************************************
1030 REM ***   MERGE SORTED ARRAYS A AND B INTO C.  ***
1040 REM
1050 REM ***        INITIALIZE ARRAY INDEXES.       ***
1060 AINDX = 1
1070 BINDX = 1
1080 CINDX = 1
1090 REM
1100 REM *** MERGE UNTIL ALL OF ONE ARRAY IS READ. ***
1110 WHILE (AINDX <= ASIZE) AND (BINDX <= BSIZE)
1120      IF A(AINDX) < B(BINDX) THEN C(CINDX) = A(AINDX)\
             AINDX = AINDX + 1 ELSE C(CINDX) = B(BINDX)\
             BINDX = BINDX + 1
1130      CINDX = CINDX + 1
1140 NEXT
1150 REM
1160 REM *** ADD REMAINING ITEMS TO END OF NEW ARRAY. ***
1170 WHILE AINDXC <= ASIZE
1180      C(CINDX) = A(AINDX)
1190      AINDX = AINDX + 1
1200      CINDX = CINDX + 1
1210 NEXT
1220 REM
1230 WHILE BINDX <= BSIZE
1240      C(CINDX) = B(BINDX)
1250      BINDX = BINDX + 1
1260      CINDX = CINDX + 1
1270 NEXT
1280 RETURN
```

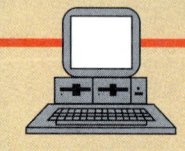

DIFFERENCES

Apple:	No WHILE loop; No IF/THEN/ELSE.
IBM/Microsoft:	1140 WEND; 1210 WEND; 1270 WEND; multiple statements separated by colons.
Macintosh/Microsoft:	1140 WEND; 1210 WEND; 1270 WEND; multiple statements separated by colons.

Searching

Sequential Search

An array search consists of examining the contents of an array until a desired value or values are found. For example, you may want to know the number of scores greater than 89 in an array QUIZ containing forty test scores. The following segment performs this task:

```
50 CNT = 0
60 FOR I = 1 TO 40
70    IF QUIZ(I) > 89 THEN CNT = CNT + 1
80 NEXT I
```

The variable CNT holds a count of the scores greater than 89. The loop is set up to check the value of each array element in numeric order, and the count is incremented only if the score being checked is greater than 89.

Another type of search might involve locating a single value. Suppose you wanted information regarding the August 19th concert at the local concert hall. The computer might prompt you to enter the date of the concert in which you are interested. It then would search an array of concert dates until it matched the given date. Finally, the computer would access the corresponding values from the arrays containing the rest of the concert information and display those values on the terminal screen.

Note that if more than one array holds corresponding (related) data, the data must be contained in the same relative position in each array. In other words, if the desired date matches the third element of the date array, the third elements of the other arrays are also accessed. This process is shown in Figure 9–10.

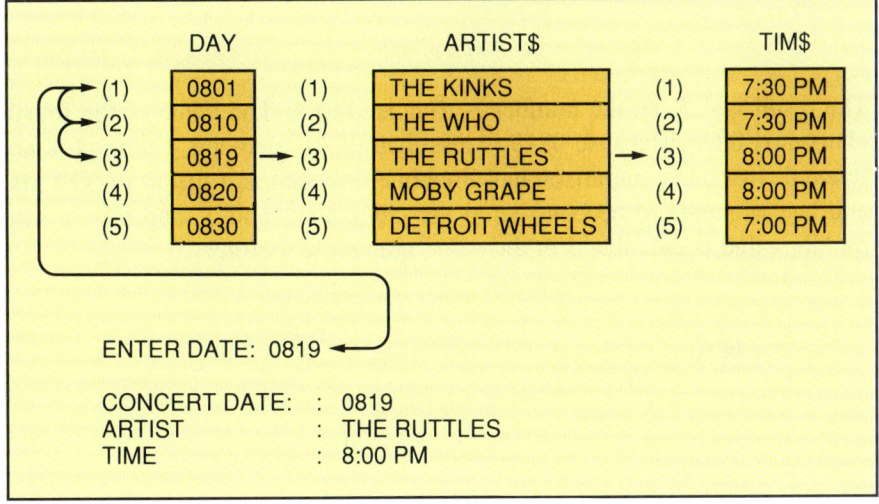

FIGURE 9–10
Concert Information Example

Sequential search
A search that examines elements from first to last in numeric order.

Both the searches just described are **sequential searches.** This type of search examines the first element, then the second element, then the third, and so on in numeric sequence until the desired element is found or the end of the array is reached. This type of search is adequate for a relatively small number of items (fewer than 100, generally speaking), but becomes slow with larger arrays. If the elements in an array can first be arranged in an ascending or descending order, the binary search is much faster and more efficient.

Binary Search

Binary search
A search that repeatedly divides a sorted array, eliminating the half not containing the target.

A **binary search** divides a sorted array into portions, eliminating those portions that do not contain the desired value. It first finds the middle value of a list and checks to see if the desired value is greater. Because the list is in order, half the list can thus be immediately eliminated. The portion of the list containing the desired value is then divided again according to a new middle value and is checked to see which half contains the desired value. This process continues until one of the middle values equals the desired value.

Consider the example of the concert dates array. The dates are listed in ascending order. (The numbers are coded to reflect the month and date as MMDD.) The array DAY can be pictured like this, with pointers at the first and last elements to be considered:

0801	0810	0819	0820	0821	0825	0828	0830
↑							↑

The desired date is 0819. To determine the middle, the subscripts of the first and last array elements are added and divided by 2.

$$\frac{1 + 8}{2} = \frac{9}{2} = 4.5$$

The result is 4.5, so the number is truncated to 4. The value of the fourth element is 0820. Because 0819 is less than 0820, elements 4 through 8 are ignored. Just one comparison has already eliminated half the array. The first and last elements to be considered are elements 1 and 3, and now a new middle value is calculated in the same manner as before:

0801	0810	0819	0820	0821	0825	0828	0830
↑		↑					

$$\frac{1 + 3}{2} = 2$$

The second element is now the middle value used to compare with the desired date 0819. Since 0810 is less than 0819, DAY(1) and DAY(2) can be ignored, and a new middle value is calculated:

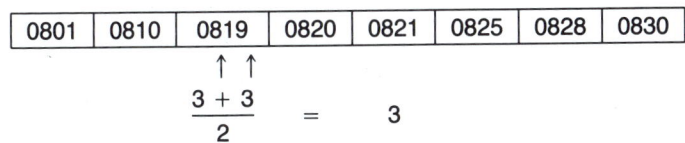

When DAY(3) is checked against 0819, the two values are found to be equal, and the search is over.

Figure 9–11 shows a subroutine that performs a binary search for a given date and prints the needed information. The WHILE loop of lines 1110 through 1140 performs the search as long as (1) the desired value does not match the value of the middle element (i.e., the desired value has not been found), and (2) the lower limit of the search is less than or equal to the upper limit. If the search has examined the first or last element of the array and still has not found the value, either the lower or upper limit will next be moved past the end of the array when line 1120 is executed. This condition indicates that the desired value is not located in the array. When the loop has terminated, this condition is checked in line 1150, and a message is printed if necessary. Otherwise, the appropriate concert information is printed.

A binary search is more efficient than a sequential search because it can find a given value with far fewer comparisons. For example, with an array of 1,000 elements, the maximum number of comparisons a binary search needs to make to find a specified element is 10. If the desired value is the last one in the array, a sequential search requires 1,000 comparisons.

Learning Check

1. A(n) _____ _____ consists of examining the elements of an array, from beginning to end, until the desired value or values are found.
2. In a sequential search of this list, how many values will be examined before 236 is located?

   12 44 103 177 236 582 978 1235

3. If a binary search is made of the above list, how many values will be examined before 236 is located?
4. A sequential search is faster than a binary search when searching large arrays. True or false?
5. Must a list be in order to do a sequential search? Must a list be in order to do a binary search?

Answers

1. sequential search 2. 5 3. 3 4. False 5. no; yes

FIGURE 9–11 Binary Search Subroutine

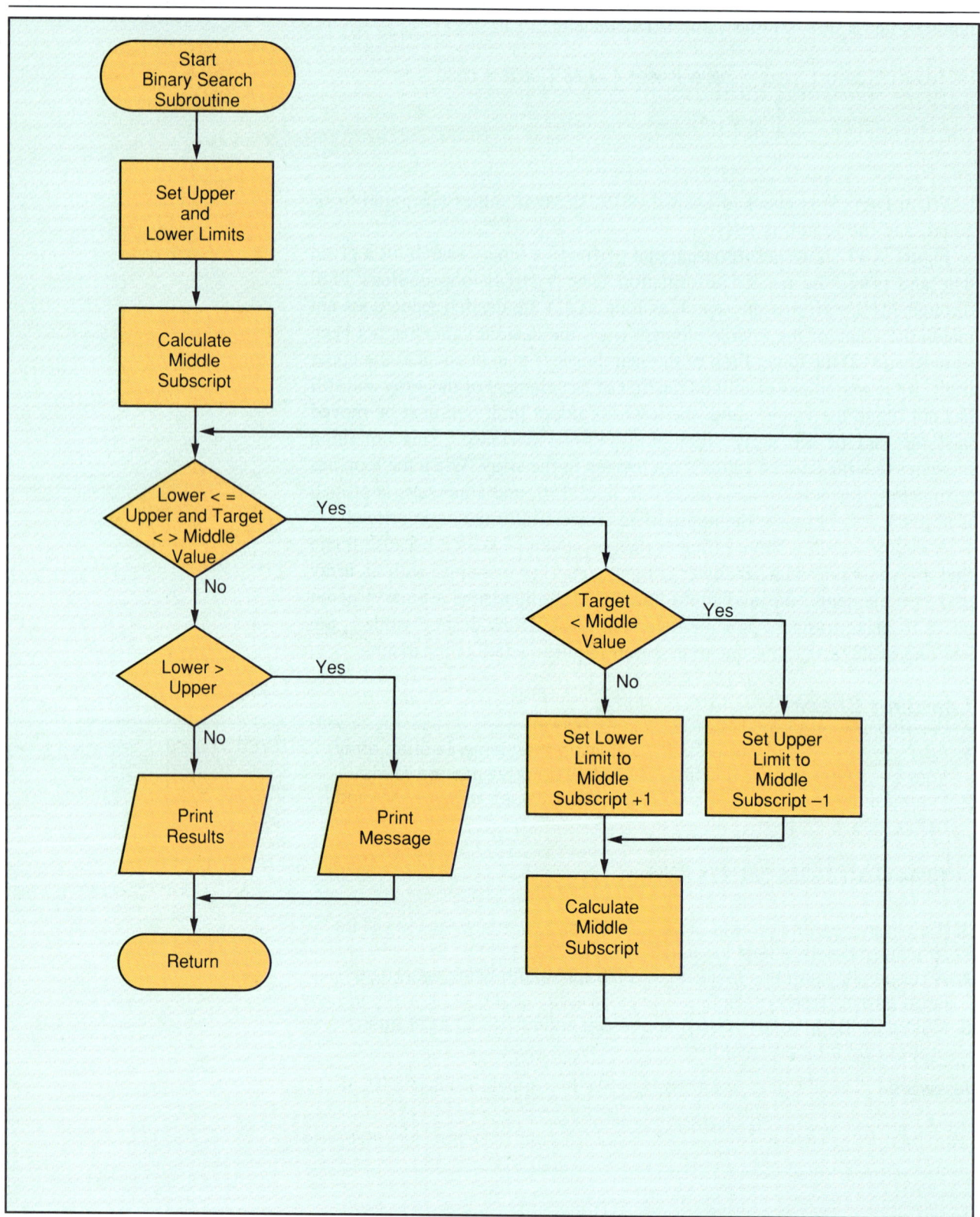

FIGURE 9–11 *Continued*

```
1000 REM ***********************************************
1010 REM ***          BINARY SEARCH SUBROUTINE       ***
1020 REM ***********************************************
1030 REM ***     SEARCH FOR GIVEN DATE AND PRINT     ***
1040 REM ***           INFORMATION IF FOUND.         ***
1050 REM
1060 UPPER = 8
1070 LOWER = 1
1080 MDL = INT(( UPPER + LOWER ) / 2 )
1090 REM
1100 REM *** LOOP UNTIL VALUE FOUND OR ENTIRE LIST CHECKED. ***
1110 WHILE ( LOWER <= UPPER ) AND ( DA <> DAY(MDL) )
1120      IF DA < DAY(MDL) THEN UPPER = MDL - 1
             ELSE LOWER = MDL + 1
1130      MDL = INT (( UPPER + LOWER ) / 2 )
1140 NEXT
1150 IF LOWER > UPPER THEN PRINT "NO CONCERT SCHEDULED" \ GOTO 1190
1160 PRINT "CONCERT DATE";DA
1170 PRINT "ARTIST:";ARTIST$(MDL)
1180 PRINT "TIME:";TIM$(MDL)
1190 RETURN
```

DIFFERENCES

Apple:	No WHILE loop; No IF/THEN/ELSE.
IBM/Microsoft:	1140 WEND; multiple statements use colons.
Macintosh/Microsoft:	1140 WEND; multiple statements use colons.

A Programming Problem

Problem Definition

The scorekeepers of the Centrovian Open Ice Skating Championships need a program to determine the winner of the final round. Each competitor is given six scores, of which the highest and lowest are discarded. The remaining four scores are then averaged to obtain the final score. The maximum score for each event is 6.0. Write a program that will read the names and scores of ten finalists and produce a listing of the skaters' names and final scores in order of finish. Sample input and needed output are shown in the following table.

Input:

BALDUCCI, G.	5.7	5.3	5.1	5.0	4.7	4.8
CREED, A.	3.1	4.9	4.1	3.7	4.6	3.9
WILLIAMS, E.	4.1	5.3	4.9	4.4	3.9	5.4
HAMILTON, S.	5.1	5.7	5.6	5.5	4.4	5.3
LORD, P.	5.9	4.8	5.5	5.0	5.7	5.7
STRAVINSKY, I.	5.1	4.7	4.1	3.1	4.6	5.0
MONTALBAN, R.	5.1	5.1	4.9	3.4	5.5	5.3
SCHELL, M.	4.9	4.3	5.2	4.5	4.6	4.9
CRANSTON, T.	6.0	6.0	5.7	5.8	5.9	5.9
CROWLEY, S.	4.3	5.2	5.9	5.3	4.3	6.0

Needed Output:

PLACE	NAME	SCORE
1	CRANSTON, T.	5.8
.	.	.
.	.	.
.	.	.

Solution Design

The problem provides us with seven items of data for each skater—a name and six scores—and asks for a list of names and averages, sorted by average. Once the data items have been read (the first step), there are two basic operations that must be performed in order to produce the listing: the averages must be calculated, and these averages with their associated names must be sorted. Thus, the problem can be broken into four major tasks: (1) read the data, (2) calculate the averages, (3) sort the names and averages, and (4) print the sorted information. The stepwise refinement is shown in Figure 9–12 and the structure chart in Figure 9–13.

The input for this problem consists of two types of data, alphabetic and numeric, so two arrays must be used to store them. The output calls for the names already stored plus a new set of values, the averages, so another array can be used to store these averages. In calculating the averages, variables

FIGURE 9–12
Stepwise Refinement of Skating Scores Problem

General Problem: Calculate and list the final results of the ten skating finalists.
Level 1
   A. Read names and scores
   B. Calculate averages
   C. Sort by averages
   D. Print results

FIGURE 9–13 Structure Chart for Skating Scores Problem

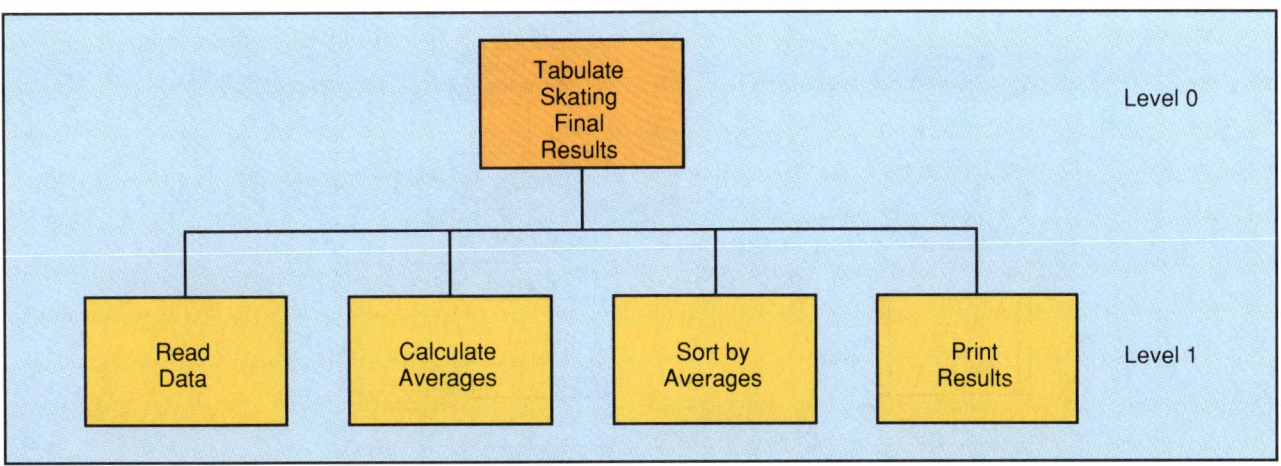

will also be needed to keep track of the high and low scores. The main variables needed can be summarized as follows.

Input variables	
array of names	(SKNM$)
array of scores	(PTS)
Program variables	
high score for a competitor	(HI)
low score for a competitor	(LO)
total of four scores	(TPTS)
Output variables	
array of averages	(AVG)

In order to calculate the averages, a search must be done on the six scores of each skater to find the high and low scores. The scores are not in order, so the sequential search is used.

A sort is required in the third step of our algorithm. A descending-order bubble sort could be effective here, because the number of items to be sorted is relatively small. A crucial point is that, as the averages are rearranged, the corresponding skater's name must be carried with each average. This means, for example, that the average for the fourth skater (SKNM$(4)) must be stored in AVG(4).

The Program

The program of Figure 9–14 shows the solution to the problem. Line 140 of the main program reserves space for a two-dimensional array for the scores. Each row of array PTS contains the scores for one skater, so ten rows with six columns each are needed.

FIGURE 9–14 Skating Scores Program

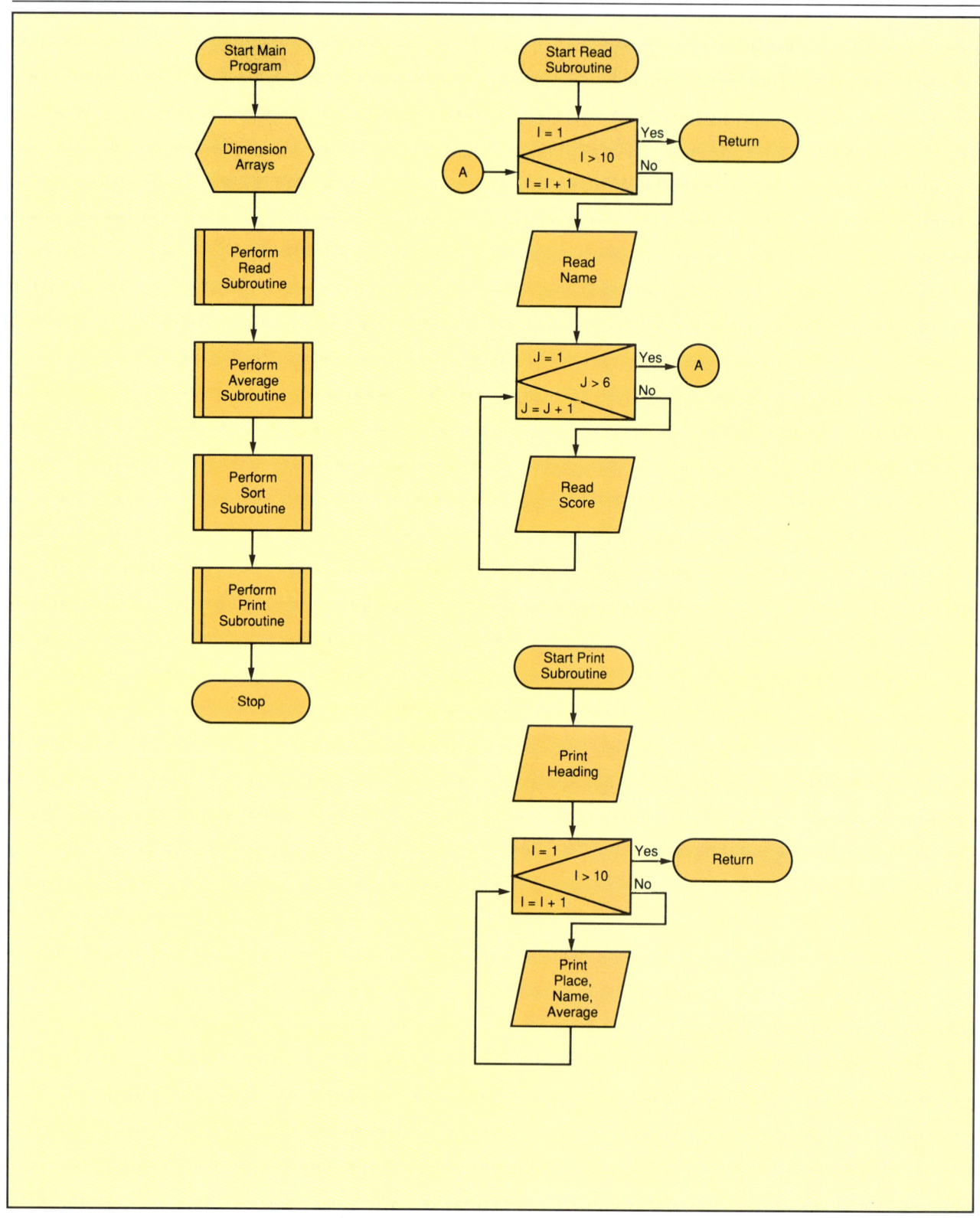

ARRAYS 385

FIGURE 9-14 *Continued*

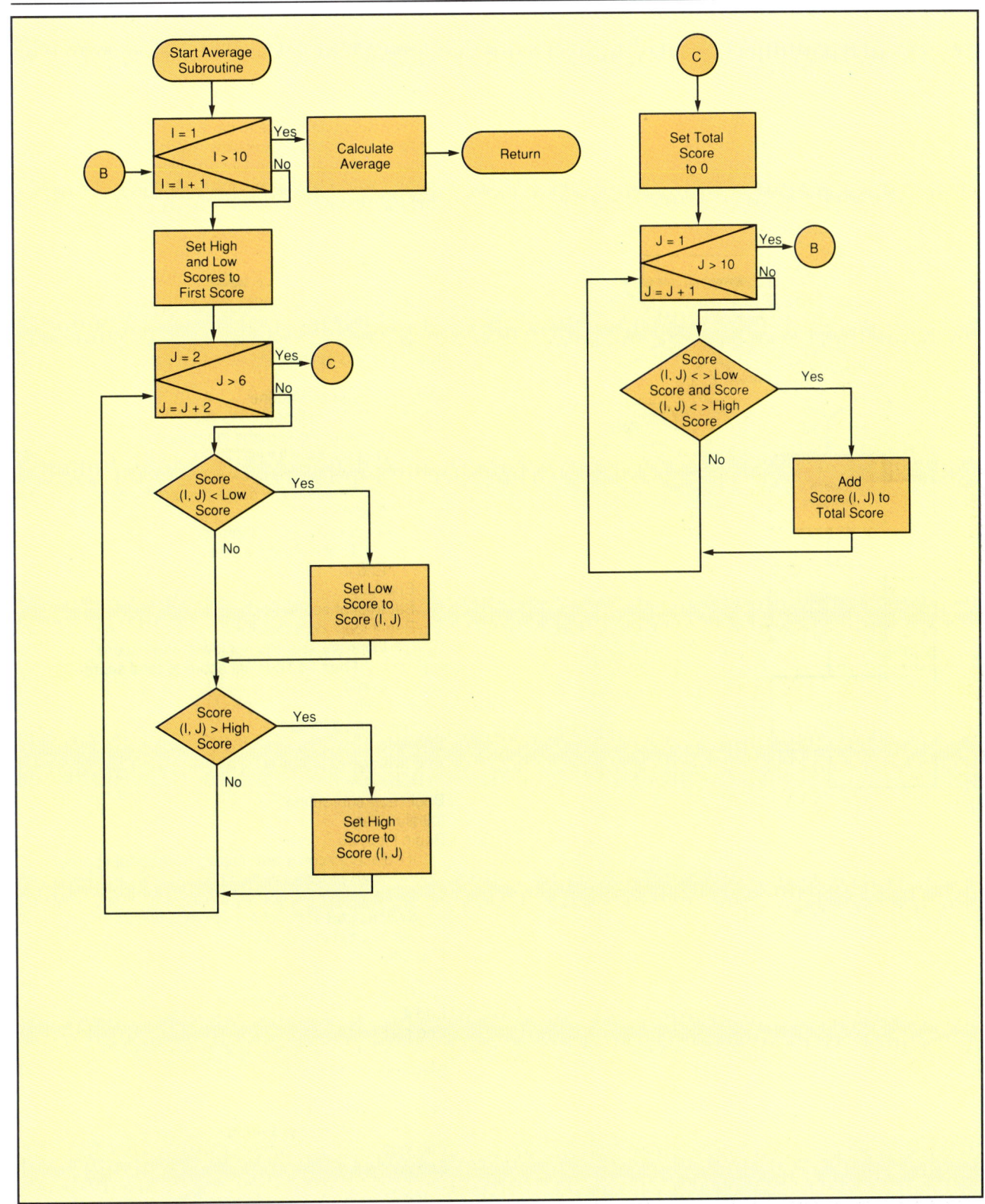

FIGURE 9–14 *Continued*

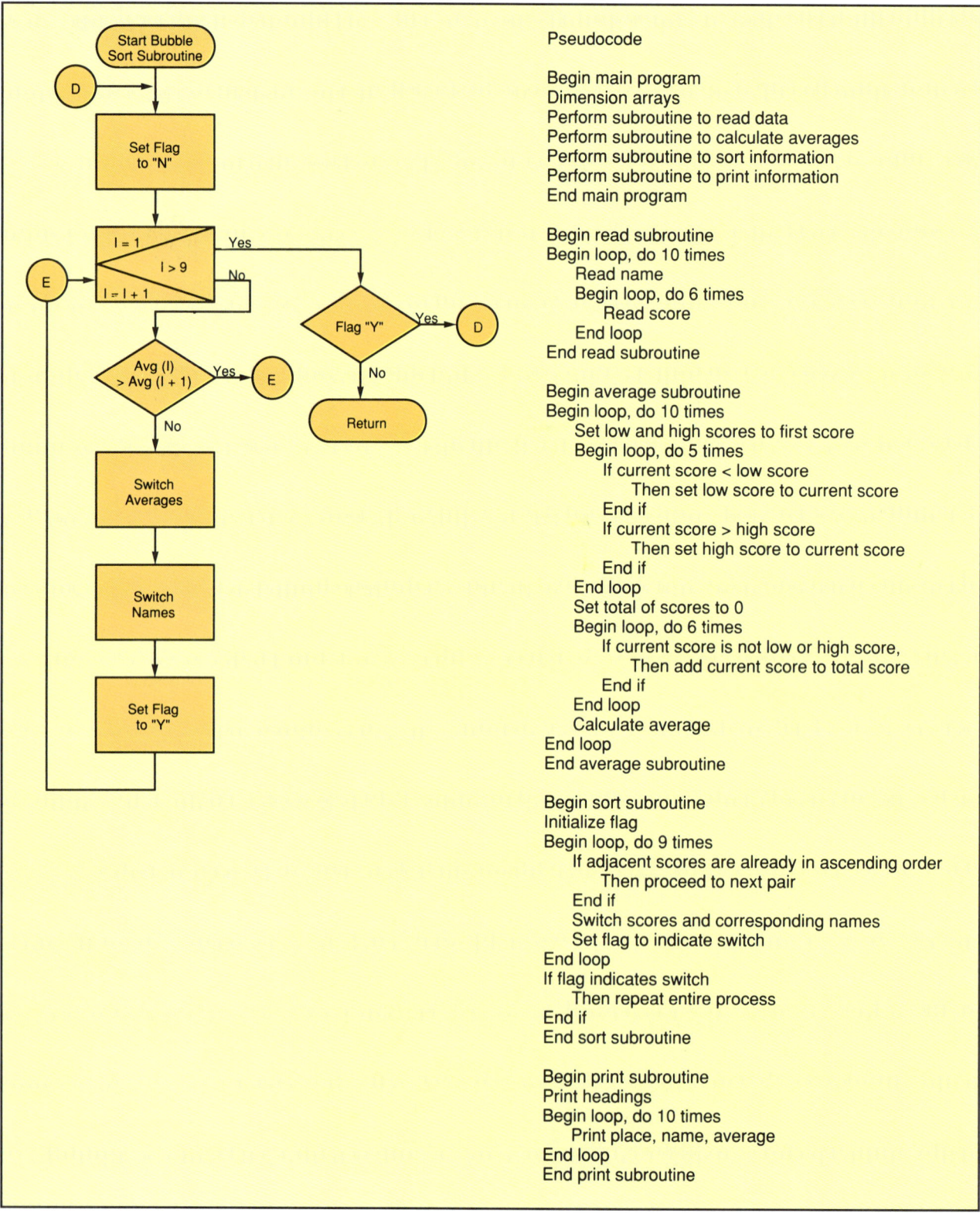

FIGURE 9–14 Continued

```
10     REM ***              SKATING FINAL RESULTS              ***
20     REM
30     REM *** THIS PROGRAM COMPUTES THE AVERAGES OF SKATING    ***
40     REM *** SCORES, USING SIX SCORES AND DROPPING THE LOW    ***
50     REM *** AND HIGH SCORES. IT THEN SORTS ALL THE AVERAGE   ***
60     REM *** SCORES IN ASCENDING ORDER.                       ***
70     REM *** MAJOR VARIABLES:                                 ***
80     REM ***      SKNM$         ARRAY OF SKATERS NAMES        ***
90     REM ***      PTS           ARRAY OF SCORES               ***
100    REM ***      AVG           ARRAY OF AVERAGES             ***
110    REM ***      HI,LO         HIGHEST/LOWEST SCORES         ***
120    REM
130    REM *** DIMENSION THE ARRAYS. ***
140    DIM SKNM$(10),PTS(10,6),AVG(10)
150    REM
160    REM *** READ NAMES AND SCORES. ***
170    GOSUB 1000
180    REM
190    REM *** CALCULATE FINAL AVERAGE. ***
200    GOSUB 2000
210    REM
220    REM *** SORT BY AVERAGE. ***
230    GOSUB 3000
240    REM
250    REM *** PRINT RESULTS. ***
260    GOSUB 4000
270    GOTO 9999
1000   REM ***********************************************************
1010   REM ***                 SUBROUTINE READ                     ***
1020   REM ***********************************************************
1030   REM ***     READ THE NAMES AND SIX SCORES.                  ***
1040   REM
1050   FOR I = 1 TO 10
1060       READ SKNM$(I)
1070       FOR J = 1 TO 6
1080           READ PTS(I,J)
1090       NEXT J
1100   NEXT I
1110   RETURN
2000   REM ***********************************************************
2010   REM ***                SUBROUTINE AVERAGE                   ***
2020   REM ***********************************************************
2030   REM ***    DROP HIGH/LOW SCORES, THEN AVERAGE SCORE.        ***
2040   REM
2050   FOR I = 1 TO 10
2060       HI = PTS(I,1)
2070       LO = PTS(I,1)
2080       FOR J = 2 TO 6
2090           IF PTS(I,J) < LO THEN LO = PTS(I,J)
2100           IF PTS(I,J) > HI THEN HI = PTS(I,J)
2110       NEXT J
```

FIGURE 9–14 *Continued*

```
2120        REM
2130        REM *** AVERAGE REMAINING SCORES. ***
2140        TPTS = 0
2150        FOR J = 1 TO 6
2160           IF PTS(I,J) <> LO OR PTS(I,J) <> HI THEN
                  TPTS = TPTS + PTS(I,J)
2170        NEXT J
2180        AVG(I) = TPTS / 4
2190 NEXT I
2200 RETURN
3000 REM ************************************************************
3010 REM ***               SUBROUTINE BUBBLE SORT                 ***
3020 REM ************************************************************
3030 REM ***        SORT AVERAGES IN ASCENDING ORDER.             ***
3040 REM
3050 SWITCH$ = "N"
3060 FOR I = 1 TO 9
3070      IF AVG(I) > AVG(I + 1) THEN 3150
3080      TEMP = AVG(I)
3090      STEMP$ = SKNM$(I)
3100      AVG(I) = AVG(I + 1)
3110      SKNM$(I) = SKNM$(I + 1)
3120      AVG(I + 1) = TEMP
3130      SKNM$(I + 1) = STEMP$
3140      SWITCH$ = "Y"
3150 NEXT I
3160 IF SWITCH$ = "Y" THEN 3050
3170 RETURN
4000 REM ************************************************************
4010 REM ***                  SUBROUTINE PRINT                    ***
4020 REM ************************************************************
4030 REM ***      PRINT THE HEADINGS AND THE RESULTS.             ***
4040 REM
4050 PRINT "PLACE";TAB(10);"NAME";TAB(30);"SCORE"
4060 PRINT
4070 FOR I = 1 TO 10
4080     PRINT I;TAB(10);SKNM$(I);TAB(30);AVG(I)
4090 NEXT I
4100 RETURN
4200 REM
4210 REM ***   DATA STATEMENTS   ***
4220 DATA "BALDUCCI,G",5.7,5.3,5.1,5.0,4.7,4.8
4230 DATA "CREED,A",3.1,4.9,4.1,3.7,4.6,3.9
4240 DATA "WILLIAMS,E.",4.1,5.3,4.9,4.4,3.9,5.4
4250 DATA "HAMILTON,S",5.1,5.7,5.6,5.5,4.4,5.3
4260 DATA "LORD,P",5.9,4.8,5.5,5.0,5.7,5.7
4270 DATA "STRAVINSKY,I",5.1,4.7,4.1,3.1,4.6,5.0
4280 DATA "MONTALBAN,R",5.1,5.1,4.9,3.4,5.5,5.3
4290 DATA "SCHELL,M",4.9,4.3,5.2,4.5,4.6,4.9
4300 DATA "CRANSTON,T",6.0,6.0,5.7,5.8,5.9,5.9
4310 DATA "CROWLEY,S",4.3,5.2,5.9,5.3,4.3,6.0
9999 END
```

FIGURE 9-14 Continued

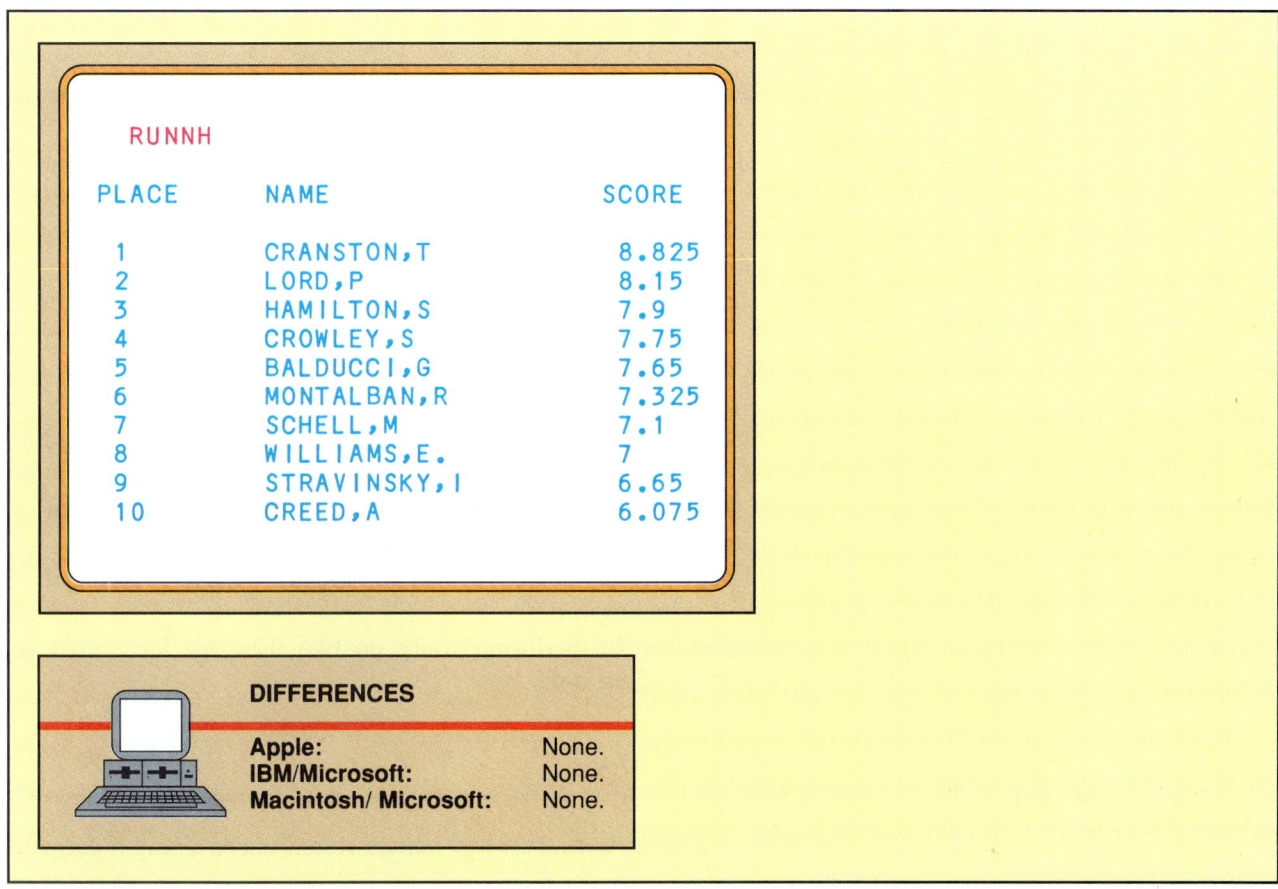

The first subroutine called by the main program reads the names and scores to their respective arrays. The second subroutine finds the average score of each skater. It does this by performing a sequential search on each row of the scores array (array PTS) in lines 2050 through 2110. When the low and high scores for the row have been found, lines 2150 through 2170 add all the scores for that row, except the low and high scores, to the total. Then the average for that row is calculated.

The sorting of the final averages is performed in the bubble sort of the third subroutine. Notice that the flag indicating that a switch has been made can be a string variable, as in line 3050. The actual value stored in the flag is unimportant; the critical factor is whether that value is changed during the sort.

The condition AVG(I) > AVG(I + 1) in line 3070 causes the averages to be sorted from highest to lowest. Every time an average is moved, its corresponding name from the array SKNM$ is also moved. The sorted results are printed by the fourth subroutine in lines 4000 through 4090.

Avoiding Common Programming Mistakes

When programming with arrays, keep the following points in mind.

- Remember that only numbers can be stored in numeric variable arrays and only character strings can be stored in string variable arrays.
- The BASIC system automatically reserves room for only eleven elements if a one-dimensional array is not declared in a DIM statement, and eleven rows and columns for a two-dimensional array. It is good programming practice to dimension all arrays, regardless of their size.
- A DIM statement must appear before the array that it dimensions is used in the program.
- Remember that the first subscript refers to the rows of an array and the second subscript refers to its columns.
- Array subscripts can vary in the program from 0 to the limit declared in the DIM statement, but no subscript can exceed that limit.
- A name used for a two-dimensional array cannot be used for a one-dimensional array in the same program.
- In order to use a binary search, the data in the array must be arranged in ascending or descending order.
- A merge sort can be performed only on two lists that are sorted in ascending or descending order.

Summary Points

- An array is a collection of related values stored under a single variable name.
- Individual array elements can be accessed by using subscripts.
- A subscript of an array element can be any legal numeric expression.
- The DIM statement sets up storage for arrays and must appear before the first reference to the array it describes.
- Array manipulation is carried out through the use of loops.
- A two-dimensional array stores values as a table, grouped into rows and columns.
- The first subscript of a two-dimensional array refers to the element's row and the second subscript to the column.
- The bubble sort places elements of an array in ascending or descending order by comparing adjacent elements.
- The Shell sort is a more efficient method of ordering large arrays than the bubble sort.
- The merge sort combines two sorted lists into one larger, sorted list.
- A sequential search of an array consists of examining each element in the array until the desired value is located.
- To perform a binary search, the array elements must be arranged in ascending or descending order.

Review Questions

1. What is an array?
2. Variables that refer to specific elements in an array are called _____ variables, whereas simple variables are called _____ variables.
3. Give two advantages of using arrays.
4. What is a subscript?
5. Where must the DIM statement appear in a program?
6. When an array is not dimensioned, its subscripts can vary in value from 0 to _____.
7. Only one array can be dimensioned in a DIM statement. True or false?
8. Assume X = 1, Y = 2, and Z = 3. What are the values of the variables A(X), A(Y − X), and A(X * Z) if array A contains the following values?

Array A

11
42
37
90
17

9. The _____ statements are an efficient method of manipulating arrays.
10. Write a program segment that will sum the ten values of a one-dimensional array of ten elements.
11. Write a segment that will sum all the values contained in a two-dimensional array of ten rows and five columns.
12. Describe how the bubble sort works.
13. How many times should the loop in a bubble sort execute?
14. Explain how the Shell sort works.
15. Which is more efficient in dealing with large arrays, the bubble or Shell sort, and why?
16. Write a segment that will total the columns of an array whose DIM statement follows, putting the sums of the columns in a one-dimensional array SUMS:

   10 DIM X(15,20)

17. How is a sequential search performed?
18. Which search is more efficient in dealing with large arrays, the binary or sequential, and why?
19. The _____ sort combines two sorted lists into a single sorted list.
20. How does a binary search work?

Debugging Exercises

Identify the following programs or program segments that contain errors, and debug them.

1. ```
10 REM *** READS DATA TO ARRAY A. ***
20 FOR I = 1 TO 20
30   INPUT A(I)
40 NEXT I
99 END
```

2. ```
10 REM *** READ 10 NUMBERS TO AN ARRAY. ***
20 DIM B(10)
30 FOR I = 1 TO 10
40     READ B
50 NEXT I
60 DATA 10,20,30,40,50
70 DATA 60,70,80,90,100
```

3. ```
10 REM *** PRINT THE VALUES STORED IN ARRAY X. ***
20 DIM X(10)
30 FOR J = 1 TO 11
40   PRINT X(J)
50 NEXT J
```

4. ```
10 REM *** TOTAL ELEMENTS OF ARRAY. ***
20 DIM X(10)
30 T = 0
40 FOR I = 1 TO 10
50     T = T + X(1)
60 NEXT I
```

5. ```
20 REM *** ADD ELEMENTS OF ARRAYS A AND B. ***
30 FOR J = 1 TO 10
40   C = A(J) + B(J)
50 NEXT J
```

6. ```
30 DIM X(5,4)
40 REM *** ADD COLUMN 1. ***
50 SUM = 0
60 FOR J = 1 TO 4
70     SUM = X(1,J)
80 NEXT J
```

7. ```
10 REM *** READ THE CONTENTS OF THE 2-DIMENSIONAL ARRAY X. ***
20 DIM X(5,4)
30 FOR I = 1 TO 4
40   FOR J = 1 TO 5
50   READ X(I,J)
60   NEXT J
70 NEXT I
```
```

8.  ```
    10  DIM X(26)
    20  REM *** BUBBLE SORT NUMBERS IN ***
    30  REM *** ASCENDING ORDER.        ***
    40  F = 0
    50  FOR I = 1 TO 26
    60     IF X(I) <= X(I + 1) THEN 100
    70     T = X(I)
    80     X(I) = X(I + 1)
    90     X(I + 1) = T
    100    F = 1
    110 NEXT I
    120 IF F = 1 THEN 30
    ```

9.  ```
    10  REM *** SHELL SORT. ***
    20  N = 10
    30  G = INT(N / 2)
    40  WHILE G <> 0
    50     F = 1
    60     FOR J = 1 TO (N - G)
    70        IF N(J) <= N(J + G) THEN 120
    80        M = N(J)
    90        N(J) = N(J + G)
    100       N(J + G) = M
    110       F = 0
    120    NEXT J
    130    IF F = 0 THEN 60
    140    G = INT(G / 2)
    150 NEXT
    ```

10. ```
    10  REM *** BINARY SEARCH. ***
    20  DIM S$(50)
    30  N$ = "268-66-9843"
    40  U = 50
    50  L = 1
    60  MDL = INT((U + L) / 2)
    70  WHILE (L <= U) AND (N$ <> S$(MDL))
    80     IF N$ < S$(MDL) THEN L = MDL - 1
    90     MDL = INT((U + L) / 2)
    100 NEXT
    110 IF L > U THEN PRINT "INVALID NUMBER" \ GOTO 999
    120 PRINT "SOCIAL SECURITY NUMBER FOUND"
    999 END
    ```

Additional Programming Problems

Level 1

1. Write a segment that reads the following data to a one-dimensional array and then prints it:

20, 22, 45, 60, 24, 16
    ```

2. Write a FOR/NEXT loop that prints every other element in an array of thirty elements.

3. Write a segment that adds the elements of an array of twenty elements and prints the total.

4. The array X contains fifty numbers. Write a FOR/NEXT loop that will print all the numbers that are greater than 20 and less than 40, using a sequential search.

5. Read twelve numbers to array A and twelve numbers to array B. Compute the product of the corresponding elements of the two arrays, and place the results in array C. Print a table similar to the following at the end of your program:

A	B	C
2	3	6
7	2	14

6. Write a program that reads the numbers 1 through 20, assigning the even numbers to the array EVEN and the odd numbers to the array ODD. Use a FOR/NEXT loop that will assign an even number and odd number each time it executes, and total the values in each array.

Your output should look something like this:

EVEN NUMBERS	ODD NUMBERS
X	X
X	X
X	X
XXX	XXX

7. The planet Uranus has five known satellites. You are to write a program that will read the satellite names to two arrays and merge them so that the output looks like this:

SATELLITES

MIRANDA
ARIEL
UMBRIEL
TITANIA
OBERON

Use the READ/DATA statements to enter data for the following arrays:

Array 1	Array 2
Miranda	Ariel
Umbriel	Titania
Oberon	

8. The computer department has asked you to produce a computer dictionary for them. The department has given you a list of the words and definitions to print in an alphabetical list. The department has not specified a format for the output, so you can use whatever format you wish. The list of words and definitions follows:

BASIC—A programming language for beginners.
Byte—A unit of storage made up of bits.
Microcomputer—A very small computer.
Secondary storage—External storage such as disks.
Field—A meaningful item of data.

9. The Casket Company needs a program to list its employees' names and I.D. numbers in ascending order by I.D. number. Use a bubble sort for the following data:

I.D. Number	Name
467217	Alston, M.
624719	Cioffari, R.
784609	Chilson, D.
290013	Sergent, D.
502977	Layman, F.
207827	Kock, D.
389662	Wymer, E.
443279	Toalston, A.
302621	Kehmer, C.
196325	McKee, K.

10. Write a program to sort ten U.S. cities into alphabetical order and print them. Use the following input:

Input

Los Angeles
Chicago
Detroit
New York City
Dallas
Cleveland
Boston
Washington
Miami
Denver

Level 2

1. The Subterranean Art Gallery is preparing for its annual auction held in Washington Square. The *Village Voice* is preparing a circular containing information concerning the paintings to be auctioned:

Painting	Artist	Value in Millions
Starry Night	Van Gogh	5.5
Last Words	Picasso	3.8
Why?	Monika	.0005
Self Portrait	Dylan	1.2
Prodigal Son	Rembrandt	4.9
Call Me Abbie	Hoffman	3.6
Yippie Sandwich	Reubens	.08

They have hired you to write a program that will input the above data, sort the information into alphabetical order by the artists' names, and print the information.

2. Steven Williams is writing a composition about the thirteenth president of the United States, Millard Fillmore. He needs to know the years in which Fillmore held office. You are to write a program that will search for Fillmore and print the years. Use a two-dimensional array to store the following data:

Adams	1797–1801
Arthur	1881–1885
Buchanan	1857–1861
Coolidge	1923–1929
Fillmore	1850–1853
Garfield	1881–1881
Hayes	1877–1881
Jackson	1829–1837
Jefferson	1801–1809
Kennedy	1961–1963

The output should look like this:

THE LATE MILLARD FILLMORE WAS THE SECOND VICE PRESIDENT TO INHERIT THE PRESIDENCY. HE WAS IN OFFICE FROM __X__ .

3. Tomorrow marks the first annual University Talent Contest. The judges have asked you to write a report listing each contestant (in order of his or her score) and the score that contestant received. Use the bubble sort to arrange scores from highest to lowest. The data consists of the contestants' names and scores:

McKinniss, S.	73.9
Bulas, Y.	47.0
Jones, B.	79.8
Busch, P.	89.7
Taylor, E.	86.7
Loren, S.	91.5
Bardot, B.	69.3
Welch, W.	72.2

4. The Klingons have captured Spock, science officer of the U.S.S. Enterprise. Captain Kirk has broken into their prison colony to free him. He has reached the computer that possesses information concerning all of the prisoners, including their cell numbers. Write a program to read the following data to arrays, alphabetize the data by name, and print information regarding a prisoner when his or her name is entered. Use a binary search routine in your program to speed Captain Kirk's search for Spock.

Prisoner	**Ship**	**Cell #**
Kenobi	Falcon	328
Spock	Enterprise	562
Yoda	None	122
Mudd	Pleasure Dome	222
Khan	Botony Bay	009
Jetson	Astrofly	468
Rogers	Galaxy 2	727
Koenig	Alpher	999
Adama	Galactic	987
Who	Tardis	585

5. A department store is having a close-out sale on all its merchandise. Write a program that will store all its prices and discounts in one array, then calculate the corresponding sale prices and store them in a second array. Print the original prices, the discount rates, and the corresponding sale prices.

PRICE	DISCOUNT	SALES PRICE
3.50	.25	x.xx
4.00	.50	x.xx
5.25	.25	x.xx
6.00	.30	x.xx

6. The New York Times needs to determine the standings for the Patrick Division of the NHL. Six teams are included in the Division. Their names, wins, and losses are as follows:

Pittsburgh Penguins	2	13
Washington Capitals	8	7
Philadelphia Flyers	7	8
New York Rangers	8	7
New York Islanders	10	5
New Jersey Devils	0	15

Sort the data in descending order by wins, and print the results.

7. Write a program that will randomly pick ten numbers between 1 and 200. Print the numbers in their original sequence and in ascending order. Use the Shell sort. The output should have the following format:

```
ORIGINAL ORDER
     X
     X
     X
     X
ASCENDING ORDER
     X
     X
     X
     X
```

8. Write a program that will randomly generate ten numbers between 1 and 10 and assign them to an array. Print the array with an asterisk beside each 5. Use a sequential search. The output should have this format:

```
10 RANDOM NUMBERS
       X
       X
       .
       .
       .
      5*
       .
       .
      5*
       X
```

9. Toys Unlimited and Playthings, Inc. are merging. The two companies want a program to merge their inventory, keeping it in alphabetical order. Use the following data:

Toys Unlimited	**Playthings, Inc.**
Barbie	Monopoly
Clue	Lite Bright

Parcheesi	Hearts
Pound Puppy	Operation
Memory	
Speak and Spell	

10. Iowa State University set up two sections of advanced Latin, both scheduled to meet at 8 A.M. Many of the students found this class too early to attend, so they dropped out. Seven students were left in one class and nine in the other, so the university decided to combine the two classes. Now it needs a program to merge the two lists of remaining students, keeping them in alphabetical order. Use the following data:

Class A	**Class B**
Baez	Andrews
Christoph	Cohn
Guthrie	Farina
Miller	Garcia
Mooser	Kim
Smothers	Pontello
Travers	Seeger
	Tallman
	Wahl

Level 3

1. The world-renowned detective, Hercules Poireau, is investing the robbery of a university professor known to his students as "Big Boy." Poireau has drawn up a list of suspects (Big Boy's former students), their present occupations, possible motives, and the places they claim to have been at the time of the robbery.

Suspect	**Occupation**	**Motive**	**Place**
Carstens, C.	Computer Programmer	Pizza money	Her wedding
Rehmer, T.	Drifter	Travel money	Party
Bertsch, S.	Gemologist	Grades	Skiing in Alps
Costa, M.	Professor	Personal problems	Office
Bulas, M.	Interior Decorator	Money for debts	Saks Fifth Ave.
Toth, D.	Bartender	Revenge	Out of town

Write a program that will read this information to arrays, alphabetize the data according to the suspects' names with a bubble sort, and print the information in the format shown here.

2. Gary Mueller has hired you to keep track of his band's payroll. Write a program that will read the following information to three arrays:

Section	Number of Musicians	Hourly Pay Rate
Bongos	3	$10.00
Horns	10	$ 5.50
Guitars	4	$ 9.50
Strings	6	$ 7.50
Maracas	20	$ 3.65

Before printing the payroll in a format similar to that shown, sort all three arrays in descending order according to the pay rate.

3. A cryptogram is a coded message formed by substituting a code character for each letter in the original message. The substitution is performed uniformly throughout the original message; that is, if *A* is equal to *Z*, every occurrence of *A* will be replaced by a *Z*. All punctuation remains unchanged. Write a program that will read a list of letters in the form of coded text and output the uncoded message. Use the code below:

Code: A B C D E F G H I J K L M N O P Q R S T U V W X Y Z
Actual Letter: Z N Y O X P W V Q U R T S A M B L C K D J E I F H G

For example, if your data looked like this:
Y
V
Q
Q
D
then your output would look like this:
H
E
L
L
O

4. The Movie Maniacs' Association is conducting a survey of 150 moviegoers to see which movie they would pick as their all-time favorite. The association would like you to write a program to show the results of the survey. The program should use INPUT statements to enter the data. Also, the program should print a report of the survey, giving the name of the movie, the percentage of votes it received, and the number of votes it received. At the end of the report, print the total number of votes (150). Use the following data:

Out of Africa	34
Childs' Play	14
Gorillas in the Mist	36
Wall Street	15

The Babysitter	24	
Funny Farm	14	
License to Drive	13	

5. Conner Video, Inc. operates three video games in four different arcades. Mr. Connor has received the following table of data concerning the number of games played at each of the four arcades:

Arcade	Star Wars	Donkey Kong	Q-bert
Video Madness	100	250	200
Sappy Sam's	500	600	700
Krazy Kevin	200	225	230
City Arcade	120	520	500

Mr. Connor would like to know how many games were played at each arcade, how many games per video were played, and the total number of games played together. The output should include the preceding table.

6. A university would like a program that will generate a report regarding enrollment in three of its colleges. The program should use the following data:

	College		
Year	Business	Education	Music
1982	548	426	321
1983	593	447	203
1984	641	430	346
1985	650	398	401

The report should indicate what percentage of each year's total enrollment is enrolled in each college. The total enrollment for each year should also be indicated. The format for the report is as follows:

ENROLLMENT PERCENTAGE FOR EACH YEAR

YEAR	BUSINESS	MUSIC	EDUCATION	TOTAL
1982	XX.XX%	XXXX%	XX.XX%	XXXX
1983				
1984				
1985				

7. Junior Johnson likes to play with computers, and now he wants a program that will keep track of all his baseball cards. He is tired of looking through all his cards whenever he wants to know something about a certain player. He would like to be able to enter the player's name and have the computer print the player's team, the number of games he has played, the number of at bats, the number of RBIs, and the player's batting average. The output should look like this:

```
NAME: Last name, first initial
CLUB: Club name
GAMES: XX
AT BATS: XXX
RBI'S: XX
AVERAGE: 0.XXX
```

Use this data:

Player	Club	Games	At Bats	RBIs	Average
Ramos	Expos	26	41	3	0.195
Hisle	Brewers	27	87	11	0.230
Driessen	Reds	82	233	33	0.236
Bonnel	Blue Jays	66	227	28	0.220
Murcer	Yankees	50	117	24	0.260
Ayala	Orioles	44	86	13	0.279

The players, clubs, games, at bats, RBIs, and averages should be in separate arrays. The data items for each player should be in the same position in their respective arrays as the position of the corresponding player. Test the program by entering any of the player's names and checking the output against the data list.

8. Write a program to provide the weather reporter with a list of major cities and their high temperatures for the day. The program should arrange the cities in alphabetical order using a Shell sort. The weather reporter should then be able to request a city and have its high temperature printed. Use a binary search to find the requested city. Here is the data:

City	Temperature
Miami	92
New York	80
Chicago	86
Denver	78
Los Angeles	83
Houston	95
Boston	73
Fresno	85

9. The Adams Restaurant Supply Company wants a program that will keep track of the inventory of five items for its three outlet locations. These items and their starting quantities are given below:

	Outlet		
	1	2	3
Chef's Knife	133	107	90
Food Processor	69	53	42
Mixer	83	68	21
Chopping Block	140	121	94
Soup Kettle	85	71	50

The program should be able to indicate the current inventory of any item. It must also provide a means of updating the inventory when a sale occurs.

10. Write a program that will print the intersection of two arrays, that is, the numbers common to both arrays. Array A should consist of ten numbers and array B of eight numbers. Use READ/DATA statements to enter the data. The output should have the following format:

INTERSECTING NUMBERS
    X
    X
    X
    X

CHAPTER 10

DATA FILES

Objectives

After studying this chapter you will be able to:
- Define a file, a record, and a field.
- Explain the various types of file organization.
- Describe the various methods of accessing a file.
- Explain what secondary storage is and how it relates to files.
- Write to and read from a sequential file using sequential access.
- Write to and read from a relative file using random access.

Outline

Overview
What Is a File?
File Organization
Methods of Accessing Files
Secondary Storage
Using Sequential Files with
    Sequential Access
    Creating and Writing to a
        Sequential File
    Reading from a Sequential File
    VAX
        Creating or Accessing a File
        Writing Data to a File
        Closing a File
        Reading a File
    Apple
        Creating or Accessing a File
        Writing Data to a File
        Closing a File
        Reading a File

IBM/Microsoft and
    Macintosh/Microsoft
    Creating or Accessing a File
    Writing Data to a File
    Closing a File
    Reading a File
Using Relative Files with Random
    Access
    VAX
        Creating or Accessing a File
        Writing Data to a File
        Closing a File
        Reading a File
    Apple
        Creating or Accessing a File
        Writing Data to a File
        Closing a File
        Reading a File

IBM/Microsoft and
    Macintosh/Microsoft
    Creating or Accessing a File
    Writing Data to a File
    Closing a File
    Reading a File
A Programming Problem
    Problem Definition
    Solution Design
    The Programs
Avoiding Common Programming
    Mistakes
Summary Points
Review Questions
Debugging Exercises
Additional Programming Problems
    Level 1
    Level 2
    Level 3

Overview

Up to this point, we have been storing data in variables using either DATA statements or INPUT statements. The storage locations of these variables are in the primary storage unit of the computer. This method of storing data is adequate for some applications, but not for others.

Suppose that a large amount of data needs to be stored. Two problems arise: the data is difficult to organize, and the computer's primary storage unit may be too small to hold all of it. For instance, a large insurance corporation needs many pieces of data for each of its policyholders. This data might include the policyholder's name, address, age, social security number, the type of policy, the amount of the policy, what the policy covers, and so on. The amount of main memory in the corporation's computer would almost certainly be too small to store all of this data, and the data would not be organized in a useful fashion.

Another problem also arises. What if the same data needs to be accessed by more than one program? For example, the data used by the accounting department in one program might need to be used by the sales department in a different program. It would not be efficient to have duplicate DATA statements in both programs, and updating all the DATA statements would likely result in some errors.

Using files can help to solve these problems. A **file** is a collection of related data items organized in a meaningful way and kept in secondary storage. In this chapter, you will learn to use files in BASIC programs. Unfortunately, however, there is no standardized method for performing operations on files. Many BASIC implementations include unique file manipulation commands, although the principles on which these commands are based are similar. We will discuss the general concepts of file handling before explaining how the necessary commands are implemented on each of the BASIC systems discussed here.

File
A collection of related data items, organized in a meaningful way and kept in secondary storage.

What Is a File?

Files provide an alternate means of organizing and storing related data. A major advantage of using files is that they make use of secondary storage, which is virtually unlimited; thus the problem of inadequate space in the primary storage unit is solved. Another advantage is that the data contained in a file can be organized and stored using a variety of methods, depending on the needs of the user. Also, many users can access the same file. Thus, data can be used more efficiently, and updating data is simpler and less error-prone.

Files have one major disadvantage. It takes longer to retrieve data stored in a file than data stored in the computer's primary storage unit. When using files, the computer must locate the data in secondary storage, move it into the primary storage unit, and then retrieve it. Nevertheless, the advantages of greater storage space and data organization outweigh this disadvantage of slower program execution.

There are two major divisions within a file. The smallest of these divisions, the **field,** contains a single unit of information. A student's name is an example of a field value. Fields are grouped together to form the second major division, the **record.** A record consists of one or more fields that describe a single entity. Therefore, a record might contain a name field, a course field, and a grade field; together, these fields would constitute a student's record for a single course. The finished product, a file, consists of a group of records. An example of a file is a group of student records for a single class, each containing a name field, a course field, and a grade field.

A computer file can be compared to a drawer in a filing cabinet. A particular file drawer usually contains related information about one general topic. For example, it might contain information about a company's employees. A computer file also contains information about a single subject. Within each file cabinet drawer there are probably folders, each containing information regarding a single employee. Records for computer files also contain information about individual entities. Each record in a file drawer folder consists of a collection of individual pieces of information, such as an employee's name, address, and so on. Each field in a computer file also contains a single piece of information. Figure 10-1 illustrates this concept.

Field
The smallest division within a file, consisting of a single unit of information. Fields group together to form records.

Record
One or more fields that together describe a single entity. Records group together to form files.

FIGURE 10-1
Parts of a File

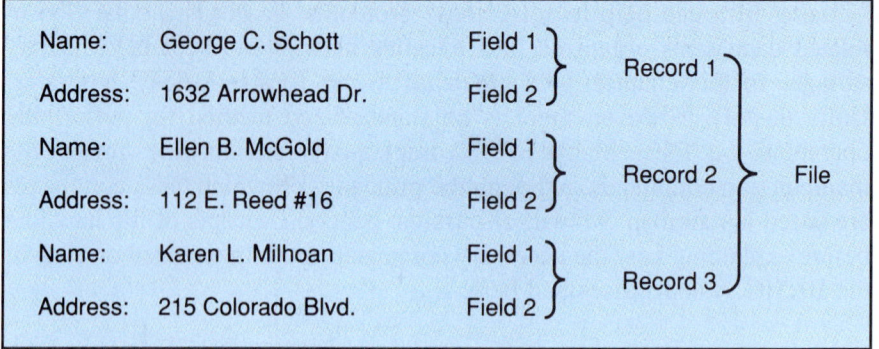

Now that the divisions of a computer file have been explained, the organization within a file can be described. In many companies or organizations, special filing systems are used. For example, the records within a file cabinet might be arranged alphabetically or from the oldest to the newest. Computer records can also be organized in several different ways. This organization of records within a file is referred to as **file organization.**

File organization
The method used to arrange records within a file.

File Organization

The method used to organize records within a file determines how these records will be stored and retrieved by the BASIC system. The method of organization is specified when a file is created. Three possible methods of file organization are implemented on BASIC systems, although some systems allow only two of them to be used.

The first method of organization, **sequential organization,** stores records in the order in which they are written. In order to access a record with sequential organization, all preceding records must be accessed before the needed record can be accessed. Therefore, if the fifth record of a file needs to be accessed, the first four records must be sequentially accessed first.

Sequential organization
Records are stored in the same order in which they are written to the file.

To help in understanding this concept, imagine four rooms, each with one door that connects it to the room next to it:

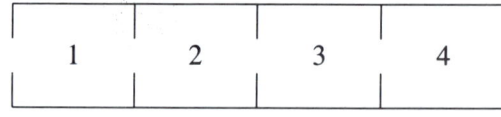

In order for a person to enter the third room, he or she must open the door at the left and walk through the first room, open the next door and walk through the second room, and then open the third door and walk through the third room. This concept is analogous to sequential organization of files.

The second method of organization, **relative organization,** stores each record in a numbered location in secondary storage. A record can be

Relative organization
Each record is stored in a numbered location.

accessed either in order from the first record to the needed record, or directly (randomly) by using the record's numbered location. Now imagine that the four connected rooms have a hallway adjacent to them. Each room still has a door that connects it to the next room, but now each room also has another door that enters into the hallway:

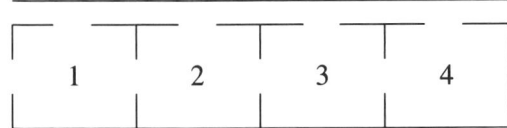

In order for a person to enter the third room, he or she can walk through the first two rooms and enter the third room, or enter the hallway and open the door to the third room. This concept is similar to that of relative organization of computer files.

The third method of file organization, **indexed organization,** stores records according to a primary key. A **primary key** is a field that uniquely identifies a particular record and by which that record is accessed. Records cannot be accessed by their physical order when using indexed organization. The primary key field of each record must be different from that of every other record in the file. An example of a primary key is a person's social security number. Because no two people have the same social security number, an individual's record can be uniquely identified by this value.

Records in a file using indexed organization may contain more than one key. The additional keys, called **secondary keys,** are unique or non-unique fields that can also be used to access and retrieve records. However, a record must be accessed through its primary key before the secondary key can be used.

Let's now compare indexed organization with our analogy of the four rooms. The rooms now have no doors between them; there is only the hallway with a door entering into each room. In order for a person to find a specific room, he or she must know the room number (that is, the primary key value). By knowing the room number, a person can find the needed room and enter it. This concept is illustrated as follows:

Indexed organization
Records are stored according to a primary key.

Primary key
A field that uniquely identifies a particular record; the record can then be accessed by this field.

Secondary key
A field that can be used to access a record after it has been accessed through its primary key.

Because records are organized within files using different methods, one might think that the retrieval of records would differ according to method. This is not the case, however; only two access methods exist. One access method can be used with all three types of file organization, and the other can be used with two types of file organization. We will discuss these access methods in the next section.

Learning Check

1. _____ make up _____, which make up a file.
2. Name the type of file organization that uses a key in order to access its records.
3. Name the type of file organization in which records must be sequentially ordered.
4. Name the type of file organization in which records are stored in numbered locations.
5. Give three reasons for using files.

Answers

1. Fields; records 2. Indexed organization. 3. Sequential organization. 4. Relative organization. 5. (1) Space in the computer's primary storage unit is limited. (2) Files make it easier to organize large amounts of data. (3) Files allow any number of programs to access the same data.

Methods of Accessing Files

Access method
A way in which the computer transmits data between secondary storage and the primary storage unit.

Random access
Accessing a record directly by means of a record location number or a primary key.

Sequential access
Accessing a record by accessing all records sequentially until the needed record is reached.

An **access method** is a way in which the computer transmits data between secondary storage and the primary storage unit when reading data to or writing data from a file. Two types of access methods are used in BASIC: random access and sequential access.

Random access allows the BASIC program, not the manner in which the file is organized, to control which record is to be accessed. The record is accessed directly because the program specifies which record is to be retrieved. A record location number is used if the record is in a relative file, and a key value is used if the record is in an indexed file. Random access cannot be used with a record in a sequential file, because there is no primary key field or record location number by which to access it.

The other access method, **sequential access,** retrieves a record based on its sequential position within the file. Sequential access uses the physical ordering of the sequential file, the position number of the relative file, or the key value of the indexed file to access a record sequentially. Note that a sequential file is not the same as sequential access. The term *sequential file* refers to the organization of a file, whereas *sequential access* refers to the manner in which individual records within the file are retrieved.

The next section discusses the type of secondary storage medium that is used by the computer to store the file. The type of medium is an important factor in file organization and access.

Secondary Storage

Secondary storage refers to storage media outside the primary storage unit on which files are permanently kept. Some forms of secondary storage

FIGURE 10–2 Read/Write Head

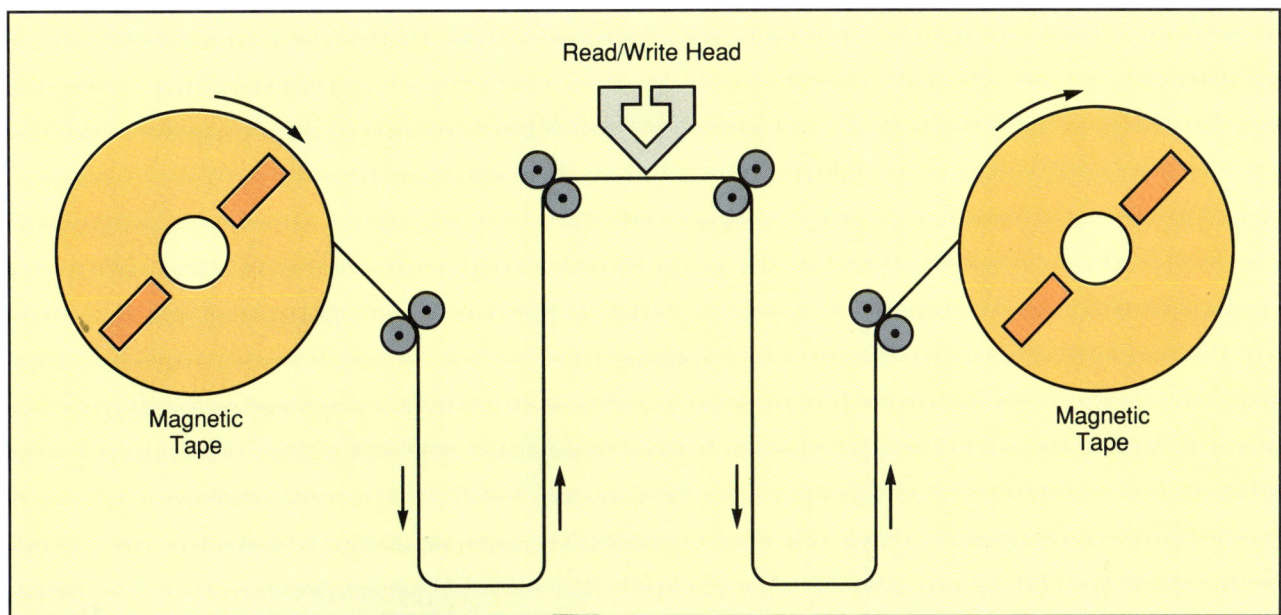

media are magnetic tapes, magnetic disks, and floppy diskettes. Home computers such as the Macintosh, Apple, and IBM PC most frequently use floppy diskettes. Larger computers, such as the VAX, use magnetic tapes or disks.

A reel of magnetic tape looks similar to a reel of movie film. Magnetic tape is usually 2,400 feet long and is spun by a tape drive, as shown in Figure 10–2. Because of the design of the tape drive, records must be read sequentially. The read/write head, which performs the actual reading and writing of the data, cannot skip to a particular record on the tape; the tape must spin until the read/write head locates the needed record. Figure 10–3 shows how records are stored on magnetic tape.

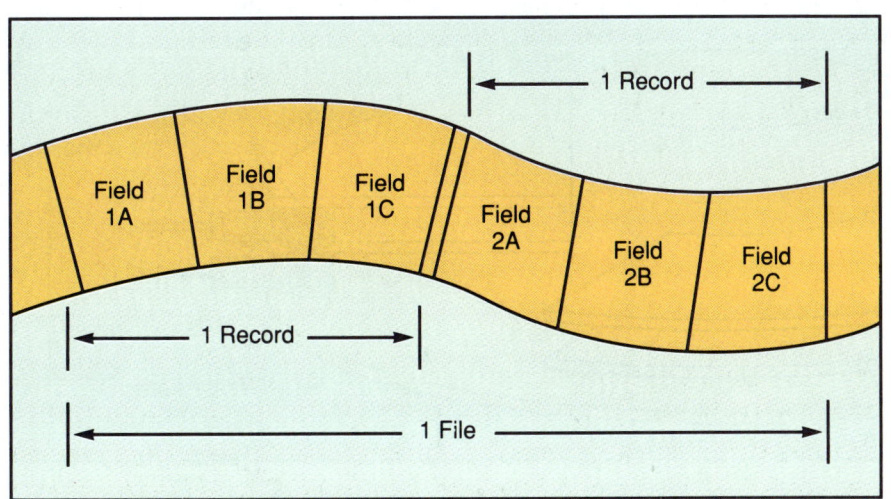

FIGURE 10–3
Data Storage on Magnetic Tape

FIGURE 10–4
Data Storage on Magnetic Disk

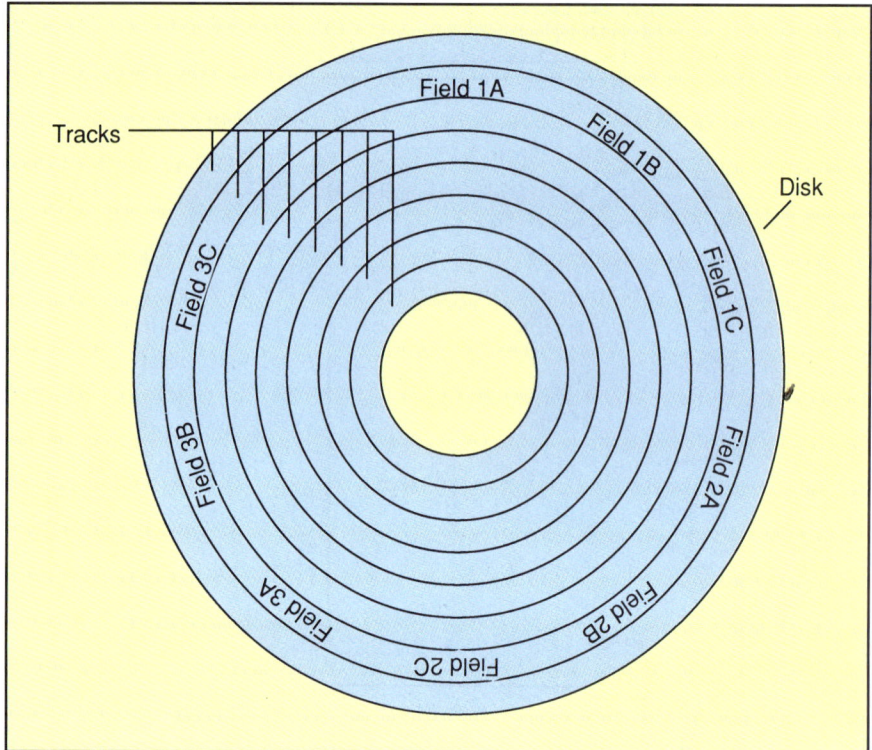

A magnetic disk looks like a record album. Data is stored on the disk in tracks, which are series of concentric circles on the surface of the magnetic disk (see Figure 10–4). A collection of concentric disk tracks with the same radius is called a *cylinder.* Both cylinders and tracks are numbered. A group of disks is a *disk pack,* which looks like a stack of record albums with a spindle passing through the middle, as shown in Figure 10–5. Notice that

FIGURE 10–5 A Disk Pack

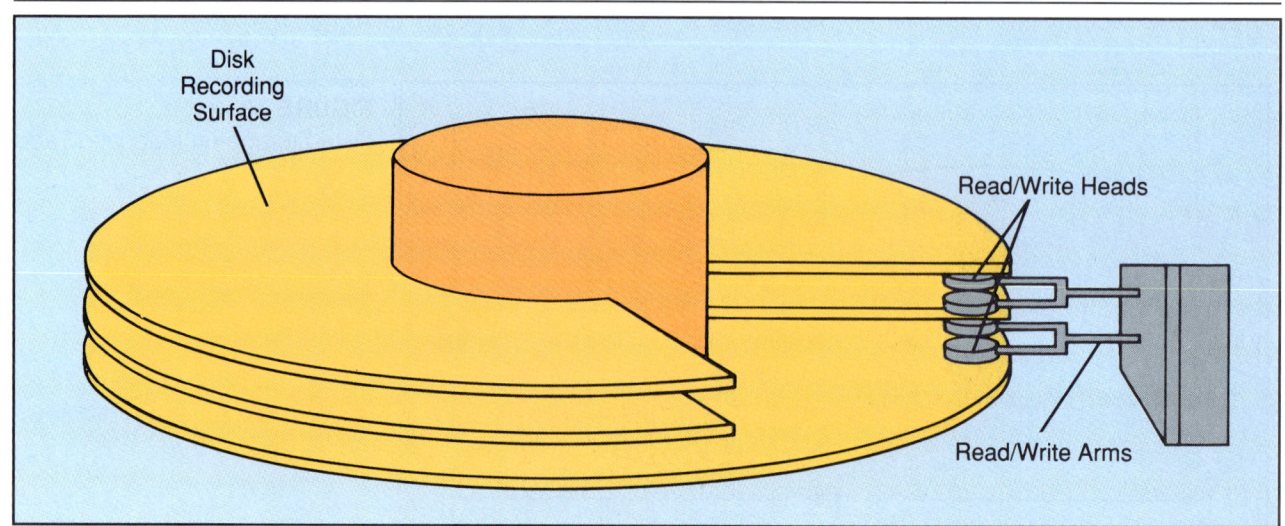

there are two read/write heads for each disk: one for the upper surface and one for the lower surface. (The top and bottom disk in the disk pack each have only one read/write head for control purposes.) The read/write arm, which holds the read/write heads, can move backward and forward, and the disk pack can rotate on the spindle as well. By using the numbered tracks and cylinders and the movement of the disk pack, the computer can find a record randomly or sequentially.

A floppy diskette (Figure 10–6) looks like a small record album in its cover. To locate a record, the computer uses tracks that are located on the diskette. Each track is divided into sectors. The diskette contains an index hole, which the computer uses to calculate the location of a particular sector by timing the diskette's rotation. Figure 10–7 shows the parts of a floppy diskette.

Data file programs never have to specify the physical address when accessing a record. However, the file organization and the access method must be determined before the program is written. Not all file organizations can be used with all access methods on all types of secondary storage, as shown in Figure 10–8.

Using Sequential Files with Sequential Access

Now that we have explained the general concepts of what a file is, how it is organized, and how it is stored, we can describe specific applications. This

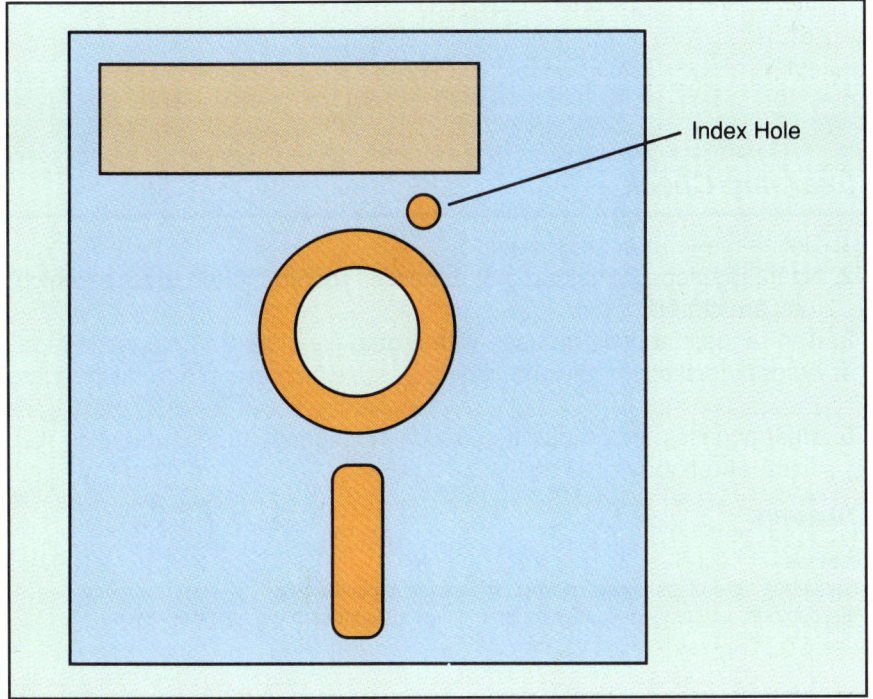

FIGURE 10–6
A Floppy Diskette

FIGURE 10–7
Parts of a Floppy Diskette

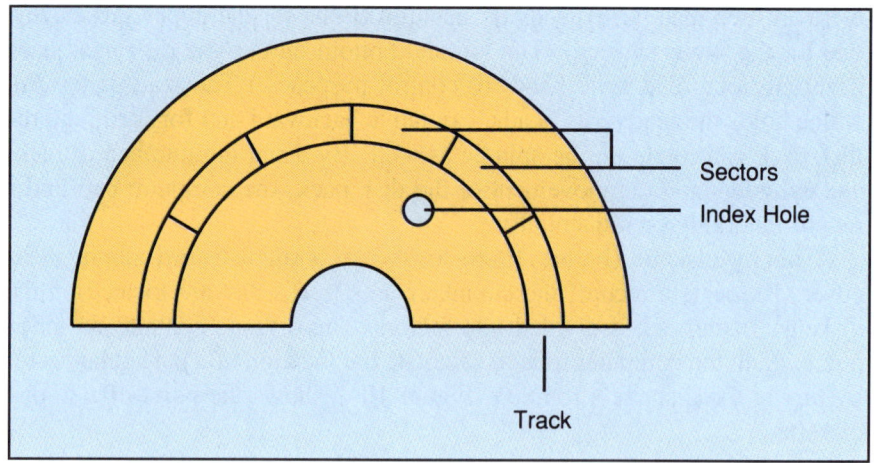

FIGURE 10–8
Possible Combinations of Storage Media, File Organizations, and Access Methods

File Organization	Access Method	Storage Media
Sequential	Sequential	Tape, Disk, Diskette
Relative	Random or Sequential	Disk, Diskette
Indexed	Random or Sequential	Disk

Learning Check

1. Define the term *access method*.
2. Name the access method that accesses records in the order in which they are stored.
3. Can random access be used with a data file stored on magnetic tape?
4. A floppy diskette is divided into _____, which are in turn divided into _____.
5. What access method can be used with magnetic tapes, magnetic disks, and floppy diskettes?

Answers

1. The way in which the computer transmits data between secondary storage and the primary storage unit. 2. Sequential access. 3. No. 4. tracks; sectors 5. Sequential access.

chapter will not explain how to use all of the possible file organizations with all the types of BASIC systems presented in this textbook. An entire book could be written on this subject. We will explain only the most frequently used combinations: sequential files with sequential access and relative files with random access.

In sequential files, records are stored in the order in which they were written to the file. Therefore, when a programmer needs to write to or read from a sequential file, all records that precede the needed one must be accessed first. There are three general steps for writing to a file and three general steps for reading from a file. These steps apply to all computers using sequential files with sequential access and are explained in the following sections.

Creating and Writing to a Sequential File

The three basic steps for creating and writing to a sequential file are as follows:

1. In order for a program to access it, the file must be opened. When opening a file, the programmer must tell the computer the name of the file to which data is to be output. If no file with that name already exists, the computer will set up a location on tape or disk for a new file. If a file of the stated name already exists, the computer prepares this file to be accessed.
2. Data is written to the file. After the file is opened, data must be written to a buffer (that is, a temporary storage location in main memory) and then transferred to the designated file.
3. The file must be closed. Once all of the data has been written to a file, the file must be closed; otherwise, the data in the file will be lost. Closing a file also indicates to the computer that the use of the file is finished for the present time.

Reading from a Sequential File

The three basic steps used when reading from a sequential file are as follows:

1. The file must be opened. The computer locates the stated file and prepares it to be read.
2. Data is read from the file. Once the file is opened, data is read to a buffer in main memory. Next, the data is copied from the buffer to a variable. Numeric data must be placed in numeric variables and string data in string variables.
3. The file is closed. As when writing to a file, the file is closed so the data will not be lost.

First, we will explain the use of files on the VAX. Information regarding the Apple, IBM/Microsoft and Macintosh/Microsoft implementations will follow. Refer to the section that relates to your computer system.

VAX

Creating or Accessing a File The general format for the OPEN statement on the VAX is as follows:

line# OPEN ''filename'' AS FILE #filenumber

If the file called *filename* does not already exist, a new file is created; if this file does exist, this statement allows it to be accessed. *Filenumber* represents an integer that provides an additional reference to the file. The programmer can type the symbol # and the file number instead of typing the entire file name in the statements following the OPEN statement.

In this section, we will write a sample program that will create a file. The OPEN statement will look like this:

```
10 OPEN "COMMITTEE" AS FILE #2
```

This statement opens a file named COMMITTEE as file #2.

Writing Data to a File After the file has been opened, data can be written to it. The basic format for the statement to write to a file is as follows:

line# PRINT #filenumber,expression

Filenumber is the integer value that was given to the file in the OPEN statement; *expression* can be a string variable, numeric variable, string value, or numeric value. Because a sequential file is simply a long list of data, the computer needs to know where one data item ends and the next one begins. Pressing the return key at the end of each PRINT statement indicates to the computer the end of the data item. Our sample program thus far looks like this:

```
10 OPEN "COMMITTEE" AS FILE #2
20 PRINT #2,"CAROL ALSTON"
30 PRINT #2,15
40 PRINT #2,"DAVE MCDONALD"
50 PRINT #2,10
60 PRINT #2,"SUSIE URBANK"
70 PRINT #2,10
80 PRINT #2,"FRED ZIMMERMAN"
90 PRINT #2,8
```

This program segment causes eight data items to be written to the file named COMMITTEE.

Closing a File The file must be closed so that the data in the file will be saved permanently. The basic format for the statement to close a file is

line# CLOSE #filenumber

Once again, *filenumber* is the integer value declared in the OPEN statement for the file. The complete program is as follows:

```
10   REM *** A SEQUENTIAL FILE, NAMED COMMITTEE, IS CREATED IN THIS
20   REM *** PROGRAM.  COMMITTEE CONTAINS EACH COMMITTEE MEMBER'S
30   REM *** NAME, AND HOURS AVAILABLE TO WORK.
40   REM
50   OPEN "COMMITTEE" AS FILE #2
60   PRINT #2,"CAROL ALSTON"
70   PRINT #2,15
80   PRINT #2,"DAVE MCDONALD"
90   PRINT #2,10
100  PRINT #2,"SUSIE URBANK"
110  PRINT #2,10
120  PRINT #2,"FRED ZIMMERMAN"
130  PRINT #2,8
140  CLOSE #2
999  END
```

When this program is executed, it will create and save a file named COMMITTEE.

Reading a File The general format for a statement to read a file is

line# INPUT #filenumber,variable1[,variable2]...

The INPUT statement moves one or more data items from secondary storage into the listed variables. Here is a program that would read and print the data in the file COMMITTEE:

```
10   REM *** THE SEQUENTIAL FILE COMMITTEE IS READ AND THE DATA
20   REM *** FROM THE FILE IS PRINTED.
30   REM *** MAJOR VARIABLES:
40   REM ***     PERSON$    COMMITTEE MEMBER'S NAME
50   REM ***     HOURS      HOURS PER WEEK THE MEMBER CAN WORK
60   REM
70   OPEN "COMMITTEE" AS FILE #2
80   FOR L = 1 TO 4
90      INPUT #2,PERSON$(L)
100     PRINT "MEMBER: ";PERSON$(L)
110     INPUT #2,HOURS(L)
120     PRINT "HOURS: ";HOURS(L)
130     PRINT
140  NEXT L
150  CLOSE #2
999  END
```

Apple

Creating or Accessing a File Data files, referred to as *text files* by Apple, are stored on floppy diskettes. In order to access the disk for text files, the user must press the CTRL key and the D key together. An alternative method of accessing files is to have the program reference a string variable that has been set equal to CHR$(4), the ASCII code character for <CTRL><D>. Usually this variable is called *D$*. The following statement should come at the beginning of a text file program:

```
10 D$ = CHR$(4)
```

Next, the file must be opened. The general format for the OPEN statement on the Apple is

line# PRINT <CTRL><D>variable;"OPEN filename"

The clause "PRINT <CTRL><D>variable" tells the computer that a file on a floppy disk is going to be accessed. OPEN opens the file, and *filename* (which can be up to thirty characters long and must begin with a letter) identifies the file. A program to create a file named COMMITTEE would start with these statements:

```
10 D$ = CHR$(4)
20 PRINT D$;"OPEN COMMITTEE"
```

COMMITTEE is now listed in the files catalog with a T beside it. The T indicates to the user that COMMITTEE is a text file.

Writing Data to a File Once a file has been created, data can be written to it. The general format for this statement is

line# PRINT <CTRL><D>variable;"WRITE filename"

This statement indicates to the computer that the disk, not the screen or the printer, is to be written to. *Filename* is the same *filename* used in the OPEN statement. The format for the second statement, which actually prints the data to the floppy disk, is

line# PRINT expression

Expression can be a string variable, a numeric variable, a string value, or a numeric value. Because a sequential file is simply a long list of data, the computer cannot determine where one data item ends and the next one begins. Pressing the return key at the end of this statement tells the computer where the end of a field is. We will now write four records, each containing two fields (a character string field and a numeric field), to the file COMMITTEE:

```
10  D$ = CHR$(4)
20  PRINT D$;"OPEN COMMITTEE"
30  PRINT D$;"WRITE COMMITTEE"
40  PRINT "CAROL ALSTON"
50  PRINT 15
60  PRINT "DAVE MCDONALD"
70  PRINT 10
80  PRINT "SUSIE URBANK"
90  PRINT 10
100 PRINT "FRED ZIMMERMAN"
110 PRINT 8
```

Closing a File   Once all of the data has been written to the text file, the file must be closed, or the data will be lost. The general format of the CLOSE statement is

line# PRINT <CTRL><D>variable;''CLOSE [filename]''

The brackets around *filename* indicate that it is optional. If no filename is specified, then all the opened text files will be closed; if a filename is specified, only that file will be closed. The finished program to create file COMMITTEE follows:

```
10  REM *** IN THIS PROGRAM A TEXT FILE, COMMITTEE, IS CREATED.
20  REM *** TWO FIELDS EXIST IN EACH RECORD OF THIS FILE. THE
30  REM *** FIRST CONTAINS THE COMMITTEE MEMBER'S NAME, AND THE
40  REM *** SECOND CONTAINS THE NUMBER OF HOURS THE COMMITTEE
50  REM *** MEMBER IS AVAILABLE TO WORK PER WEEK.
60  D$ = CHR$(4)
70  PRINT D$;"OPEN COMMITTEE"
80  PRINT D$;"WRITE COMMITTEE"
90  PRINT "CAROL ALSTON"
100 PRINT 15
110 PRINT "DAVE MCDONALD"
120 PRINT 10
130 PRINT "SUSIE URBANK"
140 PRINT 10
150 PRINT "FRED ZIMMERMAN"
160 PRINT 8
170 PRINT D$;"CLOSE COMMITTEE"
999 END
```

Reading a File   In order to read data from a file, two statements must be used. The first is the READ statement, the general format of which is

line# PRINT <CTRL><D>variable;''READ filename''

This statement identifies the disk file that is to be read. The data items are read to variables using an INPUT statement:

line# INPUT variable1[,variable2]...

A program that reads the data stored in the COMMITTEE text file follows:

```
10  REM *** THE DATA FROM THE COMMITTEE FILE IS SEQUENTIALLY
20  REM *** READ AND THEN PRINTED.
30  REM *** MAJOR VARIABLES:
40  REM ***     P$      PERSON'S NAME
50  REM ***     H       HOURS PER WEEK AVAILABLE TO WORK
60  REM
70  D$ = CHR$(4)
80  PRINT D$;"OPEN COMMITTEE"
90  PRINT D$;"READ COMMITTEE"
100 FOR L = 1 TO 4
110    INPUT P$(L)
120    PRINT "MEMBER: ";P$(L)
130    INPUT H(L)
140    PRINT "HOURS: ";H(L)
150    PRINT
160    PRINT
170 NEXT L
180 PRINT D$;"CLOSE COMMITTEE"
999 END
```

Line 80 tells the computer that the data is stored in text file COMMITTEE. Lines 110 and 130 read the data items from the text file to the array elements P$(L) and H(L). The FOR/NEXT loop, which will be executed four times, causes the contents of all four records in this file to be printed on the monitor screen.

IBM/Microsoft and Macintosh/Microsoft

For our purposes here, using sequential files with sequential access is similar for IBM/Microsoft BASIC and Macintosh/Microsoft BASIC. Therefore, we will discuss these two implementations together, noting any differences.

Creating or Accessing a File The statement that opens a data file for creation or access has the following general format. Remember that the use of line numbers is optional with Macintosh/Microsoft BASIC (See Appendix I for more details).

line# OPEN ''filename'' FOR mode AS #filenumber [LEN = buffer-size]

Filename identifies the file. The OPEN statement checks secondary storage to determine if the stated file already exists; if it does, it is prepared to be accessed. If it does not exist, a new file is created.

Mode defines how the file is to be accessed; for sequential files, its value can be OUTPUT, INPUT, or APPEND. OUTPUT indicates sequential output mode, and it is used when writing data to a file. INPUT indicates sequential input mode, and it is used when reading data from a file. APPEND indicates a sequential output mode, and it prepares the file to have data added to the end of it. Be very careful to use the APPEND mode when you are adding data to the end of an already existing file. If the OUTPUT mode is used instead, the previous contents of the file will be erased.

Filenumber, which is an integer value, provides the programmer with a shorthand method of identifying the file.

In this section we will write a sample program to create a file named COMMITTEE. The OPEN statement will look like this:

```
10 OPEN "COMMITTEE" FOR OUTPUT AS #2
```

This statement opens file COMMITTEE for OUTPUT (that is, to be written to) as file #2.

Writing Data to a File In order to write data to a new file, the OPEN statement must be set to OUTPUT. Then the PRINT statement with the following format is used:

line# PRINT #filenumber expression 1[,expression 2]…

This statement writes data to a file in secondary storage. Notice that its syntax is the same as that for a PRINT statement that writes output to the monitor screen, except that *filenumber* must be specified. *Filenumber* is the same integer value that was declared in the OPEN statement. Each of the stated expressions can be either a string value, a numeric value, a string variable, or a numeric variable. These expressions are written to the file.

The following program will write four records (each with two fields, the first a character string and the second an integer) to the file COMMITTEE.

```
10 OPEN "COMMITTEE" FOR OUTPUT AS #2
20 PRINT #2,"CAROL ALSTON"
30 PRINT #2,15
40 PRINT #2,"DAVE MCDONALD"
50 PRINT #2,10
60 PRINT #2,"SUSIE URBANK"
70 PRINT #2,10
80 PRINT #2,"FRED ZIMMERMAN"
90 PRINT #2,8
```

Closing a File Once there is no more data to be written to a file, it must be closed so that its contents will be permanently saved. The general format of the CLOSE statement is

line# CLOSE #filenumber1[,#filenumber2]…

Once again, *filenumber* must be the number specified in the OPEN statement. As indicated, one or more files can be closed in a single CLOSE statement. The complete program to create COMMITTEE is as follows:

```
10  REM *** A SEQUENTIAL FILE, NAMED COMMITTEE, IS CREATED IN
20  REM *** THIS PROGRAM.  COMMITTEE CONTAINS EACH MEMBER'S
30  REM *** NAME AND HOURS AVAILABLE TO WORK.
40  REM
50  OPEN "COMMITTEE" FOR OUTPUT AS #2
60  PRINT #2,"CAROL ALSTON"
70  PRINT #2,15
80  PRINT #2,"DAVE MCDONALD"
90  PRINT #2,10
100 PRINT #2,"SUSIE URBANK"
110 PRINT #2,10
120 PRINT #2,"FRED ZIMMERMAN"
130 PRINT #2,8
140 CLOSE #2
999 END
```

Reading a File In order for a program to read from a sequential file, the mode of the OPEN statement must be set to INPUT. This mode indicates to the computer that a file is going to be read. The next step is to use the INPUT statement, which has the following general format:

line# INPUT #filenumber,variable1[,variable2]...

Filenumber refers to the number of the file being read. The data read will be stored in the variables listed; each field in the file will be stored in a separate variable. If the field contains a numeric value, it must be read to a numeric variable; it if is a string value, it must be read to a string variable. The following program reads the COMMITTEE file:

```
10  REM *** THE SEQUENTIAL FILE, COMMITTEE, IS READ AND THE
20  REM *** DATA FROM THE FILE IS PRINTED.
30  REM *** MAJOR VARIABLES:
40  REM ***     PERSON$     COMMITTE MEMBER'S NAME
50  REM ***     HOURS       HOURS PER WEEK THE MEMBER CAN WORK
60  REM
70  OPEN "COMMITTEE" FOR INPUT AS #2
80  FOR L = 1 TO 4
90     INPUT #2,PERSON$(L)
100    PRINT "MEMBER: ";PERSON$(L)
110    INPUT #2,HOURS(L)
120    PRINT "HOURS: ";HOURS(L)
130    PRINT
140 NEXT L
150 CLOSE #2
999 END
```

Using Relative Files with Random Access

The same steps for reading and writing a file that are used with sequential files are used with relative files. However, the statement that writes to or reads from the file must specify the record location. Remember that a relative file consists of records in numbered locations: location 1 contains the first record relative to the start of the file, location 2 contains the second record, and so on. Because the record locations are numbered, records do not have to be read or written in sequential order. The records are still in sequential order from the beginning of the file, however, so they can be sequentially accessed.

Relative files that use random access are referred to as *random files* by all the BASIC systems. Random files will be explained for the VAX, Apple, IBM, and Macintosh.

VAX

Before a random file is opened, a buffer must be created in memory. A *buffer* is a space set aside in main memory that contains a record read from secondary storage or a record that will be written to secondary storage. The MAP statement establishes and names this buffer, and also describes the fields contained in each of the records in the file. It lists the variables into which each of these fields will be placed. The general format of the MAP statement is

line# MAP (buffer-name) fieldtype fieldname [,fieldtype fieldname]...

Buffer-name is the name given to the buffer. *Fieldname* is the name of each field in the record. Each field must be preceded by its data type, which is dependent on the type of values the field will contain. We will use three data types here: STRING (for fields containing string values), WORD (for fields containing integer values), and SINGLE (for fields containing real values). If a STRING field is used, it must be assigned a length. An example of a MAP statement follows:

10 MAP (BUFF1) STRING P$ = 16, WORD H

The variable P$ can contain a string with up to sixteen characters, whereas H can contain an integer value.

Creating or Accessing a File Now that the buffer exists, a file can be opened for creation or access by using the OPEN statement. The OPEN statement contains many keywords and can be very complicated. Thus, only a general format for the statement will be given here. For a more complete discussion of the OPEN statement, consult your system manual. The general format for the OPEN statement is

line# OPEN "filename" FOR mode AS FILE #filenumber

ORGANIZATION file-type FIXED, $\begin{cases} \text{MAP map-name} \\ \text{RECORD SIZE numeric expression} \end{cases}$

Filename is enclosed in quotation marks and assigns a name to the file. *Mode* can be either INPUT or OUTPUT. FOR INPUT requires that the specified file already exists, and FOR OUTPUT creates a new file named *filename*. *Filenumber* is an integer value that will be used as a shorthand reference to the file later in the program. *File-type* is either SEQUENTIAL or RELATIVE. If the SEQUENTIAL option is used, the records are arranged sequentially by the order of input. The RELATIVE option causes the records to be arranged by numbered positions within the file.

FIXED specifies that the records are of a fixed length. This length is determined by the last clause, which has two options: *MAP map-name,* or *RECORD SIZE numeric-expression*. *MAP map-name* references a previously-defined map buffer. The map buffer referenced defines the buffer that will be used to store the file's data temporarily, and defines the amount of data that will be stored for a record. Therefore, the *MAP map-name* clause can be used to define the record size. If no *MAP map-name* clause is specified, then the maximum length of records (in characters) in the file must be specified using the *RECORD SIZE numeric-expression* clause.

We will use the statements covered so far to begin creating a random file that will contain the names of a group of people who are on a committee. The first field in each record will contain the member's name (maximum length of 16 characters), and the second field will contain the number of hours per week that member is available to work on the committee (maximum length of 2 characters). This is how our program would look thus far:

```
10 MAP (BUFF1) STRING P$ = 16,WORD H
20 OPEN "GROUP" FOR OUTPUT AS FILE #2, ORGANIZATION
      RELATIVE FIXED, MAP BUFF1
```

Writing Data to a File Data is written to a file by means of the PUT statement. Its general format is as follows:

line# PUT #filenumber[,RECORD record-number]

Filenumber, which is the same *filenumber* declared in the OPEN statement, refers to the file being written to. *Record-number* is the relative location of the record. Note that the ''RECORD record-number'' clause is optional. If this clause is used, the record will be placed in the *record-number* position; if the clause is not used, the record is written to the next sequential position. Using these two statements, our sample program thus far looks like this:

```
10   REM *** A RANDOM FILE, NAMED GROUP, IS CREATED.  TWO FIELDS
20   REM *** EXIST IN EACH RECORD OF THIS FILE.  THE FIRST CONTAINS
30   REM *** THE COMMITTEE MEMBER'S NAME, AND THE SECOND CONTAINS
40   REM *** THE NUMBER OF HOURS THE COMMITTEE MEMBER IS AVAILABLE
50   REM *** TO WORK PER WEEK.
60   REM *** MAJOR VARIABLES:
```

```
 70 REM ***    P$   COMMITTEE MEMBER'S NAME
 80 REM ***    H    HOURS AVAILABLE TO WORK
 90 REM
100 MAP (BUFF1) STRING P$ = 16,WORD H
110 OPEN "GROUP" FOR OUTPUT AS FILE #2, ORGANIZATION
       RELATIVE FIXED, MAP BUFF1
120 P$ = "CAROL ALSTON"
130 H = 15
140 PUT #2,RECORD 1
150 P$ = "DAVE MCDONALD"
160 H = 10
170 PUT #2,RECORD 2
180 P$ = "SUSIE URBANK"
190 H = 10
200 PUT #2,RECORD 3
210 P$ = "FRED ZIMMERMAN"
220 H = 8
230 PUT #2,RECORD 4
```

This program segment writes four records to the file GROUP.

Closing a File A file is closed by using the CLOSE statement, the general format of which is as follows:

line# CLOSE #filenumber1[,#filenumber2]...

Notice that more than one file can be closed at a time if necessary. The final program that creates file GROUP is as follows:

```
 10 REM *** A RANDOM FILE, NAMED GROUP, IS CREATED.  TWO FIELDS
 20 REM *** EXIST IN EACH RECORD OF THIS FILE.  THE FIRST CONTAINS
 30 REM *** THE COMMITTEE MEMBER'S NAME, AND THE SECOND CONTAINS
 40 REM *** THE NUMBER OF HOURS THE COMMITTEE MEMBER IS AVAILABLE
 50 REM *** TO WORK PER WEEK.
 60 REM *** MAJOR VARIABLES:
 70 REM ***    P$   COMMITTEE MEMBER'S NAME
 80 REM ***    H    HOURS AVAILABLE TO WORK
 90 REM
100 MAP (BUFF1) STRING P$ = 16,WORD H
110 OPEN "GROUP" FOR OUTPUT AS FILE #2, ORGANIZATION
       RELATIVE FIXED, MAP BUFF1
120 P$ = "CAROL ALSTON"
130 H = 15
140 PUT #2,RECORD 1
150 P$ = "DAVE MCDONALD"
160 H = 10
170 PUT #2,RECORD 2
180 P$ = "SUSIE URBANK"
190 H = 10
200 PUT #2,RECORD 3
210 P$ = "FRED ZIMMERMAN"
220 H = 8
230 PUT #2, RECORD 4
240 CLOSE #2
999 END
```

In order to update a specific record and leave the rest of the file unchanged, the new field values must be entered, and an UPDATE statement is used as shown here:

```
120 UPDATE #2
```

Reading a File The GET statement is used to read a record from a file into a buffer. The general format of the GET statement as it will be used here is as follows:

line# GET #filenumber,RECORD numeric-expression

Filenumber refers to the file to be accessed, as already specified in the OPEN statement. *Numeric-expression* is the relative position of the needed record from the start of the file. The following program reads and prints the third record from the previous program:

```
10  REM *** RECORD 3 FROM THE RANDOM FILE NAMED GROUP IS ACCESSED.
20  REM *** DATA FROM THAT RECORD IS THEN PRINTED.
30  REM *** MAJOR VARIABLES:
40  REM ***      P$      COMMITTEE MEMBER'S NAME
50  REM ***      H       HOURS AVAILABLE
60  REM
70  MAP (BUFF1) STRING P$ = 16, WORD H
80  OPEN "GROUP" FOR INPUT AS FILE #2, ORGANIZATION
        RELATIVE FIXED,MAP BUFF1
90  GET #2,RECORD 3
100 PRINT P$,H
110 CLOSE #2
999 END
```

Apple

Creating or Accessing a File For a relative file as for a sequential file, a disk control variable must be defined so that the program can access the floppy diskette. The ASCII representation of <CTRL><D>, CHR$(4), must be used. A string variable can be assigned the value of <CTRL><D> to make it easier for the programmer to perform this task. The variable D$ is assigned this value in the following statement:

```
10 LET D$ = CHR$(4)
```

Now the file can be opened. The general format for the OPEN statement is

line# PRINT <CTRL><D>variable; "OPEN filename,L
    record-length"

The clause PRINT <CTRL><D> variable accesses the floppy diskette, and OPEN opens the file specified by *filename. Filename* must begin with a letter, and it can be up to thirty characters in length. The letter L indicates that the record length is to be specified, and *record-length* (the total number of characters in a record) must be an integer value between 1 and 32,767. No record in a file can exceed this number of characters.

We will write a sample program to create a file named GROUP. Each record in GROUP has a maximum length of eighteen characters. The first two statements of this program will look like this:

```
10 D$ = CHR$(4)
20 PRINT D$;"OPEN GROUP,L18"
```

Writing Data to a File Now that the file is opened, data can be written to it. On the Apple, data can be written to a file in either numeric or character form. Problems can arise when writing numeric data to a random file, however, so it is much easier to convert the numeric data to string data before storing it in the text file. We will follow this practice here.

The STR$ function can be used to convert the numeric data into character form. Two statements must be used to write data to a text file. The first statement is

line# PRINT <CTRL><D>variable;"WRITE filename,R"; record-number

Record-number indicates which record is being written to. Thus, each time a new record within a file is being written to, the value of *record-number* must be changed so that a previous record will not be accidentally written over. The statement that actually writes the data to the file is

line# PRINT expression

Expression can be a numeric value, a string value, a numeric variable, or a string variable. We could write four records to a file GROUP like this:

```
10   D$ = CHR$(4)
20   PRINT D$;"OPEN GROUP,L18"
30   PRINT D$;"WRITE GROUP,R";1
40   PRINT "CAROL ALSTON    "
50   H$ = STR$(15)
60   PRINT H$
70   PRINT D$;"WRITE GROUP,R";2
80   PRINT "DAVE MCDONALD   "
90   H$ = STR$(10)
100  PRINT H$
110  PRINT D$;"WRITE GROUP,R";3
120  PRINT "SUSIE URBANK    "
130  H$ = STR$(10)
140  PRINT H$
150  PRINT D$;"WRITE GROUP,R";4
160  PRINT "FRED ZIMMERMAN  "
170  H$ = STR$(8)
180  PRINT H$
```

Note that each record has eighteen characters: Sixteen for the name string and two for the hours string (H$). The statement

50 H$ = STR$(15)

converts the hours (15) to a string value and assigns it to H$.

Closing a File   The CLOSE statement for a relative file is the same as for a sequential file. Its format is as follows:

line# PRINT <CTRL><D>variable;"CLOSE [filename]"

The *filename* is optional, as indicated by the brackets. If no filename is included in the statement, all open files are closed; if one is included, just the specified file is closed. Here is the entire program to write four records to the GROUP file:

```
10   D$ = CHR$(4)
20   PRINT D$;"OPEN GROUP,L18"
30   PRINT D$;"WRITE GROUP,R";1
40   PRINT "CAROL ALSTON    "
50   H$ = STR$(15)
60   PRINT H$
70   PRINT D$;"WRITE GROUP,R";2
80   PRINT "DAVE MCDONALD   "
90   H$ = STR$(10)
100  PRINT H$
110  PRINT D$;"WRITE GROUP,R";3
120  PRINT "SUSIE URBANK    "
130  H$ = STR$(10)
140  PRINT H$
150  PRINT D$;"WRITE GROUP,R";4
160  PRINT "FRED ZIMMERMAN  "
170  H$ = STR$(8)
180  PRINT H$
190  PRINT D$;"CLOSE GROUP"
999  END
```

Reading a File   In order to read data from a text file, two statements must be used. The first statement specifies which record is to be read, by including a record number, and the second statement places the specified data item from the record into a variable. The formats for these statements are as follows:

line# PRINT <CTRL><D> variable; "READ filename,R"; record-number
line# INPUT variable 1[,variable2]...

Here is a program that will read and print record number 3 from the GROUP file:

```
10  REM *** RECORD 3 FROM THE RANDOM FILE NAMED GROUP IS
20  REM *** ACCESSED.  THE DATA FROM THAT RECORD IS THEN
30  REM *** PRINTED. ***
40  REM *** MAJOR VARIABLES:
50  REM ***    P$     COMMITTEE MEMBER'S NAME
60  REM ***    H$     NUMBER OF HOURS AVAILABLE TO WORK
70  REM ***    H      NUMBER OF HOURS IN NUMERIC FORM
80  REM
90  D$ = CHR$(4)
100 PRINT D$;"OPEN GROUP,L18"
110 PRINT D$;"READ GROUP,R";3
120 INPUT P$
130 INPUT H$
140 H = VAL(H$)
150 PRINT P$,H
160 PRINT D$;"CLOSE GROUP"
999 END
```

Line 110 specifies which record is to be read from by using the number 3. Lines 120 and 130 place the data items into variables *P$* and *H$*, respectively. Note that the character string data contained in *H$* is converted back to numeric data by using the VAL function. This step makes it possible to perform calculations on *H* if necessary. In line 150, *P$* and *H* are printed.

IBM/Microsoft and Macintosh/Microsoft

For our purposes here, the statements for using random files with IBM/Microsoft and Macintosh/Microsoft are the same, except that line numbers are optional on the Macintosh.

Creating or Accessing a File In order to create a new random file or access an old one, the OPEN statement must be used. Its general format is

line# OPEN "filename" AS #filenumber LEN = buffer-size

Filename is a character string variable that names the file. *Filenumber*, an integer value, provides a quick means of referring to the filename in later statements within the program. Note that a mode is not specified in the OPEN statement, as it was for the sequential file. This is because input and output of a random file is the default value for the mode. LEN is followed by *buffer-size*, which states the maximum number of characters in a record.

The following example of the OPEN statement will open a file named GROUP, in which each record is eighteen characters long:

```
10 OPEN "GROUP" AS #2 LEN = 18
```

Once the length of a record is declared by specifying the *buffer-size*, the length of each field in the record must also be declared. The FIELD statement declares the length of each field in the record. Its general format is line# FIELD #filenumber,fieldwidth AS fieldname [,fieldwidth AS fieldname]...

The *filenumber* is the integer value given to the file in the OPEN statement. *Fieldwidth*, an integer value, declares how long the field named *fieldname* will be. *Fieldname* is a string variable.

Every field in a record must be declared in the FIELD statement. If we wish to write a program to create a file named GROUP with two fields, one sixteen characters long and the other two characters long, the first two statements will look like this:

```
10 OPEN "GROUP" AS #2 LEN = 18
20 FIELD #2,16 AS P$,2 AS H$
```

Writing Data to a File In order to write data to a file, each data item must be in character form, and each *fieldname* from the FIELD statement must have a value written to it. One of the following three functions must be used to convert numbers to character values:

MKI$(integer number)
MKS$(single-precision real number)
MKD$(double-precision real number)

Notice that a different function must be used to convert each type of number. MKI$ produces a character string of length 2 and is used when an integer value is being converted. MKS$ results in a character string of length 4 and is used when converting single-precision real numbers. MKD$ results in a character string of length 8 and is used when converting double-precision real numbers. So far in this text, we have only used single-precision real numbers when dealing with real values. If you wish to learn about double-precision real numbers, refer to your system documentation. An example of each of these functions is shown below:

MKI$	MKS$	MKD$
40 X% = 12	40 X = 12.5	40 X# = 12.5
50 MKI$(X%)	50 MKS$(X)	50 MKD$(X#)

Once the numbers are in string form, they must be padded with blanks so that the character string is the same length as the buffer into which it is to be read. (Remember that the buffer was declared as a fixed length in the FIELD statement.) The LSET and RSET commands insert blanks along with the character string. LSET left-justifies the character string within the field, and RSET right-justifies it. For example, if the field M$ has a length of 10, the following statement would cause the character string MEREDITH followed by two blanks to be assigned to M$:

```
150 LSET M$ = "MEREDITH"
```

The following statement would cause two blanks followed by MEREDITH to be assigned to M$:

```
160 RSET M$ = "MEREDITH"
```

The general formats of these statements are as follows:

line # LSET string-variable = string-expression
line# RSET string-variable = string-expression

If the READ/DATA statements, assignment statement, or INPUT statement must be used to define a field, a variable other than the field variable must be used. The field variable must then be assigned the value of this other variable using the LSET or RSET command.

Once fields have been converted into strings and given values, the PUT statement copies the record currently in the buffer to the file. Its general format is

line# PUT #filenumber[,record-number]

Record-number, an integer value in the range 1 through 32,767, identifies the numbered record location at which the record should be placed. If the *record-number* clause is omitted, the next numbered location is used.

We will now add the statements necessary to read four records to our program to create the GROUP file:

```
10   OPEN "GROUP" AS #2 LEN = 18
20   FIELD #2,16 AS P$,2 AS H$
30   LSET P$ = "CAROL ALSTON"
40   LSET H$ = MKI$(15)
50   PUT #2,1
60   LSET P$ = "DAVE MCDONALD"
70   LSET H$ = MKI$(10)
80   PUT #2,2
90   LSET P$ = "SUSIE URBANK"
100  LSET H$ = MKI$(10)
110  PUT #2,3
120  LSET P$ = "FRED ZIMMERMAN"
130  LSET H$ = MKI$(8)
140  PUT #2,4
```

Closing a File The same statement is used to close a random file that was used to close a sequential file. Thus the general format for the CLOSE statement is as follows:

line# CLOSE #filenumber1[,#filenumber2]...

Here is the finished program to create file GROUP:

```
10  REM *** A RANDOM FILE, NAMED GROUP, IS CREATED.  TWO FIELDS
20  REM *** EXIST IN EACH RECORD OF THIS FILE.  THE FIRST
30  REM *** CONTAINS THE COMMITTEE MEMBER'S NAME, AND THE SECOND
40  REM *** CONTAINS THE NUMBER OF HOURS THE COMMITTEE MEMBER
50  REM *** IS AVAILABLE TO WORK PER WEEK.
60  REM *** MAJOR VARIABLES:
70  REM ***     P$    COMMITTEE MEMBER'S NAME
80  REM ***     H$    HOURS AVAILABLE TO WORK
90  REM
100 OPEN "GROUP" AS #2 LEN = 18
110 FIELD #2,16 AS P$,2 AS H$
120 LSET P$ = "CAROL ALSTON"
130 LSET H$ = MKI$(15)
140 PUT #2,1
150 LSET P$ = "DAVE MCDONALD"
160 LSET H$ = MKI$(10)
170 PUT #2,2
180 LSET P$ = "SUSIE URBANK"
190 LSET H$ = MKI$(10)
200 PUT #2,3
210 LSET P$ = "FRED ZIMMERMAN"
220 LSET H$ = MKI$(8)
230 PUT #2,4
240 CLOSE #2
999 END
```

Reading a File In order to read a record from a file, the record must be moved from secondary storage to a buffer. The GET statement performs this operation:

line# GET #filenumber[,record-number]

Record-number is the numbered record position of the needed record. If it is omitted, the next record in the sequence is retrieved.

Because all the data retrieved from the file is in character form, the numbers need to be converted back to numeric form if they are to be used in calculations. The three functions that do this are

CVI(2-character string)
CVS(4-character string)
CVD(8-character string)

CVI is used when converting back to an integer value; CVS is used when converting back to a single-precision real number; CVD is used when converting back to a double-precision real number. The following program reads the third record in the GROUP file:

```
10  REM *** RECORD 3 FROM THE RANDOM FILE NAMED GROUP IS
20  REM *** ACCESSED.  THE DATA FROM THAT RECORD IS THEN
30  REM *** PRINTED.
40  REM *** MAJOR VARIABLE:
```

```
50  REM ***     P$    COMMITTEE MEMBER'S NAME
60  REM ***     H$    HOURS FIELD IN GROUP FILE
70  REM ***     HOURS = NUMERIC FORM OF H$
80  REM
90  OPEN "GROUP" AS #2 LEN = 18
100 FIELD #2,16 AS P$,2 AS H$
110 GET #2,3
120 HOURS = CVI(H$)
130 PRINT P$,HOURS
140 CLOSE #2
999 END
```

A Programming Problem

Problem Definition

Winston Bank, a small-town bank, would like to make more efficient use of its computer. The manager would like a relative file to keep track of customer accounts. A relative file can be updated quickly and efficiently, and either random or sequential processing can be used. The user should be able to enter new records or update old records in the file by entering the data at the keyboard. This program will be written to run on a VAX computer.

Solution Design

Two programs will need to be written. The first will create a relative file containing all customer information, and the second will access the data in this file so that savings and checking account balances can be updated.

We will first discuss the program needed to create the file. This program needs to perform three main tasks: (1) the file has to be opened, with the necessary fields specified; (2) the records must be written to the file; and (3) the file has to be closed. The stepwise refinement and structure chart are shown in Figure 10–9 and Figure 10–10, respectively.

The input needed for this program will be the necessary data for each customer. This data will be written to a relative file, of which each record will contain the following seven fields:

customer's name	(N$)
customer's street address	(A$)
city	(C$)
state	(ST$)
zip code	(Z$)
checking account balance	(CH)
savings account balance	(S)

This program can be written using prompts to ask the user to enter the appropriate data to each field until the desired number of records has been added.

FIGURE 10–9
Stepwise Refinement of Creating Bank Customer Data File Problem

General Problem: Create a data file containing data on bank customers
Level 1
  A. Open customer file
  B. Write data to file
  C. Close file

FIGURE 10–10
Structure Chart for Creating Bank Customer Data File Problem

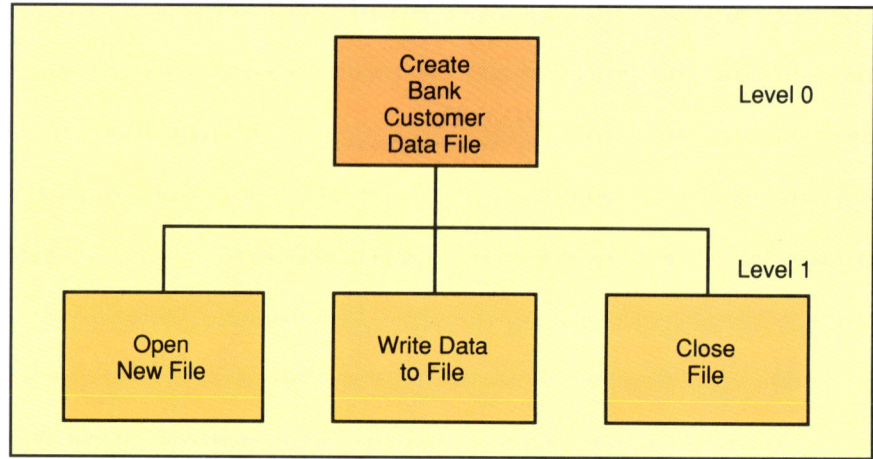

The second program is more complicated. The record that needs to be updated must be directly accessed and then correctly modified. Therefore, the major steps in this program are (1) opening the file, (2) accessing the correct record and updating it, and (3) closing the file.

When updating the file, one of two actions will occur: either the checking account balance will be modified, or the savings account balance will be modified. Because each of these actions will require a number of steps, they will be listed as separate substeps under Step 2. Refer to the stepwise refinement in Figure 10–11 and the structure chart in Figure 10–12.

FIGURE 10–11
Stepwise Refinement of Updating Bank Customer Data File Problem

General Problem: Update checking and savings account data file
Level 1
  A. Open file
  B. Access and update the correct record
  C. Close file
Level 2
  B.1. Upate savings account
  B.2. Update checking account

DATA FILES **435**

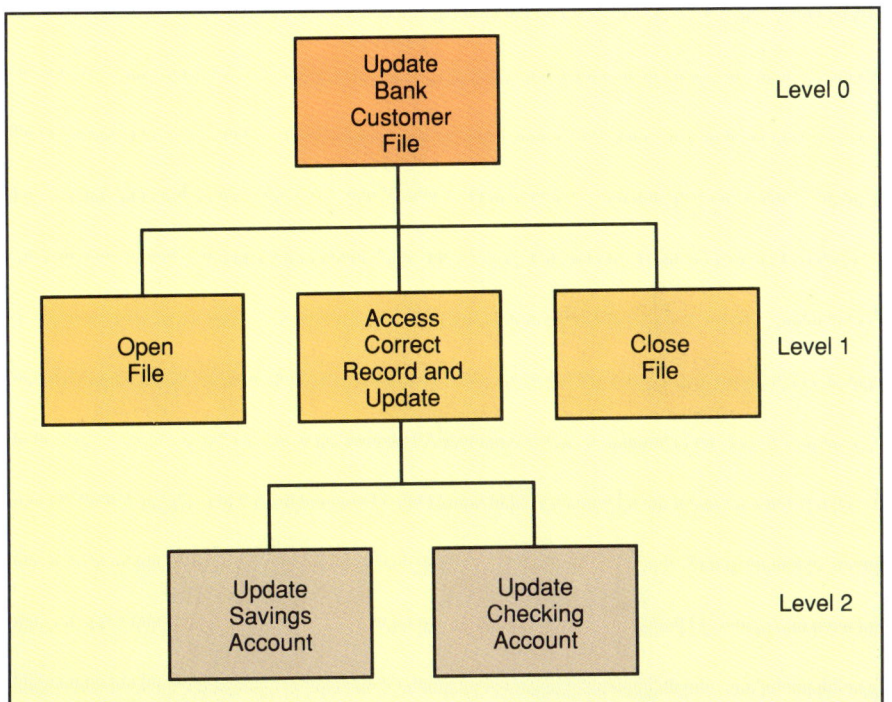

FIGURE 10–12
Structure Chart for Updating Bank Customer Data File Problem

The Programs

The program to create the bank customer data file is shown in Figure 10–13. Because it is a relatively short program and each of the three tasks specified in the structure chart consists of only a few lines of code, the program has not been divided into subroutines. Each of the seven fields is listed in the MAP statement in line 160. The file ACCT is opened for output as a relative file in line 170. Using a relative file will allow the user to access the needed record directly in the second program, which will update any specified record within the file.

When this program is executed, the user is first asked to state the number of records that will be entered. Then a FOR/NEXT loop is used to prompt the user to enter the needed data for each record. The file is closed in line 380.

The purpose of the second program (shown in Figure 10–14) is to access and update records in the file created by the first program. Therefore, the file ACCT is opened for input in line 230. In line 280, the user is prompted to enter the number of the record to be accessed. It is then necessary to determine the type of transaction to be performed; an S is entered for a savings transaction and a C for a checking transaction. Next, the user is asked if the transaction is a withdrawal (W) or a deposit (D). Lastly, the user is prompted to enter the amount of the transaction. Line 320 performs a GET to place the needed record in main memory so that it can be updated. The IF statement in line 330 causes the necessary subroutine to be called to

FIGURE 10–13 Program to Create a Bank Customer Data File

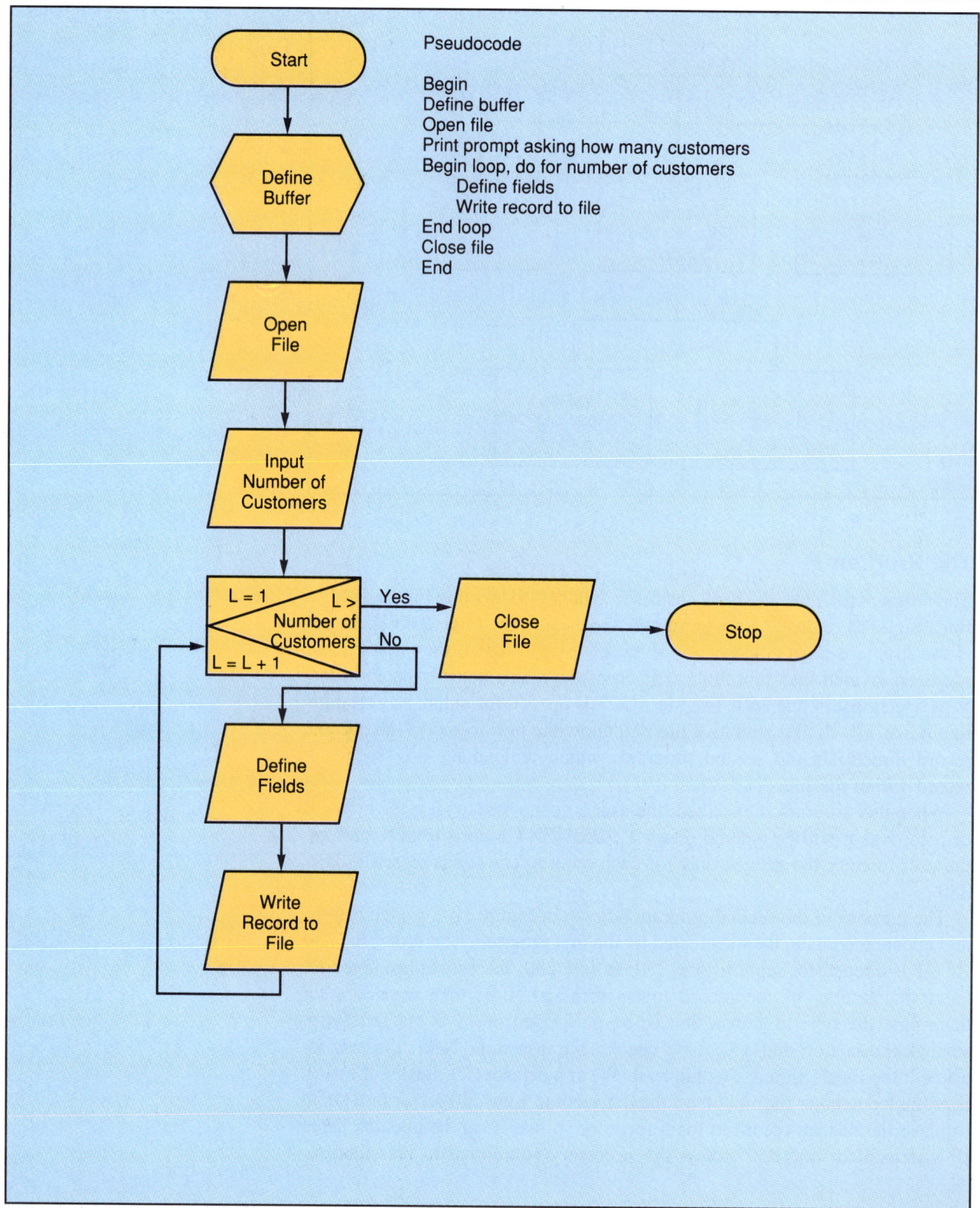

FIGURE 10–13 *Continued*

```
10  REM ***         CREATION OF RANDOM BANK CUSTOMERS FILE     ***
20  REM
30  REM *** INFORMATION ABOUT EACH BANK CUSTOMER IS STORED IN A ***
40  REM *** RANDOM FILE NAMED CUSTOMERS.  EACH RECORD CONTAINS  ***
50  REM *** THE FOLLOWING FIELDS:                               ***
60  REM ***      N$    THE CUSTOMER'S NAME                      ***
70  REM ***      A$    CUSTOMER'S STREET ADDRESS                ***
80  REM ***      C$    CITY                                     ***
90  REM ***      ST$   STATE                                    ***
100 REM ***      Z$    ZIP CODE                                 ***
110 REM ***      CH    CHECKING ACCOUNT BALANCE                 ***
120 REM ***      S     SAVINGS ACCOUNT BALANCE                  ***
130 REM *** MAJOR VARIABLES:                                    ***
140 REM ***      BC   # OF CUSTOMERS TO BE ENTERED INTO THE FILE ***
150 REM
160 MAP (CUST) STRING N$ = 20, STRING A$ = 20, STRING C$ = 10,
        STRING ST$ = 2, STRING Z$ = 5, SINGLE CH, SINGLE S
170 OPEN "ACCT" FOR OUTPUT AS FILE #1, ORGANIZATION RELATIVE FIXED,
        MAP CUST
180 PRINT
190 PRINT "HOW MANY CUSTOMERS WILL BE ENTERED INTO THE FILE?"
200 INPUT BC
210 FOR L = 1 TO BC
220    PRINT \ PRINT
230    INPUT "CUSTOMER'S NAME ";N$
240    PRINT
250    INPUT "STREET ADDRESS ";A$
260    PRINT
270    INPUT "CITY ";C$
280    PRINT
290    INPUT "STATE ";ST$
300    PRINT
310    INPUT "ZIP CODE ";Z$
320    PRINT
330    INPUT "CHECKING ACCOUNT BALANCE ";CH
340    PRINT
350    INPUT "SAVINGS ACCOUNT BALANCE ";S
360    PUT #1, RECORD L
370 NEXT L
380 CLOSE #1
999 END
```

```
RUNNH

HOW MANY CUSTOMERS WILL BE ENTERED INTO THE FILE?
? 3
```

FIGURE 10–13 *Continued*

```
CUSTOMER'S NAME ? JOANNE KOHNE
STREET ADDRESS ? 1791 PRESTON AVE
CITY ? AKRON
STATE ? OH
ZIP CODE ? 44313
CHECKING ACCOUNT BALANCE ? 300.45
SAVINGS ACCOUNT BALANCE ? 1000.34

CUSTOMER'S NAME ? KATIE MANSON
STREET ADDRESS ? 4683 QUICK RD
CITY ? PENINSULA
STATE ? OH
ZIP CODE ? 44264
CHECKING ACCOUNT BALANCE ? 250.50
SAVINGS ACCOUNT BALANCE ? 100.46

CUSTOMER'S NAME ? MANDY OFSTEAD
STREET ADDRESS ? 1135 BROOKPARK DR
CITY ? CUYAHOGA FALLS
STATE ? OH
ZIP CODE ? 44313
CHECKING ACCOUNT BALANCE ? 170.98
SAVINGS ACCOUNT BALANCE ? 4000.03
```

DATA FILES   439

FIGURE 10-14 Program to Update Bank Customer Data File

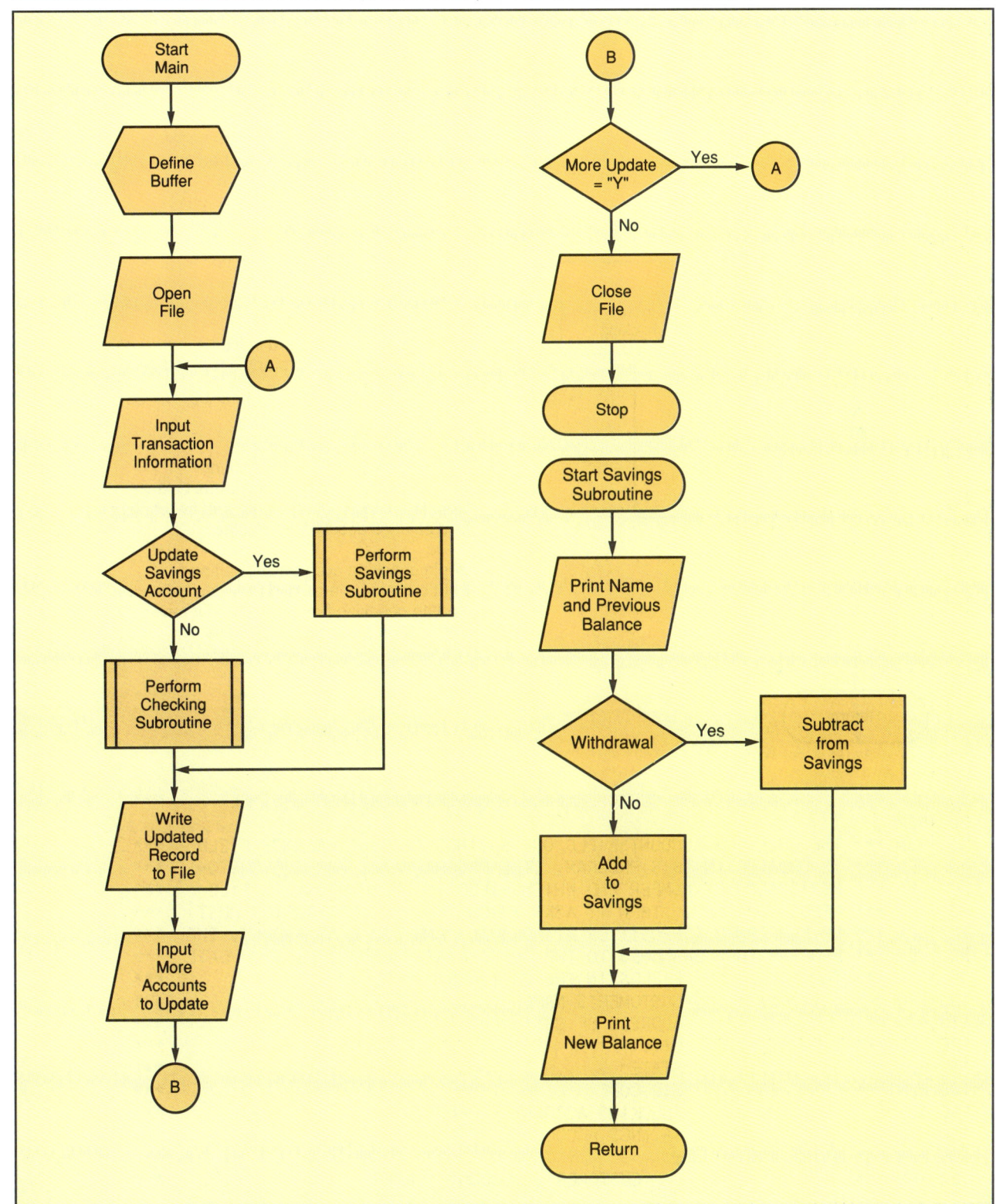

FIGURE 10-14 *Continued*

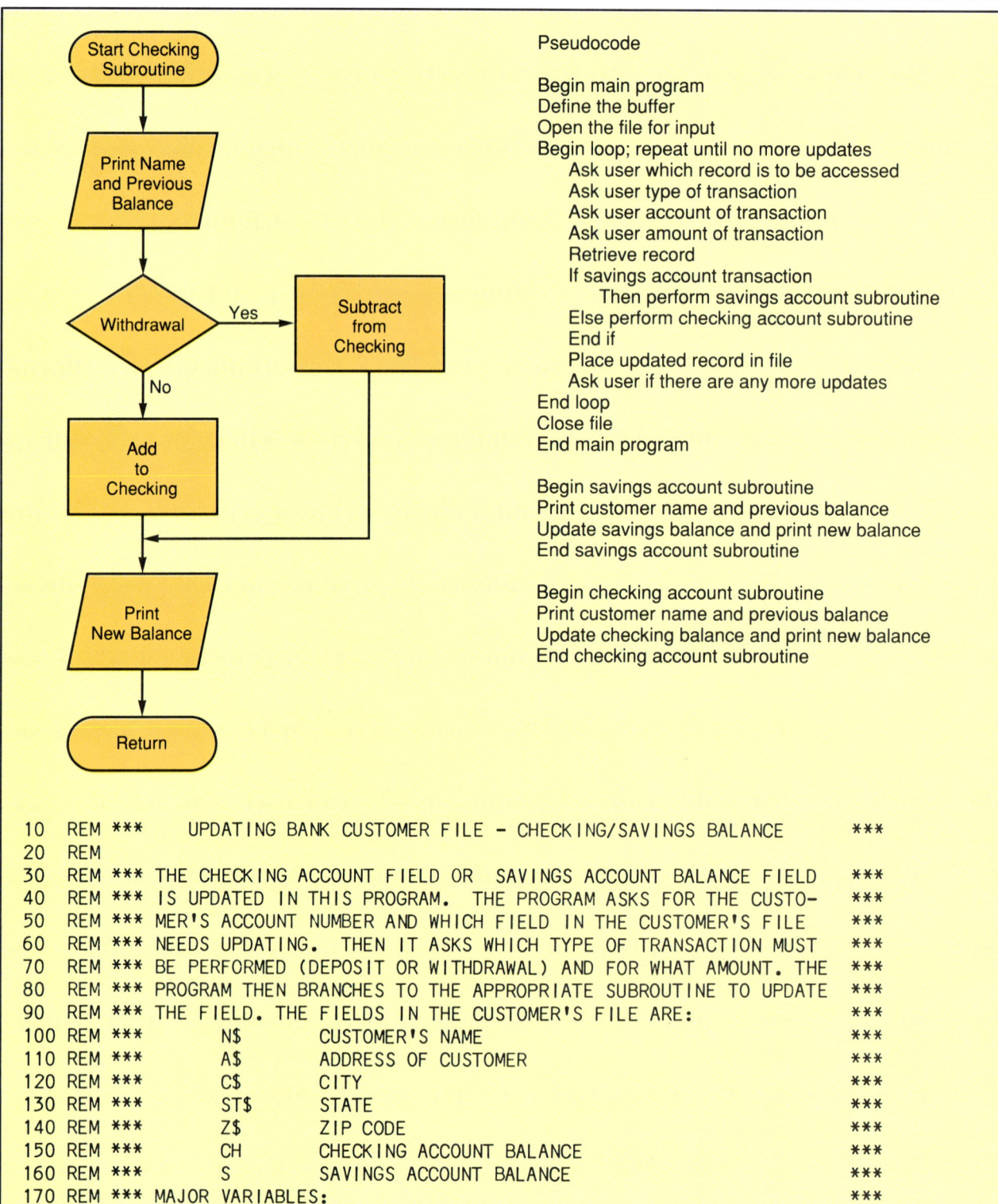

Pseudocode

Begin main program
Define the buffer
Open the file for input
Begin loop; repeat until no more updates
    Ask user which record is to be accessed
    Ask user type of transaction
    Ask user account of transaction
    Ask user amount of transaction
    Retrieve record
    If savings account transaction
        Then perform savings account subroutine
    Else perform checking account subroutine
    End if
    Place updated record in file
    Ask user if there are any more updates
End loop
Close file
End main program

Begin savings account subroutine
Print customer name and previous balance
Update savings balance and print new balance
End savings account subroutine

Begin checking account subroutine
Print customer name and previous balance
Update checking balance and print new balance
End checking account subroutine

```
10  REM ***      UPDATING BANK CUSTOMER FILE - CHECKING/SAVINGS BALANCE     ***
20  REM
30  REM *** THE CHECKING ACCOUNT FIELD OR  SAVINGS ACCOUNT BALANCE FIELD    ***
40  REM *** IS UPDATED IN THIS PROGRAM.  THE PROGRAM ASKS FOR THE CUSTO-    ***
50  REM *** MER'S ACCOUNT NUMBER AND WHICH FIELD IN THE CUSTOMER'S FILE     ***
60  REM *** NEEDS UPDATING.  THEN IT ASKS WHICH TYPE OF TRANSACTION MUST    ***
70  REM *** BE PERFORMED (DEPOSIT OR WITHDRAWAL) AND FOR WHAT AMOUNT. THE   ***
80  REM *** PROGRAM THEN BRANCHES TO THE APPROPRIATE SUBROUTINE TO UPDATE   ***
90  REM *** THE FIELD. THE FIELDS IN THE CUSTOMER'S FILE ARE:               ***
100 REM ***       N$        CUSTOMER'S NAME                                 ***
110 REM ***       A$        ADDRESS OF CUSTOMER                             ***
120 REM ***       C$        CITY                                            ***
130 REM ***       ST$       STATE                                           ***
140 REM ***       Z$        ZIP CODE                                        ***
150 REM ***       CH        CHECKING ACCOUNT BALANCE                        ***
160 REM ***       S         SAVINGS ACCOUNT BALANCE                         ***
170 REM *** MAJOR VARIABLES:                                                ***
180 REM ***       CN             CUSTOMER'S ACCOUNT NUMBER                  ***
```

FIGURE 10–14 *Continued*

```
190 REM ***     TRANSACTION$        WITHDRAWAL OR DEPOSIT                 ***
200 REM ***     AMOUNT              AMOUNT OF TRANSACTION                 ***
210 REM
220 MAP (CUST) STRING N$ = 20, STRING A$ = 20, STRING C$ = 10,
        STRING ST$ = 2, STRING Z$ = 5, SINGLE CH, SINGLE S
230 OPEN "ACCT" FOR INPUT AS FILE #1, ORGANIZATION RELATIVE FIXED, MAP CUST
240 REM
250 REM *** UPDATE THE CUSTOMERS' ACCOUNTS. ***
260 AN$ = "Y"
270 WHILE AN$ = "Y"
280     INPUT "ENTER THE ACCOUNT NUMBER ";CN
290     INPUT "ENTER TRANSACTION TYPE (Withdrawal/Deposit) ";TRANSACTION$
300     INPUT "ENTER TRANSACTION ACCOUNT (Saving/Checking) ";ACCOUNT$
310     INPUT "ENTER TRANSACTION AMOUNT ";AMOUNT
320     GET #1,RECORD CN
330     IF ACCOUNT$ = "S" THEN GOSUB 1000 ELSE GOSUB 2000
340     UPDATE #1
350     PRINT
360     INPUT "ARE THERE MORE ACCOUNTS TO UPDATE ";AN$
370     AN$ = LEFT$(AN$,1)
380     PRINT
390 NEXT
400 CLOSE #1
410 GOTO 9999
1000 REM ******************************************************************
1010 REM ***                SUBROUTINE UPDATE SAVINGS BALANCE           ***
1020 REM ******************************************************************
1030 REM *** THIS SUBROUTINE UPDATES THE SAVINGS ACCOUNT BALANCE.       ***
1040 REM
1050 PRINT
1060 PRINT "CUSTOMER'S NAME: ";N$
1070 PRINT "PREVIOUS BALANCE: ";S
1080 IF TRANSACTION$ = "W" THEN S = S - AMOUNT ELSE S = S + AMOUNT
1090 PRINT "NEW BALANCE: ";S
1100 RETURN
2000 REM ******************************************************************
2010 REM ***                SUBROUTINE UPDATE CHECKING BALANCE          ***
2020 REM ******************************************************************
2030 REM *** THIS SUBROUTINE UPDATES THE CHECKING ACCOUNT BALANCE.      ***
2040 REM
2050 PRINT
2060 PRINT "CUSTOMER'S NAME:";N$
2070 PRINT "PREVIOUS BALANCE: ";CH
2080 IF TRANSACTION$ = "W" THEN CH = CH - AMOUNT ELSE CH = CH + AMOUNT
2090 PRINT "NEW BALANCE: ";CH
2100 RETURN
9999 END
```

FIGURE 10-14 *Continued*

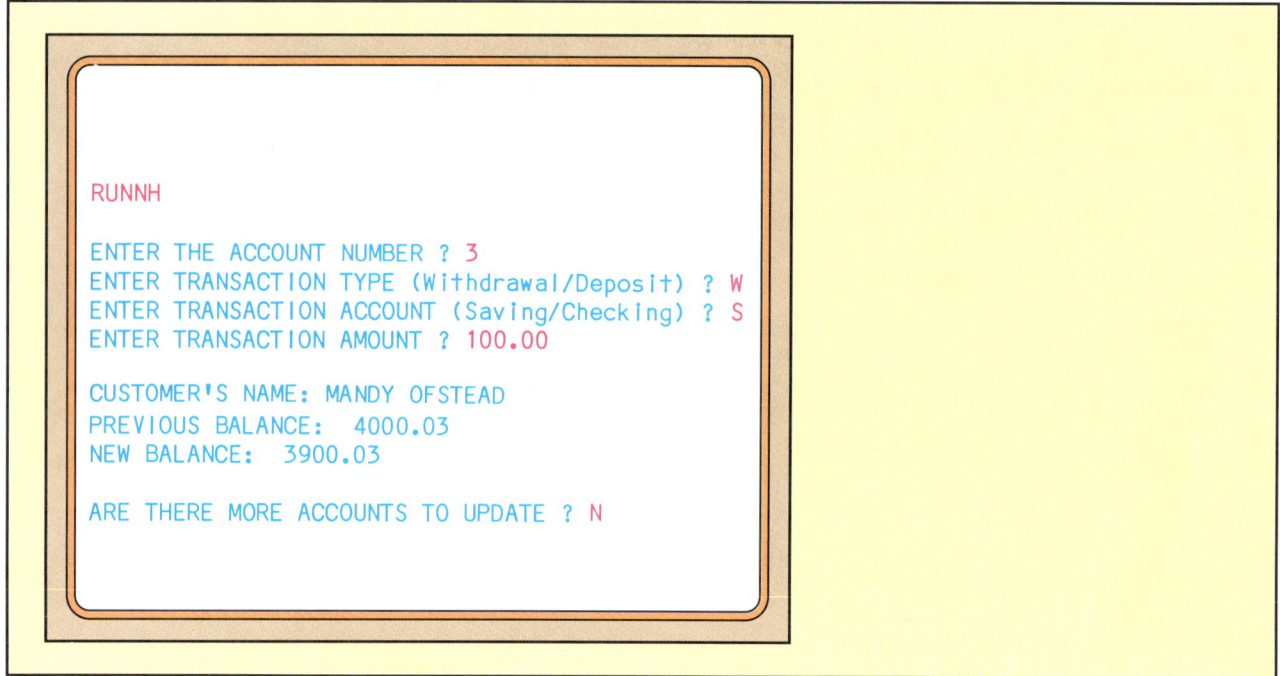

update the correct account. When control is returned to the main program, the UPDATE statement in line 340 places this new information in the correct record position. The user is then asked if there are more accounts to be updated; if there are, program control branches to the top of the loop; otherwise the file is closed and program execution terminates.

Avoiding Common Programming Mistakes

- Make sure a file is closed when it is no longer being used. This step prevents data from being lost.
- If a mode must be specified, remember that the output mode is used for writing data to a file, and the input mode is used for reading data from a file.
- Do not use a file number in a program that is different from the one specified in the OPEN statement.

Summary Points

- Files are used to organize large amounts of data. Because they are kept in secondary storage, they solve the problem of limited space in the computer's primary storage unit.

- A given file can be accessed by many different programs.
- Files are divided into records, which in turn are divided into fields.
- Files can be organized in one of three ways: sequential organization, relative organization, or indexed organization.
- In sequential organization, records are stored in a sequence, one after another.
- In relative organization, each record is stored in a numbered location.
- When indexed organization is used, records are stored according to a primary key that uniquely identifies each record.
- Two access methods exist: random access and sequential access.
- Random access allows a program to access a particular record within a file directly, regardless of its position.
- Sequential access retrieves a record based on the record's sequential order within the file. If it is necessary to access the fifth record, for example, records 1 through 4 must be accessed first.
- Secondary storage media are a factor in determining the type of file organization and access method that will be used.
- Before a file can be accessed, it must be opened.
- When processing is completed on a file, it must be closed so that its contents are not lost.
- No standardized method exists among the various BASIC systems for performing operations on files. Therefore, it is necessary to become familiar with the specific statements used on your system.

Review Questions

1. What is a file?
2. What are the advantages and disadvantages of using a data file?
3. Name the divisions of a file, explain how they are related to each other, and give an example of each.
4. Explain sequential file organization.
5. Explain relative file organization.
6. Explain indexed file organization.
7. What is a primary key?
8. What is meant by an access method?
9. Differentiate between random access and sequential access.
10. What is secondary storage?
11. Give the definition of a read/write head.
12. Name two parts of a disk pack that help the read/write heads locate a record.
13. Why can a magnetic tape contain only sequential files?
14. What types of file organization use random access?
15. What are the general steps in writing to a sequential file?
16. What are the general steps in reading data from a sequential file?
17. Why must a file be closed?

18. What is a buffer?
19. What are the differences between writing a record to a sequential file and writing a record to a relative file?
20. What is a cylinder?

Debugging Exercises

Identify the following programs and program segments that contain errors, and debug them. These exercises are written for the VAX BASIC implementation of files.

1. ```
   10 REM *** READ TWO NAMES TO SEQUENTIAL FILE WINNERS. ***
   20 OPEN "WINNERS" AS FILE #1
   30 PRINT #1;"ELIZABETH LITTLER"
   40 PRINT #1;"KEN MINNS"
   50 CLOSE #1
   99 END
   ```

2. ```
   10 REM *** CREATE PAYSCALE FILE. ***
   20 MAP (BUFF) J$ = 20, WORD PS = 5
   30 OPEN "PAYSCALE" FOR OUTPUT AS FILE #4 ORGANIZATION
          RELATIVE FIXED, MAP BUFF
   40 FOR I = 1 TO 4
   50     PRINT "JOB TITLE?"
   60     INPUT J$
   70     PRINT "HOURLY WAGE?"
   80     INPUT PS
   90     PUT #4, RECORD I
   100 NEXT I
   110 CLOSE #4
   999 END
   ```

3. ```
   10 MAP (BUFF) STRING S$ = 20, STRING A$ = 20
   20 OPEN "SUBSCRIBERS" FOR OUPUT AS FILE #4, ORGANIZATION
          RELATIVE FIXED, MAP BUFF
   30 FOR X = 1 TO 20
   40     GET #4, RECORD X
   50     PRINT S$
   60     PRINT A$
   70     PRINT
   80     PRINT
   90 NEXT X
   99 END
   ```

4. ```
   10 REM *** CREATE INGREDIENTS FILE. ***
   20 OPEN "INGREDIENTS" AS FILE #3
   30 FOR S = 1 TO 10
   40     READ I$
   50     PRINT #3,S
   60 NEXT S
   70 CLOSE #3
   99 END
   ```

5. ```
10 OPEN "SCALE" AS FILE #1
20 FOR S = 1 TO 10
30   INPUT #1 SALES$(S)
40   INPUT NUMBERSOLD(S)
50 NEXT S
60 CLOSE #1
99 END
```

6. ```
10  REM *** CREATE SEQUENTIAL FILE UNIVERSITIES. ***
20  OPEN "UNIVERSITIES" AS FILE #3
30  INPUT "IOWA STATE UNIVERSITY";U$
40  PRINT #3,RECORD 1
50  INPUT "COLORADO STATE UNIVERSITY";U$
60  PRINT #3,RECORD 1
70  INPUT "OHIO STATE UNIVERSITY"
80  PRINT #3,RECORD 2
90  CLOSE #3
99  END
```

7. ```
10 REM *** CREATE FILE AND READ DATA TO IT. ***
20 MAP (BUFF) STRING I$ = 10,WORD IN,WORD Q
30 OPEN "INVENTORY" FOR OUTPUT AS FILE #3,ORGANIZATION
        RELATIVE FIXED,MAP BUFF
40 PRINT #3,"PAPER"
50 PRINT #3,00167
60 PRINT #3,121
70 PRINT #3,"PENS"
80 PRINT #3,12372
90 PRINT #3,75
100 PRINT #3,"ERASERS"
110 PRINT #3,63192
120 PRINT #3,10
130 CLOSE #3
999 END
```

8. ```
10 REM *** READ FILE RECORDS.  IF DATE = 7/23/86,
20 REM *** THEN PRINT RECORD.
30 OPEN "RESERVATIONS" AS FILE #4
40 FOR X = 1 TO 100
50    INPUT #2,D$,N$,T$
60    IF D$ = "7/23/86" THEN PRINT N$,T$
70 NEXT X
80 CLOSE #2
99 END
```

9. ```
10 REM *** DISPLAY INFORMATION ON A REQUESTED EVENT.
20 MAP (BUFF) STRING E$ = 15, STRING DTE$ = 8, WORD T$ = 5
30 OPEN "OLYMPICS" FOR INPUT AS FILE #1, ORGANIZATION
        RELATIVE FIXED, MAP BUFF
40 PRINT "WHICH EVENT WOULD YOU LIKE TO SEE?"
50 INPUT EVENT$
60 FOR M = 1 TO 30
70   GET #1, RECORD M
80   IF E$ = EVENT$ THEN PRINT DTE$,T$
90 NEXT M
99 END
```
```

10.
```
10 REM *** ENTER RESULTS OF SURVEY INTO THE FILE RESPONSES.
20 MAP (BUFF) STRING P$ = 10,STRING UP$ = 4
30 OPEN "RESPONSES" FOR OUPUT AS FILE #3, ORGANIZATION
        RELATIVE FIXED, MAP BUFF
40 INPUT "COKE";P$
50 INPUT "48%";UP$
60 PUT #3,RECORD 1
70 INPUT "PEPSI";P$
80 INPUT "54%";UP$
90 CLOSE #3
99 END
```

Additional Programming Problems

Level 1

1. Create a sequential file for Western Company's inventory:

Product Name	Unit Price	On Hand	In Order
AAA123	$4.82	50	30
BBB213	$9.73	70	20
CCC312	$5.00	20	10
DDD195	$4.35	60	20
EEE332	$0.55	90	30

Then write the contents of the file to the terminal screen with appropriate headings.

2. Using the file created in problem 1, determine the value of inventory on hand for each item and the total inventory value. Print these values to the terminal screen using appropriate headings.

3. Create a file named STUD to store the following information:

Name	Major	Year	GPA
Adams, B.	Business	Freshman	3.5
Benson, J.	Fishery	Junior	2.98
Fetter, M.	Math	Sophomore	4.0
Hossy, S.	History	Junior	3.9
Zienta, Y.	English	Sophomore	3.03

4. The secretary needs a list of all students who qualify for the dean's list—those with a GPA of 3.5 and above. Use the file created in problem 3 as the data to create this list. The output should be printed to the terminal screen with appropriate headings.

5. Create a data file on all the phonograph albums in your home record library. For each album, the following data items should be used:

Manufacturer's Identification	Artist's Name	Album Title	Composer	Music Type
BA7674	Brian Adams	Heaven	Brian Adams	Rock-n-Roll
23-1665	Paul Manz	In Dulci Jubilo	J.S. Bach	Classical
AL8439	Alabama	40 Hours a Week	Alabama	Country

6. The Happy Hedonist Health Club needs a program to keep track of its members. Create a sequential file containing the name and sex of each member. Allow this data to be entered while the program is running. When a user is finished entering the data, close the file.

7. Access the file in problem 6. Print a list of all the male club members.

8. Write a program to allow Gary to keep track of odd jobs he does for neighbors and the amount of money they owe him for each job. Create a sequential file of records containing the following data:

Name	Job	Time
Hall	Mowing	3.5
Ling	Babysitting	5.0
Brandt	Gardening	2.0

9. Gary charges $3.50 an hour for doing any kind of odd job. Write a program that computes how much money each neighbor owes him (see problem 8) and then outputs the neighbors' names, the type of job he did for each neighbor, and the amount owed to Gary.

10. Allow Gary to search the file created in problem 8. Ask him to enter the customer's name and the number of records in the file. Then search the file for all records containing that customer's name, and print the record to the terminal screen.

Level 2

1. Write a program to determine if a student is eligible for driver's education at Washington High School. Read ten students' names, ages, and grade point averages. To qualify for driver's education, a student must be at least fifteen years old and have a minimum grade point average of 2.5. Print all eligible students' records to a sequential file. Create your own data for this program. Then access the file and print it to the terminal screen.

2. General Hospital would like a file created that consists of the name, address, balance due, and date of last payments for its patients. After creating the file, print its contents. Use the following data:

Name	Address	Balance	Last Payment
Tom Schneider	163 State Street	$2020.72	3/10/88
Jane Jones	319 Arch Street	$ 150.80	1/11/89
Harry Person	21 Frazer Ave.	$ 72.81	4/12/89
Philip Barth	1104 Berchard Ave.	$1095.43	9/4/88
Sam Duke	28460 Lane	$1102.10	2/6/89

3. General Hospital would like to send a letter of payment notice to all patients who owe them more than $1,000.00 and have not made a payment since January 1, 1989. Create a program to write these patients' names, addresses, and balances due from the file created in problem 2.

4. Write a program that creates a random file containing the following data:

Name	Age	Social Security #	Telephone Number
Minnie Ha	74	189-47-3362	846-3592
Candy Thrun	18	294-70-3352	542-6806
Rhea Curshron	33	262-01-1005	354-9164
Indigo Bunting	28	364-60-3323	346-9649
Die Vilope	49	103-08-0019	555-8987

5. Write a program using a random file to keep track of the items for sale at the Hoboken Hardware Store. Each record in the file should contain the inventory number, the name of the item, and the quantity of that item on hand. Allow the owner to make as many entries as needed. Use the following sample data to test your program.

Inventory Number	Name	Quantity in Stock
235	Hammers	89
479	Clamps	252
091	Rakes	47
531	Hooks	1276

6. Write a program to allow the file created in problem 5 to be accessed. Allow the user to enter a record number. The contents of this record should be printed with appropriate labels.

7. Write a program to keep track of fines for the school library. Create a random relative file of records that contains the name of the student, the title of the book, and the amount of the fine. Fines are $0.20 a day for regular books and $0.50 for reserved books. Allow the user to enter as many records as needed.

8. Reopen the file from problem 7, and allow the librarian to access a given record by its record number. Print the record with appropriate labels.

9. Get Rich Quick is having a $1,000,000 sweepstakes contest. The drawing will be on May 1st. Entry blanks for the contest will be shipped to a list of subscribers who receive *Make Money* magazine. The subscribers are

Name	Address			
	Street	City	State	Zip Code
Wanda Win	234 Pennsylvania Ave.	Richmond	VA	63214
Semore Dinero	196 S. Main St.	Bradner	OH	43402
Tim Schaeffer	1164 Newton Ave.	Los Angeles	CA	06123
Cindy Ofstead	1294 Quick Road	Boston	MA	04121
George Gersh	596 E. Mantana Dr.	Ft. Collins	CO	82615
Sue Smith	421 Maybelle Rd.	Honolulu	HI	64213

Write a program that creates a random file, inserts the data, and prints it after the file has been created.

10. It is May 1st. Get Rich Quick must now draw a name to find the recipient of the $1,000,000 prize. Write a program that reads the names from the random file created in problem 9 and then randomly chooses a winner. The winner's name should be printed to the terminal screen.

Level 3

1. Create a sequential file with the following information:

Acct #	L. Name	F. Name	Sex	City	State	Height	Birthday
86439	Stein	Franklin	M	Scary	Penn	90	08/10/43
74822	Fletch	Sarah	F	Fremont	Ohio	68	08/16/63
94391	Hetrick	Rick	M	Oakroot	Ohio	75	04/04/62
74391	Macwitz	Clara	F	Shy	Iowa	61	03/11/52
84965	Lopez	Maria	F	El Paso	Texas	66	02/19/61

2. Print the average age and the average height of all females, as well as the average age and the average height of all males, from the file created in problem 1.

3. Given the following account numbers from the data of problem 1, write a program to produce a list of their names, addresses and birthdates. Print them in the stated order:

Account Numbers

74391
86439
84965

4. The Sleazy Room Hotel has rooms numbered from 101 through 999. The manager wants to use a random file to record the status of each room. When a guest checks in, FULL is to be written to the file if the chosen room is unoccupied. Determine the record number by subtracting 100 from the room number assigned to a guest. When a guest checks out, EMPTY should be written in the record for that room. The program should print to the terminal screen the status of any chosen room when a guest is checking in.

5. Tom Jennings wants to create a file that will enable him to keep track of travel expenses for his business trips. Possible expenses that may occur are

Airfare
Motel/Hotel
Food
Entertainment
Car Rental
Tips

Tom usually takes four trips per year. So far this year, Tom has gone on three business trips:

	Trip 1	Trip 2	Trip 3
Airfare	$239.00	$186.50	$280.00
Motel	$187.50	$72.98	$223.89
Food	$93.98	$39.62	$158.69
Entertainment	$56.20	$21.32	$73.52
Car Rental	$72.30	$0.00	$109.98
Tips	$28.60	$18.10	$49.60

The file is to include the individual trip expenses, so allow for the fourth trip.

6. Tom is on a set expense account. He is planning his fourth trip and wants to know how much money he has left to spend in each expense category:

Allocated Expenses

Airfare	$1000.00
Motel	$ 750.00
Food	$ 800.00
Entertainment	$ 250.00
Car Rental	$ 350.00
Tips	$ 150.00

The output should list how much Tom can spend in each expense category for his fourth trip.

7. The Roadrunners' baseball club has just computerized its entire operation. However, the club needs specific software. The Roadrunners' owner has just called you to write a payroll program. The sequential file must contain the following data:

Name	Address				Gross Pay
Sam Slugger	275 Sax Ave.	Phoenix	AZ	65243	$2000.00
Bob Debench	6292 Lily Dr.	Phoenix	AZ	65242	$900.00
Semore Flies	5432 Brookside Rd.	Smalltown	AZ	65101	$1000.00
Casey Jones	61 Strike St.	Smalltown	AZ	65101	$1500.00
Mickey Hitcher	8756 Norton Rd.	Phoenix	AZ	65242	$1580.00
Jeff Spitbol	281 Sax Ave.	Phoenix	AZ	65619	$2500.00
Sidney Shorter	111 Mandalay Rd.	Kalvin	AZ	65621	$1500.00
Lenny Leadoff	276 Wooster St.	Mayberry	AZ	65633	$2100.00
George Slide	1822 Brookside Dr.	Smalltown	AZ	65101	$2000.00

8. Now a program must be written, using the data in problem 7, that prints the players' paychecks. State taxes are 6 percent of the gross pay, social security taxes are 6.5 percent, and city taxes are 2 percent. The output should look like this:

```
Date: _____
Amount: _____
Name: _____
Amount: _____
Signature: _____
```

9. Cinema Movie Theater must report to the main headquarters how many tickets were sold each month for a particular movie, and whether these tickets were sold at a regular or discounted rate. Write a program that creates a random file. Each record should contain the name of the movie, the number of tickets sold at the matinee, and the number of tickets sold at regular rates. The data for last week, which was the beginning of the month, were as follows:

	Number Sold	
Movie	**Matinee**	**Regular**
License to Drive	200	400
Wall Street	145	538
A Fish Called Wanda	103	590

10. Write a program that will enable an employee of Cinema Movie Theater (See problem 9) to add the number of tickets sold that day to the totals in the file and then store the new totals. On the Monday of week 2, the number of tickets sold were as follows:

	Number Sold	
Movie	**Matinee**	**Regular**
License to Drive	50	200
Wall Street	25	200
A Fish Called Wanda	30	100

CHAPTER
11

PROGRAM TESTING AND WRITING USER-FRIENDLY PROGRAMS

Objectives

After studying this chapter you will be able to:
- Name four advantages of using structured programming.
- Explain the term program style and list some characteristics of programs with good style.
- Name the two basic categories of program errors.
- Use program tracing to locate and correct logic errors.
- Define error trapping, and use it when writing programs.
- Discuss the difference between complete program testing and selective program testing.
- Use selective program testing to test programs that you have written.
- Explain the characteristics of a user-friendly program.
- Write programs that are user-friendly.
- Write programs that use control breaks to output summary information.

Outline

Overview
More on Structured Programming
Program Style
  Documentation
    The Use of Blank Lines and
      Spaces
The Two Types of Program Errors

Syntax Errors
  Logic Errors
Program Testing Methods
Report Writing
Printer Control Characters
Writing User-Friendly Programs
A Programming Problem

Summary Points
Review Questions
Debugging Exercises
Additional Programming Problems
  Level 1
  Level 2

Overview

This chapter discusses the features of a program that make it easy for both the programmer and the user to understand and use. Program style, mentioned previously, will be reviewed here. The computer is not affected by the style of a program. It can execute a program with poor style just as efficiently as one with good style. Using good style is for the benefit of people.

Despite the many advantages of structured programming, programs rarely work correctly the first time they are executed. This chapter will introduce some proven methods for locating and correcting program errors. These techniques will help you test your programs in an efficient, logical manner.

More on Structured Programming

We have discussed two basic characteristics of structured programming. The first characteristic is that the logic of a structured program is easy to follow. For example, structures such as the FOR/NEXT and WHILE loops are used whenever possible instead of the GOTO statement. The second basic characteristic is that the problem solution is developed using top-down design. A structure chart is developed to show the levels of refinement. When the program is actually coded, each module in the structure chart is implemented as a subroutine (except for those involving only a few lines of code, which may be left in the main program). This procedure results in a program that is divided into subroutines, each performing a specific task.

A program written using these techniques has a number of advantages over an unstructured program. Some of the major ones are:

- The logic of the program is easy to follow.
- The programmer is able to use his or her time efficiently.
- The program is easy to modify and maintain (that is, to keep in working order). Programmers in business and industry must often make changes to

programs that someone else wrote. It is much easier to make changes to a structured program than to an unstructured one.
- The program is more likely to be error-free than an unstructured program. If there are errors, they are generally easier to locate and correct.

Program Style

As previously mentioned, the purpose of using good program style is to make a program as easy as possible to read and understand. A program with good style has the following characteristics:

- It is well documented.
- Blank spaces have been used to make the program easy to read and understand.
- The variables in the program have been given descriptive names.

We have already discussed the importance of using descriptive variable names. Documentation and the use of blank spaces have been mentioned briefly and will be discussed further here.

Documentation

Documentation consists of any written descriptions and explanations of a program or information related to the program's use. It can be divided into two categories: external and internal. **External documentation** consists of any reference or user's manuals that are associated with the program; it is separate from the program. Often external documentation is printed in paper form. Structure charts and flowcharts are examples of external documentation used to explain the program graphically. **Internal documentation** consists of any comments (REM statements) that are placed within the program itself. In this chapter, we will be concerned only with internal documentation.

Thorough documentation helps greatly in debugging programs. The programmer may think he or she will remember how a specific subroutine works, but this may not be true, particularly if it is contained within a large program. Furthermore, thorough documentation is essential when a program needs to be modified at a later date. This is especially true in business, where the original programmer may be long gone by the time the program needs to be changed.

Internal documentation appears in two basic places within the program: at the beginning of the program and within the body of the program.

After the program title comes the beginning documentation, which explains the program as a whole. The purpose of the program is stated here, and its input, output, and major variables are explained. Study the program in Figure 11–1. As the beginning documentation states, this program

External documentation
Written descriptions or explanations of a program that are external to the program itself.

Internal documentation
Comments placed within the program that explain it to people.

FIGURE 11–1 Documenting a Simple Program

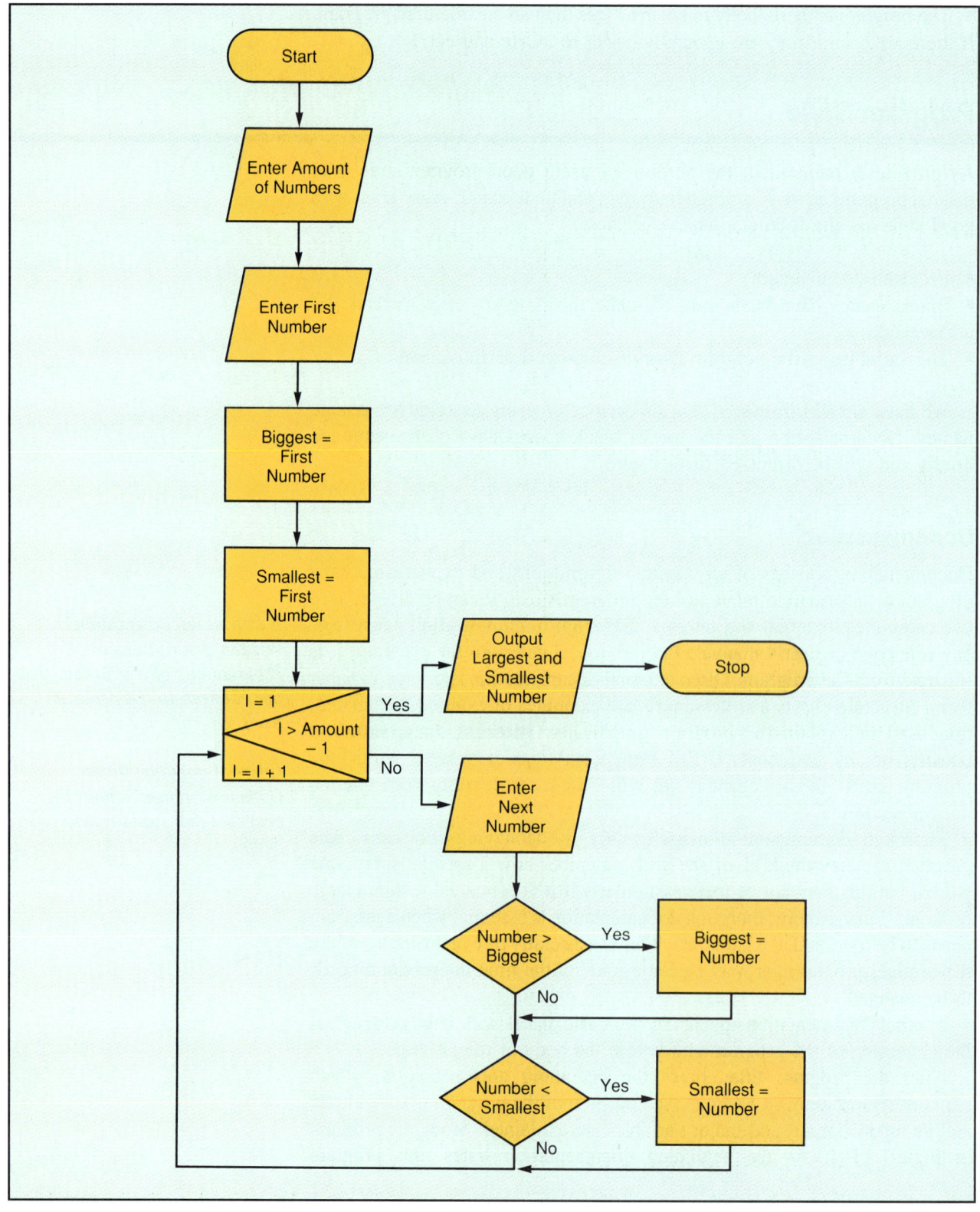

FIGURE 11-1 *Continued*

```
10  REM *** DETERMINE LARGEST AND SMALLEST NUMBER IN A SERIES. ***
20  REM ***     MAJOR VARIABLES:                                ***
30  REM ***         NMBR       THE NUMBER CURRENTLY BEING READ  ***
40  REM ***         AMT        HOW MANY NUMBERS ARE TO BE INPUT ***
50  REM ***         BIGGEST    CURRENT LARGEST NUMBER           ***
60  REM ***         SMALLEST   CURRENT SMALLEST NUMBER          ***
70  REM ***
80  REM *** DETERMINE HOW MANY NUMBERS WILL BE READ. ***
90  INPUT "HOW MANY NUMBERS ARE THERE";AMT
100 REM *** READ FIRST NUMBER AND SET BIGGEST AND SMALLEST TO IT. ***
110 INPUT "ENTER THE FIRST NUMBER";NMBR
120 BIGGEST  = NMBR
130 SMALLEST = NMBR
140 REM
150 REM *** READ REST OF NUMBERS. ***
160 FOR I = 1 TO (AMT - 1)
170    INPUT "ENTER THE NEXT NUMBER";NMBR
180    REM *** IF NUMBER IS LARGER THAN BIGGEST, ASSIGN IT TO BIGGEST. ***
190    IF NMBR > BIGGEST THEN BIGGEST = NMBR
200    REM *** IF NUMBER IS SMALLER THAN SMALLEST, ASSIGN IT TO SMALLEST. ***
210    IF NMBR < SMALLEST THEN SMALLEST = NMBR
220 NEXT I
235 REM
240 REM *** PRINT LARGEST AND SMALLEST NUMBERS. ***
250 PRINT "THE LARGEST NUMBER IS ";BIGGEST
260 PRINT "THE SMALLEST NUMBER IS ";SMALLEST
999 END
```

```
RUNNH

HOW MANY NUMBERS ARE THERE? 6
ENTER THE FIRST NUMBER? 23
ENTER THE NEXT NUMBER? 27
ENTER THE NEXT NUMBER? 6
ENTER THE NEXT NUMBER? 45
ENTER THE NEXT NUMBER? 60
ENTER THE NEXT NUMBER? 17
THE LARGEST NUMBER IS  60
THE SMALLEST NUMBER IS  6
```

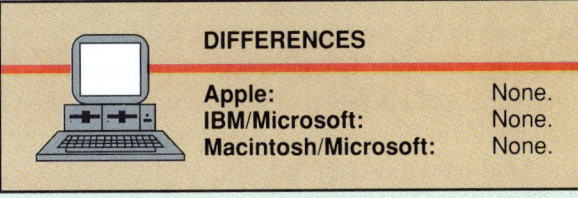

DIFFERENCES

Apple:	None.
IBM/Microsoft:	None.
Macintosh/Microsoft:	None.

determines the largest and smallest numbers in a sequence of numbers. Each of the major variables is listed along with its purpose. Notice that the loop control variable I is not listed here; it is not necessary to explain minor variables such as this, because their purposes are limited and generally self-evident within the program.

Documentation that is placed within the body of a program is usually brief, consisting of no more than a couple of lines. Look at the comment before the first INPUT statement in Figure 11–1:

```
80 REM *** DETERMINE HOW MANY NUMBERS WILL BE READ. ***
```

This comment briefly explains that the INPUT statement following it asks the user how many numbers will be entered and then reads the response. Comments should be used to explain the purpose of control statements. The following statement briefly explains the purpose of the FOR/NEXT loop:

```
140 REM *** READ REST OF NUMBERS. ***
```

Similar short comments have been placed throughout this program. These help the reader to identify what is happening in the program.

The Use of Blank Lines and Spaces

Imagine an essay written for an English class that has no paragraphs, margins, or blank lines. The essay would be a sheet of paper filled with sentence after sentence. It would not be easy to read or understand. Certainly it would not be enjoyable to read and would not receive a good grade.

A programmer should attempt to make a program as easy to read as a well-written English essay. Although the use of blank lines and spacing make no difference to the computer, they can make a great deal of difference to humans.

The word REM can be used alone on a line to separate sections of a program. This is particularly useful for separating subroutines from one another. Also, REM statements containing asterisks (or other characters such as the underscore) can be used to separate these sections visually. You may choose to follow the style used in this textbook or develop your own. The main idea is to make it easy for the reader to identify sections within the program.

Spaces within BASIC statements can also improve readability as shown in Figure 11–2. As far as the computer is concerned, it is not necessary to leave spaces between variables and operators. The computer would be able to execute all of the statements in Figure 11–2, but those on the right side are easier for humans to read than those on the left.

Without Spacing	With Spacing
AMT=AMT+(AMT*PERCENT)	AMT = AMT + (AMT * PERCENT)
WHILE(COUNT<>100)OR(X*Y>10)	WHILE (COUNT < > 100) OR (X * Y > 10)
IF A$="S" THEN TTL=TTL+1	IF A$ = "S" THEN TTL = TTL + 1

FIGURE 11–2
Using Spacing to Make Statements More Readable

Learning Check

1. A structure chart is an example of _____ _____.
2. Comments within a program are called _____ _____.
3. Name the two main places where comments are used in a program.

Answers

1. external documentation 2. internal documentation 3. At the beginning of the program, and within the body of the program.

A Tale of Two Bugs

The story of the first computer bug has become a legend. In the summer of 1945, something went wrong with the Mark II, a large electromechanical device used by the Department of Defense. Although the machine was not working properly, the operating personnel could find no obvious problem. A continued search revealed a large moth that had been beaten to death by one of the electromechanical relays. The moth was pulled out with tweezers and taped to a log book (now exhibited in the Naval Museum at the Naval Surface Weapons Center, Dahlgren, Virginia). "From then on," said Commodore Grace Hopper, one of the people working with the machine, "when the officer came in to ask if we were accomplishing anything, we told him we were 'debugging' the computer." Thus the phrases "bugs in the program" and "debugging the program" became popular in describing programming errors.

Few people realize, however, that the use of the word "bug" to mean an error is more than 100 years old. Thomas Alva Edison used the word in a letter to Theodore Puskas, Edison's representative in France, on November 13, 1878. He wrote:

> I have the right principle and am on the right track, but time, hard work, and some good luck are necessary too. It has been just so in all of my inventions. The first step is an intuition, and comes with a burst, then difficulties arise—this thing gives out and then that—"bugs"—as such little faults and difficulties are called—show themselves and months of intense watching, study and labor are requisite before commercial success—or failure—is certainly reached.

The Two Types of Program Errors

Program errors can be divided into two broad categories: syntax and logic. Each of these types will be discussed, along with techniques for avoiding and correcting them.

Syntax Errors

The most common type of error for beginning programmers is the syntax error. Fortunately, it is also the easiest type of error to locate and correct. **Syntax errors** are violations of the grammatical rules of a programming language. Mistyping a word is the most frequent cause of syntax errors. Consider the following statement:

```
120 IS X >= 8 THEN PRINT X
```

The typing error in this statement can easily be spotted and can be corrected by reentering the line as follows:

```
120 IF X >= 8 THEN PRINT X
```

Most syntax errors can be caught by careful proofreading. All syntax errors must be corrected before a program can be executed.

Syntax error
A violation of the grammatical rules of a language.

Logic Errors

Logic errors are flaws in the algorithm that has been developed to solve a programming problem. These errors can be divided into two categories: those that cause the program to stop executing prematurely (**run-time errors**), and those in which program execution terminates properly but the output is incorrect.

There are many logic errors that can cause a program to stop executing prematurely. For example, the following statement will cause a run-time error because the computer will not allow division by zero:

```
230 AMT = 887.0 / 0
```

In this example the error may seem obvious, but suppose this program segment were rewritten to look like this:

```
220 INPUT "ENTER THE DIVISOR";DIV
230 AMT = 887.0 / DIV
```

In this case, the program is dependent upon the user to enter a number that can be used as a divisor. The programmer should rewrite this program

Logic error
A flaw in an algorithm developed to solve a programming problem.

Run-time error
A logic error that causes program execution to stop prematurely.

segment so that if the user enters an unusable value, such as zero, he or she will be asked to reenter the divisor. It could be done like this:

```
20 INPUT "ENTER THE DIVISOR";DIV
30 WHILE DIV = 0
40    PRINT "DIVISION BY ZERO IS NOT ALLOWED."
50    INPUT "PLEASE ENTER A DIVISOR OTHER THAN ZERO";DIV
60 NEXT
70 AMT = TTL / DIV
```

This WHILE loop will be executed only if the user enters a zero. In that case, the user will be asked to reenter the number. This new number will then be checked to make certain it is not also a zero. This technique is referred to as **error trapping.** The program has been written in such a way that the error (which in this case is caused by invalid input) is trapped. Program execution cannot continue until the user enters a value for DIV that can be used by the program.

Error trapping
Writing a program in such a way that it "traps" errors such as invalid data.

The most difficult aspect of run-time errors is that often they do not show up every time a program is executed. In the preceding example, the program will continue to execute correctly so long as a zero is not entered for the value of DIV. Figure 11–3 lists some common run-time errors.

The program in Figure 11–4 contains the second type of logic error, which causes incorrect output. The loop in this program is supposed to execute N times, but because the controlling condition is incorrectly stated, it executes only N − 1 times. Line 20 is correctly written as follows:

```
20 WHILE LOOP <= N
```

```
Division by zero.

Attempting to assign a character value to a numeric variable.

Attempting to transfer control to a nonexistent line number.

Attempting to use an array subscript larger than the maximum stated in the DIM statement (or greater than 10, if no DIM statement has been used).
```

FIGURE 11–3
Common Run-Time Errors

```
10 LOOP = 1
20 WHILE LOOP < N
30    PRINT "THIS LOOP SHOULD EXECUTE N TIMES"
40    PRINT "IT REALLY EXECUTES N - 1 TIMES."
50    PRINT "LOOK AT THE TEST IN THE WHILE"
60    PRINT "EXPRESSION FOR THE REASON (HINT: <)."
70    LOOP = LOOP + 1
80 NEXT
```

FIGURE 11–4
Off-By-One Error

Program Testing Methods

It has been estimated that about 80 percent of professional programmers' time is spent in testing and modifying programs that have already been written. Even after the programmer thinks that a program is working correctly, it is difficult, if not impossible, to determine if it will always work properly with all types of data. The ability of a program to work properly regardless of the data entered to it is referred to as its **reliability. Program testing** is the process of systematically checking a program to determine its reliability.

All of the various methods of testing programs for errors can be divided into two categories: static testing and run-time testing. *Static testing* involves examining the text of the program itself for errors. One type of static testing is *desk checking,* which was discussed in Chapter 2. Programmers sometimes say they are "playing computer" when they desk-check a program. They are trying to mentally trace through the program, following the same steps the computer would follow during program execution. This type of testing can be used to locate both syntax and logic errors. Before entering a program into the computer, it is a good idea to do some desk checking with some sample data. A few extra minutes spent at this stage of program development can save hours of debugging later.

Run-time testing takes place while the program is executing. One type of run-time testing is **program tracing,** which involves inserting PRINT statements into the program at locations where the programmer suspects that incorrect results are being calculated. This process helps the programmer pinpoint errors or flaws in the program's algorithm.

Look at the program at the top of Figure 11–5, which is supposed to calculate the following:

$$N + (N - 1) + (N - 2) + \ldots$$

When the value 3 is entered to this program, the output value of SUM is 3. We can calculate the correct output by hand and determine that it should be 6. One way of determining what is wrong is by examining the values of NMBR and SUM each time through the loop. This is done by inserting the following statement right before the end of the loop:

```
95 PRINT "NMBR = ";NMBR,"SUM = ";SUM
```

Doing this will demonstrate that the value of SUM is 2 at the end of the first loop execution, when in fact it should be 3. This error occurs because the value of NMBR is decremented *before* it is added to SUM rather than afterward. The program at the bottom of Figure 11–5 shows how the program is correctly written. By using program tracing, we were able to pinpoint the logic error in this program.

Reliability
The ability of a program to work properly regardless of the data entered to it.

Program testing
Systematically checking a program to determine its reliability.

Program tracing
A method of locating program errors by inserting PRINT statements to check the values of specific variables.

FIGURE 11–5 Locating an Error By Using Program Tracing

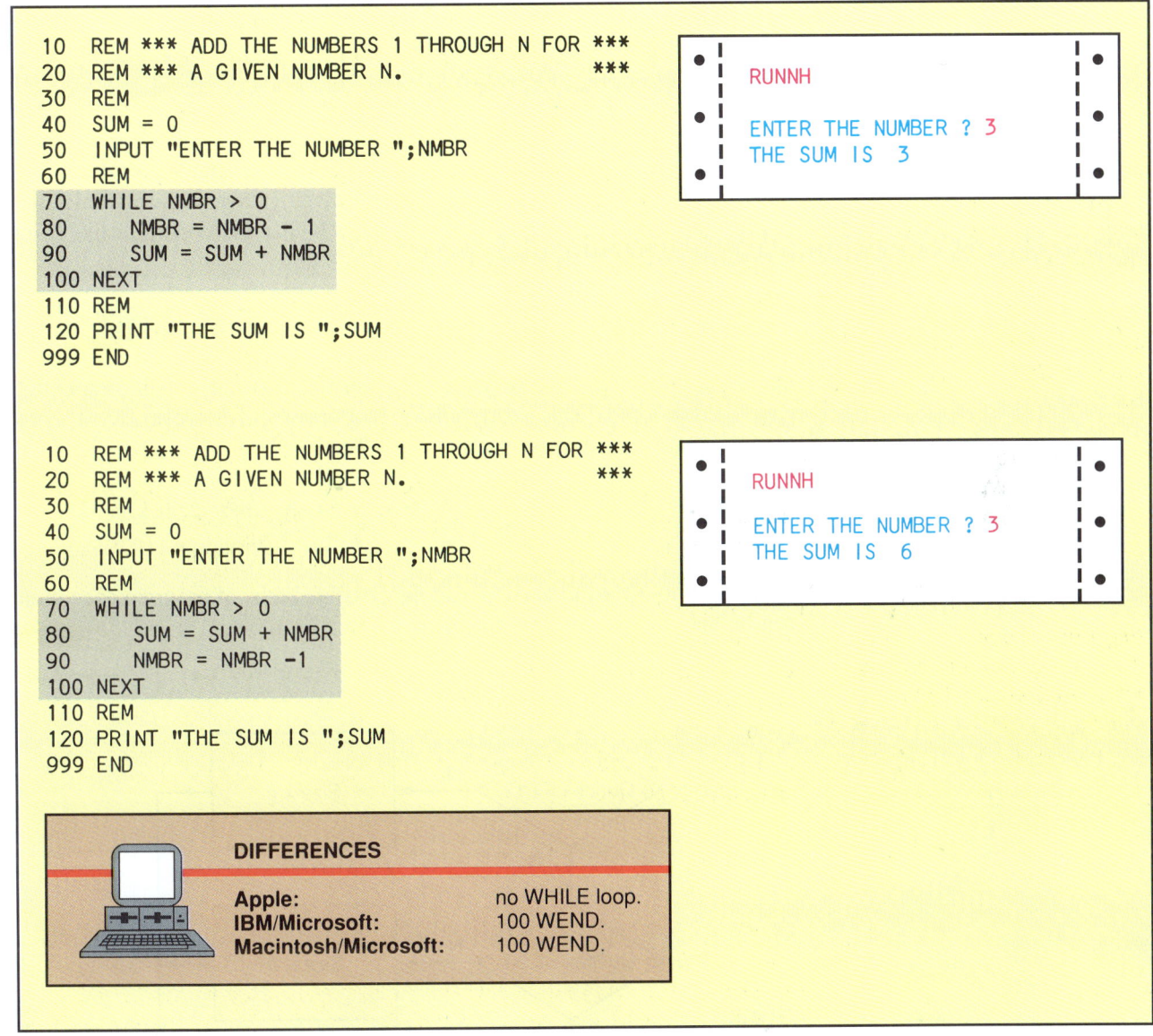

Program testing falls into two basic categories: complete program testing and selective program testing. **Complete program testing** involves testing all possible paths of execution in the program. This approach is possible only with very small programs. The number of possible paths in moderate to large programs is so great that the complete testing approach is not practical. **Selective program testing,** which involves testing the program using data with specific characteristics, is therefore normally used to determine if a program obtains correct results. One method of selective

Complete program testing
Testing all possible paths of program execution.

Selective program testing
Testing a program using data with specific characteristics.

testing is to make certain that a program works properly for boundary cases. *Boundary cases* are data that fall at the very extremes of the legal range of allowable data. Consider the following IF/THEN statement:

```
50 IF AGE > 21 THEN PRINT "THIS PERSON IS AN ADULT."
```

The purpose of this segment is to print the "adult" message if the person is 21 years of age or over. If we tested this segment by assigning a value of 21 to AGE (21 is at the boundary of the adult range), however, we would find that no message was printed. The problem is that the condition has been improperly stated. It is correctly written like this:

```
50 IF AGE >= 21 THEN PRINT "THIS PERSON IS AN ADULT."
```

Checking the boundary case helped us determine that the condition was not expressed properly. This procedure is more involved, however, for a more complex program segment such as the following:

```
70 IF OUNCES >= 12 THEN IF OUNCES >= 20 THEN SIZE$ = "A"
   ELSE SIZE$ = "B" ELSE SIZE$ = "C"
```

Drawing a flowchart to visualize all the possible paths of program execution can be helpful. Here is the flowchart for this example:

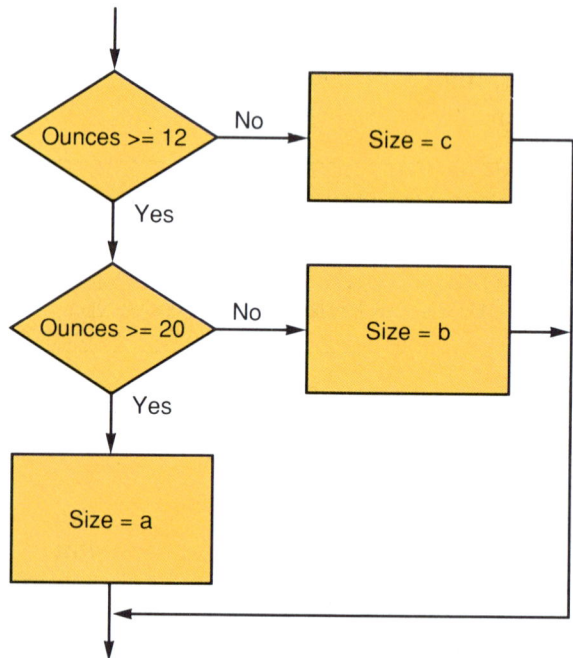

From this flowchart, we can determine that the following boundary values should be assigned to variable OUNCES for testing purposes: 12, 11, 19, and 20. If the program assigns the correct value to SIZE for each of these cases, we can be fairly certain that this IF/THEN/ELSE statement is working properly.

Report Writing

In business, computer programs often need to be written to generate reports. For example, a company might need an end-of-the-year fiscal report showing expenses and profits for each of its departments. Another example would be an accounts receivable report for a company that itemized the amount owed by each of its customers. These reports often involve summarizing information in order to give the reader an overall analysis of large quantities of data. Writing a report of this type often involves reading data that is stored in a file and printing this data plus various summary information.

To illustrate report writing, we will develop a program that prints monthly accounts receivable information for the W. R. Horton Advertising Agency. The company has a sequential file that contains all of the data needed for the program. Each record in the file consists of a customer's name, account number, and the amount of a single bill. These files are arranged numerically by the account number. The program that is to be written must perform the following tasks:

1. Read each record until the end of the file is reached.
2. Write the customer's account number, name, and the amount of each bill.
3. Total all bills due on a single account, and print this information.
4. Total all bills for all accounts, and print this information.

The structure chart for this program is shown in Figure 11–6. An example of data that might be stored in the input file follows.

```
14792
JANNING ELECTRIC
89.47
14792
JANNING ELECTRIC
37.65
19002
BERK INSURANCE
112.86
19002
BERK INSURANCE
43.89
19002
BERK INSURANCE
86.60
24605
COLUMBIA TRAVEL
185.42
```

FIGURE 11-6 Structure Chart for Accounts Receivable Program

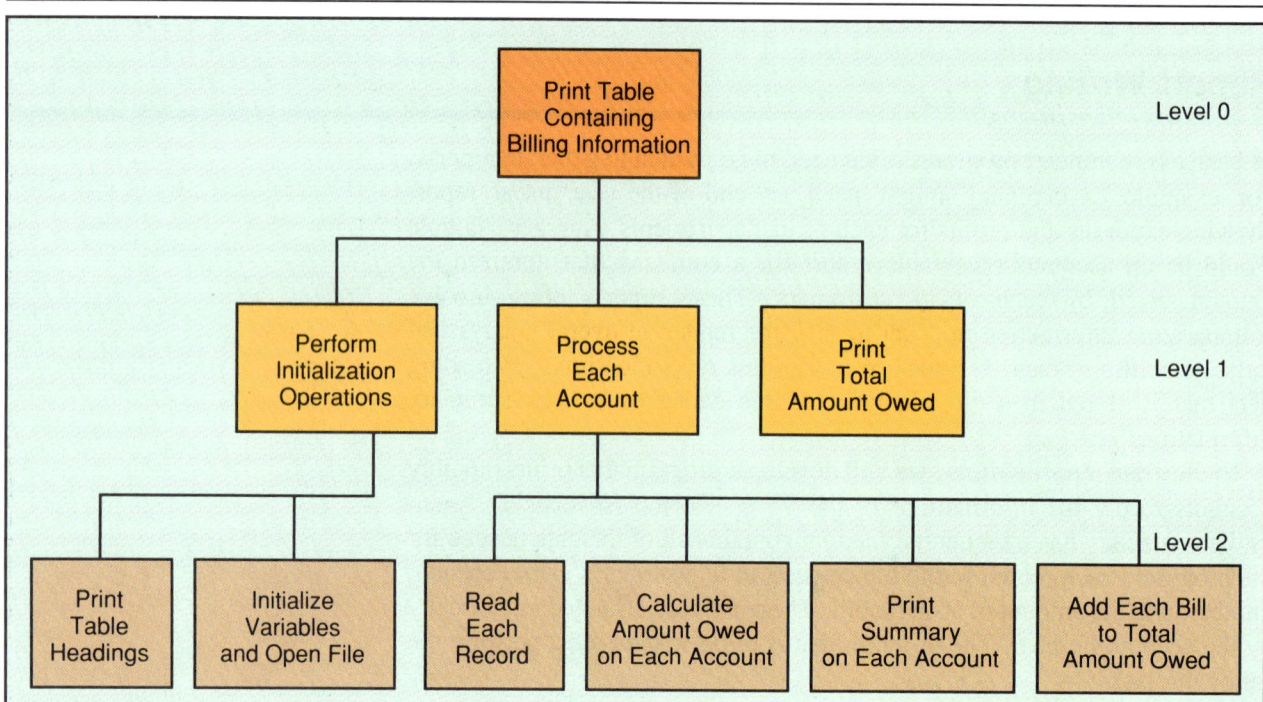

Control break
The situation that occurs when there is a change in the value of a specified field in a record.

Notice that the customers' accounts are in order by account number and that all the bills for a given customer are stored sequentially. In order to determine when data on a new account has been read, the program will need to determine if a given account number is identical to the one in the previous record. If the account numbers do not match, it will be necessary for a control break to occur. A **control break** occurs when there is a change in the value of a specified field. In the case of the accounts receivable program, a control break will occur when an account number is read that is different than the number in the record immediately preceding it. Two control breaks will occur when the data file shown above is processed; the first one when account number 19002 is first encountered and the second when account number 24605 is encountered.

Therefore, the program must be written so that the value of the account number in the previous record is compared to that of the current record. If they differ, the summary information on the previous account will be printed. Also, the variable used to store the total amount owed by a particular company will need to be reinitialized to zero in preparation to summing the amount owed on the next account. Otherwise, the amount of the bill stored in the previous record will simply be added to the total amount owed on the current account.

Study the completed program in Figure 11-7. First, the subroutine starting at line 1000 is called to open the input file, initialize the necessary

PROGRAM TESTING AND WRITING USER-FRIENDLY PROGRAMS 467

FIGURE 11-7 Accounts Receivable Program

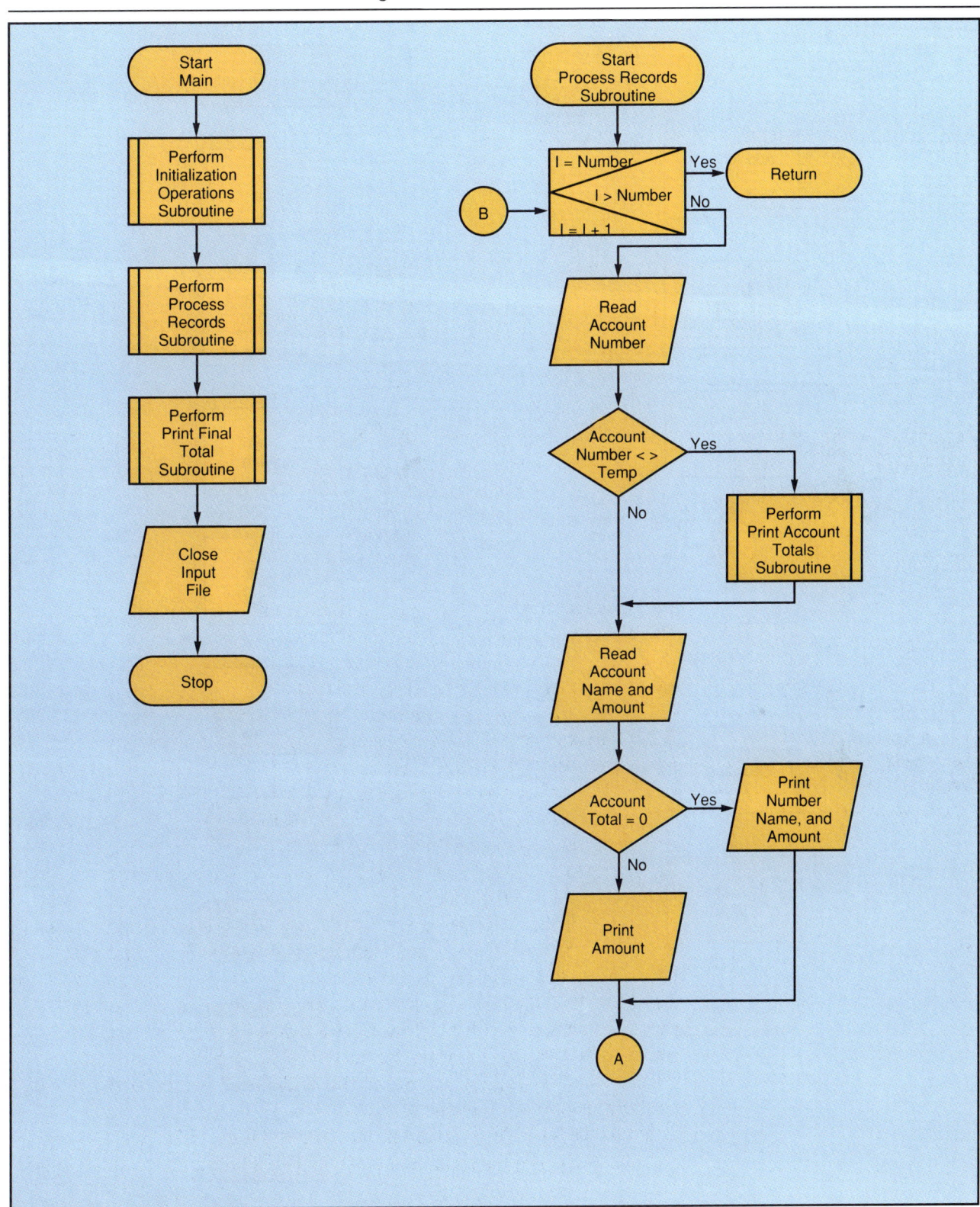

FIGURE 11–7 *Continued*

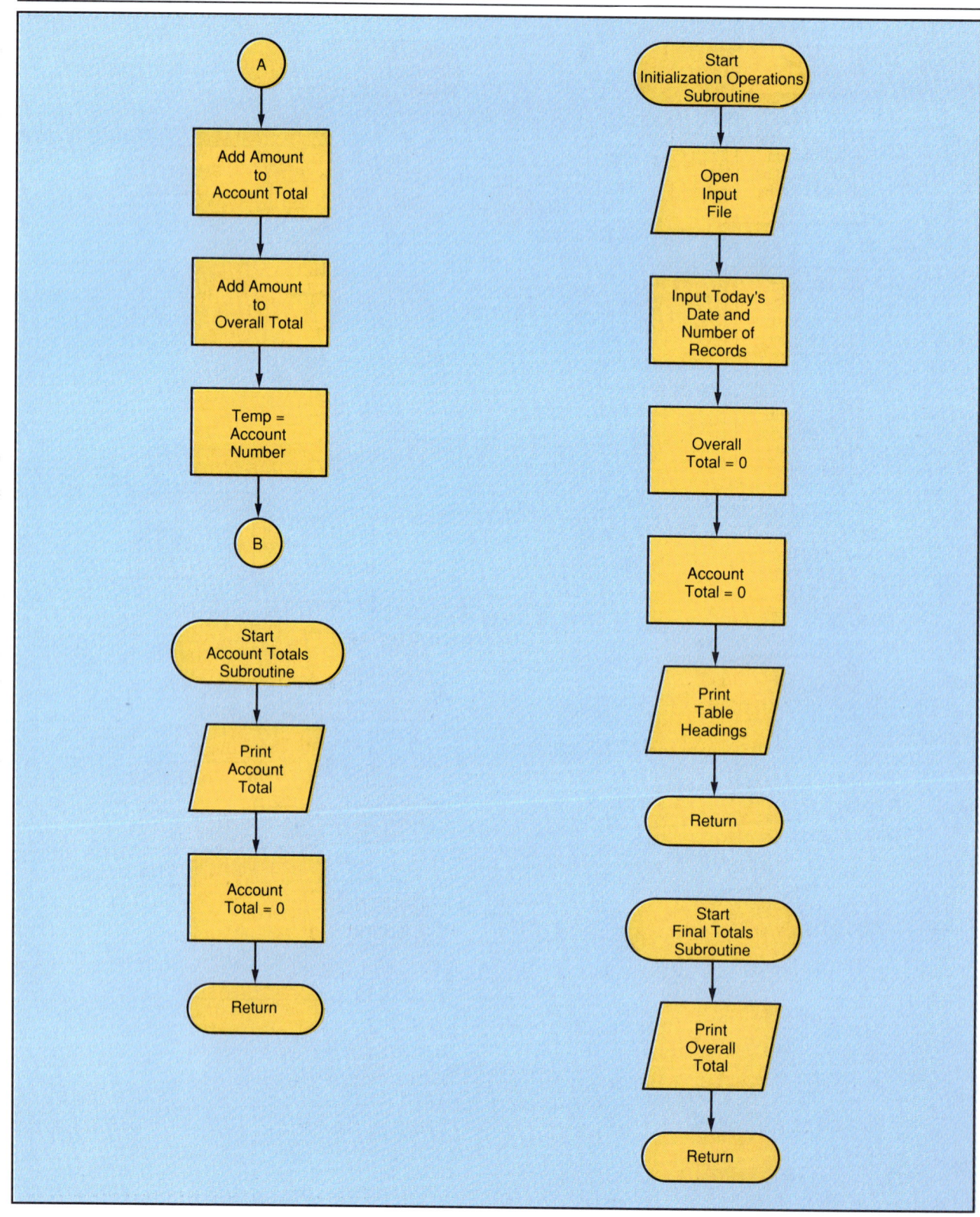

FIGURE 11–7 *Continued*

```
10   REM ***             ACCOUNTS RECEIVABLE PROGRAM              ***
20   REM
30   REM *** THIS PROGRAM PREPARES AN ACCOUNTS RECEIVABLE ***
40   REM *** REPORT FOR THE R. W. HORTON ADVERTISING      ***
50   REM *** AGENCY.  EACH CUSTOMER'S BILLING RECORDS ARE ***
60   REM *** READ FROM A SEQUENTIAL FILE.  THIS INFORMA-  ***
70   REM *** TION IS THEN PRINTED ALONG WITH THE TOTAL    ***
80   REM *** AMOUNT OWED BY THE CUSTOMER AND THE TOTAL OF ***
90   REM *** ALL CUSTOMERS' ACCOUNTS.                     ***
100  REM
110  REM *** MAJOR VARIABLES:                             ***
120  REM ***     ATNMBR        ACCOUNT NUMBER             ***
130  REM ***     ANME$         NAME OF THE COMPANY        ***
140  REM ***     AMT           AMOUNT OF THE BILL         ***
150  REM ***     TTL           TOTAL OF ALL ACCOUNTS      ***
160  REM ***     TACCT         TOTAL OF EACH ACCOUNT      ***
170  REM
180  REM *** PERFORM INITIALIZATION OPERATIONS.
190  GOSUB 1000
200  REM
210  REM *** PERFORM PROCESS RECORDS.
220  GOSUB 2000
230  REM
240  REM *** PERFORM PRINT FINAL TOTAL.
250  GOSUB 4000
260  CLOSE #2
270  GOTO 9999
1000 REM ************************************************************
1010 REM ***              INITIALIZATION OPERATIONS              ***
1020 REM ************************************************************
1030 REM OPEN INPUT FILE AND INITIALIZE VARIABLES.          ***
1040 REM
1050 OPEN "BILLING" AS FILE #2
1060 INPUT "ENTER TODAY'S DATE";DTE$
1070 INPUT "HOW MANY RECORDS ARE IN THE INPUT FILE";NMBR
1080 TTL = 0
1090 TACCT = 0
1100 REM *** PRINT HEADINGS.
1110 PRINT
1120 H$ = "'CCCCCCCCCCCCCCCCCCCCCCCCCCCCCCCCCCCCCCCC"
1130 PRINT USING H$;"R. W. HORTON ADVERTISING AGENCY"
1140 PRINT
1150 PRINT USING H$;"ACCOUNTS RECEIVABLE REPORT"
1160 PRINT
1170 PRINT USING H$;DTE$
1180 PRINT
1190 RETURN
2000 REM ************************************************************
2010 REM ***                    PROCESS RECORDS                 ***
2020 REM ************************************************************
2030 REM
```

FIGURE 11–7 *Continued*

```
2040 REM *** READ EACH RECORDS AND UPDATE TOTAL AMOUNTS.      ***
2050 FOR I = 1 TO NMBR
2060     INPUT #2,ATNMBR
2070     IF I = 1 THEN TEMP = ATNMBR
2080     IF ATNMBR <> TEMP THEN GOSUB 3000
2090     INPUT #2,ANME$
2100     INPUT #2,AMT
2110     L1$ = "#####      'LLLLLLLLLLLLLLLLLLLLL  $###,###.##"
2120     L2$ = "                                   $###,###.##"
2130     IF TACCT = 0 THEN PRINT USING L1$,ATNMBR,ANME$,AMT
             ELSE PRINT USING L2$,AMT
2140     TACCT = TACCT + AMT
2150     TTL = TTL + AMT
2160     TEMP = ATNMBR
2170 NEXT I
2180 REM *** PRINT AMOUNT OWED ON LAST ACCOUNT PROCESSED.
2190 GOSUB 3000
2200 RETURN
3000 REM **********************************************************
3010 REM ***                  PRINT ACCOUNT TOTALS              ***
3020 REM **********************************************************
3030 REM *** PRINT TOTAL AMOUNT OWED ON CURRENT ACCOUNT.    ***
3040 PRINT
3050 L3$ = "'LLLLLLLLLLLLLLLLLLLLLLLL #####    $###,##.##"
3060 PRINT USING L3$;"**TOTAL OWED ON ACCOUNT",TEMP,TACCT
3070 PRINT
3080 TACCT = 0
3090 RETURN
4000 REM **********************************************************
4010 REM ***                  PRINT FINAL TOTAL                 ***
4020 REM **********************************************************
4030 REM
4040 REM *** PRINT TOTAL AMOUNT OWED ON ALL ACCOUNTS.       ***
4050 PRINT USING H$,"_____"
4060 PRINT
4070 L4$ = "'LLLLLLLLLLLLLLLLLLLLLLLLLLLL    $###,###.##"
4080 PRINT USING L4$;"***TOTAL OF ALL ACCOUNTS",TTL
4090 RETURN
9999 END
```

FIGURE 11-7 Continued

```
RUNNH

ENTER TODAY'S DATE? 4/28/89
HOW MANY RECORDS ARE IN THE INPUT FILE? 6

          R. W. HORTON ADVERTISING AGENCY

             ACCOUNTS RECEIVABLE REPORT

                     4/28/89

  14792      JANNING ELECTRIC         $      89.47
                                      $      37.65

**TOTAL OWED ON ACCOUNT    14792      $     127.12

  19002      BERK INSURANCE           $     112.86
                                      $      43.89
                                      $      86.60

**TOTAL OWED ON ACCOUNT    19002      $     243.35

  24605      COLUMBIA TRAVEL          $     185.42

**TOTAL OWED ON ACCOUNT    24605      $     185.42
             _____

***TOTAL OF ALL ACCOUNTS              $     555.89
```

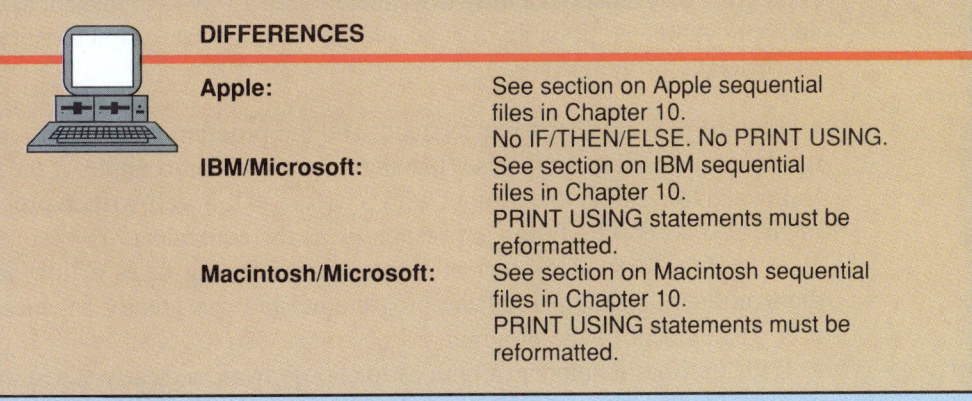

DIFFERENCES

Apple: See section on Apple sequential files in Chapter 10. No IF/THEN/ELSE. No PRINT USING.

IBM/Microsoft: See section on IBM sequential files in Chapter 10. PRINT USING statements must be reformatted.

Macintosh/Microsoft: See section on Macintosh sequential files in Chapter 10. PRINT USING statements must be reformatted.

variables, and print the report headings. The subroutine starting at line 2000 is called to read each record. Notice that the account number of the previous record is stored in the variable TEMP. TEMP is compared to the current account number (ATNMBR) and if these values do not match, the subroutine starting at line 3000 is called to print the total amount owed by the previous account. As each record is read, the amount owed is added to the total owed by that account and the total of all of the accounts. After all of the records are processed, the overall total amount owed is printed, and program execution terminates.

Printer Control Characters

Today most printers have special features that allow the programmer to control the manner in which output is printed in a variety of ways. Special control characters are placed within a program and sent to the printer by means of a PRINT statement. The particular control characters used depend on the printer being used. For example, on the Epson MX-80, a printer that is commonly used with microcomputers, the statement, 20 PRINT CHR$(10), causes the paper to advance one line, leaving a blank line. This advance occurs because the line feed character is ASCII code 10. These printer control characters can be used to cause output to be printed in different type styles such as compressing the print, underlining the output, and printing it in superscript and subscript. Some examples of different type styles are shown in Figure 11–8. Consult your printer manual for details on this subject. You will need to experiment to become proficient in the use of printer control characters.

Writing User-Friendly Programs

User-friendly
Describes a program that is designed to be easy and enjoyable for people to use.

A program that is **user-friendly** is written in such a way as to make it as easy and enjoyable as possible for people to use. Some characteristics of user-friendly programs are

- The prompts are easy to understand, and the program is written to make it as easy as possible for the user to enter responses. For example, if the user is directed to respond to a prompt with a y (for yes), a well-written program might also accept the following responses as the equivalent: Y, Yes, yeah, YES, and so forth. This sort of careful programming takes a little more thoughtfulness on the part of the programmer but can greatly enhance the user's enjoyment of the program.
- If the user has a number of options to choose from, a clearly stated menu should list all of these options and the codes necessary for choosing them.
- The program should be able to handle invalid input and print a polite error message. If the program is interactive, the user should be prompted to reenter the necessary input.

> This is a line of type in NORMAL mode.
>
> This is a line of type in COMPRESSED mode.
>
> **This is a line of type in BOLDED mode.**
>
> <u>This is a line of type in underline mode.</u>
>
> This is a line of type in superscript mode.

FIGURE 11–8
Examples of Different Printer Type Models

By writing programs that can handle a wide variety of invalid user input properly, many run-time errors and logic errors can be avoided. For example, if the data to be entered should be within a given range, the computer should check it to make certain it meets the specified requirements before the program continues. If it does not meet those requirements, an error message should be printed, and the user should be prompted to reenter the data. Below is a program segment in which the user is supposed to enter a digit representing a day of the week:

```
100 INPUT "ENTER AN INTEGER REPRESENTING THE DAY (1-7)";DY$
110 WHILE (ASCII(DY$) < 49) OR (ASCII(DY$) > 55)
120    PRINT "THE NUMBER MUST BE BETWEEN 1 AND 7."
130    INPUT "PLEASE REENTER THE DAY";DY$
140 NEXT
```

Learning Check

1. Errors caused by not following the rules of a language are _____ errors.
2. _____ errors occur when there is a flaw in a program's algorithm.
3. In _____ _____, PRINT statements are inserted at strategic points within the program to determine the value of specific variables at these points.
4. Logic errors always cause programs to stop executing prematurely. True or false?
5. _____ program testing involves testing all possible paths of execution in a program.

Answers

1. syntax 2. Logic 3. program tracing 4. False 5. Complete

The value that the user enters should be an integer. However, the value is read to the string variable *DY$*, so that a run-time error will be avoided if a noninteger value is accidentally entered. The ASCII value of the character is checked to make certain that it falls within the 1 through 7 range. Programs that are user-friendly should be able to handle any type of invalid data.

The program designed in the following section ("A Programming Problem") illustrates the characteristics of a user-friendly program.

A Programming Problem

This section will be somewhat different from that in previous chapters. Rather than developing a new program, we will discuss how the program that was developed at the end of Chapter 7 might be tested to determine that it works properly. Figure 11–9 contains the program; it has been modified so that it is capable of handling invalid user input properly.

First spend a few moments looking at the layout of this program. Notice that blank REM statements have been used to separate main sections of the program. Lines of asterisks have been used to separate the subroutines and make their starting locations easy to find.

The main program begins by transferring control to subroutine INPUT, starting at line 1000. The purpose of this subroutine is to allow the user to enter the data needed by the program; each response is checked for its validity. Notice that in line 1060 the price of the book is stored in the character variable PRICE$. The purpose of assigning this value (which should be numeric) to a character variable is to prevent program execution from terminating prematurely if the user incorrectly enters non-numeric data.

Next, program execution transfers to subroutine PRICE CHECK, starting at line 7000. This subroutine calls subroutine CHARACTER CHECK to make certain that each character in the string PRICE$ is either a numeric digit or a period (the only values allowed in a real number). If this is true, the VAL function is used to convert PRICE$ to a numeric value in line 7140. If the value entered is not a number, the user is prompted to reenter the book price, and program control once again transfers to CHARACTER CHECK to determine if this new value is a valid number.

In line 1140, the user is asked to enter the book type code, which should be a 1, 2, or 3. Notice that this code is read to a character variable, CODE$. Once again, this is to protect the program if the user incorrectly enters non-numeric data. Next, the program calls subroutine CODE CHECK, starting at line 5000. The statement at line 5060 checks to see if the value entered is more than one character in length or is outside the range 1 through 3. If it is invalid, the user is prompted to reenter the code. Once a usable code has been entered, program control passes back to line 1180, where this code is changed from a character to a numeric value.

FIGURE 11–9 Program BOOKCOST

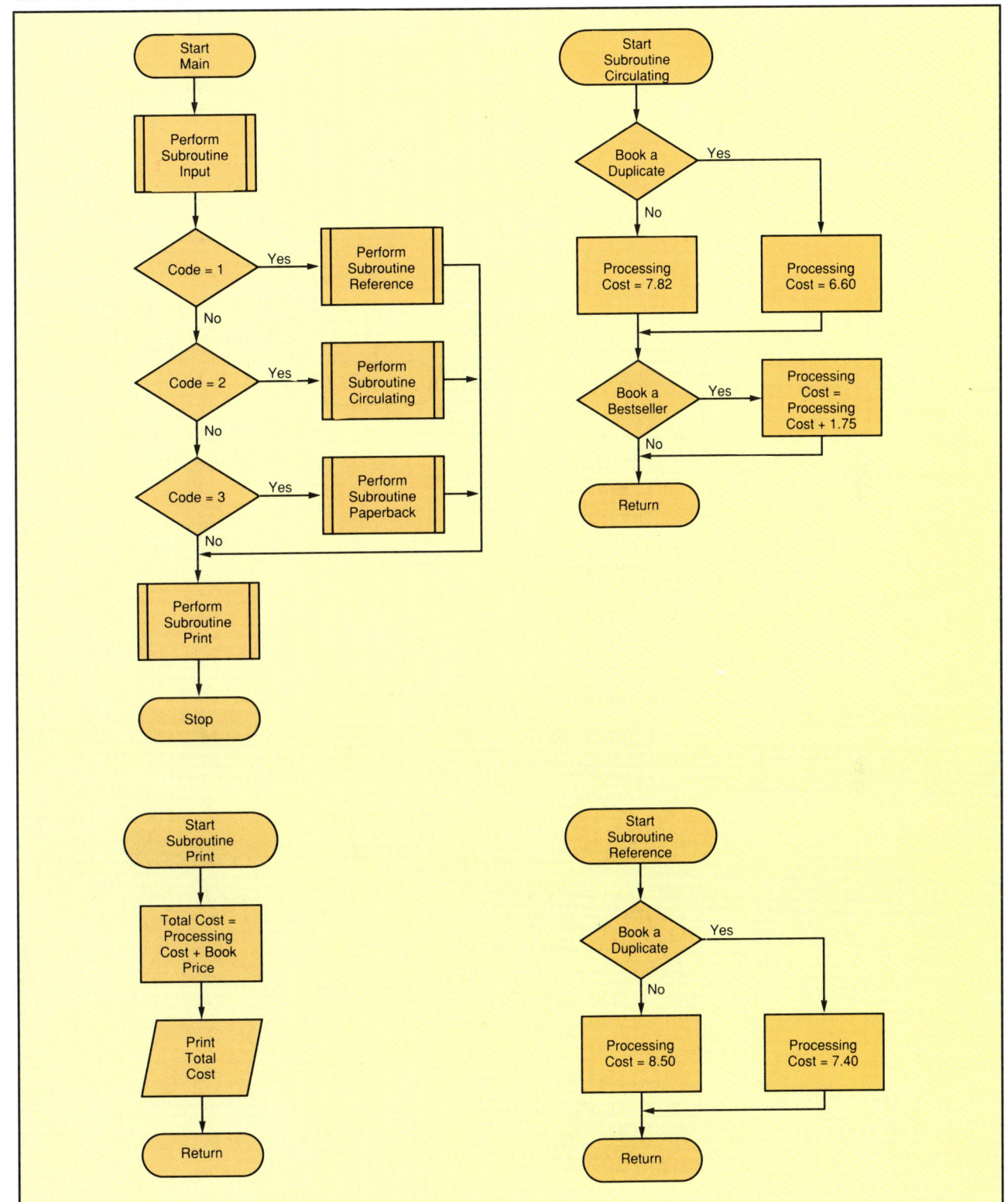

FIGURE 11–9 *Continued*

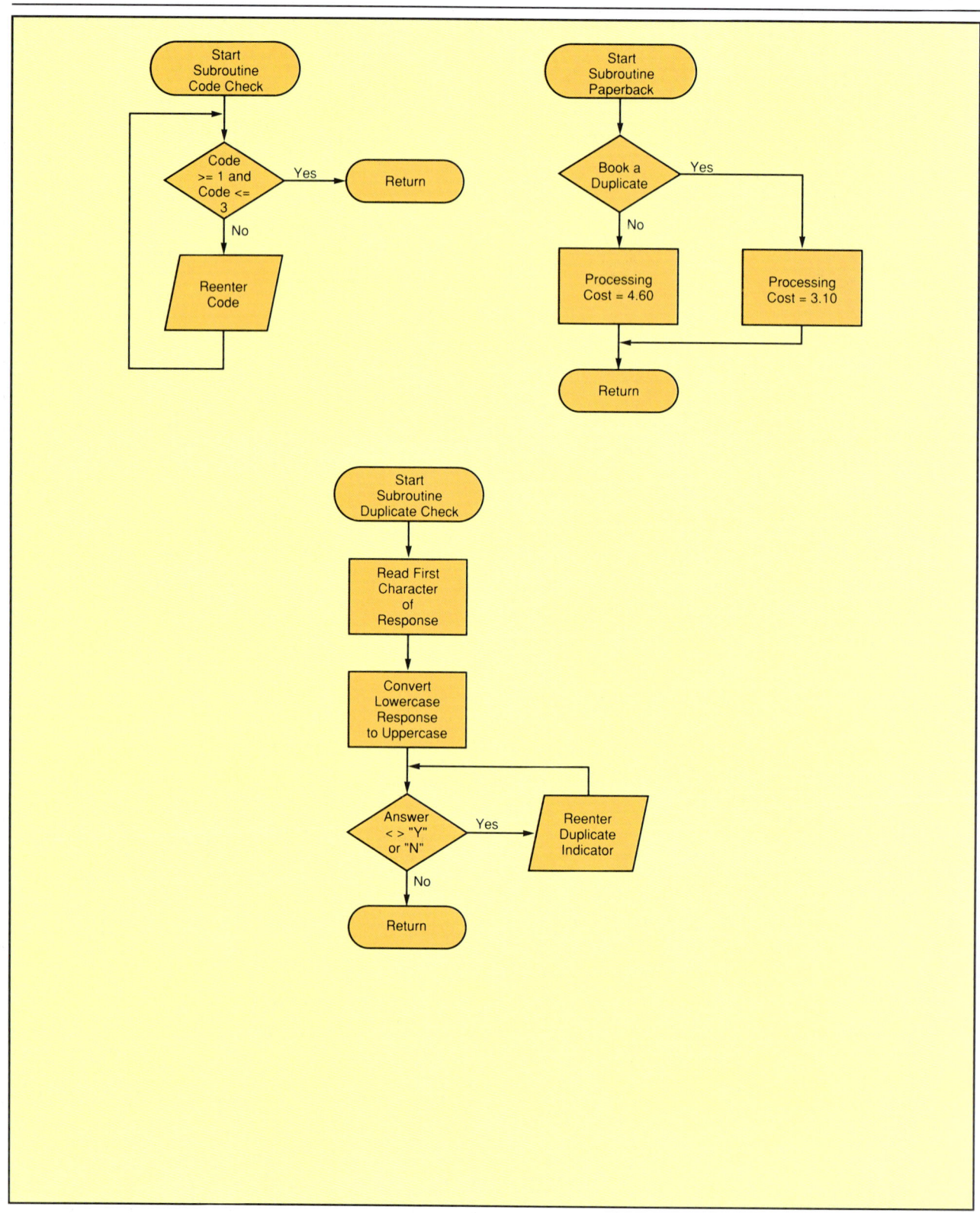

FIGURE 11-9 Continued

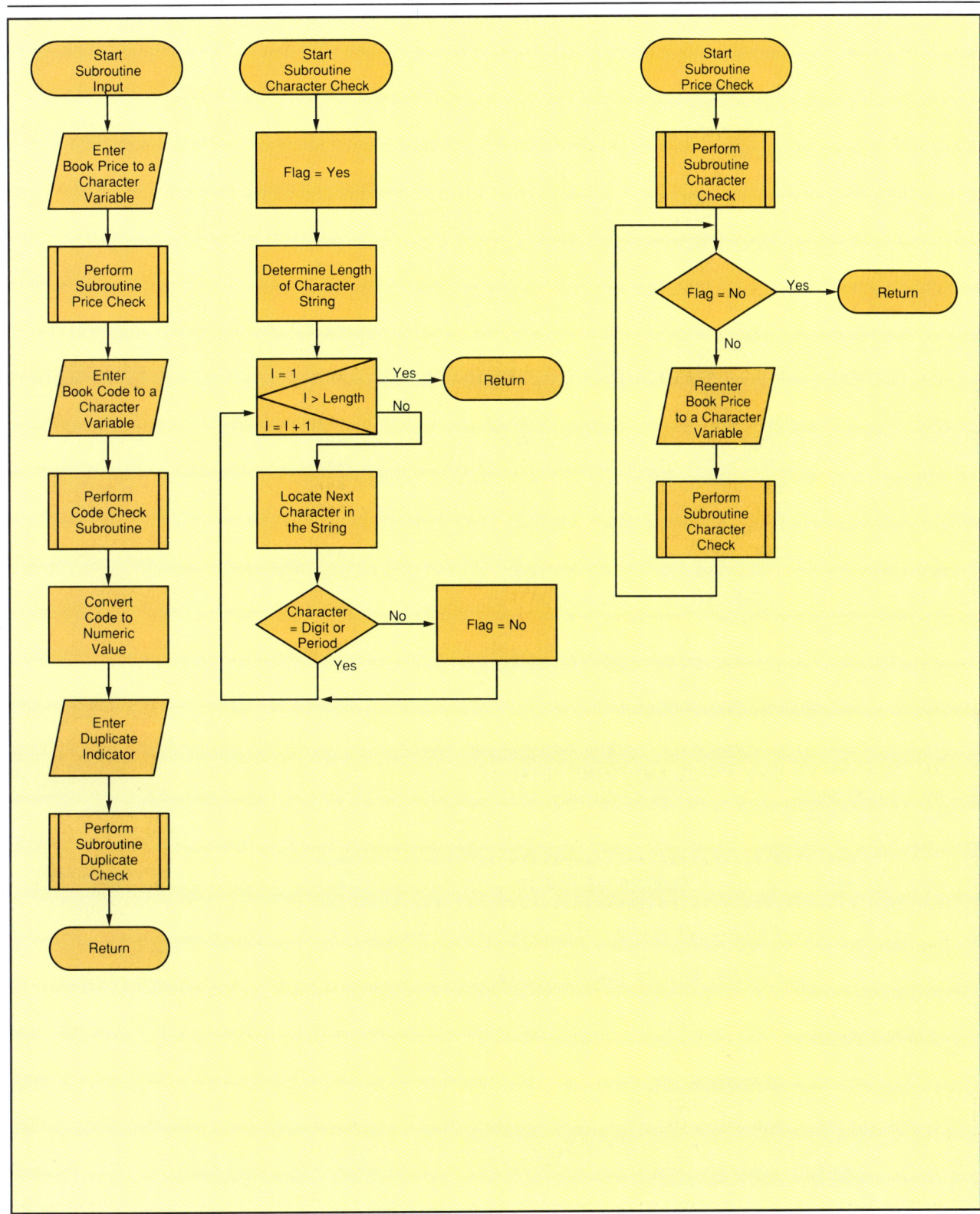

FIGURE 11–9 Continued

```
10    REM ***                     PROGRAM BOOKCOST                ***
20    REM
30    REM ***    THIS PROGRAM CALCULATES THE TOTAL COST OF         ***
40    REM ***    A BOOK. THE TOTAL COST IS OBTAINED BY             ***
50    REM ***    ADDING THE PRICE OF THE BOOK TO THE PRO-          ***
60    REM ***    CESSING COST, WHICH IS BASED ON THE TYPE.         ***
70    REM ***        1.  REFERENCE BOOK                            ***
80    REM ***              NOT A DUPLICATE    $8.50                ***
90    REM ***              DUPLICATE          $7.40                ***
100   REM ***        2.  CIRCULATING BOOK                          ***
110   REM ***              NOT A DUPLICATE    $7.82                ***
120   REM ***              DUPLICATE          $6.60                ***
130   REM ***              BESTSELLER         $1.75                ***
140   REM ***        3.  PAPERBACK                                 ***
150   REM ***              NOT A DUPLICATE    $4.60                ***
160   REM ***              DUPLICATE          $3.10                ***
170   REM
180   REM ***    MAJOR VARIABLES:                                  ***
190   REM ***      PRICE          PRICE OF THE BOOK                ***
200   REM ***      CODE           TYPE OF BOOK AS ABOVE            ***
210   REM ***      DUP$           IS BOOK A DUPLICATE(Y/N)?        ***
220   REM ***      PRCST          PROCESSING COST                  ***
230   REM ***      SELLER$        IS BOOK A BESTSELLER(Y/N)?       ***
240   REM ***      TTCST          TOTAL COST OF BOOK               ***
250   REM
260   REM *** CALL SUBROUTINE TO ENTER DATA.
270   GOSUB 1000
280   REM
290   REM *** CALL APPROPRIATE SUBROUTINE TO CALCULATE
300   REM *** THE PROCESSING COST.
310   ON CODE GOSUB 2000,3000,4000
320   REM
330   REM *** CALL SUBROUTINE TO ADD PROCESSING COST
340   REM *** TO BOOK PRICE AND PRINT TOTAL COST.
350   GOSUB 9000
360   GOTO 9999
1000  REM
1010  REM *******************************************************
1020  REM ***                 SUBROUTINE INPUT                ***
1030  REM *******************************************************
1040  REM *** SUBROUTINE TO ALLOW USER TO ENTER DATA.         ***
1050  REM
1060  INPUT "ENTER PRICE OF THE BOOK";PRICE$
1070  REM
1080  REM *** CHECK FOR INVALID PRICE.
1090  GOSUB 7010
1100  PRINT
1110  PRINT "1 - REFERENCE BOOK "
1120  PRINT "2 - CIRCULATING BOOK "
1130  PRINT "3 - PAPERBACK "
1140  PRINT "ENTER TYPE CODE FOR THE BOOK, USING THE CODES LISTED ABOVE ";
      CODE$
```

FIGURE 11–9 Continued

```
1150 REM
1160 REM *** CHECK FOR INVALID CODE.
1170 GOSUB 5010
1180 CODE = VAL(CODE$)
1190 INPUT "IS BOOK A DUPLICATE (Y/N)";DUP$
1200 AN$ = DUP$
1210 REM
1220 REM *** CHECK FOR INVALID RESPONSE.
1230 GOSUB 6010
1240 DUP$ = AN$
1250 RETURN
2000 REM
2010 REM ***********************************************************
2020 REM ***                 SUBROUTINE REFERENCE              ***
2030 REM ***********************************************************
2040 REM *** SUBROUTINE TO CALCULATE PROCESSING COST OF        ***
2050 REM *** REFERENCE BOOK.                                   ***
2060 REM
2070 IF DUP$ = "Y" THEN PRCST = 7.40 ELSE PRCST = 8.50
2080 RETURN
3000 REM
3010 REM ***********************************************************
3020 REM ***                 SUBROUTINE CIRCULATING            ***
3030 REM ***********************************************************
3040 REM *** SUBROUTINE TO CALCULATE PROCESSING COST OF        ***
3050 REM *** CIRCULATING BOOK.                                 ***
3060 REM
3070 IF DUP$ = "Y" THEN PRCST = 6.60 ELSE PRCST = 7.82
3080 INPUT "IS THE BOOK A BESTSELLER (Y/N) ";SELLER$
3090 AN$ = SELLER$
3100 REM
3110 REM *** CHECK FOR INVALID RESPONSE.
3120 GOSUB 6010
3130 SELLER$ = AN$
3140 IF SELLER$ = "Y" THEN PRCST = PRCST + 1.75
3150 RETURN
4000 REM
4010 REM ***********************************************************
4020 REM ***                 SUBROUTINE PAPERBACK              ***
4030 REM ***********************************************************
4040 REM *** SUBROUTINE TO CALCULATE PROCESSING COST OF        ***
4050 REM *** PAPERBACK BOOK.                                   ***
4060 REM
4070 IF DUP$ = "Y" THEN PRCST = 3.10 ELSE PRCST = 4.60
4080 RETURN
5000 REM
5010 REM ***********************************************************
5020 REM ***                 SUBROUTINE CODE CHECK             ***
5030 REM ***********************************************************
5040 REM ***    ALLOW CODE TO BE REENTERED IF INVALID.         ***
5050 REM
```

FIGURE 11–9 *Continued*

```
5060 WHILE LEN(CODE$) > 1 OR ASCII(CODE$) < 49 OR ASCII(CODE$) > 51
5070    PRINT
5080    INPUT "TYPE CODE MUST BE 1, 2, OR 3. PLEASE REENTER CODE: ";CODE$
5090 NEXT
5100 PRINT
5110 RETURN
6000 REM
6010 REM ***********************************************************
6020 REM ***            SUBROUTINE DUPLICATE CHECK              ***
6030 REM ***********************************************************
6040 REM *** ALLOW USER RESPONSE TO BE REENTERED IF             ***
6050 REM *** INVALID.                                            ***
6060 REM
6070 AN$ = LEFT$(AN$,1)
6080 NUMDUP = ASCII(AN$)
6090 IF NUMDUP > 96 THEN AN$ = CHR$(NUMDUP - 32)
6100 WHILE AN$ <> "Y" AND AN$ <> "N"
6110    PRINT
6120    INPUT "PLEASE ENTER A 'Y' OR 'N' ";AN$
6130    AN$ = LEFT$(AN$,1)
6140    NUMDUP = ASCII(AN$)
6150    IF NUMDUP > 96 THEN AN$ = CHR$(NUMDUP - 32)
6160 NEXT
6170 PRINT
6180 RETURN
7000 REM
7010 REM ***********************************************************
7020 REM ***              SUBROUTINE PRICE CHECK                ***
7030 REM ***********************************************************
7040 REM *** ALLOW PRICE TO BE REENTERED IF INVALID.            ***
7050 REM
7060 GOSUB 8000
7070 REM
7080 REM *** REENTER PRICE UNTIL VALID.
7090 WHILE OK$ = "N"
7100    PRINT
7110    INPUT "PLEASE ENTER ONLY DIGITS AND A DECIMAL POINT ";PRICE$
7120    GOSUB 8000
7130 NEXT
7140 PRICE = VAL(PRICE$)
7150 RETURN
8000 REM
8010 REM ***********************************************************
8020 REM ***            SUBROUTINE CHARACTER CHECK              ***
8030 REM ***********************************************************
8040 REM *** CHECK THE CHARACTERS IN THE PRICE TO               ***
8050 REM *** MAKE SURE IT CONSISTS ONLY OF DIGITS AND A         ***
8060 REM *** DECIMAL POINT.                                      ***
8070 REM
8080 OK$ = "Y"
8090 LNGTH = LEN(PRICE$)
```

FIGURE 11–9 Continued

```
8100 REM
8110 REM *** CHECK EACH CHARACTER OF PRICE.
8120 FOR I = 1 TO LNGTH
8130    DIG$ = MID$(PRICE$,I,1)
8140    IF (ASCII(DIG$) <> 46) AND ((ASCII(DIG$) < 48) OR
        (ASCII(DIG$) > 57)) THEN OK$ = "N"
8150 NEXT I
8160 RETURN
9000 REM
9010 REM ************************************************
9020 REM ***             SUBROUTINE PRINT             ***
9030 REM ************************************************
9040 REM *** SUBROUTINE TO CALCULATE AND PRINT TOTAL  ***
9050 REM *** COST.                                    ***
9060 REM
9070 TTCST = PRCST + PRICE
9080 PRINT
9090 PRINT USING "\                    \ $$##.##";"***  TOTAL COST:",
     TTCST
9100 RETURN
9999 END
```

```
RUNNH

ENTER PRICE OF THE BOOK? 5.98

1 - REFERENCE BOOK
2 - CIRCULATING BOOK
3 - PAPERBACK
ENTER TYPE CODE FOR THE BOOK, USING THE CODES LISTED ABOVE

TYPE CODE MUST BE 1, 2, OR 3. PLEASE REENTER CODE: ? 3

IS BOOK A DUPLICATE (Y/N)? Y


***  TOTAL COST:         $9.08
```

DIFFERENCES

Apple:	No IF/THEN/ELSE; no WHILE/NEXT; no PRINT USING; all ASCII should be ASC.
IBM/Microsoft:	All WHILE/NEXT should be WHILE/WEND; all ASCII should be ASC.
Macintosh/Microsoft:	All WHILE/NEXT should be WHILE/WEND; all ASCII should be ASC.

There are two places in this program where the user is expected to enter a response of Y or N: at lines 1190 and 3080. In both of these cases, the program calls the subroutine DUPLICATE CHECK, which starts at line 6000. The purpose of this subroutine is to accommodate the possibility that the user might enter a lowercase y or n or a word starting with a Y, N, y or n (such as yes or no). The subroutine accomplishes this by using the LEFT$ function to assign only the first character of the string to AN$ in line 6070. In line 6080, the ASCII value of this character is checked to see if it is lowercase; if it is, the response is converted to its uppercase equivalent. The WHILE loop starting in line 6100 allows the user to reenter the duplicate indicator if the value stored in AN$ is not equal to a Y or an N.

Let's now discuss how this program might be tested to determine its reliability. First, we can determine if the program works properly if non-numeric data is entered for the book price. For example, if the value $32.50 is entered as the price, the user should be prompted to reenter the price (the dollar sign is invalid input). Next, we can check to see if the program works properly when invalid data is entered for the type code. Because the type code should be a 1, 2, or 3, we might first check to determine if the program works properly for values that are non-numeric, such as "a", "large", or "*". Then we can check to see if it works properly for integers outside the range 1 through 3, such as −1 or 8. It is especially important to check the boundary cases 0 and 4. Another good idea is to see if it works properly for numbers that have a valid starting integer but are more than one digit in length, such as 15, 23, and 38.9.

In each of these cases, the program should prompt the user to reenter the type code until a valid code is entered. If the program is able to handle these situations properly, we can then check to make certain that the program does in fact execute correctly when a valid type code is entered. Because there are only three valid codes (1, 2, or 3), we can easily test each of them.

The prompts that require a response of Y or N in lines 1190 and 3080 should be checked to make certain that they work properly for both upper- and lowercase letters, and also for words starting with either a Y or an N.

Now we want to make certain that the program obtains the correct total for the book cost. Therefore, each of the following combinations needs to be checked:

Reference book	**Circulating book**	**Paperback book**
duplicate/nonduplicate	duplicate/nonduplicate bestseller/nonbestseller	duplicate/ nonduplicate

This test involves running the program with eight different sets of data to test each of the possible paths of execution. The total price obtained in each of these cases must be checked for correctness. If the program works for each of these possibilities, we can be reasonably certain that it is working properly.

The testing procedure described here is time-consuming for a program of any significant length, but it can save many future problems and help in the development of a well-written, user-friendly program.

Summary Points

- Structured programming uses loop structures such as the FOR/NEXT and WHILE/NEXT rather than GOTO statements. Also, structured programs of any significant length are divided into subroutines that perform specific tasks. Some of the advantages of writing structured programs are that the logic of the finished program is easy to follow; the programmer's time is used efficiently; the resulting program is easy to modify and maintain; and the program is more likely to be error-free than an unstructured program.
- Good program style is used to make a program easier for people to understand. The computer is not affected by the style of a program.
- Programs with good style are well documented, make good use of blank spaces, and use meaningful variable names.
- Documentation may be either internal (within the program) or external (outside the program, such as a user's manual printed on paper). Internal documentation should be used to explain what is happening in a program.
- Syntax and logic errors are the two basic types of program errors.
- Syntax errors can often be avoided by careful typing and proofreading of the program before it is executed.
- Logic errors are caused by flaws in the program's algorithm. There are two types of logic errors: run-time errors, which cause execution to stop prematurely, and errors in which program execution terminates properly but the output is not always correct.
- Program testing is the process of systematically checking a program to determine its reliability, that is, its ability to work properly at all times.
- Complete program testing, which is generally impractical, involves testing all possible paths of execution of a program. Selective program testing involves testing programs using data with specific characteristics. When selective testing is used, programs are usually checked to determine if they work properly for boundary cases (that is, data at the very extremes of valid ranges).
- Report writing is used in business to print tables of information, such as financial reports.
- The style of printer output can be altered by using control characters. These characters, which vary depending on the type of printer being used, can cause output to be printed in many different modes, such as italics, boldface, or underlined.
- User-friendly programs are written so that they are easy and pleasant for people to use. They also are able to handle invalid data in appropriate ways.

Review Questions

1. Name four advantages of using structured programming techniques.
2. Why should programmers use good programming style?
3. Give three characteristics of a program with good style.
4. What is the difference between internal and external documentation?
5. Give some examples of external documentation.
6. What information should be included in the documentation at the beginning of a program?
7. What is the purpose of using blank spaces within BASIC statements?
8. What are the two categories of program errors?
9. What is the most common cause of syntax errors?
10. How can syntax errors be avoided?
11. What are the two categories of logic errors?
12. List several common run-time errors.
13. Explain how error trapping is used to protect a program from invalid data.
14. Explain how program tracing can be used to locate run-time errors.
15. What is the difference between complete program testing and selective program testing?
16. Define the term *reliability* as applied to programs.
17. Why is complete program testing generally not feasible?
18. What is meant by testing the boundary cases when using selective testing?
19. Define the term *user-friendly*.
20. List some characteristics of user-friendly programs.

Debugging Exercises

Identify the following programs and program segments that contain errors, and debug them.

1.
```
10 FOR K = 1 TO N
20   T = K * 10
30    PRINT T
40 NEXT K
99 END
```

2.
```
10 REM *** READ THREE NUMBERS AND MULTIPLY THEM TOGETHER. ***
20 READ A,B,C
30 PRING A * B * C
99 END
```

3.
```
10 REM *** READ LIST OF VALUES UNTIL FIRST VALUE (C) IS ***
20 REM *** SMALLER THAN SECOND (D).                      ***
30 READ C D
40 IF C = D OR C > D THEN GOTO 30
50 PRINT "C IS LESS THAN D";D C
60 DATA 5,5,5,4,8,5,5,6
99 END
```

4. ```
10 REM *** PRINT ADDRESS IF IT IS ON AN AVENUE (AVE). ***
20 READ ST$
30 FOR B = 1 TO LEN(ST$) - 3
40   IF MID$(ST$,B,1) = "AVE" THEN 60
50 NEXT B
60 PRINT ST$
70 DATA JACKSON ST.
99 END
```

5. ```
10 REM *** READ AND DISPLAY A PERSON'S NAME AND ADDRESS. ***
20 READ NME$,S$,CTY$,ST$,ZCDE
30 ADRS$ = CTY$ + " " + ST$ + " " + ZCDE
40 PRINT NME$
50 PRINT S$
60 PRINT ADRS$
70 DATA ELAINE JOHNSON, 1704 CARBON ST., TULSA,
       WYOMING,49023
99 END
```

6. ```
10 REM *** READ A SERIES OF TWO VALUES AND PRINT THE LARGER ONE.
20 READ X,Y
30 IF X > Y THEN 40
40 PRINT "Y IS GREATER THAN X" \ GOTO 20
50 PRINT "X IS GREATER THAN Y" \ GOTO 20
60 DATA 10,9,20,21,17
99 END
```

7. ```
10 READ PHRASE$
20 IF PHRASE$ = "LAST" GOTO 99
30 FOR I = 1 TO 10
40     PRINT LEFT$(PHRASE$,I,1)
50 NEXT I
60 PRINT
70 GOTO 10
80 DATA "I AM HAPPY","TOMMORROW IS COMING","LAST"
99 END
```

8. ```
10 FOR I = 1 TO 10
20   FOR J = 1 TO 20
30   T = T + J / K
40   NEXT J
50   PRINT T
60 NEXT T
99 END
```

9. ```
10 REM *** COMPUTE AN AVERAGE. ***
20 REM *** AVE = AVERAGE          ***
30 A = 3
40 B = 27
50 COMPUTE THE AVERAGE.
60 (A + B) / 2 = AVE
70 PRINT "THE AVERAGE IS";AVE
99 END
```

10. ```
10 FOR I = 1 TO 20
20   IF X > 10 THEN 10
30 IF X < 11 THEN PRINT X
40   X = X + 2
50 NEXT I
99 END
```
```

11.
```
10  REM *** PROGRAM TO SQUARE 3 SUCCESSIVE VALUES. ***
20  PRINT "SQUARING THREE SUCCESSIVE VALUES"
30  INPUT "WHAT IS THE FIRST VALUE";VLUE
40  PRINT "VALUE","VALUE SQUARED"
50  FOR I = 1 TO 3
60      SQ = VLUE ^ 2
70      TT = TT + SQ
80      VLUE = VLUE + 1
90      PRINT VLUE,SQ
100 NEXT I
110 PRINT "TOTAL OF SQUARED VALUES IS ";TT
120 INPUT " DO YOU WANT TO TRY AGAIN (Y/N)";A
130 IF A = Y THEN 40
999 END
```

12.
```
10  REM *** READ AND PRINT A LIST OF 4 NAMES. ***
20  DIM AGE(4),NME$(4)
30  I = 0
40  WHILE I <= 4
50      I = I + 1
60      READ AGE(I),NME$(I)
70      PRINT AGE(I),NME$(I)
80  NEXT I
90  DATA "HONEY",10,"TODD",25
100 DATA "J.J.",21,"JIM",17
999 END
```

13.
```
210 REM *** FIND THE PRODUCT OF THE ELEMENTS ***
220 REM *** IN A 3 X 3 ARRAY.                 ***
230 REM
240 PROD = 0
250 FOR I = 1 TO 3
260     FOR J = 1 TO 3
270         PROD = PROD * X(I,J)
280     NEXT J
290 NEXT I
```

14.
```
10 REM *** OUTPUT THE STRING CDEF. ***
20 READ A$,B$
30 A = STR$(A$)
40 A = A + 3
50 A$ = VAL(A)
60 C$ = A$ + B$
70 PRINT C$
80 DATA ABC,DEF
99 END
```

15.
```
10 REM *** READ AND PRINT A LIST OF VALUES. ***
20 FOR I = 1 TO 20 STEP -2
30     READ N
40     IF N > 15 THEN 50
50     PRINT N
60 NEXT
70 DATA 9,1,18,26,3,2,4,20,28,52
99 END
```

16.
```
10 Y = 12.96
20 R = FNAB(Y)
30 PRINT R
40 REM *** FUNCTION TO ROUND NUMBER TO NEAREST TENTH. ***
50 FNAB(X) = INT(X + 0.005) * 100) / 100
99 END
```

17.
```
10 REM *** SORT THE STUDENTS IN BIOLOGY 101 ***
20 REM *** INTO ALPHABETICAL ORDER BY NAME. ***
30 DIM STUD$(15)
40 REM *** READ NAMES. ***
50 FOR I = 1 TO 15
60     INPUT STUD$(I)
70 NEXT I
80 REM
90 REM *** BUBBLE SORT ***
100 F = 0
110 FOR I = 1 TO 14
120    IF STUD$(I) <= STUD$(I + 1) THEN 170
130    STUD$(I) = STUD$(I + 1)
140    TEMP$ = STUD$(I)
150    STUD$(I + 1) = TEMP$
160    F = 1
170 NEXT I
180 IF F = 1 THEN 100
190 PRINT "LIST SORTED"
```

18.
```
10   REM *** STORE ALL NAMES BEGINNING WITH ***
20   REM *** LETTERS A - J IN ARRAY CUST.    ***
30   REM
40   DIM CUST$(20)
50   I = 1
60   INPUT NAM$
70   WHILE NAM$ <> "DONE"
80      INPUT NAM$
90      LTTR$ = LEFT$(NAM$,1)
100     IF LTTR$ >= "A" AND LTTR$ <= "J" THEN CUST$(I) = NAM$
110  NEXT
120  FOR J = 1 TO I
130     PRINT CUST$(J)
140  NEXT J
999  END
```

19.
```
20   REM *** PRINT TABLE CONTAINING SALES DATA. ***
30   DIM SALE(10,5)
40   PRINT TAB(15);"TOTAL SALES"
50   PRINT
60   PRINT TAB(10);"MAIN STORE";
          TAB(20);"FIRST QUARTER"
70   PRINT
80   FOR T = 1 TO 5
90      FOR S = 1 TO 10
100        PRINT "    ";TAB(10);SALE(T,S);
110     NEXT S
120     PRINT
130  NEXT T
```

20. The following program's output should be as follows:

```
$ 18.49      $ 6.53      $ 8.71
  21.47        4.93        5.22

GRAND TOTAL OF ALL AMOUNTS: $ 65.35
```

Correct the program so the output is formatted as above.

```
10 READ FAMT,SAMT,TAMT
20 PRINT "$";FAMT,"$";SAMT,"$";TAMT
30 READ SFAMT,SSAMT,STAMT
40 PRINT SFAMT,SSAMT,STAMT
50 TT = FAMT + SAMT + TAMT + SFAMT + SSAMT + STAMT
60 PRINT "GRAND TOTAL OF ALL AMOUNTS: " "$";TT
70 DATA 18.49,6.53,8.71
80 DATA 21.47,4.93,5.22
99 END
```

Additional Programming Problems

The following programs have syntax and/or logic errors. Find and correct these errors.

Level 1

1.
```
10  REM ********************************************
20  REM *** THIS PROGRAM READS THE NAMES OF CITIES OR ***
30  REM *** VACATION SPOTS AND THE DISTANCES BETWEEN  ***
40  REM *** EACH CITY. A LIST OF THE VACATION PLANS   ***
50  REM *** IS PRINTED WITH NAMES, DISTANCES AND      ***
60  REM *** TRAVEL TIME.                              ***
70  REM *** MAJOR VARIABLES:                          ***
80  REM ***    CITIES$    ARRAY OF VACATION SPOTS     ***
90  REM ***    TRAVTIM    ARRAY OF TRAVEL TIMES       ***
100 REM ***    MILES      NUMBER OF MILES TRAVELED    ***
110 REM ***    TMILES     LOG OF MILES TRAVELED       ***
120 REM
130 DIM CITIES$(4),TRAVTIM(4),TMILES(4)
140 REM
150 PRINT "THIS PROGRAM WILL HELP YOU TO PLAN A TRIP "
160 PRINT "TO 4 CITIES OR VACATION SPOTS. THINK OF "
170 PRINT "4 PLACES YOU WOULD LIKE TO VISIT, THE ORDER"
180 PRINT "IN WHICH YOU WANT TO VISIT THEM, AND THE "
190 PRINT "DISTANCE BETWEEN EACH PLACE."
200 REM
210 REM *** READ CITIES AND DISTANCES ***
220 FOR I = 1 TO 4
230    PRINT "CITY OR PLACE ";I;" IS"
240    INPUT CITIES$(I)
```

```
250     IF I = 1 THEN PRINT "DISTANCE TO ";CITIES$(I);":"
            \ INPUT MILES \    TMILES(I) = MILES
            ELSE PRINT "DISTANCE TO ";CITIES$(I);" FROM ";CITIES$(I - 1);":"
            \ INPUT MILES \ TMILES(I) = MILES
260     TRAVTIM(I) = MILES * 55
270 NEXT I
280 REM
290 REM *** VACATION PLAN PRINTED - PLACE, DISTANCE ***
300 REM *** BETWEEN SPOTS, TIME                     ***
310 PRINT
320 PRINT TAB(15);"YOUR VACATION PLANS"
330 PRINT TAB(7);"PLACE";TAB(19);"DISTANCE";TAB(35);"TRAVEL TIME"
340 PRINT
350 FOR J = 1 TO 4
360     PRINT TAB(7);CITIES$(I);TAB(19);TMILES(I);TAB(35);TRAVTIM(I)
370 NEXT J
999 END
```

2.
```
10    REM *** CALCULATE THE LEATHER NEEDED TO COVER  ***
20    REM *** SPORTS BALLS FOR ACME, INC.            ***
30    REM
40    REM *** DEFINE FUNCTION TO COMPUTE SURFACE     ***
50    REM *** OF THE BALL.                           ***
60    DEF FNA(RA) = 4 * 3.1415 * X ^ 2
70    REM
80    REM *** INPUT BALL RADII AND NUMBERS. ***
90    GOSUB 1000
1000 REM *******************************************
1010 REM ***           SUBROUTINE INPUT          ***
1020 REM *******************************************
1030 REM
1040 MRE$ = "Y"
1050 WHILE MRE$ = "Y"
1060    INPUT "ENTER THE RADII OF BALL(INCHES): ";RA
1070    INPUT "ENTER THE NUMBER OF BALLS: ";NM
1080    GOSUB 2000
1090    INPUT "DO YOU WANT TO CONTINUE (Y/N) ";MRE$
1100 NEXT
1110 RETURN
2000 REM *******************************************
2010 REM ***           SUBROUTINE CALCULATE      ***
2020 REM *******************************************
2030 REM *** TOTAL AREA = NUMBER * AREA            ***
2040 REM *** 1296 INCHES = 1 SQUARE YARD           ***
2050 REM
2060 AREA = FNA(RA)
2070 TAREA = AREA / 1296
2080 PRINT "TOTAL AREA (SQ. YARDS): ";TAREA
2090 RETURN
9999 END
```

Level 2

1.  ```
    10   REM *** THIS PROGRAM READS A LIST OF INTEGERS   ***
    20   REM *** TYPED AT THE KEYBOARD ONE AT A TIME,    ***
    30   REM *** AND DETERMINES IF THEY ARE ODD OR EVEN. ***
    40   REM *** THEN ALL THE ODD NUMBERS ARE ADDED TO-  ***
    50   REM *** GETHER AND THE EVEN NUMBERS ARE ADDED   ***
    60   REM *** TOGETHER. THESE TWO SUMS ARE PRINTED.   ***
    70   REM *** MAJOR VARIABLES:                        ***
    80   REM ***      ESUM    SUM OF EVEN NUMBERS        ***
    90   REM ***      OSUM    SUM OF ODD NUMBERS         ***
    100  REM ***      NMBR    INTEGER ENTERED            ***
    110  REM ***      QUANT   NUMBER OF INTEGERS         ***
    120  REM ***      EVEN$   IS INTEGER ODD?            ***
    130  REM
    140  ESUM = 0
    150  OSUM = 0
    160  INPUT "HOW MANY NUMBERS ARE THERE ";QUANT
    170  REM
    180  REM *** ENTER EACH NUMBER AND ASSIGN IT TO ***
    190  REM *** THE APPROPRIATE SUM.               ***
    200  PRINT "ENTER THE NUMBERS"
    210  FOR I = 1 TO QUANT
    220     INPUT (NMBR)
    230     GOSUB 1000
    240     IF EVEN$ = "Y" THEN ESUM = ESUM + NMBR
               ELSE OSUM = OSUM + NMBR
    250  NEXT I
    260  PRINT
    270  PRINT "THE SUM OF THE EVEN NUMBERS IS ";ESUM
    280  PRINT "THE SUM OF THE ODD NUMBERS IS ";OSUM
    290  GOTO 9999
    1000 REM ********************************************
    1010 REM ***             SUBROUTINE TEST          ***
    1020 REM ********************************************
    1030 REM *** DETERMINE IF INTEGER IS EVEN OR ODD. ***
    1040 REM
    1050 X = NMBR / 2 - INT(NMBR / 2)
    1060 IF X = <> THEN EVEN$ = "Y" ELSE EVEN$ = "N"
    1070 RETURN
    9999 END
    ```

2.  ```
    10   REM *** THIS PROGRAM PRINTS THE SELECTIONS ON A   ***
    20   REM *** JUKEBOX AND ALLOWS THE USER TO DELETE     ***
    30   REM *** SELECTIONS AS DESIRED, GIVEN THE LOCATION ***
    40   REM *** OF THE TUNE IN THE LIST.                  ***
    50   REM *** MAJOR VARIABLES:                          ***
    60   REM ***      TUNE$   ARRAY OF SELECTIONS          ***
    70   REM ***      SNG$    TUNE ENTERED BY USER         ***
    80   REM ***      CAN$    IS TUNE TO BE DELETED?       ***
    90   REM ***      QUANT   NUMBER OF TUNES              ***
    100  DIM TUNE$(20)
    110  REM *** ENTER THE TUNES. ***
    120  GOSUB 1000
    130  REM *** PRINT THE TUNE LIST. ***
    ```

```
140     GOSUB 2000
150  REM *** ALLOW THE USER TO REMOVE SELECTIONS. ***
160     GOSUB 3000
170  REM *** PRINT THE FINAL LIST. ***
180     GOSUB 2000
190     GOTO 9999
1000 REM ***************************************************
1010 REM ***                 SUBROUTINE INPUT            ***
1020 REM ***************************************************
1030 PRINT "ENTER UP TO 20 TUNES. TYPE 'XX' TO STOP "
1040 I = 1
1050 INPUT SNG$
1060 WHILE SNG$ <> "XY" AND I <= 20
1070     TUNE$(I) = SNG$
1080     I = I + 1
1090     INPUT SNG$
1100 NEXT
1110 QUANT = I
1120 RETURN
2000 REM ***************************************************
2010 REM ***                 SUBROUTINE PRINT            ***
2020 REM ***************************************************
2030 REM *** PRINT THE SELECTION LIST.  ***
2040 PRINT "SELECTION LIST "
2050 FOR I = 1 TO QUANT
2060     PRINT I;".";TUNE$(I)
2070 NEXT I
2080 RETURN
3000 REM ***************************************************
3010 REM ***                 SUBROUTINE DELETE           ***
3020 REM ***************************************************
3030 REM *** ALLOW USER TO DELETE A SELECTION. ***
3040 INPUT "WOULD YOU LIKE TO REMOVE A SELECTION ";CAN$
3050 INPUT "WHAT IS ITS POSITION IN THE LIST ";NM
3060 WHILE CAN$ = "Y" AND QUANT > 0
3070     FOR I = NM TO QUANT - 1
3080         TUNE$(I) = TUNE$(I + 1)
3090     NEXT I
3100     TUNE$(I + 1) = " "
3110     QUANT = QUANT - 1
3120     GOSUB 2000
3130     INPUT "WOULD YOU LIKE TO REMOVE A SELECTION ";CAN$
3140 NEXT
9999 END
```

CHAPTER 12

MATRIX COMMANDS

Objectives

After studying this chapter, you will be able to:
- Explain and use the MAT READ and MAT PRINT commands.
- Explain and use the MAT command with math operations.
- Explain and use the MAT command with math functions.

Outline

Overview
Matrix Input/Output
Matrix Mathematics
   Addition and Subtraction
   Matrix Multiplication
   Scalar Multiplication
   Replacement
Matrix Functions
   Initialization

The Identity Matrix
Transposition
Inversion
A Programming Problem
   Problem Definition
   Solution Design
   The Program
Avoiding Common Programming
   Mistakes

Summary Points
Review Questions
Debugging Exercises
Additional Programming Problems
   Level 1
   Level 2
   Level 3

Overview

Matrix
An array.

A matrix can be either a list or a table of data; essentially, the term **matrix** is just another name for an array. Some implementations of the BASIC language have a set of matrix statements that provide convenient, easy ways to perform array operations and functions on arrays containing numeric data. Unfortunately, many BASIC systems do not include these commands. Of the systems discussed in our text, only the VAX provides these statements.

This chapter explains the various matrix commands that are commonly used. Table 12–1 defines these typical matrix statements (X, Y, and Z are all matrices). Notice that one keyword found in each command is the word MAT. The MAT commands contribute to the efficiency of a program because they enable the programmer to perform operations on an entire array in one statement, rather than managing the individual elements of an array by means of a loop.

Before an array is used in a MAT command, it should first be dimensioned by means of the DIM statement.

TABLE 12–1 Matrix Statements

OPERATION	BASIC STATEMENT	FUNCTION	ARRAY MANIPULATION
Dimension	DIM X(2,2), Y(2,2), Z(2,2)	Establish matrix size	X = 2×2; Y = 2×2; Z = 2×2
Input/Output	MAT READ X	Read data values to matrix X from DATA statements	X $\begin{vmatrix} 1 & 2 \\ -4 & 5 \end{vmatrix}$
	MAT INPUT Y	Enter data values to matrix Y at keyboard	Y $\begin{vmatrix} 5 & 6 \\ 8 & 9 \end{vmatrix}$

TABLE 12–1 Continued

OPERATION	BASIC STATEMENT	FUNCTION	ARRAY MANIPULATION
Input/Output	MAT PRINT X,	Print matrix X row by row	$\begin{vmatrix} 1 & 2 \\ -4 & 5 \end{vmatrix}$
Replacement	MAT Z = X	Assign matrix elements on right side of equal sign to corresponding elements of matrix on left side of equal sign	$Z = \begin{vmatrix} 1 & 2 \\ -4 & 5 \end{vmatrix}$
Addition	MAT Z = X + Y	Add corresponding elements of Y to X and place result in Z	$\begin{matrix} Z & X & Y \end{matrix}$ $\begin{vmatrix} 6 & 8 \\ 4 & 14 \end{vmatrix} = \begin{vmatrix} 1 & 2 \\ -4 & 5 \end{vmatrix} + \begin{vmatrix} 5 & 6 \\ 8 & 9 \end{vmatrix}$
Subtraction	MAT Z = X − Y	Subtract corresponding elements of Y from X and place result in Z	$\begin{matrix} Z & X & Y \end{matrix}$ $\begin{vmatrix} -4 & -4 \\ -12 & -4 \end{vmatrix} = \begin{vmatrix} 1 & 2 \\ -4 & 5 \end{vmatrix} - \begin{vmatrix} 5 & 6 \\ 8 & 9 \end{vmatrix}$
Multiplication	MAT Z = X * Y	Store products of X and Y in Z (see MATRIX MULTIPLICATION section for details)	$\begin{matrix} Z & X & Y \end{matrix}$ $\begin{vmatrix} 21 & 24 \\ 20 & 21 \end{vmatrix} = \begin{vmatrix} 1 & 2 \\ -4 & 5 \end{vmatrix} * \begin{vmatrix} 5 & 6 \\ 8 & 9 \end{vmatrix}$
Scalar Multiplication	MAT Z = (2) * X	Multiply each element in X by 2 and place in Z	$\begin{matrix} Z & & X \end{matrix}$ $\begin{vmatrix} 2 & 4 \\ -8 & 10 \end{vmatrix} = 2 * \begin{vmatrix} 1 & 2 \\ -4 & 5 \end{vmatrix}$
Initialization	MAT Z = ZER	Initialize elements of Z to zero	Z $\begin{vmatrix} 0 & 0 \\ 0 & 0 \end{vmatrix}$
	MAT Z = CON	Initialize elements of Z to 1	Z $\begin{vmatrix} 1 & 1 \\ 1 & 1 \end{vmatrix}$
Identity	MAT Z = IDN	Creates the identity matrix	Z $\begin{vmatrix} 1 & 0 \\ 0 & 1 \end{vmatrix}$
Transposition	MAT Z = TRN(X)	Enter the transposition of X to Z	Z $\begin{vmatrix} 1 & -4 \\ 2 & 5 \end{vmatrix}$
Inversion	MAT Z = INV(X)	Enter the inverse of X to Z	Z $\begin{vmatrix} 0.038 & -0.15 \\ 0.031 & 0.08 \end{vmatrix}$

Matrix Input/Output

To read data to a matrix, we can use the MAT READ or MAT INPUT statements. The general format of these statements is as follows:

line# MAT READ matrix name
line# MAT INPUT matrix name

Assume there exists a matrix X, with the following elements:

$$\begin{vmatrix} 64 & 22 & 20 \\ 95 & 45 & 23 \end{vmatrix}$$

The following statements could be used to read this data to matrix X:

```
10 DIM X(2,3)
20 MAT READ X
30 DATA 64,22,20,95,45,23
```

The MAT READ command causes the computer to read the data in row order according to the dimensions assigned to the matrix. That is, all of the first row is read to the matrix, then all of the second row, and so on. All of the positions in the array must be filled when MAT commands are used; otherwise, an "out of data" error message will result. If there are more data items than positions in the matrix, the extra data is left unread.

The MAT READ statement is equivalent to a READ within nested FOR/NEXT statements, as shown here:

Array Input with MAT Statement

```
10 DIM A(2,3)
20 MAT READ A
30 DATA 64,22,20,43,45,23
99 END
```

Array Input with Nested FOR/NEXT Statements

```
10 DIM A(2,3)
20 FOR I = 1 TO 2
30    FOR J = 1 TO 3
40       READ A(I,J)
50    NEXT J
60 NEXT I
70 DATA 64,22,20,43,45,23
99 END
```

Similarly, we can use a MAT INPUT statement to enter data at the keyboard:

```
10 DIM A(2,3)
20 MAT INPUT A
```

A MAT PRINT statement can be used to print a matrix in row order. The MAT PRINT statement has the following format:

line# MAT PRINT matrix name

Thus, the statement

```
10 MAT PRINT A,
```

is equivalent to the following statements:

```
10 FOR I = 1 TO 2
20    FOR J = 1 TO 3
30       PRINT A(I,J),
40    NEXT J
50    PRINT
60 NEXT I
```

The example in Figure 12–1 illustrates the use of the MAT INPUT statement to enter data to a 3 × 3 matrix, and the use of the MAT PRINT statement to output the matrix.

Notice that line 70 ends with a comma, which causes the output to be printed in matrix form. If we omit the comma, the output looks like this:

```
7
9
45
6
12
2
54
1
0
```

Although the output is formatted differently, the matrix values are still printed in row order.

Learning Check

1. The term _____ is another name for an array.
2. The _____ and _____ statements are used to read data to a matrix.
3. Data is entered to a matrix in _____ order.
4. To enter data to a matrix at the keyboard, the _____ statement is used.
5. The following statements are equivalent to what MAT statement?

    ```
    10 FOR I = 1 TO 3
    20    FOR J = 1 TO 4
    30       PRINT A(I,J),
    40    NEXT J
    50    PRINT
    60 NEXT I
    ```

Answers

1. matrix 2. MAT READ, MAT INPUT 3. row 4. MAT INPUT 5. 10 MAT PRINT A,

FIGURE 12–1 The MAT INPUT and MAT PRINT Statements

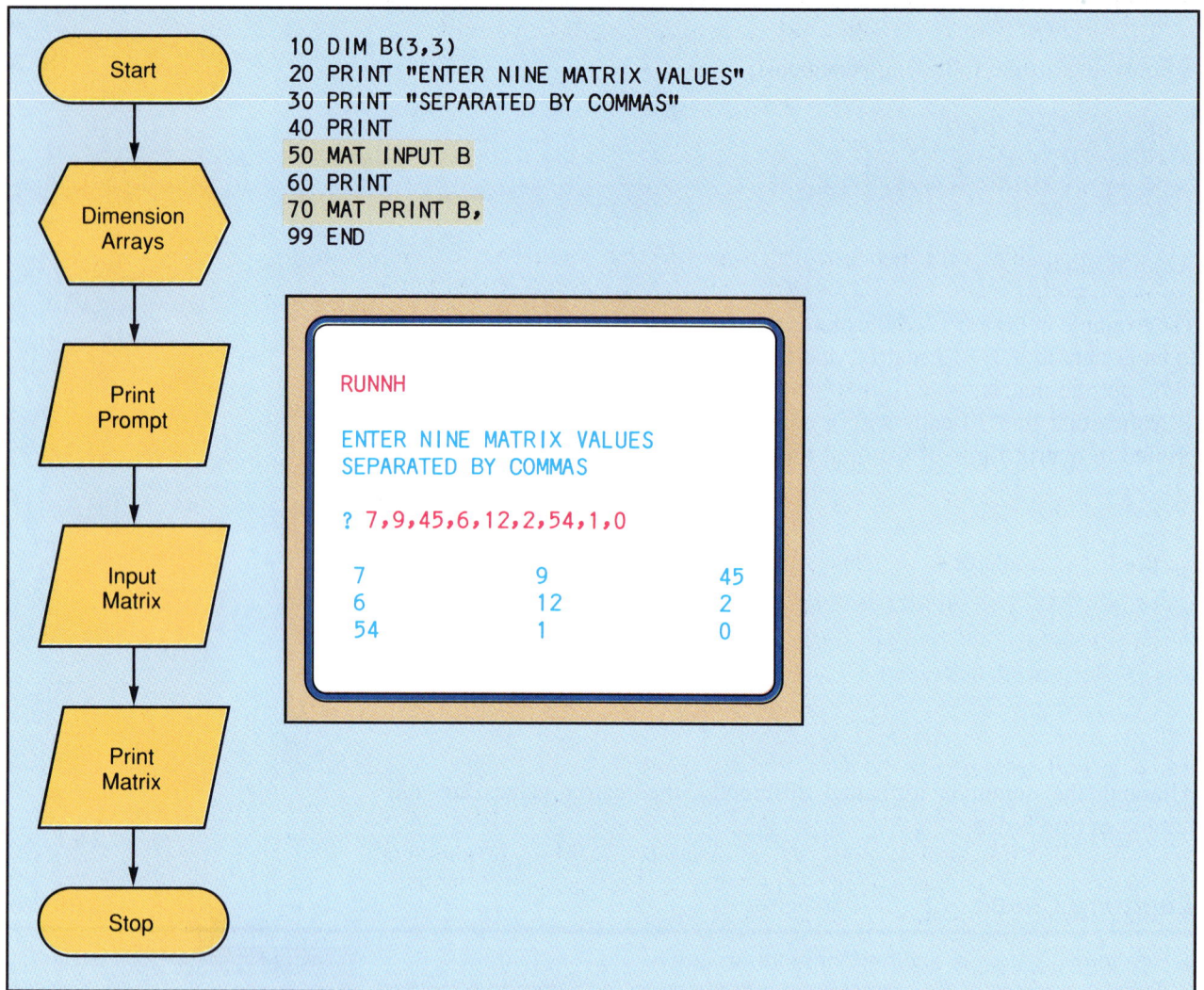

Matrix Mathematics

Although matrices are often used merely to store values, they can also be added, subtracted, multiplied, and made equivalent to one another. However, when using MAT commands, only one of these operations can be performed at a time. Thus, the following statement is invalid:

```
20 MAT X = A + B + C
```

Addition and Subtraction

Two matrices must have the same dimensions if they are to be added or subtracted. For example, the following arrays have the same number of rows (3) and the same number of columns (2):

```
10 DIM X(3,2),Y(3,2),Z(3,2)
20 MAT Y = X + Z
30 MAT Y = Y - Z
```

The corresponding elements of one matrix are added to (or subtracted from) those of another matrix. Notice that the same matrix can be referred to on both sides of the equal sign, just as with other variables:

$$\text{Matrix Y} \quad \text{Matrix X} \quad \text{Matrix Z}$$

$$\begin{vmatrix} 16 & 20 \\ 2 & 3 \\ 5 & 6 \end{vmatrix} = \begin{vmatrix} 7 & 9 \\ 1 & 3 \\ 2 & 4 \end{vmatrix} + \begin{vmatrix} 9 & 11 \\ 1 & 0 \\ 3 & 2 \end{vmatrix}$$

$$\text{Matrix Y} \quad \text{Matrix Y} \quad \text{Matrix Z}$$

$$\begin{vmatrix} 7 & 9 \\ 1 & 3 \\ 2 & 4 \end{vmatrix} = \begin{vmatrix} 16 & 20 \\ 2 & 3 \\ 5 & 6 \end{vmatrix} - \begin{vmatrix} 9 & 11 \\ 1 & 0 \\ 3 & 2 \end{vmatrix}$$

Matrix Multiplication

For two matrices to be multiplied, the number of columns of the first matrix must be equal to the number of rows of the second matrix. The resulting product matrix has the same number of rows as the first matrix and the same number of columns as the second one. Examples are given in the following table:

Dimensions for Matrix Multiplication			
Matrix	**First**	**Second**	**Result**
Valid Dimensions	(4×5)	(5×2)	(4×2)
	(2×3)	(3×4)	(2×4)
Invalid Dimensions	(2×4)	(3×2)	—
	(3×2)	(3×7)	—

The multiplication of two matrices follows a particular formula, which is illustrated by the following example:

$$\begin{array}{cc} \text{Matrix B} & \text{Matrix C} \\ \begin{vmatrix} b_1 & b_2 \\ b_3 & b_4 \\ b_5 & b_6 \end{vmatrix} * & \begin{vmatrix} c_1 & c_2 & c_3 \\ c_4 & c_5 & c_6 \end{vmatrix} \end{array} = \begin{array}{c} \text{Product Matrix} \\ \begin{array}{ccc} \text{column 1} & \text{column 2} & \text{column 3} \end{array} \\ \begin{vmatrix} b_1c_1+b_2c_4 & b_1c_2+b_2c_5 & b_1c_3+b_2c_6 \\ b_3c_1+b_4c_4 & b_3c_2+b_4c_5 & b_3c_3+b4c_6 \\ b_5c_1+b_6c_4 & b_5c_2+b_6c_5 & b_5c_3+b_6c_6 \end{vmatrix} \end{array}$$

The product matrix is derived by addition of the products of the row elements of the first matrix times the column elements of the second matrix.

Suppose we have the following statements:

```
10 DIM A(3,3),B(3,2),C(2,3)
20 MAT A = B * C
```

$$\begin{array}{ccc} \text{Matrix A} & \text{Matrix B} & \text{Matrix C} \\ \begin{vmatrix} ? & ? & ? \\ ? & ? & ? \\ ? & ? & ? \end{vmatrix} = & \begin{vmatrix} 5 & 6 \\ 7 & 8 \\ 9 & 10 \end{vmatrix} * & \begin{vmatrix} 1 & 2 & 3 \\ 4 & 5 & 6 \end{vmatrix} \\ 3 \times 3 & 3 \times 2 & 2 \times 3 \end{array}$$

To determine the value of the element in the first row, first column of array A, multiply all of the elements of row 1 of matrix B times their corresponding elements in column 1 of matrix C, and add these products together. Proceed in the same way to get the other elements of matrix A:

$$\begin{array}{c} \text{Matrix A} \\ \begin{array}{ccc} \text{col.1} & \text{col.2} & \text{col.3} \end{array} \\ \begin{vmatrix} 29 & 40 & 51 \\ 39 & 54 & 69 \\ 49 & 68 & 87 \end{vmatrix} = \begin{array}{ccc} \text{col.1} & \text{col.2} & \text{col.3} \end{array} \\ \begin{vmatrix} (5*1)+(6*4) & (5*2)+(6*5) & (5*3)+(6*6) \\ (7*1)+(8*4) & (7*2)+(8*5) & (7*3)+(8*6) \\ (9*1)+(10*4) & (9*2)+(10*5) & (9*3)+(10*6) \end{vmatrix} \end{array}$$

Note: The same matrix cannot appear on both sides of the equal sign in matrix multiplication.

Scalar Multiplication

A matrix can be multiplied by a *scalar value* (a single numeric constant, variable, or expression) enclosed in parentheses. Each element of the matrix is multiplied by this value as shown:

```
10 MAT E = (2) * E
```

Matrix E   **Matrix E**

$$\begin{vmatrix} 10 & 12 \\ 14 & 16 \\ 18 & 20 \end{vmatrix} = 2 * \begin{vmatrix} 5 & 6 \\ 7 & 8 \\ 9 & 10 \end{vmatrix}$$

Replacement

The replacement operation is much like an assignment statement. The elements of the matrix appearing on the left side of the equal sign are set equal to the corresponding elements of the matrix on the right side. The matrices must have the same dimensions, of course. For example:

```
10 DIM A(2,4),B(2,4)
20 MAT A = B
```

Matrix A   **Matrix B**

$$\begin{vmatrix} 10 & 20 & 50 & 60 \\ 30 & 40 & 70 & 80 \end{vmatrix} = \begin{vmatrix} 10 & 20 & 50 & 60 \\ 30 & 40 & 70 & 80 \end{vmatrix}$$

Matrix Functions

In addition to the basic math operations already discussed, the MAT statements also include the following functions:

1. Initialization
2. Identity
3. Transposition
4. Inversion

Initialization

It is often necessary to initialize variables to specific values. The same can be done with matrices. To initialize all the elements of an array to 0, use the ZER function as shown:

```
10 DIM A(4,2)
20 MAT A = ZER
```

Matrix A

$$\begin{vmatrix} 0 & 0 \\ 0 & 0 \\ 0 & 0 \\ 0 & 0 \end{vmatrix}$$

We can also use a MAT command to initialize all the elements of an array to 1, by means of the CON function:

```
10 DIM B(2,4)
20 MAT B = CON
```

Matrix B

$$\begin{vmatrix} 1 & 1 & 1 & 1 \\ 1 & 1 & 1 & 1 \end{vmatrix}$$

The Identity Matrix

Any matrix multiplied by the identity matrix yields itself. The following statements create an identity (IDN) matrix:

```
10 DIM T(4,4)
20 MAT T = IDN
```

The diagonal of an identity matrix contains 1s, and all other elements are 0s:

Matrix T

$$\begin{vmatrix} 1 & 0 & 0 & 0 \\ 0 & 1 & 0 & 0 \\ 0 & 0 & 1 & 0 \\ 0 & 0 & 0 & 1 \end{vmatrix}$$

Note that when the IDN function is used, the number of rows in the matrix must be equal to the number of columns.

Transposition

When a matrix is transposed, the rows of the old matrix become the columns of the new matrix. For example:

```
10 MAT M = TRN(T)
```

If T looks like this:

$$\begin{vmatrix} 1 & 2 \\ 3 & 4 \\ 5 & 6 \\ 7 & 8 \end{vmatrix}$$

then the transposition of T looks like this:

$$\begin{vmatrix} 1 & 3 & 5 & 7 \\ 2 & 4 & 6 & 8 \end{vmatrix}$$

You must be careful that the dimensions of the matrix that will contain the transposed matrix values are the reverse of the dimensions of the matrix to be transposed. In the preceding example, T is a 4 × 2 matrix. Therefore, M (which is to contain the transposition of T) must be a 2 × 4 matrix.

Inversion

One of the most powerful matrix commands is the inverse function. It often is used to solve simultaneous linear equations. The inverse of A is usually written A^{-1}. The usefulness of the inverse function comes from the fact that A multiplied by its inverse yields the identity matrix. (See ''A Programming Problem'' for an example of its use.) For example, assume the matrix A contains these values:

Matrix A

$$\begin{vmatrix} 4 & 0 & 0 \\ 0 & 0 & 2 \\ 0 & 8 & 0 \end{vmatrix}$$

The following statements assign the inverse of this matrix (A^{-1}) to the matrix B and print B:

```
30 MAT B = INV(A)
40 PRINT TAB(9);"B"
50 MAT PRINT B,
```

RUNNH

```
            B
.25         0           0
0           0           .125
0           .5          0
```

The original matrix A, multiplied by its inverse B, produces the identity matrix of A:

```
60 MAT C = A * B
70 PRINT TAB(9);"C"
80 MAT PRINT C,
```

RUNNH

```
            C
1           0           0
0           1           0
0           0           1
```

Use your knowledge of matrix multiplication to verify this result.

Learning Check

1. To add or subtract two matrices, they must have _____.
2. The same matrix cannot be referred to on both sides of the equal sign when performing matrix multiplication. True or false?
3. When multiplying two matrices, the resulting matrix will have the same number of _____ as the first matrix and the same number of _____ as the second one.
4. 10 MAT A = B + C * D is a valid MAT statement. True or false?
5. Give the statements needed to create an identity matrix for a matrix with two rows and two columns.
6. _____ is the process whereby the rows of the old matrix become the columns of the new matrix.
7. Matrix X multiplied by its _____ yields the identity matrix.
8. Give the statements that initialize a 2 × 4 matrix to 0.

Answers

1. the same dimensions 2. True 3. rows, columns 4. False
5. 10 DIM X(2,2)   6. Transposition 7. Inverse 8. 10 DIM X(2,4)
   20 MAT X = IDN   20 MAT X = ZER

A Programming Problem

Problem Definition

A program is needed that uses MAT commands to solve three linear equations with three unknowns. This type of problem is very common in statistics, the sciences, engineering, and the area of business administration called operations research. Our method for solving this problem can easily be expanded for use with higher numbers of equations and unknowns.

In this example, we want to find the values X_1, X_2, and X_3 that will simultaneously satisfy the following three equations:

$$14X_1 - X_2 + 3X_3 = 21$$
$$4X_1 - X_2 + 2X_3 = 8$$
$$X_1 + 2X_2 - 3X_3 = -4$$

Solution Design

If we look at this problem in terms of matrices, we can analyze the three equations in the following manner. Let's place the coefficients of each equation in the matrix C:

$$C = \begin{vmatrix} 14 & -1 & 3 \\ 4 & -1 & 2 \\ 1 & 2 & -3 \end{vmatrix}$$

The three unknowns are placed in the matrix X:

$$X = \begin{vmatrix} X_1 \\ X_2 \\ X_3 \end{vmatrix}$$

Finally, we place the results of the equations in matrix R:

$$R = \begin{vmatrix} 21 \\ 8 \\ -4 \end{vmatrix}$$

The resulting matrix math operation follows. Use your knowledge of the matrix multiplication formula to verify that this operation yields the original equations.

$$\begin{vmatrix} 14 & -1 & 3 \\ 4 & -1 & 2 \\ 1 & 2 & -3 \end{vmatrix} * \begin{vmatrix} X_1 \\ X_2 \\ X_3 \end{vmatrix} = \begin{vmatrix} 21 \\ 8 \\ -4 \end{vmatrix}$$

In matrix notation, the three equations can be written as follows:

$CX = R$

We can use the inverse of matrix C to solve this problem in the following steps:

1. Multiply both sides by the inverse of C (C^{-1}):

$C^{-1} CX = C^{-1} R$

In order to obtain the integer values that solve this equation, it is necessary to round the values in the inverse matrix to the nearest integer.

2. Notice that $C^{-1}C$ yields the identity matrix:

$$\begin{vmatrix} 1 & 0 & 0 \\ 0 & 1 & 0 \\ 0 & 0 & 1 \end{vmatrix}$$

Therefore,

$IX = C^{-1} R$

where I represents the identity matrix. Remember that any matrix multiplied by the identity matrix yields itself:

$X = C^{-1} R$

FIGURE 12–2
Stepwise Refinement of Linear Equations Problem

> **General Problem:** Find the values of X1, X2, and X3 that will simultaneously solve 3 equations.
>
> **Level 1**
>   A. Read coefficients and results to arrays
>   B. Calculate inverse array and print
>   C. Calculate and print the identity matrix
>   D. Calculate and print the solution

As the above statement shows, all we have to do to find the matrix X is to multiply matrix R by the inverse of matrix C.

The stepwise refinement and structure chart for this problem are shown in Figures 12–2 and 12–3.

The Program

Figure 12–4 shows the complete program. Line 90 sets the dimensions of the arrays (matrices) C, X, R, I, and D.

Line 110 reads data to the coefficient matrix, C, and line 160 prints C. Line 120 reads data to the result matrix, R. Line 180 makes I the inverse of C. I is then printed by line 260. Notice that lines 190 through 230 use the INT function to round each element of Matrix I. (To illustrate better how the inverse works, lines 280 through 310 multiply C by its own inverse and print the result—the identity matrix.) Line 330 calculates the solution (three unknowns, X_1, X_2, and X_3) by multiplying R by the inverse of C. The solution is printed by line 360.

The output of the program displays the coefficient matrix C, its inverse, and these two multiplied by each other to correctly produce the identity

FIGURE 12–3 Structure Chart for Linear Equations Problem

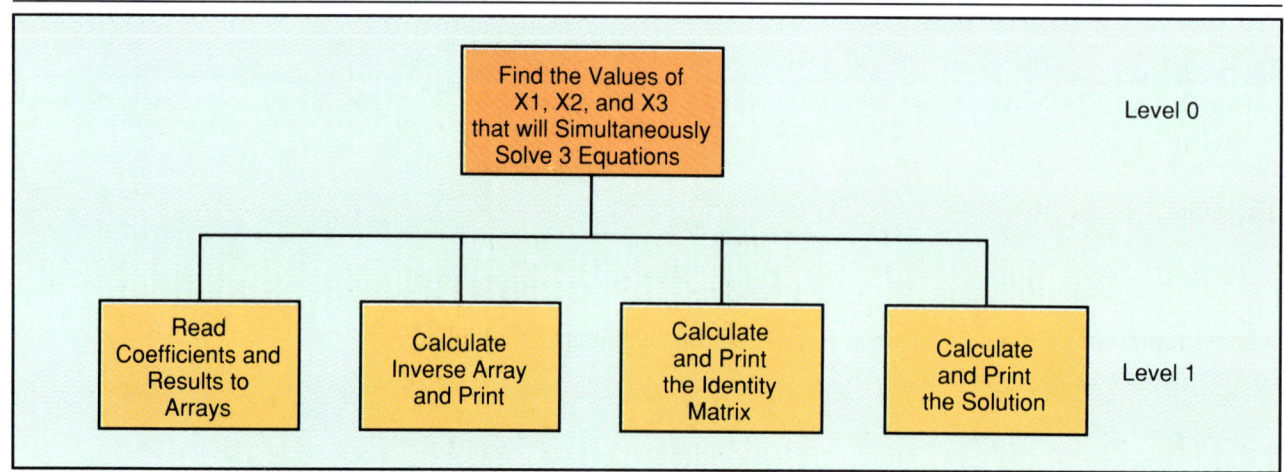

FIGURE 12–4 Linear Equations Program

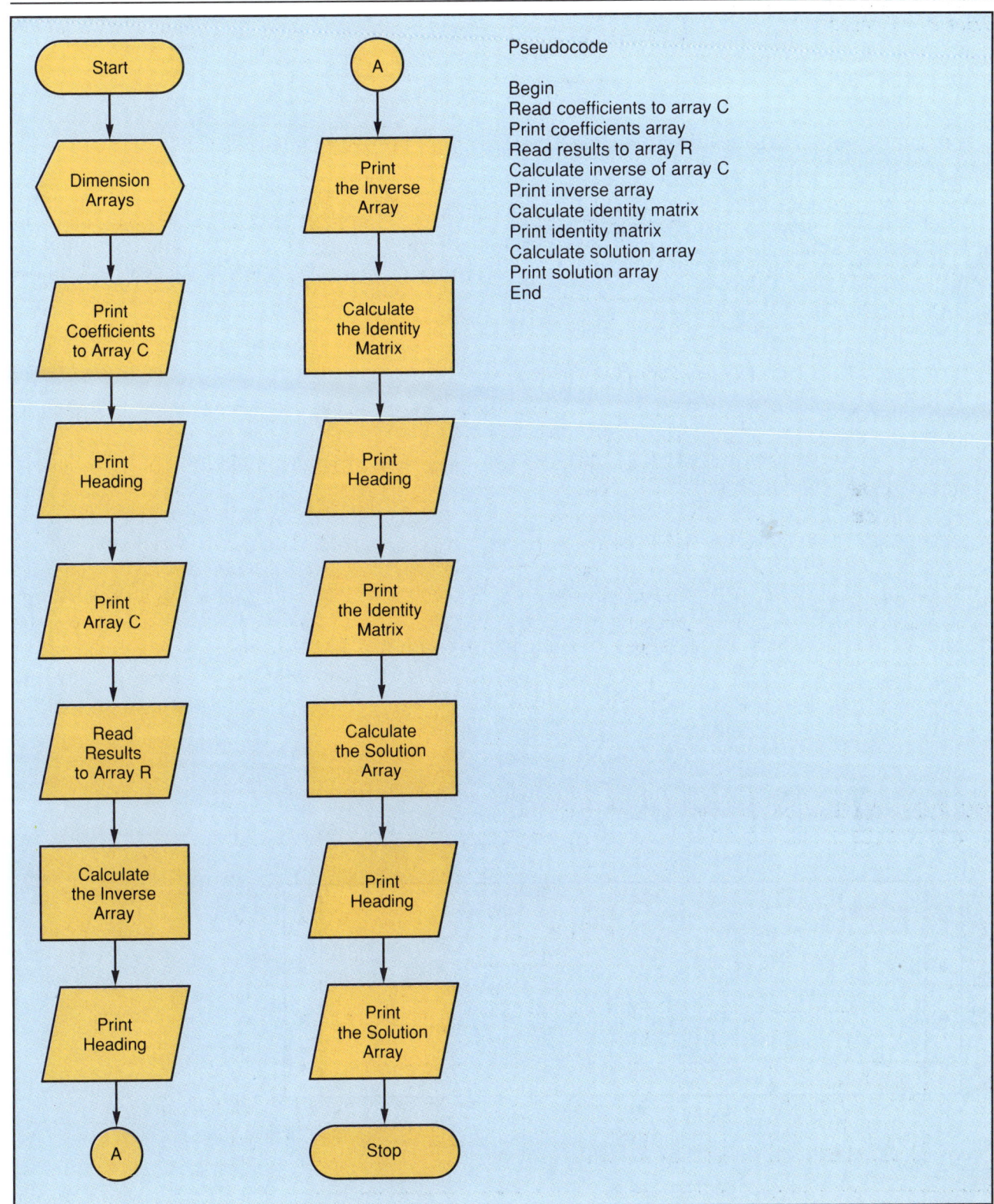

FIGURE 12–4 Continued

```
10   REM ***   THIS PROGRAM SOLVES A LINEAR EQUATION.   ***
20   REM ***   MAJOR VARIABLES:                         ***
30   REM ***     C   COEFFICIENT ARRAY                  ***
40   REM ***     X   ARRAY OF UNKNOWNS                  ***
50   REM ***     R   RESULTS ARRAY                      ***
60   REM ***     I   INVERSE OF C                       ***
70   REM
80   REM *** DIMENSION THE ARRAYS. ***
90   DIM C(3,3), X(3,1), R(3,1), I(3,3), D(3,3)
100  REM *** READ C AND R MATRICES. ***
110  MAT READ C
120  MAT READ R
130  PRINT
140  PRINT
150  PRINT "THE COEFFICIENT MATRIX -- C"
160  MAT PRINT C,
170  REM *** FIND INVERSE OF MATRIX C. ***
180  MAT I = INV(C)
190  FOR C1 = 1 TO 3
200     FOR C2 = 1 TO 3
210        I(C1,C2) = INT(I(C1,C2) + 0.5)
220     NEXT C2
230  NEXT C1
240  PRINT
250  PRINT "INVERSE OF MATRIX C"
260  MAT PRINT I,
270  REM *** PROVE IDENTITY FUNCTION. ***
280  MAT D = I * C
290  PRINT
300  PRINT "INVERSE OF C TIMES C SHOULD BE IDENTITY MATRIX."
310  MAT PRINT D,
320  REM *** DETERMINE SOLUTIONS. ***
330  MAT X = I * R
340  PRINT
350  PRINT "SOLUTION -- MATRIX X"
360  MAT PRINT X,
370  REM *** DATA STATEMENTS ***
380  DATA 14,-1,3,4,-1,2,1,2,-3,21,8,-4
999  END
```

```
RUNNH


THE COEFFICIENT MATRIX -- C
 14              -1               3
  4              -1               2
  1               2              -3
```

FIGURE 12–4 *Continued*

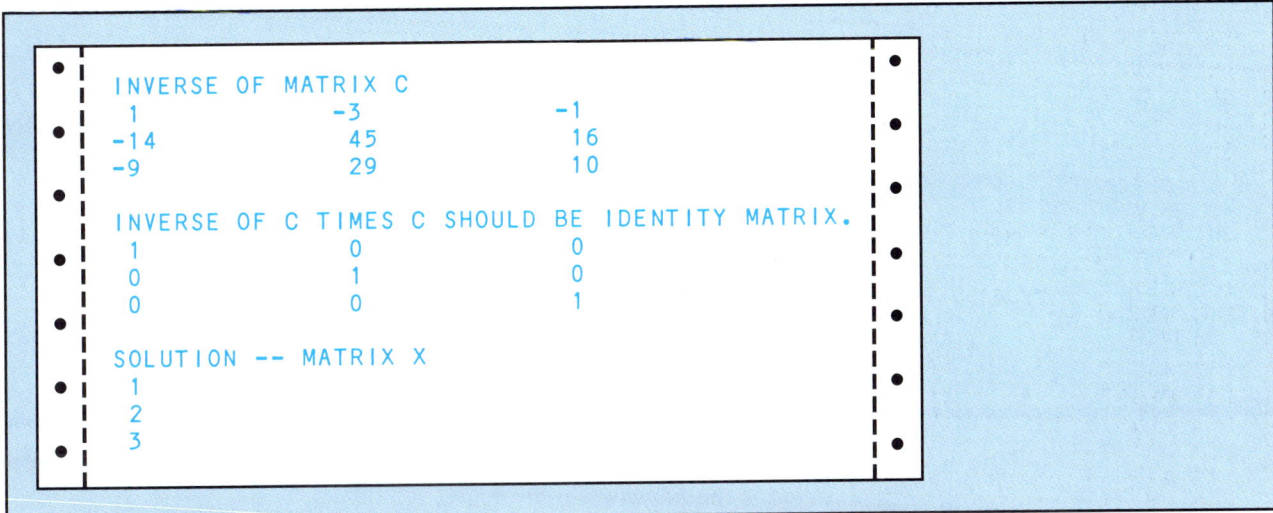

matrix. The solution shows that $X_1 = 1$, $X_2 = 2$, and $X_3 = 3$. You can verify the results by putting these values back into the original equations and observing that these numbers do indeed satisfy the equations.

Avoiding Common Programming Mistakes

- An array should appear in a DIM statement before it is used in a MAT command.
- To avoid an "out of data" error message, make sure that all the positions of a matrix are filled.
- Remember that only one MAT command can be performed at a time.
- Be sure to place the scalar value in parentheses in scalar multiplication.
- Be aware of the dimension requirements for arrays used in the various operations and functions. (For instance, the dimensions of the new matrix that contains the transposed matrix values are the reverse of the dimensions of the matrix to be transposed.)

Summary Points

- A matrix is another name for an array.
- Some implementations of BASIC provide MAT statements to simplify array operations.
- The MAT READ and MAT PRINT statements read and print data in row order.
- The MAT INPUT statement permits data to be entered to a matrix at the keyboard.

- There are MAT commands that perform the mathematical manipulations of addition, subtraction, multiplication, scalar multiplication, and replacement.
- Various dimension requirements are placed on arrays used with the MAT operations and functions.
- The ZER function initializes each element of a matrix to 0; the CON function initializes each element of a matrix to 1.
- The IDN function creates an identity matrix.
- To transpose a matrix, the TRN function is used.
- Matrix inversion is achieved by the INV function.
- A matrix multiplied by its inverse yields the identity matrix.

Review Questions

1. What is a matrix?
2. What is the keyword in all matrix commands?
3. How do the MAT READ and MAT INPUT commands read data?
4. What statement will reserve space for a 4 × 5 matrix called M?
5. What statement will print the matrix M in matrix table form?
6. What restriction is placed on matrices involved in addition, subtraction, and replacement?
7. How are matrices added?
8. When can a matrix appear on both sides of an equal sign?
9. What restriction is placed on the multiplication of matrices?
10. If matrix A is 3 × 5 and B is 5 × 4, what are the dimensions of matrix C, which is A * B?
11. Explain how one matrix is multiplied by another.
12. What is a scalar value, and how do you multiply a matrix by a scalar value?
13. What command initializes an array to 0?
14. What does the statement MAT A = CON do?
15. What is an identity matrix?
16. How do you create an identity matrix, and what restrictions are placed on its dimensions?
17. What is the transposition of a matrix?
18. What are the dimensions of matrix B, if MAT B = TRN(A), where A is a 2 × 3 matrix?
19. What is the inverse of a matrix, and what command will invert matrix X?
20. Why is the inverse of a matrix useful?

Debugging Exercises

Identify the following programs and program segments that contain errors and debug them.

1.
```
10 MAT READ A
20 MAT PRINT A,
30 DATA 10,20,30,40,50,60
```
2.
```
10 DIM X(3,2)
20 MAT READ X
30 MAT PRINT X
40 DATA 2,0,3,9,6
```
3.
```
10 REM *** ADD MATRICES A AND B AND PLACE IN C. ***
20 DIM A(2,3),B(2,3),C(2,3)
30 PRINT "INPUT MATRIX A"
40 MAT INPUT A
50 PRINT "INPUT MATRIX B"
60 MAT INPUT B
70 C = A + B
80 MAT PRINT C,
```
4.
```
10 REM *** SUBTRACT MATRIX B FROM A AND STORE RESULT IN C. ***
20 DIM A(2,3),B(2,3),C(2,3)
30 MAT READ A
40 MAT READ X
50 MAT C = A - B
60 REM *** PRINT RESULTING MATRIX. ***
70 MAT PRINT C,
80 DATA 1,2,3,4,5,6,7,8,9,10,11,12
```
5.
```
10 REM *** MULTIPLY MATRIX X BY Y AND STORE IN Z. ***
20 DIM X(2,4),Y(4,3),Z(4,3)
30 MAT INPUT X
40 MAT INPUT Y
50 MAT Z = X * Y
60 MAT PRINT Z,
```
6.
```
10 REM *** MULTIPLY A BY B AND STORE RESULT IN C. ***
20 DIM A(2,3),B(3,4),C(2,4)
30 MAT INPUT A
40 MAT INPUT B
50 MAT C = A * B
60 MAT PRINT C,
```
7.
```
10 REM *** MULTIPLY MATRIX X BY THE SCALAR VALUE 6. ***
20 DIM X(3,3)
30 MAT READ X
40 MAT X = 6 * X
50 MAT PRINT X,
60 DATA 22,20,6,3,7,5,9,3,4
```
8.
```
10 REM *** INITIALIZE ALL ELEMENTS OF A TO ONE. ***
20 DIM A(4,3)
30 MAT A = ONE
40 MAT PRINT X,
```
9.
```
10 REM *** SET X TO THE IDENTITY MATRIX. ***
20 DIM X(3,4)
30 MAT X = IDN
40 MAT PRINT X,
```
10.
```
10 REM *** TRANSPOSE MATRIX B AND PLACE IN A. ***
20 DIM A(5,4),B(5,4)
30 MAT INPUT B
40 MAT A TRN(B)
50 MAT PRINT A
```

Additional Programming Problems

Level 1

1. Write a program segment to read the following array, using the MAT READ statement:

$$\begin{vmatrix} 78 & 17 \\ 42 & 90 \\ 33 & 49 \end{vmatrix}$$

Then print this matrix, using the MAT PRINT statement.

2. Write a program segment using the MAT INPUT statement to allow the user to enter data to a 5 × 5 matrix.

3. Write a program segment to create an identity matrix with dimensions 6 × 6.

4. Write a program segment to multiply the following matrix by 4. Print the resulting matrix.

$$\begin{vmatrix} 12 & 19 & 49 \\ 0 & 77 & 50 \\ 106 & 18 & 85 \end{vmatrix}$$

5. Write a program segment to add the following two matrices and print the resulting matrix:

$$\begin{vmatrix} 7 & 10 & 8 \\ 1 & 12 & 44 \end{vmatrix} + \begin{vmatrix} 19 & 0 & 4 \\ 2 & 7 & 50 \end{vmatrix}$$

6. Write a program to transpose matrix M and store the result in matrix N. Then print matrices M and N.

Matrix M

$$\begin{vmatrix} 4.8 & 17.0 & 6.5 \\ 12.1 & 11.0 & 10.9 \\ 17.6 & 18.8 & 9.2 \end{vmatrix}$$

7. Write a program to multiply the following two matrices and print the resulting matrix:

$$\begin{vmatrix} 2 & 3.9 \\ 7 & 15 \\ 0 & 19 \end{vmatrix} * \begin{vmatrix} 7.5 & 5 & 4.6 \\ 8 & 6.2 & 10.3 \end{vmatrix}$$

8. Read your own data to a 4 × 2 matrix. Use the initialization command,

CON, to add 1 to each element of the matrix. Print both the original and incremented matrices.

9. Write a program that allows the user to enter data to a 4 × 4 matrix called D. Then use a single statement to copy this matrix D to matrix E. Print E.

10. Write a program to read matrix M. Find the inverse of M and then print both matrices.

Matrix M

$$\begin{vmatrix} 4 & 12 & 1 \\ 42 & 17 & 68 \\ 80 & 3 & 0 \end{vmatrix}$$

Level 2

1. Write a program to do the following:
  a. Add matrix A to matrix B.

Matrix A   **Matrix B**

$$\begin{vmatrix} 2 & 4 \\ 9 & 7 \end{vmatrix} \quad \begin{vmatrix} 16 & 10 \\ 7 & 12 \end{vmatrix}$$

  b. Multiply the resulting matrix by 2.
  c. Transpose the resulting matrix, and print this new matrix.

2. Assume that A is a 2 × 4 matrix, B is a 4 × 3 matrix, and C is a 3 × 3 matrix. Write a program, using your own data, which will verify the following equation:

$$(A * B)C = A(B * C)$$

3. Given the following matrix A, write a program to print A and to compute and print its transposition and inverse (A^{-1}). Then multiply A by A^{-1} and A^{-1} by A, and print the results. Can you explain these results?

$$A = \begin{vmatrix} 1 & 2 & 3 \\ -9 & 8 & 7 \\ -2 & 5 & -7 \end{vmatrix}$$

4. Write a program to read the distances in yards given in array Y. Then convert these distances to feet and then to inches. Print all three matrices with appropriate labels.

Array Y

$$\begin{vmatrix} 14 & 2.5 & 3 \\ 6 & 20 & 17 \end{vmatrix}$$

5. Epstein's Department Store is having a sale. All items are discounted by 15 percent. The current prices of these items are listed below. Write a program that will print a labeled listing of the sale prices.

Sweaters	Jeans	Mittens	Socks	Galoshes
25.95	22.00	5.80	2.29	19.89

6. Write a program to read your own data to a 5 × 5 matrix. Find the inverse of this matrix and then multiply the two matrices together. Place the result in a third matrix. Print all three matrices with appropriate labels at the end of the program.

7. Mr. Brown teaches a class in computer science. He decided to curve the grades at the end of the semester by adding five points to each test. Write a program to compute the new grades for Mr. Brown. The grades are now as follows:

Student	Test 1	Test 2	Test 3
Alice	70	65	73
Joe	81	79	74
Bob	93	95	89
Sue	87	83	85
Peg	54	63	70

8. Find the values of X and Y that will simultaneously satisfy these two equations:

$$Y + 3X = 15$$
$$4Y + X = 16$$

9. Find the values of A and B that will simultaneously satisfy these two equations:

$$10A + 3B = 51$$
$$2B + 2A = 34$$

10. The White Snowmobile Company sells three models of snowmobiles (regular, super, and deluxe) in two colors (red and blue). The snowmobile sales for January and February are recorded here. Compute the total and average sales for each type of snowmobile.

January	Regular	Super	Deluxe
Red	3	5	2
Blue	1	4	1

February	Regular	Super	Deluxe
Red	7	2	3
Blue	4	1	6

Level 3

1. Smiley's Pizza Pub determines the price of its pizzas by size (10-, 14-, or 16-inch) and number of toppings (a maximum of three). Their prices are as follows:

	10"	14"	16"
1 topping	4.00	5.90	7.20
2 toppings	4.50	6.40	8.00
3 toppings	4.85	6.85	8.75

Print a matrix that will give the prices of the above pizzas after a 6 percent sales tax has been added.

2. An insurance company has the following income and expenses over a three-month period. Write a program that calculates the company's monthly profit. Also, determine the amount of cash to be reserved for Christmas bonuses based on 10 percent of the monthly profit. (Hint: Use two 1×3 matrices.)

	October	November	December
Income	22,247	25,475	34,628
Expenses	17,753	19,091	23,152

3. Write a program that uses MAT commands to calculate paychecks at Kinko's Duck Farm. All employees make $6.50 per hour. They are paid time-and-a-half for any hours they work over 40. Here is the data:

	George	Monica	Herman	Irene
Hours	42	45	40	50

Print a matrix showing how much each employee's paycheck should be. Label it appropriately.

4. The following matrix contains the diameters of eight circles. Write a program that will:
  a. Read and print the matrix.
  b. Print a matrix containing the radii of these circles.
  c. Print a matrix containing the circumferences of these circles.

4.5	8.2	1.0	3.7
6.9	10.0	5.1	7.6

5. Michelle always serves the same four items at her parties: soda pop, chips, hot dogs, and cookies. Allow her to enter a matrix containing the amount of each item needed per guest. Then allow her to enter the number of guests, and multiply this number by the matrix. Print the resulting matrix so that Michelle will know how much of each item to buy.

6. Dr. Dadfar, a professor of archeology, is heading an expedition to Greece, and wishes to take with him as assistants the five students with the highest final scores. The final score for each student is the average of the following scores:

Student	Tests	Lab	Project	Exam
Mamud	97	93	99	92
Angelita	68	50	75	88
Tony	88	99	95	98
Tom	62	40	78	72
Monica	94	86	92	94
Anisa	87	73	63	82
Irene	68	79	87	75
Eickle	88	92	62	94

Before averaging the four scores to calculate the final score, Dr. Dadfar is adding 5 percent to the project scores. Write a program to calculate and print the final score for each student.

7. Felicia's Fragrances, a perfume boutique, sold the following number of 3-ounce bottles of perfume for the standard price of $11.95 each:

Fragrance	December	January
Floral	150	75
Sports	100	32
Evening	125	61

Write a program to calculate and print the total income for each fragrance category in December (allowing for a sale of 20 percent off all fragrances that month), in January, and the average for the two months.

8. The Waite Public Library would like to know the total of each type of book (paperback, general, or magazine) checked out over a three-month period from all three of its branches. The following are the statistics for each branch. Print a table listing totals per month of each type of book. Then print a table containing the averages per month for each type of book.

	Branch 1			Branch 2			Branch 3		
	July	Aug.	Sept.	July	Aug.	Sept.	July	Aug.	Sept.
Paperback	387	419	622	202	322	585	345	405	609
General	692	520	810	604	501	723	606	487	791
Magazine	140	93	155	90	78	106	120	84	142

9. The Fairlawn Racquet Club just held its annual family tennis tournament. Points were awarded based on the number of matches won. The highest-scoring families are listed in the following table:

Family	Husband	Points	Wife	Points	Child	Points
Rostov	Anthony	10	Monica	1	Tony	5
Springsteen	Bruce	6	Yvonne	2	Gabriel	2
Bulas	Robert	7	Lesley	6	Anne	3
Tully	Mark	3	Kate	0	Levi	4
Dylan	Bob	0	Joan	5	Oliver	1

The three scores earned by each family are added together to calculate the final score awarded to each family. Before calculating this final score the children's scores are doubled, and the scores of the wives are incremented by 1.

Write a program that will print a roster of the final scores awarded to each family, including appropriate headings. Be sure to use at least one matrix function in your program.

10. The demand for a product is given by the equation $100p - q = 300$. The supply of that same product is given by the equation $100p + q = 500$. In these equations, p stands for the price of the product, and q stands for the number of units demanded or supplied. Write a program to find p and q so that all products produced will be sold. That is, solve the simultaneous linear equations for p and q. (Hint: See ''A Programming Problem'' at the end of this chapter.)

APPENDIX A

RESERVED WORDS

VAX BASIC

ABORT	FIELD	LINPUT	POS
ABS	FILE	LOCKED	POS$
ALL	FILL	LOG	PPS
AND	FILL$	LOG10	PRIMARY
APPEND	FIND	LSA	PRINT
AS	FIX	MAP	PUT
ASCII	FNEND	MAR%	RAD$
ATN	FNEXIT	MARGIN	RANDOMIZE
BY	FOR	MAT	RCTRLC
CALL	FROM	MID$	RCTRLO
CHAIN	GE	MOD	READ
CHR$	GET	MOD%	RECORD
CLK$	GO	MODE	RECORDSIZE
CLOSE	GOSUB	MODIFY	REM
COMMON	GOTO	MOVE	RESET
CONT	GT	NAME	RESTORE
COS	IDN	NEXT	RESUME
CTRLC	IF	NEW	RETURN
DAT$	IFEND	NOCHANGES	RIGHT$
DATA	IFMORE	NODATA	RND
DATE	IMAGE	NODUPLICATES	SCRATCH
DEF	IMP	NOECHO	SEG$
DEL	INPUT	NONE	SGN
DELETE	INSTR	NOSPAN	SIN
DIM	INT	NOT	SLEEP
ECHO	INV	NUL$	SP
EDIT$	INVALID	NUM	SPACE$
ELSE	KEY	ON	SPAN
END	KILL	ONERROR	SQR
EXP	LEFT	OPEN	SQRT
EQV	LEFT$	OR	STATUS
ERR	LEN	OUTPUT	STEP
ERROR	LET	PAGE	STOP
EXP	LINO	PI	STR$

STREAM	TIME	UNLESS	VPS%
SUB	TIME$	UNLOCK	WAIT
SUBEXIT	TRM$	UNTIL	WHILE
SYS	TRN	UPDATE	WITH
TAB	TO	USR$	XLATE
TAN	UNALIGNED	VAL	XOR
THEN			

Apple/Applesoft BASIC

ABS	GR	NOT	SCRN(
ABD	HCOLOR=	NOTRACE	SGN
AND	HGR	ON	SHLOAD
ASC	HGR2	ONERR	SIN
AT	HIMEM:	OR	SPC(
ATN	HLIN	PDL	SPEED=
CALL	HOME	PEEK	SQR
CHR$	HPLOT	PLOT	STEP
CLEAR	HTAB	POKE	STOP
COLOR=	IF	POP	STORE
CONT	IN#	POS	STR$
COS	INPUT	PRINT	TAB(
DATA	INT	PR#	TAN
DEF	INVERSE	READ	TEXT
DEL	LEFT$	RECALL	THEN
DIM	LEN	REM	TO
END	LET	RESTORE	TRACE
EXP	LIST	RESUME	USR
FLASH	LOAD	RETURN	VAL
FN	LOG	RIGHT$	VLIN
FOR	LOMEM:	RND	VTAB
FRE	MID$	ROT=	WAIT
GET	NEW	RUN	XDRAW
GOSUB	NEXT	SAVE	
GOTO	NORMAL	SCALE=	

The following Apple DOS commands are considered reserved words only when used in immediate mode or in a PRINT statement beginning with a CTRL-D character.

APPEND	CLOSE	LOCK	RUN
BLOAD	DELETE	OPEN	SAVE
BRUN	EXEC	POSITION	UNLOCK
BSAVE	INIT	READ	VERIFY
CHAIN	LOAD	RENAME	WRITE

IBM/Microsoft BASIC

ABS	EQV	LPRINT	RND
AND	ERASE	LSET	RSET
ASC	ERDEV	MERGE	RUN
ATN	ERDEV$	MID$	SAVE
AUTO	ERL	MKDIR	SCREEN
BEEP	ERR	MKD$	SGN
BLOAD	ERROR	MKI$	SHELL
BSAVE	EXP	MKS$	SIN
CALL	FIELD	MOD	SOUND
CDBL	FILES	MOTOR	SPACE$
CHAIN	FIX	NAME	SPC(
CHDIR	FN*xxxxxxxx*	NEW	SQR
CHR$	FOR	NEXT	STEP
CINT	FRE	NOT	STICK
CIRCLE	GET	OCT$	STOP
CLEAR	GOSUB	OFF	STR$
CLOSE	GOTO	ON	STRIG
CLS	HEX$	OPEN	STRING$
COLOR	IF	OPTION	SWAP
COM	IMP	OR	SYSTEM
COMMON	INKEY$	OUT	TAB(
CONT	INP	PAINT	TAN
COS	INPUT	PEEK	THEN
CSNG	INPUT#	PEN	TIME$
CSRLIN	INPUT$	PLAY	TIMER
CVD	INSTR	PMAP	TO
CVI	INT	POINT	TROFF
CVS	INTER$	POKE	TRON
DATA	IOCTL	POS	USING
DATE$	IOCTL$	PRESET	USR
DEF	KEY	PRINT	VAL
DEFDBL	KILL	PRINT#	VARPTR
DEFINT	LEFT$	PSET	VARPTR$
DEFSNG	LEN	PUT	VIEW
DEFSTR	LET	RANDOMIZE	WAIT
DELETE	LINE	READ	WEND
DIM	LIST	REM	WHILE
DRAW	LLIST	RENUM	WIDTH
EDIT	LOAD	RESET	WINDOW
ELSE	LOC	RESTORE	WRITE
END	LOCATE	RESUME	WRITE#
ENVIRON	LOF	RETURN	XOR
ENVIRON$	LOG	RIGHT$	
EOF	LPOS	RMDIR	

Macintosh/Microsoft BASIC

ABS	EOF	INVERTOVAL	OUTPUT
ALL	EQV	INVERTPOLY	PAINTARC
AND	ERASE	INVERTRECT	PAINTOVAL
APPEND	ERASEARC	INVERTROUNDRECT	PAINTPOLY
AS	ERASEOVAL	KILL	PAINTRECT
ASC	ERASEPOLY	LBOUND	PAINTROUNDRECT
ATN	ERASERECT	LCOPY	PEEK
BACKPAT	ERASEROUNDRECT	LEFT$	PENMODE
BASE	ERL	LEN	PENNORMAL
BEEP	ERR	LET	PENPAT
BREAK	ERROR	LIBRARY	PENSIZE
BUTTON	EXIT	LINE	PICTURE
CALL	EXP	LINETO	POINT
CDBL	FIELD	LIST	POKE
CHAIN	FILES	LLIST	POS
CHR$	FILLARC	LOAD	PRESET
CINT	FILLOVAL	LOC	PRINT
CIRCLE	FILLPOLY	LOCATE	PSET
CLEAR	FILLRECT	LOF	PTAB
CLOSE	FILLROUNDRECT	LOG	PUT
CLS	FIX	LPOS	RANDOMIZE
COMMON	FN	LPRINT	READ
CONT	FOR	LSET	REM
COS	FRAMEARC	MENU	RESET
CSNG	FRAMEOVAL	MERGE	RESTORE
CSRLIN	FRAMEPOLY	MID$	RESUME
CVD	FRAMERECT	MKD$	RETURN
CVDBCD	FRAMEROUNDRECT	MKI$	RIGHT$
CVI	FRE	MKS$	RND
CVS	GET	MOD	RSET
CVSBCD	GETPEN	MOUSE	RUN
DATA	GOSUB	MOVE	SAVE
DATE$	GOTO	MOVETO	SCROLL
DEF	HEX$	NAME	SETCURSOR
DEFDBL	HIDECURSOR	NEW	SGN
DEFINT	HIDEPEN	NEXT	SHARED
DEFSNG	IF	NOT	SHOWCURSOR
DEFSTR	IMP	OBSCURECURSOR	SHOWPEN
DELETE	INITCURSOR	OCT$	SIN
DIALOG	INKEY$	OFF	SOUND
DIM	INPUT	ON	SPACE$
EDIT	INSTR	OPEN	SPC
ELSE	INT	OPTION	SQR
END	INVERTARC	OR	STATIC

STEP	TEXTFACE	TROFF	WAIT
STOP	TEXTFONT	TRON	WAVE
STR$	TEXTMODE	UBOUND	WEND
STRING$	TEXTSIZE	UCASE$	WHILE
SWAP	THEN	USING	WIDTH
SYSTEM	TIME	USR	WINDOW
TAB	TIMER	VAL	WRITE
TAN	TO	VARPTR	XOR

APPENDIX

BASIC OPERATORS

Arithmetic

    ^   (exponentiation)
    +   (unary; the sign used alone with a number)
    −   (unary; the sign used alone with a number)
    *   (multiplication)
    /   (division)
    +   (addition)
    −   (subtraction)

String

    +   (concatenation)

Relational

=	<=
<> or ><	>
<	>=

Boolean

NOT
AND
OR

Order of Precedence

1. Exponentiation
2. Unary plus and minus
3. Multiplication and division
4. Addition and subtraction
5. Concatenation
6. Relational operators
7. NOT
8. AND
9. OR

APPENDIX C

NUMERIC FUNCTIONS

Function	Operation
ABS(X)	Absolute value of X
ATN(X)	Trigonometric arctangent of X radians
COS(X)	Trigonometric cosine of X radians
EXP(X)	e^x
INT(X)	Greatest integer less than or equal to X
LOG(X)	Natural logarithm (if $x = e^y$, LOG(X) = Y)
RND	Random number between 0 and 1
SGN(X)	Sign of X: +1 if X > 0, 0 if X = 0, −1 if X < 0
SIN(X)	Trigonometric sine of X radians
SQR(X)	Square root of X
TAN(X)	Trigonometric tangent of X radians

APPENDIX

STRING FUNCTIONS

Function	Operation	Example
string1 + string2	Concatenation; joins two strings	"KUNG" + "FU" is "KUNGFU"
ASCII(string) or ASC(string)	Returns the ASCII code for the first character in the string.	If A$ = "DOG", THEN ASCII(A$) is 68
CHR$(integer expression)	Returns the string representation of the ASCII code of the expression.	CHR$(68) is "D"
LEFT$(string, integer expression)	Returns the number of leftmost characters of a string specified by the expression.	LEFT$("ABCD",2) is "AB"
LEN(string)	Returns the length of a string.	IF N$ = "HI THERE", THEN LEN(N$) is 8
MID$(string, expression1, expression2)	Starting with the character at expression1, returns the number of characters specified by expression2.	MID$("MARIE",2,3) is "ARI"
RIGHT$(string, expression)	VAX system: Returns the rightmost characters of a string, starting with the character specified by the expression.	RIGHT$("ABCDE",2) is BCDE
	Microcomputers: Returns the number of rightmost characters specified by the expression.	RIGHT$("ABCDE",2) is "DE"
STR$(expression)	Converts a number to its string equivalent.	STR$(123) is "123"
VAL(string)	Returns the numeric value of a number string.	IF N$ = "352 63", THEN VAL(N$) is 35263

APPENDIX

ASCII CODE

Below is a list of commonly used ASCII code characters.

	CHAR		CHAR		CHAR		CHAR		CHAR		CHAR
32	SPC	48	0	64	@	80	P	96	`	112	p
33	!	49	1	65	A	81	Q	97	a	113	q
34	"	50	2	66	B	82	R	98	b	114	r
35	#	51	3	67	C	83	S	99	c	115	s
36	$	52	4	68	D	84	T	100	d	116	t
37	%	53	5	69	E	85	U	101	e	117	u
38	&	54	6	70	F	86	V	102	f	118	v
39	'	55	7	71	G	87	W	103	g	119	w
40	(	56	8	72	H	88	X	104	h	120	x
41	)	57	9	73	I	89	Y	105	i	121	y
42	*	58	:	74	J	90	Z	106	j	122	z
43	+	59	;	75	K	91	[	107	k	123	{
44	,	60	<	76	L	92	\	108	l	124	|
45	-	61	=	77	M	93	]	109	m	125	}
46	.	62	>	78	N	94	^	110	n	126	~
47	/	63	?	79	O	95	_	111	o	127	DEL

APPENDIX

GETTING STARTED ON THE VAX

The computer used to run the programs in this text is one of the VAX 8500 series, a VAX 8530. This computer uses the VMS operating system. It can contain up to several million bytes of addressable internal storage for programs. The implementation of BASIC used is VAX BASIC, Version 3.2.

Instructions for accessing the VAX depend heavily on the type of terminal being used. Two popular CRT terminals are discussed here: the VT100 and VT220. The manufacturer's user guides provide further hardware information.

Signing On

On both the VT100 and VT220, the power switch (toggle variety) is at the lower left on the back of the video monitor. To turn on the VT100, flip the power switch up. On the VT220, press the "1" on the power switch down.

When the power is on and the cursor (a solid rectangular box) appears at the top left of the screen, hit the <RETURN> key to initiate the link between the terminal and the computer. A message similar to the following will appear:

Welcome to the VAX 8500 (NodeName) VMS version 4.6

Username:

This is the system log in prompt. Now the system needs some identification information so it can locate your account (that is, your space in the system). After you supply each requested data item, press the <RETURN> key to let the system know that you have finished. Enter your username, and then your password:

Username: MANDELL
Password:

Notice that the characters you type as your password do not appear on the screen. This helps keep your password a secret to protect your account from unauthorized access by others.

527

After you have properly logged in, the computer responds with some opening messages. For example:

```
Last Interactive login on Thursday, 25-AUG-1988 8:22
```

If the computer is down, either a "temporarily unavailable" message will appear, or there will be no response to your log in request.

System Commands

The commands in this section must be executed at the system prompt ($) and not in the BASIC environment. Some commonly used system commands are listed below.

Signing Off

To sign off the system, type

```
$LOGOUT
```

After the computer acknowledges your message, turn off the terminal.

Displaying the Files in Your Account

To list the files in your account, type

```
$DIR
```

The names of your files will appear:

```
Directory DISK$USER5:[ACCT.MANDELL]

LOGIN.COM;1    PROG1.BAS;1    PROG2.BAS;1
```

Deleting a File

To remove a file from your account, use

```
$DEL PROG1.BAS;1
```

You must include all the punctuation and the version number (the number after the semicolon).

The HELP Facility

A system HELP facility allows you to obtain information on different system commands. To get a list of available HELP topics, type

$HELP

To exit the HELP facility, hit the <RETURN> key until the system prompt returns.

The Keyboard

The VT220 keyboard includes a few more options than the VT100. If you have used a typewriter, you will find both models relatively easy to use, with a little additional instruction.

Both keyboards allow entry of all standard text characters plus some additional symbols. By pressing the <SHIFT> key, you can enter the upper symbol on those keys that have two symbols. To do this, hold down the <SHIFT> key while pressing the key with the desired symbol. The shift key can also be used to produce all uppercase letters by pressing the <CAPS LOCK> (VT100) or <LOCK> (VT220) key. On the VT100, the <CAPS LOCK> key remains depressed while activated. On the VT220, the "Lock" visual indicator light at the upper right of the keyboard remains lit. To switch back to lowercase, press the <CAPS LOCK> or <LOCK> key again.

The <CTRL> key is always used with other keys. By itself, this key does nothing. See your user's manual for the control characters created when <CTRL> is pressed with particular keys.

The following table lists some special keys on the VT100 and VT220 keyboards.

Function	VT100 Key	VT220
Stops the display, so that output doesn't scroll off the top. Press this key again to resume scrolling.	NO SCROLL (lower left)	HOLD SCREEN (upper left)
Informs the computer that you have finished entering a command or a program statement.	RETURN (right end of keypad)	RETURN (right end of keypad)
Eliminates the last character typed.	DELETE (right end of main keypad)	⟨X⟩ (right end of main keypad)
Moves cursor back one space.	BACK SPACE (just below → character)	F12 (BS) (on the top row—function key)
Moves the cursor to the beginning of the next eight-column field.	TAB	TAB

Function	VT100 Key	VT220
Curser arrows used to move the cursor in the desired direction.	↑ ↓ ← →	↑ ← ↓ →
Activates the command recall feature that allows you to scan the last group of commands and hit <RETURN> to execute a specified command again.	Not available	↑ ↓

Each key also has a special feature: when the key is held down for about a second, a stream of characters will be printed until the key is released. The auxiliary, or numeric, keypad at the right end of both the VT100 and VT220 is not used in the VAX BASIC environment.

Working in the VAX BASIC Environment

To use the BASIC language, just type BASIC <RETURN> after the system prompt ($). When the computer is prepared to accept BASIC commands, it responds with the prompt Ready.

```
$ BASIC
VAX BASIC V3.2

Ready
```

The HELP Facility

Once you have entered the VAX BASIC environment, you can select any command from the list of available BASIC commands. To display the list of HELP topics, type HELP. For example, if you want information on how to use the END statement, enter the following command:

```
HELP END
```

Information concerning the END statement will be displayed. To exit the HELP facility, press the <RETURN> key repeatedly until the READY prompt appears.

Entering a New Program

To create a program, type NEW. The computer then asks for a name for the new program:

```
NEW
New file name--IRENE.1

Ready
```

If you press <RETURN> without supplying a name, the computer will call the program NONAME. You can then proceed to type in your program.

Saving and Loading a Program

Because you already assigned a name to your program in the NEW command, no name must be given when saving your program. Simply type

```
SAVE

Ready
```

The system will save the program on disk under the name given in the NEW command.

To load a program that is in secondary storage back into the computer's main memory, use the OLD command:

```
OLD IRENE.1

Ready
```

After the computer again responds with the Ready prompt, you can list your program or execute it.

Executing a Program

Two commands can be used to execute a program: RUN and RUNNH. The first command (RUN) displays the program output along with some system information, whereas the RUNNH (RUN-No Heading) displays only the program output.

Leaving the BASIC Environment

If you are in BASIC and wish to return to the system prompt ($), type EXIT, then press <RETURN>. The computer will respond with a "$" prompt.

APPENDIX G

GETTING STARTED ON THE APPLE IIe AND APPLE IIgs

Both the Apple IIe and the Apple IIgs contain Applesoft BASIC. This version of BASIC does not contain all the control statements available on the VAX system; for example, there is no WHILE loop or IF/THEN/ELSE statement (only an IF/THEN statement). The chapters discussing these statements explain how they can be simulated in Applesoft BASIC.

Starting BASIC on the Apple IIe

On the Apple IIe the power switch is located on the left rear portion of the computer. An external monitor is required, so you also must remember to turn the power on to this device. The switch is at the upper right of the monitor. Insert the disk operating system (DOS) disk before turning the computer on. (When the disk drive "boots" the DOS, it loads from the diskette the instructions that tell the computer how to manage disk operations such as saving a program on a disk.) The computer automatically "comes up" in Applesoft BASIC, indicated by the following prompt:

]

Starting BASIC on the Apple IIgs

Insert the Apple IIgs system disk into the disk drive and turn the computer on. The power switch is on the left rear side of the computer. In addition, you must turn on the power switch for the monitor. It is on the upper right side of the monitor. The monitor brightness and contrast dials are below the power switch. After the system disk is booted, the names of the files on the disk will appear on the screen. Use the mouse to "double click" (click twice rapidly) on the file named "BASIS.System." You will then be in Applesoft BASIC as indicated by the BASIC prompt.

]

Keyboard

The Apple IIe and the Apple IIGS keyboards contain all the standard keyboard characters. On the Apple IIe, all commands must be entered in uppercase letters. Therefore, when entering BASIC programs on the IIe, press the <CAPS LOCK> key to use only uppercase mode. The Apple IIGS allows BASIC commands to be entered in either upper or lowercase letters. The <SHIFT> key can be used to enter the upper symbol on those keys that contain two symbols. For example, to enter an asterisk (*), hold down the <SHIFT> key and press the * key.

The <CONTROL> key does nothing by itself; when used with other keys, however, it produces additional control characters. A few of these sequences are listed in the following section. Check your reference manual to find the uses of other combinations.

Specialized Keys

When one of the keys in the following box is pressed, BASIC performs a specific function rather than accepting the key as keyboard data.

Key	Function
Return	Enters the line.
Reset	While holding down the <CONTROL> key, press <RESET> to stop program execution.
🍎	To restart the computer, as if you had turned the power off and back on, press <CONTROL>, the < 🍎 > key, and <RESET> at the same time.
↑ ↓ ← →	These keys move the cursor in the indicated directions.

Manipulating Programs

Programs are commonly accessed from disk on this system.

When the] prompt appears, you may begin programming in BASIC. Type NEW, press <RETURN>, and then you may begin typing your program. The NEW command erases any program that might still reside in memory and thereby avoids combining it with the new program.

] NEW

The Apple has a convenient file-by-name catalog system. To save an Applesoft program—for example, one named PROGRAM1—on disk, type the following:

```
]SAVE PROGRAM1
```

and press <RETURN>. To load the same program from disk, type this:

```
]LOAD PROGRAM1
```

and press <RETURN>. You can now run the program. Alternatively, you can type RUN PROGRAM1 without first loading the program; this causes the DOS both to load and to run the program.

Special Features

When using Applesoft BASIC, it is important to remember that only the first two characters of a variable name are recognized by the computer. Therefore, Applesoft BASIC sees the variable names ST$ and STD$ as being identical. In addition, any variable name that contains an embedded reserved word is invalid. For example, BRUN is an invalid name because it contains the reserved word RUN.

To obtain a listing of all of the files on a disk, enter

```
]CATALOG
```

Use the DELETE command to remove a program from a disk, For example, if you have a program named PROGRAM1 that you no longer want, enter the following command:

```
]DELETE PROGRAM1
```

Programs can be printed on paper by entering the command

```
]PR#1
```

If you list a program after entering this command, it will be transferred to the printer rather than being displayed on the monitor screen. To switch back to the monitor, type in

```
]PR#0
```

Anything you type in will now appear on the monitor rather than on paper.

Applesoft BASIC "comes up" in 40-column mode. This means that each line can have a maximum of 40 characters on it. To switch to 80-column mode, enter

]PR#3

Notice that the characters are smaller and closer together than in 40-column mode. If you have an Apple IIe, it must be equipped with a special 80-column card in order for you to use 80-column mode.

When writing interactive programs, you may wish to clear the monitor screen before having any prompt or program output displayed. This can be done by using the statement

10 HOME

Each key has a repeat feature: when the key is held down for more than a second, a stream of that character will be printed until you release the key.

APPENDIX

GETTING STARTED WITH IBM BASIC AND MICROSOFT GW-BASIC

Microsoft DOS and IBM DOS come with BASIC. IBM DOS is the version of DOS developed by Microsoft Corporation to be used with the IBM family of personal computers, whereas Microsoft DOS is used with IBM-compatible computers. The version of BASIC that comes with Microsoft DOS is referrred to as GW-BASIC. However, the BASIC is virtually the same for both types of systems.

Starting the Computer

For the purposes of this discussion, we will assume that you are accessing BASIC by using a floppy disk drive. If you are using a hard disk, the commands will vary slightly. Place the DOS diskette in Drive A and turn on the computer. The power switch for the IBM is at the right rear of the machine. Remember to turn on the monitor and, if necessary, adjust the brightness dial. As soon as the computer is on, it will attempt to load the DOS. Once the DOS has been booted, or loaded, the computer asks for the date and time. If you do not wish to enter the date and/or time, merely press the <⏎> (Enter) key after the prompts, which will be similar to the following:

```
A>date
Current date is Tue  1-01-1980
Enter new date (mm-dd-yy):

A>time
Current time is  0:00:44.48
Enter new time:
```

After you respond to the time prompt and press <⏎>, the computer responds with a display similar to the following:

```
Microsoft(R) MS-DOS(R)  Version 3.30
         (C) Copyright Microsoft Corp 1981-1987

A>
```

The A> is the system prompt. Simply type BASIC (for an IBM) or GWBASIC (for an IBM-compatible) and press <↵>. The BASIC prompt will appear:

Ok

Now you are ready to enter your program.

Keyboard

The IBM keyboard allows entry of all standard characters plus some special symbols that are not found on a regular typewriter, such as ^, [, and]. The shift key is marked with the symbol ⇧. While holding down the shift key, you may enter the upper symbol on any key that has two symbols. The shift keys produce uppercase letters when used with the A through Z keys. The <Caps Lock> key causes uppercase letters to be produced every time an A through Z key is pressed. While the <Caps Lock> key is on, press the shift key to type a letter in lowercase. To switch back to lowercase mode, press the <Caps Lock> key once again. In addition to the shift keys, the <Ctrl> and <Alt> keys may be used with many other keys to enter characters or perform specific functions (check your manual).

Specialized Keys

When one of the keys shown in the following box is pressed, BASIC performs a specific function rather than accepting the key as keyboard data:

Key	Function
↵	Carriage return key; usually must be pressed to enter information into the computer.
←	Backspace key (located above the carriage return key); moves the cursor one position left and erases that character.
PrtSc	Print screen key; when pressed along with the shift key, causes whatever appears on the screen to be printed on the printer.
Home	Moves the cursor to the upper left corner of the screen.
↑	Moves the cursor up one line.
↓	Moves the cursor down one line.
←	Moves the cursor one character to the left, but does not erase (located below the 4 on the numeric keyboard).
→	Moves the cursor one position to the right.
End	Moves the cursor to the end of the logical line.

Ins	Allows characters to be inserted in the statement at the current cursor position. Press it again to return to normal operation mode.
Del	Deletes the character at the current cursor position.
Esc	Causes the entire logical line to be erased from the screen; the line is not passed to BASIC for processing.
⇤⇥	Tab; moves the cursor to the next tab stop. (Tab stops occur every eight characters.)

Special Features

The IBM keyboard consists of three sections: the normal typewriter area, the function keys, and the numeric keyboard. Each key has a repeat feature, which causes it to repeat as long as the key is pressed.

The function key section (F1 through F10) is located on the left side of the keyboard. The function keys can be set to type any sequence of characters automatically. Some have already been assigned frequently used commands, but these can be changed.

The numeric keyboard, similar to a calculator keyboard, is found on the right side of the keyboard. Pressing the <NUM LOCK> key shifts the numeric keypad so that it can be used to type the numbers 0 through 9 and the decimal point. Pressing <NUM LOCK> again returns the keypad to its cursor-control mode.

When writing interactive programs, you may wish to clear the monitor screen before having any prompts displayed on the screen. This is done by using the CLS statement as shown below:

```
120 CLS
```

This will cause any previous text, such as a listing of a program, to be removed from the screen.

Manipulating Programs

BASIC uses a convenient file-by-name system to keep track of the programs stored on disk. If you are at the BASIC prompt, enter the following command to get a listing of the programs stored on disk:

```
FILES
```

If you are at the system prompt (A>), enter the following command instead:

```
DIR
```

To save a program (for example, one named TESTS), type the following:

```
SAVE "TESTS"
```

The length of the program file name should be less than or equal to eight characters. Do not embed any spaces within the program name. If you type the FILES command after saving ''TESTS,'' you will see that this program has been saved under the name TESTS.BAS. The BASIC system has supplied the extension .BAS to indicate that TESTS is a BASIC program.

In order to save and also protect a program, type:

```
SAVE "TEST",P
```

This command qualifier allows the program to be loaded and run but not listed.

To save the program in ASCII format, type

```
SAVE "TEST",A
```

Now the program is saved in text (or ASCII) format, and a word processor can be used to edit it. To load the program from a disk, type

```
LOAD "TESTS"
```

The ending quotation marks are optional. You can now list and/or run the program.

If you are in BASIC and wish to delete the program named TESTS, enter the following command:

```
KILL "TESTS.BAS"
```

Notice that it is necessary to include the extension ''.BAS'' in the KILL command.

Exiting BASIC

If you are in BASIC and wish to stop, just turn off the computer and the monitor. If, however, you wish to return to the system level, type SYSTEM and press < ↵ >. The system prompt A> indicates a successful return.

APPENDIX

GETTING STARTED ON THE MACINTOSH

The implementation of BASIC used on the Macintosh for this textbook is Microsoft 2.0.

Starting the Computer

Turn on the Macintosh power switch, which is located on the lower left side of the back of the terminal. Now place the Microsoft BASIC disk in the disk drive. When the screen comes on, you will be in the "Finder" or monitor mode. On the lower half of the screen you will see several icons, or symbols, representing the various forms of BASIC that are available for use; choose the one that best fills your needs. For the programs in this book, Decimal BASIC is the most suitable version. The "mouse," or control box, is a feature of the Macintosh that requires some explanation. It works like a remote control: you move the box in the direction you wish the screen's cursor-arrow to go. Once you have maneuvered the cursor arrow over the appropriate icon, "double-click" the button on the mouse by pressing the button twice, rapidly. The computer will now load the chosen version of Microsoft BASIC. The Command window, appearing at the bottom of the screen, indicates that you are now in BASIC.

As an alternative, the Finder will also display a box at the top of the screen containing the icons of the programs already in memory. To load the program and its appropriate version of BASIC at the same time, simply double-click the program's symbol. The computer will come up in BASIC with the program already loaded.

The Microsoft BASIC Screen

Regions

The Microsoft BASIC screen has four main regions:

1. Menu bar (located at the top of the screen)
2. Command window (appears at the bottom of the screen)
3. Output window (the left portion of the screen)
4. List window (appears on the right side of the screen when activated)

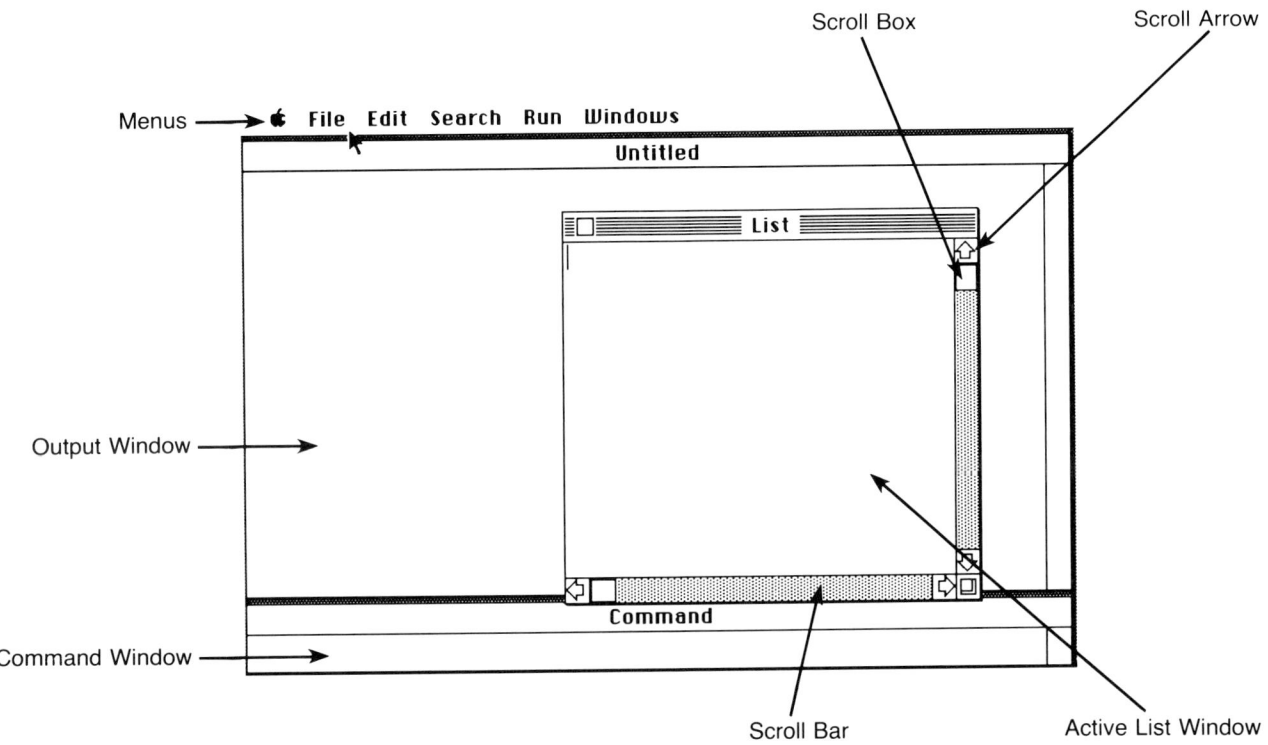

Menu Bar

The Menu Bar allows you to choose one of six menus and to gain access to the commands they contain: Apple, File, Edit, Search, Run, and Windows.

- *Apple Menu:* Contains Macintosh desk accessories.
- *File Menu:* Contains seven BASIC commands that deal with program files.
- *Edit Menu:* Contains three commands used to edit programs.
- *Search Menu:* Contains six editing commands.
- *Run Menu:* Contains six commands concerning program execution.
- *Window Menu:* Contains four commands that open windows.

Windows

To make any of the windows active, you must click the mouse button while the cursor is in the window. To close a window, simply click in the "close box," located in the upper left corner of each window. If you use the mouse to "drag" (to hold the button down while moving the mouse), the title bar will move any window around the screen. In the same way, by dragging the size box (lower right corner of the window), you can change the size of the box.

BASIC commands may be entered in the Command window and will be executed immediately; however, these commands are not stored in memory and are lost immediately after execution. The Output window displays the output of a program when it is run. When the command is given to list a program, the List window appears, displaying the program listing.

Use of the Screen

Many of the commands supplied by the menus for use with the mouse can instead be entered to the computer by manually typing the command in the Command window, with the same results.

Manipulating Programs

Before typing a program, click the File menu and then click the New command, listed under the File menu:

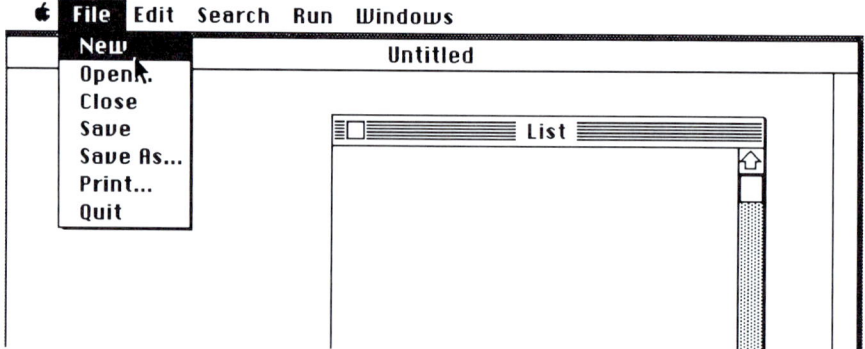

The List window is now active, and you can type your program in this window. You may want to enlarge the List window before typing the program. Another option is to activate the Command window and type NEW in this window:

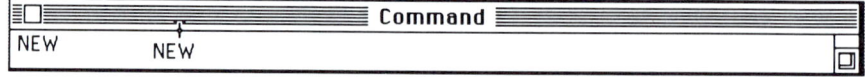

Then press <RETURN>.

To save a program named Monica, for example, click the File menu and then click the Save As . . . command. A dialog box will appear, requesting a name for the program. At this point, move the cursor into the space provided, type Monica, and press the <RETURN> key.

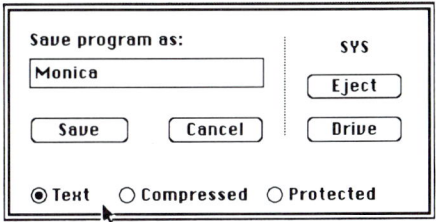

You can also type SAVE "Monica" in the Command window (note that the file name must be in double quotation marks) and press <RETURN> to get the same results:

SAVE "Monica"

To store the program in protected format, type

SAVE "Monica",P

and then <RETURN>. This command qualifier prevents the program from being listed at a later time.

To load an old program, click the Open command in the File menu, which will display all the programs in memory. Click the program you wish to load, and then click the Open box again. The program is now loaded and can be listed or run. Optionally, type LOAD "Monica" in the Command window:

LOAD "Monica"

Press <RETURN>. Type the following statement:

LOAD "Monica",R

Press <RETURN> to load and run a program automatically.

To list a program, you may want to enlarge the List window first: just click the List window title bar twice. To list a program, click the Window menu and then click the Show List command, which is listed under the Window menu.

If your program is longer than the screen, see Additional Features for scrolling control. Instead of using the Window menu, you can list a program by activating the Command window, typing LIST in the window, and then pressing <RETURN>.

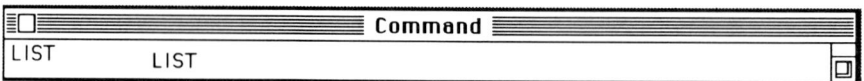

As with the other program-manipulating commands, you have two options to run a program: you can use the mouse and menu features, or you can type the command manually.

To use the menu option, click the Window menu and then click Show Output, which is found in the Window menu:

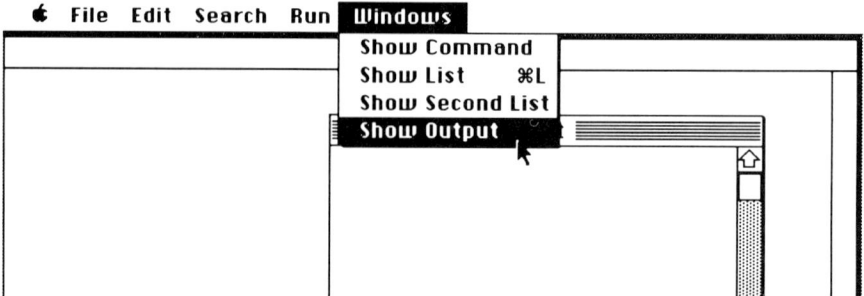

You then need to click the Run menu, and click Start, found in the Run menu.

When the program is running, all windows are hidden except for the untitled window, which is used to display the output.

When the output window is filled with output, it scrolls, eliminating the display of the topmost line of output to make room for a new line of output at the bottom of the output window.

Your other option for running a program is to use the command window and type RUN in the window, then press <RETURN>:

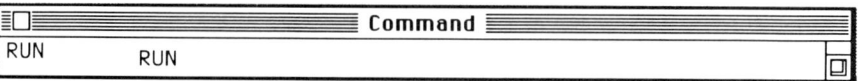

As with the other method, the program's output will be displayed and all other windows will be hidden.

Exiting BASIC

If you are in BASIC and wish to return to the Finder, click the Quit command under the File menu. As an alternative, you may type SYSTEM in the Command window and press <RETURN>:

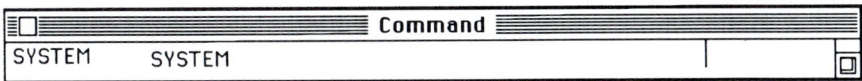

Once in the Finder, double-click the Eject command under the File menu to eject your disk. Turn off the power.

Keyboard

The Macintosh keyboard contains all of the standard keyboard characters. The <SHIFT> key can be used to enter the upper symbol on those keys that contain two symbols. To type only in uppercase, depress the <CAPS LOCK> key. Press the <CAPS LOCK> key once again to return to the lowercase mode.

Specialized Keys

When one of the keys listed in the following box is pressed, BASIC performs a specific function rather than accepting the key as standard keyboard data.

Key	Function
Return	Enters a line to the computer.
Backspace	Deletes the character at the current cursor position.
Tab	Can be set to move the cursor to set positions.

Additional Features

Scrolling Control

When a program is listed (and the List window is therefore active), and it exceeds the screen's height, it scrolls off the top of the screen. Likewise, if a line is longer than the screen's width, you cannot see the entire line. In either situation, use of the scroll boxes becomes necessary. The horizontal scroll boxes are located on the right side of the List window, and the vertical scroll boxes are located on the bottom of the List window.

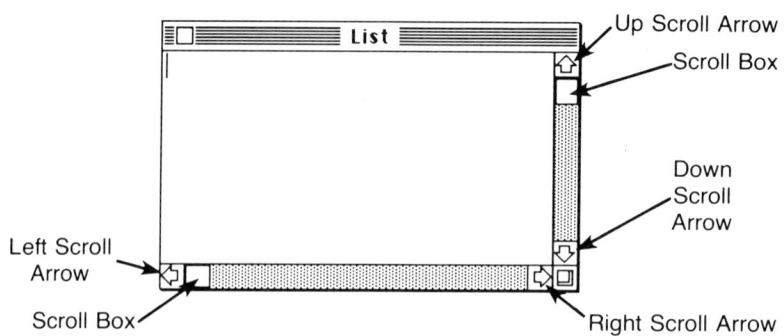

To move up or down in the listing, press the mouse button when the mouse pointer is on the up or down scroll arrow. To move left or right in the listing, press the mouse button on the left or right scroll arrow. To move large intervals (rather than line by line) vertically or horizontally through a listing, press the mouse button on the horizontal or vertical scroll bar and drag the box (still holding down the mouse button.)

Output scrolling is controlled in an entirely different manner. To stop scrolling an output, it is necessary to click the Run menu and then click Suspend, which is found in the Run menu.

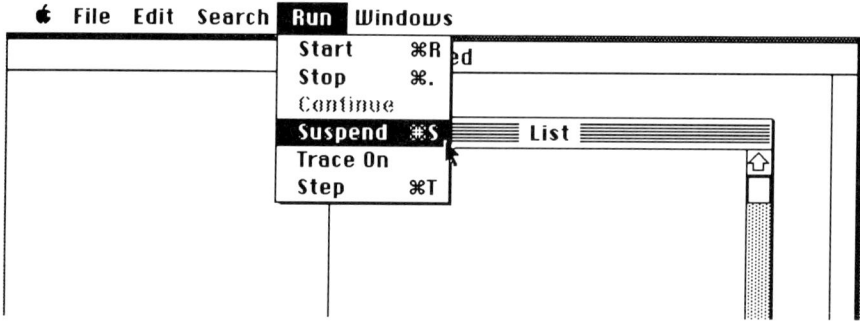

This halts the program output listing. To continue processing, simply click the Run menu again. Then click the command Continue, which is found in the Run menu.

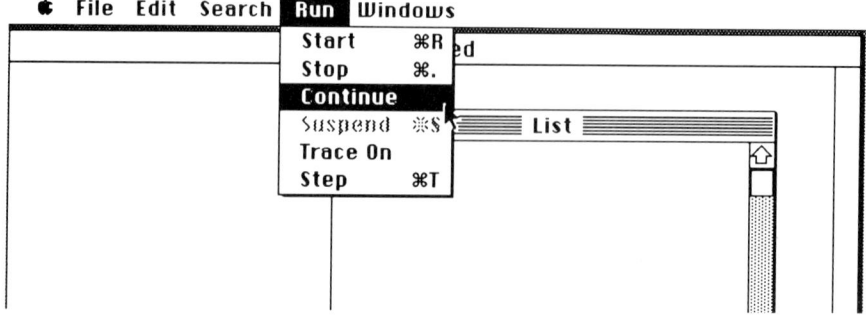

This method applies regardless of whether Run was initiated from the menu or the Command window.

Screen Factor

When a window is enlarged to occupy the entire screen, the screen can display up to 16 horizontal lines. The number of characters that can be printed on one line of the screen varies, because reserved words are boldfaced and thus occupy more space than variable names and numbers. For example, the first of the following two examples will occupy less space than the second, even though each has 24 characters, because IF, THEN, and PRINT will be boldfaced in the second statement, whereas only PRINT will be boldfaced in the first statememt:

```
100 PRINT "MY NAME IS SARAH"
110 IF DONE THEN PRINT "YES"
```

A line is not limited to the screen width; it can have up to 255 characters. When a line exceeds the screen width, the Macintosh automatically scrolls to the left.

Line Numbers

Line numbers are optional in Microsoft BASIC on the Macintosh. If line numbers are used, however, the minimum line number is 0 and the maximum line number is 65529.

Print Zones and Width

The Macintosh enables the user to set the print zone width, and in turn the number of print zones per line, via the WIDTH command. Print zone width is entirely up to the user. To set it to 10, you would need to type the following statement:

```
100 WIDTH,10
```

It is possible to specify an output device and a print line width in the WIDTH command. These values default to SCREEN and 255 respectively, which is acceptable for our purposes here. If you wish to change the output device and/or line width, refer to your manual.

The number of print zones per line depends on the value you set for the zone width. Line width defaults to 255, and we set the zone width to 10 in the previous example, so in this case there will be 25.5 zones per line. If zone width is set to 14 (WIDTH,14) there are 18.5 print zones per line, again assuming the line width default value of 255.

When the following statement is executed, the print zone width will become 25 spaces and there will be 10.2 zones per line:

```
100 WIDTH,25
```

GLOSSARY

Access method A way in which the computer transmits data between secondary storage and the primary storage unit.

Algorithm The sequence of steps needed to solve a problem. Each step must be listed in the order in which it is to be performed.

Alphanumeric data Any combination of letters, digits, and/or special characters.

Application program A program written to meet a specific user need.

Argument A value used by a function to obtain its final result.

Arithmetic/logic unit (ALU) The component of the central processing unit that performs mathematical computations and logical operations.

Array An ordered collection of related data items. A single variable name is used to refer to the entire collection of items.

Assembly language A programming language that uses symbolic names rather than the 0s and 1s of machine language; like machine language, it is dependent upon the type of computer being used.

Assignment Statement A BASIC statement that causes a value to be stored in a variable.

Auxiliary storage See Secondary storage.

Batch processing Processing in which jobs are grouped together and processed in a continuous stream without user intervention.

Binary representation See Machine language.

Binary search A search that repeatedly divides a sorted array into halves, comparing the target to the middle element and eliminating the portion that does not contain the target.

Boolean operator See Logical operator.

Bottom-up design A method of problem solving that proceeds from the specific to the general.

Branching Altering of the normal flow of execution.

Bubble sort A sort that progressively arranges the elements of an array in ascending or descending order by making a series of comparisons of the adjacent array values and exchanging values that are out of order.

Built-in-function See Library function.

Call To cause a subroutine to be executed.

Central processing unit (CPU) The "brain" of the computer, composed of three parts: the control unit, the arithmetic/logic unit, and the primary storage unit.

Character string A group of alphanumeric characters enclosed in quotation marks.

Coding The process of writing a problem solution in a programming language.

Collating sequence The order the computer assigns to the set of characters that it is capable of recognizing. This order is dependent upon the computer system being used, and it enables the computer to make comparisons.

Compiler A language translation program that translates the entire source program into machine language before program execution begins.

Complete program testing Testing all possible paths of program execution.

Computer An electronic machine that is capable of processing data in a wide variety of ways. Its speed, accuracy, and storage and retrieval capabilities make it extremely useful.

Concatenation The joining of data items, such as character strings, to form a single item.

Conditional transfer Program control is transferred to another point only if a stated condition is satisfied.

Constant A value that cannot change during program execution.
Control break Occurs when there is a change in the value of a specified field of a file.
Control statements Statements that allow the programmer to alter the order in which program instructions are executed.
Control unit The part of the central processing unit that governs the actions of the various components of the computer.
Counter A method of loop control in which a numeric variable is assigned a specific value that is tested each time the loop is executed until the desired number of repetitions is reached.
Conversational mode *See* Inquiry-and-response mode.

Data Facts that have not been organized in a meaningful way.
Data list A single list containing the values in all of the data statements in a program. The values appear in the list in the order in which they occur in the program.
Debug To locate and correct program errors.
Decision structure *See* Conditional transfer.
Descriptive variable name A name that describes the variable it represents.
Desk checking A method of tracing through a program by hand to check the correctness of the syntax and logic.
Direct mode command *See* Immediate mode command.
Documentation Comments that explain a program to people; documentation is ignored by the computer.
Double-alternative decision step A decision step in which a specific action is taken if a stated condition is true and otherwise a different action is taken.
Driver program A program of which the main purpose is to call subroutines, which do the actual work of the program.

Element An individual value stored in an array.
Endless loop *See* Infinite loop.
Error trapping The technique of writing a program in such a way that it "traps" or catches input errors, such as invalid data.

Execution The process by which the computer carries out the instructions submitted to it.
External documentation Written descriptions or explanations of a program that are external to the program itself.

Field The smallest division within a file, consisting of a single unit of information. Fields group together to form records.
File A collection of related data items, organized in a meaningful way and kept in secondary storage.
File organization The method used to arrange records within a file. There are three types of file organization: sequential organization, relative organization, and indexed organization.
Flowchart A graphic representation of the solution to a programming problem.
Function A subprogram that performs a specific task and results in a single value.

Hard copy Output printed on paper.
Hardware The physical components of a computer.
Hierarchy of operations The order in which arithmetic operations are performed. In BASIC the order is (1) anything in parentheses, (2) exponentiation, (3) multiplication and division, and (4) addition and subtraction.
High-level language A programming language that uses English-like statements that must be translated into machine language before execution.

Immediate-mode command A command executed as soon as the RETURN key is pressed; it is used without line numbers.
Index *See* Subscript.
Indexed organization Records are stored according to a primary key.
Indirect mode The mode in which statements are not executed until the RUN command is given. The statements must have line numbers.
Infinite loop A loop with no exit point.
Information Data that has been processed so that it is meaningful to the user.
Input Data that is entered into the computer for processing.

Inquiry-and-response mode A mode of operation in which the program asks a question and the user enters a response.

Interactive processing Processing in which the user is able to communicate directly with the computer during program execution.

Internal documenation Comments placed within the program that explain it to people.

Internal storage *See* Primary storage unit.

Interpreter A language translation program that translates the source program into machine language and executes it a line at a time.

Intrinsic Function *See* Library function.

Library function A function that is prewritten as part of the language.

Line number A number preceding a BASIC statement that is used to reference that statement and determine its order of execution.

Literal An expression containing any combination of letters, numbers, and/or special characters.

Logic error A flaw in an algorithm developed to solve a programming problem.

Logical operator An operator that acts on one or more conditions to produce a value of true or false.

Loop A structure that allows a given section of a program to be repeated as many times as necessary.

Loop body The statement(s) that constitute the action to be performed by the loop.

Loop control variable A variable of which the value is used to determine the number of loop repetitions.

Machine language The only instructions that the computer is able to execute directly; consists of combinations of 0s and 1s that represent on and off electrical states. Machine language is different for each type of computer.

Main memory *See* Primary storage unit.

Mainframe A large computer commonly used in business and industry.

Matrix An array.

Menu A screen display of a program's functions. The user enters a code at the keyboard to make a selection.

Merge sort A sort that combines two sorted arrays into a single sorted array.

Microcomputer The smallest and least expensive computer currently available. Microcomputers have a smaller primary storage unit than other types of computers.

Minicomputer A computer that has many of the capabilities of a mainframe but is generally lower-priced and has a smaller primary storage unit.

Module *See* Subprogram.

Numeric constant A number that is contained within a BASIC statement.

Numeric variable A variable used to store a number.

Object program The executable instructions created when the source program is translated into machine language.

Predefined function *See* Library function.

Primary key A field that uniquely identifies a particular record; the record can then be accessed by this field.

Primary memory *See* Primary storage unit.

Primary storage unit The component of the central processing unit that temporarily stores programs, data, and results.

Program A sequence of step-by-step instructions that a computer can use to solve a problem.

Program style A way of writing a program that affects the ease with which people are able to read and understand it.

Program testing Systematically checking a program to determine its reliability.

Program tracing A method of locating program errors by inserting PRINT statements to check the values of specific variables.

Programming The process of writing instructions for a computer to use to solve a problem.

Programming language A language that a programmer can use to give instructions to a computer. These languages can be divided into three broad categories: machine, assembly, and high-level.

Programming process The steps used to develop a solution to a programming problem.

Prompt A message telling the user that data should be entered at this point.

Pseudocode An English-like description of a program's logic.

Random A term describing a set (such as a set of numbers) in which every member has an equal chance of occurring.

Random access Accessing a record directly by means of a record location number or a primary key.

Record One or more fields that together describe a single entity. Records group together to form files.

Relational symbol A symbol used to compare two values.

Relative organization A method of organization in which each record is stored in a numbered location.

Reliability The ability of a program to work properly regardless of the data entered to it.

Reserved word A word that has a specific meaning to the BASIC system and therefore cannot be used as a variable name.

Run-time error A logic error that causes program execution to stop prematurely.

Scrolling The process in which lines move vertically on the terminal screen.

Secondary key A field that can be used to access a record after it has been accessed through its primary key.

Secondary storage Storage that is used to supplement the primary storage unit. Because it is external to the computer, it takes longer to access than primary storage, but it is less costly.

Selective program testing Testing a program using data with specific characteristics.

Sentinel value *See* Trailer value.

Sequential access Accessing all records sequentially until the needed record is reached.

Sequential organization A method of organization in which records are stored in the same order in which they are written to a file.

Sequential search A search that examines elements from first to last in numeric order.

Shell sort A sort that groups elements separated by a chosen gap into sublists, ordering each sublist independently. The chosen gap is progressively diminished until the entire list is sorted.

Single-alternative decision step A decision step in which a specific action is taken if a stated condition is true and otherwise execution proceeds to the next statement.

Soft copy Output displayed on a terminal screen.

Software A program or a series of programs.

Source program A sequence of instructions, written in either assembly or a high-level language, that must be translated into machine language before execution.

Spaghetti program A program with convoluted logic, often resulting from the use of numerous GOTO statements.

Stepwise refinement The process used in top-down design to divide a problem into smaller and smaller subproblems.

String variable A variable used to store a character string.

Structure chart A diagram that visually illustrates how a problem solution has been developed using stepwise refinement.

Structured programming A method of programming in which programs have easy-to-follow logic and are divided into subprograms, each designed to perform a specific task.

Stub A subroutine containing only a PRINT statement, which indicates that the subroutine has not yet been implemented, and a RETURN statement. Stubs are used when implementing a program in a top-down fashion.

Subprogram A distinct part of a larger program; designed to perform a specific task. In structured programming, subprograms are used to make a program's logic easier to follow.

Subroutine A module in a BASIC program containing a sequence of statements designed to perform a specific task; it follows the main program.

Subscript A value enclosed in parentheses that identifies the position in an array of a particular element.

Subscripted variable A variable that refers to a specific element of an array.

Supercomputer The largest, fastest type of computer currently available, capable of doing at least 100 million arithmetic operations per second.

Syntax The grammatical rules of a language.

Syntax error A violation of the grammatical rules of a language.

System program A program that coordinates the operation of computer circuitry and helps the computer run quickly and efficiently.

Time-sharing system A system with many terminals connected to a central computer that divides its time among the users.

Top-down design A method of solving a problem that proceeds from the general to the specific.

Trailer value A method of controlling a loop in which a unique value signals the termination of the loop.

Unary operator An operator used with one operand.

Unconditional transfer Control is always passed elsewhere, regardless of any program conditions.

Unsubscripted variable A simple variable; one that does not refer to an array element.

User-defined function A function that is written by the programmer.

User-friendly Describes a program that is designed to be easy and enjoyable for people to use.

Variable A storage location containing a value that can change during program execution.

Variable name The name used to represent the memory location where a variable is stored.

INDEX

ABS function, 284, 325
Access method, 410, 413, 443
    See also Opening a sequential/random file
Accumulator, 12
Addition, 2, 54
    in hierarchy of operations, 56
    matrix and, 498, 499, 510
Address (storage), 5, 10, 46–47
    assembly language and, 11
Algorithm, 22
    logic errors and, 460, 483
    pseudocode as type of, 29
Alphanumeric data, 45
American Standard Code for Information Interchange (ASCII), 123, 124, 531
AND operator, 201–205
APPEND mode, 420–421
Apple system
    common BASIC commands, functions, statements in, 561–562
    FOR/NEXT loop in, 183
    getting started on, 539–542
    no IF/THEN/ELSE statement in, 125
    no WHILE loop in, 195, 196
    ON/GOTO statement in, 136
    printing numbers in, 86
    random files in, 426–429
    random number function in, 287
    reserved words in, 50
    sequential files in, 417–420
    spaces around numbers in, 86
    special features in, 534–535
    specialized keys in, 540
    text files in, 417
Applesoft BASIC, 532, 534
Application programs, 9
Argument, 278–279, 324
    dummy, 313
    user-defined functions and, 309–316
Arithmetic expressions, 54–55, 63
    hierarchy of operations in, 55–56
    in IF/THEN statement, 122
    printing value of, 58–59
    and remark statement, 52
    See also Expressions
Arithmetic formula, 53

Arithmetic operations/functions, 2, 561
Arithmetic operators, 54–55, 201, 523
Arithmetic/logic unit (ALU), 4
Arrays, 337–403
    adding columns of, 354
    adding rows of, 351–354
    dimensioning, 341–342, 390
    index, 339
    multi-dimensional, 347, 355–359, 390
    one-dimensional, 342–347, 390
    performing calculations on elements of, 344–347
    printing contents of, 343–344
    reading data to, 342–343
    subscripted/unsubscripted variables, 340
    subscripts, 339–340, 390
    two-dimensional, 347–355, 390
    versus loop, 338–339
    See also Matrix
ASC function, 299
ASCII (American Standard Code for Information Interchange), 123, 124, 531
ASCII function, 297–303, 325
Assembler, 12
Assembly language, 9, 11–12
Assignment statement, 53–56, 63, 501
Asterisks (in REM statements), 51, 458
Auxiliary storage, 5

Backslashes, 98
BASIC
    Applesoft, 532, 534
    background on, 13
    commands. *See* Commands (BASIC)
    file operations, versus other systems, 407, 410
    fundamentals of programming in, 36–64
    grammatical rules in, 13. *See also* Syntax
    as high-level language, 12
    interpreters/compilers used by most programs in, 14
    vs. machine languages, 12
    older versions of, 13
    reference card for, 561–562
    statements. *See* Statements (BASIC)

Batch processing, 14–15
Beginner's All-purpose Symbolic Instruction Code. *See* BASIC
Binary codes, 10, 11
Binary representation, 9–10
Binary search, 378–381, 390
    versus sequential, 379
Bits, 10
Blanks
    in character strings, 46
    in IF/THEN statement, 124
    in IF/THEN/ELSE statement, 130
    to improve program style/readability, 58, 455, 458–459, 483
    in numeric variables, 48
    See also Spaces
Boldface, 483
Boolean operators, 201. *See also* Logical operators
Bottom-up design, 25–26
Boundary cases, 464, 483
Braces, 121
Branching, 118, 212
    infinite loops and, 143
    menus and, 137–140
    in writing subroutines, 231, 232, 245
Bubble sort, 360–367, 390
Buffer, 415, 423, 429
Business applications, 7

Carriage control, 36–37
CATALOG command (in Apple system), 541
Central processing unit (CPU), 4, 14, 15
Changing programs. *See* Modifying programs
Character string constants, 45–46, 53
    in IF/THEN statement, 122, 123–124
    maximum length of, 46
Character string literals, 57–58, 63
Character string variables
    DATA and READ statements and, 82
    INPUT statement and, 77
    See also String variable
CHR$ function, 297–303, 325
Classroom applications, 9

553

CLOSE statement
    random files and, 425, 431
    sequential files and, 419, 421
Closing a random file
    Apple system, 428
    IBM/Macintosh system, 431–432
    VAX system, 425–426
Closing a sequential file
    Apple system, 419
    IBM/Macintosh system, 421–422
    VAX system, 416–417
COBOL, 12
Coding, 31
Collating sequence, 123
Colon, 98
Columns (printing), 93
Commands (BASIC), 36–40
    common, 560
    direct-mode, 36–37, 40, 63
    file handling, 407
    immediate-mode, 36–37
    indirect-mode, 40
    See also Statements (BASIC)
Commas
    DATA statements and, 81
    INPUT statement and, 77, 78
    in line numbers, 41
    in numeric constants, 44
    in PRINT statement, 56–57, 87, 88, 106
Comments, 31, 53, 63
    to document program, 53
    to improve program style, 455, 458
    See also Remark (REM) statement
Comparison, 26. *See also* Decision step
Comparison operations, 2
Compiler, 12, 14
Complete program testing, 463–464, 483
Compressed print, 472
Computer
    components of, 3–6
    defined, 2
    home, 7
    as problem-solving tool, 20
    types of operations of, 2–3
Computer systems
    classification of, 6–9
    time-sharing, 15
CON function, 502, 510
Concatenation, 291–293, 325
Conditional transfer, 120–140
Connection symbol, 27
Constants, 44–46
    in IF/THEN statement, 122
Control break, 466
Control characters (for printer), 472, 483
Control statements, 117–156
    avoiding common mistakes in, 155
    defined, 118
    looping and, 142

Control unit, 4
Conversational mode, 81
Correcting a line, 42
Counters, 142, 146–147, 172
    testing, 146
    FOR/NEXT loop and, 172, 173, 185
Cray Research, Inc., 7
Cray X-MP computer, 7
Creating a file. *See* Opening a sequential/random file
Cursor arrows, in VAX system, 530
Cylinder, 412

Dartmouth College, 13
Data
    defined, 3
    documentation and, 21
    organization of, 407
Data files, 405–451
    See also Files
Data list, 82
DATA statement, 81–83, 106
    compared to INPUT statement, 84–85
    limitations of, 406
Data values, 82–85, 106
Debugging, 32
    documentation as aid to, 455
    GOTO statement and, 119
    origin of term, 459
    stubs and, 248
    See also Program testing
Decimal point, 44, 45
    in variable names, 49
Decision step, 26, 120–140
    double-alternative, 120–121, 127
    single-alternative, 120, 121, 122
Decision symbol, 27
DEF statement, 309–316, 326
Defining problem, 20–21
Definition (DEF) statement, 309–316, 326
Deleting a program
    in Apple system, 534
    in IBM system, 539
    in VAX system, 528
Descriptive variable names, 47
Designing solution, 22–31
Desk checking, 31, 194, 462
DIM statement, 341–342
    MAT command and, 494, 509
    See also Dimension statement
Dimension (DIM) statement, 341–342, 510
    MAT command and, 494, 509
DIR command (in IBM system), 538
Direct-mode commands, 36–37, 40, 63
    See also Immediate-mode commands
Disk drive, 3, 4, 5
Disk pack, 112, 413
Disks, 5. *See also* Floppy disks/diskette
Displaying a file, in VAX system, 528
Divide-and-conquer method, 23

Division, 2, 54
    in hierarchy of operations, 56
Documentation/documenting, 31, 50–53
    beginning, 455
    defined, 50
    external/internal, 455, 483
    a problem, 20–21
    program style and, 455–458, 483
    a solution, 22–31
Dollar sign
    in PRINT USING statement, 94
    in string variable name, 49
DOS (disk operating system), 532, 536
Double-alternative decision step, 120–121, 127
Driver program, 244
Dummy arguments, 313

E (the letter), 45
Edison, Thomas Alva, 459
Education applications, 9
Elements, 339, 390
END statement, 36, 50, 59, 63
    DATA statements and, 81
    vs. STOP statement, 257
    in writing subroutines, 232
Endless loop, 143. *See also* Infinite loop
ENTER (or RETURN) key, 36–37, 63
Entering/submitting a program, 31–32, 37
    in Apple system, 534
    in VAX system, 530–531
Entry and exit points, 185
Equal to/not equal to (symbols), 122, 324
Error checking, 258. *See also* Invalid data/input
Error message
    DATA and READ statements and, 82
    INPUT statement and, 78–79
        OUT OF DATA, 82, 496, 509
    regarding invalid data, 252, 267
    regarding ON/GOTO statement, 136, 137
    in user-friendly programs, 472
    in writing subroutines, 238
Error-trapping, 461
Errors. *See* Programming errors
Exclamation point, to mark beginning of comment, 53
Executable statements, 44, 119
Execution, 2, 39–40
    by batch vs. interactive processing, 14–15
    FOR/NEXT and WHILE loops for improved, 196
    machine language and ease of, 12
    order of, 26, 41. *See also* Sequence
    program structures and, 26
    REM statements and, 50
    translation necessary before, 14

unexpected flow of, 155
in VAX system, 531
EXIT command, in VAX system, 531
Exit point, 185
Exiting BASIC
in IBM system, 539
in Macintosh system, 545
in VAX system, 531
Exponential functions, 280, 325
Exponential notation, 44
Exponential value, 45
Exponentiation, 54
in hierarchy of operations, 56
Expressions
random files and, 427
sequential files and, 416, 418
See also Arithmetic expressions
External documentation, 455, 483

Field, 407, 443
Fieldname, 423, 430
Fieldwidth, 430
File organization, 408–410
access methods and, 413, 443
primary/secondary keys and, 409
File-type, 424
Filename
random files and, 424, 426–427, 428, 429
sequential files and, 416, 418, 419, 420
Filenumber
random files and, 424, 426, 429
sequential files and, 416, 417, 421, 422
Files, 407–408, 443
text, 417
disadvantage of, 407
methods of accessing, 410
random, 423. See also Relative organization, with random access
relative. See Relative organization
sequential. See Sequential organization
See also Data files
See also File organization
Finder (in Macintosh system), 540, 545
Floating-point numbers, 44
Floppy disks/diskettes, 5, 411, 543
Flowchart, 27–29, 455
assignment statement symbol in, 53
END statement symbol in, 59
example of, 464
of FOR/NEXT loop, 182
for loop, 173–174
showing multiple entry and exit points, 185
PRINT statement symbol in, 56
See also Structure charts
FOR statement, 177, 178, 214
as entry point, 185
loop body and, 184, 212

FOR/NEXT loop, 174–190
avoiding common mistakes in, 212–214
compared to WHILE loop, 196
entry and exit points in, 185
flowchart for, 182
nested. See Nested FOR/NEXT loops/statements
processing steps of, 177–182
program logic and, 196
rules for avoiding errors, 182–185
tasks done efficiently by, 185
sequential files and, 420
vs. GOTO statement, 454, 483
Format control characters, in PRINT USING statement, 93, 95, 98
Formatting, 21
FORTRAN, 12
Fractions, 44
Freezing (a listing), 38
Function call, 278–279
Functions, 277–335
absolute value (ABS), 284, 325
ASC, 299
ASCII, 297–303, 325
CHR$, 297–303, 325
common BASIC, 561
CON, 502, 510
exponential, 280, 325
integer (INT), 281–283, 325
intrinsic (predefined), 278
inverse (INV), 503, 510
LEFT$ and RIGHT$, 294–295, 325
length (LEN), 293–294, 325
library. See Library functions
matrix, 501–503, 510
MID$, 295–297, 325
natural logarithm (LOG), 280, 325
numeric, 279–291, 324–325, 527
random number (RND), 284–290, 324
sign (SGN), 284, 325
SPC, 92–93
square root (SQR), 280–281, 325
STR$, 303–309
string, 279, 291–309, 325, 529
TAB, 89–92, 106
trigonometric, 279–280, 324
user-defined, 278, 309–316, 325
VAL, 303, 309
ZER, 501, 510

Games, 9
General-purpose programming language, 13
GOSUB statement, 230, 231
common errors regarding, 267
GOTO statement, 118–120
computed. See ON/GOTO statement
vs. FOR/NEXT and WHILE loops, 454, 483
vs. GOSUB, 231
in loops, 143, 178, 196–200

spaghetti program resulting from numerous, 196
writing subroutines and, 231, 232
Greater than (symbol), 122
GW-BASIC, 536–539

Hard disk, 536
Hard disks, 5, 536
Hardware, 3–4
HELP facility, in VAX system, 528–529, 530
Hierarchy of operations, 55
High vs. low electronic states, 10
High-level language, 9, 12
storage locations and, 47
translation of, 14
Home computers, 7
Hopper, Grace, 459

IBM BASIC, 536–539
IBM DOS, 536
IBM system, 90, 92, 98
common BASIC commands, functions, statements in, 561–562
function key section in, 538
getting started in, 536–539
IF/THEN/ELSE statement in, 125, 125
modularization and, 244
ON/GOTO statement in, 136
random files in, 429–435
random number function in, 287–288
sequential files in, 420–422
special features in, 545
specialized keys in, 544–545
WHILE loop in, 195, 196
Identity (IDN) matrix, 502, 503, 510
IDN matrix, 502, 510
IF/THEN statement, 121–125
logical operators and, 201–205
in loop, 178
nested, 130–135, 155
in subroutines, 246
IF/THEN/ELSE statement, 125–130
nested, 130–135, 155
Immediate-mode commands, 36–37. See also Direct-mode commands
Incrementing counter/variable, 146, 173
in WHILE loop, 195
Indents, 190
Index, 339
Index hole, 413
Indexed organization, 409
Indirect-mode commands, 40
Infinite loop, 143, 155
step values and, 184
from WHILE loop, 195, 214
Information, defined, 3
Initial values, 177, 182, 183, 196, 212
number of loop executions and, 185, 212

Initialization, 501–502, 510
Initializing counter/variable, 146, 172, 173
　　in WHILE loop, 195, 196, 214
Input
　　defined, 3
　　devices, 3–4
　　documentation of, 21
　　symbol, 27
　　variables, 48
INPUT mode, 420–421, 424, 442
INPUT statement, 76–79
　　avoiding common mistakes in, 106
　　compared to DATA/READ statements, 84–85
　　limitations of, 406
　　printing prompts for user before, 79–81, 106
　　sequential files and, 417, 419, 422
　　trailer values and, 143, 155
Inquiry-and-response mode, 81
Inserting a line, 42
Instructions (BASIC), 40, 43
　　remarks to explain, 51–52
　　See also Statements (BASIC)
INT function, 281–283, 324, 325
Integer constants, 45
Integer functions, 281–283, 325
Integer variables, 48, 49
Interactive processing, 14–15
Interactive program
　　in Apple system, 535
　　checking for invalid data in, 248, 267
　　in IBM system, 538
　　in user-friendly programs, 472
Internal documentation, 455, 483
Internal storage, 5
Interpreter, 12, 14
Intrinsic (predefined) functions, 278
INV function, 510
　　See also Inversion
Invalid data/input
　　checking for, 248–258, 267
　　in user-friendly programs, 472, 473–474
Inverse (INV) function, 503, 510
Inversion (INV) function, 503, 510
Italics, 483

Kemeny, John, 13
Keyboard, 3
　　in Apple system, 533, 535
　　in IBM system, 537–538
　　in Macintosh system, 545
　　in VAX system, 529–530
Kurtz, Thomas, 13

Labels, line numbers as, 41
LEFT$ function, 294–295, 325
LEN function, 293–294, 325
Length (LEN) function, 293–294, 325
Less than (symbol), 122

LET, 36, 50, 53–56
Library functions, 278–309, 324–325
　　numeric, 279–291, 324–325
　　string, 279, 291–309, 325
Light pen, 3, 4
Line numbers, 40–43
　　avoiding common mistakes in, 63, 267
　　to improve readability, 51
　　in writing subroutines, 231, 232, 235, 238, 267
LIST command, 36, 37–38
Listing a program, 37–38
　　in Apple system, 534
　　in IBM system, 538
Lists, 494. See also Matrix
Literal, 57
LOAD command, 36, 39
Loading a program, 39
　　in Apple system, 534
　　in IBM system, 539
　　in Macintosh system, 543
　　in VAX system, 531
LOG function, 280, 325
Logarithm (LOG) function, 280, 325
Logic (of program), 29, 31, 32
　　errors caused by nested IF statements, 155
　　GOTO statement and, 119, 196
　　modularization and, 230
　　parentheses and, 214
　　printing prompts and, 81
　　READ statements and, 81
　　single entry and exit points and, 185
　　structured programming and, 454, 483
Logic errors, 32, 460–461, 483
　　avoided, 473
　　desk checking for, 462
Logical operations, 2, 4
Logical operators, 201–205, 230
　　order of precedence of, 203–204, 214
Loop body, 172
　　FOR statement and, 184, 212
　　in WHILE loop, 195
Loop control variable, 172
　　in FOR/NEXT loop, 177, 183–184, 185, 212
　　in nested FOR/NEXT loops, 190–191
　　resetting, 184, 212
　　in WHILE loop, 196, 214
Loop/looping, 26, 140–147, 172–227
　　avoiding common mistakes in, 212–214
　　boundaries of, 173
　　counters. See Counters
　　elements of, 172–174
　　flowchart for, 173
　　FOR/NEXT loop, 174–190
　　GOTO statement in, 178, 196–200
　　IF/THEN statement in, 178
　　importance of, 196–201
　　infinite (endless), 143, 155
　　MAT command to avoid, 494

　　single entry and exit points in, 185
　　trailer values, 142, 143–145, 155
　　versus arrays, 338–339
　　WHILE loop, 194–196
Low vs. high electronic states, 10
Low-level language, 11–12

Machine language, 9–11
　　storage address and, 47
　　translation of high-level language into, 14
Macintosh system, 98
　　common BASIC commands, functions, statements in, 561–562
　　getting started in, 540–547
　　IF/THEN/ELSE statement in, 125, 128–130
　　line numbers in, 41
　　modularization and, 244
　　ON/GOTO statement in, 136
　　random files in, 429–435
　　random number function in, 287–288
　　sequential files in, 420–422
　　special features in, 545–547
　　specialized keys in, 545
　　TAB function in, 92
　　WHILE loop in, 195, 196
Magnetic disk, 5, 6, 411, 412–413
Magnetic tape, 5, 6, 411
Main memory, 5
Mainframes, 7, 15
Mantissa, 45
Manuals, 455
Map buffer, 424
MAP map-name, 424
Mark II, 459
MAT command, 494, 509
　　to initialize, 502, 510
　　See also Matrix commands
MAT INPUT statement, 496, 497, 509
MAT PRINT statement, 497, 509
MAT READ statement, 496, 509
Mathematical computations, 4
Mathematics, matrix, 498–501, 509, 510
Matrix, 494, 509
　　functions, 501–503, 510
　　mathematics, 498–501, 509, 510
　　See also Arrays
Matrix (MAT) commands, 493–517
Medicine applications, 9
Memory, 5
Memory locations. See Address (storage)
Menu bar (in Macintosh system), 541
Menus, 137–140
　　modularization and, 247
　　in user-friendly programs, 472
Merge sort, 369–376, 390
Microcomputers, 7–9, 15
Microsoft Version 2.0, 547
Microsoft Corporation, 536
Microsoft DOS, 536

Microsoft GW-BASIC, 536–539
MID$ function, 295–297, 325
Minicomputers, 7, 15
Minus sign, 45, 86
Modes
    conversational/inquiry-and-response, 81
    direct/indirect/immediate, 36–37, 40, 63
    input/output/append, 420–421, 424, 442
    random files and, 424, 442
    sequential files and, 420–421, 442
Modifying programs, 462
    structured programming and, 455, 483
Modularization, 13, 230–268
    checking for invalid data and, 248–258
    importance of, 230
    menus and, 247
    structure charts for, 230–244
    stubs and, 247–248
    top-down design and, 247
    See also Subroutines
Modules, 13, 230, 454
Mouse (in Macintosh system), 540, 542
Multi-dimensional arrays, 347, 355–359, 390
Multiple entry points, 185
Multiple statements on single physical line, 98–99
Multiplication, 2, 54
    in hierarchy of operations, 56
    matrix and, 498, 499–500, 510
    matrix and scalar, 500–501, 509, 510

Naming a program, 37, 38–39
Natural logarithm function, 280, 325
Naval Museum, 459
Negative numbers, 44, 45
Negative step value, 178, 182
Nested FOR/NEXT loops/statements, 190–194, 214
    MAT READ statement and, 496
    program logic and, 196
    single entry and exit points in, 191
Nested IF statements, 130–135, 155
Nested parentheses, 55
NEW command, 36, 63
    in Apple system, 533
    in Macintosh system, 542
    in VAX system, 530, 531
New program
    in Apple system, 534
    in VAX system, 530–531
NEXT statement, 177, 178, 195, 214
    as exit point, 185
Nonexecutable statements, 44, 50, 119
    DATA statements, 81
    in writing subroutines, 231, 232
NOT operator, 201–205
Numbers
    floating-point, 44
    negative vs. positive, 44

    numeric constants, 44
    PRINT USING statement for printing columns of, 93
    real vs. integers, 44
    signs for, 44, 45, 86
    See also Line numbers
Numeric constants, 44–45, 53
    in arithmetic expressions, 54
    in IF/THEN statement, 122
Numeric functions, 279–291, 324–325, 527
Numeric literals, 57, 58
Numeric variables, 48–49, 53
    in arithmetic expressions, 54
    in IF/THEN statement, 122
    INPUT statement and, 78, 79
Numeric-expression, 424, 426

Object program, 14
Off bit, 10
OLD command, 36, 39, 537
On bit, 10
ON/GOSUB statement, 230, 231, 232–239, 244
    common errors regarding, 267
    menus and, 247
ON/GOTO statement, 135–137, 155
    menus and, 137–140
    vs. ON/GOSUB, 235, 238
One-dimensional arrays, 342–347, 390
OPEN statement
    random files and, 423
    sequential files and, 416, 418, 421, 422
Opening a random file
    Apple system, 426–427
    IBM/Macintosh system, 429–430
    VAX system, 423–424
Opening a sequential file, 415
    Apple system, 417–418
    IBM/Macintosh system, 420–421
    VAX system, 416
Operators, 44, 201, 523
    arithmetic, 54–55, 201
    logical (Boolean), 201–205, 230
    relational, 122, 201
    unary, 202
OR operator, 201–205
Order of execution, 26
    altering, 41
    See also Sequence
Order of precedence (of logical operators), 203–204, 214
OUT OF DATA message, 82, 496, 509
Output, 4, 21
    devices, 4, 5–6
    symbol, 27
    variables, 48
OUTPUT mode, 420–421, 424, 442

Parentheses
    to alter precedence of logical operators, 203–204, 214

    in arithmetic expressions, 55
    for readability, 201, 214
Pascal, 12
Pass, 360
Percent sign, in integer variable names, 48
Periods, in variable names, 48
Physical line (defined), 128
Plus sign, 45, 86
Positive numbers, 44, 45
Predefined functions, 278
Preparation symbol, 27
Primary key, 409
Primary memory, 5
Primary storage, 4, 5–6, 46–47
    limitations of, 407, 408
PRINT statement, 36, 50, 56–59
    avoiding common mistakes in, 106
    commas in, 87, 88
    to control printer output, 472, 483
    print zones in, 87–89
    program tracing with, 462
    prompts for user and, 79–81
    semicolon in, 85–86
    sequential files and, 421
    SPC function and, 92–93
    TAB function and, 89–92
PRINT USING statement, 93–98
Print zones, 87–89
    avoiding common mistakes in, 106
Printer, 4, 5
    control characters, 472, 483
Printing, 85–98
    columns, 93
    multiple statements on single physical line, 98–99
    PRINT USING statement, 93–98
    semicolon in, 85–86
    SPC function and, 92–93
    TAB function and, 89–92
    using the print zones, 87–89
Problem solving, 20
    structured, 20–34
    top-down design vs. bottom-up, 23–26
Process symbol, 27
Program
    application vs. system, 9
    commercial, 9
    defined, 2
    modifying. *See* Modifying programs
    object, 14
    source, 14
    See also Application program; System program
Program structures, 26
Program style, 454, 455–459, 483
Program testing, 32
    complete versus selective, 463–464, 483
    defined, 462
    methods of, 462–465, 483
    necessity of, 454
    static and run-time, 462

Program tracing, 462
Program variable, 48
Programming
  defined, 9
  fundamentals of BASIC, 36–64
  process, 20–33
  See also Structured programming
Programming errors, 31–32
  defining and documenting problem clearly to reduce, 21
  debugging and testing to eliminate, 32
  infinite loop as cause of, 143
  locating, 32
  logic, 32, 460–461, 483
  machine language and, 12
  reduced by structured programming, 455, 483
  rules for avoiding, 63, 106, 155, 324, 442
  rules for avoiding in arrays/matrices, 390, 509
  rules for avoiding in looping, 212–214
  run-time, 460–461, 483
  single entry and exit points and, 185
  story of the first computer "bug," 459
  reduced by structured programming, 13
  stubs to reduce, 247–248
  syntax, 460, 483
  subroutines to reduce, 245, 267, 454
  typing vs. logic, 32
  WHILE loop (common error in), 214
Programming languages, 9–12
  defined, 2
  general-purpose, 13
Prompt, 79–81, 106
  in user-friendly programs, 472
Pseudocode, 29–30
Puskas, Theodore, 459
PUT statement, 424

Question mark, INPUT statement and, 77, 78
QUIT command, in Macintosh system, 545
Quotation marks, 39, 45, 53
  DATA statements and, 81
  INPUT statement and, 78
  PRINT statement and, 57, 58, 63

Random access, 410, 415, 422–442, 443
Random files, 423–442
Random number function, 284–290, 324
RANDOMIZE statement, 287–289, 324
  See also RND function
READ statement, 81–83, 106
  compared to INPUT statement, 84–85
  MAT READ statement and, 496
  sequential files and, 419
  trailer values and, 143, 155
Read/write heads, 413

Readability, 55
  blanks for, 58, 455, 458–459, 483
  FOR/NEXT and WHILE loops and, 196
  with IF/THEN/ELSE statement, 130
  line numbers for, 51
  in nested FOR/NEXT loops, 190
  in numeric values, 86
  parentheses for, 201, 214
  program style and, 455
  in writing subroutines, 232
Reading a random file
  Apple system, 428–429
  IBM/Macintosh system, 432–435
  VAX system, 426
Reading a sequential file, 415
  Apple system, 419–420
  IBM/Macintosh, 422
  VAX system, 417
Real constants, 44–45
Real numeric variables, 48, 49
Record, 407, 443
RECORD SIZE numeric-expression, 424
Record-length, 427
Record-number, 424, 427, 431, 432
Regions (in Macintosh system), 540–541
Relational operators, 122, 201
Relational symbol, 122
RELATIVE option, 424
Relative organization, 408, 443
  with random access, 415, 422–442
Reliability, 462
REM statements, 36, 44, 50–53
  asterisks in, 51, 458
  avoiding common mistakes in, 63
  to improve program style, 455, 458
  See also Remark statement
Remark (REM) statement, 50, 51–52
  See also Comments; REM statements
Repetitive task, 26. *See also* Loop/looping
Replacement operation, 501, 510
Report writing, 465–472, 483
Reserved words, 49–50, 63, 518–522
  INPUT, 77
  LET, 54
  PRINT, 57
  REM, 50, 63
  TAB, 90, 106
RESTORE statement, 83–84
Retrieval operations, 3, 407, 409
  types of, 410
RETURN (or ENTER) key, 36–37, 63
RETURN statement, 231, 238, 246, 267
RIGHT$ function, 294–295, 325
RND function, 284–290, 324
  See also RANDOMIZE statement
Row order, 496, 497
RUN command, 36, 39, 40, 531
  in Macintosh system, 544
RUN-No Headings, 39, 531

Run-time errors, 460–461, 483
  avoided, 473
Run-time testing, 462
RUNNH command, 39, 40, 531

SAVE command, 36, 38, 63, 531
Saving a program, 3, 37, 38–39
  in Apple system, 534
  in IBM system, 539
  in Macintosh system, 542–543
  in VAX system, 531
Scalar multiplication, 500–501, 509, 510
Scalar value, 500, 509
Scientific applications, 7
Scientific notation, 44
Scrolling, 38
  in Macintosh system, 545–547
Searching, 377–381
  binary, 378–381, 390
  binary vs. sequential, 379
  sequential, 377–378, 390
Secondary keys, 409
Secondary storage, 5, 6, 407, 410–413
  file organization and access and, 410, 413, 414, 443
Sectors, 413
Seed, 284, 286
Selective program testing, 463–464, 483
Semicolon, PRINT statement and, 85–86
Sentinel value, 143. *See also* Trailer value
Sequence, 26
  flowchart, 27
  line numbers and, 41
Sequential access, 410, 413–422, 443
SEQUENTIAL option, 424
Sequential organization, 408, 443
  with sequential access, 413–422
Sequential search, 377–378, 390
  versus binary, 379
SGN function, 284, 325
Shell, Donald, 367
Shell sort, 367–369, 390
Sign (SGN) function, 284, 325
Signing on/off, in VAX system, 527–528
Single entry and exit points, 185, 245
  in nested FOR/NEXT loops, 191
  for subroutines, 245–246, 267
Single-alternative decision step, 120, 121, 122
Single-exit point principle, 246, 267
Soft copy, 5
Software, 9
Sorting, 360–376, 390
  bubble, 360–367, 390
  merge, 369–376, 390
  Shell, 367–369, 390
Source program, 14
SPACE (SPC) function, 92–93

Spaces
    in line numbers, 41
    in numeric values, 86
    See also Blanks
Spaghetti program, 196
SPC function, 92–93
Spindle, 413
SQR function, 280–281, 325
Square root function, 280–281, 325
Statements (BASIC), 36, 40–50
    assignment, 53–56, 63, 501
    CLOSE. See CLOSE statement
    common, 561
    components, 43–50
    control, 117–156
    DATA. See DATA statement
    definition (DEF), 309–316, 326
    dimension (DIM), 341–342, 390
    END. See END statement
    executable vs. nonexecutable, 44
    MAT. See Matrix (MAT) commands
    OPEN. See OPEN statement
    simple, 50–59
Static testing, 462
Step values, 177, 178, 182, 183, 212
    infinite loop and, 184
STOP statement, 257
Storage (and retrieval), 3, 407, 409
    internal, 5
    primary. See Primary storage
    problems with, 406, 407
    secondary. See Secondary storage
    See also Address (storage)
Storage locations, 5, 46–47
    PRINT statement and, 57
    relative organization and, 408–409, 414
STR$ function, 303–309
    See also String (STR$) functions
String constant, 53
    See also Character string constant
String (STR$) functions, 279, 291–309, 325, 529
    common BASIC, 560
String variables, 48, 49, 53
    in IF/THEN statement, 122, 123–124
    See also Character string variable
Structure chart, 239–244, 454, 455
    See also Flowchart
Structured problem solving, 20–34
Structured programming, 13, 230, 454–455, 483
    GOTO statement to be avoided in, 196
    single entry and exit points in, 185, 245, 267
    See also Structured problem solving
Stub, 247–248
Submitting/entering a program, 31–32, 37
Subprograms, 13
Subroutine symbol, 27

Subroutines, 13, 230
    to improve program style, 454, 483
    menus and, 247
    to reduce errors, 245, 267, 454
    separating, 458
    top-down development and, 247
    writing, 231–246
Subscripted variables, 340
Subscripts, 339–340, 390, 472
Subtraction, 2, 54
    in hierarchy of operations, 56
    matrix and, 498, 499, 510
Supercomputers, 7
Superscripts, 472
Symbols
    flowchart, 27. See also Flowchart subheadings
    relational, 122
Syntax, 29, 31
Syntax errors, 460, 483
    desk checking for, 462
SYSTEM command
    in IBM system, 539
    in Macintosh system, 545
System programs, 9
    compiler or interpreter, 12, 14

TAB function, 89–92
    avoiding common mistakes in, 106
Tables, 494
    PRINT USING statement for printing, 93
    See also Matrix
Tape drive, 3, 4, 5, 411
Terminal screen, 4, 5, 165
    VT100 and VT220, 527
Terminal symbol, 27, 59
Terminal values, 177, 182, 183, 196, 212
    number of loop executions and, 185, 212
Testing a program. See Program testing
Text files, 417, 428
THEN clause, 201
Time-sharing systems, 15
Top-down design, 23–25
    vs. bottom-up, 25–26
    to improve program style, 454, 483
    subroutines and, 247
Tracks, 413
Trailer values, 142, 143–145, 155
    FOR/NEXT loop and, 196
    WHILE loop and, 196
Transferring control, 118–140, 155
    from loop body statement to FOR statement, 184
Translation, 14, 15
Transposition, 502–503, 510
Trigonometric functions, 279–280, 324

Two-dimensional arrays, 347–355, 390
Type styles, 472 , 483

Unary operator, 202
Unconditional transfer, 118–120
Underlining, 472, 483
    PRINT statement and, 57–58
    in variable names, 48
Unsubscripted variables, 340
User's manuals, 455
User-defined functions, 278, 309–316, 325
User-friendly programs, 472–474

VAL function, 303–309
Values
    constant, 44
    variables and, 47
Variable names, 47, 63, 455, 483
    documentation to explain, 50
    reserved words and, 49–50
Variables, 44, 46–49, 63
    in arrays, 340
    in IF/THEN statement, 122
    INPUT statement and, 77
    in PRINT statement, 85–86
    printing value of, 57
VAX 8500 series, 527
VAX 8530, 527
VAX BASIC, Version 3.2, 527
VAX system
    versus Apple, 532
    commands in, 528–529
    comments in, 53
    common BASIC commands, functions, statements in, 561–562
    END statement in, 59, 247
    format control characters in, 98
    getting started on, 527–531
    IF/THEN/ELSE statement in, 125
    line numbers in, 41, 257
    matrix statements in, 494
    multiple statements on single physical line in, 98–99
    NEW command in, 37
    OLD command in, 39
    ON/GOTO statement in, 135, 136
    print zones in, 87
    random files in, 423–426
    random number function in, 287
    RIGHT$ function in, 295, 325
    SAVE command in, 38
    sequential files in, 416–417
    STOP statement in, 257
    subroutines in, 232, 238
    TAB function in, 90
    VAL function in, 309
    variable names in, 48, 49
    WHILE loop in, 194–195
VMS operating system, 527

VT100 terminal, 527–529
VT220 terminal, 527–529

WEND statement, 195, 196, 214
WHILE loop, 194–196
    avoiding common mistakes in, 212–214
    to check for invalid data, 248
    compared to FOR/NEXT loop, 196
    vs. GOTO statement, 454, 483
    program logic and, 196
WHILE statement, 195, 214

WHILE/NEXT statements, 195, 196
WHILE/WEND statements, 195, 196
Windows (in Macintosh system), 541–542
Word processing, 9
Wrap around, 128, 130
Writing a program, 31, 36
    printing prompts to simplify, 81
Writing to a random file
    Apple system, 427–428
    IBM/Macintosh system, 430–431
    VAX system, 424–425

Writing to a sequential file, 415
    Apple system, 418–419
    IBM/Macintosh system, 421
    VAX system, 416
Writing subroutines. *See* subroutines
Writing user-friendly programs, 472–473, 483

ZER function, 501, 510

BASIC Reference Card ▪ Steven L. Mandell
BASIC Programming Today: A Structured Approach

Common BASIC Commands

Command	Explanation	System
LIST	Displays on screen entire program currently in main memory.	All systems*
LOAD program	Transfers specified program from secondary storage to main memory.	Macintosh, IBM, Apple**
NEW program	Clears a portion of main memory and assigns the specified name to the new program.	VAX system
NEW	Clears a portion of main memory in preparation for a new program to be entered.	Macintosh, IBM, Apple
OLD program	Transfers specified program from secondary storage to main memory.	VAX system
RUN	Executes program currently in main memory.	All systems
SAVE	Writes program currently in main memory to secondary storage.	VAX system
SAVE program	Writes program currently in main memory to secondary storage under specified name.	Macintosh, IBM, Apple**

Common Arithmetic Functions

Function	Purpose	System
ABS(X)	Returns the absolute value of X.	All systems*
INT(X)	Largest integer less than or equal to X.	All systems
RND	Random number between 0 and 1.	VAX system, IBM, Macintosh
RND(X)	Random number between 0 and 1.	Apple
SQR(X)	Square root of X.	All systems

Common String Functions

String Function	Operation	Example	System
ASCII(string)	Returns the ASCII code for the first character in the string.	If A$=DOG then ASCII(A$) is 68	VAX system
ASC(string)	Returns the ASCII code for the first character in the string.	If A$=DOG then ASC(A$) is 68	IBM, Apple, Macintosh
LEN(string)	Returns length of a string.	if H$ is HI THERE, then LEN(H$) is 8	All systems*
STR$(expression)	Converts a real number to a string.	STR$(12.34) returns the string 12.34	All systems
VAL(expression)	Converts a numeric string expression to its numeric equivalent.	VAL("12.34") returns 12.34	All systems
stringA + stringB	Concatenates two strings.	NIGHT + MARE is NIGHTMARE	All systems

*VAX, Macintosh, IBM, Apple
**On the IBM and Macintosh, the program name must be enclosed in double quotes.

Common BASIC Statements

Statement	Explanation	Example	System
DIM	Sets dimensions for arrays.	10 DIM ITEM$(25)	All systems*
END	Stops program execution.	9999 END	All systems
FOR/NEXT	Sets up a loop that is executed a stated number of times.	250 FOR X = 1 TO 20 STEP 2 400 NEXT X	All systems
GOSUB	Transfers control from the calling program to subroutine.	260 GOSUB 1000	All systems
GOTO	Unconditional transfer of control.	160 GOTO 250	All systems
IF/THEN	Conditional transfer of control.	430 IF NME$ = "DONE" THEN 550	All systems
IF/THEN/ELSE	Conditional transfer of control to one of two execution paths.	430 IF NM$ = "DONE" THEN 550 ELSE 220	VAX system, IBM, Macintosh
INPUT	Allows user to enter data during program execution.	50 INPUT NME$,AGE	All systems
LET	Assignment statement (the word LET is optional).	100 TOTAL = TOTAL + 1	All systems
ON/GOSUB	Transfers control to one of several subroutines, based on the evaluation of a mathematical expression.	250 ON X GOSUB 100,200	All systems
ON/GOTO	Transfers control to other statements, based on the evaluation of a mathematical expression.	190 ON X GOTO 120,140	All systems
PRINT	Displays or prints the results of computer processing.	130 PRINT "NAME", PAY	All systems
PRINT USING	Permits flexibility in formatting output.	100 PRINT USING F$;PAY	VAX system, IBM, Macintosh
READ/DATA	Reads data from the data list to variables.	100 READ NME$, HRS 800 DATA SMITH, 40	All systems
REM	Used to indicate documentation.	100 REM COMPUTE PAY	All systems
RESTORE	Causes next READ statement to assign values from beginning of data list.	200 RESTORE	All systems
RETURN	Transfers control from a subroutine back to the calling program.	1500 RETURN	All systems
TAB	Prints output in a specified column.	100 PRINT TAB(15); "NAME"; TAB(25);"ADDRESS"	All systems
WHILE/NEXT	Executes a loop as long as a stated condition is true.	120 WHILE CNT < 50 230 NEXT	VAX system
WHILE/WEND	Executes a loop as long as a stated condition is true.	150 WHILE CNT < 50 240 WEND	.IBM, Macintosh

*VAX, Macintosh, IBM, Apple